D1558634

SEAN O'CASEY'S
AUTOBIOGRAPHIES

SEAN O'CASEY'S AUTOBIOGRAPHIES

An Annotated Index

Robert G. Lowery
Foreword by David Krause

GREENWOOD PRESS
Westport, Connecticut • London, England

Library of Congress Cataloging in Publication Data

Lowery, Robert G., 1941-
  Sean O'Casey's autobiographies.

  Bibliography: p.
  1. O'Casey, Sean, 1880-1964—Dictionaries, indexes,
etc. 2. O'Casey, Sean, 1880-1964—Biography—Indexes.
3. Dramatists, Irish—20th century—Biography—Indexes.
I. Title.
PR6029.C33Z459   1983   016.822'912 [B]   83-826
ISBN 0-313-23765-4 (lib. bdg.)

Library of Congress Catalog Card Number 83-826
ISBN: 0-313-23765-4

First published in 1983

Greenwood Press
A division of Congressional Information Service, Inc.
88 Post Road West
Westport, Connecticut 06881

Printed in the United States of America

10 9 8 7 6 5 4 3 2 1

To Pat, who is one of God's good people.

He would splash his thoughts over what he had seen and heard; keep eyes and ears open to see and hear what life did, what life had to say, and how life said it; life drunk or sober; life sickly or sturdy; life sensible or half demented; life well-off or poor; life on its knees in prayer, or shouting up a wild curse to heaven's centre.

—Sean O'Casey
Inishfallen, Fare Thee Well

CONTENTS

FOREWORD

Like all works of art, Sean O'Casey's autobiography functions on many diverse levels of experience. It is structured in a flexible form with a variety of literary techniques and dramatized voices, with a wide ranging context of historical crises and personal imperatives, and with an extensive series of private and public fantasies suspended in streams of consciousness. On the immediate level of response, of course, it is the narrative and dramatic tale of his growing up angry and lyrical in dirty Victorian Dublin during the last two decades of the nineteenth century. On the symbolic level it is an impressionistic tale of his creative and socialist awakening, and of the awakening of Irish literature and politics, through the first half of the twentieth century. Finally, it is also an epic tale of the artist as child and man rendered in a fictive design that is at once mythic and authentic. The events of his life generally and specifically happened as he described them, but the viable form in which they are described is a changing and shaping structure that did not exist until he created it as an imaginative extension of reality. The result is a revelation of autobiography through fiction and fiction through autobiography.

Myth and reality are fused in the story of O'Casey's life. Perhaps one approach to the secret of his art, in his plays as well as in his autobiography, may be found precisely in his Blakean fusion of opposites, in his determination to draw connections between disparate forms, emotions, and events: the yoking of the comic and the tragic, the lyric and the ironic, the epic and the mundane, the melodramatic and the satiric, the historic and the idealistic— infinite combinations of realistic and mythic correspondences.

O'Casey created his world of correspondences with a texture of felt life that is projected as vividly and intensely as the autobiographical London of Dickens or the autobiographical Dublin of Joyce. Only that artistic process can fully illuminate the life process. As we respond to the epic story of O'Casey's early years of pain and struggle, we perceive the compensatory power and rage of the half-blind young man behind the artist; we perceive the common laborer and poor Protestant among predominantly poor Catholics fighting to assert his reaction to injustice through his socialist idealism; we perceive the self-educated dramatist eagerly discovering the shape and sound of words that were to become his weapons of liberation. And through it all he invariably reflected in his nature a paradoxical correspondence of pity and pride. Pity for human suffering always moved him profoundly, and if he inherited his depth of compassion from his mother, by contrast he followed his father in his fierce pride as an autodidact who above all worshipped books and the glory of their knowledge.

His father was known as the austere scholar of Lower Dorset Street, and although O'Casey was only a boy of six when his father died, the memory of the man was transfixed in his mind when in the first volume of the auto-biography he reached back fifty-three years to draw a sharply etched portrait of Michael Casey in which the father anticipates the son as one "liked by many, a little feared by all who knew him, having a sometime gentle, sometime fierce habit of criticism, and famed by all as one who spat out his thoughts in the middle of a body's face." And the son might have been gazing into the same mirror when he went on to describe his father's proud love of learning: "A scholar he was to all, who was for ever poring over deep books, with a fine knowledge of Latin, and a keen desire that others should love learning for its own sake, as he did."

It would be difficult to read the autobiography without recognizing O'Casey's intense dedication to learning for its own sake, for the pride and pleasure of presenting all the acquired and recalled knowledge of a lifetime as a vital aspect of his story. Nevertheless, he was a pragmatist and he wanted learning to serve as an enlightening and liberating element in the lives of the poor whose unfortunate circumstances were the direct result of ignorance as well as exploitation. Furthermore, to humanize the portrait, there is also an easily recognizable tone of self-congratulation in his love of learning for the sake of Sean, the self-made Sean in an alien world who David-like armed himself with his considerable knowledge as if it were a slingshot to bring down the Goliaths in his life. If this fantasy reveals a streak of the romantic puritan in his nature, it is only one of his many dominant and seemingly disparate traits. His ego was as large as his heart. After a long life of ordeals and defeats tempered by victories of the spirit, perhaps he had earned the right to present a heroic and narcississtic image of himself, for he was in his wholeness a man of sufficient stature to possess the vision of an artist, the conscience of a proletarian, the irreverence of a jester, and the passion of a scholar.

It would be difficult to measure the incredibly vast range and depth of his knowledge, which he displays and even flaunts on every page of the six-volume autobiography by invoking and celebrating the names of people, places, events, poems, songs, and books. These multiple layers of reference are more than a catalogue of information: they provide the rooted framework of associations and connections that constantly resonate throughout the story; they constitute the topographical design of the autobiography. The topography of O'Casey's world is as organic as the cetology of Melville's world. Furthermore, there is a very relevant Celtic connection. In the spirit of the old Gaelic *Dinnshenchas*, the topographical naming and exalting of places and people in ancient Ireland, O'Casey is following a traditional genre that invests his writing with the bardic echoes of Celtic Ireland, and he continues the association by celebrating the topographical correspondences in contemporary Ireland and the broad scope of modern history. He is an unmistakable product of his Irish heritage, but he is also an artisan and citizen of the world.

No reader in or outside of Ireland could be expected to have in his mind, or on his library shelf, a key to all the topographical references and allusions in the autobiography. But now, at long last, twenty-nine years after the completion of the final volume in 1954, and nineteen years after the death of O'Casey in 1964, we have been provided with such an indispensable key or concordance, conceived and researched and organized by the indefatigable Robert Lowery. Thanks to the special dedication of Lowery, a versatile historian and editor and scholar who shares O'Casey's vision and love of learning, we are now able to explore and have at our fingertips all the associations and correspondences mentioned or submerged in the text and to follow the original order and time span of the major incidents in all the volumes. It must be stressed, however, that Lowery's valuable book is intended to be an aid, not a substitute, for O'Casey's autobiography. O'Casey's story speaks for itself and can be read on its own ground, but if it is taken with Lowery as a *vade mecum*, the reader's levels of knowledge and pleasure will certainly be increased.

Always the artist intent upon imposing an original shape on the raw material of his life, O'Casey had to be oblique as well as direct in his writing. He was determined not to follow the usual conventions of autobiography. Instead of clogging the narrative with vital statistics and dates, he omitted or took poetic liberties with such information. Instead of being restricted by the chronological order of events, he introduced the technical innovations of a modern novelist and often suspended or shifted clock and calendar time in order to pursue the irregular or overlapping time patterns and surrealities of the mind. With the possible exception of George Moore in *Hail and Farewell*, few writers have exploited as many fictional strategies in the genre of autobiography as O'Casey has. Joyce, by contrast, went the other way and exploited infinite permutations of autobiographical strategy in his fiction. Moore influenced Joyce and both influenced O'Casey in their mythic and comic metamorphoses of their own lives. Nevertheless, as an apt and instinctive disciple, O'Casey went on to create his own unorthodox and irreverent techniques in the telling of his life story.

The existence of Robert Lowery's book should encourage readers and students to explore many of those old and new techniques and to launch an in-depth examination of O'Casey's ultimate achievement as a unique auto-biographer. Once when he was asked about some symbolic meaning in his work, O'Casey replied, "I must have builded better than I knew." Confronted now by the sheer magnitude of Lowery's book, one is tempted to say that O'Casey builded better than we knew.

David Krause

ACKNOWLEDGMENTS

Like most great ideas this project had its origin over a few pints in a pub. On a snowy February night in 1976 in Hempstead, Long Island, several O'Casey scholars were relaxing, having participated in the first "Sean O'Casey Conference." On that night at least two of them agreed that, apart from a socialist revolution, what the world needed was an annotated index to O'Casey's autobiographies.

Many people helped with this project: with over 4,000 items to define and annotate it could not have been otherwise. Foremost were the faithful few: Maureen Murphy, David Krause and Bernard Benstock. Dr. Murphy was patient, guiding, and always a phone call away with answers to my persistent inquiries. Dr. Krause became a warm and close friend and a critical advisor during the long months of the project, taking valuable time off from his important work with O'Casey's letters to encourage me and to urge the project onward. Dr. Benstock's camaradarie became a source of inspiration, and his critical eye for scholarship kept me from dumb errors. This troika suffered my frustrations and shared my joys: One in Three and Three in One.

Eternal gratitude and thanks are given to: Sean's beautiful bride, Eileen, who constantly gives us a portrait of Sean's good taste; Ronald Ayling, who saw the beginnings; John and Kate O'Riordan, whose red roses always bloom; Tom and Alice Buggy, who answered the knock at the door; Alf MacLochlainn, who was truly a national librarian; Bill Maroldo, whose letters from afar stirred the still waters; Jack Lindsay, the crimson in the Union Jack: Gearoid O Clerigh, Irish consul general, a Gael's Gael; Seamus Scully and Deirdre Henchy, Ireland's proud past and shining future; those at the Abbey Theatre, especially Deirdre McQuillan, Tomas MacAnna, the late Bill Foley, the late Angela Newman, and Philip O'Flynn—warm and generous; E. J. Dumay and Co. and Manuel and Carmela Moya, the French Connection; Brooks Atkinson, Irving Stone, Michael Yeats, Gabriel Fallon, and Elie

Siegmeister, who were there; Hofstra University's History and English departments, especially John Moore, Lynn Thorn, George Jackson, Edward Dunbaugh, John Marcus, and Allan Davis; and the staff and librarians of the world's halls of healing, including Stony Brook and Hofstra university libraries, the National Library of Ireland, Suffolk Community College, the American Irish Historical Society, and the New York Public Library, with special thanks to Lola Szladits.

Acknowledgment is gratefully made to many others who had a part of the whole: Weldon Thornton, Thomas Staley, Emmet Larkin, Barbara Brothers, Patrick Galvin, John Frayne, Shari Benstock, Robert Hogan, Edward Mikhail, David Clark, Richard Finneran, Mary Fitzgerald Finneran, Rhona and Michael Kenneally, Karl Bottigheimer, Elisabeth Freundlich, Heinz Zaslawski, Donal Nevin, Doris da Rin, Richard Kain, Claire McCabe, Augustine Martin, Alvin Boretz, Aaron Godfrey, James Carens, Stanley Weintraub, F.S.L. Lyons, and, from far off battles and happy times many years ago, Louis Williams.

Special thanks to The Macmillan Press Ltd. and Humanities Press for permission to reprint portions of this index which first appeared in *An O'Casey Annual*, nos. 1 and 2.

Finally, generous acknowledgment is made to my dear wife, Pat, to whom these labors are lovingly dedicated.

INTRODUCTION

Sean O'Casey's autobiographies were published in six volumes between 1939 and 1954. The first four books—*I Knock at the Door* (1939), *Pictures in the Hallway* (1942), *Drums under the Windows* (1946), and *Inishfallen, Fare Thee Well* (1949)—were the Irish books, covering his life from birth in 1880 to self-imposed exile in 1926. The last two volumes—*Rose and Crown* (1952) and *Sunset and Evening Star* (1954)—traced the period from his arrival in England to approximately 1952. O'Casey died in 1964.

One critic noted that O'Casey's autobiographies were not so much a portrait of an emerging writer as they were "life regained, relived passionately with all the intensity of a man still fiercely engaged."[1] And, indeed, the books do reflect the development of an extraordinary man and all the emotional excitement of twentieth-century Europe and Ireland. For the first part of his life, O'Casey was witness to or participant in the major events that shaped modern Ireland: the struggles to regain a lost language, literature and heritage; the birth of a dynamic labor movement and its subsequent betrayal; and the nationalist Easter Rising, War of Independence, and Kafkaesque Civil War—events which claimed the flower of a generation including many of O'Casey's friends. He watched the poor and unemployed march off to the trenches in Belgium and France, and watched them return spiritually and physically scarred. He hailed the Russian Revolution and shared the dreams and hopes of the many for land, peace, and bread.

The flowering of O'Casey's artistry neatly divides his eighty-four years of life. After 1922, O'Casey the dramatist developed his talent. His first plays saved Ireland's national theatre, the Abbey, from bankruptcy, and his fame mounted. But disillusioned by a Dublin that spurned his finest effort, *The Plough and the Stars*, he left for England where he married, raised a family, and wrote the majority of his plays. He cultivated new friends—George Bernard Shaw, Augustus John and others—but retained the comradeship of his Dublin "butties" with whom he often shared memories of "far-off battles, long ago."

His drama changed as he began to explore and experiment with new styles and forms that bewildered many of his earlier admirers. But his commitment to the best in human values remained. He heard the war drums in Spain, Italy, and Germany, and felt the sufferings of thousands of refugees from the charred ruins of English cities and Europe's camps who poured into the West Country. Passing sixty-five years, he renewed his commitment to the vitality of youth and the challenge and beauty of life, for life to O'Casey was perpetually "a lament in one ear maybe, but always a song in the other."

He left behind fourteen full-length and nine one-act plays, several books of critical essays, many thousands of letters to friends he never met around the world, and six dynamic volumes of autobiography. Few of his plays were ordinary. Many occasioned riots, turmoil, attempted kidnappings, pious condemnations, and bombing threats. They were banned in Boston, burned in Limerick, and shouted down in Vienna and Berlin. Yet, two of them, *The Plough and the Stars* and *Juno and the Paycock*, are critically judged to be among the best plays in modern drama. His essays, his "blasts and benedictions," were equally controversial and predictably banned as he condemned bigotry, ignorance, disease, the Church and State, and anything else that demeaned the dignity of Man and art. Though he always felt inadequate as an essayist, his "Under the Greenwood Tree He Died" must be considered one of the most poignant and moving essays in modern prose. The bulk of his letters were written to relatively unknown people, but they have about them a quality reminiscent of the correspondence of an eighteenth-century society for which letters were the means of thrashing out important issues. And upon his death in 1964, the *New York Times* editorialized that his autobiographies were "one of the most memorable works of this century,"[2] a fitting tribute to one of the most memorable men of the century.

There are several ways of approaching O'Casey's autobiographies, two of which will be discussed here. Objectively, they comprise six books, half a million words, and span nearly seventy-five years of the playwright's life. The author takes liberties with style, form and substance, and alternates between factual accounts and imaginative reworking of events. The lyrical Biblical and Elizabethan language is at times overpowering, and has prompted such critics as Brooks Atkinson to comment several times that O'Casey wrote "the most glorious English prose of his time."[3] There is also what Hubert Nicholsen called O'Casey's "horn of plenty":[4] a prodigious knowledge of songs, plays, literature, poetry, Catholic and Protestant symbolism, Dublin geography, and a few thousand years of Irish and world history.

Artistically, the books have an epic quality. They fulfill what Roy Pascal calls "a search for one's inner meaning,"[5] and contribute significantly to the genre of autobiography. They are, as Pascal wrote of Wells's *Experiments in Autobiography*, "another contribution to his life's works, not a resume of it."[6] The artistic interpretation of the autobiographies has increasingly become the mainstay of O'Casey criticism, thanks to the efforts of Ronald Ayling. According to this view, the autobiographies should not be viewed "primarily as source material" for the dramatist's life or "as being no more than a personal memoir," but "as a work of art in its own right." The dramatist has "recreated his early life with the balanced detachment of a novelist, while yet communicating the enthusiasms and commitments of his protagonist with a vivid immediacy."[7] One is tempted, therefore, to use as the epitome of criticism the reply of a novelist, Joseph Conrad, to a researcher, with one minor substitution: "After all, I am a writer of fiction [substitute: dramatist], and it is not what actually happened but the manner of presenting it that settles the literary and even the moral worth of my work."[8] The artistic view almost always equates O'Casey's autobiographies with Joyce, if not in substance then in Conrad's "manner of presenting it." Ayling writes, "It is as if *A Portrait of the Artist as a Young Man* were to be assessed only in terms of how well it reflected Joyce's early life."[9]

But there are a few problems that cannot be solved by viewing O'Casey's autobiographies through an artistic prism, problems which have to be understood to fully appreciate the stature of the books. The artistic perspective must be combined with a historical approach, for if the artistry of the books overshadows their historical qualities much of their power is negated. O'Casey's life-story is the history of modern Ireland. He incorporates every important historical event as if it were part of his own life because he felt himself part of the developing history of Ireland. By the use of a variety of devices, primarily literary, he expanded that Life into a World. If much of the power of the autobiographies is derived from its lyrical writing and its epiphanies, it is also true that it achieves some remarkable insights into the journey of twentieth-century working-class Man.

The historical approach to the autobiographies is necessary to solve what Pascal called "the central and most complicated problem of autobiography"— its truth or falsity. This, he writes, is "the really troubling question [that] affects the central theme of autobiography. We like to ask, does the author's representation of himself as a personality correspond to what we can get to know of him through other evidence? It is a question that can never be asked regarding a work of art."[10]

A historic approach to the autobiographies must combine a rigorous examination of the books with a sensitive understanding of their artistic worth. Unlike the artistic critic, though, the historian is not ultimately concerned with literary form or inner growth but in factual and verifiable truth, that is, truth which can be documented and augmented by other sources (which in turn have to be verified) and used to illuminate a period or a person's life. The historical approach is not primarily interested in the autobiographer's exposure of his soul so much as it is concerned with the reliability of what is exposed.

One criterion used in historial studies with an autobiography is that any autobiography is a suspicious document because it is usually written long after the fact. It is both a primary and a secondary souce, though: primary because it is written by one with first-hand knowledge, but secondary because it is written from a reflective perspective. In that sense it may be twice autobiographical: first, as relating actual details of a subject's life or period, and second, as reflecting the subject's state of consciousness at the time of writing. This criterion is used with all historical documents and writings, and it is a useful tool for filtering out contemporary standards imposed upon the past. For instance, Gibbon's masterful *The History of the Decline and Fall of the Roman Empire* almost becomes a primary source for the last twenty-five years of the eighteenth century, the period in which it was written, for that was a period in which England's empire was threatened by the American, French, and Irish revolutions.

Historians must study problems and ask questions. If they are good historians they will ask questions which will be answerable. With O'Casey's autobiographies, we must ask many questions. What is there to be verified? How do the books compare with his other writings on the same subjects at the time of writing and of the time he is writing about? How do they compare with other documents of the same period? Were they written entirely from first-hand knowledge, or did he use the writings of others to refresh his memory? What was O'Casey's state of mind at the time of writing?

All of these questions cannot be dealt with here, but a few examples may serve as illustrations. Basic to the historicism of the autobiographies is an understanding of Irish life. One cannot miss the upheavals O'Casey recorded in his books: the fall of Parnell, the Literary Renaissance, the 1913 Lockout, and the Easter Rising, War of Independence and Civil War. But what might be missed are the fundamentals of the Dublin experience. Though Ireland was undergoing revolutionary changes between 1880 and 1926, there were evolutionary and more subtle transformations taking place in a less noticeable fashion. For instance, the names of streets, buildings, bridges, and even towns changed. Streets and bridges assumed more patriotic names, buildings went up and came down, especially during the war years. Kingstown became Dun Laoghaire, and Queenstown became Cobh. These changes are reflected in O'Casey's autobiographies. For example, O'Casey uses Carlisle Bridge until

Drums when he begins calling it O'Connell Bridge, its modern name since 1882. Rutland Square is used until *Inishfallen* when he switches to Parnell Square. Sackville Street and O'Connell Street are used interchangeably throughout the six books, a reflection of old habits which die hard. But O'Connell Street is not mentioned until *Drums*, evidence of O'Casey's historical intent. In this very basic and fundamental exercise, O'Casey renders a historical service to students of Dublin life; more of a service, one might add, than Joyce's *Ulysses*. For, while one might indeed be able to rebuild Dublin using Joyce, it would be a static city. One gains a greater sense of the change, development and continuity in the city from O'Casey's autobiographies.

O'Casey's portrait of Dublin is fairly easy to verify. Using a representative selection of *Thoms* directories, one can get the sense of the streets down which he trod, the shops where he stopped to visit, the sights at which he marveled, and the town he loved so much. In this respect, the accuracy of the books is phenomenal. We cannot imagine O'Casey sitting down with a directory of Dublin and writing his memoirs. But he gained the same effect as if he had. He returned to Dublin only twice after his departure in 1926, and these were hardly research trips. The degree to which he retained a living memory of the city, including the most intimate and seemingly inconsequential details, is an example of his ability to exercise almost total recall—a demonstration which should be kept in mind as the books are read.

Another of the more interesting historical aspects of the autobiographies is the sources the playwright used. It is important to know whether or not O'Casey was writing from personal knowledge. If he was, then his version of events can be given greater credence than if he used secondary sources. For instance, there is no evidence that O'Casey ever knew Walter MacDonald, whom he eloquently defended in the "Silence" chapter in *Inishfallen*. Instead, O'Casey used as his entire source MacDonald's book, *Reminiscences of a Maynooth Professor*, which was published posthumously in 1925. The same might be said for his defense of Michael O'Hickey, from the "Lost Leader" chapter in *Drums*. But here the evidence is less conclusive because O'Hickey's pamphlet, "Irish in the New University—Or Else!," was widely distributed, and it may have been the subject of debates in the Gaelic League during O'Casey's time with them.

Strange and odd sources appear in the autobiographies, none of which O'Casey cites. For instance, he used Margot Asquith's *Autobiography* (1920, 1922) for parts of "St. Vincent Provides a Bed" in *Drums*, describing the book only as "a British source." In the "Inishfallen, Fare Thee Well" chapter of the fourth book, we find him appearing to quote a Lamb of Newry and a Dr. Kenny. As O'Casey put it:

> . . . Lamb of Newry and Dr. Kenny ventured to say, "they would not take a
> Catholic University, if the present hierarchy had anything to do with it. . . ."

Actually, O'Casey never read what Lamb or Kenny said. He is quoting from a
little-known book, *Five Years in Ireland,* by Michael McCarthy, who wrote:

> The Parnellites utter some plain truths about the church—some of them, Mr.
> Lamb of Newry and the late Dr. Kenny, go so far as to say they would not take
> a Catholic University if the present hierarchy had anything to do with it.[11]

One source used in the "Dublin's Glittering Guy" chapter in *Inishfallen* was
Monk Gibbon's introduction to AE (George Russell)'s writings, *The Living
Torch* (1937). We know from his letters that O'Casey ordered the book,[12]
and we know that he read it and used it because he quotes from it (without
attribution) several times in the chapter. These quotes are italicized so we
know the playwright is using another source, but when he recites a long list of
paintings, sculptures, and medallions done of AE, he leaves us with the
impression that this list was compiled from personal knowledge. In fact,
O'Casey copied the list almost verbatim from Gibbon's introduction, and it is
doubtful O'Casey ever saw the items in question. There is no doubt that
O'Casey knew AE reasonably well, at least after the 1913 Lockout when
Russell wrote his famous letter defending the strikers. But we might surmise
that O'Casey gave AE a wide berth and had little time for him. Certainly he
did not know him intimately.

Fortunately, O'Casey lived in Dublin in exciting times, and there is no end
of memoirs and documents to compare with his autobiographies. Yet he
himself is also a document of those years. His early writings, which were
gathered in *Feathers from a Green Crow,* may be used to analyze sections of
Drums and *Inishfallen.* His *Story of the Irish Citizen Army* is probably more
valuable for historical purposes than the last few chapters of *Drums;* for in
writing *Story,* the preface notes that he used "materials, carefully gathered
together from original manuscripts in his possession, from notes recorded
during the organising period of the Army, and from contemplation of events
in which the author participated." This short statement gives two important
facts: (1) that O'Casey used original material, and (2) that he participated in
many events of the ICA which he further described more eloquently though
less factually in *Drums.* (In Micheal O Maolain's account of "The Raid," he
alludes to some incriminating documents O'Casey had with him. These were
almost surely the ones used in writing *Story,* but we may assume they were
too dangerous to keep and were destroyed afterwards.) *Story* is important for
another reason. In this pamphlet O'Casey writes more or less as an observer,

and the account is complete with names, dates, events, and even the time of day. This, of course, contrasts dramatically with the style of the autobiographies. It is evidence, though, that O'Casey was capable of objectifying a situation when it was necessary, and that the obscurity of hard, historical data in the autobiographies is by design and not because of a vagueness of memory.

For this period, the autobiographies are interesting for what they do not include. In his early writings, one of his articles (21 February 1914) accuses Padraic Pearse of crossing picket lines during the Lockout. This charge is not repeated in *Drums*. There, Pearse is presented in glossier tones, evidence not only of O'Casey's reflective perspective but also of his increased admiration for Pearse. Also not included is the ideological change O'Casey underwent on the National question. In *Drums* he accurately records his opposition to any kind of united front between labor and the nationalists. This is a faithful portrayal of his feeling at the time in question, but it did not correspond to his view at the time of writing the chapters (early 1940s). As early as 1937 he could write: "National Freedom must, unfortunately, come before Communism. I am speaking at a gathering here [Wales] next Tuesday, & hope I may persuade some who haven't yet joined the National Movement to fight for a flag, and a government of their own."[13] There is, then, on one hand an awareness that an earlier statement may have been rash or at least unproven, and, on the other hand, an obligation to be conscientious to the times.

Documentation of O'Casey's accounts of events can be found in the memoirs of the period. For instance, his efforts to obtain a St. Patrick's Day service in Gaelic at St. Kevin's church ("Gaelstroem," *Drums*) are substantiated by Desmond Fitzgerald, who wrote: "I certainly regarded Sean O'Casey as a familiar figure. But I did not think of him as a dramatist or a writer. I knew rather about his enthusiasm for High Anglicanism, of the visits he had paid with [Ernest] Blythe to Church of Ireland dignitaries to get them to have a service in Irish on St. Patrick's Day."[14] The account of his mother's funeral ("Mrs. Casside Takes a Holiday," *Inishfallen*) is the same as he told Lady Gregory only a short time after 1919, and which she recorded in her journals. Desmond Fitzgerald's *Remembering Sion* (1934) and John Devoy's *Recollections of an Irish Rebel* (1929) present portraits of the dramatist which are even more flamboyant and flattering than O'Casey's self-portrait. (It was flattering to be called "disgruntled" by Devoy.)

It is well to keep in mind that no picture of O'Casey is likely to be entirely accurate, whether it presents him in a good or bad light, whether it documents or refutes the autobiographies, or whether it is scholarly or unscholarly. He was a man who had staunch defenders and fierce enemies. His writings and statements had a polarization effect on all who paid any attention to him. His autobiographies, the first two of which were banned in Ireland, created deep resentment in his native country. For every hero or institution he blasted, the critics fired back an equal number of salvos. He was accused of poor-mouthing, or exaggerating his poverty, and of being out of touch with reality. Equally, his defenders were, and are, polarized. They have always found it terribly difficult to be objective about the man. They have never apologized for this condition, nor should they. The passion and intensity that O'Casey continues to evoke are part of knowing and understanding him.

Why has Pascal's question—"We like to ask, does the author's representation of himself as a personality correspond to what we can get to know of him through other evidence?"—gone unanswered for so long? Perhaps the answer is that critics basically have been uninterested in separating fact from fiction in the autobiographies. The twenty-nine years since the last volume was published have produced only rudimentary efforts. This is due partly to the lack of necessity and partly to O'Casey's style. No full-scale biography of the dramatist has been attempted and his own writings have been allowed to stand relatively unexamined. A major drawback has undoubtedly been O'Casey's own cavalier attitude toward dates and other vital statistics. O'Casey's style, though, has been the major obstacle. Scholars and critics have not been helped by the dramatist's use of literary devices to illustrate, delineate, or expand a point or event. The use of allegory, verse, melodrama, puns, imaginative parades, characterization and dream sequences, and fantasy in general are better suited to the novelist and the dramatist rather than to the writing of factual autobiography. It is these devices which, though undoubtedly contributing to the artistic merits of the books, have probably been the greatest barrier to sorting out the truth from the fiction. Of these, fantasy and O'Casey's literary imagination are two primary areas for discussion.

It should be understood that although O'Casey thoroughly enjoyed writing fantasy, he was frequently called upon by critics (and his publisher) to document the factual, historical aspects of his works. In his own mind he was quite able to separate the one from the other even if it did not come across on paper. From his statements, we know that some things were meant to be fictional fantasy and others were meant to be historically factual. For instance, about his highly-regarded play, *Cock-a-Doodle Dandy*, he wrote: "In spite of the *fanciful* nature of the play, almost all the incidents are *factual*."[15] And about his autobiographies he wrote: "Bar the obvious *fantasy*, they are an *accurate* portrayal of men and things, there with you and here with me."[16] If, then, as Ayling commented, O'Casey "wrote realistically without relinquishing his love of fantasy,"[17] it is also true that he wrote fantasy without losing his grip on reality. For despite the fanciful nature of the books, O'Casey's life was grounded in reality. He was an acute observer of life with its attendent joys and tragedies, and he could never retire from the day-to-day realities of living. If he had an opiate it was life—life today and life tomorrow.

O'Casey's imaginative powers are another disorienting device for students of the autobiographies. For some reason, an imaginative writer is often assumed to be living in a world of imagination. The mistake, though, is to equate imagination with fantasy and to equate the two with fiction. Although the fiction is there in the fantasy it is erroneous to see his imaginative powers in the same light. To O'Casey, imagination was as much a part of the reality of life as was a lack of imagination. Imagination was that intangible essence of greatness and a formless surge of energy that emanated from the grander moments in life. It was present in all great figures and moments from the past as well as in the vigorous dynamism that flowed from the life of the working class. It was vital to life and, as a tool, vital to the writer. Technique, he once wrote,

> is useful and important, the marshalling of a play within a limited allowance of time and space; but imagination is all: it is the focus of all achievements by man; it sparked the American Revolution, it began the discovery of Evolution in the mind of Darwin, it flamed forth from the mind of Lenin, inspired Shakespeare's plays and all his songs; and it is the burning core of form and eloquence which is present in a fine play, novel, painting, and musical creation. . . . but the dramatist must make his imagination serve him; he must control it; if he doesn't, it will make all the difference between an interesting but disorderly play and a fine work of art.[18]

There can be little doubt that O'Casey brought this manner of writing—realism plus imagination—to everything he wrote. "Every play," he wrote,

> in whatever form, however written, must deal in one way or another with the life of the people meeting the dramatist who writes it, of those whom he has worked with, lived with, and of those whom he has watched in every conceivable way within the locality where he has lived himself. He weaves all these things through his mind, through his imagination, using the technique of the stage to place there what is called a play—a pattern of words and movement, either in poetry or prose, which must, if it is to be a fine work, bring to all who see or hear a new and an exciting experience.[19]

The chapters in the autobiographies which are clearly fictional or quasi-truthful are designed to raise issues that are specific and pointed. They serve a structural purpose by appearing at junctures in O'Casey's life and in Ireland's history. Although the dialogue is imaginary, it gives voice to issues and ideas in language that is effective and evocative. For example, the "Song of the Shift" chapter in *Drums* gives an account of the hysterical response of Ireland's protectors of literary good taste, the Gaelic League, to Synge's *Playboy of the Western World*, and foreshadows the response to O'Casey's own play, *The Plough and the Stars*, in the same theatre twenty years later. It is a critical juncture for O'Casey and for Ireland because while it opens the eyes of a future dramatist to the problems he will one day face, it closes the eyes of the masses of demonstrators to the integrity of art. Ireland has given O'Casey a message: only those plays which present the country at its finest will be tolerated. Fortunately, he chose to ignore the message.

"Song of the Shift" is fictional in the sense that the event did not take place exactly as O'Casey describes it. It has more to do with the story line of an emerging Ireland and an emerging O'Casey. But it need not detract from the specifics of the historical reality. Pascal writes: "All autobiographies must, like novels, have a story structure. But it would be wrong to suppose that this imposes a regrettable limitation on their truthfulness, . . . It is their mode of presenting truth."[20]

The story of an emerging O'Casey naturally raises the question of his talent as a dramatist and its relationship to the autobiographies. It should be said that it is rare for any writer to excel in more than one genre, for the skills and techniques of one have different demands from that of another. Most writers spend their entire lives mastering one skill and occasionally experimenting with another. But few earn the sentiments expressed by the aforementioned *New York Times* editorial. Of the Irish writers, only O'Casey, Oscar Wilde, and John Millington Synge appear to have bridged the gap between fruitless experimentation and great art. (O'Casey would include George Bernard Shaw in this group, but many critics would not.) Others, like James Joyce and Oliver St. John Gogarty, were reasonably proficient at more than one genre, but neither writer's "other works" would be regarded as great literature.

The critics themselves are often a stumbling block for an appreciation of "other works." With O'Casey's autobiographies, the books, more often than not, are viewed as an extension of his drama and not always on their own merits. Eric Bentley wrote, "Though diffuse, and over-full of self-pity and proletarian snobbery, the autobiography may be almost as good as people say it is; even so, it is *ersatz*: and *the best passages are scenes from plays that will never be written*."[21]

Padraic Colum must have been reading the same scenes, for he commented: "That quality which his plays have exceptionally and which is the making of them as audience-holders *he has transferred to his narratives*, and it gives certain scenes a dimension that is not in other biographical writing."[22] Gogarty, in his review of *I Knock at the Door*, found "parts where the dramatist merges into the lyricist at the cost of the dramatic mask."[23]

There is good reason for some of this criticism. One of the most striking similarities between the plays and autobiographies is O'Casey's gift of characterization, so famously noted by Lady Gregory. The majority of O'Casey's intimate characters come to life: his mother, sister and brothers, Ayamonn O'Farrel, "Mild Millie," and the Jewish glazier to mention a few.[24] Others can be found in his plays, like "The Girl He Left Behind Him" as Shelia Moorneen in *Red Roses for Me*; Richard Brannigan and Barney Conway as Brannigan in *The Star Turns Red* (as well as his fellow workers on the Great Northern Railway of Ireland in the same play); and of course O'Casey himself. Moreover, one chapter, "The Raid," in *Inishfallen*, parallels *The Shadow of a Gunman*, and parts of two others (in *Drums* and *Sunset*) appear in *Red Roses* and *The Bishop's Bonfire*. Additionally, there is a similar mixture of extreme realism and brilliant fantasy. And finally, there is a similar vision: sympathy for the oppressed, condemnation for the oppressor, and a lust for all parts of life.

But, however much O'Casey's dramatic skills helped with the writing of the autobiographies, there is a danger in assuming too close an overlapping of the two. O'Casey started his career in his early twenties writing satiric prose,[25] and it was not for another fifteen years that he wrote his first major play. He was always interested in drama, of course, and as an adolescent was greatly influenced by Shakespeare and Dion Boucicault. But his reading habits of those early years also included essayists and historians such as John Ruskin, Ralph Waldo Emerson, Thomas Carlyle, and John Locke, and novelists like Charles Dickens, Honoré Balzac, James Fenimore Cooper, and Victor Hugo—most of whom had an equal influence on him.[26] This list does not include perhaps *the* greatest influence on his style, the Bible. His first published book, *The Story of the Irish Citizen Army*, appeared only a few years before he began writing his first major play, and after an interval of about nine years, during which he wrote almost no serious prose, he announced his intention of beginning the autobiographies.[27] In other words, after only four major plays, O'Casey began once again seriously to think of the narrative, with the majority of his plays still unwritten. There is no reason to doubt that O'Casey's loyalty was to the stage. But, as I've tried to show, there is good reason to doubt that his prose was merely an extension of his dramaturgy.

This index deals with the real, the surreal, the fact, and the fiction in O'Casey's autobiographies. It is intended to be a tool for further studies of the books by enabling students and scholars to have a handy companion to consult. It has been compiled to use with "books in hand," and it is not a substitute of any kind. It is an annotated index to the autobiographies.

For the purpose of this study, I have indexed the American edition (all U.S. editions have the same pagination) and the PAN (United Kingdom) paperback edition. The latter was chosen because it was the latest large printing (from 1971), and if it is not in print when this appears, it should still be easier to obtain than the first British editions or the two-volume Macmillan paperback printing (1963). Moreover, the PAN edition incorporates all the changes from the first printings. In 1981, Macmillan (London) reprinted a commemorative edition of the books in two volumes, using the negatives (which were enlarged) from the PAN edition. It, too, can be used with this index.

There are differences between the U.S. and U.K. editions; although, it should be emphasized, not enough to make a major difference one way or the other. The differences are primarily in the area of punctuation and capitalization, but there are a few instances where a name or sentence has been deleted or added. To some extent, these problems determined the methodology of the editor. For instance, the same word is sometimes capitalized in one edition but not in the other. As an example, the word Bible is capitalized in all five entries in *Drums* but in only one of three in the U.S. printing; and in all six entries in PAN's *Sunset and Evening Star* but in only one of six in the U.S. edition. Since I have relied on capitalization to identify proper nouns the resulting problem is obvious.

Various words, and sometimes whole lines and paragraphs, are either misspelled, replaced or added in one edition and not in the other. For instance, "Mrs. Gogan," a character in *The Plough and the Stars*, is given as "Grogan" in the U.S. edition but corrected in the PAN printing. "Aldhelm" is incorrectly spelled in the PAN edition. "Garnett" is given two names, Edward and David (father and son), in all printings of *Inishfallen* and O'Casey apparently means the same person. The chapter title, "House of the Living," in *Drums* (U.S.) is given as "Home of the Living" in PAN. The former appeared in the first British edition though it appears as the latter in the two-volume Macmillan edition, PAN's obvious model. T. C. Murray's name is deleted in a *Sunset* passage (PAN) and the words, "there is nothing to show his identity" are inserted. In the PAN edition (also in the first British edition), there is a line that reads:

> He would leave Lady Gregory watching wild swans rising from the lake, or walking in her Seven Woods of Coole; and the lesser writers, too. . . .

The corresponding line in the U.S. edition reads:

> He would leave Lady Gregory in her Seven Woods of Coole; and the lesser writers, too. . . .

How much of this is O'Casey and how much is the result of careless editing is difficult to ascertain. Most of the inconsistencies occur in the last four books when O'Casey was past sixty—and in the case of *Rose and Crown* and *Sunset* past seventy—years of age. His eyes, bad at their best, may have missed items that would have been caught by someone with better eyesight. The Murray deletion was almost surely O'Casey's wish. He and Murray clashed as far back as 1940[28] and O'Casey may have felt compelled to withdraw his name. The other major differences may have also had O'Casey's hand behind them, such as the change in a chapter title.

There is one deletion, though, which must be attributed to American censorship. In the "Silence" chapter in *Inishfallen*, there is a quote from Cardinal Spellman which is present in all British editions and absent from all American editions. The paragraph begins:

> And they ask, preach, even command tolerance in others than themselves. "The Federal council of Christian Churches who have persuaded President Truman to withdraw the American Envoy, Myron Taylor, from the Holy See, are guilty of intolerance," said Cardinal Spellman. This is a kettle black as hell calling another one as black as night. Catholics are canonically forbidden. . . .

In the American editions this reads:

> And they ask, preach, even command tolerance in others than themselves. Catholics are canonically forbidden. . . .

This deletion should not be surprising. *Inishfallen*, the only autobiographical volume to win any kind of award, was published in 1949 when the United States was in the midst of "witch-hunts," the growth of which was to become McCarthyism, George Kennan's "containment" of Communism policy, and the Cold War. Cardinal Spellman was an immensely powerful spokesman for the right wing, and the publishers obviously felt it was unwise to provoke reactionary forces. The irony of it all is that the deletion occurs in a chapter involving the silencing of a progressive priest, Walter MacDonald, by the Catholic hierarchy.

One central point emerges from this study: there have been several changes in the autobiographies since they first appeared. Moreover, there are several differences between the various editions. Rather than continue reprinting, and by definition repeating, the same errors, it seems sensible to call for a new edition which incorporates all of O'Casey's changes and corrects what are clearly misprints, typographical errors, and differences.

Another major problem that arose in compiling the index was handling

O'Casey's style. The playwright frequently used titles of works for his own
purposes. For example the titles of Daniel Corkery's well-known books, *The
Hidden Ireland* and *The Hounds of Banba*, were used by O'Casey to mean
other things than Corkery intended. In one case the "hidden Ireland"
(O'Casey's non-capitalization) was used to personify Dublin's slums and the
precarious life of the working class. Similarly the "hounds of Banba" were the
Gaelic Leaguers baying at the heels of Walter MacDonald and Michael
O'Hickey. Users of this index should therefore not assume that a title entry of
a song, book, poem, or play is necessarily a discussion of that work. It may be
only O'Casey's use to illustrate a point.

The problem of names invariably confronts the student of O'Casey's
autobiographies. A minor problem is that O'Casey failed to give proper first
names, such as using Dan for Daniel or Bob for Robert. In these cases and in
order to prevent repetition I have used the full proper name in the initial
entry. More difficult, at least for the indexer, is the deliberate misspelling of
last names, such as Loug, Log, and Lug for Cardinal Michael Logue. No easy
formula exists for indexing these variants without cluttering the manuscript
with countless entries listing variables. In general the variants are not so
different as to make the entire name unrecognizable, so I have listed the
proper name in its alphabetical order and the variants within the annotation,
unless the variant is the only name used (see for instance "Markoni").
Sometimes O'Casey used approximations of Irish names. For instance he
always referred to William Patrick Ryan as "O'Ryan" and to Patrick Kearney
as "Cearney." Outside the autobiographies I have found instances where
O'Casey called Ryan by his Irish name, Liam O Riann. Similarly, Kearney's
Irish name is O Cearnaigh, and since he was allegedly one of O'Casey's
instructors in the Irish language, this is probably the name by which O'Casey
knew him. Ryan is listed under Ryan and Kearney is listed under Cearney.

Some decision had to be made about including the bric-a-brac, the
hundreds of minor characters, stores, streets, towns, and states mentioned in
the autobiographies. I decided on the basis of their importance to the books
and to O'Casey's life and plays. I have listed the stores, streets, and towns of
Ireland and England, O'Casey's two residences, but have excluded some
similar material from the United States and other countries. Moreover, nearly
all of the dramatist's childhood friends are excluded except those who figure
prominently (such as George Middleton). On the other hand, none of his
workmates are excluded because there is evidence that he used their charac-
teristics in *The Star Turns Red*. Arizona, New Mexico, Massachusetts, and
Pennsylvania are mentioned in the books but only the latter two have been
listed. Massachusetts is important because of the *Within the Gates* controversy
and because O'Casey visited Harvard University. O'Casey also visited

Pennsylvania, at the home of the American producer of his play, and in Philadelphia where he was reunited with Kitty Curling, one of the actresses in the premiere of *The Plough and the Stars*.

Annotations of the entries have been kept uniformly simple. I have found little reason to extrapolate beyond identification and context in the majority of cases, and it is beyond the scope of this study to treat every entry in minute detail. Where necessary I have referred the reader to more complete explanations. I have tried to avoid repeating data given by O'Casey except where no other information is available. In relatively few cases the words, "appears as," precede the annotation to designate this void. Biographical annotations have been given in the style of *Webster's Biographical Dictionary* (1966). Where appropriate they are slanted towards an Irish context (e.g. Gladstone and Churchill). I have excluded some biographical material of universally known subjects simply because of their prominence and to avoid pedantry. To avoid repetition I have listed the dates of play and book publication only under the author entry. Production dates, such as those by the Abbey Theatre, are given under the theatre entry. Cited works without authorship are the works of O'Casey and may be found in the bibliography.

O'Casey's style has necessitated special arrangements. Songs, poems (as well as partial quotations from both), newspapers, journals, and other items are integral parts of the autobiographies, and I have included several appendices to handle these.

Appendix I: Songs and tunes are listed alphabetically.

Appendix II: Throughout the books, O'Casey sets lines from poems, songs and essays *apart* from the body of the text. In general they are always noticeable though rarely are they titled; they are listed as they appear.

Appendix III: O'Casey also incorporates lines from or allusions to songs and poems *into* the body of his writing. They are almost always less distinguishable than the entries of appendices I and II. I have also used this appendix to identify items that are not indexable in the conventional sense; they are listed as they appear.

Appendix IV: Newspapers and journals are listed alphabetically.

Appendix V: O'Casey's works—plays, books and articles—mentioned or alluded to are listed alphabetically.

Appendix VI: Essential data on O'Casey including age, place of employment, and residence portrayed in the respective chapters are broken down chapter-by-chapter.

Appendix VII: Bibliography.

Throughout this study, the first numbers refer to the PAN edition; those numbers in parentheses are from the U.S. edition. Roman numerals refer to the respective book:

I: *I Knock at the Door*

II: *Pictures in the Hallway*

III: *Drums under the Windows*

IV: *Inishfallen, Fare Thee Well*

V: *Rose and Crown*

VI: *Sunset and Evening Star.*

NOTES

1. Roy Pascal, *Design and Truth in Autobiography* (Cambridge, Mass.: Harvard University Press, 1960), p. 151.

2. *New York Times*, 25 September 1964, p. 40.

3. Brooks Atkinson, in a review of *Inishfallen, Fare Thee Well, New York Times*, 27 February 1949. See also his reviews of other volumes in the same paper, 22 September 1946, 14 September 1952, and 11 November 1954.

4. Hubert Nicholson, "O'Casey's Horn of Plenty," in Ronald Ayling, ed., *Sean O'Casey*, Modern Judgments Series (Nashville, Tenn.: Aurora Publishers, Inc., 1969), p. 207.

5. Pascal, p. 182.

6. Ibid., p. 193.

7. Ayling, Introduction to *Sean O'Casey*, pp. 33, 39.

8. Quoted by Pascal, p. 182.

9. Ayling, Introduction to *Sean O'Casey*, p. 35.

10. Pascal, pp. 16, 188.

11. Michael McCarthy, *Five Years in Ireland* (Dublin, 1902), p. 73.

12. Sean O'Casey, *Letters of Sean O'Casey*, vol. I, ed. David Krause (London, Cassells, 1976), p. 684.

13. Ibid., pp. 677-78.

14. Desmond Fitzgerald, *Memoirs of Desmond Fitzgerald* (Dublin, 1968), p. 21.

15. Sean O'Casey, "Cockadoodle Doo," in *Blasts and Benedictions*, ed. Ronald Ayling (London: Macmillan, 1967), p. 145, emphasis added.

16. Sean O'Casey to Frank Hugh O'Donnell, University of Delaware Special Collections, emphasis added.

17. Ronald Ayling, *Continuity and Innovation in Sean O'Casey's Drama* (Austria: Institut fur Englische Sprache und Literatur, Universitat Salzburg, 1976), p. 49.

18. Sean O'Casey, "Art Is the Song of Life," in *Blasts and Benedictions*, p. 78.

19. Ibid.

20. Pascal, p. 187.

21. Eric Bentley, *New Republic*, 12 October 1952, emphasis added.

22. Padraic Colum, "Sean O'Casey's Narratives," in *Sean O'Casey*, p. 226, emphasis added.

23. O'Casey, *Letters*, p. 783.

24. See Jim Scrimgeour, "Characterization in the Autobiographies," *Sean O'Casey Review*, 4, no. 1 (Fall 1977): 57-65.

25. In a letter to Brooks Atkinson (*Letters*, p. 792), O'Casey writes that it was his first article (a "satiric fantasy") which convinced him that he could write.

26. O'Casey gives an extensive reading list in his *Pictures in the Hallway* (New York: Macmillan, 1942), p. 187.

27. In an interview with the *Observer*, 6 October 1929, O'Casey said: "I have also written part of an autobiography." This is undoubtedly the first public mention of it.

28. O'Casey, *Letters*, pp. 876-77.

SEAN O'CASEY'S
AUTOBIOGRAPHIES

ANNOTATED INDEX

A

AARON'S ROD
In the Old Testament, a rod which turned into a serpent and by which Aaron surpassed the performances of the Egyptian magician before Pharaoh (Exodus 8:10).

II: 69	(101)
III: 32, 222	(39, 330)
V: 31	(31)

ABBEY STREET
Lower, Middle and Upper.

II: 22, 127, 133	(26, 194, 204)
IV: 75, 285	(95, 395)

ABBEY THEATRE
Most famous of Dublin theatres and center of the Irish dramatic movement. Founded (1899) by Yeats, Lady Gregory and the Fay Brothers, the Abbey sought to present Irish plays by Irish dramatists on Irish subjects with Irish actors and actresses. The Abbey has been the scene of several of O'Casey's premieres including: The Shadow of a Gunman (12 April 1923), Kathleen Listens In (1 October 1923), Juno and the Paycock (3 March 1924), Nannie's Night Out (29 September 1924), The Plough and the Stars (8 February 1926), and The End of the Beginning (8 February 1937). For a closer look at the dramatist and his relationship with the Abbey, see Ronald Ayling's article, "Sean O'Casey and the Abbey Theatre, Dublin," in Dalhousie Review, Spring 1972. For a complete record of O'Casey's plays at the Abbey (through 1979), see Sean O'Casey, Centenary Essays (1980).

III:	and Playboy riots (see SYNGE)	121, 124-8	(176, 181-6)
	and Shaw*	174	(257)
IV:	as one of four symbols		
	in O'Casey's life	76	(98)
	returns The Frost and the Flower	114	(152)
	comments on The Harvest Festival	115	(153)
	and Gunman premiere	122-4, 168-9	(163-5, 229-30)

MORE

ABBEY THEATRE (cont.)

description of	167-8	(227-8)
and Juno premiere	170, 187	(231-2, 255)
and Plough premiere	127, 172-7,	(170, 235-41,
	280-1	387-9)
	V: 235	(V: 315)
and Man and Superman affair		
(revived 10 August 1925)	183-4, 280	(249-50, 388)
V: and rejection of Silver Tassie	31-4, 38, 40-1	(32-6, 41, 45)
(see Letters, I, pp. 225-326)	VI: 161, 180	(VI: 226, 254)
and production of Tassie		
(opened 12 August 1935)	46-52	(53-61)
and Within the Gates	44	(49)
and Juno (see SINCLAIR, ARTHUR)	105-6	(136-7)
and tours	108, 121-2	(140, 157-8)
VI: and Gate Theatre	78	(104-5)
and Bealtaine*	79	(105)

Mentioned: IV: 117-8, 144, 164, 194,   (156, 195, 223, 266, 275,
               201, 260, 283, 285   360, 391, 394)
           V: 18, 43, 54, 75, 116, 118 (15, 48, 64, 93, 151, 154)
          VI: 108, 215   (148, 309)

ABDEL - KADAR
c.1807 - 1883. Algerian Arab leader against French colonialism. O'Casey's
description of him is directly from the first verse of Thomas Davis's*
song, "Ballad of Freedom."

III: 32-3   (41)

ABDIEL
The seraph in John Milton's* Paradise Lost.

II: 121   (187)

ABELARD, PIERRE
1079 - 1142. French philosopher and theologian whose secret marriage
to Heloise has been a theme for many works of literature.

V: 193, 204   (258, 273)
VI: 133   (184)

ABERCORN HOSPITAL
This is almost surely Adelaide Hospital.* O'Casey lived at 18 Abercorn
Road.

I: 12   (6)

ABERCORNS
Scottish peerage borne by members of the Hamilton family. One of the
latest, Albert Edward Hamilton (1869-1953), was governor of Northern
Ireland (1922-45).

IV: 274   (380)

ABRAHAM, ISAAC AND JOSEPH
From the Bible. Abraham was the traditional patriarch of the Jews and
the father of Isaac, who in turn was the father of Joseph.

VI: 32   (36)

ACHILLES
In Greek mythology, son of Peleus and Thetis; bravest, handsomest and
swiftest of the army of Agamemnon. See also HYDE PARK (#).

I: 76   (111)
V: 77#   (97#)

ACT OF UNION
An act (1800) which merged the English and Irish parliaments following
a widespread outbreak of rebellion by the United Irishmen* against
England. Throughout the 19th century, repeal of the Act of Union was
one of primary demands of Irish separatist movements.

III: 15   (13)

ACTS OF THE APOSTLES
In the Bible, a book of the New Testament written by Luke. It is a
history of the early progress of Christianity after the ascension of
Christ.

IV: 265   (366)

ACTON, LORD JOHN
1834 - 1902. English historian and leader of liberal English Catholics
who were hostile to the dogma of papal infallibility.

IV: 252   (348)
V: 142   (187)

ADAM AND EVE
Sometimes one is given without the other.

III: 123, 177, 179, 180-6, 242   (179, 260, 264-75, 362)
IV: 227   (312)
V: 144   (189-90)
VI: 51, 56, 70, 159, 196   (64, 72, 92-3, 223, 279)

ADAMI, MADAME
Pianist who often assisted O'Casey with the music in his plays and as
accompanist at rehearsals.

V: 125-6   (162-5)

ADELAIDE HOSPITAL
Located on Peter Street, Dublin. Designed for Protestants only with a
capacity of 135 beds, although its dispensaries were open to the poor
of all religions. O'Casey mistakenly calls it Abercorn Hospital.#

I: 12#   (6#)
II: 149-53   (229-42)
III: 246, 258   (368, 386)

ADDISON, JOSEPH
1672 - 1719. Celebrated English essayist and poet.

IV: 170   (231)

ADELPHI TERRACE
George Bernard Shaw's* home (#10), from 1896 to 1927. Located in
London overlooking Victoria Gardens and Victoria Embankment.

VI: 164   (231)

AENGUS OG
In Irish mythology, son of the Dagda* and the Irish god of love.
Accompanied by four birds flying over his head.

III: 65, 129   (90, 187)

AESCHYLUS
525 - 456 B.C. Celebrated Greek dramatist.

V: 103   (133)

AESCULAPIUS
In Greek mythology, the god of medicine. Son of Apollo* and Coronis.*

I: 10   (3)

AFGHANISTAN/AFGHAN 'N BURMAN MEDALS
O'Casey is referring (#) to the ribbons from a series of 19th century
British campaigns in Afghanistan and Burma. There were wars in both
countries from the 1830s to the 1890s resulting from British attempts
to "pacify" the two nations.

I: 68, 158#   (97, 244#)

AFRICA
VI: 23, 130, 176   (22, 181, 249)

AGATE, JAMES
1877 - 1947. Dramatic critic for the London Sunday Times (1923-47) and
the most powerful English critic of his day. The title of O'Casey's
book, The Flying Wasp (1937), is taken from Agate's statement: "There is
a nest of wasps that must be smoked out because it is doing the theatre
infinite harm." According to Agate, his name is mentioned in Wasp 166
times (his office boy counted them). For more on O'Casey and Agate,
see Letters, I, pp. 657-66. For more on the Purple Dust controversy (#),
see Agate's article in the Sunday Times, 19 April 1942, and O'Casey's
reply, 26 April and 10 May.

V: 23, 25, 26   (21, 23-4, 25)
VI: 117-8#, 163, 164   (161-2#, 230, 231)
My Theatre Talks (1933) V: 20 (17)

AGHADOE
Irish town near Killarney in Co. Kerry.

III: 61   (85)

AGRICOLA, GNAEUS JULIUS
37 - 93. Roman soldier. Subject of Tacitus's _Agricola_.

II: 88   (131)

AHERNE, JOHN
More usually found as Owen Aherne. With Michael Robartes* the symbolic
antinomous personages who figure prominently in many of Yeats's* works.

V: 87   (110)

AIDEEN'S GRAVE
Poem by Samuel Ferguson.* In Irish mythology Aideen was the wife of
Oscar and daughter-in-law of Oisin.* She was buried at Ben Edar (Howth)
where a large dolmen was raised over her grave.

V: 173   (230)

ALABAMA
In its context O'Casey refers to its well-know reputation as a place
of inequity and suppression of blacks.

V: 231-3   (311-13)

ALADDIN
From _The Arabian Nights Entertainment_.

IV: 235   (325)

ALBAN
Ancient name for Scotland.

V: 93   (119)

ALBERT HALL
In Kensington Gore, the largest concert hall in London.

VI: 115   (158)

ALBERT,PRINCE
A reference to the Albert Memorial in Hyde Park, London. Unveiled
(1876) for Albert Francis Charles Augustus Emmanuel of Saxe-Coburg-Gotha
(1819 - 1861), husband of Queen Victoria.* In his article, "Culture Inc."
in _Under a Colored Cap_, O'Casey refers to the Albert Memorial as a
"gigantic empire and colonial Peter Pan."

V: 77   (97)

ALBIGENSES
Heretical sect of the 12th and 13th centuries against which a crusade
was launched.

II: 221   (343)

ALCANTARA
Town in western Spain which once belonged to the Knights of Alcantara,
a military-religious order.

IV: 221   (304)

ALCIBIADES
450 - 404 B.C. Athenian captain in Shakespeare's* play, Timon of Athens.

II: 108   (164)

ALCUIN
735 - 804. English theologian and scholar.

VI: 204   (291)

ALDBOROUGH BARRACKS
The Aldborough House in Portland Row in northeast Dublin. Built (1798)
by Lord Aldborough and used a military barracks.

III: 41   (53)

ALDHELM
c.640 - 709. English scholar and author of Latin verse and a treatise
on Latin prosody, including his famous 101 riddles.

VI: 204   (291)

ALEXANDER THE GREAT
356 - 323 B.C. Macedonian ruler and conquerer of most of his known world.

II: 88   (131)

ALEXANDRA
1844 - 1925. Eldest daughter of Christian IX of Denmark. Queen consort
of Edward VII* of England whom she married (1863) when he was Prince of
Wales.

I: 181   (279)

ALFRED
849 - 899. Called Alfred the Great after wars (866) against invading
Danes. Sovereign of England and active in compiling laws and promoting
scholarship.

V: 163   (216)

ALICE IN WONDERLAND
Also given as BLUNDERLAND (#). From Alice's Adventures in Wonderland
(1865) by Lewis Carroll (1832 - 1898). See also the line: "through
the looking glass," VI: 116 (159).

IV: 96   (126)
VI: 142#   (198#)

ALINGTON, CYRIL ARGENTINE
1872 - 1955. Dean of Durham University, England, and author of several
popular fictional works.

V: 143   (189)

ALL FOR IRELAND LEAGUE
Founded (1909) by independent Irish nationalists who were led by William
O'Brien,* Tim Healy,* and others who were dissatisfied with the efforts
of John Redmond's* Irish Parliamentary Party to gain Home Rule.

III: 14, 102   (12, 146)

ALL SAINTS CHURCH
Church of All Saints on Phibsborough Road, Dublin.

III: 207   (307)

ALLGOOD, SARA
1883 - 1950. Abbey Theatre actress who studied with Frank J. Fay and
joined the Abbey in 1903. Appeared in many productions of the Abbey
where she had a long illustrous career before leaving for Hollywood.
In O'Casey's premieres, she played the roles of Juno in Juno and the
Paycock and the Irish Nannie in Nannie's Night Out. Her last stage
appearance was opposite Barry Fitzgerald* in Juno in New York (1940).

IV: 185-6   (253)

ALMA-TADEMA, SIR LAWRENCE
1836 - 1912. Dutch painter whose work dealt with Frankish subjects
and (after 1865) studies of Greek and Roman life.

VI: 202   (288)

ALOYSIUS, FATHER
Capuchin priest. Bearer, with Father Augustine, of surrender orders from
Pearse* to Thomas MacDonagh* (at Jacob's factory) after the capitulation
of the G.P.O. in the Easter Rising. With James Connolly at the time of
his death. See his "Personal Recollections" in Capuchin Annual, 1966.

III: 282   (423)

AMALEKITES
In the Bible, ancient nomads who were doomed to destruction after the
attack on the Israelites under Joshua.

I: 93   (138)

AMALFI, ARCHBISHOPRIC OF
The Italian town of Amalfi, an archbishopric. O'Casey is alluding to
Webster's* play, The Duchess of Malfi.

IV: 254   (351)

AMERICAN CONSTITUTION
II: 88   (131)
V: 181   (240)

AMERICAN VICTORY LOAN
The "Victory Fund," established in the U.S. by Irish and Irish-American
groups during the Irish War of Independence (1918-21). Two of the central organizations directing the several millions of dollars collected
were the Friends of Irish Freedom and the American Committee for Relief
in Ireland. Much of the money passed into the account of the Free State
government after the signing of the Anglo-Irish Treaty.

IV: 157   (213)

AMERSHAM
Town in Buckinghamshire, England.

V: 133, 137   (175, 180)

AMIENS STREET
In east central Dublin, leading northeast from the Custom House.

II: 55   (78)

AMIENS STREET STATION
Now Connolly Station. Terminal of the Great Northern Railway (where
O'Casey worked) with trains to Belfast and the north of Ireland.

II: 170   (261)

AMSTERDAM
V: 94   (120)

ANCIENT OF DAYS
A term mentioned three times in the Bible (Daniel 7:9, 13, 22) as a
title of God in his capacity as Judge of the World. Also found in
AE's* poem, "Hope in Failure."

IV: 196   (269)

ANCIENT ORDER OF HIBERNIANS
One of the oldest of Irish organizations and presently a fraternal order
limited to Catholics. Progressive Irish, like O'Casey, regarded it as
a sectarian organization similar to its Protestant counterpart, the
Orange Order.

III: 65, 152   (90, 224)

ANDERSON, JOHN
1896 - 1943. American dramatic critic for the New York Evening Post
(1924) and the New York Journal (from 1928).

V: 181   (241)

ANDREIEV, LEONID N.
1871 - 1919. Russian novelist, short story writer and dramatist. First
stories published by Maxim Gorky. Bitter opponent of the Bolshevik
Revolution (1917).

The Life of Man (1906) IV: 125   (167)

ANDROMEDA
In Greek legend, the daughter of Cepheus and Cassiopeia who was offered
as a sacrifice to a sea monster but was rescued by Perseus.

IV: 136   (183)

ANGELS OF MONS
Novel (1915) by Arthur Machen (1863 - 1947), Welsh short story writer.

VI: 156   (274)

ANGUS OF THE GOLDEN HAIR
In Irish mythology, the Celtic god of youth, beauty and poetry.

IV: 200   (274)

ANJOU
French noble family established in the 9th century.

V: 187-8   (249-50)

ANNA LIFFEY MINSTREL TROUPE
Late 19th century Dublin dramatic and minstrel group.

II: 132   (203)

ANNA LIVIA PLURABELLE
In Dublin, the River Liffey.*

III: 114, 141   (165, 206)
IV: 92   (121)
VI: 69   (91)

ANNABEL LEE
Probably from the poem of the same name by Edgar Allen Poe (1809 - 1849).

V: 158   (209)

ANTHONY OF AGHADOE
Probably a variant on St. Anthony.*

IV: 67   (85)

ANTHONY, MARK
One of the triumvirs after Caesar's death in Shakespeare's Julius Caesar.

II: 131   (202)

ANTRIM
County in the north of Ireland and site of a major battle in the
1798 Rebellion.

IV: 66   (82)
VI: 76   (102)

APOLLO
In Greek and Roman mythology, one of the great Olympian gods.

VI: 71   (94)

APPIAN WAY
In Ranelagh, on the outskirts of Dublin, leading into Leeson Street.

IV: 105   (138)

APPLESEED, JOHNNY
Nickname of John Chapman (1774 - 1847), American pioneer and subject
of many legends for allegedly ranging over the country and planting
apple seeds.

V: 180   (239)
VI: 177   (250)

APPRENTICE BOYS
A group of thirteen Protestant boys who shut the gates (12 August 1689)
of the Derry garrison against James II's* troups which began the Siege
of Derry.✣ Still celebrated every year by the Orange Order.

III: 189   (280)

ARABI PASHA
c.1841 - 1911. Egyptian revolutionary and leader of rebel forces
against England at Tell el-Kebir (1882).

I: 75   (109)

ARABIA
III: 273   (410)
IV: 31   (33)

ARABIAN NIGHTS ENTERTAINMENT, THE
Ancient collection of tales of Persian, Indian and Arabian origin, held
together by Scheherazade, the story teller.

IV: 235, 274   (325, 379)
VI: 90   (121)

ARAN ISLANDS
Off the west coast of Ireland and one of the last Gaelic-speaking areas
of the country.

III: 101, 228   (145, 340)
V: 174   (231)

ARCHBISHOP OF CANTERBURY
William Cosmo Gordon Lang, first baron of Lambeth. 1865 - 1945. O'Casey
may be alluding (#) to Lang's sudden recovery from fifth-nerve neuralgia,
acute fibrositis and shingles in 1932, coinciding with the victory of
the Conservative Party in the election.

V: 77#, 112   (96#, 146)

ARCHER, WILLIAM
1856 - 1924. British dramatic critic and translator of Ibsen (1906-08).
Dramatic critic for London Figaro, World, Tribune and Nation.

V: 23-4   (22-3)
The Old Drama and the New (1923) V: 24, 234   (22-3, 314)

ARDAGH/ARDAGH CHALICE
Irish town near Killarney. Site of the Ardagh Chalice,an ancient
ecclesiastical treasure of metal work.

III: 201   (298)
VI: 216   (309)

ARDEE
In Irish, Ath Fherdia, the place in Co. Louth where Ferdia* died.

III: 242   (361)

ARDILAUN, LORD
Sir Arthur Edward Guinness. 1840 - 1915. Famous Irish brewer and benefactor to Dublin and the Church of Ireland. O'Casey refers to the opening of St. Stephen's Green in Dublin as a public park which was made
possible, in part, by Guinness who secured legislation (1877) opening
the grounds to the public and who also financed much of the landscaping
costs.

III: 103   (149)
IV: 274   (379)

ARDRAHAN
Irish hamlet in Co. Galway on the Galway-Limerick Road. Eight miles
north of Gort.

III: 103   (148)
IV: 131   (176)

ARGO
A Bristol steamship which was usually moored at the Custom House quay
in Dublin.

II: 106   (161)

ARIOSTO, LODOVICO
1474 - 1533. Noted Italian poet.

III: 183   (270)

ARISTOTLE
III: 62   (86)
IV: 227   (313)
VI: 205   (293)

ARMAGH
County in the north of Ireland and Ireland's ecclesiastical center.

III: 106, 132, 155, 176, 202, 240   (152, 194, 227, 260, 298, 358)
IV: 13, 68, 150, 274   (8, 86, 203, 379)
V: 165   (218)

ARMSTRONG, ARTHUR
Appears as a manager of the Olympic Theatre, Dublin.

III: 14   (8)

ARNAUD, YVONNE
1892 - 1958. French-born actress who spent her professional life in
London. Outstanding performances include Mrs. Pepys in And So to Bed
and the Duchess of Tann in The Improper Duchess.

V: 26   (26)

ARNHEM
In the Netherlands, site of important battles in World War I and II.

IV: 17   (12)

ARNOLD, SIDNEY
Appears as a member of the Socialist Party of Ireland.*

IV: 14   (8)

ARNOTT & CO.
Drapery firm at 11-15 Henry Street, Dublin, from which the uniforms for
the Irish Citizen Army* were order. The uniforms were dark green (darker
than those of the Irish Volunteers) and members wore a slough hat with
one side turned up and pinned with a Red Hand union badge. Members paid
for them by weekly contribution. Before the uniforms, rank and file
members wore linen armlets with "I.C.A." embroidered on them. Officers
wore red armbands.

II: 71, 116, 160   (105, 176, 247)
III: 228, 229   (340-2)

ARRAH-NA-POGUE COELI
Arrah-na-Pogue is the title of a play by Dion Boucicault.* Ara Coeli is
the residence of the archbishop of Armagh, Co. Armagh, Ireland.

IV: 263   (364)

ARTANE REFORMATORY
The O'Brien Institute for Destitute Catholic Children in Artane.

III: 188   (278)

ARTEGALL
Personification of justice in Edmund Spenser's* Faerie Queen.

V: 77, 214   (97, 286)

ARTFUL DODGER
In Dickens's* Oliver Twist, the character Jack Dawkins who leads Oliver
to Fagin.

VI: 209   (298)

ARTICLES OF ASSOCIATION
Also known as the Anglo-Irish Treaty and most frequently referred to
simply as "The Treaty." Signed (6 December 1921) by representatives of
the Irish Free State and the British government, the treaty consisted
of 18 articles, few of which were not hotly contested by the Irish
representatives when it was presented for ratification. The most controversial articles were: the oath to be taken by the parliamentary
representatives in Ireland and the acceptance of the Government of Ireland Act (1920) which created Northern Ireland. The Free State's
ratification of the treaty plunged Ireland into a civil war. The full
text of the treaty is given in Macardle, The Irish Republic. See also
DOCUMENT NO. 2 and TREATY.

IV: 83   (106)

AS OTHERS SEE US
Short sketch (1926) by Ronald Jeans (1887 - ?), English dramatist.

V: 20   (17)

ASCHAM, ROGER
1515 - 1568. English scholar and author of an influential treatise on
practical education, The Scholemaster (1570).

VI: 61   (79)

ASHE, THOMAS
1885 - 1917. As an officer in the Irish Volunteers in the Easter Rising,
Ashe led an attack against Ashbourne police barracks. He was arrested,
sentenced to life imprisonment, but released during a general amnesty.
He was arrested again in August 1917 and sentenced to one year imprisonment in Mountjoy Jail. On September 17, he began a hunger strike and
died on September 25 from forced feedings and beatings. O'Casey's early
publications eulogized his friend in two laments: Thomas Ashe and The
Sacrifice of Thomas Ashe (both 1918).

IV: 16, 18   (11, 13)

ASIA
VI: 23, 130   (22, 181)

ASQUITH, HERBERT HENRY
1852 - 1928. English politician and prime minister (1908-16). Quashed
Irish Home Rule efforts at the outbreak of World War I by forestalling
MORE

ASQUITH (cont.)

implementation of a Home Rule bill. In 1926 he presented O'Casey with
the Hawthornden Prize for <u>Juno and the Paycock</u>. For his remarks see
<u>The Times</u>, 24 March 1926.

III: 248-9, 254, 267   (371-2, 380-1, 400)

ASQUITH, MARGARET
1864 - 1945. Second wife (from 1894) of Herbert Asquith.* Author and
activist in English politics. Margot Asquith is the "English authority"
quoted in "St. Vincent Provides a Bed," though O'Casey misquotes her. It
should be "standing up on their chairs" rather than "cheers." (#) The
source is her <u>Autobiography</u> (1920), the chapter "The Veto of the House
of Lords."

III: 250#, 255   (373#, 381)

ASSOCIATION OF NATIONAL SCHOOLTEACHERS
Probably the Irish National Teachers Organization at 9 Gardiner Place,
Dublin, which was founded in 1868. See O'Casey's article, "Room for the
Teachers," in <u>Feathers from a Green Crow</u>.

III: 155   (227)

ASSYRIA, KING OF
Sennacherib, king of Assyria (705-681 B.C.), who invaded Palestine,
capturing many Judah cities (2 Kings 18:13), was repelled but later
launched another campaign against Jerusalem (2 Kings 19).

V: 91   (116)

ASTON'S QUAY
In Dublin across the River Liffey from Bachelor's Walk.

IV: 232   (320)

ASTOR, LADY
Vicountess Nancy Langhorne. 1879 - 1964. First woman to sit in the
British Parliament. See O'Casey's letters to her in <u>Letters</u>, I.

V: 131   (172)

ATAHUALPA
c.1500 - 1533. Last Inca king of Peru. Killed by Pizarro when he refused to become a Christian.

III: 90   (129)

ATHANASIAN CREED
Christian creed in Europe about 400 A.D. relating to the Trinity and the
Incarnation. O'Casey also gives its Latin name, <u>Quicunque Vult</u>.

I: 117   (177)
II: 231   (358)
IV: 227   (313)
VI: 58   (74-5)

ATHENS
II: 88, 221   (132, 342)
V: 238   (321)

ATHENRY
Irish town in Co. Galway.

IV: 129, 131, 192, 194   (172, 175, 262, 265)

ATHLONE
Irish town in Co. Westmeath on the Shannon River. The Siege of Athlone
(#) occurred during the Jacobite Wars when a dozen men held the bridge
entering the city against the army of William of Orange in 1691.

II: 236#   (367#)
III: 32#   (39#)
VI: 25   (25)

ATKINSON, J. BROOKS
b. 1894. Dramatic critic for the New York Times (1925-60) and a close
friend of the O'Caseys. Author of over 60 articles, essays and reviews
on the dramatist which were collected in Sean O'Casey, From Times Past,
Robert G. Lowery, ed. (1982).

V: 239   (322)
Once Around the Sun (1951) VI: 173   (245)

ATTLEE, CLEMENT
1883 - 1967. English politician and prime minister (1945-51).

V: 93, 94, 165   (120, 218)
VI: 81   (108)

ATTWATER, DONALD
b.1892. Author of several books on the Catholic Church, its saints,
and various other religious topics. O'Casey is quoting from Attwater's
article in Studies (December 1939).

The Catholic Eastern Churches (1937) V: 226-7   (304)

AUGHRIM, BATTLE OF
In Co. Galway, a decisive Irish defeat by the forces of William III*
under General Codert Ginkel* over those of James II* under General St.
Ruth.* The defeat at the Pass of Aughrim forced the Irish army to re-
group at Limerick, and shortly thereafter (3 October 1691), the Treaty
of Limerick was signed, ending the Jacobite Wars in Ireland.

II: 87, 236   (130, 367)
III: 37   (48)
VI: 120   (165)

AUNGIER STREET
In south Dublin near Dublin Castle. Birthplace of Irish poet, Thomas
Moore.*

I: 49   (67)

AURICULA, FATHER
Character in O'Casey's half-mythical exploration of religion. An auricular confession is the confession of one's sins privately to a confessor rather than publicly.

V: 152-3, 158   (200-2, 209)

AUSTIN FRIARS
Friars Hermits of the Order of St. Augustine of Hippo. Founded 1253.

V: 74   (92)

AUXILIARIES
The Auxiliary Division of the Royal Irish Constabulary, more familiarly known as "the Auxies." They were special British forces stationed in Ireland during the Irish War of Independence to deal with I.R.A. rebels, and were as tough and ruthless as the Black and Tans.* Their commanding officer, Brigadier-General E. F. Crozier, resigned his post rather than continue leading what he described as a drunken and insubordinate body of men. Formed in 1920.

IV: 63, 64, 68   (52, 53, 56)
V: 224   (301)

AYOT ST. LAWRENCE
George Bernard Shaw's* home in Herefordshire, England, where he lived from 1906 until his death in 1950.

VI: 175, 183, 184, 185   (247, 260, 261, 262, 263)

AZRAEL
Found in various Judaic and Islamic writings as the angel who separates the soul from the body at the moment of death.

IV: 54   (65)

B

BABBITT, LAND OF
From the character, George F. Babbitt, in Sinclair Lewis's novel, Babbitt (1922); a business or professional man conforming unthinkingly to bourgeois standards.

V: 180   (239)

BABEL
In the Old Testament, the Tower of Babel was built in the valley of Shinar by the descendants of Noah who sought a way to reach heaven. In O'Casey's play, Cock-a-Doodle Dandy (1949), there is a character named Shanaar.

IV: 265   (366)
V: 186   (248)

BABYLON/BABYLONIANS
II: 87, 88, 231   (131, 358)
V: 135   (178)

BACH, JOHANN SEBASTIAN
IV: 23   (20)
VI: 175   (247)

BACHELOR'S WALK
In Dublin, on the north bank of the River Liffey. Here British forces
(Socttish Borderers) fired into an unarmed crowd in July, 1914, killing
and wounding several Irish civilians. "Remember Bachelor's Walk" became
a slogan of Irish republicans in the ensuing years.

II: 126   (193)

BACKS, THE
At Cambridge University, a stretch of the Cam river running along the
backs of several colleges.

VI: 50, 52   (63, 65)

BAGGOT STREET
In south Dublin, north of the Grand Canal.

IV: 20   (17)

BAGNAL, DICK
Appears as one of O'Casey's fellow workers.

III: 22   (24)

BAKECOBS
Variant on the bakery of Jacobs.*

III: 104   (149)

BALAAM
In the Bible, a diviner summoned by Moabite king Balak to curse the
Israelites. (Numbers 22-24)

V: 50   (58)

BALACLAVA
In Russia, where O'Casey's uncle was wounded during the Crimean War.*

V: 36   (39)
VI: 103   (142)

BALDWIN, STANLEY
1867 - 1947. English politician. Prime minister (1923-4, 1924-9, 1935-7).

V: 77-88, 91, 92, 94, 100   (96-110, 117, 118, 121, 128)

BALFOUR, ARTHUR JAMES
1848 - 1930. British politician. Conservative M.P. and prime minister
(1902-05). Author of Balfour Declaration (1917) favoring establishment
of Jewish homeland in Palestine.

III: 75, 76, 248   (106-7, 371)
IV: 275   (380)
VI: 165   (233)

BALL, JOHN
d.1381. English priest and expounder of doctrines of Wycliffe; influential in Wat Tyler's* rebellion for which he was executed.

VI: 102   (140)

BALL, SIR ROBERT S.
1840 - 1913. Noted Irish astronomer and mathematician.

The Story of the Heavens (1885) II: 87, 122   (130, 187)

BALLAGHADERREEN
Cathedral town in the Diocese of Achonry. According to O'Casey's notebooks, a "Ballaghaderreen policeman" was "one from this tiny town in
a wild part of Mayo, the far west. Such a one, as distinct from a
Dublin man, would be mystified by what he saw passing, looming up before
him in the cool mist of the morning." (Eileen O'Casey, Sean, pp. 278-9)

V: 89   (113)

BALLINA
Irish town in Co. Mayo. Captured by the French during the 1798 Rebellion.

I: 42   (54)

BALLINAMUCK
Irish town in Co. Longford. Site of the French army defeat during the
1798 Rebellion.

III: 101   (145)

BALLIOL COLLEGE
Constituent college of Oxford University.

III: 248   (371)

BALLYBOUGH
Northeastern suburb of Dublin. The Ballybough Bridge is over the River
Tolka at the eastern end of Clonliffe Road and dates from 1488.

II: 205   (318)
III: 206   (305)

BALLYNEETY
Irish town in Co. Limerick. Where Sarsfield* broke up the train of
William of Orange* before the Siege of Limerick.*

II: 236   (367)

BALLYNOY, BESSIE
Appears as a neighbor of O'Casey at 35 Mountjoy Square, Dublin. She is
a composite of two women O'Casey knew. According to Cowasjee, one of
the women was Mrs. Schweppe of the same address. However, in a review
of Cowasjee's book, Ronald Ayling disputes this assertion (see Drama
Survey, Fall 1965).

IV: 50-63   (66-78)

BALLYRAGGETT HOUSE
Unknown.

II: 136   (208)

BALLYVOURNEY
Irish town in Co. Cork.

III: 101, 151   (145, 222)
V: 238   (321)
VI: 76   (101)

BALOR OF THE EVIL EYE/OF THE BLOWS
Irish mythological figure. One of the gods of death and of the under-
world. So named because the gaze of his one eye could slay those on
whom he looked in anger. Killed by his grandson, Lugh of the Long
Arm.*

III: 33, 65   (41, 90)
VI: 63   (82)

BALZAC, HONORE
II: 122   (187)
IV: 75   (95)

BANAGHER
Irish town in Co. Offaly.

III: 106   (152)

BANBA/BANBANIANS
Legendary first settlers of Ireland with her sisters Erin and Fotha.
Known as the Queen of the Tuatha de Danann, a mythical prehistoric
race of heroes. Often used as a poetic name for Ireland and a word
which O'Casey might use derisively. Banba was also the name of a monthly
journal of the Keating Branch of the Gaelic League which was hostile to
the Executive Committee of the League.

III: 32, 142, 152, 174   (40, 209, 224, 257)
V: 172   (230)

BANBA HALL
20 Rutland (Parnell) Square, Dublin, a center for nationalist activities
during the early part of the 20th century.

III: 206   (305)

BANCROFT, SIR SQUIRE
1841 - 1926. English actor and prominent theatre manager. According
to O'Casey, Bancroft died the day O'Casey entered the Garrick Club
(19 April).

V: 22   (19-20)

BANK OF IRELAND
Located at College Green, Dublin. Until 1800, the Parliament House
of Ireland.

I: 58, 181-2   (81, 280)
II: 67   (98)
III: 14, 172, 276   (12, 254, 413)
IV: 90-1, 149   (118, 201)
V: 39   (43)
VI: 139, 207   (195, 295)

BANNERMAN, SIR HENRY CAMPBELL
1836 - 1908. British politician. Chief secretary for Ireland (1884-85);
prime minister (1905-08). Supported Gladstone's* Home Rule policies.

III: 248   (371)
VI: 165   (233)

BANTRY BAY
Site of French landing in Co. Cork with a contingent of soldiers who
supported the United Irishmen in the 1798 Rebellion. Alluded to in
the first line of the popular Irish song, "The Shan Van Vocht," as
"The French are on the bay."

I: 178   (274)
III: 158   (233)
IV: 177   (241)

BARDOLPH
Companion of Falstaff in Shakespeare's* plays.

V: 23   (20)

BARLOW, SEAN
Noted stage designer, scene painter, settings expert and occasional
Abbey Theatre actor who was with the Abbey at its inception (1904).

IV: 184   (250-1)

BARRETT, STIFFUN
Stephen J. Barrett, treasurer of the Gaelic League (from 1898). d.1921.
Barrett was a landlord of a house in Blessington Street, Dublin, and
was attacked in the Irish Worker as "The Modern Gael" (18 January 1913).

III: 111   (161)

BARROW
Irish river in Leinster province.

IV: 233   (321)

BARRY, FATHER ROBERT
Parish priest of Oldcastle, Co. Meath.

III: 154   (226)

BASTILLE
The prison tower in Paris,the storming of which in July 1789 signaled
the beginnings of the French Revolution.

III: 17, 32, 188   (17, 40, 278)
V: 83   (105)

BASUTONIANS
From Basutoland, South Africa. Allies of England in the Boer War.

II: 198   (305)

BATH
City and county borough in southwest England in Somersetshire. An
ancient health resort and one of the leading spas of England.

V: 111   (145)
VI: 56   (71)

BATTERSEA/BATTERSEA COUNCIL/BATTERSEA PARK
A borough in south London of about 2307 acres and where O'Casey resided
from September 1934 to September 1938. The council was composed of the
mayor, nine aldermen, and 45 councillors. Battersea Park was a favorite
place of training for athletes, and it contained a small lake bordered
by sub-tropical gardens. O'Casey's room at 49 Overstrand Mansions
overlooked the park, and he frequently used the park for walks. O'Casey
alludes to Chesterton* in Battersea. Chesterton moved to Battersea
in the summer of 1901. For more, see F. A. Lea, The Wild Knight of
Battersea: C. K. Chesterton (1945).

V: 109, 180   (142, 239)
VI: 9-21, 41   (1-19, 49, 50)

BATTLES, DAISY
Appears as a woman whom O'Casey met during a demonstration against the
Boer War.*

II: 198-209   (307-23)

BAUDIER, FATHER PERE
Author of a series of articles for Revue des Sciences Ecclesiastiques
(1887) which Walter MacDonald* used in his defense at Maynooth College.

IV: 248   (342)

BAWN, COLLEEN
The name of songs, books, and the personification of Ireland. O'Casey
uses it here to identify Eily O'Connor, a character in Boucicault's*
play, The Colleen Bawn.

II: 45   (64)

BAYLIS, LILIAN
1874 - 1937. English theatre manager; founder of the Old Vic and
Sadler's Wells.

V: 128-30   (167-70)

BEACONSFIELD
Small residential district in Buckingham, England. Chesterton* lived
on Grove Road (1909-35) where he wrote his Father Brown crime stories.

VI: 16   (12)

BEANN EDAIR
Ben Edar, Irish for Hill of Howth.*

III: 242   (361)

BEARDSLEY, AUBREY
1872 - 1898. English illustrator and art editor of the Yellow Book.

V: 10   (3)

BEAUFORT, LADY MARGARET
1443 - 1509. Generous patron of education. Enriched foundations that
opened as Christ's College, Cambridge.

V: 14   (9)

BECHUANALANDIANS
From Bechuanaland, South Africa. Allies of England in the Boer War.*

II: 198   (305)

BEETHOVEN LUDWIG VAN
For an example of Shaw's* criticism (#), see Bentley, Shaw on Music,
pp. 83-9.

III: 168   (247)
IV: 23   (20)
V: 190   (235)
VI: 174#, 175   (245#, 247)
Symphony in C   V: 162   (214)
Ninth Symphony in D Minor VI: 37   (43)

BEGGARS BUSH BARRACKS
Before 1922, a British army barracks in south Dublin. First barracks
to be taken over by Free State soldiers after the Anglo-Irish Treaty.

II: 155   .   (239)

BELFAST
II: 50, 165, 170, 175   (72, 254, 261, 271)
III: 26, 101, 103, 104, 169,   (30, 145, 148, 249, 280,
189, 225, 229   336, 341)
V: 82, 88, 89, 105-6, 109, 159 (104, 112, 113, 136-7, 141,
160, 165, 217   210, 212, 219, 291)

BELGIUM
Appears mainly in reference to the two world wars. In World War I,
British recruiters and Allied propaganda frequently sensationalized the
alleged atrocities committed by the Germans in Belgium. In Catholic
countries, the slogan, "Save Catholic Belgium," was used as a recruiting
device. In World War II, the Germans invaded Belgium on 10 May 1940
and forced a surrender after an 18 day campaign.

III: 267   (400)
VI: 123   (170-1)

BELGRADE
III: 19, 123   (19, 179)

BELGRAVE ROAD
In Rathmines, south of Dublin.

IV: 105   (138)

BELL, CLIVE
1881 - 1964. Leading English art critic and author of several books.

IV: 199   (273)

BELLARMINE, ROBERT
1542 - 1621. Italian prelate and controversialist. Known primarily
for his theological disputes with James I of England.

V: 221   (297)

BELLOC, HILAIRE
1870 - 1953. One of O'Casey's beta noires. English author of essays,
verse, novels, biography and criticism. Like his friend Chesterton,*
a noted convert to Catholicism for which he wrote many articles.

III: 152   (224)
IV: 160, 246, 248, 254   (218, 339, 351, 359-60, 361, 377)
260, 261, 273
V: 192   (256-7)
VI: 169-71, 178   (239-42, 251)
Europe and the Faith (1920) V: 191 (254)

BELLS OF ST. MARY'S
Probably an allusion to the film of the same name (1945) which O'Casey
often ridiculed because of its glossy portrayal of the Irish clergy.

IV: 273   (377)
VI: 10, 191   (2, 271)

BELVEDERE, EARLS OF
Peerage of the Rochford family. For whom Belvedere College, Dublin, was
named.

III: 70   (98)

BEN BULBEN
The mountain near the grave of Yeats* in Co. Sligo, Ireland.

V: 52   (61)

BENAVENTE, MARTINEZ JACINTO
1866 - 1954. Spanish dramatist and translator of Shakespeare and others.
Nobel Prize for literature in 1922.

Passion Flower (1913)   IV: 125   (167)

BENNETT, ARNOLD
1867 - 1931. English novelist and dramatist. Treated in infinite
detail the squalid life of the "Five Towns" centers of the pottery
industry.

V: 213   (286)

BENSON, NICHOLAS
Nicholas Beaver. c.1867 - 1907. Husband of O'Casey's sister, Isabella
("Ella"). Born in Wexford, he was the son of a color sergeant whom he
followed by enlisting in the British army for a 12 year term at the age
of 15. Beaver served part of his enlistment at South Aldershot Military
Camp, England, and rose to the rank of lance corporal. Discharged in
1893, he obtained employment as a porter on the Great Northern Railway
in Dublin where he eventually became head of its parcel department.
Died of a brain disease, 10 November, after a long illness. Source:
Margulies, The Early Life of Sean O'Casey.

I: 55-6, 67-77, 185-6   (76-8, 96-112, 286-7)
II: 155-6   (239-40)
III: 51-6, 65, 67, 68, 73, 100   (71-7, 91, 93, 95, 103, 144)

BERCHTESGADEN
Bavarian town and site of Hitler's summer home.

VI: 116, 151   (160, 209)

BERESFORD, LORD
Charles William de la Poer. 1846 - 1919. British naval officer active
in Egyptian campaigns (1882-85). Advocate of large naval programs.

III: 87, 94   (124, 135)

BERESFORD PLACE
In Dublin, running into Butt Bridge and around the Custom House. Named
for John Beresford, chief commissioner of the Revenue (1780-1802).

IV: 168, 285   (228, 395)

BERGIN'S
Dublin pub at 46 Amiens Street, owned by Daniel L. Bergin, who was
also an alderman for the North Dock Ward.

II: 55   (78)

BERKELEY, BISHOP GEORGE
1685 - 1753. Irish philosopher (one of the few).

I: 35   (44)
V: 45   (51)

BERKELEY STREET CHAPEL
St. Joseph's Catholic Church, 10-13 Berkeley Street, Dublin.

IV: 101   (132)

BERLIN
The riots to which O'Casey refers (#) occurred during a performance
(20 June 1953) of The Silver Tassie which was directed by Fritz Kortner
(translated by Elisabeth Freundlich). The riots were directed against
the play and against the return of Kortner, who was Jewish, to the
Berlin theatre.

VI: 118, 150, 155, 195#   (163, 209, 217, 277#)

BERNARD, DEAN JOHN HENRY
1860 - 1927. Irish churchman. Archbishop of Dublin (1915-19); provost
of Trinity College (1919-27).

III: 147   (216)

BETHLEHEM
II: 23, 171   (26, 263)
V: 74   (92)
VI: 51, 90   (63, 122)

BEWLEY & DRAPER'S
Manufacturers of mineral water, wholesale druggists, wine merchants
and ink manufacturers at 23-27 Mary Street, Dublin.

III: 104   (149)

BHAGAVAD-GITA
Important Hindu philosophical and religious book of metaphysics and
ethics.

IV: 216   (297)

BIBLE
There are hundreds of allusions to the Bible and to people and events
in it in the autobiographies. This entry lists only those pages where
the book is specifically mentioned by name.

I: 14, 92, 95-6, 97, 98, 113, 114-5,   (10, 136, 140, 142, 143, 144,
117, 125, 144   145, 170, 171, 175, 176, 188,
                                         220)
II: 23, 29, 32, 33, 79, 88, 223, 230, 237(27, 36, 37, 42, 43, 118, 131,
                                         346, 358, 368)

III: 27, 37, 70, 84, 241   (32, 47, 99, 120, 359)
                                                      MORE

BIBLE (cont.)

IV: 133, 244, 265   (178, 336, 366)
V: 29, 91, 143   (29, 116, 189)
VI: 37, 50, 70, 126, 196   (42, 43, 63, 92, 175, 279)

BIDDY
Common name for a street hawker.

II: 87, 91-9, 112   (130, 138-49, 170-1)

BIG BEN
The famous bell in the clock tower of the British House of Parliaments.

III: 255   (381)
IV: 283   (391)
V: 123   (160)

BIG TREE, THE
Dublin pub at 35-39 Lower Dorset Street.

II: 40, 54   (55, 78)

BIGGAR, FRANCIS JOSEPH
1863 - ? Patron and supporter of the Irish literary movement. Member,
Supreme Council of the Irish Republican Brotherhood.*

III: 106   (153)

BILL
Appears as a foreman, probably on the Great Northern Railway of Ireland.

III: 192-3   (284-5)

BINN'S BRIDGE
In Dublin, crosses the Royal Canal where Lower Dorset Street moves into
Lower Drumcondra Road.

II: 55, 103   (78, 156)
IV: 215   (296)

BIRCH AAR
Beirt Fhear, Irish for "two men," was the pseudonym of Seamas O Dubh-
ghaill (1885 - 1929), an Irish writer who was active in the language
movement.

III: 133,149   (194, 219)

BIRDS OF DIAMOND GLORY
From AE's poem, "The Hour of the King," verse three.

IV: 196   (269)

BIRMINGHAM
English town in Warwickshire.

VI: 195   (277)

BIRRELL, AUGUSTINE
1850 - 1933. English politician. Chief secretary for Ireland (1907-16).
Responsible for the Irish University Act (1908), creating the National
University of Ireland. One of O'Casey's earliest articles attacked
Birrell for his meddling in the Irish education system. See "Sound the
Loud Trumpet" in Feathers from a Green Crow.

III: 23, 31   (26, 39)

BLACK AND TANS
British soldiers in Ireland during the War of Independence. So named for
their mixture of uniform colors: black berets, green shirts and khaki
trousers. They were usually recruited from unemployed veterans of World
War I and, by 1920, they numbered 7000. The Tans, as they were unpopularly
called, were known for their harsh, brutal and terrorist tactics against
Irish civilians.

IV:42-4, 51-4, 56, 59, 61, 64, 65, 90   (49-52, 61-5, 69, 74-6, 79-82, 117,
95, 97, 105, 107, 111, 131   124, 128, 139, 142, 146, 175)
V: 76, 224   (96, 301)

BLACK AND WHITE ASSEMBLY OF CENSORIANS
Censors are notorious for their views that literature is either good or
bad -- black or white. For an example of O'Casey's experiences see under
his works, I Knock at the Door and Pictures in the Hallway. See also
CENSORSHIP BOARD.

III: 153   (224)

BLACK PRINCE
Edward of England, Duke of Aquitain.1330 - 1376. Hero of the rout of
French forces at the Battle of Crecy (26 August 1346).

I: 50   (68)

BLACKER, COLONEL WILLIAM
1777 - 1855. Author of many books and composer of several Irish ballads.

II: 235   (364)

BLACKSHIRTS
British fascists led by Oswald Mosley* in the 1930s. Their counterparts
in Ireland were known as Blueshirts.

VI: 115   (158, 159)

BLACKSOD BAY
In Co. Mayo, 65 miles north of Galway Bay.

III: 15   (14)

BLACKWOOD, WILLIAM
1876 - 1942. Noted editor of Blackwood's Magazine.

V: 58-9   (70)

BLAKE, WILLIAM
1757 - 1827. Celebrated English artist, poet and mystic. O'Casey
alludes (#) to Chesterton's* study, William Blake (1910).

IV: 199, 206   (272, 283)
V: 79   (99)
VI: 16#, 168#   (11#, 236#)

BLAND, HUBERT
1856 - 1914. British socialist. Author of several studies for the
Fabian Society. A short notice of his death appeared in the Irish
Worker (18 April).

Can a Catholic Be a Socialist?   III: 16   (15)

BLANQUIERE BRIDGE
In north Dublin, immediately south of Mountjoy Prison.

IV: 64   (79)

BLEEDING HORSE
Dublin pub at 24-25 Camden Street. Owned by Andrew Wren. So named
because of its huge painting of a white horse being bled for veterinary
purposes on the exterior wall facing the traffic going out of Dublin
to Rathmines.

II: 54   (78)

BLIND ASYLUM
The National Institution and Molyneux Asylum for the Female Blind of
Ireland, Leeson Park, Co. Dublin. For Protestants only. In 1896 it had
52 inmates.

I: 108   (162)

BLOK, ALEXSANDR A.
1880 - 1921. Russian symbolist poet. Greatly influenced by the Russian
revolutions of 1905 and 1917 (October). O'Casey's allusions are to the
final line of Blok's most famous poem, The Twelve, a celebration of the
1917 Revolution.

VI: 176   (249)

BLOOMSBURY
A favorite residential section in west central London for artists and
writers during the 1920s.

V: 11, 129   (4, 168)

BLUE LION
Dublin pub on Great Britain (Parnell) Street. Used in O'Casey's play,
The Shadow of a Gunman (Act II).

IV: 195   (268)

BLUE-COAT SCHOOL
In Dublin (#), King's Hospital, the oldest public (U.S.: private) school
in Ireland (founded 1670). So named because the boys wore a long blue
coat girded at the loin with a leather belt. In London (##), the school
was formerly on Newgate Street at Christ's Hospital. It was moved in
1902 to Horsham, Sussex. The Christ's Hospital location was the site of
a Grey Friars monastery, to which O'Casey alludes.

I: 186#   (287#)
V: 74##   (92##)

BLYTHE, ERNEST
1889 - 1975. One of O'Casey's earliest friends in the language movement.
Later (1906 by Blythe's account) he was recruited into the Irish Republican Brotherhood by O'Casey. In the Irish Free State government, Blythe
was Minister of Finance (1922-32) and was instrumental in obtaining the
first annual grant for the Abbey Theatre (July 1925). Director of the
Abbey from 1935 to 1972. A fierce administrator.

III: 147   (215)
V: 122   (159)

BOADICEA, BATTLE OF
One of the many spellings of Boudicca. Ancient British revolt against
the Romans (11 A.D.) which was led by the Queen of the Icene (Norfolk),
Boudicca. She was defeated and killed by Paulinus. Dramatized in
Webster's* Bonduca (1647), O'Casey's likely source.

V: 77   (96)

BOANN
Irish mythology, Boanna (River Boyne), mother of Angus Og.* Treated by
Lady Gregory* in her Cuchulain of Muirthemne.

II: 235   (364)

BOAR'S HILL
In Oxford, England. Yeats* visited John Masefield here in 1930 for the
30th anniversary of their first meeting.

V: 119, 120   (155, 156)

BOCCANEROS
Genoese family of statesmen, soldiers and financiers of 14th century
Italy.

III: 136   (199)

BODENSTOWN
In Co. Kildare, the burial spot of Wolfe Tone.* Annual marches to
the gravesite in June are an Irish republican tradition. See O'Casey's
articles in Feathers from a Green Crow: "A Day in Bodenstown" and "Tone's
Grave."

II: 190   (294)
III: 162, 175, 228, 231, 242 (239, 259, 340, 344, 361)

BOEOTIA
In Greece. An important ancient center of civilization.

V: 192   (255)

BOER REPUBLICS/BOER WAR
The South African War, also known as the Anglo-Boer War or Boer War,
was fought between Great Britain and the two Boer republics, the South
African Republic (Transva 1) and the Orange Free State, between October
1899 and May 1902. As is evident from O'Casey's narrative, the Irish
people generally supported the Boers and resisted British attempts at
recruitment.

II: 197-8, 200-1, 204   (305-6, 309, 311, 315)
III: 26, 164, 269   (30, 241, 403)
V: 36   (39)
VI: 103   (142)

BOHEMIAN GIRL, THE
Opera (1843) by Michael William Balfe (1808-1870).

II: 45   (63)

BOLAND, HARRY
1887 - 1922. Dublin tailor and energetic organizer for Sinn Fein.*
Close associate and friend of deValera*; active in the Easter Rising
for which he was imprisoned. Sent to the United States to report on
Irish-American organizations and support. Envoy to Washington until
the Treaty* which he opposed. Killed by Free State troops (30 July).

IV: 82   (106)

BOLAND'S
Dublin bakers at 134-136 Capel Street.

I: 85   (125)

BOLSHEVIK REVOLUTION
Socialist revolution (1917) in Russia led by Lenin and Trotsky. By
his own words O'Casey supported the revolution from its beginnings
as did many other Irish men and women. See also COMMUNISM, SOCIALISM
and SOVIET UNION.

IV: 230   (318)
V: 77   (97)
VI: 118-9, 213-16   (163, 305-09)

BOLTON STREET
East of Henrietta Street in north Dublin.

I: 169   (260)

BONA MORS CONFRATERNITY
Known also as "Confraternity of Our Lord Jesus Christ Dying on the Cross,
and of the Most Blessed Virgin Mary, His sorrowful Mother," a Catholic
spiritual association founded (1648) by Vincent Corafa, who was known
for his attentions to the suffering and dying victims of the plague.

VI: 209   (299)

BOND STREET
Famous thoroughfare between Oxford Street and Picadilly in London.

V: 60   (72)

BONNIE PRINCE CHARLIE
Charles Edward Stuart (1720 - 1788). English prince who was known as
the "Young Pretender." Headed the famous Jacobite Rising in Scotland
(1745).

IV: 11   (4)

BONNINGTON, SIR RALPH BLOOMFIELD
The famous physician in Shaw's* play, The Doctor's Dilemma (1906).

VI: 89   (121)

BOOK OF BALLYMOTE
Irish anthology (c.1390) produced in Sligo by several scribes. It
contains the Book of Invasions and several histories, legends and
genealogies of ancient Ireland.

III: 101   (146)

BOOK OF BOOKS
The Bible.*

I: 95, 97, 98   (140, 144, 145)

BOOK OF FENAGH
Medieval Irish manuscript edited by R.A.S. Macalister.

III: 285   (427)

BOOK OF THE GREEN AND GOLDEN SLUMBERS
Mocking allusion. "Golden Slumbers Kiss Your Eyes" is a lullaby, to
the air of "May Fair," by Thomas Dekker.

VI: 10   (3)

BOOK OF KELLS
One of Ireland's national treasures. An illustrated copy of the gospels
in Latin in the library of Trinity College.

III: 18, 22, 101, 200   (18, 25, 146, 297)
IV: 72, 165   (91, 223)

BOOK OF LISMORE
Ancient Irish book compiled about 1411 which has been translated by
various scholars.

IV: 165   (223)

BOOK OF MacDURNAN
The Gospels of MacDurnan, a medieval Irish book of the four gospels.

III: 22   (25)

BOOK OF MONASTERBOICE
Either the Short Book of Monasterboice or the Books of Flann of Monasterboice. Both are ancient (before 1100) Irish volumes.

III: 285   (427)

BOOK OF THE OLD DUN (and DONE) COW
Book of the Dun Cow (Leabhar na h-Uidhre). One of the earliest trans-
scriptions of Irish literature (c.1100). Contains the legend of Tuan
MacCarell, the reappearance of Cuchulain,* and romantic prose tales.

III: 101, 200   (146, 297)

BOOK OF O'MONEY
O'Casey is alluding to the links between the Church (Holy books) and
financial matters.

III: 200   (297)

BOOK OF THE REVISED VERSION OF CATHLEEN'S THORNY WAY
The line, "Cathleen ni Houlihan, your way's a thorny way," is from
Eithna Carbery's poem, "The Passing of the Gael." O'Casey uses the
line several times in his play, The Shadow of a Gunman.

III: 201   (297)

BOOK OF THE RIPE AND EDIFYING THOUGHTS IN THE HEAD OF KINSALE
Perhaps an allusion to the English meaning of the Irish word, Ceann-
saile, the head of the brine (highest point of a river tide).

III: 200   (297)

BOOK OF WISDOM
Biblical book written in the 2nd and 1st centuries B.C. containing
a defense of the Jewish way of life and chronicling the special
providence of God in the history of Israel.

IV: 265   (366)

BOOKS OF THE VEDA
Primary class of Hindu sacred writings.

IV: 216   (297)

BOONE, DANIEL
V: 180   (239)

BOOTERSTOWN
Suburb of Dublin.

II: 117   (179)

BOOTH, GENERAL WILLIAM BRANWELL
1856 - 1929. Son of the founder of the Salvation Army. Chief organizer
and chief of staff (1880-1912) and general of the army (1912-29).

II: 171   (262)
VI: 51   (63)

BORRIS-IN-OSSORY THING AT ARMS
Borris-in-Ossory is an Irish town in Co. Laoighis. "Thing at arms"
is a play on King at Arms, a heraldic official who looked after such
matters as protocol, coats of arms, etc.

V: 39   (43)

BORROW, GEORGE
1803 - 1881. English author and linguist.

V: 93   (119)
VI:118   (163)
Lavengro (1851) III: 207   (308)
Romany Rhye (1857 III: 219   (326)

BORTHWICK, NORMA
Gaelic League official and assistant to Eoin MacNeill* on An Claidheamh
Soluis. Co-founder (with Margaret O'Rahilly) of the Irish Book Company
and instrumental in modernizing Irish texts.

III: 151   (222)

BORU, BRIAN
See BRIAN BORU

BOSTON
For more on O'Casey's troubles with Boston, see his article, "The
Church Tries to Close the Gates," in Blasts and Benedictions.

V: 174, 202-07, 222, 231, 233   (231, 270-7, 298, 311, 313)

BOSTON COLLEGE
American college in Chestnut Hill. In 1935, a number of their Jesuit
teachers led the campaign to ban O'Casey's Within the Gates.

V: 202   (270)

BOSWORTH, BATTLE OF
Important historical battle between King Richard III and Henry Tudor
(22 August 1485) which ended the War of the Roses. Climax of Shakespeare's* play, Richard III.

V: 188   (251)
VI: 77   (102)

BOTANIC AVENUE
In Glasnevin, north of Dublin, off Lower Drumcondra Road.

II: 63   (91-2)

BOTANIC GARDENS
Public garden of 50 acres in Glasnevin, north of Dublin. Founded (1790)
by the Royal Dublin Society.

II: 63   (92)

BOTHA, LOUIS
1862 - 1919. Boer general and first prime minister of Transvaal (1907).
Also the first prime minister of the Union of South Africa (1910-19).

II: 198   (306)
III: 164, 269   (241, 403)

BOTOLPH
Appears as a clerk at Leedom, Hampton chandler company, Dublin.

II: 84-9   (125-33)

BOUCICAULT, DION
c.1822 - 1890. Irish dramatist who was a prominent influence in O'Casey's
drama.

II: 24   (28-9)
IV: 125, 168   (167, 228)
The Colleen Bawn (1860) II: 23   (28)
                        IV: 184   (251)
The Octoroon (1859)   II: 23, 132, 133 (28, 202, 204)
The Shaughraun (1874)   II: 23, 132, 134 (28, 202, 206)
                        IV: 168, 184, 285 (228, 251, 395)
Arragh-na-Pogue (1864) II: 132   (203)
                        III: 120   (174)
SEE ALSO: BAWN, COLLEEN   MOYA
            CONN THE SHAUGHRAUN   O'GRADY
            COPPALEEN, MYLES NA   O'NEILL, ARTE
            DOLAN, FATHER   SCUDDER, SALEM
            DUFF, HARVEY   SHAUN THE POST
            FFOLLIOTT, ROBERT   SUIL-A-BEG
            KINCHELLA, CORRY   SUIL-A-MORE CASTLE
            McCLUSKEY, JACOB   WICKLOW WEDDING

BOURBONS
French royal family dating from the 9th century.

IV: 265   (366)

BOW
From the popular nursery rhyme, "Bells of London," the last line of
which refers to "the Great Bells of Bow."

VI: 191   (271)

BOW LANE
In south Dublin, heading into Aungier Street. II: 31 (40)

BOWERY
A section of lower Manhattan in New York City known as a gathering place
for the "down-and-outs" of society. Popularized most extensively by
Walt Whitman.*

III: 25   (29)

BOY BLEW
Allusion to the famous Blue Boy painting (1779) by Thomas Gainsborough.

III: 111   (160)

BOY CORPS OF EMAIN MACHA
In the Tain, a band of 150 boys, sons of province chieftains, who went
to the aid of the men of Ulster. All were slain in battle. This idea
of a band of young boys sitting at the feet of their teacher was one of
the basic concepts of Pearse's* St. Enda's.*

III: 237, 240   (354, 358)

BOYD, ALICE
Appears as a young Presbyterian girl who worked with O'Casey at
Leedom, Hampton chandler company.

II: 101-3, 108, 109, 111, 112-16   (153-6, 164, 166, 170, 171-7)

BOYD, MR.
Thoms 1888 lists a "Mr. H. Boyd" as the principal at Central Model
School #2 (male).

I: 65   (93)

BOYLAN, ANDREW
Minister at Maynooth (Thoms 1880) and bishop of Kilmore (1907-10).

IV: 241   (333)

BOYLE, CAPTAIN JACK
Juno's* husband in O'Casey's play, Juno and the Paycock. A braggart and
buffoon full of comic mendacities and defenses.

IV: 171   (232)

BOYLE, MARY
Daughter of Juno and Jack Boyle in Juno and the Paycock.

V: 203   (272)

BOYNE RIVER
In Leinster province flowing into the Irish Sea. The scene of the
historical defeat of James II* by William of Orange* in 1690. Memorial-
ized in song and verse and regarded as a symbol of the defeat of Irish
nationalism and still commemorated each July 12 by Protestant groups.

I: 143   (219)
II: 57, 228-37   (82, 355-69)
III: 22-3, 37, 135, 145, 174 (25-6, 48, 197, 212-13, 257)

BOYS OF ORMAND QUAY
In the 1790s, a deadly rivalry developed between the Liberty Boys --
tailors and weavers of the Coombe -- and the Ormand Boys -- butchers
who lived in Ormand Market. Witnesses reported daily battles between
the two groups which engulfed the area around Ormand Quay, closing
all shops and compelling others to stay out of the area.

I: 160   (246)
III: 231   (344)
IV: 256   (354)

BOYS, RICHARD C.
Harvard student and captain of the basketball team who organized his
fellow students in protest against the banning of Within the Gates.
See Letters, I, pp. 533 ff.

V: 205   (275)

BRABANT
Belgian province containing Brussels.

III: 285   (427)

BRADFORD
English county borough and manufacturing city in Yorkshire.

II: 192   (296)

BRADY, "DIAMOND" JIM
1856 - 1917. Ostentatious American financier.

V: 68-9   (83, 85)

BRADY, JIM
One of the leaders of the secret Irish organization, the Invincibles,*
who was hanged for his part in the assassination of Cavendish* and
Burke* at Phoenix Park. Executed on May 14 1883. See "Lines Written on
the Execution of Joe Brady" in Healy, ed., Old Irish Street Ballads, I.

I: 75   (108)
II: 35, 37-9   (46, 50-3)
V: 51   (59)

BRADY'S LANE
Presently Irvine Terrace in north Dublin around the corner from St. Barnabas' Church.

I: 131, 132-3, 149   (198, 199, 229)

BRAHMIN
Brahma, the supreme god of Hindu mythology. Subject of poems by Emerson, AE and others.

IV: 125   (167)
V: 144   (190)

BRAHMS, JOHANNES
O'Casey is only partially correct in his evaluation of Shaw's* judgement of Brahms. During Shaw's term as a music critic (1888-94), he sided with the Wagnerian circles and violently deprecated Brahms. In 1936, though, he recanted and admitted that his earlier remarks were "hasty" and "silly."

VI: 174, 177   (245, 250)

BRANDYBURGERS
From Brandenburg, therefore Germans. During the Jacobite Wars, William of Orange* had a large contingent of German soldiers fighting for him, arriving in Ireland in April and May 1690. For O'Casey's allusion see the song, I: 33-4 (40-1).

II: 228   (354)

BRANCKER, SIR WILLIAM SEFTON
1877 - 1930. English military officer and organizer of the National Air Surface. First recipient of the Air Force Cross (1918); air vice-marshall (1924). Killed in the airship disaster, "R.101."

V: 69   (85)

BRANNIGAN, RICHARD
Former member of the Orange Order who became a stalwart supporter and member of the Gaelic League and Irish Citizen Army council. Elected, with Markiewicz,* treasurer of the I.C.A. (22 March 1914). At the same election, O'Casey was appointed secretary. In O'Casey's play, The Star Turns Red, the character Brannigan is a composite of Brannigan and Barney Conway.*

III: 225, 229   (335, 341)

BRAQUE, GEORGES
1882 - 1963. French painter and one of the founders of Cubism.

IV: 206   (283)

BRASENOSE COLLEGE
Constituent college of Oxford University.

III: 248   (371)

BRASE, FRITZ
d.1940. Bandmaster of the 1st Grenadier Guards in Berlin (1911-18).
Accepted post (February 1923) as director of the Irish Army School of
Music, Portobello Barracks.

IV: 151   (205)

BREAD STREET/CRIPPLEGATE
In London, the birth and burial places of John Milton.*

VI: 197   (281)

BREEN, DAN
1894 - 1969. Irish guerilla hero of the Irish War of Independence
(1918-21). Joined the Irish Volunteers in 1914 and became one of the
leading I.R.A. commanders. Later a member of the Irish Dail. Sent a
letter of condolence to Eileen O'Casey when the dramatist died.

IV: 92   (120)

BREEN, FATHER JIMMY
Republican priest from Tralee. According to John H. Whyte, Leaders and
Men of the Easter Rising: Dublin 1916, Breen "was in the confidence of
Pearse and Stack about the plans to land arms from the Aud."

III: 261   (391)

BREENBORUVIANS
Though this seems to be a pun on the above two entries, it is more
closely tied to Brian Boru.*

III: 153   (224)

BREHON LAWS
Ancient Irish laws. Derived from the term brehon which was applied to
the lawgiver. In existence as living law in parts of Ireland until the
16th century.

III: 120, 160   (174, 235)

BRENNAN, CAPTAIN
Member of the Irish Citizen Army in O'Casey's play, The Plough and the
Stars.

IV: 173   (235)

BRIAN BORU
Dublin pub owned by J. M. Ryan at 1 Prospect Terrace, north of the
Crossguns Bridge.

II: 55   (78)

BRIAN BORU
926 - 1014. Legendary 9th century warrior and Ireland's first national
hero. King of Ireland (1002-14). Killed after defeating the Danes
at the Battle of Clontarf. Subject of many tales and ballads through
the ages. A Brian Boru harp (#) is the golden-colored harp on the
label of Guinness beer.

II: 186-8   (287-91)
III: 24, 33, 103, 112#, 146, 155, 226#   (27, 41, 148, 162#, 214, 229,
                                    336#)
IV: 9#, 145-6   (1#, 196-7)
VI: 206   (294)

BRIAN'S SON
Murrough, killed (1014) at the Battle of Clontarf. The chess game
incident between Murrough and Mailmurra to which O'Casey refers is
rooted in Irish legend and is in most history books detailing the
period.

II: 187   (288)

BRIDGE OF SIGHS
The best known bridge of this name is Ponte de Sospiri, Venice. O'Casey,
however, is referring to a bridge of the same name at St. John's College,
Cambridge University, which leads to the Third Court.

VI: 52   (65)

BRIEUX, EUGENE
1852 - 1932. French dramatist. The volume of plays containing the
Shaw introduction was published in 1907.

IV: 232   (320)

BRIGHTON
Town in Sussex, England.

II: 11   (8)

BRITISH ASSOCIATION
Probably the British Association for Advancement of Science.

IV: 211   (289)

BRITISH COUNCIL
Established (November 1934) primarily to "Make the life and thought
of British peoples more widely known abroad." The tour to which O'Casey
refers occurred 1936-39.

VI: 107   (147-8)

BRITOMART, LADY
Lady Britomart Undershaft is the daughter of the Earl of Stevenage and
wife of armaments millionaire Andrew Undershaft in Shaw's Major Barbara.

V: 77, 214   (97, 286)

BRIXHAM
Town in Devon, England.

VI: 80   (107)

BROADBENT, TOM
The partner of Larry Doyle in Shaw's John Bull's Other Island.

III: 173   (256)

BROADSTONE STATION
In Dublin on Phibsborough Road, the Midland Great Western Railway terminal. Now the C.I.E. Bus and Road Freight depot.

III: 141   (207)

BROADWAY
V: 183   (243)
VI: 142   (198)

BRODAR
A leader from Man who conspired with Gormaliath* to dispose of Brian
Boru.* Brodar fought as an ally with Brian during the battle of
Clontarf, but entered the command tent after the battle and killed him.

II: 188   (290-1)
III: 103   (148)

BRONTE SISTERS
Emily (1818 - 1848), Charlotte (1816 - 1855) and Anne (1820 - 1849).
O'Casey is probably referring to Chesterton's* chapter on Charlotte
Bronte in his Twelve Types (1902).

VI: 168   (237)

BRONX
New York City.

V: 235-6   (316-7)

BROOKE, BASIL
1876 - 1945. British politician. Prime minister, Northern Ireland
(1943).

V: 165   (218)

BROOKLYN
For many years the home of Whitman.* O'Casey's allusion to the "camp
of the lost brigade" is a reference to Whitman's poem, "The Centenarian's
Story," in his Drum-Taps, lines 109-112.

V: 179   (238)
VI: 142   (198)

BROWN, RUDMOSE
Thomas B. Rudmose-Brown, 1878 - 1942. Professor of romance languages
at Trinity College. Author of several works on French literature and
poetry. See his obituary, Dublin Magazine, v. 17, no. 3, 1942.

IV: 149   (201)

BROWN SHIRTS
See also BLACKSHIRTS.

VI: 118   (163)

BROWNE AND NOLAN
Dublin publishers at 24-25 Nassau Street in south Dublin.

III: 135   (197)

BROWNING, ROBERT
1818 - 1889. English poet and author of several verse plays. The
Sunset passages allude to Chesterton's* work, Robert Browning (1903).
See also PIPPA.

III: 169   (249-50)
VI: 15, 168   (10, 236)
Bells and Pomegranates (1841-46) III: 84   (120)

BRUCE
Robert VIII. 1274 - 1329. King and liberator of Scotland.
See also Appendix III, this page.

III: 33   (41)

BRUGHA, CATHAL
1874 - 1922. Irish patriot killed in the Civil War. Known especially
for his rigorous military mind, discipline and bravery. He was an
early member of the Gaelic League and the Irish Volunteers, and was
second in command at the South Dublin Union during the Easter Rising.

IV: 93-4, 100   (122, 131)

BRUNSWICK STREET
In north Dublin, running parallel to North King Street.

IV: 285   (395)

BRUTUS, MARCUS
c.84 - 43 B.C. One of Caesar's noted assassins.

II: 131, 132   (201, 203)

BUCHANAN, JACK
1891 - 1957. Scottish-born actor who appeared in several Broadway
plays (mainly musicals), films and revues as a tap-dancing star.

V: 70   (86)

BUCKFASTLEIGH
In Devon, England. The Benedictine abbey to which O'Casey refers was
rebuilt (1907-32) by monks. It is a Cistercian abbey situated in
the wooded valley of the Dart river and manufactures confectionary
of which honey, from the monastic bees, is the chief ingredient.

VI: 70   (92)

BUCKINGHAM PLACE/BUCKINGHAMSHIRE
Buckingham Palace (#) is the London residence of the British sovereign.

IV: 218#   (300#)
V: 75, 109, 208   (94, 141, 278)
VI: 72, 139-40#   (96, 194-5#)

BUDDHA
IV: 45, 216   (53, 297)
V: 124, 141, 168, 201, 221   (161, 185, 223, 268, 296)
VI: 54, 105, 161, 220   (68, 144, 227, 315)

BUG RIVER
In east Poland. Site of a major World War II battle.

VI: 119   (164-5)

BULAWAYONIANS
From Southern Rhodesia. Allies of England in the Boer War.

II: 198   (305)

BULLER, SIR REDVERS
1839 - 1908. British general and briefly commander in chief in the
Boer War. Forced to retire because of his indiscreet replies to
criticism of war failures. According to a letter from O'Casey to Ronald
Ayling, his brother, Tom, served under Buller in the Boer War.

II: 197, 200   (305, 310)
III: 41   (54)

BUNKER HILL
Outside Boston, where the opening shots of the American Revolution were
fired (17 June 1775).

II: 12   (9)
IV: 275   (380)
V: 83, 179, 180   (105, 238, 240)

BUNYAN, JOHN
1628 - 1688. English preacher and author who was frequently imprisoned
for preaching without a licence. His most famous work (given below)
was written while in prison.

Pilgrim's Progress (pub. 1678) II: 122   (187)
                               IV: 257   (355)
                               VI: 65   (85)

BURKE, EDMOND
1729 - 1797. Conservative Irish-born statesman and philosopher on
current affairs. One of his most influential works was Reflections
on the French Revolution.(1790).

V: 45   (51)

BURKE, THOMAS HENRY
1829 - 1882. Irish undersecretary for Ireland and one of the victims
of the Invincibles.*

I: 75   (108)
II: 38, 54   (51, 78)

BURMA
The first entries are allusions to the three Anglo-Burmese Wars (1824-
26, 1852, 1852-85) which resulted in the piecemeal annexation of the
country by England. The second refers to Orwell's* service as a
British civil servant.

I: 68, 158-9   (97, 244-5)
VI: 101   (139)

BURNABY, COLONEL FREDERICK G.
1852 - 1885. Famous English cavalry officer and correspondent for the
London Times who traveled with Gordon* in the Sudan and other places,
sending back colorful dispatches.

I: 158   (243)

BURNHAM BEECHES
In Bucks, England, three miles east of Maidenhead. A large area of
beautifully wooded health resorts bought by the London Corporation (1879).

V: 208   (278)

BURNS, CHARLES WESLEY
Wesleyan bishop who joined with other zealots to ban the Boston production of O'Casey's play, Within the Gates (1934).

V: 202, 206   (270, 276)

BURNS, JOHN
1853 - 1943. Major British socialist leader and trade union organizer.
M.P.(1892-1918); cabinet member (1905-14) from which he resigned at
the outbreak of World War I. Spoke in Dublin during the 1913 Lockout.

VI: 15   (10)

BURNS, ROBERT
1759 - 1795. Scottish national poet and one of O'Casey's favorites.
For more, see the indexes to appendices I and II.

I: 35   (43)
III: 38   (49)

BURREN, HILLS OF
In Co. Clare, Ireland. Historically, the name of a barony, the ancient
territory of the O'Lochlainns, ancient kings of Ireland.

IV: 143   (193)
V: 173   (230)

BUTLER, HUBERT
Irish Protestant from Kilkenny who sparked the "Papal Nuncio Incident"
at a meeting of the International Affairs Association* in Dublin by
referring to the reactionary policies of Cardinal Stepinac.* This
angered the papal nuncio who left the meeting. Butler was subsequently
the target of Catholic persecution and vilification by the press and by
the Kilkenny County Council,and was forced to resign from several
positions. (October 1952)

VI: 210, 211   (300)

BUTLER, ORMOND
Variant on the Irish family of Butler whose members were earls, marquises and dukes of Ormonde.

III: 37   (47)

BUTLER, SAMUEL
1835 - 1902. English satirist and author of works on family
life in mid-Victorian England.

The Way of All Flesh (wr. 1873-85, pub. 1903) III: 207   (308)

BUTLER, SIR WILLIAM F.
1838 - 1901. British army general and commander of troops at Alexandria
(1890-93) and during the Boer War.

V: 168   (222)

BUTLER'S
George Butler, manufacturers of musical instruments at 34 Bachelor's
Walk in Dublin.

III: 154   (227)

BUTLIN'S
An Irish holiday camp in Co. Meath with recreational facilities.

V: 74-5   (93)

BUTT BRIDGE
Furtherest east of Dublin bridges across the River Liffey.

II: 130   (189)

BUTTE, MONTANA
V: 172   (229)

BYRNE, ALFIE
See FAIR OF FAIRS

BYRON (Lord), GEORGE GORDON
1788 - 1824. English poet and champion of liberty during the European
reactionary period following Napoleon's downfall. Joined Greek insurgents in their struggle for independence where he died of malaria.
See also the index to Appendix III.

II: 122   (187)
Don Juan (1819-24) VI: 37   (43)

BYZANTIUM
O'Casey's reference is to Yeats's* poem, "Sailing to Byzantium."

V: 75, 87   (93, 111)

C

C.I.D.
The Criminal Investigation Division of the Dublin Metropolitan Police.

IV: 103, 188   (135, 257)

CADE, JACK
d.1450. English rebel and leader of the Kentish rebellion in protest
against court corruption and oppressive taxation. Shakespeare's* rebel
in 2 Henry VI.

V: 209   (279)

CADOGANS/CADOGAN SQUARE and GARDENS
Irish peerage family dating from the 17th century of whom several were
active in the British army and politics. The latest, George Henry
Cadogan (1840 - 1915), was lord lieutenant of Ireland (1895-1902). In
London, Cadogan Square is off Sloane Street and is the site of the
Cadogan Botanical Gardens.

IV: 274   (380)
VI: 25   (25)

CAER-LUD
Ancient name for Ludgate, near Fleet Street, in the heart of London.

VI: 76   (102)

CAESAR, JULIUS
II: 88, 120   (131, 184)
V: 29   (29)
VI: 81, 202   (108, 228)

CAFFREY, THOMAS
One of the Invincibles.*

II: 37   (50)

CAHIRCIVEEN
Irish town in Co. Kerry. Birthplace of Daniel O'Connell.*

III: 101   (146)
VI: 76   (102)

CAIN/ABEL
IV: 97   (127)
VI: 196   (279)

CALABRIA
Region of the toe of the Italian boot with, historically, large feudal
estates and a poor peasantry.

V: 112   (145)

CALAHORRA
Historical city in northern Spain. Site of an unsuccessful siege by
Pompey (76 B.C.) during his war with the rebel Sertorius.

II: 221   (343)

CALDY ISLAND
Island off the southwest coast of Wales and the site of a 12th century
Benedictine monastery.

V: 78   (99)

CALENDAR OF THE CULDEES
From Oengus, the Culdee (c.800 - 850), author of the Feilire, a
calendar of saints and festivals with a verse for each day of the year.

III: 202   (299)

CALIBAN
A deformed slave from Shakespeare's* play, The Tempest.

V: 25   (23)

CALVIN, JOHN
1509 - 1564. French theologian and Reformation zealot whose writings
and excesses became known as Calvinism.

V: 221   (297)

CAM RIVER
In east central England flowing past Cambridge University.

VI: 44, 50, 65   (54, 63, 85)

CAMAC/WILLIAMS
The latter may be J. E. Williams, an official of the Amalgamated Society
of Railway Servants (A.S.R.S.), which would account for "the letters
after their name." Camac may have been an associate.

III: 120   (174

CAMBRIDGE UNIVERSITY
Major university in England with over 20 constituent colleges. In
February 1936, O'Casey spoke there as a guest of the Shirley Society
of St. Catherine's College. His talk was entitled, "The Holy Ghost
Leaves England." Published in Letters, I, pp. 603-05.

III: 143	(210)
IV: 237, 260	(327, 359)
V: 13, 151, 181	(7, 199, 240)
VI: 44-67, 73	(53-88, 97)

CAMPANIA
This may have been the British naval ship, the first seaplane carrier,
which was commanded by Oliver Swann (1878 - 1948) who later became an
important figure in the development of the Royal Air Force.

III: 140   (206)

CANAAN
In Biblical history, the land promised by God to Abraham (Genesis 12).

II: 10, 21	(6, 23)
III: 48	(65)
VI: 11	(4)

CANADA

I:68	(97)
IV: 15	(10)
V: 36, 85, 121	(39, 108, 157)
VI: 195	(278)

CANNING
Any from this prominent English family, all of whom were active in
English politics. One of the most noted was George Canning (1770 -
1827), an English liberal statesman prominent at the Congress of Vienna.

IV: 183   (249)

CANNON, BROOKES, AND ODGERS
Appear as local land agents in London.

VI: 182   (258)

CANONS MINOR/MAJOR/REGULAR

III: 152	(224)
V: 74	(92)

CANOSSA
Small village and castle in Italy. O'Casey is referring to the scene
of the penance of Henry IV of Germany before Pope Gregory VIII (January
1077) to rescind the excommunication imposed by the Pope. It is said
that Henry stood for three days in the snow outside the castle before
the Pope would grant absolution.

IV: 262   (361)

CANTRELL & COCHRANE
Mineral and table water manufacturers based in London with offices in
Belfast and Dublin (2-4 Nassau Place).

III: 103   (149)

CAOCAUN, MR.
Fictitious name. In Irish, caochan = mole or blind person. His real
name was Miggins. O'Casey also changed the name of the estate. (Letters,
II, p. 277.)

III: 144   (211)

CAPEL STREET
Major thoroughfare in Dublin which butts into the River Liffey at
Grattan's Bridge.

I: 170   (261)
II: 55   (78)
IV: 229   (315)

CAPPADOCIA
Ancient geographical section in Asia Minor and birthplace of celebrated
ecclesiastics.

III: 89   (127)

CAPRI
Resort isle off the coast of Italy.

V: 75   (93)

CAPUCHIN ANNUALS (1942)
Thick paper-bound annual publication of the Dublin Capuchins, edited
by Father Senan, O.F.M. The photo to which O'Casey refers appeared in
the article, "Religious Orders of Men in Ireland," pp. 487-521.

V: 230-1   (310)

CARBERY, EITHNE
1866 - 1911. Pen name of Anna MacManus nee Johnston, Irish poet and
editor, who wrote many poems for The Nation and United Ireland. See
Appendix I and II.

Four Winds of Freedom (1902) III: 82   (116)

CARDIFF
Capital city of Wales.

VI: 73   (97)

CARDINAL
Cardinal Thomas Wolsey (1475 - 1530), archbishop of York in Shakespeare's
play, Henry VIII.

II: 131, 132   (202)

CAREY, JAMES
1845 - 1883. Noted Irish informer on the Invincibles * and treasurer
of the Irish Republican Brotherhood. After the assassination of Burke*
and Cavendish,* Carey was arrested 13 January 1883) and, with 16 others,
was charged with conspiracy to murder public officials. He turned
state's evidence (13 February) and revealed the details of the plot.
He left Dublin (6 July) with his wife and family and, using the name
of Poer, sailed towards Africa. However, he was followed and killed
(29 July) by Patrick O'Donnell, a bricklayer who in turn was captured,
returned to England, and executed (17 December).

II: 34   (45)

CARLISLE BRIDGE
The original name for O'Connell Bridge, Dublin. Built 1794, the name
was changed in 1882.

I: 181   (279-80)

CARLOW
Irish county in Leinster province.

II: 38   (51)

CARMELITES
One of the four principal orders of the mendicant friars of the Catholic
Church.

V: 83   (105)

CAROLINA, NORTH and SOUTH
III: 113   (164)

CARPENTER, WALTER
Dublin socialist active in the Irish Transport and General Workers'
Union.* Publicly supported the Russian Revolution and the establishment
of several local Irish "soviets" in the 1920s. Founding member,
Communist Party of Ireland (1921) and a friend of O'Casey.

III: 269-70   (404-5)
IV: 12   (6)

CARR, DARGAVILLE
Appears as a senior partner at Harmsworth's Irish Agency.

II: 210, 213-14   (324-5, 331-2)

CARR, DR. THOMAS J.
1839 - 1917. Professor of theology, dean and vice-president of Maynooth
College. Editor, <u>Irish Ecclesiastical Record</u> (1880-83); bishop of
Galway (1883-86); archbishop of Melbourne (from 1886).

IV: 241-2   (332-4)

CARRICKBEG
Small Irish town in Co. Waterford.

III: 140, 142   (205, 208)

CARRICKFERGUS
Irish town in Co. Antrim.

III: 140   (205)

CARSON, SIR EDWARD HENRY
1854 - 1935. British politician. M.P. (1892 - 1921); first lord of
the admiralty (1917). As a Conservative M.P., Carson fought against
Home Rule and, failing that, for the exclusion of Ulster from independence from England. In 1913, he organized the Ulster Volunteers which
was countered by the Irish Volunteers. It is now generally recognized
that Carson was a pawn in the efforts to maintain the power of the Tories.

V: 81-3, 85, 87, 88, 91   (103-04, 108, 110, 112, 113, 117)

CARY
Appears as a senior messenger at Leedom, Hampton chandler company.
Spelled CAREY in latter entry.

II: 105, 123   (149-50, 188)

CARZEN OF THE PAPES
See FAIR OF FAIRS

CASABIANCA
Familiar narrative poem (1829) by Felicia Dorthea Hemans (1793 - 1935),
her most famous work. Its opening line is the noted "The boy stood on
the burning deck," for which see I: 39 (51) and III: 39 (50). "Casabianca" is one of O'Casey's fictitious saints in his play, The Bishop's
Bonfire.

V: 142   (188)

CASELANAGAN
This and all the other names with it comes from Reeves, Ecclesiastical
History of Down, Connor, and Dromore, a book O'Casey apparently read
since the names are listed in the same order. The passage concerns the
founding of the monastery of Iobhair Cinn Tragh, in the county of
Down, in 1144. Fourteen years later, Maurice O Loughlin,king of Ireland,
endowed the monastery with various lands. The following list is of names
O'Casey gives and their present names according to Reeves: Enacratha
(Carnmean); Cromglean (nothing in Reeves, but possibly Crumlin); Casel-
lanagan (Castle Enigan); Lissinelle (now included in Sheeptown); Croa,
Druimfornact (Crobane and Croreagh); Letir (nothing in Reeves); Cor-
cragh (Corcreeghy); Fidglassayn (Conlea and Greenan); Tirmorgonnean
(Turmore); Cimocul (Carnacally).

V: 164   (217)

CASEMENT, ROGER
1864 - 1916. Irish patriot who distinguished himself as an investiga-
tor for the British government into the conduct of the rubber trade in
Upper Congo (1903) and into the atrocities by the Anglo-Peruvian Amazon
Company (1910). Knighted in 1910. He joined the Irish nationalists in
opposing participation by Irish men and women in World War I and jour-
neyed to Berlin to organize Irish prisoners of war into an Irish Brigade.
While there, he arranged for the sale of arms for the expected Rising
in Ireland, but he was captured on his return. O'Casey is using Tyburn*
in the figurative sense. Casement was taken to Ardfert Barracks on
April 21 and to England on April 22. From then until May 15, he was in
military custody in the Tower of London. He was hanged August 3 in
Pentonville Prison.

III: 271   (407)

CASHEL
Irish episcopal city in Co. Tipperary and an ancient seat of kings.
Where St. Patrick used the shamrock to explain the Trinity.

III: 132, 285   (194, 427)

CASSIDE, ARCHIE
Isaac Archer Casey. 1873 - 1931. O'Casey's brother. Born at 6
Upper Dorset Street, Dublin. Office boy, Daily Express (c.1888);
married Johanna Fairtlough (April 1900) in the Pro-Cathedral; converted
to Catholicism and changed name to Joseph. Sales clerk, Health In-
surance Section, Irish Transport and General Workers' Union; helped
organize the union dramatic society (Liberty Hall Players). Left
Dublin to Liverpool in 1916. Variety of jobs including foreman of
an autoparts factory and in Dunlop rubber factory. Source: Margulies,
The Early Life of Sean O'Casey.

PAN
I: 22-3, 27, 38, 48, 49, 55-8, 60-3, 65, 80-1, 85, 91, 105, 106, 151,
156, 168, 185, 186, 189

II: 7-11, 17-18, 20, 22-6, 46-7, 49-54, 57, 62, 64-5, 87, 131-3, 136
142-3, 154, 160, 209-11

IV: 22, 168, 184
U.S.
I: 21-3, 30, 49, 65, 67, 76-82, 84-9, 93, 118, 126, 134, 157, 158, 159,
232, 240, 258, 286, 287, 291

II: 2-7, 17-19, 22, 23, 25-32, 66, 70-78, 81, 90, 92, 94-5, 130, 201-03,
208, 218-19, 237, 246, 324-6

IV: 20, 228-9, 251

CASSIDE, ELLA
Isabella Charlotte Casey Beaver. 1865 - 1918. O'Casey's sister. Born
at 22 Wellington Street, Dublin. Graduated with honors (1882), Central
Model Schools.* Graduated from Teachers Training College, Marlborough
Street, Dublin (1884). Principal teacher at St. Mary's Infant School,
20 Dominick Street, Dublin (1885-?). Married Nicholas Beaver (see
BENSON, NICHOLAS) March 7, 1889, at St. Mary's Church. Buried at
MORE

CASSIDE, ELLA (cont.)

Mount Jerome Cemetery, Dublin. Source: Margulies, The Early Life of Sean O'Casey.

PAN

I: 22-3, 34, 35, 36, 38, 48-52, 54-63, 67-8, 70-1, 73, 76-9, 185-9

II: 21, 22, 24, 65-6, 84, 154, 185

III: 44-5, 50-5, 67-8, 73, 80-2, 86-8, 91-100, 209

IV: 21, 22-3, 38, 217, 286

U.S.

I: 21-3, 42, 43, 44, 48, 65-71, 75-88, 95-6, 101-2, 105, 109-15, 286-91

II: 24, 25, 28, 95-7, 125, 237, 285

III: 57-9, 70-5, 93-5, 103, 114-17, 122-5, 130-44, 310

IV: 18, 20, 42, 299, 396

CASSIDE, MICHAEL
Michael Casey. c.1837 - 1886. O'Casey's father. Born in Co. Limerick.
Arrived in Dublin in 1863 and lived at 22 Chamber Street. Married
Susan Archer (27 January 1863) at St. Catherine's Church on Thomas
Street. At the time of the marriage he was a clerk with the Irish Church
Mission. At night he moonlighted as an assistant teacher at a night
school run by the Society of Church Mission. Died September 6. Buried
at Mount Jerome Cemetery, Dublin. Source: Margulies, The Early Life of
Sean O'Casey.

PAN

I: 12, 14, 17, 18, 29, 33 ff.-70, 87, 97, 154, 175, 176, 185

II: 9, 17, 24, 27, 28, 30, 31, 37, 70, 87, 121

III: 35, 100, 210

IV: 31, 34

U.S.

I: 6, 9-10, 14, 15, 33, 40 ff.- 99, 128, 147, 236, 270, 271, 286

II: 5, 18, 28, 34, 36, 38, 39, 50, 103, 130, 185

III: 44, 144, 311

IV: 33, 36

CASSIDE, MICK
Michael Harding Casey. 1865 - 1947. O'Casey's brother. Born at 22
Wellington Street, Dublin. Civil service employee at the post office.
Joined Royal Engineers, British army (1887-94). Regained his job at the
post office (1894). Rejoined Royal Engineers (1915). Received disability
pension (1920). Source: Margulies, The Early Life of Sean O'Casey.

MORE

CASSIDE, MICK (cont.)

<u>PAN</u>
I: 36, 48, 49, 57-69, 78, 186

II: 17, 23, 28-9, 30, 53-63, 84, 143, 154, 157

III: 38, 67

IV: 22, 39-41, 44, 46-7, 225-6, 284, 286

VI: 77

<u>U.S.</u>
I: 44, 65, 67, 79-98, 112, 287

II: 17, 27, 35-6, 76, 78-92, 125, 220, 242, 246

III: 49, 93

IV: 20, 45-7, 52, 54-5, 310-11, 393, 396

VI: 103

CASSIDE, SUSAN
Susan Archer Casey. c.1835 - 1918. O'Casey's mother. Married Michael
Casey.* Resident at 22 Wellington Street; to 23½ Dorset Street; to 57
Wellington Street; to 6 Upper Dorset Street; to 85 Upper Dorset Street
(1879); to 9 Innishfallen Parade (c.1882); to 20 Lower Dominick Street
(c.1888); to 25 Hawthorne Terrace (1889); to 18 Abercorn Road. Died
9 November. Buried at Mount Jerome Cemetery, Dublin. Source: Margulies,
<u>The Early Life of Sean O'Casey</u>.
<u>PAN</u>
I: 9-23, 27-8, 37-8, 40-1, 45-63, 67-70, 73, 77-8, 84-5, 93, 98-9,
104-13, 117-18, 122-5, 127, 143, 147, 150-6, 168-87, 189

II: 7-11, 17-18, 20, 21-2, 24, 26-8, 30, 37, 41-6, 64-5, 69-71, 83-4,
101, 109, 117, 137, 144-50, 154, 158-9, 174, 183, 184-5, 189, 193,
195, 210, 240

III: 27, 28, 29, 43-5, 52, 67, 80, 82, 87, 88, 90-3, 97, 206-10, 215,
277

IV: 20-41, 45-6, 94, 126

V: 40, 221

VI: 71-2, 76, 223
<u>U.S.</u>
I: 1-23, 30-1, 48-9, 52-3, 61-90, 95-9, 105, 112-14, 123, 137, 147-8,
157-70, 177, 185-8, 189, 192, 220, 225, 231-8, 240, 259-89, 291

II: 1-7, 18, 23, 24-5, 33-6, 50, 57-65, 94-5, 102-04, 124-5, 158, 166,
179, 211, 221-31, 236, 243, 244, 268, 281, 285, 293, 298, 301, 325, 372

III: 32, 34, 35, 56-9, 71, 94, 114, 117, 124, 126, 130-3, 139, 305-11,
320, 415

MORE

CASSIDE, SUSAN (cont.)

IV: 16-47, 52-3, 124, 169

V: 44, 296

VI: 93-4, 102, 319

CASSIDE, TOM
Tom Casey. 1869 - 1914. O'Casey's brother. Born at 23½ Dorset Street,
Dublin. Civil service employee at the post office. Member, Royal
Dublin Fusiliers (1887-94), British army. Regained job at the post
office (1894). Recalled to service for Boer War (1899). Married Mary
Kelly, 1903 (see COOLEY, AGATHA). Died 6 February. Source: Margulies,
The Early Life of Sean O'Casey.
                                        PAN
I: 38, 48, 50, 55-70, 78, 186

II: 23, 28-9, 46-64, 84, 128, 143-54, 157-8, 160, 197

III: 25-47, 100, 209

IV: 21, 22-3, 286

V: 221
                                        U.S.
I: 49, 65, 67, 76-100, 112, 287

II: 27, 35-6, 66-92, 125, 196, 220-37, 242, 246, 305

III: 30-63, 144, 309

IV: 18, 20, 396

V: 296

CASSIDY, HOPALONG
Fictional cowboy character in films and comic books. Primarily identified with William Boyd (b.1895), a leading man in silent films and
later a star in television and motion pictures.

VI: 16   (12)

CASSINO
Town and commune in central Italy. Site of Monte Cassino, founded by
the Benedictine Order and one of the most famous monasteries in the world.

IV: 80   (103)

CASSIUS, GAIUS
Chief conspirator against Caesar.*

II: 132   (203)

CASTLEREAGH, VISCOUNT ROBERT STEWART
1769 - 1822. English politician. Chief secretary for Ireland (1799-1801) and one of the chief architects of the Act of Union.* Leader of the coalition against Napoleon. O'Casey's allusion is to Castlereagh's suicide by cutting his own throat.

V: 76   (95)

CAT N' CAGE
Well known Dublin pub at 74 Upper Drumcondra Road in north Dublin. Established 1750.

II: 46, 52-62, 172   (66, 74-89, 265)

CATHLÉEN, DAUGHTER OF HOULIHAN
More popularly expressed as simply "Cathleen ni Houlihan." An allegorical name for Ireland which is rooted in folklore. Subject of poems and translations by Mangan* and O'Grady* and a play by Yeats.*See also BANBA and DARK ROSALEEN.

III: 14, 21, 80, 123, 127, 129, 143,   (11, 23, 113, 179, 184, 185,
161, 213, 225, 226, 235, 270, 282, 287   188, 209, 238, 315, 336, 351,
                                         405, 424, 431)
IV: 148, 176, 177, 284   (201, 240, 393)
VI: 29, 104, 108-11   (31, 143, 148-53)

CATHOLIC ASSOCIATION
The best known association of this sort was founded by Daniel O'Connell* and supported by the Irish clergy (probably O'Casey's point) to promote the political emancipation of Irish Catholics (1823-29). Achieved its objective with the Catholic Emancipation Act (1829).

III: 112   (162)

CATHOLIC ENCYCLOPEDIA
The U.S.- edited Catholic Encyclopedia (1907-14), the most significant Catholic reference book for more than a half century.

V: 192-3, 196   (257, 261)

CATHOLIC HERALDANGELIST/TIMERIANS
Variants on the two Catholic newspapers, Catholic Herald and Catholic Times. Magennis* is referred to as a "herald angel."

III: 152, 153   (224)

CATHOLIC TRUTH SOCIETY
Publishers of Catholic educational material in a number of English-speaking countries. In Dublin, it was located at 24 Upper Sackville (O'Connell) Street. Also in Liverpool (#).

IV: 195   (266)
V: 142#   (188#)
VI: 195   (278)

CATHOLIC YOUNG MEN'S SOCIETY
According to Krause's Sean O'Casey, the production of The Silver Tassie
by the Abbey Theatre in Dublin in 1935 produced the following resolution
by the Dublin C.Y.M.S. (29 North Frederick Street):

> That we condemn vehemently the dramatic work of the Abbey Theatre
> in so far as it infringes the canons of Christian reverence or
> human decency and so far as it infringes the nation's prestige at
> home and abroad.

In a footnote, Krause continues: "A week later, Mr. J. Costeloe, hon-
orary secretary of the National Council of the Federation of the Catholic Young Men's Societies, wrote a letter to the Irish Press (3 September 1935), stating that his Council has passed a resolution against the
Abbey Theatre's production of the play: 'The action of the Galway branch
has the wholehearted support of the National Council of the C.Y.M.S.'"

III: 118	(172)
V: 50, 52	(57, 61)
VI: 215	(309)

CAT'S CRADLE
Play (1926) by A. P. Stuart which appeared at the Criterion Theatre,
London, April 1926.

V: 20	(16)

CATTLE DRIVING MOVEMENT
The Gaelic League and the Irish-Ireland movements, to whom the Tain
(see TAWN BO COOLEY) was the Book of Books.

III: 105	(152)

CATTLE RAID OF COOLEY
The English title of Tain Bo Cualagne (see TAWN BO COOLEY).

III: 236, 240	(352, 358)

CATULLUS, GAIUS VALERIUS
84 - 54 B.C. Regarded as one of the greatest lyric poets of Rome.

VI: 202	(288)

CAVAN
Inland Irish county in Ulster province.

VI: 221	(317)

CAVE HILL
Hill north of Belfast with three caves in it. In the 1790s, it was a
secret meeting place for the United Irishmen.*

III: 103	(148)
IV: 66	(82)
V: 217	(291)

CAVENDISH, LORD FREDERICK CHARLES
1836 - 1882. Chief secretary for Ireland (1882). Assassinated, with
undersecretary Burke,* by the Invincibles* in Phoenix Park, Dublin.

I: 75   (108)
II: 38, 54   (51-2, 78)

CAVENDISH ROW
In north Dublin, off Great Britain (Parnell) Street.

I: 22, 49   (22, 66)
II: 77   (115)
IV: 285   (394)

CEARNEY, PEADER
(Kearney or O Cearnaigh) 1883 - 1942. Irish playwright and song
writer. Author of lyrics to the Irish national anthem, "The Soldier's
Song." Said to have taught Irish to O'Casey in 1907 (see Cleeve,
Dictionary of Irish Writers). Kearney worked as a prop man with the
Abbey, wrote poetry, plays, painted and was the author of many popular
rebel songs. He was active in the Easter Rising, the Irish Republican
Brotherhood, and on the Free State side during the Civil War. Brendan
Behan's uncle.

III: 164   (242)

CENOTAPH
The Whitehall (London) monument which is dedicated to the dead English
soldiers of both world wars. Designed by Sir Edwin Lutyens.

VI: 114   (157)

CENSORSHIP BOARD
The Irish Censorship of Publications Board which banned many of O'Casey's
books, including Within the Gates (4 December 1934), I Knock at the
Door (16 May 1939, resc. 16 December 1947), Pictures in the Hallway (16
December 1942, resc. 16 December 1947) and others. According to Blanshard, The Irish and Catholic Power, up to 1953, over 4057 books and
376 periodicals were banned in Ireland, including nearly all the great
works of modern literature. See O'Casey's Letters, I, pp. 519n, 592n
and 796n. See also MAGENNIS.

V: 45-6   (52)

CENTRAL MODEL SCHOOLS
Non-denominational schools created in Ireland in the 1850s for the pur-
pose of exhibiting improved teaching methods to surrounding schools and
for the purpose of training young teachers. The schools were "mixed"
(Protestant and Catholic), and most of the students were from lower and
middle class families. The schools were outside the control of both the
Protestant and Catholic clergy and were the objects of attack by them.
According to a letter to Horace Reynolds (Letters, I, pp. 696-700),
O'Casey attended Central Model School #2 "for a year or two."

I: 65   (92)

CENTRAL PARK
Principal park in New York City, extending from 59th to 110th Street
and from Fifth Avenue to Central Park West.

V: 196   (262)

CERBERUS
In Greek mythology, the watchdog at the entrance to Hades, the infernal
regions.

IV: 233   (321)

CEZANNE, PAUL
1839 - 1906. French painter. A leader of post-impressionism who ex-
celled in still-life and landscape.

IV: 170, 186, 206, 282   (231, 254, 283, 391)
Boy in the Red Waist Coat   VI: 74   (98)

CHALFONT ST. GILES
English village about 20 miles northwest of London. From 1931 to 1934,
O'Casey lived in a bungalow called Hillcrest which was almost opposite
Milton's* former home.

V: 133, 134, 138   (174, 175, 181-2)

CHAMBER'S DICTIONARY
One of the many reference books published in the 19th and 20th centuries
by Chambers & Chambers Publishing firm, London and Edinburgh.

II: 122   (187)

CHAMBERLAIN, NEVILLE
1869 - 1940. British politician. Best known for his capitulation to
Hitler and the infamous Munich Pact (1938). Chamberlain's speech (#) ,
"A Go-Getter for Peace," took place at the annual Lord Mayor's banquet
in the Guildhall, London (9 November 1938), and was an explanation of
the Munich Pact.

VI: 22, 113-4#, 116, 118-9   (20, 155-7#, 160, 162-4)

CHANCELLOR'S
Dublin optical instrument makers at 55 Lower Sackville (O'Connell) Street.

III: 154   (227)
IV: 274   (379)

CHAPELIZOD GATE
South gate of Phoenix Park, Dublin, which leads to Chapelizod Road.

II: 39   (53)

CHARING CROSS ROAD
In central London, leading to Charing Cross and spilling into Trafalgar
Square.

V: 61   (74)

CHARLES STREET TUBERCULAR CLINIC
In Dublin, the P. F. Collier Memorial Dispensary for Prevention of
Tuberculosis, 5-6 Charles Street.

III: 245   (367)

CHARLES THE BAWDY
There is no Charles with such a title, though one deserved it.
O'Casey is probably referring to Charles the Second.*

V: 23   (21)

CHARLES THE SECOND
1630 - 1685. King (1660-85) of England, called the "Merry Monarch."
He had numerous mistresses, 13 known by name, and many illegitimate
children. There is a statue of him at the Chelsea Hospital across the
Thames from Battersea Park, London.

V: 26   (26)

CHAUCER, GEOFFREY
c.1340 - 1400. The first major English poet. O'Casey alludes to
Chaucer's civil service job of comptroller of the customs and subsidy
of wools in London (1374). Chaucer was often reduced to poverty because
of the capriciousness of pensions and gifts by rich Kentish heirs.

V: 45, 128   (51, 167)
VI: 57, 64-5, 66, 102   (73-4, 84-5, 87, 140)

CHAVANNES, PUVIS DE
1824 - 1898. French painter and muralist.

IV: 199   (273)

CHEKHOV, ANTON
1860 - 1904. Noted Russian dramatist. See O'Casey's essay, "One of the
World's Dramatists," in Blasts and Benedictions.

IV: 177, 191   (241, 261)
The Cherry Orchard (1904) III:125   (182)
Uncle Vanya (1899)   V: 11   (4)

CHELSEA
Borough in southwest London where O'Casey lived in the late 1920s.

V: 64   (78)
VI: 11   (3-4)

CHESTER
English city and county in Chesire.

III: 285   (427)
V: 9   (1)

CHESTERTON, GILBERT KEITH
1874 - 1936. English author and noted convert to Catholicism (July 1922).
O'Casey alludes to a number of subjects in Chesterton's books and articles
for which see the relevant entries in the index and appendix. He also
links Chesterton to Belloc* in several passages which stems from their
well-publicized friendship (from 1900). The first references allude to
Chesterton's noted tavern habits, to his novel The Flying Inn (1914),
and to his wife's acid comment that Chesterton only wanted to be a
"Jolly Journalist." Chesterton's medieval views on feudalism and the
Reformation (#) can be found in his Short History of England (1917).
See also:

BATTERSEA	FAIR OF FAIRS
BEACONSFIELD	NOTTING HILL GATE
DAABRUIN	RAMSGATE

III: 180-5, 242	(266-72), 361)
IV: 160, 195, 242, 248, 254#, 255#,	(218, 267, 335, 342, 351#, 352#,
258, 261, 264, 267, 273	356, 360, 365, 369, 377-8)
V: 134#, 143, 192#, 193-4	(177#, 188, 256#, 258)
VI: 10, 13, 15-16, 85, 167-71	(3, 8, 10-12, 114, 235-51)
Magic (play, 1913) VI: 168	(237)

CHEYNEY/RICHMOND
Sir John Cheyney (d.1509), encased in the North Nave Aisle in Salisbury
Cathedral.* Cheyney was the standard bearer to Henry VII at Bosworth
Field.

V: 188	(250)

CHICAGO
See the article, "Sean O'Casey Comes to Chicago," by Mary Agnes Doyle
in The Drama, December 1927.

V: 108, 109	(140)
VI: 141	(197)

CHILDERMASS DAY
Feast of the Holy Innocents, celebrated on December 28 in commemoration
of the male infants slaughtered after the birth of Christ.

VI: 37	(43)

CHILDERS, ERSKINE
1870 - 1922. Anglo-Irish author and patriot. He served in the Boer War
and as a naval intelligence officer in World War I, for which he was
awarded a D.S.C. Devoted himself thereafter to Irish independence and
was a member of the Dail (1921). Following the signing of the Anglo-
Irish Treaty, he joined those who opposed it. He was captured and executed by Free State soldier for possessing a weapon which had been given
to him by Michael Collins.* His son became president of Ireland. Author
of the well-known The Riddle of the Sands (1903) and historical articles
and books.

III: 244	(365)

CHILDREN OF LIR
In ancient Irish legend, condemned by their stepmother to be exiles.
Celebrated in many Irish poems and translations.

III: 20   (21)

CHILLINGSWORTH, WILLIAM
1602 - 1644. English theologian and controversialist. Sought to vin-
dicate the sole authority of the Bible in matters of salvation and the
individual's right to interpret it.

The Religion of Protestants (1837) I: 35   (43)

CHILTERN HILLS
Range of low hills in southwest England.

V: 133   (175)

CHINA
Most of the references are to the Chinese Revolution (1949).

V: 168   (222)
VI: 130, 176, 196   (180, 249, 278-9)

CHRIST'S COLLEGE
Constituent college of Cambridge University.

VI: 50   (63)

CHRIST'S HOSPITAL
Blue-coat school* in London.

VI: 231   (332)

CHRISTCHURCH CATHEDRAL
Cathedral of the Protestant archdiocese of Dublin and Glendalough. One
of the oldest religious sites in Ireland, dating from the Anglo-Norman
invasion (1170). Restored in 1878.

III: 70   (99)
V: 39   (43)

CHRISTIAN BROTHERS
The Christian Brothers' School was located on North Circular Road and
North Richmond Street, Dublin. The only schools not directly under
British administration, they gave unqualified support to the Gaelic
League. Many of the leaders who emerged in the early half of the 20th
century were past pupils of the Christian Brothers, including the Pearse
brothers, Eamonn Ceannt, Con Colbert, Sean Heuston, Liam Mellows, Eamonn
de Valera, Arthur Griffith, William T. Cosgrave, and Richard Mulcahy.

III: 29   (35)
IV: 115   (152)

CHRISTIAN DOCTRINE
Unknown. There were hundreds of books and pamphlets with titles like
this.

VI: 56   (71)

CHRISTIAN UNION BUILDING
In Dublin on Lower Abbey Street,housing several charitable and religious
organizations, including the Dublin Free Breakfasts for the Poor and the
Hibernian Band of Hope Union.

I: 40   (52)

CHRYSLER BUILDING
At 405 Lexington Avenue, New York City. Built (1929) for Walter Perry
Chrysler (1875 - 1940), American automobile capitalist.

V: 190   (254)

CHURCH OF IRELAND
The established church in Ireland through the first 70 years of the
19th century. Under the Act of Union,* the Church of Ireland became
part of the United Church of England and Ireland, holding a privileged
status and drawing its tithes from tenant farmers despite the fact that
only about one-eighth of the population in 1861 claimed membership in
it. The 1830s witnessed a "tithe war," though, and the church was
disestablished by the Act of Disestablishment, introduced by Gladstone*
in 1869 (became law, January 1871).

III: 148   (217)
IV: 182   (249)

CHURCH OF JERUSALEM, ALEXANDRIA, AND ANTIOCH
A reference to the shifting sites of the early Christian Church. Antioch
was the place where followers of Jesus were first called Christians after
having severed themselves from the synagogue (see Acts 11:26 and 13:1).
In Alexandria, St. Mark founded a Christian Church and the city became
a great center of Christian learning. Jerusalem is the holy city of
Judaism and Christianity and is intimately associated with Jesus.

II: 47   (67)

CHURCH OF THE TWELVE APOSTLES/PATRONS
The first reference is to the Church of St. John the Baptist, Seafield
Road, Clontarf, where O'Casey's confirmation was held. The names are
fictitious, but the Very Rev. N. D. Emerson, in The World of Sean O'Casey,
remarked: " . . . a research student from an American university . . .
asked Sean O'Casey if he had been a Roman Catholic, and O'Casey had
answered, 'No, I belong to the Church of the Twelve Apostles.' I was too
stupid at the time not to see that he meant that Rome was the Church of
St. Peter but we were the church of all the Apostles. My American friend
was no wiser, so we missed a typical O'Casey jeu d'esprit."

II: 160   (246)
III: 124   (180)

CHURCH ROAD
In north Dublin, around the corner from Abercorn Road.

III: 30   (37)

CHURCHILL, JOHN
Duke of Marlborough. 1650 - 1722. Famous British military leader and
conspirator against the Jacobites. Professed allegiance to James II,*
but was secretly committed to William of Orange.* O'Casey refers to
Churchill's leadership of England's armies against Cork and Kinsale in
1690.

V: 173   (231)

CHURCHILL, RANDOLPH
1849 - 1895. British politician and aggressive Tory. An implacable
foe of Irish Home Rule and of Gladstone.* There is no definite date
for the first usage of the statement that O'Casey correctly attributes
to Churchill -- "Ulster will fight, Ulster will be right" -- but it
was frequently heard in Churchill's speeches in Ulster during the
Home Rule crisis of 1886 when the first Home Rule Bill was introduced.
"It was," his son Winston* wrote, "one of the war-cries of the time and
sped with spirit-speed over the country."

II: 230   (357)
III: 76   (107)

CHURCHILL, WINSTON
1875 - 1965. In Irish history, Churchill does not command the respect
accorded him by others. Like his father, Randolph,* he was hostile
to every move for Irish independence (as well as to the independence
of any English colony). He was undersecretary (1905-08) and secretary
(1919-22) for the colonies. The latter period was of crucial importance
for Ireland as it involved their War of Independence. Churchill was
on the negotiating team for the Anglo-Irish Treaty* and he is credited
for bludgeoning the Irish representatives into signing or facing the
threat of "immediate, terrible war." The lone holdout, Erksine Childers,*
was characterized by Churchill as a "mischief-making murderous renegade."
In his notebooks, O'Casey compared Churchill with Bulldog Drummond.*
"Churchill had the build and look of Bulldog D," wrote O'Casey, "but he
was, of course, a very different type, full of decision, daring, imagination; vital, and a great leader; but he did bluster occasionally, and,
at times, even bullied. But in the war, he was a godsend to England."
(Sean, p. 279)

IV: 72, 73   (92-3)
V: 27, 88, 91-2, 93, 94, 100-02, 165   (27, 110, 117-21, 128-9, 218)
VI: 81, 122, 126, 136, 142, 173   (108, 168, 175, 190, 218)

CHURCHILL, MRS. WINSTON
Nee Clementine Hozier. 1885 - 1977. In the winter of 1941, shortly after
the Nazi invasion of the USSR, Mrs. Churchill issued an appeal for "Aid
to Russia" and eight million pounds were raised.

VI: 142   (199)

CICERO, MARCUS
106 - 43 B.C.   Roman statesman, orator and author.

VI: 201, 203   (286, 289)

CING BULLY OF THE BOYNE OF CONTENTION
See FAIR OF FAIRS

CIRCE
In Greek mythology, an enchantress, daughter of Helios, on the island
of Aeaea, who metamorphosed Odysseus's companions into swine.

III: 187   (276)

CISTERCIANS
Monastic order in the Catholic Church which made its appearance in
Ireland at Mellifont, Co. Louth (c. 12th century).

V: 164   (217)

CIVIC GUARD
The Irish police force, formed after the Anglo-Irish Treaty.* In 1925,
the Dublin Metropolitan Police* was integrated with the Civic Guard,
forming the present Garda Siochana. O'Casey is referring to one of
New York City's policemen, traditionally having large numbers of Irishmen.

V: 185   (247)

CIVITAS DEI
The City of God by St. Augustine.*

V: 236   (317)

The following list of clans is more representative of various famous
names in Irish history than of actual families.

    CLAN OF CAOILTE
    Caoilte MacRonain, a legendary warrior-poet of the Fianna, reputed
    to have lived for over 300 years. Central book in the Colloquy of
    the Ancients, a collection of tales belonging to the Fenian cycle
    which tells of his conversations with St. Patrick.

    III: 102   (147)

    CLAN COLEMAN
    St. Colman MacLenin, patron saint of a cathedral church at Kilmacdugh,
    near Coole and not far from Yeats's home. Readers should compare
    O'Casey's descriptions of this with Rolleston's line from Clonmacnois:
    "Many a blue-eye of Clan Colman the turf covers/ Many a snow white
    breast."

    V: 172   (229)

    CLAN OF CONN
    See CONN OF THE HUNDRED BATTLES

CLAN (cont.)

CLAN OF CORMAC
Cormac was one of the important early kings of Ireland (c. 254-c. 277). Credited with being the first legislator of Ireland, making Tara the capital of the country.

III: 102   (147)

CLAN OF DERMOT
See MacMOURROUGH OF THE CURSES, DERMOD

CLAN OF FERGUS
Fergus MacRoigh, legendary king of Ireland and friend of Cuchulain.* Married to Nessa, and was tricked into giving up his throne to Conchubar. See Yeats's* play, Deirdre (1907).

III: 102   (147)

CLAN OF FINN
See McCOOL, FINN

CLAN HUGH
Hugh MacAnimire, king of Ireland (572-598), who summoned the first national assembly after the fall of Tara.

III: 102   (147)

CLAN OF KEVIN
See ST. KEVIN

CLAN OLIVER
O'Casey is quoting from the first line, third verse, of Charles Gavan Duffy's (1816 - 1903) poem, "The Irish Rapparees."

I: 21   (21)

CLAN OWEN
Eoghan, a 2nd-century Irish king of Munster who was defeated by Conn of the Hundred Battles.*

III: 102   (147)

CLAN SASSENACH
From the Irish word, sassana = Englishman or England.

I: 21   (21)

CLANCY, CLUNE AND McKEE
Murder victims in a series of assassinations and reprisals between the British Secret Service and Irish Republican Army.   On November 21, 1920, 14 British agents were killed by Michael Collins'* special squad of soldiers.   That afternoon, the British army fired into a civilian crowd who were watching a football game at Croke Park in Dublin, killing 12 and wounding 60.   That same evening, Dick McKee (b.1893), commandant

MORE

CLANCY, CLUNE AND McKEE (cont.)

of the Dublin Brigade of the I.R.A.; Peadar Clancy (b.1888), vice-commandant; and Conor Clune (b.1893) were arrested and murdered in Dublin Castle. A British court of inquiry concluded that the three were killed "trying to escape." See the souvernir pamphlet, They Died on Bloody Sunday.

IV: 52   (63)

CLANWILLIAM
Ancient Celtic baronies in Limerick and Tipperary. There is a Clan-william House at 85 St. Stephen's Green, Dublin.

III: 70   (98)

CLARE
Irish county in Munster.

III: 156   (229)
IV: 135, 192   (182, 263)

CLARE, ANGEL
Tess's husband in Thomas Hardy's Tess of the D'Urbervilles.

V: 18   (14)

CLARE COLLEGE
Constituent college of Cambridge University.

VI: 50, 53   (63, 67)

CLARE STREET
In Dublin, next to Leinster Street and Lincoln Place.

IV: 117   (156)

CLARENCE, DUKE OF
Albert Victor Christian Edward, Duke of Clarence and Avondale. 1864 - 1892. Eldest son of Edward VII. Betrothed (1891) to Princess Mary (later Queen Mary, consort of George V) but died before marriage.

II: 26   (32)

CLARKE, AUSTIN
1896 - 1974. Major Irish poet of the 20th century. O'Casey refers to Clarke's criticisms about the opening production of The Plough and the Stars, which were in a letter to the editor, Irish Statesman, 20 February 1926.

IV: 128, 181, 185   (171, 247, 253)
VI: 208   (298)

CLARKE, THOMAS
1858 - 1916. Oldest signatory of the Irish Proclamation of Independence.
A member of the Irish Republican Brotherhood, Clarke spent nearly half
his life in British jails for revolutionary activity. He was at one time
friendly with O'Casey, but their relationship soured when O'Casey began
attacking the Irish Volunteers. In 1914, at the height of O'Casey's
attacks, Clarke, in a letter to John Devoy, described O'Casey as a
"disgruntled fellow" and blamed him for sowing disunity among the ranks.
Clarke's tobacconist's shop was located at 75a Parnell Street.

III: 161, 164-5, 223, 231, 233-4, 235, 244, 272, 286
     (236, 242, 331, 344, 348, 351, 364, 408, 430)

CLEENA, WAVES OF
The Tonn Cliodhna, on the seashore at Glandore Bay, Co. Cork. The name
derives from the legend of a Danann maiden who left the Land of Youth
with a mortal lover. She fell asleep near the bay and was swept away.
According to Lady Gregory's Gods and Fighting Men, the maiden's name
was Cliodhna of the Fair Hair. It has been the subject of several poems
and is included in the Tain.

III: 105   (151)

CLEMANTIS, FATHER
According to O'Casey's notebooks, "The real name of the visiting priest
was Father Leo, whose birth-name was McLoughlin. The order was that of
the Discalced Carmelites . . ." (Sean, p. 279)

V: 148-52, 156-8   (195-200, 206-09)

CLERY'S
Major department store in Dublin at 21-27 Sackville (O'Connell) Street.
Owned by William Martin Murphy.*

III: 191   (282)

CLIFFONEY
Irish town in Co. Sligo.

IV: 116   (153, 155)

CLITHEROE, JENNIE
Appears as a girlfriend of the young O'Casey.

I: 90, 189-90   (133, 292-3)
II: 34-5, 39, 41, 55, 82, 160 (45-6, 52, 57, 79, 122, 247)
IV: 217   (299)

CLIVE, ROBERT
1725 - 1774. British soldier and architect of the conquest of India.
Plagued by opium addiction and committed suicide.

IV: 177, 183   (242, 249)

CLONERVY, MICK
Appears as a colonel in the Free State Army.

IV: 102-05, 107-09   (134-8, 142-4)

CLONLIFFE ROAD
In Dublin, running from Lower Drumcondra Road into Poplar Row.

III: 164   (241)

CLONMACNOIS
Ancient religious center in Co. Offaly.   A bishopric from c.548,
the town was destroyed in 1552. See T. W. Rolleston's poem, "The
Dead at Clonmacnois."

VI: 216   (309)

CLONTARF
Suburb north of Dublin. Site of the ancient battle (1014) which resulted in defeat of the Danes by Irish forces under Brian Boru.* One
of the meetings to which O'Casey refers (#) is detailed in O Broin,
Revolutionary Underground, p. 149.

II: 160   (246)
III: 103, 146#, 191   (148, 214#, 282)
IV: 146   (197)

CLYDE RIVER
In northern Scotland along which, in certain areas, is heavily indus-
trialized.

I: 69   (99)

COCHRAN, CHARLES BLAKE
1872 - 1951. London producer of the world premiere of O'Casey's play,
The Silver Tassie (1928). English theatrical manager and the leading
impresario of his day. Knighted in 1948.

V: 33, 37-8, 68-70, 128-9   (35, 41, 83-7, 167-8)

COCKADOO, MOST REV. DR.
O'Casey is quoting accurately from the journal he cites except for the
obvious puns. "Bishop of Blarney" was the bishop of Cork; "Corca Dorca
jails" was Cork jail; "The Most Reverend Dr.C ockadoo, Lord Bishop of
Blarney" was the Most Rev. Dr. Cohalan, Lord Bishop of Cork; and "Free
State jails" was Cork jails. According to Phillips, The Revolution
in Ireland, Cohalan was excommunicating those who murdered policemen,
and had his pronouncements in a pastoral letter read at High Mass in
all the churches in his diocese on Sunday, 19 December 1920.

IV: 111   (147)

CODE OF ECCLESIASTICAL LAW
The Code of Canon Law (1918), the common law of the Catholic Church.

IV: 264   (365)

COERCION ACTS
Acts by the British government against rebel or disturbance activities
in Ireland. From the Act of Union* to 1887, nearly 75 Coercion Acts
were passed. They were variously titled "Public Peace Act," "Unlawful
Oaths Act," "Peace Preservation Act," etc.

III: 105   (152)

COFFEE PALACE
At 6 Townsend Street, Dublin. The Dublin Temperance Institute and
Coffee Booths and Restaurant, operated by the Dublin Total Abstinence
Society. Also the home of the Ormonde Dramatic Society, associated
(1891-99) with W. F. Fay.

II: 20, 132   (22, 203)

COFFEY
Unknown.

III: 120   (174)

COGHLAN, DANIEL
Misspelling of Daniel Cohalan. 1859 - 1952. Senior professor of dog-
matic theology at Maynooth (1886-1914), and bishop of Cork (1916-52).
See COCKADOO, MOST REV. DR.

IV: 258-9   (357)

COGLEY, MADAME D. BARNARD
1883 - 1965. Actress and founder-director, with Michael MacLiammoir,*
Hilton Edwards,* and Georoid O Lochlainn, of the Dublin Gate Theatre.*

IV: 12   (6)

COLBERT, CORNELIUS
1896 - 1916. Part of the dissident group that broke away from the
National Volunteers to form the Irish Volunteers.* Member of Fianna
Eireann and the Irish Republican Brotherhood. During the Easter Rising,
he was in charge of a unit ordered to capture Rowe's distillery.
Executed May 8.

III: 231   (344)

COLE, ALDERMAN
This may be Councillor Michael Cole of 11 Cuffe Street, Dublin, who
represented the Mansion House Ward (Thoms 1909).

III: 155   (228)

COLENSO
Village on the Tuglea River in western Natal, South Africa. Site of a
battle (December 1899) during the Boer War,* which halted General
Butler's* advance to the relief of Ladysmith. Occupied by the British
(20 February 1900).

II: 200   (310)

COLERIDGE, SAMUEL TAYLOR
1772 - 1834. Major English poet.

III: 27   (33)
IV: 206   (282)

COLE'S LANE
In Dublin, connecting Great Britain (Parnell) Street with Henry Street.

II: 92   (138)

COLESBURG
Town in Cape Province, South Africa. Scene of repeated clashes between
the Boers and British during the Boer War.*

II: 200   (310)

COLLEGE OF CARDINALS
I: 94   (139)
IV: 238   (328)

COLLEGE GREEN
Site of Trinity College.*

III: 113, 175   (163, 258)

COLLEGE OF ST. PATRICK
See MAYNOOTH

COLLEGE STREET
In south central Dublin, connecting Great Brunswick (Pearse) Street with
College Green.

I: 184   (284)

COLLIER, JOHN
1850 - 1934. English portrait painter and writer on art. The Shaw
portrait to which O'Casey refers is presently in the National Gallery
of Ireland.

VI: 173   (244)

COLLINS, MICHAEL
1890 - 1922. Hero and military leader of the Irish War of Independence.
Especially adept at evading capture and at gaining his agents' penetra-
tion into the British Secret Service. Killed during the Civil War by
anti-Treatyites at Beal-na-Blath, Co. Cork.

IV: 9, 72-3, 83-4, 87-8, 95-6)   (2, 91-3, 107-08, 113-14, 125-6)

COLUMBIA UNIVERSITY
Prestigious American university in New York City.

VI: 56   (71)

COLUMBUS, CHRISTOPHER
II: 88   (131)
III: 159   (233)

COMBINED MAZE, THE
Play (1927) by F. Vosper, adopted from the novel (1913) by May Sinclair.
Opened at the Royalty Theatre, London, January 1927.

V: 20   (17)

COMINTERN
Shortened form for the Communist International, an organization founded
(1919) "to accelerate the development of events toward world revolution"
by leading members of the Soviet Communist Party. It was abolished
during World War II (May 1943). In 1924, O'Casey's friend, James
Larkin,* was elected to its executive council and attended world
conferences in Moscow in 1924 and 1928.

VI: 94   (127)

COMMONWEALTH
As in the British Commonwealth of Nations.

V: 93   (119-20)
VI: 117, 121   (162, 167)

COMMUNISM
See also SOCIALISM and SOVIET UNION.

III: 251   (376)
IV: 90, 97, 158, 170, 224,   (117, 127, 214, 231, 308-09,
227-8, 230-1   313, 315, 318)
V: 78, 113-16, 161-2, 226, 227   (97, 148-51, 213-14, 303, 305)
VI: 68, 115-16, 118, 137, 200, 233   (89, 159, 163, 191, 285, 335)

COMMUNIST MANIFESTO
Founding statement (1848) of the modern Communist movement. Written
by Karl Marx,* it was greatly admired by O'Casey for its literary style
as well as for its content.

III: 245   (366)
V: 78, 116   (98, 151)

COMPREHENSIVE SURVEY, THE
Author unknown.

II: 87   (131)
V: 180   (240)

CONCERT ROOMS
Given as "ancient Concert Rooms" in PAN and as "Ancient Concert Rooms"
in U.S. Found frequently as Antient Concert Rooms. On Brunswick (Pearse)
Street, Dublin, a large (capacity 800) hall, home of the Irish Literary
Theatre (1899) and the Irish National Dramatic Company (1902) before
the Abbey Theatre was built (1904). Presently the Academy Cinema.

IV: 285   (395)

CONEY ISLAND
Popular amusement resort in Brooklyn.

IV: 276   (383)

CONFRATERNITIES OF BANCORIANS, INVESTORIANS, AND BROKERIANS
A variant on symbols of high finance: banks, investors and brokers.

III: 153   (224)

CONFRATERNITY OF TRUE MALTATERIANS
Variant on the Knights of Malta, the Hospitallers of St. John of Jerusalem, who is on the island of Malta.

III: 153   (225)

CONFUCIUS
III: 59   (82)
IV: 216   (297)

CONG/CROSS OF CONG/CROSSCONGOLIANS
The Cross of Cong is an ancient Irish artifact, made in Co. Roscommon
by a monk (whose name is inscribed on it) to hold a fragment of cross
on which Christ was crucified. Cong is in Galway where Rory O'Connor*
is buried. It is an ancient abbey, founded in 624, burned in 1114,
rebuilt in Norman style, abandoned in the 16th century, and restored
in the 19th century.

III: 201   (298)
IV: 165   (233)
V: 173   (230)

CONGRESS (U.S.)
II: 12   (9)

CONN OF THE HUNDRED BATTLES
First of the high kings of Ireland (125-145). His reign was marked by
assassination and turmoil. Assassinated by Tibradi Tireach.

III: 65, 102   (90, 147)
V: 172   (229)

CONN THE SHAUGHRAUN
The character, Conn O'Kelly, in Boucicault's* play, The Shaughraun.

II: 23, 132, 134, 136, 140-2   (28-9, 203, 206, 208, 216-17)

CONNAUGHT
Province in the west of Ireland. During Cromwell's* conquest, his victims were given the choice of "to hell or Connaught," at that time poor
and barely able to sustain life.

III: 103, 111, 116, 154, 155, 237   (152, 161, 169, 226, 227, 354)
IV: 11, 133, 135   (4, 178, 182)
V: 54   (84)

CONNAUGHT RANGERS
In the British army, the 88th and 94th Infantry Regiments. Active in
many campaigns throughout the 19th century and in World War I. Disband-
ed after their mutiny in India (1921), protesting Black and Tan atrocities.
Nicknamed "The Devil's Own."

III: 105   (152)

CONNELLY, MARCUS COOK
1890 - 1980. American playwright and Pulitzer Prize Winner (1920).

V: 53   (62)

CONNELLY, TERRENCE LEO
1888 - 1961. Faculty member and librarian of Boston College. Frequent
contributor to America* magazine on dramatic topics. Connelly was
bitterly opposed to O'Casey's play, Within the Gates, in Boston, and he
led the way in having it banned.   See his articles in America, 25
August 1934 and 19 January 1935.

V: 203-06   (271-6)

CONNEMARA
Mountainous region in Co. Galway. For centuries an Irish-speaking area.

I: 99   (147)
II: 209   (324)
III: 25, 122, 254, 287   (29, 177, 380, 430)
IV: 158   (214)
V: 202, 217   (269, 291)

CONNOLLY, JAMES
1868 - 1916. Founder of the Irish Socialist Republican Party (1896) and,
by virtue of his writings, the founder of the modern Irish socialist
movement. Leader of the Irish Citizen Army (1915-16) and one of the
signers of the Irish Proclamation of Independence. Executed after the
Easter Rising.

II: 179, 196, 202   (275, 302, 311)
III: 14, 19, 22, 160, 221, 224-6, 228,   (12, 21-2, 24, 235, 316, 334,
229, 244, 257, 266-70, 272, 287   336, 340-1, 364, 384, 399-408,
                                         431)
IV: 13, 49   (7, 59)
VI: 90   (122)
Socialism Made Easy   III: 16, 20 (16, 21)
Under Which Flag? (1916) III: 266   (399)

CONNOLLY, SEAN
d.1916. Abbey Theatre actor who was active in the Republican movement.
Worked with O'Casey at Eason's* and was later involved in the 1913
Strike. A member of the Irish Citizen Army, he was the first casualty
of the Easter Rising.

II: 175-7, 179   (271-3, 275-6)
III: 262-3, 276   (393-5, 414)

CONNOR, JEROME
1876 - 1943. Irish sculptor. The bust of AE to which O'Casey refers
was used as a frontispiece for John Eglinton's book, A Memoir of AE
(1937). The bust was done around 1926.

IV: 212   (291)

CONSERVATIVE PARTY (UK)
Between the world wars, the Conservatives were in power, either alone
or as the largest party in coalition governments, from 1922 to 1945,
except for two minority Labour governments (1923-24, 1929-31). The
leading Conservative figures were Stanley Baldwin and Neville Chamberlain.

V: 77-8, 85, 87, 88, 92   (96-8, 108, 111, 117)

CONSTABLE, JOHN
1776 - 1837. Major English painter who produced realistic studies of
rustic life.

II: 225-6   (349, 350-1)
III: 61, 217   (84, 322)
IV: 199   (274)
V: 15, 18, 27   (9, 14, 27)
VI: 49, 80   (61, 108)
The Cornfield (1826) III: 48 (65)
                     V: 23 (20)
Salisbury Cathedral (1831) V: 187 (249)

CONSTANTINOPLE
VI: 89-90   (121)

CONWAY
Town in Wales noted for its wall, castle and eight cylindrical towers
which were built (1284) by Edward I.

VI: 79   (107)

CONWAY, BARNEY
1882 - 1965. Dublin dockworker and friend of O'Casey from the Dublin
Strike (1913). He is part of the character "Brannigan" in O'Casey's
play, The Star Turns Red. See also BRANNIGAN, RICHARD.

V: 212   (284)
VI: 43   (52)

COO ULLA/COOCOO ULLA
Phonetic spelling of Cu Uladh,* the Hound of Ulster.

III: 133   ·   (194)
IV: 82   (106)

COOK, ELIZA
1818 - 1889. English poet. Best known for her Lays of a Wild Harp.

II: 122   (187)

COOLBANAGHER
Parish in Co. Leix.

III: 190, 211   (281, 313)

COOLE PARK
Home of Lady Gregory* in Co. Galway. O'Casey first visited Coole in
June 1924 (arrived June 7) for a week. For more on O'Casey's visit,
see the relevant entries in Lady Gregory's Journals. The "sacred tree"
on which O'Casey carved his initials is still standing (1982). It has
the initials of Augustus John, Shaw, W. B. and Jack B. Yeats, Synge,
AE, and Lady Gregory and her son, Robert. Coole Park was sold to the
Irish land commission and Department of Forestry in 1927 and destroyed
in 1941 by a building contractor for the value of the stone.

IV: 129, 132-47, 187, 192, 272, 282   (172, 177-99, 254, 262, 376, 391)
V: 43, 66   (48, 80, 81)
VI: 72   (95)

COOLEY, AGATHA
Mary Kelly, Tom Casey's* wife. A Catholic servant girl from the Dublin
suburb of Blackrock where her father had been a plumber. Married in 1903.
See Margulies, The Early Life of Sean O'Casey, pp. 37-9.

III: 26-8, 33-6, 41-7   (30-1, 41-45, 53-63)

COOMBE
Oldest district in Dublin. A dilapidated area around St. Patrick's
Cathedral.

III: 31, 63, 146   (38, 87, 215)

COONEY'S BLACKING
Cooney's Manufacturing Co. Ltd., manufacturers of mustard, laundry
blue, blackings,and black lead. 57-60 Bock Lane, Dublin (Thoms, 1896).

I: 112   (169)
II: 20   (23)

COOPER, JAMES FENIMORE
1789 - 1851. American novelist.

II: 122   (187)

COPPALEEN, MYLES NA
Character in Boucicault's* play, The Colleen Bawn.

II: 45, 132, 134, 209   (64, 203, 206, 324)
III: 120   (174)

COQUELIN, BENOIT CONSTANT
1841 - 1909. French actor, noted for his creation of the role of
Cyrano de Bergerac.

V: 181   (241)

CORCA DORCA
Corkadorgha, the mythical Gaeltacht (Irish-speaking) area that is
satirized in Myles na gCopaleen's* novel, An Beal Bocht (1941). Translated (1973) as The Poor Mouth by Patrick C. Power. See COCKADOO.

IV: 111   (147)

CORK/CORK HARBOUR
II: 88, 175   (131, 271)
III: 101, 113, 115, 118, 140, 141,   (145, 164, 168, 172, 206,
159, 189-90   233, 280-1)
IV: 70, 80, 90, 111, 146   (88, 103, 118, 146, 198)
V: 82, 171, 173, 177   (104, 228, 231, 236)

CORK HILL
Dublin street between Lord Edward and Dame streets near Dublin Castle.

I: 21   (20)
II: 27, 215   (34, 334)

CORKERY, DANIEL
1878 - 1964. Major Irish writer with a strong Catholic, nationalist
bias who heavily influenced Irish prose writing. Disapproved of
O'Casey's plays.

III: 190   (281)
Hounds of Banba (1920)   III: 142   (209)
The Hidden Ireland (1925) III: 101, 125 (145, 182)
                          IV: 118   (158)
                          V: 79   (100)

CORNHILL
London street, leading out from the National Provincial Bank.

V: 73   (91)

CORNMARKET
In southwest Dublin on High Street. At 22 Cornmarket, Lord Edward
Fitzgerald had refuge briefly before his capture during the 1798
Rebellion.

II: 215   (334)

CORNWALL
Maritime county in southwest England.

VI: 75, 76   (100, 103)

COROMBONA, VITTORIA
The "White Devil" in Webster's* tragedy of the same name.

V: 110   (143)

CORPUS CHRISTI COLLEGE
Constituent college of Cambridge University. The college of Marlowe,
Fletcher and Thomas Hobson.*

III: 248   (371)

CORPUS CHRISTI DAY
Catholic feast day in honor of the Holy Eucharist, celebrated on the
first Tuesday after Trinity Sunday.

III: 37   (47)

CORPUS CHRISTI GUILD OF COVENTRY
O'Casey is alluding to the pageantry of the Procession on Corpus Christi
Day at Coventry, England, since the 16th century. See Thomas Sharp,
A Dissertation on the Pageants or Dramatic Mysteries Anciently Performed
At Coventry, 1825, rpted. 1973.

III: 284   (427)

CORRUCKTHER, PATRON OF DANCERS
Unknown. Possibly related to Curetes who, in ancient Greek mythology,
were said to have been heavenly dancers guarding Zeus.

III: 159   (233)

CORSICAN BROTHERS, THE
Louis and Fabian de Franchi, heroes of the drama, translated from the
French by Boucicault.*

II: 133   (204)

CORTEZ, HERNANDO
1485 - 1547. Spanish conqueror of Mexico.

III: 46, 89   (61, 127)

COSGRAVE, LIAM T.
1880 - 1965. Irish politician. Member of Dail Eireann (1917); chairman of provisional government and president of the Dail (1922); president of the executive council of Irish Free State (1922-32).

IV: 150, 157, 158, 182, 282 (203, 213, 215, 249, 391)
V: 39   (44)

COSMOGONY
Probably an allusion to AE's* essay, "Celtic Cosmogony," in his book,
The Candle of Vision (1918).

III: 85   (121)

COSTELLO, JOHN A.
1891 - 1976. Irish politician. Taoiseach (1948-51, 1954-57).

VI: 29, 207   (31, 295)

COSTELLO, WARD
Appears as a student at Yale University who defended The Silver Tassie.

V: 53   (61)

COTMAN, JOHN SELL
1782 - 1842. English landscape painter and etcher. Best known for his
architectual drawings.

V: 15   (9)

COULTON, GEORGE GORDON
1858 - 1947. English historian and Cambridge University professor. His
works deal mainly with the Middle Ages and are well-respected in the
field. They do, however, have a discernible anti-Catholic bias. Spelled
COULSON in PAN (#).

IV: 237, 252   (327, 348)
V: 151, 191#, 193#   (199, 255, 258)
VI: 52, 203-04   (66, 290)
Five Centuries of Religion (1923-50) IV: 254   (351)
                                     V: 13, 167   (8, 221)
                                     VI: 91   (124)
A Premium on Falsehood   IV: 260   (359)
Infant Perdition in the Middle Ages V: 157   (208)
Four Score Years (1943)   VI: 51, 65   (64, 84)

COUNCIL OF TRENT
Catholic council gathered (1545-63) to stop the spread of the Reformation, Protestantism and their influences in all sectors of people's
lives. Their dictates extended into the area of music where only
plainsong and Gregorian chants were permitted and encouraged.

V: 85   (107)

COUNCIL OF VIENNA
Should be Council of Vienne. The 15th Ecumenical Council which ordered
the suppression of the Templars; condemned the errors of the Beghards;
and legislated for reform of the clergy (1311-12).

IV: 266   (368)

COURT THEATRE
Should be Royal Court Theatre, London, on Sloane Square. O'Casey is
alluding to the production (opened 27 May 1927) of The Shadow of a
Gunman in which Eileen O'Casey played the part of Minnie Powell, and
to the production (#) of Shaw's* Back to Methuselah (opened 5 March 1928).

V: 32, 38   (33, 41)
VI: 30#   (33#)

COURTMACSHERRY
Irish town in Co. Cork.

III: 70   (98)

COUTHON, GEORGES
1755 - 1794. French revolutionary leader and member of the legislative
assembly (1791)and the national convention (1792). Guillotined July 28
by Robespierre.*

III: 231   (344)

COVE
Cobh, Irish harbor near Cork.

III: 113   (164)

COVENT GARDEN
Area in London between the Strand and Longacre. Until recently, chiefly
known as the site of the Covent Garden Market where flowers, fruits and
vegetables have been sold since the 17th century.

V: 27   (26)

COWARD, NOEL
1899 - 1975. English actor, playwright, and composer. For more on
O'Casey's criticisms of Coward, see the sections, " Coward Codology,"
in The Flying Wasp (rpted in The Green Crow).

V: 14, 19, 69, 70   (8, 16, 85, 87)
Easy Virtue (1926)   V: 20   (16)
The Queen Was in the Parlour (1926) V:20 (16)
The Woman's Business (1925) V: 20   (16)
Bitter Sweet (1929)   V: 70   (86)

CRABBE, GEORGE
1754 - 1832. Popular English poet. Collected Works (8 vols., 1834).

II: 122   (187)

CRADDOCK, JOHN
c.1708 - 1778. Irish ecclesiastic. Bishop of Kilmore (1757-76).
Archbishop of Dublin (from 1777).

III: 70   (98)

CRAIG, GORDON
1872 - 1966. Son of Ellen Terry. English stage designer and producer.
Founded The Mask (1908), a journal devoted to the theatre.

IV: 146   (197)

CRAIG, MAY
1889 - 1972. Abbey Theatre actress. In the premiere of The Plough and
the Stars, she played the role of Mrs. Gogan.

IV: 173   (235)

CRAMER, WOOD AND CO. LTD.
Pianaforte Gallery and Music Warehouse, 4-5 Westmoreland Street, Dublin.

II: 118   (181)

CRANMER, THOMAS
1489 - 1556. English reformer and archbishop of Canterbury. Burned at
the stake for heresy.

VI: 50, 57   (63, 72, 73)

CRAUGHWELL
Irish town in Co. Galway, the closest railway station to Lady Gregory's*
home.

IV: 131   (176)

CRAWFORD, ROBERT LINDSAY
1868 - 1945. Influential Dubliner in the Orange Order. President,
Grand Lodge of Independents; editor, Ulster Guardian (1907) and Irish
Protestant. Crawford had strong labor sympathies and he supported
progressive trade unionism and the Larkin-led strike in Belfast in
1907, for which he was expelled from the Orange Order.

III: 233   (348)

CRECY-EN-PONTHIEU
Village in northern France where Edward II of England defeated Philip
VI of France in 1346.

I: 50   (68)
III: 105   (152)
V: 85   (108)

CREDE/DINNERTACH/AIDNE
In Irish legend, Crede was the daughter of King Gooary of Aidne who
fell in love with Dinertach of the Hy Fidgenti. Dinertach was wounded
17 times at the battle of Aidne, died, and was buried in the cemetery
of Colman's church (see CLAN COLMAN). O'Casey's quote is the first
two lines from "The Song of Crede, Daughter of Gooary," an anonymous
10th-century Irish poem.

VI: 203   (290)

CREENA, NORA
Maire Keating, O'Casey's girlfriend in the early 1920s. She was the
daughter of a retired police officer and is the "Maura" to whom Two
Plays (1925) is partially dedicated. O'Casey's letters to her are in
the National Library of Ireland. In O'Casey's Red Roses for Me, she is
the character "Sheila Moorneen." See the essay, "The Girl He Left
Behind Him," in The World of Sean O'Casey.

IV: 217-23, 228-31   (299-307, 315-18)

CREENA, NORA
See Appendix I.

CRIMEAN WAR
II: 27, 28, 32, 37   (33-4, 35, 41, 49)
III: 105   (152)
VI: 118   (163)

CRITICS' CIRCLE
Organization of leading dramatic critics in London. The occasion to
which O'Casey refers was the annual dinner in 1926. O'Casey elaborates
on his remarks in Letters, I, p. 662. For his comparison of London and
U.S. dramatic critics, see the essay, "Hail Columbia," in The Flying Wasp.

V: 68   (83)

CROAGH PATRICK
Irish mountain in Co. Mayo and site of pilgrimages in honor of St.
Patrick.

II: 13   (11)
III: 122   (177)
IV: 66, 68   (82, 85)
V: 217   (291)
VI: 179   (254)

CROMER, LORD MAURICE BARING
1875 - 1945. Journalist and author of poems, plays, novels and several
books on Russia and Russian literature. See Letters, I, p. 662.

V: 68   (84)

CROMWELL, OLIVER
1599 - 1658. England's "Lord Protector" and responsible for the massa-
cres in Irish towns of Drogheda and Wexford in 1649. No other Englishman has left such a scar on the Irish national consciousness. The
"Ironsides" to which O'Casey refers was a famous cavalry regiment led
by Cromwell during the English civil war. The term was afterwards
applied to his entire army.

III: 286   (429)
IV: 70   (88-9)
VI: 105, 197   (144, 145, 281)

CROMWELL, THOMAS
1485 - 1540. The servant to Cardinal Wolsey in Shakespeare's* play,
Henry VIII.

II: 132   (202)

CROMWELL ROAD
In South Kensington, London, crossing Queen's Gate, on which is located
the Victoria and Albert Museum.

V: 31   (32)

CRONJE, PIET ARNOLDUS
1840 - 1911. Commander in chief of the Boers during the Boer War.*
He was captured and held prisoner at St. Helena until the end of the war.

III: 164, 269   (241, 403)

CRONUS
In Greek mythology, a Titan, son of Uranus and Ge. Dethroned by Zeus.

IV: 157   (213)

CROSBY, HARRY LILLIS ("BING")
1904 - 1977. American singer and entertainer. Winner, Academy Award
(1944), for Going My Way, a film giving a glossy portrait of the Irish
clergy, stirring O'Casey's wrath.

V: 149-50, 232   (197-8, 312)
VI: 38, 230-1   (45, 331)

CROSS GUNS/CROSS GUNS BRIDGE
The Cross Guns pub is immediately south of the Cross Guns Bridge on
Phibsboro Road, Dublin.

II: 53-4, 63   (77-8, 92)

CROWE, EILEEN
1898 - 1978. Abbey Theatre actress. In O'Casey's premieres, she played
the role of Kathleen in Kathleen Listens In; Mary in Juno; Young Girl
in Nannie's Night Out; and a woman in The Plough and the Stars. In
the latter she refused to play the role of Mrs. Gogan because she felt
some of the lines were indecent. In a 1930 revival of the play, she
played the role of Rosie Redmond, a prostitute. Married (1925) to
F. J. McCormick.*

IV: 173, 280   (235, 387)
V: 121   (159)

CROYDON PARK
In Clontarf, northeast of Dublin. A three-acre lot with a house which
was rented by Larkin* from August 1913 until 1915. Used as a recreational center for ITGWU members. On various occasions it was used for meetings, Irish Citizen Army training and as a sports ground. Delia Larkin
looked after the management and recreational details.

III: 224, 228, 261-3   (334, 340, 392-4)

CRUACHAN, OILLOL OF/WHITE BULL OF
Cruachan is an Irish town in Co. Roscommon, now called Ratherghan. It
was the ancient capital of Connaught and is featured prominently in the
Tain. In the Tain, "Oillol" (Aillill*) is the husband of Queen Maeve*
and commander of the Knights of Clanna Morna. The White Bull was owned
by Queen Maeve.

III: 240, 242   (359, 361)
IV: 133   (179)

CRUDEN'S CONCORDANCE
Probably the oldest of biblical concordances. Published (1737) by
Alexander Cruden (1701 - 1770) and contains almost 200,000 references.
Cruden used the Authorized Version of 1611 ("King James's Version").

I: 35   (43)

CRUSADES
Series of military expeditions undertaken by the Christian powers in
the 11th, 12th and 13th centuries to recover the Holy Land from the
Muslims.

IV: 97   (127)
VI: 89-90   (121)

CU ULADH
Pseudonym of P. T. McGinley. 1857 - 1942. His Irish name was Peadar
MacFhionnghaile. Joined the Gaelic League in 1893 and became its
president (1923-25). Author of Handbook of Irish Teaching (1903) and
editor of several anthologies of Irish verse. The comments to which
O'Casey refers appeared in the Irish Independent, 21 August 1935.

V: 50   (58)

CUCHULAIN
The Irish Achilles. Legendary figure of first-century Ulster. ɪ ᴠmanti-
cized in the Tain as the defender of Ulster from Queen Maeve.* Eˉ elled
in every manly art.

II: 181, 235   (280, 364)
III: 103, 162, 237-41, 264   (148, 238, 353-60, 395)
IV: 68, 176, 270   (85, 239, 373)
V: 50, 165   (59, 218)
VI: 167   (235)

CULLEN'S HOUND
In Irish mythology, Cullen was a wealthy smith who had a ferocious dog
to guard his house. While Setanta was approaching his home, the dog
attacked him, but was killed. Thereafter Setanta was named Cuchulain,*
the Hound of Cullen.

IV: 133   (178)

CULLENITES
Probably a pun on those who took the legend of Cullen's Hound* too
seriously.

III: 153   (224)

CUMBERLAND
Maritime county in northwest England.

VI: 76   (101)

CUMBERLAND STREET
In Dublin, running into Great Brunswick (Pearse) Street.

III: 168   (247)

CUMMANN NA MBAN
Irish for Society of Women, an Irish republican organization of women --
separatist and nationalist -- which was established in June 1914.

                                                              MORE

CUMMANN NA MBAN (cont.)
Prominent in the Easter Rising and in the protests surrounding the
premiere of O'Casey's play, The Plough and the Stars.

IV: 176   (240)

CUMMINS, DR. JOSEPH DOMINICK
1882 - 1959. Chief eye surgeon of the Royal Eye and Ear Hospital, Dublin,
who treated O'Casey's ulcerated corneas for many years. O'Casey's play,
Red Roses for Me, is dedicated: "To J. D. Cummins in memory of the
grand chats around the surgery fire."

IV: 170, 174, 286   (231, 235, 398)
V: 70   (85)
VI: 84   (114)

CUNEIFORM ORDER OF IMPASSIONATE CANONS IRREGULAR
In O'Casey's notebooks,he wrote:
                    Jocular play on words. Cuneiform is, of course, name
                    of the word symbols used by Babylon and Assyria, wedge-
                    shaped, ancient, and dead . . . like the methods ɔf the
                    Orders. Impassionate as against Passionists; Irreʏular
                    -- there is no such thing as Irregular. There are Canons
                    Regular, signifying that though they be connected with
                    a cathedral, they are bound by canons or rules, therefore
                    becoming a regular Order as distinct from the ordinary
                    priest. . .
See AURICULAR, FATHER for the conclusion of this passage.

V: 149, 153, 155   (195, 202, 205)

CUNNIN MWAIL
Conan Maol, pen name of Padraig O Seaghdha. 1855 - 1928. Irish history
and language enthusiast. The name, meaning Conan the Bald, is taken
from an early Fianna hero.

III: 133   (195)

CUREHELLI, MARIAR
Marie Corelli. Pseudonym of Mary MacKay. 1855 - 1924. English writer
and a favorite of Queen Victoria. Author of over 28 novels.

II: 16   (16)

CURIE, MARJA
nee Sklodowska. 1867 - 1934. Polish-born French physicist. Winner of
Nobel Prize for chemistry (1911) and for physics (1904, shared).

IV: 277   (383)

CURLEY, DANIEL
One of the Invincibles.* See the song,"Lines Written on the Execution
of Dan Curley," in Healy's Old Irish Street Ballads, v. 1.

II: 37   (50)

CURLING, KITTY
Abbey Theatre actress. Played the role of Mollser in the premiere of
O'Casey's play, The Plough and the Stars.

V: 235   (315)

CURRAGH CAMP
Former British army camp in Co. Kildare. Used as an internment camp
for Irish Republican Army suspects.

IV: 90   (117)

CURRAN, CONSTANTINE P.
Official in the Dublin law courts and a friend of AE and Joyce. Frequent
contributor to the Irish Statesman under the initials C.P.C. Curran's
comments appeared in the foreward to The Living Torch.

IV: 210   (288)

CURRAN, SARAH
1782 - 1808. Secretly engaged to Robert Emmet* who was captured while
trying to see her. Immortalized in Thomas Moore's* poem, "She is Far
from the Land" and in Washington Irving's short story, The Broken Heart.

IV: 158   (214)

CUSHENDALL
Irish village in Co. Antrim.

VI: 76   (102)

CUSTER, GEORGE ARMSTRONG
1839 - 1876. American army officer and romanticized adventurer of the
American west. A vain man who brutally murdered and mistreated Indians,
he was killed at the Little Big Horn in South Dakota (25 June).

V: 180   (239)

CUSTOM HOUSE
Dublin official building (built 1791) on the River Liffey east of
O'Connell Street. Houses the custom and excise tax offices, the Board
of Public Works, and the Poor Law Commission. Briefly occupied by
the Irish Citizen Army during the Easter Rising.

II: 106   (161)
III: 187, 214, 271   (276, 317, 407)
V: 212   (283)

CYMRU
Wales

VI: 103, 110, 204   (142, 152, 291)

CYRUS
Either Cyrus the Elder (c.600-529 B.C.) or Cyrus the Younger (c.424-401 B.C.), both of whom are associated with ancient Persia and regarded as substantial historical figures.

II: 88   (131)

CZARS
In this case, the Romanovs, hereditary rulers of Russia before the Russian Revolution (1917).

IV: 163   (221)

CZECHOSLOVAKIA
And the Munich Crisis (1938)

VI: 114   (156)

D

D.W.D.
Dublin Whiskey Distillery Co. Ltd., 50-53 Cork Street.

III: 176   (260)

DA VINCI, LEONARDO
III: 61   (84)
The Last Supper III: 40   (52)

DAABRUIN
Chesterton's* detective priest, Father Brown. In Irish, daabruin is "brown." The model for Father Brown was Father John O'Connor of Yorkshire, a close friend of Chesterton.

III: 181-5   (266-73)

DADLANTIC CHARTER
Variant on "dad" and on the Atlantic Charter, a declaration (1941) of peace aims which was endorsed by 15 nations. Used by O'Casey to condemn the dominant role which men have played in the marriage relationship.

VI: 31   (33)

DAFFY, DEN and COCK
Two Dubliners of local fame, the latter being a football player. Den was a docker and, according to Cowasjee, Sean O'Casey, was the model for the character ,Sylvester Heegan, in The Silver Tassie.

III: 250-1   (374-5)

DAGDA MOR
Father and chief of the people of Dana* in Irish mythology. According to legend, he once ate a large pitfull of porridge and shoveled earth and gravel down his throat.

II: 235   (364)
III: 57, 212   (79, 314)

DAIL EIREANN
The popularly-elected representative chamber of the Oireachtas (National Parliament) of Ireland. The full name was adopted at the Sinn Fein convention (1917). The first Dail convened at the Dublin Mansion House (21 January 1919) with 27 of 75 members present. The remaining were either in jails or on the run. At this convention, whose proceedings were entirely in Irish, Ireland was proclaimed a republic, a provisional government was appointed, and delegates were named to the peace conference at Versailles.

IV: 11, 83, 84-5, 157   (4, 107, 108-10, 212)
VI: 221   (316-17)

DAINGEAN
Irish town in Co. Offaly.

III: 101   (145)

DALLCASSIANS
Also given in puns. Early Irish kings' household troops. Descendants of Cormac Cas, the grandson of Eoghan Mor. The name derives from a sept of east Clare, Dal Cais, whose leader, Mathgamain, captured Cashel from the Eoganachta in 964. Brian Boru's* bodyguards.

II: 187-8   (289-90)
III: 45   (60)
VI: 207   (295)

DALTON, FRANK
Celebrated Dublin actor and father of Louis Dalton, Irish playwright. He is given the name "Tommy Talton" elsewhere in the autobiographies, and the use of Dalton was probably an unintentional slip on O'Casey's part.

II: 87   (130)
IV: 285   (394)

DALY, JOXER
Cunning and comical no-account in O'Casey's play, Juno and the Paycock. One of his most memorable characters.

III: 120   (174)
V: 149   (197)

DALY, P. T.
Influential trade unionist and head of the Dublin Fire Brigade Union. An early advocate of national-based trade unions (as opposed to being affiliated with British unions, the practice to then), a member of Sinn Fein and the Irish Citizen Army, and active in the 1913 Strike. He was Larkin's* choice to succeed him after Larkin went to the U.S. (1914), but Thomas Foran* and William O'Brien* persuaded Larkin to appoint Connolly.* From then on, Daly was systematically excluded from many union activities, but he remained to fight the Foran-O'Brien clique and the trend towards strict unionism. See O'Casey's defence of Daly in Letters, I, pp. 73-4, 78-9.

III: 133   (194)

DAMASCUS
II: 234   (364)
IV: 246   (340)
VI: 51   (63)

DAME STREET
The Wall Street of Dublin. In 1905, there were 93 members of the Dublin
Stock Exchange located on this street.

I: 22, 168, 170, 183, 185   (22, 258, 261, 283, 285)
II: 201   (311)

DANA
In Irish mythology, Tuatha de Danann, "the folk of the god whose mother
is Dana," the mythical colonizers of Ireland.

III: 61, 63   (85, 87)

DANAE
Given in U.S. edition as DANAIDES. In Greek mythology, the daughter of
Acrisius of Argos and mother of Perseus by Zeus. Subject of a number of
famous paintings by Rembrandt, Titian and Correggio.

V: 129   (168)

DANES
Ancient invaders of Ireland and founder of Dublin and other Irish cities.

II: 186-7   (287-90)
V: 22   (20)

DANTE ALIGHIERI
1265 - 1321. The celebrated Italian poet. O'Casey is quoting (#) from
Dante's famous work, The Divine Comedy.

III: 183   (270)
IV: 79, 80, 82, 257#   (102-03, 105, 355#)
V: 177, 183   (235, 243)

DANTON, GEORGES JACQUES
1759 - 1794. French revolutionary. Minister of justice (1792); president of Jacobin Club (1793); guillotined by Robespierre.*

III: 231   (344)

DARIEN
On the Isthmus of Panama, site of two abortive settlements. The first
was by Spanish colonizers (1510, by Balboa). The second was a Scottish
colony, founded in 1698 by William Paterson. O'Casey's use of the word
comes from Keats's* "Sonnet: On First Looking into Chapman's Homer"
(the line: "Silent, upon a peak in Darien").

III: 46, 62, 89   (61, 86, 127)
IV: 222   (305)
V: 19, 146   (16, 193)

DARK ROSALEEN
Personification of Ireland from a 16th-century poem, "Roisin Dubh." The -
most noted translation is by Mangan.*

III: 15, 103, 235, 259, 266   (14, 149, 350, 388, 399)

DART RIVER
In Devon, England. Flows 37 miles southeast past Totnes to the English
Channel at Dartmouth.

VI: 69, 70, 80, 81, 83, 128, 129, 135, 158
(91, 92, 107, 109, 111, 177, 179, 187, 222)

D'ARTAGNON
One of the Three Musketeers, a quick-witted, high-tempered young Gascon
in Dumas's* novel (1844).

V: 91   (117)

DARTINGTON
Agricultural village in Devon, England, on the Dart river and three
miles northwest of Totnes. Birthplace of James Froude, historian.

VI: 93, 138   (126, 127, 192)

DARTINGTON HALL SCHOOL
Where O'Casey's children went to school. It is a manor house dating
from Saxon and Norman times and is presently a well-known coeducational
school and headquarters of a ballet company. The school is part of a
vast (1000 acres) estate bought (1925) by Leonard and Dorothy Elmhirst
for an experiment in rural life reconstruction.

VI: 35, 68-9, 182   (40, 90, 257)

DARTMOOR
Famous prison in Prince Town, Devon, England. Built (1806) for Napoleon's
soldiers and, since 1850, has been used for British convicts. It was
one of the prisons where Irish rebels were sent after the Easter Rising.

IV: 9   (1)

DARTRY
Area immediately north of Milltown in the southern part of Dublin.

IV: 105   (138)

DARWIN, CHARLES R.
1809 - 1882. Darwin was important in O'Casey's intellectual development. At one point, he wrote that after reading Darwin, his "life was
to begin all over again."

I: 10   (3)
III: 27, 83, 175, 176, 217   (32, 119, 259, 260, 322)
IV: 284   (393)
V: 27   (27)
VI: 49   (61)

MORE

DARWIN (cont.)

On the Origin of the Species by Means of Natural Selection (1859)
II: 122   (187)
III: 15   (14)
 VI: 57   (73)
The Descent of Man (1871)   II: 122   (187)

DATHI
Last pagan king of Ireland, reigning 23 years (404-27). A favorite
subject for many Irish poets.

II: 88   (131)

D'AUBIGNE, MERLE
1794 - 1872. Swiss Protestant theologian.

History of the Reformation (4 vols., 1835-47)   I: 35   (43)
                                               II: 17-18, 87 (18, 131)

DAUMIER, HONORE
1808 - 1879. French caricaturist. Imprisoned (1832) for his illustrations
in La Caricature which lampooned bourgeois society.

IV: 199   (273)

DAVID
From the Bible. King of Judah and Israel.

I: 141   (216)
III: 49, 83, 168   (66, 118, 247)
V: 164, 202   (216, 269)
VI: 191   (271)

DAVIS, THOMAS
1814 - 1845. Influential Irish poet and writer of patriotic songs. One
of the founders and leaders of the Young Ireland movement and of the
Nation (1842) to which he contributed many poems, songs and political
articles. O'Casey knew the works of Davis well and alludes to many of
his songs. See Appendix I, II and III. See also O'Casey's article, "The
Soul of Davis," in Feathers from a Green Crow.

III: 16, 17, 21, 126, 163, 235   (14, 17, 23, 183, 240, 350)
IV: 11, 80, 100, 131, 159   (4, 103, 132, 176, 216)

DAVITT, MICHAEL
1846 - 1906. Irish socialist and one of the founders of the Land League.*
Author of Leaves from a Prison Diary (1884) and The Fall of Feudalism
in Ireland (1904).

IV: 159, 240   (216, 331)

DAWSON STREET
In south Dublin, leading north from St. Stephen's Green.

II: 224   (348)
III: 107   (155)

DE BLACAM, AODH
1890 - 1951. Columnist for the Irish Press and writer under the name
of "Roddy the Rover." Interned by the Black and Tans for his nationalist
sympathies.

III: 10   (3)

DE GUERMANTES, MADAME
Character in Marcel Proust's (1871 - 1922) Remembrance of Things Past.
For more Proust, see SWANN'S WAY.

V: 126   (164)

DE LA REY, JACOBUS
1847 - 1914. Boer general who distinguished himself as a brilliant
commander in guerilla warfare in the Boer War.*

III: 164, 269   (241, 403)

DE LION, JACQUARD
Joseph Marie Jacquard of Lyons. 1752 - 1834. Inventor of the Jacquard
Loom which facilitated weaving of patterns.

III: 284   (427)

DE VALERA, EAMON
1882 - 1975. One of the prime movers behind the modern Irish state.
Born in the U.S. of an Irish mother and Cuban father, he returned to
Ireland at a very early age. Became a leader after the Easter Rising
(for which he was sentenced to death, though his U.S. birth succeeded
in gaining a commutation to life imprisonment). Released in 1917 during
the general amnesty. President of Sinn Fein (1917-26); president of
the Irish Volunteers (1917-22); and president of Fianna Fail* (1926-59).
President of Ireland (1959-73).
    O'Casey alludes to several features of de Valera's career, many of
which are dealt with under separate entries. De Valera was a schooled
and trained mathematician. His meeting with Lloyd George took place on
12 July 1921. His statement on the land annuities may be found in
Macardle, The Irish Republic, pp. 988-90. Delegates were dispatched to
the U.S.S.R. in the early years of the Irish Republic in an effort to
gain diplomatic recognition. O'Casey also alludes to de Valera's strong
sense of Catholicism and puritanism.

III: commentary on   161   (237, 238)
     as mathematician   244   (364)

IV: as Sinn Fein president 10   (2-3)
     commentary on   11, 158-60   (3-4, 215-17)
     meeting with Lloyd
     George*   66-73   (83-92)
     and Anglo-Irish Treaty 79, 82-4, 156-7,   (102, 106-08, 211-13,
                            182 V: 50   279 V: 58)
     and Document No. 2*   86-8, 152, 182   (113-15, 205-06, 249)
     and cease fire   148   (200)
     and land annuities   160 V: 228   (217 V: 306-07)
                                                            MORE

DE VALERA, EAMON (cont.)

V: and Baldwin*   78-80   (98-101)
     and the U.S.S.R.   83   (105)

VI: and the Irish Press*   10, 120   (3, 166)
     and Lane Pictures*   29   (31)

Mentioned: IV: 13, 151, 282   (7, 205, 391)
                V: 39, 83, 86, 159-60 (44, 106, 109, 210-12)
                VI: 194, 207   (275, 296)

DE WET, CHRISTIAN R.
1854 - 1922. Boer general who was especially successful as a guerilla
leader. He later rebelled against the South African government and
was imprisoned (1914)

II: 198   (306)
III: 26, 164, 269   (30, 241, 403)

DEACON, SEUMAS
See DEAKIN, SEUMAS

DEAD MARCH IN SAUL
From Act III of Handel's (1685 - 1759) oratorio Saul (1739). The Dead
March occurs when the Israelites discover the bodies of Saul and his son.

II: 19   (20)
III: 223   (332)

DEADWOOD DICK
Sobriquet of Richard Clarke (1845 - 1930), English-born frontiersman
of the American west.

II: 20, 149   (23, 230)

DEAKIN, SEUMAS
Given with two names, Deakin and Deacon. Member of the Supreme Council
of the Irish Republican Brotherhood and was a founding member of the
Irish Volunteers.* He owned a chemist shop on Sackville (O'Connell)
Street, over which he had a flat which he shared with Bulmer Hobson*
in 1909. He and O'Casey would frequently gather there to discuss
politics.

III: 147-8, 207-08, 232, 235   (215, 217, 242, 306-07, 347-8,
                                    351)

DECIES
In Irish mythology, Cormac MacArt's granddaughter Sgeimh Soluis (Light
of Beauty), who was asked in marriage by the son of the King of the
Decies in Co. Wexford.

III: 254   (380)

DECTORA
Character in Yeats's* play, The Shadowy Waters (1911)

V: 176   (234)

DELANY, DR.
Appears as the attending physician to O'Casey's mother. According to
Thoms 1919, there were at least five medical doctors with this name.

IV: 23, 27   (21, 27)

DELANY, MAUREEN
Abbey Theatre actress. In the premieres of O'Casey's plays, she played
the roles of Sheela in Kathleen Listens In; Polly in Nannie's Night Out;
Maisie in Juno; Bessie in The Plough and the Stars; and Lizzie in The
End of the Beginning.

V: 121   (157)

DELMEGE, LUKE
Luke Delmege (1901), a popular novel by Canon P. A. Sheehan.*

III: 133   (195)

DEMETER
In Greek mythology, daughter of Cronus and Rhea, and goddess of vege-
tation and of useful fruits.

V: 116   (151)

DEMPSEY, FATHER
Parish priest in Roscullen in Shaw's* play, John Bull's Other Island.

III: 175, 177   (258, 262)
IV: 273   (377)

DEMPSEY, L. C.
See ELOQUENT DEMPSEY

DEMPSEY'S
Dublin pub.

I: 44   (58)

DENIKIN, ANTON
1872 - 1947. Russian general and leader of White army forces against
the Bolsheviks in the Russian Civil War (1918-22). Set up a South
Russian government (1919), but failed to win popular support.

IV: 230   (318)

DENMARK
The latter reference alludes to the German invasion (April 1940).

I: 181   (279)
VI: 121   (168)

DEPRESSION
The capitalist crisis and economic collapse affecting most of the West
in varying degrees from 1929 to World War II.

IV: 211   (290)

DERBY
Annual race for three-year-olds at Epsom, England. Derby Day is the
last Wednesday in May or the first Wednesday in June.

V: 39   (44)

DERRY
Second largest city in the north of Ireland and a county in the province
of Ulster. One of the areas lost by the Treaty.* Its name was changed
(1608) when it was burned and handed over to the City of London's
corporation, becoming officially Londonderry.
    O'Casey alludes to the siege of Derry (1689) by James II.* The
inhabitants, mostly Protestants, held out for 105 days under the leadership of Rev. George Walker.* See also APPRENTICE BOYS.

II: 87   (130)
III: 189, 241, 242   (280, 361)
V: 88   (112)

DERRYNANE PARADE
In Dublin, connecting Innisfallen Parade with North Circular Road.

II: 55   (78)

DESMOND, EARLS OF
The Fitzgeralds, an ancient Irish family descending from Norman tenants.

III: 254   (380)

DESMOULINS, CAMILLE
1760 - 1794. French journalist and revolutionary leader. Deputy to
the national convention (1793); executed (5 April) by Robespierre.*

III:231   (344)

DETTINGEN
Village in Lower Franconia, Bavaria, where George II of England defeated
Marshal Adrien Mauric de Noailles (27 June 1743).

III: 252   (376)

DEVLIN, JOSEPH
1872 - 1934. Irish politician. Leader of sectarian Ancient Order of
Hibernians, Belfast branch (also known as the Board of Erin). Nicknamed
"Wee Joe."

II: 229, 232   (356, 360)
III: 65   (90)

DEVON
County in southwest England, bounded by the Bristol Channel, Somerset,
Dorset, the English Channel and Cornwall.

V: 199, 232   (266, 312)
VI: 69-83, 93, 129, 134, 135, 138-42,   (89-112, 127, 179, 186, 192-8,
144, 180-2, 184, 220, 222   201, 255-7, 262, 316, 319)

DIAMOND, BATTLE OF THE
21 September 1795. A battle between Protestant Peep of Day Boys,who
raided Catholic homes at dawn, and the Defenders, Catholics who banded
together to resist. Shortly thereafter, the first lodges of the Orange
Order* were formed.

II: 229   (335)
III: 105   (152)

DICK'S STANDARD PLAYS
Series of plays published for dramatic societies by John Dicks publishing house, London, between 1874-1907.

II: 132   (202)
V: 118   (153)

DICKENS, CHARLES
1812 - 1870. Celebrated English novelist. O'Casey alludes (#) to
Chesterton's* work, Charles Dickens (1906). See also MOLD and SQUEERS.

I: 34, 35   (42, 43)
II: 122, 124   (187, 189)
IV: 21, 191   (18, 261)
V: 18, 22, 167   (14, 20, 221)
VI: 15#, 156, 191   (10#, 218, 271)

DIES IRAE
Translated as "Day of Wrath," from the poem by Tommaso DiCelano (c.1185-
c.1255).

IV: 80   (103)
V: 157   (208)
VI: 178, 211   (252, 302)

DILISH, JIM AND JERRY
Appears as a building firm which habitually cheated on construction
specifications. In a letter to Helen Kiok (31 October 1956), O'Casey
commented: "I've often worked on a building that I knew was badly done,
away from specifications, so that the contractor could make a bigger
profit." (Sean O'Casey Review, Fall 1976) The name of the firm is
fictitious (in Irish, dilish = sweet). O'Casey first used the name of
"Bonem" which he said was a Latin approximation of the real firm
(Letters, II). John Good was one of the largest contractors in Dublin.
In Latin, bonum = good.

III: 166-8   (244-7)

DILKE, CHARLES
1843 - 1911. English politician and supporter of Irish Home Rule.

VI: 166   (233)

DILLON, ARTHUR
1670 - 1733. Irish soldier and general of the Irish Brigade in the
French army. Active in many campaigns including Fontenoy.*

III: 152   (223)

DILLON, JOHN
1851 - 1927. Irish nationalist politician. Very influential in Irish
Parliamentary Party* in the early 1900s and opposed to Sinn Fein*
policies. M.P. (1880-83, 1885-1918).

II: 12, 229, 232   (10, 356, 360)
III: 14, 75, 102, 151-2   (12, 106, 146, 222-4)
IV: 273   (378)

DING DONG DEDERO
First line from "Smith's Song" by George Sigerson (1835 - 1925), a poem
and song of anvils, bellows and blacksmiths.

III: 61   (85)
IV: 272   (377)

DINGLE
Irish town in Co. Kerry.

IV: 233   (321)

DISPENSARY
The #1 Dispensary, Langrishe Place, part of the North Dublin Union.

IV: 285   (394)

DISRAELI, BENJAMIN
1804 - 1881. Noted British statesman and author. Earl of Beaconsfield. O'Casey alludes to the large amount of patronage given by Disraeli during his long career as a British Power in Parliament, but the
term "six hundred Baronets" is just a play on Tennyson's* "noble six
hundred." See also PRIMROSE LEAGUE and TWO NATIONS.

III: 75-6   (106-07)
V: 17-18, 57, 91, 101, 168   (13, 68, 116, 130, 223)
VI: 11, 135   (4, 188)

DIXIE
VI: 142   (198)

DOCUMENT NO. 2
Eamon de Valera's* counter-offer to the Treaty,* directed to the British
and Irish governments, rejected by the pro-Treaty Dail and by the British,
which would have joined Ireland to England only by a term known as
"external association," and would have kept Ireland out of the British
Empire, at least to de Valera's satisfaction. The entire document is in
Macardle, The Irish Republic, pp. 959-63.

IV: 86-7, 90, 96, 152   (111-13, 117, 126, 205-06)

DODDER RIVER
Small river running through Irishtown, Ballsbridge and the southeast of
Dublin.

IV: 105, 231   (138, 319)

DOLAN, FATHER
Spelled DOOLAN, U.S. II: 29. Character in Boucicault's* play, The
Shaughraun.

II: 24-5, 136, 138, 140-2   (29, 208-10, 213, 215-16, 218)
IV: 184   (251)

DOLAN, MICHAEL J.
1884 - 1954. Actor and play director at the Abbey Theatre. In O'Casey's
premieres he played the roles of Tommy Owens in The Shadow of a Gunman;
Jimmy in Kathleen Listens In; director and part of Needle Nugent in Juno;
director and part of Oul' Jimmy in Nannie's Night Out; Covey in The
Plough and the Stars. Also played the role of Norton in the 1935 Abbey
production of Tassie. For more on O'Casey's quarrel with Dolan, see
Letters, I, pp. 138-40.

IV: 171, 183, 270, 280   (233, 250-1, 373, 388)

DOLPHIN'S BARN
Street and section in southwestern Dublin, west of Tenter's Field.

I: 20   (19)

DOMINICANS
See also ST. SAVIOUR'S CHURCH.

III: 168   (247)
V: 46, 74, 83   (53, 92, 105)

DOMINICK STREET, LOWER
In north Dublin, crossing Upper Dorset Street at Bolton Street. In
1888, O'Casey lived in a two-room attic flat in Lower Dominick Street
with his mother and sister.

I: 72, 115   (103, 173)
III: 168   (247)

DONALDSON, FRANK
Appears as a secretary to the Grand Loyal Orange Order in Dublin. The
name is real, for he was also editor of the Irish Protestant.

II: 227, 239   (353, 371)

DONEGAL
Northernmost county in Ireland.

III: 151   (222)

DONEGALL, EARL OF
Arthur Chichester. 1606 - 1675. Active as commander against the Irish
uprising of 1641.

III: 70   (98)

DONIEL
O'Casey is using a line from Shakespeare's play, The Merchant of Venice:
"Daniel came to judgement." It is spelled Doniel to signify a Don, or
a college professor.

V: 49   (57)

DONNELLY, THOMAS
Medical doctor at #1 Dispensary. Lived at 12 Rutland Square (Thoms 1907).
In Letters, II, p. 278, O'Casey commented: "Dr. Donnelly is the real
name. He has been dead a long time. He was forced to resign as Dispensary doctor on account of the many complaints against him."

III: 206   (306)

DONNYBROOK
Southeast duburb of Dublin. Famous for its fair, founded 1204 by King
John.

III: 13   (10)
IV: 103   (135)

DONOUGH, YELLOW-HAIRED
An unseen character in Yeats's* play, Cathleen ni Houlihan. Yeats claimed
that he got the name from an old Irish folk song, Donnchadh Ban, or
Flaxen-haired Donough,   thought to have been composed by Anthony Raftery.*

III: 143   (209)

DONOVAN, MAJOR
Unknown. Possibly Robert Donovan (1862 - 1934), professor of English,
University College Dublin (1900-34).

III: 141   (206)

DOONEY'S
Appears as a pub in Great Britain (Parnell) Street. Perhaps Mooney's.*

II: 87-90   (130-5)

DOOSARD, EDWARD
Appears as an inspector with the Quay Police. Probably a fictitious
name, although there was a Edward Doran, Guardian from the Inns Quay
Ward, North Dublin Poor Union.

II: 227-31, 236, 239   (353-8, 367, 371)

DORAN, BARNEY
"A short-armed, stout-bodied, round-headed, red-haired man . . . with
an enormous capacity for derisive, obscene, blasphemous, or merely
cruel and senseless fun" in Shaw's* play, John Bull's Other Island.

III: 175   (258-9)

DORSET STREET, UPPER and LOWER
In north Dublin, running from Bolton Street to Drumcondra Road. O'Casey
was born at 85 Upper Dorset Street, not Lower Dorset Street as he states.
The house was owned by William Lattimer and it had a valuation of 20
pounds. O'Casey's family lived there for approximately two years after
O'Casey was born. The street was named for Lionel Cranfield Sackville,
first Duke of Dorset, who was viceroy of Ireland (1731-37, 1751-55).

I: 81-2, 113, 168, 169, 185   (118-19, 170, 259, 260, 285)
II: 35, 47, 48, 54, 107   (46, 66, 67, 79, 163)
III: 168   (247)
IV: 285   (394)
VI: 218   (312)

DORSETSHIRE
County in southwest England which was closely associated with Thomas
Hardy's* works.

VI: 77   (107)

DOSTOIEVSKY, FEODOR
IV: 186, 190, 191   (255, 260, 261)
The Idiot (1868-69)   IV: 187   (255)
The Brothers Karamozov (1879-80) IV: 187   (255)

DOUAI TESTAMENT
Douay version of the Bible, an English translation of the Vulgate used
by Catholics.

I: 35   (43)

DOUGLAS, MELVYN
1901 - 1981. U.S. actor and director of the U.S. premiere of O'Casey's
play, Within the Gates.

V: 198   (264)

DOVER
In east Kent, England. In World War II it was the chief port for the
Dunkirk* evacuation.

VI: 147   (205)

DOVERGULL, ANTHONY
Anthony Deverall, owner-partner of Leedom, Hampton company, Dublin
wholesale chandlers. More often given as Mr. Anthony. In 1888, he
lived at 34-35 Moore Street, Dublin.

II: 67-9, 72-7, 79-80, 84-8, 90, 92-107, 109-30, 134, 184
(99-101, 105-13, 118-19, 126-32, 135, 138-62, 167-200, 205, 283)

DOWN
County in the north of Ireland.

V: 161, 165, 214   (212, 218, 287)

DOWNING STREET
In London. The British prime minister's residence is #10.

II: 236   (367)
III: 254   (380)
IV: 70, 77, 79   (89, 99, 102)
V: 90, 93   (115, 119)
VI: 113   (156)

DOWNPATRICK
Irish town in Co. Down. One of the oldest towns in Ireland and the
reputed burial place of St. Patrick.*

V: 164-5   (217-18)

DOYLE
Unknown.

VI: 208, 211   (297, 302)

DOYLE, ARTHUR CONAN
1859 - 1930. British physician, novelist and detective story writer.
Best known for his Sherlock Holmes stories.

V: 143   (189)

DOYLE,CORNEY AND JUDY
In Shaw's* play, John Bull's Other Island. Corney Doyle is a small-town
businessman and the father of Larry Doyle. Judy is the aunt of Larry
Doyle and a housekeeper to Corney.

III: 175, 176   (258, 259)

DOYLE, LAM
Lamb Doyle's is a well-known restaurant in the Dublin suburb of
Sandyfort.

III: 205   (303)

DRAKE, SIR FRANCIS
1540 - 1596. English navigator who made the first circumnavigation of
the globe by an Englishman. Landed in Plymouth (1580). "Drake's Drum"
(#) alludes to the poem of the same name by Henry Newbolt.

III: 249   (372)
VI: 82, 116#   (111, 159#

DREAMS OF ANGUS
Aislinge Oenguso (The Dream of Oenghus), an ancient Irish tale involving
Oenghus, son of Dadhda* and Boann.* In the dream, he is the lover who
longs for a girl he has seen only in a dream. The dream ends with the
girl and him together after a long search, flying off as swans and chant-
ing music so beautiful that all who heard it slept three days and nights.

IV: 68   (85)

DREYFUS, ALFRED
1859 - 1935. Celebrated French Jewish officer unjustly convicted of
having divulged state secrets to a foreign power. O'Casey alludes to
Chesterton's* early support of Dreyfus ("To a Certain Nation") which
later wavered (see the note to The Wild Night, 2nd edition).

VI: 168   (236)

DROGHEDA
Irish town in Co. Louth. Site of Cromwell's* massacre of Irish civilians
and where the Irish parliament met(1494) to pass Poyning's Law, making
future Irish legislation subject of English approval.

III: 48   (64)

DRUIDS
Ancient Celtic priesthood who appear in Irish and Welsh sagas as
magicians and wizards.

II: 13, 14   (11, 12)
V: 86-7   (109-10)

DRUMCLIFFE
Village on the Bundoran Road, north of Sligo near Ben Bulben.* Though
Yeats* died in France (28 January 1939),it was not until September 1948
that his body was reinterred at Drumcliffe.

VI: 216   (310)

DRUMCONDRA
Neighboring village of Dublin north of the Royal Canal.

III: 13   (10)

DRUMCONDRA ROAD
In north Dublin, leading from Lower Dorset Street into Drumcondra.

II: 69   (102)
IV: 215   (296)

DRUMMOND, BULLDOG
Chief character in several novels and a play by English novelist, Cyril
C. McNeile ("Sapper") (1880 - 1937). In O'Casey's notebooks, he wrote
of Drummond: "A celebrated but ridiculous character in the stories by
one calling himself 'Sapper.' A lusty, beefy fellow of great strength,
belonging to the upper class; daring against all kinds of spies and
criminals; never daunted -- a ridiculous and fictitious hero . . ."
(Sean, p. 279) See also CHURCHILL, WINSTON.

V: 88   (110)

DRURY LANE
In central London, site of the Drury Lane Theatre (see ROYAL THEATRE).

II: 137   (210)
V: 11   (4)

DUBLIN CASTLE
On Dame Street, Dublin. Seat of British rule in Ireland. Contained the
offices of the lord lieutenant, chief secretary and the law offices of
the Crown.

I: 21, 22, 23, 26, 75   (20, 22, 23, 24, 29, 108)
II: 39, 198, 202   (53, 306, 312)
III: 12, 108, 110, 135, 190, 270,   (9, 155, 158, 198, 280, 290-1,
276, 287   405, 414, 431)
IV: 52, 65, 90, 91, 138, 274   (62-3, 81, 118-19, 186, 379)

DUBLIN COUNCIL COMMITTEE/CORPORATION
The Dublin Corporation is the ruling municipal body of Dublin, comprising
the lord mayor, 15 aldermen and 45 town councillors (one alderman and
three councillors for each of the 15 municipal wards).

III: 103   (149)
IV: 115   (152)

DUBLIN FIRE BRIGADE
Dublin Metropolitan Brigade. In 1909, the superintendent was Captain
Purcess. The fire brigade station was on Great Brunswick (Pearse)
Street.

III: 145   (213)

DUBLIN GALLERY
See NATIONAL ART GALLERY

DUBLIN METROPOLITAN POLICE
See CIVIC GUARD

I: 67   (95)

DUBLIN MOUNTAINS
South of Dublin.

I: 80   (117)
II: 149   (229)
III: 58, 280   (80, 420)
V: 44   (50)

DUBLIN UNIVERSITY
Trinity College.*

VI: 130   (180)

DUBLIN, UNIVERSITY OF
University College Dublin, constituent college of the National University.*

IV: 255   (353)

DUBLIN'S ARCHBISHOP
Archbishop Charles McQuaid.*

VI: 31   (34)

DUCHESNE, LOUIS MARIE OLIVER
1843 - 1922. French Catholic prelate and scholar.

V: 142   (187)

DUCK, DONALD
VI: 38   (45)

DUFF, HARVEY
Police informer in Boucicault's* play, The Shaughraun.

II: 52, 132, 140-2   (74, 202, 215-19)
IV: 168, 184   (228, 251)

DUFFERIN, RACAVAN, LECALE, DONNEGOR, KINNELAERTY
Dufferin, Lecale and Kinnelaerty are baronies in Co. Down. Recavan and
Donnegor are townlands and parishes in Co. Antrim.

V: 165   (218)

DUFFY, JAMES AND SONS
Dublin publishers at 15 Wellington Quay.

V: 157   (208)

DUISKA
Appears as a Russian friend of Shaw.*

VI: 165   (233)

DUKE OF YORK THEATRE
On St. Martin's Lane, London.

V: 11   (4)

DULAC, EDMUND
1882 - ? English portraitist, designer and caricaturist. A devotee
of the Noh plays, Dulac designed several woodcuts of and for Yeats*
including the frontispiece for Yeats's A Vision.

IV: 270   (374)

DULANTY, JOHN
For many years the Irish High Commissioner in London. After 1948, when
an Irish Republic was declared and removed Ireland from the Commonwealth,
Frederick Boland became the first Irish ambassador to London. Dulanty's
address in London was York House, Regent Street.

VI: 165, 184-5   (232, 261-3)

DULEEK
Irish town in Co. Meath.

II: 232, 233, 236   (360, 362, 366)

DUMAS, ALEXANDER
1802 - 1870. French novelist and playwright. See D'ARTAGNON.

II: 122   (187)
IV: 208, 216   (286, 297)

DUN EMER GUILD
Cooperative society of artists and mechanics founded (1903) by Evelyn
Gleeson and Yeats's* two sisters, Elizabeth and Lily in Dublin. It was
in some ways a reaction against the standardization and commercialism of
early 20th century Ireland. The artists produced hand-woven carpets and
rugs, embroideries, and hand-printed books. Later (1908) became the
Cuala Press. The name, Dun Emer, is Irish for Emer's Fort, the name
Gleeson gave to the house she bought for the guild.

III: 230   (343)

DUN SCOTUS
c.1265 - 1308. Famous religious scholastic.

IV: 234   (323)

DUNBAR, WILLIAM
c.146? - c.1525. Scottish poet of the Chaucerian school.

V: 194   (259)

DUNCAN, MARY
1885 - 1960. English-born artist who spent several years (c.1908-16)
in Ireland. A Gaelic Leaguer, she adopted the name Maire Ni Dhonnchada
and executed several portrait etchings of James Stephens, Seumas
O'Sullivan and AE. O'Casey is referring to her lithograph of AE, done
in her studio, 7 North Great George's Street, Dublin, in 1912 or 1913.

IV: 212   (291)

DUNEDIN
Literary and Gaelic name for Edinburgh, Scotland.

V: 93   (119)

DUNGANNON
Irish town in Co. Tyrone. Site of the Irish Volunteers' convention
(15 February 1782) and of the Dungannon Clubs, formed (1905) by Bulmer
Hobson* and Dennis McCullough, both of the Irish Republican Brot erhood,
as a symbol of emerging Irish nationalism. The Dungannon Clubs later
merged with Sinn Fein* (1907).

II: 160   (236)

DUNGENESS
Flat headland in Kent, England, on the English Channel.

VI: 147   (205)

DUNKIRK
Coastal town in northern France. Site of the memorable evacuation of
Allied troops to England (May-June 1940) in retreat from German forces.
See also Appendix III (#).

III: 19#, 123#   (19#, 179#)
VI: 136, 145-7   (100, 202-05)

DUNPHY'S
This may be Thomas Dunphy, family grocer, 160-161 Phibsborough Road and
60 North Circular Road (Thoms 1888), near Dorset Street.

II: 48   (68)

DUNSANY, LORD
Edward John Plunkett. 1878 - 1957. Irish poet and dramatist and nephew
of Sir Horace Plunkett.* Won his reputation as a playwright with The
Glittering Gate (Abbey premiere 1907).

IV: 196   (268)

DUNSEVERIC
In Co. Antrim, Ireland, the home and castle of Connall, the Victorious,
a distinguished Ulster warrior and fosterer of Cuchulain.*

III: 101   (145)

DUTCH BLUE GUARDS
The favorite Dutch troops of William of Orange* at the Battle of the
Boyne.* The colors of Holland are blue and orange (see HOUSE OF NASSAU).
The Dutch troops were nearly all Catholic, and among their leaders were
Schomberg and Ginkle (both *).

II: 228-30   (354-7)
III: 37   (47)

DUTCH SCHOOL OF PAINTING
Late 16th and early 17th century school which broke away from Flemish
painting. Marked by an absence of religious objects and an increase in
naturalism, portraits and landscapes.

IV: 170   (231)

DWYER, MICHAEL
1771 - 1815. Irish Republican leader in the rebellions of 1798 and 1803.

III: 103   (148)

DYSON, WILLIAM HENRY
1883 - 1938. British etcher and cartoonist. For many years on the
staff of the Daily Herald (London). O'Casey refers to Dyson's full-
page cartoon on page one of the Daily Herald, 9 December 1913.

III: 214   (318)

E

EARL STREET
Immediately north of the River Liffey in central Dublin.

I: 64   (89)
II: 55   (79)

EASON'S AND SON, LTD.
At 79-80 Middle Abbey Street, Dublin. The principal newspaper and
magazine distributors in Ireland. See also JASON'S.

III: 191   (283)

EASTER RISING
The events of 24-29 April 1916, primarily in Dublin but also in scatter-
ed parts of the country. On April 24, the Monday after Easter, approximately 1100 men and women -- variously given as 85% Irish Volunteers
and 15% Irish Citizen Army -- led by Pearse and Connolly occupied
strategic positions in Dublin. The General Post Office on O'Connell
Street was the Rising's headquarters in front of which Pearse read the
Irish Proclamation. The British attacked and a bloody fight began which
lasted until April 29 when Pearse and Connolly issued orders to surrender.
Hundreds were arrested and interned in Irish and British jails. All the
signers of the Proclamation were arrested and executed. Though the
Rising had little immediate support, the executions galvanized public
opinion and the returning survivors (released the following year in
a general amnesty) provided leadership for the ensuing War of Independence. For more on O'Casey's views and analyses of the Rising and
the events leading to it, see his The Story of the Irish Citizen Army
(1919, rpted. in Feathers from a Green Crow).

III: 271-87   (407-31)

EBLANA, OUR LADY OF
Eblana was the name given (c.140 A.D.) to a region north of Dublin
by Ptolemy (c.139 161 A.D.), Greek astronomer and geographer.
P. W. Joyce, in his A Smaller Social History of Ireland, remarked that
Ptolemy "is known to have derived his information from Phoenician
authorities."

IV: 165   (224)

EBLANUS OF STOPASIDE, BISHOP
Stepaside is the name of an Irish village in the Dublin mountains in
Co. Wicklow. See EBLANA, OUR LADY OF, above.

III: 202-05   (299-304)

ECRET, FRED
Classmate of O'Casey at St. Mary's National School.

I: 117, 127-35, 141-5, 149, 172   (176, 192-205, 215-21, 228, 265)
II: 42   (58)
III: 86   (123)

EDDYSTONE
The Eddystone Rocks, a dangerous reef in the English Channel. A famous
lighthouse was erected there, first in 1699, and its beacon can be seen
for 17½ miles.

III: 249   (372)

EDEN, GARDEN OF
III: 85, 177, 179   (121, 261, 263)
IV: 227   (312)

EDGEWORTH, MARIA
1767 - 1849. Noted Irish novelist.

V: 68   (83)

EDINBURGH/EDINBURGH CASTLE
IV: 218   (300)
V: 238   (321)
VI: 73   (97)

EDWARD THE CONFESSOR
c.1002 - 1066. Last of the Anglo-Saxon (before the Normans) kings.
Founded Westminister Abbey* in which he is buried.

III: 249   (373)

EDWARD THE SEVENTH
1841 - 1910. King of Great Britain (1901-10). Visited Ireland in 1885
and 1903.

III: 37   (48)

EDWARDS, HILTON
b.1903. Irish actor and director. With Michael MacLiammoir* he founded
the Dublin Gate Theatre (1928) and has since directed over 300 plays at
that theatre and at the Gaiety Theatre.

VI: 78   (104)

EGAN, TOM
Appears as a member of the Irish Socialist Republican Party. According
to a memoir by Ronald Ayling (CKUA, University of Alberta, Canada, radio
station, April 1969), one of the models for the Covey in O'Casey's play,
The Plough and the Stars, was Tommy Egan.

III: 16-17   (15-17)

EGREMONT
The earls of Egremont, the family of Wyndham, which included George
Wyndham (1868 - 1913), chief secretary of Ireland (1900-05).

V: 18   (13)

EGYPT
Used primarily in a biblical sense, though a few references to British
campaigns.

I: 75	(99)
II: 21	(23)
III: 18, 177	(19, 261)
IV: 253	(350)
V: 10, 153, 167, 225	(3, 202, 221, 302)
VI: 188	(267)

EIREBY
Probably an allusion to Joyce's* short story, Araby (1914).

III: 114   (165)

ELIJAH
Hebrew prophet of the 9th century B.C..

I: 15   (10)

ELIOT, GEORGE
1819 - 1880. Pseudonym of Marian Evans, English novelist.

I: 35   (42)

ELIOT, THOMAS STEARNS
1888 - 1965. Celebrated American expatriate poet. The "white bones"
(#) passage is an allusion to The Waste Land (1922). See also ETERNAL
FOOTMAN, PRUFROCK, and the chapter, "A Long Ashwednesday," Rose and
Crown, pp. 120 (156) where O'Casey paraphrases Eliot's poem, Ash
Wednesday.

V: 139, 196#		(183, 261#)
VI: 199		(284)
The Criterion*	V: 175	(234)
Ash Wednesday (1930)	VI: 42	(50)
The Rock (play, 1934)	VI: 87-91	(119-24)

ELIZABETH, QUEEN
Queen Elizabeth I. 1533 - 1603. Queen of England and Ireland (from
1558),of the House of Tudor. O'Casey alludes to laws of the 14th
through the 16th centuries which frequently regulated length of dresses,
types of shoes, and mode of apparel that the nobility were allowed to
wear.

V: 195   (260)

ELIZABETH THE SECOND
b.1926. The present (1982) queen of England.

VI: 198   (281)

ELLESSDEE/ELLESDEEA
Variant on the Latin, libra, a pound; solidus, a shilling; and denarius, a penny. There was a play, L.S.D., by Arthur Pinero* at the Queen's Theatre, Dublin (23 April 1888). See also L. S. DEFENDER.

II: 81   (121)
III: 159, 191-2   (234, 283-4)

ELOQUENT DEMPSEY, THE
A play (1907) by William Boyle (1853 - 1922), Irish dramatist. Abbey premiere, 20 January 1906.

III: 120, 204   (174, 302)

ELSTREE
Motion picture studios in Hertford, England. According to O'Casey's "No Flowers for Films" (The Green Crow), he once visited Elstree with Adrian Brunel and Ivan Montague.

V: 67, 123, 124   (81, 160, 161)

EMAIN MACHA
Ancient capitol of Uladh (Ulster). The region southwest of present Co. Armagh, named after Emain, daughter of Hugh Roe, who claimed to rule in her father's right after his death. After defeating her brother, Dihorba, in battle and capturing his five sons, she ordered them to build her a palace.

III: 242   (361)
IV: 68   (86)
V: 173   (230)

EMER OF BORDA
Cuchulain's* wife, the daughter of Forgall. Found in Yeats's* play, The Only Jealousy of Emer (1919) and in "The Wooing of Emer" in the Tain.

II: 219   (340)

EMERSON, RALPH WALDO
1803 - 1882. American essayist, poet and anti-slavery activist. In a letter to Ronald Ayling, O'Casey commented that Emerson's works "had a great influence on me long before I thought of writing my first paper, longhand, for our Gaelic Club." O'Casey is quoting (#) from Emerson's Conduct of Life: Considerations by the Way.

V: 56, 178, 233   (66, 238, 314)
VI: 58, 202#   (74, 288#)
Essays (1841, 1844) III: 81 (116)

EMIL
Should be Ernil, in the parish of Mooncoin, Co. Kilkenny, Ireland.

IV: 235   (324)

EMMANUEL COLLEGE
Constituent college of Cambridge University.

III: 248   (371)
VI: 50   (63)

EMMET, ROBERT
1778 - 1803. Leader of the Irish Rebellion of 1803. His stirring oration
at his trial is one of the most famous in Irish history. O'Casey alludes
(#) to Emmet's view on private property which is probably from Connolly's
Labour in Irish History:

>   It is . . . worthy to note that in the name of the
>   "Provisional Government of Ireland" the first article
>   decrees the wholesale confiscation of church property
>   and the nationalizing of the same,and the third and
>   fourth decrees forbid and declare void the transfer of
>   all landed property, bonds, debitures, and public
>   securities until the national government is established
>   and the national will upon them is declared.

Emmet's Fort (##) was at St. Enda's College.* In his Political Writings,
Pearse* wrote: "In the room in which I work at St. Enda's College,
Robert Emmet is said often to have sat . . . at an angle of our boundary
wall there is a little fortified lodge called Emmet's Fort."

II: 27, 206   (34-5, 319)
III: 75, 190#, 248, 287##   (106, 281#, 372, 430##)
IV: 100, 158, 273   (132, 214, 377)
V: 76   (95)

EMPIRE STATE BUILDING
V: 190   (254)

EMPLOYERS FEDERATION
The Dublin Employers Federation, Ltd. Formed (1911) to "meet combination with combination." Its impetus came from William Martin Murphy*
and its ranks swelled to 404 employers by the time of the 1913 Strike.
It was supported by the Catholic hierarchy, the British administration
in Ireland, and the press. Its model was the earlier (1909) Employers
Federation of Cork. Employees of Federation members were forced, under
penalty of dischargement, to take the following oath:

>   I hereby undertake to carry out all instructions given
>   to me by or on behalf of my employers, and, further, I
>   agree to immediately resign my membership (if a member);
>   and I further undertake that I will not join or in any
>   way support this union.

III: 190   (280)

ENNIS, THOMAS
General and commander of Free State troops during the artillery bombard-
ment of entrenched Irish Republicans in the Four Courts building (28 June
1922).

IV: 92   (120-1)

EPHRAIM
One of the 12 tribes of Israel; so called from its founder, Ephraim, son of Joseph.

I: 66   (93)

ERASMUS, DESIDERIUS
1466 - 1536. Dutch scholar who worked to promote reforms in the Catholic Church.

II: 87   (131)

EREWHON, LAND OF
Anagram for "nowhere." Samuel Butler's (1835 - 1902) utopian novel.

III: 113   (163)
VI: 85   (115)

ERIN'S HOPE BAND
Unknown.

III: 154, 155   (227)

ERRISHCOOL, JIM
Fictitious name. In a letter to Thomas Mark (Letters, II, p. 560), O'Casey wrote: "Errishcool is a manufactured name from two words often appearing in the Irish names of places."

IV: 188   (257-8)

ERVINE, ST. JOHN GREER
1883 - 1971. Irish playwright, novelist, and dramatic critic. Manager of the Abbey Theatre (1915); professor of dramatic literature, Royal Society of Literature (1933-36). See also O'Casey's article, "Mr. Ervine's Cry for the Critics" in The Flying Wasp.

IV: 158   (215)
V: 38, 69   (42, 85)
Mary, Mary Quite Contrary (1923) IV: 124, 171   (165, 232)

ESSEX BRIDGE
Original name for the Grattan Bridge (from 1775). Changed c.1888. The principal bridge across the River Liffey until Carlisle Bridge* was built.

I: 170   (261)

ETAIN
In Irish mythology, the horse/sun goddess, Etain Echraide, consort of the sun god. Heroine of the tale, The Wooing of Etain.

V: 86   (109)

ETERNAL FOOTMAN
From a line in T. S. Eliot's* The Love Song of J. Alfred Prufrock:*
"And I have seen the eternal Footman hold my coat, and snicker."

VI: 137   (190)

ETHELBERT, ALFRED AND EDWIN
Characters in T. S. Eliot's* play, The Rock.

VI: 90-1   (122-3)

ETON
In Buckingham, England. One of the most famous public (U.S.: private)
schools. Founded by Henry VI (1440).

III: 248   (371)
VI: 23, 24, 25, 189, 201, 231   (22, 24, 268, 286, 331-2)

EUCLID
c.323 - 285 B.C. Famous Greek mathematician and physicist.

I: 189   (292)

EUSTON STATION
In London.

V: 9-10   (2-3)

EVA OF THE NATION
Mary Eva Kelly (1826 - 1910) who used her middle name while writing
poetry for The Nation. Also used the name "Fionnuala."

IV: 158   (214)

EVANS, FEEMY
Also "Euphemia," a prostitute in Shaw's* play, The Shewing-Up of Blanco
Posnet.

VI: 16, 189   (12, 269)

EVERYMAN'S ENCYCLOPEDIA
First edition, 1913, ed. by Andrew Boyle, 12 vols. (London and New York).

VI: 200-01   (286)

EXETER
County borough and cathedral city, county seat of Devon, England.

VI: 81   (108)

EXHIBITION, INTERNATIONAL AND NATIONAL
Irish International Exhibition at Herbert Park, Ballsbridge, from 4 May
to 9 November, 1907. The incident to which O'Casey refers is probably
the same one mentioned by O Fearail in his The Story of Conradh na
Gaeilge (Gaelic League):
                    A proposal was made that an International Exhibition
MORE

EXHIBITION (cont.)

> be held in Dublin in 1907. Conradh na Gaeilge opposed
> it and called it "The Police Aided Exhibition." The
> grounds for An Conradh's objection was that it would
> bring in foreign goods and do little to increase home
> manufacturers. Instead, An Conradh proposed that a
> national exhibition be held which would display infor-
> mation on all the industries in Ireland . . .

III: 155-6   (228-9)

F

FABER, FATHER FREDERICK WILLIAM
1814 - 1863. English priest and hymn writer. Best known for "The Pilgrims of the Night" and "Land Beyond the Sea."

V: 90   (114)

FAGAN, JAMES BERNARD
1873 - 1933. English playwright and producer. Director of the Festival
Theatre (1929); responsible for many productions by the Irish Players.*

IV: 177, 180   (241, 245)
V: 11-13, 22-7, 55, 59-61, 129   (3-6, 19-26, 65, 71-3, 168)
And So to Bed (1926) V: 11, 26, 59-60   (3, 24, 71-2)

FAGAN, MICHAEL
Member of the Invincibles.*

II: 37   (50)

FAIR
Most of the following "fairs" are not real but are allusions to other
items. For another view of O'Casey's use of fairs, see his article,
"Come to the Fair," in The Green Crow.

> FAIR IN THE VALLEY OF SQUINTING WINDOWS
> Allusion to Brinsley Macnamara's* novel, The Valley of the Squinting
> Windows (1918).

III: 285   (428)

> FAIR OF CLAPPING OF HANDS
> As a guess, an allusion to Psalm 47:1, "O clap your hands, all ye
> people; shout unto God with the voice of triumph." In III: 12 (9)
> O'Casey uses the phrase: "clapping of white hands."

> FAIR OF FAIRS OF BLESSED SAINTS
> There were 12 disciples of Jesus, though O'Casey gives 13.

III: 285-6   (428-9)

> CING BULLY OF THE BOYNE OF CONTENTION
> Variant on several things. In Irish, "cing" would be pronounced

MORE

FAIR (cont.)

"king"; Bully is King William* whose prominence in Irish history
rests on the Battle of the Boyne;* the "Boyne of Contention" alludes
to that battle which has been a bone of contention.

CARZEN OF THE PAPES
Obvious variant on "Tarzan of the Apes," a fictional character crea-
ted by Edgar Rice Burroughs (1875 - 1950), but also a variant on
Lord Edward Carson* and on the word "papist," an often used synonym
for Catholic. For a time, Carson ruled the north of Ireland like
Tarzan ruled the jungle.

MISHE LEMASS MORE
In Irish a common manner of signing letters is "Is mise, le meas
more," meaning "I am yours with great respect." It would be accorded "sainthood" in O'Casey's satire because it was frequently the
extent of many Irish-Irelanders' knowledge of the Irish language.
An alternative would be "I am the great Lemass" (Sean Lemass, notable
Irish governmental leader.)

A TALBOT A TALBOT
See TALBOT, MATT. The use of the letter "A" may be in the style of
Thomas a Kempis, author of The Imitation of Christ.* The double use
of the name may signify a Catholic litany or come from the rhyme,
"A tisket, a tasket."

LILY BULLERO
See LILY BULLERO

SHANTEE OHKAY
See O'KELLY, SEAN T.

RODDY THE SHROVER
See DE CLACOM, AODH and RODDY THE ROVER

IRISH SWEEP WHO BEAT MIRACULOUS MELODY FROM A DRUM
See HOSPITAL SWEEP. The winning ticket is pulled from a drum.

ELFIE BYRNE OF BALLYBLANDUS
Alfie Byrne (1882 - 1956), lord mayor of Dublin (1930-38, 1954-55),
one of Dublin's most colorful characters. This is also a variant
on the Irish song, "Billy Byrne of Ballymanus." "Elfie" may be an
allusion to the old, blind minstrel in Chesterton's* Ballad of the
White Horse.

GUFFER GAFFNEY
See GAFFNEY, FATHER

PRAYBOY OF THE FESTERIN' WORLD
Variant on Synge's* play, The Playboy of the Western World

BILLORA ET LABORA O'BRIEN
Pun on the Latin, Laborare est orare (To labor is to pray), the
ancient motto of the Benedictine monks. See O'BRIEN, WILLIAM

FAIR (cont.)

GEE KIAORIA JESTERTON, THE LAUGHING DEWINE
G. K. Chesterton,* a noted convert to Catholicism ("dewine") and a
play on Emile Commaert's book on Chesterton, The Laughing Prophet
(1937). "Wine" is probably an allusion to Chesterton's reputation
as a wine critic. (See his poems, Wine, Water,and Song, 1915)
"Kiaoria" is an allusion to the Greek, "Kyria Eleison," Lord have
mercy, a phrase found in the Mass.

FAIR OF THE FOGGY DEW
Variant on the Irish song of rebellion, "The Foggy Dew," for which see
Appendix I.

III: 285   (428)

FAIR OF GARMAIN
In Irish mythology, Garman was the son of Glas, a mortal who abducted
Mesca the goddess. O'Casey may be referring to the famous Fair of
Carman (Wexford).

III: 285   (428)

FAIR OF OPENING EYES
Unknown.

III: 285   (428)

FAIR OF TELLTOWN
"Telltown" is from the ancient Tailltin* in Co. Meath, a hill near the
Blackwater River where the mythical hero, Lugh of the Long Hand,*
instituted public games and fairs which took place annually down to
the 12th century. Revived in 1924. See the chapter "Fairs" in
The Story of the Irish Race.

III: 285   (428)

FAIR OF THE VALLEY LAY SMILING BEFORE ME
From the line of the song, "The Song of O'Ruark," by Thomas Moore.*
See Appendix I.

III: 285   (428)

FAIRBEELY, JOSEPHINE
Johanna Fairtlough, Archie Casey's* wife. Married in April 1900 at the
Dublin Pro-Cathedral. Her brother, William Fairtlough, was active in
labor and nationalist circles and held several offices in the Irish
Transport and General Workers' Union.

II: 210   (325)

FALLON, GABRIEL
1898 - 1980. Abbey Theatre actor and dramatic critic. Directed plays
for Dublin Drama League and various amateur societies (from 1929);
lecturer in Theatre Arts, University College Dublin (1963-64); member,
board of directors, Abbey Theatre (1959-74); governor of the Royal
MORE

FALLON (cont.)

Irish Academy of Music (1971-75);   author of <u>Sean O'Casey, The Man I
Knew</u> (1965) and <u>The Abbey and the Actor</u> (1969).   In O'Casey's premieres,
he played the roles of Mr. Gallagher in <u>The Shadow of a Gunman</u>; Man in
the Kilts in <u>Kathleen Listens In</u>; Charlie Bentham in <u>Juno</u>; Oul' Joe in
<u>Nannie's Night Out</u>; and Captain Brennan in <u>The Plough and the Stars</u>.

IV: 124, 173   (166, 235)

FALLON, PADRAIC
1905 - 1974.   Irish poet and playwright.   Successfully treated Irish
legends and an author of critical works.

VI: 208   (297-8)

FALSTAFF, SIR JOHN
Regarded as the most substantial comic character to grace a stage.   In
Shakespeare's* <u>1 Henry IV</u>, <u>2 Henry IV</u> and <u>The Merry Wives of Windsor</u>.

I: 34   (42)
V: 11, 18, 114   (4, 14, 149)

FARADAY, MICHAEL
1791 - 1867.   English chemist and physicist who made important discoveries
relating to electricity.

IV: 277, 282   (383, 390)

FARELLA
Unknow.

III: 151-2   (222-4)

FARMER OAK, SERGEANT TROY, MARTY SOUTH, DIGGORY VENN, BILL BREWER, JAN
STEWER, PETER GURNEY, PETER DAVY, DAN'L WHIDDON, HARRY HAWK, UNCLE TOM
COBLEY
The first four are characters from Thomas Hardy's* novels.   The rest are
from the well-known Devonshire ballad, "Widdecombe Fair."

VI: 153   (214)

FARMER OAK,
Gabriel Oak, a small farmer in <u>Far from the Madding Crowd</u> (1874).

SERGEANT TROY
Francis Troy, a sergeant in the 11th Dragoons in <u>Far from the
Madding Crowd</u> (1874).

MARTY SOUTH
Daughter of John South in <u>The Woodlanders</u> (1887).

DIGGORY VENN
Traveling salesman in <u>The Return of the Native</u> (1878).

BILL BREWER, et. al.

MORE

BILL BREWER, et. al. (cont.)

Cobley was a substantial yeoman of Spreyton, Devon, who died at the end of the 18th century. His companions on the famous ride to Widdecombe Fair also come from the Spreyton district. The last verse of the song reads:

And all the long night he heard shirling and groans,
And all the long night he heard shirling and groans,
From Tom Pearce's old mare in her rattling bones
And from Bill Brewer, Jan Stewer, Peter Gurney, Peter
Davy, Dan'l Whiddon,
Harry Hawk, old Uncle Tom Cobbley and all.

Chorus: Old Uncle Tom Cobbley and all.

FARR, FLORENCE
1860 - 1917. British actress, producer and manager. First to produce Shaw's* Arms and the Man (1894) and Yeats's* The Land of Heart's Desire (1894) in London. Created the part of Alell in Yeats's The Countess Cathleen (1899).

IV: 138   (186)

FARRELL, JAY JAY
John J. Farrell, alderman and Poor Law Guardian for the North Dock Ward, Dublin. (Thoms, 1909). Lived at 53 Talbot Street. Dublin lord mayor (1911). The "Jay Jay," a play on the initials, was also used by "Nix" in his "Pembroke Notes," Irish Worker, 6 December 1913.

III: 106, 108   (153-4, 156)

FARRELL, PATSY
Young Irish laborer in Shaw's* play, John Bull's Other Island.

III: 175, 176   (258, 259)

FARRELLY, J.P., J.P.
Thoms (1888) does not list a J. P. Farrelly for this time, though O'Casey could have had in mind O. P. Farrelly, a grocer and wine merchant at 44-45 Middle Gardiner Street. He was not, however, a justice of the peace or a poor law guardian. Over 20 years later, though, a "Councillor J. P. Farrelly" was prominent in a controversy featured in the 17 June 1911 issue of the Irish Worker. In O'Casey's letter (12 October 1913) in the Irish Worker, he lists a "J. P. Farrelly, Esq. Lower Sheriff Street" as a subscriber to the Women and Children Relief Fund (contribution, 2 pounds).

I: 124   (186)

FARRELLY, THOMAS
Rev. Farrelly was the bursar at Maynooth (Thoms, 1880).

IV: 240   (331)

FASHODA AFFAIR
A dispute (1898) between Great Britain and France involving Fashoda
(renamed Kodok in 1904) on the Nile River, which severely strained
relations between the two nations.

II: 170   (261)

FATIMA
Regarded as the "Lourdes of Portugal" since the "miracle" of 1917.

IV: 197, 277   (270, 384)
VI: 156   (218)

FAUGH A BALLAGH BOYS
From the Irish, fag an bealach = clear the way or road. Though O'Casey
ascribes this to the Connaught Rangers* it more properly belongs to the
87th or Royal Irish Fusiliers who allegedly used the war cry during the
Peninsular Wars.

III: 105   (152)

FEARALLY, OONA
Agnes M. O'Farrelly (d.1951), professor of modern Irish poetry, Univer-
sity College Dublin. Principal, Gaelic Training College, Clochanelly,
Co. Donegal. Also given as OONI NI MERRILLY.

III: 111, 140, 142   (160, 206, 208)

FEARCEARTAIS
Of doubtful historicity. In Irish, fior=truth, ceart=right, and
fios=wisdom, or "man of equity, justice and law."

V: 86   (109)

FEARON, JAMES
Irish labor leader from Cork. Credited by Larkin* with the idea of a
"citizen army." Fearon organized 800 men into a "civil army" in Cork
in 1908 (see EMPLOYERS FEDERATION) as part of the National Union of
Dock Workers. O'Casey's description of Fearon incorporates the Irish
song, "The Ould Plaid Shawl" (see Appendix I).

III: 120   (174)

FECKIMGUMOY, PATRON OF SEELOTS
Two Irish words: feicim=I see and a corruption of machaire=a plain.
Or, I see plainly.

III: 159   (233)

FEDAMORE, SENATOR
Fictitious name. In a letter to Thomas Mark (Letters, II, p. 560),
O'Casey commented: "Fedamore is a town . . . in Limerick from which
a famous team of hurlers came, who held the Championship for years."

IV: 188-9   (257-8)

FEEGILE
Probably the small town of Feakle, Co. Clare, known as the birthplace
of Brian Merriman.*

II: 186   (287)

FEENY, FATHER LEONARD, S. J.
1898 - 1978. American Jesuit from Boston who taught that there was no
salvation without explicit membership in the visible unity of the Catholic Church, and that only Catholics could be saved. Subject of the
letter, Suprema haec sacra, issued by the Holy Office of the Vatican
(8 August 1949), which silenced him. An anti-Semite, Feeney was excommunicated in 1953. See New York Times, 1 February 1978.

VI: 58   (75)

FENIANS
Used almost entirely to refer to the Irish Republican Brotherhood,*
who took the name from the Fianna, warriors who served Finn McCool* in
the 3rd century.

I: 10, 22, 75, 87, 151, 175   (3, 21, 108, 128, 232, 270-1)
II: 36, 59, 139-41, 160, 177, 196,   (48, 85, 214-16, 246, 272-3,
235, 238   303, 365, 369)
III: 65, 105, 128, 133, 146, 234   (90, 151-2, 186, 195, 214, 350)
IV: 103, 113, 165   (136, 150, 224)
V: 85   (107)

FERDIAH
In the Tain, Ferdiah is chosen by Queen Maeve* to fight Cuchulain* when
she attempts the invasion of Ulster. Once a close comrade and foster-
brother of Cuchulain, Ferdiah is killed at the famous "Combat of the
Ford."

III: 103, 238, 241   (148, 355, 359)
VI: 167   (235)

FERGHIL, THE SHINING ONE
Of doubtful historicity. Gile is Irish for "bright."

V: 86   (109)

FERGUS OF THE KINDLY TONGUE
Fergus MacRoigh, who was occasionally called "Fergus Honeymouth."
See CLAN FERGUS.

III: 286   (429)

FERGUSON, SAMUEL
1810 - 1886. Irish antiquary and major poet. See appendixes I, II, and
III.

IV: 100   (131)
"The Fair Hills of Ireland" III: 201   (297)

FERMANAGH FUSILIERS
The Fermanagh Militia, 3rd Battalion of the Royal Inniskilling Fusiliers
in the British army.

I: 159-62, 164-5, 166   (245-9, 253, 254)

FEWS, THE
Baronies in Armagh and Waterford. One of the most notable was Hugh
O'Neill of the Fews (c.1540 - 1616).

IV: 68   (86)

FFOLLIOTT, ROBERT
Character in Boucicault's* play, The Shaughraun.

II: 140-1   (214-16)

FIANNA
The Fianna have traditionally represented Ireland's standing army,
comprising the flower of her young men. O'Casey uses the symbol for
youth which is consistent with those who headed Na Fianna Eireann, the
Boy Scouts or Young Guard of Erin, founded (1909) by Countess Markiewicz.*
The Fianna has commanded the organizational abilities of several prominent Irish soldiers, including Sean Heuston and Liam Mellows.* Headquartered at 77 Aungier Street, Dublin.

IV: 81   (104)
V: 173   (230)

FIANNA FAIL
Irish for "Soldiers of Destiny." Eamon de Valera's* political party
and the dominant party in political circles since 1927. Organized
(1926) after the Civil War for the purpose of entering the Irish parliament and striking down many of the strictures of the Treaty.* This
tactic met with strong opposition from the anti-Treaty Republicans whose
means to the same end was in armed struggle. Also given as DE VALERA'S
PARTY.

IV: 65, 72, 103, 160   (81, 91, 136, 217)
V: 83   (105)
VI: 194   (276)

FIDELITY
Possibly Fidelity Guarantee Association Company, 118 Grafton Street,
Dublin.

III: 276   (414)

FIFTH AVENUE
New York City.

V: 200   (267)

FILM COMPANY
British International Pictures, producers of the film version of Juno
and the Paycock, directed by Alfred Hitchcock,* released in 1930. For
a review of the film, see New York Times, 29 June 1930.

V: 66   (81)

FINDLATER, ALEXANDER
Alexander Findlater and Co. Ltd., grocers, tea and wine merchants at
28-32 Upper Sackville (O'Connell) Street with several outlets in Dublin.

I: 176-7   (272)

FINDOBHAIR
In the Tain, the beautiful daughter of Queen Maeve* who promised to
marry the man defeating Cuchulain.*

III: 238   (355)

FINGAL
Area north of Dublin where the Danes settled. The word means the
territory (fine) of the Galls or foreigners.

III: 238   (356)
IV: 274   (379)

FINGLAS
Neighboring village of Dublin, north of the Royal Canal.

I: 80   (118)
II: 55   (78)
III: 156, 159   (230, 234)
IV: 120   (159)

FINNIGAN, DEFENDER FIDO
Variant on the Latin words for "Defender of the Faith" (traditionally
the British sovereign), Fidei Defensor. See also L. S. D. DEFENDER OF
THE FAITH.

III: 120   (174)

FINNEGAN'S WAKE
Since this is coupled with Lannigan's Ball,* it is probably a reference
to the song, for which see Appendix I.

III: 129   (188)

FINTAN
In Irish mythology, a man who accompanied Cessair, the supposed granddaughter of Noah, when she fled to Ireland to escape the flood.

V: 201   (268)

FITZALAN, EARL OF
Edmund Bernard Fitzalan-Howard. 1855 - 1947. Viceroy of Ireland
(1921-22). From a long line of English Catholic nobility.

IV: 91   (118-19)

FITZGERALD, BARRY
1888 - 1961. Real name, William Shields. Abbey Theatre and film actor
who was a friend of O'Casey. In his will, Fitzgerald left the O'Caseys
several thousand pounds. In the premieres of O'Casey's plays, Fitzgerald played the roles of Thornton in Nannie's Night Out; Captain Boyle
in Juno and the Paycock; and Fluther Good in The Plough and the Stars.
He also played Fluther in the film version of The Plough.

IV: 124-5, 167, 171-3, 175, 183   (165-6, 227, 232-5, 239, 249)
V: 121-2   (157)

FITZGERALD, SIR EDWARD
Not to be confused with Lord Edward Fitzgerald, United Irishman hero,
who is not mentioned in O'Casey's autobiographies. This Fitzgerald was
a Cork magistrate, alderman for the South Ward, and lived at Geraldine
Place, St. Finn Barr (Thoms, 1909).

III: 190   (280)

FITZHENRY, MAILER
d.1220. Justiciar of Ireland. A bastard son of King Henry I, he
accompanied Fitzstephen on a trip to Ireland where he stayed (from 1169)
and became active in the invasion of Ossary and other engagements.
Appointed (1200) to "the care and custody of all Ireland."

IV: 91   (119)

FITZWILLIAM MUSEUM
At Cambridge University. Built in 1837-47, the museum contains the
manuscript of Keats's* "Ode to a Nightingale."

VI: 52   (65-6)

FITZWILLIAM SQUARE
In south Dublin. O'Casey is referring to 42 Fitzwilliam Place where
James Stephens* lived.

IV: 205   (282)

FIVE CHAMPIONS OF CHRISTENDOM
Unknown.

IV: 236, 243   (326, 336)

FLANDERS
County divided between Belgium and France. Site of frequent fighting
in both world wars.

III: 105, 252, 267, 268   (152, 376, 400, 402)
VI: 123   (170)

FLECKER, HERMAN JAMES ELROY
1884 - 1915. English poet and playwright. O'Casey is referring to
Flecker's fullest achievement, The Golden Journey of Samarkand (1913).

V: 75   (93)

FLEETWAY HOUSE
On Fleet Street, London. Location of several newspaper publishing houses.

V: 58   (70)

FLETCHER, REV. CANON ARTHUR HENRY
1867 - 1949. Curate of St. Barnabas Church, Dublin (1896-98).

II: 148-53, 158-61, 189, 193-7,   (228-36, 244-7, 291-3,
223-4, 236   297-301, 347, 358)
III: 39   (50)

FLETCHER, BRAMWELL
b.1904. Actor who played the Dreamer in the New York City production
of Within the Gates (1934).

V: 198   (264)

FLETCHER, REV. WILLIAM DUDLEY
1863 - 1948. Rector at Kilbanagher, Laois (1907-27); canon at St.
Laseuans (1927-46). Fletcher contributed two articles (#) to the
Irish Worker (22 November, 13 December 1913).

III: 39, 190#, 211   (50, 281#, 313)

FLIGHT OF THE EARL
Allusion to the "Flight of the Earls," a period in Irish history
(1595-1603) which left Ireland virtually leaderless. Until the 1590s,
Ulster was in the hands of Irish lords, who had succeeded in diminish-
ing English influence. However, the Tudor conquest -- which opened the
doors to the colonialization of Ulster -- proved so crushing that
thousands of earls were forced to flee. The most noted of these was
Hugh O'Neill.*

IV: 91   (119)

FLOGGING BILL
A reference to the Public Safety (Emergency Powers) Bill, sent from
the Dail for a second reading in the Senate on 26 July 1923. The bill
carried a flogging measure and Yeats* apparently voted for it.

V: 224   (301)

FLYNN, PETER
"Uncle Peter" in O'Casey's play, The Plough and the Stars.

IV: 173   (235)

FOLEY, MICHAEL
This probably the Foley Typewriter Company, once located at 25 Bache-
lor's Walk and advertising itself as the "Irish-Ireland Firm." When
O'Casey bought his typewriter, it had moved to 83 Abbey Street, Dublin.

IV: 75   (95)

FONTENOY
One of the many engagements (11 May 1745) in the War of Austrian
Succession. Six regiments of the Irish Brigade in the French Army have
been given various degrees of credit for turning the tide of battle,
and for inflicting one of England's greatest military disasters of the
18th century.

III: 152, 252   (233, 376)

FORAN, THOMAS
General president of the Irish Transport and General Workers' Union
(1909-39) and vice-chairman of the Irish Citizen Army. With William
O'Brien* he was one of the most powerful Irish labor leaders from the
early 1920s. Concentrated on trade union rather than political issues
and was an opponent of Larkin* and of the Larkin faction in the union.

III: 261   (391)

FORBES-ROBERTSON, JEAN
1905 - 1962. Daughter of the noted English actor, Sir Johnston Forbes-
Robertson. O'Casey's allusion is to the London production of Uncle
Vanya by Anton Chekhov,in which the actress played the role of Sonya
(March 1926).

V: 11   (4)

FORD, FORD MADOX
1873 - 1939. Noted English writer of poems and novels.

VI: 199-200, 203   (283-4, 289)

FORD, HENRY
1863 - 1947. American capitalist and automobile manufacturer. Bitter
opponent of trade unions.

VI: 90   (122)

FORD, JOHN
1586 - 1639. English dramatist.

IV: 126   (168)

FORD OF THE HURDLES
English translation of Ath Cliath, the Irish name for Dublin.

V: 76   (95)

FORTUNE THEATRE
Small London theatre in Russell Street. Presented a season of O'Casey
plays in 1927 which were produced by J. B. Fagan.* O'Casey alludes to
the 12 May 1926 production of Juno and the Paycock (given as "first play,"
the first London production) which had been transfered from the Fortune
to the Royalty Theatre.*

V: 11, 54   (3-4, 65)

FORTY-NINERS
Term applied to the fortune seekers who poured into California after
the discovery of gold there (1848-49).

VI: 10   (3)

FOUNTAINS ABBEY
In Yorkshire, one of England's loveliest ruins.

VI: 70   (92)

FOUR COURTS
On Inn Quay, Dublin, home of the Irish Courts of Justice and its record
center. Site of a dramatic struggle (1922) between Free State soldiers
and anti-Treaty Republicans. The latter occupied the building from
April until June. On June 27, the Free State began to shell the building
and continued until June 30. Centuries of documents and records were
destroyed.

II: 165, 217, 218   (255, 336, 338)
III: 271   (407)
IV: 92, 93   (120, 121)

FOX, RALPH M.
1899 - 1969. Author, journalist and drama critic of the Dublin
Evening Mail (1939-62). Author of biographies of Connolly,* Larkin,*
and the History of the Irish Citizen Army (1943). Fox's comments
appeared in the article, "The Drama of the Dregs," in the Irish Statesman, August 1928.

IV: 181   (247)

FOXE, JOHN
1516 - 1587. Known primarily for his book on Christian martyrs (Book
of Martyrs -- O'Casey), History of the Acts and Monuments of the Christian Martyrs (c.1560).

I: 35   (43)

FOXFORD
Irish village in Co. Mayo which, during the 19th century, had a thriving
handwoven industry.

III: 103   (148)

FOXROCK
Neighboring village six miles southeast of Dublin.

IV: 117   (156)

FRA ANGELICO
Giovanni da Fiesole. 1387 - 1455. Italian Dominican friar and painter.
O'Casey alludes (#) to Christ Ascending and Christ Greeted by Two Bro-
thers.

II: 225-6#   (349#)
IV: 199, 200   (274)

FRAGONARD, JEAN HONORE
1732 - 1806. French painter and engraver.

II: 226   (351)
IV: 170   (231)

FRANCE
See also BANTRY BAY, BASTILLE, FRANCO-PRUSSIAN WAR, FRENCH REVOLUTION,
and SHAN VAN VOCHT.

I: 178, 181   (274, 279)
II: 19   (20)
III: 158   (233)
IV: 97, 254-5, 263, 279   (127, 351-2, 364, 386)
V: 54, 83, 162, 182, 219, 226   (63, 105, 215, 242, 294, 303)
VI: 13, 16, 22, 113, 118, 119, 123,   (7, 11, 20, 155, 163, 164, 170,
127, 145, 182, 203, 212   176, 202, 258, 290, 304)

FRANCE, ANATOLE
1844 - 1924. French novelist, critic and poet. One of O'Casey's
favorites.

III: 175   (259)

FRANCISCANS
Members of the Order of Friars Minor observing the unmodified rule of
the first order of St. Francis of Assisi. Given also as GREY FRIARS (#).

V: 73-4#, 83   (92#, 105)
VI: 86   (117)

FRANCO, FRANCISCO
1892 - 1975. Spanish dictator who overthrew the Republican government
during a bitter civil war (1936-39).

V: 127   (166)

FRANCO-PRUSSIAN WAR
From 1870 to 1871 between France and Germany which resulted in the
unification of Germany.

III: 269   (403)

FRANKLIN, BENJAMIN
1706 - 1790. American statesman, inventor, scientist,and author.

II: 88   (131)

FRAZER, JAMES GEORGE
1854 - 1941. Scottish anthropologist. Author of The Golden Bough
(1890, revised 1900), a study of the development of religion.

III: 175   (259)
The Golden Bough III: 85, 186   (122, 275)
                   V: 14, 22   (8, 20)

FREE, MICKEY
Michael Free, the servant in Charles Lever's (1806 - 1872) novel,
Charles O'Malley (1841).

III: 133   (195)

FREE STATE ARMY/FREE STATERS
According to Macardle's Irish Republic: "These anti-Treaty Volunteers
reserved for their own army henceforth the title 'Irish Republican
Army,' and referred to the pro-Treaty forces as 'Beggars Bush troops,'
or the 'Free State Army.' The Provisional Government and its supporters
indignantly objected to the term 'Free State Army'; they continued to
refer to the pro-Treaty forces as the Irish Republican Army, representing those obeying the new executive as mutineers."

IV: 89, 90, 94, 96, 100, 102, 104-05,   (116, 118, 123, 126, 131, 134,
107, 111, 112, 120, 121   137-8, 142, 147-8, 160-1)
V: 44   (50)

FREE STATE GOVERNMENT, PROVISIONAL
The government ruling Ireland immediately after the Treaty*; created
by article 17 of the Articles of Association.*

IV: 89, 95, 98, 109-10, 154   (115, 125, 129, 145-6, 208)

FREE STATE PARTY
Cumann na nGaedheal, launched in 1923 for the pro-Treaty forces which
ruled the Free State government until 1932 when it was replaced by
Fianna Fail.* Founded and headed by W. T. Cosgrave.* Progenitor of
the Fine Gael party.

IV: 151, 157, 169   (205, 213, 230)

FREEMASONS
Protestant fraternal organization which has been condemned by the
Catholic Church as anti-Catholic. See the article, "The Freemasons,"
by Terence de Vere White in Secret Societies in Ireland.

IV: 97   (127)

FRENCH COMMUNARDS
Properly, the French Communards are the Paris Communes of the French
Revolution.or of the Paris Commune of 1871. O'Casey, however, is
referring to Adam Mickiewicz's* celebration of the 1848 Risings in France
which witnessed the bloodiest street fighting in Europe and which overthrew King Louis Philippe.

III: 194, 269   (287, 403)
VI: 85   (114)

FRENCH, GENERAL JOHN DENTON P.
1852 - 1925. British field marshal and commander of British forces in
Great Britain (from 1916). Best known in Ireland for his pursuit of
Irish Republicans with a brutal intensity. O'Casey refers to French's
Boer War* exploits when French achieved fame as a cavalry commander.

II: 200-01   (390-10)

FRENCH REVOLUTION
See also BASTILLE, COUTHON, DANTON, DESMOULINS, ROBESPIERRE, and ST.
JUST.

IV: 254-5, 263   (351-2, 364)
V: 83, 219, 226   (105, 294, 303)
VI: 16   (11)

FRENCH, SAMUEL
Publishers of plays and acting editions in London and New York. In
1932, O'Casey was forced to sell half the amateur rights to The Shadow
of a Gunman, Juno and the Paycock and The Plough and the Stars to this
company. See Letters, I, p. 449n.

V: 108, 118, 119   (140, 153, 154)

FRIENDLY SONS OF ST. PATRICK
Fraternal organization of Irish men and women, established in the U.S.
during the American Revolution.

III: 158, 159   (232, 234)

FROBISHER, ST. MARTIN
1535 - 1594. English mariner who commanded an expedition in search of
the Northwest Passage (1576).

III: 249   (372)

FRONGOCH
British internment camp in Wales where insurrectionists of the Easter
Rising were transported following the collapse of the Rising.

IV: 9   (1)

FURNISS, FATHER
Dublin priest and author of hymnals and books on catechism.

The Sight of Hell (1875)   V: 157   (208)

G

GAD
One of the 12 tribes of Israel, occupying the region west of the
Jordan.

II: 230, 239   (357, 371)

GAEDHILGE
Irish for the Gaelic language. O'Casey's interest in the language dates
from his early 20s when he began a process of self-education (see
CEARNEY). After joining the Gaelic League* he changed his name from
John Casey to Sean O Cathasaigh, its Irish form. See his articles,
"Down with the Gaedhilge!" and "A Language Controversy" in Feathers
from a Green Crow.

III: 20, 21, 111, 201   (21, 22, 160, 297)

GAELIC ATHLETIC ASSOCIATION
Irish organization founded (1884) by Michael Cusack (1847 - 1907),
dedicated to the revival of Irish sports. See HURLING LEAGUE.

III: 171   (251)

GAELIC LEAGUE
Irish organization founded (1893) by Douglas Hyde* and others, dedicated
to the revival of the Irish language and literature. Although it was
avowedly non-political, nearly all the Irish revolutionaries of the
1910-20 period were members or associated with its activities in one
way or another. Its headquarters in Dublin were at 25 Rutland (Parnell)
Square. According to Cowasjee, O'Casey joined the Gaelic League in 1903.
He was apparently a member of the Drumcondra Branch which he joined in
1906, for which he became secretary (Letters, I, chronology). See
O'Casey's articles, "The Gaelic League in Dublin" and "The Gaelic Movement Today," in Feathers from a Green Crow.

II: 171, 175-7, 215   (262, 270-5, 333)

                           PAN
III: 12, 13, 18, 23-5, 48, 66, 68, 82, 87, 105, 107, 110, 114, 118,
     120, 123-6, 133, 136, 140, 144, 145, 147, 148-51, 154, 162, 171
     172, 213, 225, 266
                           U.S.
     9-10, 19, 26-7, 29, 64, 92, 95, 117, 125, 151, 155, 160, 165,
     172, 175, 180-4, 194, 199, 205, 210, 212-13, 215, 218-22, 226,
     238, 244, 253, 255, 313, 316, 335-6

IV: 10, 30, 82, 234, 249, 276, 286   (3, 31, 106, 323, 344, 381,
                                           396)
V: 50   (58)

GAELIC LEAGUE, BRANCHES OF
Central Branch   III: 150   (220)
                            IV: 10   (3)
Drumcondra Branch   III: 145   (213)
Keating Branch   III: 156, 157, 159 (229, 231, 234)

GAELIC LEAGUE, BRANCHES OF (cont.)

Kilkenny Branch	III: 154	(226)
Rory O'Moore Branch	III: 143	(210)
St. Margaret's Branch	III: 145	(213)

GAELIC LEAGUE EXECUTIVE
Ruling body of the Gaelic League, having 56 members who were elected annually. They generally held meetings once a month in Dublin.

III: 145, 147, 148   (212, 215, 218)

GAFFNEY, REV. MICHAEL HENRY
Dominican priest and playwright who led the protest against O'Casey's play, The Silver Tassie, when it was produced at the Abbey Theatre in 1935. See the exchanges in Letters, I, pp. 418-19, 576-77.

II: 47   (67)
III: 124, 286   (181, 429)

GAIETY THEATRE
In Dublin on King Street. An old theatre (opened 1871) which offered opera, musical comedy and drama, it attracted some of the best English companies. O'Casey's play, The Silver Tassie, appeared there in 1947, directed by Ria Mooney and Josephine Alberria.

V: 52   (61)

GALILEE
I: 41   (54)
IV: 221   (305)

GALILEO
1565 - 1642. Noted Italian physicist and astronomer.

III: 62   (86)

GALLEHER, MR.
Appears as a Catholic assistant in the Central Model Schools.*

I: 65-6   (93)

GALVIN, PATRICK
b.1927. Irish dramatist, journalist and balladeer. O'Casey's comments were in response to a review Galvin wrote of O'Casey's one-act plays which were to be performed at the London Unity Theatre. The review was scheduled to appear in the Tribune and in the Irish Democrat, but never did for some unknown reason. Galvin had, however, sent copies of the review to O'Casey. Galvin edited a poetry magazine, Chanticleer.

VI: 220-3   (316-19)

GALVIN'S
Dublin pub at 129-131 Capel Street which was owned by the Galvin Brothers.

II: 55   (78)

GALWAY
County in the west of Ireland.

III: 15, 101, 115, 118, 122, 133,   (14, 145, 168, 172, 177, 195,
189, 230, 285   280, 343, 427)
IV: 80, 129, 130, 131, 133, 135,   (103, 172, 174-5, 178, 182-3,
136, 192, 241   187, 262-3)
V: 50, 172-3, 177   (57, 229-31, 236)

GALWAY, UNIVERSITY OF
In Co. Galway, Ireland.   Constituent college of the National University
of Ireland.*

V: 52   (61)

GANDHI, MAHATMA
1869 - 1948.   Indian nationalist leader.

VI: 186, 187   (264, 265)

GANNON, REV. P. J.
Noted Irish Jesuit.   Gannon's comments appeared in the article, "The
World Crisis and the Catholic Situation," Studies, December 1939.

V: 226   (304)

GAP OF DUNLOE
In Co. Kerry, Ireland.   A defile running between the Macgillicuddy
Reeks and the Purple Mountain group.

I: 113   (171)

GARDINER, STEPHEN
c.1483 - 1555.   English prelate and politician.   Supported prosecution
of Protestants during Mary's regime, but tried to save Cranmer.*

An Explication and Assertion of the True Catholic Fayth, touching the
most blessed sacrement of the aulter with a confutation of a booke
written agaynst the same (by Cranmer)   (1551)   VI: 57   (73)

GARDINER STREET
In north Dublin.

III: 168, 207   (247, 306)

GARGAN, DR. DENIS
1819 - 1903.   Professor at Maynooth College. Lecturer on ecclesiastical
history (1859); vice-president (1885) and president (1894) of Maynooth.

IV: 237   (326)

GARIBALDI, GIUSEPPE
1807 - 1882.   Italian patriot and leader of struggle for Italian nation-
hood.

VI: 91   (124)

GARNETT
Though O'Casey gives the names of Edward and David to this person on two separate occasions, he probably means the same person. Edward Garnett (1868 - 1937) was an English writer as was his son, David (1892 - 1981), who was the winner of the Hawthornden and James Tait Black memorial prizes (1923). Best guess is David.

IV: 127, 173   (169-70, 236)

GARRICK CLUB
First organized by the luminaries of England. Its present clubhouse stands on Rose Street, London (since 1864), and offers one of the best theatre libraries in the world.

V: 22-3, 26-8   (19-20, 25-7)

GARRICK, DAVID
1717 - 1779. Regarded as one of the greatest Shakespearean actors in the history of the English stage.

V: 22   (20)
VI: 164   (231)

GASQUET, CARDINAL FRANCIS AIDAN
1846 - 1929. English Catholic prelate.

IV: 242, 260   (335, 359)

GASSNER, JOHN W.
1903 - 1967. Sterling professor of dramatic literature at Yale University (from 1956). Author and editor of many books on drama including The Selected Plays on Sean O'Casey (1956).

VI: 56   (71)

GATACRE, SIR WILLIAM FORBES
1843 - 1906. British general who commanded the 3rd Division of the South African Field Force (1899-1900) in the Boer War.* Defeated at Stormberg (11 December 1899).

II: 200   (310)

GATE THEATRE
Dublin theatre on Cavendish Row. Founded (1928) by Michael MacLiammoir,* Hilton Edwards* and others, and opened in the Peacock Theatre, an annex of the Abbey. The name is in recognition of the assistance given by Peter Godfrey of the London Gate Theatre. In the period 1935-39, they made several trips abroad, including to Cairo and Alexandria, Belgrade, Sofia, Bucharest, etc. In February 1930, the theatre moved to new premesis in the Rotunda on Parnell Square.

VI: 73, 78, 107   (97, 104, 105, 148)

GAUGUIN, EUGENE HENRI PAUL
1848 - 1903. French painter who was one of the main founders of the symbolist school of Pont-Aven.

VI: 73-4   (97-9)

GAUMALFRY
Probably a play on several Irish and English words: gamal means simpleton, fool, etc; alfratis means rascal, rogue; and the English "galimalfry," meaning medley or jumble. The word gaum (now English/ Irish slang) is frequently used for gamal.

IV: 269   (372)

GAURA
Irish town in Co. Meath.

V: 173   (230)

gCOPALEEN, MILES NA
One of the pseudonyms of Briain O Nuallain (1912 - 1966), Irish writer. Used over his satirical column in the Irish Times. Some of his works appeared under the name Flann O'Brien.

V: 53   (62)
VI: 210   (301)

GDYNIA
Polish port city near Gdansk.

VI: 114   (157)

GENERAL STRIKE
In England, 3-12 May 1926, in sympathy with the coal miners' strike (1 May), which involved about 2½ million of the 6 million trade unionists of Britain. The miner' union continued its strike until 19 November, when it surrendered unconditionally.

V: 55-8, 94   (65-8, 120)
VI: 87   (118)

GEORGE, DAVID LLOYD
1863 - 1945. British politician of Welsh parentage. Prime minister (1916-22). He arranged the conference with Irish leaders which resulted in the creation of the Irish Free State and Northern Ireland. See also DE VALERA, EAMON.

IV: 66-72   (83-93)

GERAGHTY, FATHER BRIAN
The comments to which O'Casey alludes appeared in the February 1952 number of Far East.

VI: 130-1   (181)

GERALDINES
The Irish family of Fitzgerald, comprising earls of Desmond and Kildare. The hereditary enemies of the Butler family, comprising dukes of Ormonde. See also "THE GERALDINES," Appendix I.

III: 139   (204)
IV: 232-3   (321)

GERMANY
I: 180-1   (278-9)
V: 36, 228   (39, 307)
VI: 113-15, 119, 123, 143, 203   (155-9, 164, 170, 200, 290)

GERONTIUS
fl.390. Deacon at Milan under Ambrose. He had an extraordinary dream of being on the verge of death, but could see beyond the veil. Newman's Dream of Gerontius was turned into an oratorio by Elgar.

III: 103   (148)

GERRARDS CROSS
Town in Buckinghamshire, England, near Chalfont St. Giles.

V: 140-5   (184-92)

GERSON, JEAN DE CHARLIER
1363 - 1429. French theologian and mystic who attempted to forward church unity and ecclesiastical reforms.

V: 196   (261)

GHENGIST AND HOARSA
Hengist and Horsa, legendary figures, leaders of the first Saxons to settle in England (c.449).

III: 249   (373)

GIACOSA, GIUSEPPE
1847 - 1906. After Verga, Italy's most famous dramatist.

Falling Leaves IV: 125   (167)

GIBBON, EDWARD
1737 - 1794. Noted British historian.

VI: 202   (288)
The History of the Decline and Fall of the Roman Empire I: 35 (43)

GIBBON, WILLIAM (MONK)
b.1896. Irish poet who is best known for his early love poems. O'Casey is quoting from Gibbon's introduction to The Living Torch (1937), a collection of AE's* writings. O'Casey ordered the book on 2 November 1937 (see Letters, I, p. 684). See O'Casey's essay, "Censorship," in Blasts and Benedictions.

IV: 197, 209   (270, 288)

GILBERT, DONALD
1900 - 1961. British sculptor. The bronze to which O'Casey refers
was executed in October-November 1933. Gilbert wrote a two-page letter
describing AE's setting and it is printed in Denson's George W. Russell,
pp. 250-1.

IV: 212   (291)

GILDEROY
Noted robber and cattle stealer of Perthshire who was hanged at
Gallowlee near Edinburgh (July 1638). His real name was said to have
been Patrick Mcgregor. See "MY HANDSOME GILDEROY" (#), Appendix I.

I: 21   (21)
VI: 143-4#   (201#)

GINKEL, GENERAL CODERT
1644 - 1703. Dutch-born general in the British service. Accompanied
William of Orange* to England (1688) and the winner of victories at
Aughrim and Limerick (1691) in Ireland during the Jacobite Wars.

V: 173   (231)

GIORGIONE
c.1478 - 1511. Chief master painter of the Venetian school in his day.
See also VAYNUS.

V: 18   (14)
The Tempest   IV: 201   (276)
The Sleeping Venus   IV: 201   (276)
                         VI: 73-4   (97-8)

GISH, LILLIAN
b.1893. American actress. Played the role of the Young Whore in the
U.S. premiere of O'Casey's play, Within the Gates.

V: 198, 239   (264, 322)
VI: 9   (1)

GLADSTONE, WILLIAM
1809 - 1898. British politician active for many years on behalf of
Irish Home Rule. Prime minister (1868-74, 1880-85, 1886, 1892-94).

I: 76   (109, 110)
II: 12-13, 16, 229   (9-10, 16, 356)
III: 75   (106)
IV: 159, 240   (215, 332)
VI: 27, 166   (28, 233)

GLASNEVIN
Neighboring village north of Dublin. Site of the National Cemetery.

II: 55, 57, 58   (78, 82, 84)
III: 46, 100   (61, 143)

GLASNEVIN ROAD
In Glasnevin, north of Dublin, east of the Botanic Gardens.

II: 63   (92)

GLAZIER, JOHN
Appears as a foreman in the Great Western Railway goods store. He is
mentioned in O'Casey's letter to Rev. Robert S. Griffin (Letters, II,
p. 635).

II: 228-32, 236, 239   (353-9, 366-7, 371)

GLEN MAWMA, BATTLE OF
The battle of Mama, a decisive battle (999) which resulted in the defeat of the Dublin Norse and the king of Leinster by Brian Boru.*

II: 187   (289)

GLENCREE REFORMATORY
St. Kevin's Reformatory, Glencree, Co. Wicklow.

III: 188   (278)

GLENDALOUGH
Site of a former Irish monastery in Co. Wicklow, founded (c.570) by
St. Kevin,* and center of a famous pilgrimage (until the 19th century)
to celebrate the feast of St. Kevin (June 3). Glendalough's seven
churches are Trinity Church, the Cathedral, St. Kevin's Kitchen, Our
Lady's Chapel, Royal Cemetery Church, the Priory of St. Saviour,
Teampull-na-Skellig, and the Ivy Church.

V: 161   (213)

GLOUCESTER, DUKE OF
The fourth son of Richard Plantagenet, Duke of York and later Richard
III. "That valiant crookback prodigy" in Shakespeare's 2 Henry VI,
3 Henry VI and Richard III.

II: 20, 21, 25, 131   (22, 23, 31, 201)

GLOUCESTER STREET
In cenral Dublin, south of the City Quay.

III: 165, 168   (242, 247)

GLOUCESTERSHIRE
County and borough in western England.

VI: 77   (102)

GLYNN, SIR JOSEPH
1869 - 1951. Member (1899-1919) and chairman (1902-12), Galway County
Council. Author of several pamphlets for the Catholic Truth Society.

Life of Matt Talbot (1925)   IV: 165-6   (224-6)

GOD
"may be but a shout in the street" (from Joyce's <u>Ulysses</u>).

V: 219   (294)

GOETHE, JOHANN WOLFGANG VON
1749 - 1832. The noted German poet, novelist and dramatist.

II: 223   (345)
III: 280   (421)
IV: 282   (390)

GOG/MAGOG
In British legend, the sole survivors of a monstrous brood, the offspring
of demons and the 33 daughters of Emperor Diocletian. In the Bible,
Gog and Magog symbolize all future enemies of God. It is also the name
given to two 14-foot statues in the London Guildhall.

VI: 113, 114   (156)

GOGAN, JENNIE
Spelled "Grogan" in U.S.# Character in O'Casey's play, <u>The Plough and</u>
<u>the Stars</u>.

IV: 173, 280   (235#, 387)

GOGARTY, OLIVER ST. JOHN
1878 - 1957. Irish physician, poet and writer. Senator (1922-36),
Irish Free State. Called by Yeats "one of the great lyric poets of our
age." The play to which O'Casey alludes, <u>Blight</u>, was written by "Alpha
and Omega" (Gogarty and Joseph O'Connor) and opened at the Abbey Theatre
on 11 December 1917. According to James Carens, the play is "99 and 99/
100 % pure Gogary." The review of <u>I Knock at the Door</u> (#) appeared in
the <u>Observer</u> (12 March 1939) , not the <u>Sunday Times</u>, and is reprinted in
<u>Letters</u>, I, pp. 782-6.

IV: 194, 205   (265-6, 282)
V: 217   (291)
VI: 79, 106, 196#, 204#, 211 (106, 146, 278#, 291#, 302)
<u>Blight</u> (1917)   IV: 114   (152)

GOLDEN DAWN
Order of the Golden Dawn, a theosophical and occultist society in London
and Dublin. Within its middle ranks were people such as Yeats,* Maude
Gonne,* Annie Horniman* and Florence Farr.* Yeats was initiated as a
Hermetic student on 7 March 1890.

V: 73   (91)

GOLDSMITH, OLIVER
1728 - 1774. Noted Irish poet, playwright and novelist.

II: 122, 185, 190   (187, 285, 293)
V: 45   (51)
VI: 202   (288)
<u>The Deserted Village</u> (1770) II: 184   (285)

GOLLANCZ, VICTOR
1893 - 1967. British publisher and activist. Founder of his own publishing house (1928) and a sponsor of numerous humanitarian causes.
Founder, Left Book Club, which at its peak (April 1939) had 60,000 members. He and O'Casey were members of the General Council of the Unity
Theatre, London. Knighted in 1965.

VI: 105   (145)

GOMARAWL, T.
From the Irish word, gomeril = a boob. Also a one-act play, Gomeril
(1909), by Rutherford Mayne.

III: 192, 193   (284, 285)

GOOD, FLUTHER
In The Plough and the Stars, one of O'Casey's greatest comedic characters.
Based in part on one John Good who entered a libel suit against O'Casey
in 1938. See Ronald Ayling, "Sean O'Casey, The Writer Behind His Critics,"
Drama Survey, 1964.

IV: 173, 175, 271-2   (236, 239, 375-6)
V: 46, 141, 142   (52, 186, 187)
VI: 16   (12)

GONNE, MAUD
1866 - 1953. Irish patriot and heroine of many of Yeats's* lyrics and
plays. Married (1903) Major John McBride.* O'Casey's reference to her
being "the colonel's daughter still" (#) refers to her father, Colonel
Thomas Gonne, an assistant adjutant general in Dublin.

II: 202   (312)
III: 212-13   (315)
IV: 178-9#, 180   (243#, 245)

GONZAGA, SISTER
Appears as a nurse in St. Vincent's Hospital.*

III: 246, 252-3   (368, 378)

GORDON, GENERAL CHARLES GEORGE
1833 - 1885. Famous British soldier who was best known for his adventures
while suppressing the Taiping Rebellion (1863-64) and at Khartoum (1884).

I: 76   (109, 110)
V: 167-8   (221-3)

GORE, CHARLES
1853 - 1932. Anglican prelate. Bishop of Oxford (1911-19). A leader
in the Anglo-Catholic movement.

V: 13   (8)

GORMLAITH
c.880 - 946. Daughter of Flann Sinna and wife of, successively, Cormac
MacDullinan; Carrol, King of Leinster; and Nial Glundubh. Her checkered
life has been a theme for many poems.

II: 187   (288)

GORT
Irish town in Co. Galway, near the home of Lady Gregory.*

IV: 129, 131, 142, 143, 192   (172, 176, 192, 193, 262)

GOSLING, HARRY
1861 - 1930. English trade union leader and social democrat. President
(1910-21), National Transport Workers' Federation.

III: 214   (318)

GOVERNMENT OF THE CHURCH IN THE FOURTH CENTURY
Should be Government of the Church in the First Century, an essay submitted by Father Moran to the faculty at Maynooth for a degree.

IV: 251   (347)

GOWAN, FATHER
One of Walter MacDonald's* teachers at St. Kiernan's College.

IV: 238   (328)

GOWER, JOHN
c.1325 - 1408. English poet whose principal work was Confessionamantis
(1386).

Vox Clamantis (1381)   VI: 102   (140)

GOYA, LUCIENTES Y, FRANCISCO JOSE
1746 - 1828. Noted Spanish painter.

III: 217   (322)
IV: 75, 170   (95, 231)
V: 18   (14)

GRAFTON STREET
Fashionable street in south Dublin.

I: 184   (283)
II: 162   (249)
III: 108   (156)
IV: 216   (297)

GRAHAMS
Highlander regiment in the British army. In 1888, the 2nd Battalion,
Gordon Highlanders regiment, was stationed in Ireland.

I: 159-62, 165   (245-9, 254-5)

GRAND NATIONAL
The English steeplechase run annually at Aintree near Liverpool.

III: 171   (252)

GRANGEGORMAN
Region north of Dublin comprising five townlands. Site of the Richmond
District Lunatic Asylum (now St. Brendan's Mental Hospital, since 1921).

III: 55, 207   (76, 307)

GRANT'S TOMB
Burial mausoleum on Riverside Drive in New York City of Ulysses S. Grant
(1822 - 1885), 18th president of the U.S.

V: 179   (238)

GRANTABRIGGE
The old name for Cambridge, England. The word means "bridge over the
river Cam."

VI: 44   (54)

GRATTAN, HENRY
1746 - 1820. Irish politician. Member of the Irish parliament (1775-97,
1800) and of the British parliament (1805-20). Because of his influence,
the Irish parliament became known as "Grattan's Parliament."

II: 28   (35)
III: 75   (105)
V: 76   (95)

GRAY, BETSY
Irish patriot and one of the heroines of the 1798 Rebellion. Killed at
Ballynohinik (13 June) during a retreat. Subject of many songs.

IV: 158   (214)

GRAY, DORIAN
From the novel, The Picture of Dorian Gray (1891), by Oscar Wilde.*

IV: 40   (45)

GRAY, THOMAS
1716 - 1771. English poet. Elegy Written in a Country Churchyard.

I: 35   (43)
II: 122   (187)

GRAYBURN, LIEUTENANT JOHN
Scotsman whom O'Casey knew as a boy while the O'Caseys lived at Hillcrest,
Chalfont St. Giles, England. Grayburn's parents lived in Gerrards Cross,
and his nanny used to bring him to Hillcrest to play with O'Casey's son,
Breon. Grayburn was killed in World War II and was awared the Victoria
Cross. To whom Oak Leaves and Lavender is dedicated.

IV: 17-18   (12-13)

GREAT BRITAIN STREET
Now Parnell Street (since 1911).

I: 180	(278)
II: 67, 88, 127	(98, 132, 194)
IV: 195	(268)

GREAT NORTHERN RAILWAY OF IRELAND
Where O'Casey worked as a common laborer for nine years (1902-December
1911). He wrote a series of articles exposing working conditions on
the railroad which were reprinted in Feathers from a Green Crow. See
also Letters, I, p. 10n and p. 12n.

II: 165, 171   (254, 262)

GREAT RUSSELL STREET
In central London, on which is located the British Museum.

V: 11   (4)

GREAT WESTERN RAILWAY GOOD STORE
The Great Southern and Western Railroad Co. office and terminus, Military
Road, Dublin.

II: 228   (353)

GREAT WHITE WAY
Once popular name for Broadway.*

| IV: 196 | (269) |
| V: 183, 184 | (244) |

GREECE
I: 145	(223)
IV: 136, 213, 236, 265	(183, 293, 326, 366)
V: 116, 178	(151, 238)

GREEN BUSHES
Three-act play (1857?) by John Baldwin Buckstone (1807 - 1879). For a
review of the play, see "The Green Bushes at the Queen's Theatre" in
Towards a National Theatre, Robert Hogan, editor.

IV: 184   (251)

GREENE, GRAHAM
b.1904. English writer and author of novels, reviews, articles, and
screenplays.

VI: 168, 188		(237, 267)
The Heart of the Matter (novel 1948)	V: 52	(61)
Brighton Rock (novel 1938)	V: 203	(272)

GREENO, NORA
See CREENA, NORA.

III: 133   (194)

GREGORY, LADY AUGUSTA
1859 - 1932. Playwright, co-founder of the Abbey Theatre, author of
many books on poetry, folklore and drama, and a witness to or participant
in all the major dramatic events of the first 30 years of the Irish dramatic movement. A good friend of O'Casey, she encouraged him in the early
years and was an inadvertent victim in the Silver Tassie controversy.
For more on their relationship see the essays by Ayling and Fitzgerald in
Sean O'Casey, Centenary Essays, and "The Lady Gregory Letters to Sean O'-
Casey," in Modern Drama, May 1965. See also:

MORE

GREGORY, LADY AUGUSTA (cont.)

Works:

The Keening of Kilcash	IV: 139	(187)
Kincora (1905)	IV: 145, 146	(196, 197)
The Jackdaw (1909)	IV: 114-15	(152)
Cuchulain of Murhevna (1902)	IV: 133	(179)
The Dragon (1923)	IV: 167	(227)

GREGORY, MARGRET
Lady Gregory's daughter-in-law, wife of Robert Gregory.* Artist who illustrated Lady Gregory's Kiltartan Wonder Book (1910). Lived in London and spent holidays in Coole.

V: 97   (124)
VI: 25   (25)

GREGORY, ROBERT
1881 - 1918. Lady Gregory's son. Educated at Harrow and at New College, Oxford. Joined Connaught Rangers* (1915) and the Royal Flying Corps (1916). Awarded Chevalier of the Legion d'Honneur and a Military Cross (1917). Killed (23 January) on the Italian front. Yeats's* poems, "In Memory," "An Irish Airman Foresees his Death,""Shepherd and Goatherd," and "Reprisals" are on Robert Gregory.

I   139, 146   (188, 197)
V: 36, 220   (39, 295)

GRESHAM HOTEL
In Dublin at 20-23 Sackville (O'Connell) Street. For many years, it was a headquarters for the Nationalist Party.

III: 114   (164-5

GREY, SIR EDWARD
1862 - 1933. Secretary of state for foreign affairs (1905-16); consolidated Triple Entent and took an important part in negotiations of Balkan problems at the London Peace Conference (1912-13). For the context of O'Casey's remarks, see ASQUITH, MARGARET.

III: 250   (373)

GREY, EDWIN DROOP
Fictional name. Neither it nor the poems O'Casey mentions ever appeared in the Irish Statesman. There was, however, an Edmund Dwyer Grey, owner of the Freeman's Journal.

IV: 195-201, 204, 207-11, 215   (268-76, 280, 285-9, 296)

GREY, MARY
Stage name of Ada Bryant. Married (1914) J. B. Fagin.* Lived at 16 Cambridge Street, London.

V: 11, 129   (4, 168)

GREY, ZANE
1875 - 1939. American novelist specializing in western adventure stories.

IV: 195, 208, 210, 216   (266, 286, 289, 297)

GREY OF MACHA
One of Cuchulain's* two chariot horses. Cuchulain saw it emerge from the grey lake at Slieve Fuad, seized it around the neck, and was carried all over Ireland.

II: 235   (364)

GRIFFIN, CARDINAL BERNARD
1899 - 1956. English prelate. Archbishop of Westminister (1943); cardinal (1946).

V: 151   (199)
VI: 31   (34)

GRIFFIN, EDWARD MORGAN
d.1923. Rector of St. Barnabas Church, Dublin (1899-1918). To whom O'Casey's Pictures in the Hallway is dedicated. One of Griffin's daughters spoke to David Krause about her remembrances of O'Casey many years after her father died. That conversation is recorded in the article, "Toward the End," reprinted in The Sting and the Twinkle.

II: 223, 226-7, 232, 239-40   (346, 351-2, 360, 372-3)
III: 27, 36, 39, 40-3, 84, 96-8,   (32, 46, 50-5, 120, 139-41,
100, 149, 216   144, 218-19, 320-1)
IV: 33, 255, 286   (35, 352, 396)

GRIFFITH, ARTHUR
1872 - 1922. Irish nationalist and founder-editor of The United Irishman (1899). His initial ideas centered around the establishment of a dual monarchy between England and Ireland similar to his interpretation of the arrangement between Austria and Hungary (see THE RESURRECTION OF HUNGARY). Founded Sinn Fein,* though later claimants to the name differed markedly with Griffith. He supported the Irish Volunteers,* but took no part the Easter Rising.* Elected vice-president of the Irish Republic (1918) while interned by British authorities; leader of the Irish delegation which signed the Treaty; elected president of Dail Eireann* (1922). O'Casey's distrust of Griffith stems from Griffith's constant attacks on Yeats, Synge and the Abbey Theatre , and his vilification of Larkin and the labor movement. See also HELEN OF EIREANN.

II: 198, 202   (302, 312)
III: 15-16, 17-24, 50, 65, 126, 133-4,   (13-15, 17-24, 26, 27, 67, 90,
151, 157, 160, 161, 213, 242-4   183, 195-6, 221, 231, 236, 238,
                                            316, 362-4)
IV: 9-11, 72, 83, 85, 87, 95, 158   (2-4, 92, 107, 109, 113, 125-6,
                                            215)

GRIFFITHIANS, THE 1872 COMPANY OF
The year 1872 is notable only as the year of Griffith's* birth. O'Casey
appears to be referring to Griffith's noted support of the Irish
Volunteers (see VOLUNTEERS OF 1782) whose centenary was widely celebrated
in 1882, not 1872. O'Casey does, however, use the correct date in III:
20 (22).

III: 153   (224)

GROSVENOR SQUARE
Fashionable square in London, east of Hyde Park.

III: 250   (372)

GUERNICA
Spanish town which was bombed in April 1937 by German planes. The re-
sulting slaughter of innocent women and children became a symbol of
Fascist terror. Subject of a famous painting by Picasso.*

V: 128   (167)

GUINNESS
Used mainly to identify the beer rather than the family of brewers in
Dublin. See McGUINNESS.

III: 36, 65, 70, 103   (45, 90, 99, 151)
V: 47   (53)

GULLED OF DREAMY JERONTIUS
See GERONTIUS.

III: 153   (224)

GUY'S HOPSITAL
In London, on St. Thomas's Street, south of the River Thames. Founded
(1721) by Thomas Guy.

III: 250   (374)

GWENN, EDMUND
1875 - 1959. English actor, noted for his portrayal of working class
characters.

V: 26, 60   (26, 72)

GWYNN, STEPHEN
1864 - 1950. Irish writer and nationalist. Author of historical, cultural, literary and poetry books, studies and reviews. Founding member,
Irish Academy of Letters.*

V: 92-3   (118)

GYRA, SHELIA NEE
In Ethna Carberry's* poem of the same name, an allegorical name for
Ireland. Also a poem (trans.) by Mangan.*

III: 174   (257)

H

HACKETT, REV. RICHARD
Professor of logic and ethics at Maynooth College (Thoms 1880).

IV: 237, 241   (326, 333-4)

HAFFICAN, MATT
Elderly peasant farmer in Shaw's* play, John Bull's Other Island.

III: 176   (259)
IV: 273   (377)

HAGGERTY, PADDY
From the song, "Paddy Heggarty's Leather Breeches," for which see Appendix I.

III: 101   (146)

HAGUE, THE
City in the Netherlands and site of several international peace conferences in the late 19th and early 20th centuries. O'Casey alludes to the 1907 conference where among the issues discussed was the regulation of land warfare.

III: 227   (338)

HALES, GENERAL SEAN
Deputy of the provisional Irish parliament who was assassinated (7 December 1922) for voting for a resolution which gave the Free State army the power to execute captured Irish Republican Army suspects.

IV: 95   (125)

HAMLET
Prince of Denmark in Shakespeare's* play, Hamlet.

I: 71   (102)
V: 36-7   (39-40)

HANNA'S SHOP
Probably Hanna's Book Shop in Nassau Street, owned by Arthur Hannah, a friend of Yeats. Cowasjee claims this book shop is the "Dublin Book Shop" at 32 Bachelor's Walk. The street is correct, but the name is not. Thoms (1896) does not list a book shop at that address; only at # 8 and 23. It is possible that O'Casey is confusing addresses as he did with Webb's.*

II: 122, 126-7   (186, 193-4)

HANNIBAL
247 B.C. - 183 B.C. Noted Carthaginian general.

II: 88   (131)

HANS ANDERSON SHELTERS
Pun on the London air raid shelters named for Sir John Anderson (1882 -
1959), British civil servant in charge of air raid preparations in
World War II. The shelters were portable, steel-mesh with steel tops
and iron bottoms, and could hold two adults.

VI: 148, 156   (207, 219)

HARDIE, KEIR JAMES
1856 - 1915. Scottish socialist and labor leader. Secretary of
Scottish Miners' Federation (1866); chairman, Scottish Labour Party
(1888); M.P. (1892-95, 1900-15); first leader of the Labour Party in
parliament (1906-07). Hardie spoke in Dublin during the 1913 Strike.

VI: 90, 219   (122, 314)

HARDY, THOMAS
1840 - 1928. English novelist and one of O'Casey's favorites. See
also FARMER OAK.

The Dynasts (1904-08), allusion to	IV: 136	(183-4)
Tess of the D'Ubervilles (1891)	V: 18	(14)
	VI: 153	(214)
Jude the Obscure (1895)	V: 18	(14)

HARMSWORTH, ALFRED
1865 - 1922. English newspaper magnate. Acquired The Times in 1908.
Active in English politics, supporting a vigorous prosecution of World
War I and also Lloyd George. Active in bringing about the Treaty.*

II: 213-16, 223   (330-5, 345)

HARMSWORTH IRISH AGENCY
In Dublin, one of the firms which handled distribution of newspapers in
Ireland. O'Casey worked there briefly for 5 shillings a week.

II: 209-10, 212   (324-5, 328)

HAROLD'S CROSS
South Dublin suburb, where the Yeats family lived (1885-87) at 10 Ash-
field Terrace and, where is located Mt. Jerome Cemetery.*

II: 117   (179)

HARROD'S LTD.
Famous London department store in Knightsbridge.

V: 62   (75)

HARROW
Famous public (U.S., private) school in Middlesex, England.

III: 249   (371)
VI: 25, 189, 201, 231   (24, 268, 286, 332)

HARVARD POETRY SOCIETY/HARVARD UNIVERSITY
On 16 November 1934, O'Casey gave the Morris Gray Poetry Talk in Fogg
Museum at Harvard University. His talk was entitled "The Old Drama and
the New."

IV: 211   (290)
V: 181, 203-04, 233-4   (240, 274-5, 314)
VI: 44, 73   (53, 97)

HARVEY, BOB
Appears as a fellow worker with O'Casey on the Great Northern Railway
Company.*

III: 9, 11, 21   (5, 7, 22)

HAUPTMANN, GERHART
1862 - 1946. German dramatist.

The Weavers (1892)   V: 116   (151)

HAWK'S WELL, THE
At the Hawk's Well, a play by Yeats.* There was a performance of this
play in Yeats's home (82 Merrion Square) on Monday, 31 March 1924. See
Yeats's invitation to O'Casey in Letters, I, p. 108.

IV: 269   (372-3)

HAYADAWN, MARY NI
Mary Hayden. 1862 - 1942. Professor of modern Irish history at Uni-
versity College, Dublin (1911-38), and for many years on the Gaelic
League executive board.

III: 111   (160)

HEAL'S
London fabric store at 196 Tottenham Court Road.

V: 61   (74)

HEALY, REV. DR. JOHN
Professor of moral theology at Maynooth College (Thoms, 1880).

IV: 240   (332)

HEALY, TIMOTHY MICHAEL
1855 - 1931. Irish nationalist politician. First governor-general of
the Irish Free State (1922-27). O'Casey's ardent dislike of Healy stems
from Healy's actions during the Parnell* crisis, when he virtually de-
serted Parnell as well as the Home Rule movement. See also UNCLE TIM'S
CABIN.

II: 11, 12, 17, 57-8   (6, 8, 10, 83)
III: 14, 62, 75, 102, 244   (12, 86, 106, 146, 365)
IV: 150-1, 153, 156, 158, 241, 249, 273   (203-04, 207, 211, 214, 332-3,
249, 273   343, 344, 378)
V: 81, 82   (102, 103)

HEARD, GERALD HENRY
1899 - 1971. English writer and literary editor of <u>The Realist</u>.

VI: 162   (227)

HECTOR
In Greek legend, the son of Priam and Hecuba. A principal character
in <u>The Iliad</u>.

II: 88   (131)

HELEN OF EIREANN
In Irish legend, Devorgilla, wife of Tiernan O'Ruarce. In this case,
however, O'Casey is referring to Maud Gonne,* about whom a critical
editorial appeared in the <u>Irish Figaro</u> (7 April 1900), written by
Ramsay Colles. Griffith* took exception, attacked Colles, was arrested,
and served a month in jail.

III: 18   (18)

HELEN OF TROY
In Greek legend, the wife of Menelaus, king of Sparta, and daughter of
Zeus and Leda. Celebrated for her beauty and for her flight, which
caused the Trojan War.

II: 120   (184)
III: 92, 94, 126, 193   (133, 135, 184, 285)

HELENA
Regarded by Coleridge to be Shakespeare's* "loveliest character." In
<u>All's Well That Ends Well</u>.

VI: 226   (325)

HELGA
British warship which sailed up the River Liffey during the Easter
Rising and shelled parts of Dublin.

III: 277   (416)
IV: 12   (5)

HENCHY, R. J.
Secretary of the Protestant Orphan Society, Dublin, the agency which
adopted the youngest son of O'Casey's sister, Isabella. Factual name.

III: 215-19   (319-25)

HENDERSON, NEVILLE
1882 - 1942. British ambassador to Germany (1937-39). Author of <u>The
Mission That Failed</u> (1940).

VI: 116   (160)

HENESSEY'S
Dublin pub at 70 Great Britain (Parnell) Street, owned by James Henessey.

I: 44   (58)

HENN, THOMAS R.
1901 - 1974. Distinguished scholar who had a long career at Cambridge
University.   In his Five Arches (1980), he noted that it was he who
invited O'Casey to give the Cambridge talk.

VI: 54   (68)

HENRY, PAUL
1877 - 1959. Irish artist. Studied in Paris at Whistler's studio and
settled in Connemara.

IV: 198   (272)

HENRY STREET
In north central Dublin. Severely damaged during the Easter Rising.

II: 65, 67, 103, 126, 127   (95, 99, 156, 193, 194)
III: 200   (295)

HENRY THE EIGHTH
1491 - 1547. King (from 1509) from house of Tudor.* Declared king of
Ireland (1541) by the Irish parliament. Executor of Thomas More (1535).

III: 37   (47)
V: 218, 226   (292, 304)

HENRY THE SIXTH
1421 - 1471. Weak king of England. Succeeded to the throne at the age
of nine months. Killed by Richard of Gloucester. In Shakespeare's* 1,
2, and 3 Henry VI.

II: 20, 21, 131   (22, 23, 201)

HENRY THE THIRD
1551 - 1589. As Duke of Anjou, credited with winning several battles
(1569). Elected king of Poland (1573); became king of France (1574).

V: 188   (250)

HERCULES
In Greek and Roman mythology, a mighty hero of strength and courage.
O'Casey's references involve the famous 12 labors of Hercules, in which
he died to expiate his crimes.

III: 35   (44)
VI: 204   (291)

HERMITAGE
In Rathfarnham,* the house of St. Enda's School.*

III: 190, 287   (281, 430)

HEROD
Herod Antipas, ruler of Judea at the time of Christ's birth.

VI: 37   (43)

HEWSON, MR.
An official at Leedom, Hampton chandler company, Dublin.

II: 74-6, 79, 85, 88, 90, 99, 100, 101-2, 104-5, 112, 113, 116, 128-30
    (110-13, 118-19, 127-8, 131, 135, 150-1, 154, 157-8, 170-2, 195-9)

HEYSHAM
In Lancashire, England, terminal of Irish Sea ships to Belfast.

V: 159   (210)

HIAWATHA
From the narrative poem (1855) by Henry Wadsworth Longfellow (1807 -
1882), American poet.

VI: 177   (251)

HIBERNIA
Probably the Hibernia Bank Ltd., 23-27 College Green, Dublin.

IV: 276   (414)

HIBERNIAN ACADEMY
The Royal Hibernian Academy of Painting, Sculpture, and Architecture,
15 Ely Place, Dublin. Founded in 1823. Burned and destroyed during
the Easter Rising.

IV: 212   (291)

HIBERNIAN BIBLE SOCIETY
At 10 Upper Sackville (O'Connell) Street. Its purpose was "to encourage
wider circulation of the Holy Scripture, without note or comment, in
Ireland." Founded in 1806.

II: 227   (352)

HIDDEN IRELAND
See CORKERY, DANIEL

HIGGINS, FREDERICK ROBERT
1896 - 1941. Irish poet and dramatist, and editor of several economic
and literary journals. A director of the Abbey theatre (from 1935).
Founding member, Irish Academy of Letters.* Higgins' comment (#) on
The Plough were in a letter to the editor, Irish Statesman, 6 March
1926. The reference to AE's portrait (##) is to a pastel (1911) by
Mathilde de C., which was in Higgins' possession.

IV: 127-8#, 181#, 212##   (169-70#, 247#, 291##)
V: 54, 122   (63, 159)

HILL STREET
In north Dublin, an extension of Temple Street from Hardwicke Place.

II: 131, 159   (210, 244)

HILLOLEURUS AND ARDALAUNUS
The first is unknown.For the second, see ARDILAUN, LORD.

III: 159   (233)

HILLS OF DUBLIN/DUBLIN HILLS
Small group of hills south of Dublin. "Hills of Dublin" was also the
title of a collection of poetry, published by An Philibin (1917).

III: 164   (241)
IV: 105   (138)

HILLSBOROUGH
Possibly Wills Hill, earl of Hillsborough. 1718 - 1793. English
politician. Favored union of England and Ireland.

III: 70   (98)

HINSLEY, ARCHBISHOP ARTHUR
1865 - 1943. English Catholic prelate. Archbishop of Westminister
(from 1935); cardinal (1937). Staunch advocate of British imperialism.

IV: 242   (335)
V: 78   (99)

HITCHCOCK, ALFRED
1899 - 1981. American film director (born in Britain). Responsible
for the filming of Juno (1930) from O'Casey's Juno and the Paycock.
For more of O'Casey on Hitchcock, see the article, "No Flowers for
Films," in The Green Crow. See also FILM COMPANY.

V: 123-5   (160-2)

HITLER, ADOLPH
V: 127, 228   (167, 301)
VI: 114-15, 116, 118, 121-4, 126, 137, (156-60, 163-5, 167, 169-71,
138, 143, 144, 145, 150, 160, 190   174, 189, 191, 192, 199-202,
                                        210, 271, 272)

HOBSON, BULMER
1883 - 1969. Irish nationalist. Editor (1912) of Irish Freedom*;
secretary, Irish Volunteers (1914); author of History of the Irish
Volunteers (1918). During the Easter Rising, Hobson was detained by
Irish Republicans because of his questionable support.

III: 160-1, 164, 231, 232, 244, 271-2   (236-7, 242, 344, 346, 364, 407)

HOBSON, THOMAS
c.1544 - 1630. English carrier and keeper of a livery stable at Cambridge. Subject of two kindly poems by Milton* and an essay by Steele.

VI: 197   (281)

HOEY'S COURT
In central Dublin, south of the River Liffey. Birthplace of Swift.*

V: 76   (95)

HOFER, ANDREAS
1767 - 1810. Tyrolese patriot who led the rebellion against the Bavarian government of the Tyrol (1809). See also Appendix III, this
page number.

III: 33   (41)

HOGAN, DR. JOHN
Professor of modern languages (1895) and president of Maynooth College
(1914). One of the judges in the O'Hickey* case.

V: 258-9   (357-8)

HOGARTH, WILLIAM
1697 - 1764. English painter and engraver. O'Casey is probably referring to such Hogarth paintings as Beer Street and Gin Lane.

V: 23, 111   (20, 144)

HOLLOWAY, JOSEPH
1861 - 1944. Compulsive Dublin theatre-goer for 50 years, and architect
of the Abbey Theatre (1904). Holloway allegedly attended every
production at the Abbey in his lifetime. He left these impressions
in the form of a diary which covers 221 volumes. See Joseph Holloway's
Abbey Theatre.

IV: 281   (389)

HOLLYWOOD
In his article, "No Flowers for Films," in The Green Crow, O'Casey
writes more about his experiences with Hollywood. In one case,
he turned down $100,000 to write the scenario for Thomas Wolfe's
book, Look Homeward Angel! (See his letter to William Herndon, Letters,
II, pp. 204-05.)

I: 9   (2)
V: 123, 124, 209   (160, 161, 279)

HOLMES, SHERLOCK
Arthur Conan Doyle's* fictional sleuth.

V: 197, 227   (263, 305)

HOLY ROOD
Allusion to Yeats's* poem, "Red Hanrahan's Song About Ireland."

III: 80, 127   (111, 185)
VI: 108   (149)

HOLYHEAD
In Wales, the chief port for the Dublin passenger run.

V: 9   (1)

HOME GUARD
In England, a volunteer force raised early in World War II which was
trained for defense against threatened invasion.

VI: 138, 148, 151   (192, 206, 211)

HOME RULE/HOME RULE BILL
There were three important Home Rule Bills (#) initiated during the
first half of O'Casey's life. The first (1886),introduced by Gladstone*,
failed by a narrow margin in the House of Commons. The second (1893)
passed the House of Commons, but was rejected in the House of Lords.
The last, in 1914, passed both houses in September, but it was suspended
for the duration of the war. This last bill was what Yeats was probably
referring to in his poem, "Easter 1916," when he wrote that "England
may yet keep faith." Home Rule crises invariably gave rise to sectarian
slogans, including the Protestant-inspired "Home Rule is Rome Rule."

I: 15, 23, 58, 74, 175   (11, 23, 81, 107, 270)
II: 229#   (356#)
III: 105#, 248, 254#   (152#, 372, 380#)

HOOVER, HERBERT C.
1874 - 1964. The 31st president of the U.S. See also WILBUR.

IV: 212   (292)

HOPKINSON, HENRY THOMAS
b.1905. English author of essays and short stories. Editor, Picture
Post* (1940-50). See Letters, I, pp. 806-07.

V: 223   (300)

HORACE
65 B.C. - 8 B.C. Roman lyric poet and satirist.

VI: 200, 201, 202   (285, 286, 287)
Dulce Ridentem Lalagen Amabo, Dulce Loquentem VI: 199   (283)

HORNIMAN, ANN ELIZABETH
1860 - 1937. Owner and restorer of the Abbey Theatre, which the Irish
National Literary Society had free use of (1904-10). Owned and managed
the Gaiety Theatre, London (1908-21).

IV: 144, 281   (195, 389)

HORSE GUARDS BLUE
See LIFE GUARDS RED.

HORSE SHOW
The annual Irish horse show in the first week of August, sponsored by
the Royal Dublin Society at their agricultural premises in Ballsbridge,
outside Dublin.

IV: 154   (209)

HORSES OF DEA
Dea is the De Danaans, the people of the Goddess Dana in Irish mythology.

III: 57   (79)

HORSES OF EMAIN
Chariot horses of Cuchulain.*

III: 57   (79)

HOSPITALS SWEEPS
The Irish Hospitals' Sweepstakes.

VI: 215   (308)

HOSPICE FOR THE DYING
Our Lady's Hospice for the Dy.ing, Harold's Cross, Co. Dublin. Primarily intended for the poor of all religions. Accommodated 110 patients.

IV: 118, 119, 121   (157, 158, 159, 161)

HOUSE OF COMMONS
In the British parliament.

I: 74, 75, 174   (107, 109, 269)
III: 151, 248, 254   (222, 371, 381)
V: 59, 92   (71, 117)
VI: 28, 48, 90, 219   (29, 60, 122, 314)

HOUSE OF LORDS
In the British parliament.

III: 248   (371)
VI: 48   (59)

HOUSE OF MECKLENBURG-SCHWERIN
Claims to be the oldest sovereign house in the West (from c.1100). It
became Mecklenburg-Schwerin in 1701. One of the most recent descendants
is Queen Wilhelmina of the Netherlands. Mecklenburg Street was Dublin's
red-light district. Its name was changed to Tyrone Street (1887), and
later to Railway Street.

I: 181   (279)

HOUSE OF NASSAU
Family in Europe which derived its name from a county near the Rhine
(c.1250). The first line of Orange-Nassau, from which the Orange Order*
derives its name, was established (1544) by William the Silent.

II: 239   (371)

HOWSOM, REV. VINCENT
Vicar of an East End London church. Credited with rewriting the part of
Bert, the foreman of the workers, in Eliot's* The Rock.

VI: 90   (122)

HOWTH

Howth Hill is on a promontory on the north side of the entrance to
Dublin Bay, about eight miles east of Dublin. The Howth landing (26
July 1914) involved a large consignment of arms (900 mauser rifles and
26,000 rounds of ammunition) for the Irish Volunteers. The shipment
was brought in by Erskine Childers,* Mary Spring-Rice,* and others on
Childers' yacht, the Asgard. The British intercepted the Volunteers,
and, in the ensuing conflict, three civilians were killed and 32
others were wounded at Bachelor's Walk.*

II: 188	(290)
III: 261-6, 281	(391-8, 422)
V: 56, 173	(66, 230)

HUDSON RIVER
In west New York, forming part of the New York-New Jersey border.

V: 179   (238)

HUDSON THEATRE
In New York City at 139 West 44th Street. The letter is clearly bogus
since Juno was never performed at the Hudson. The Plough, however, had
its U.S. premiere there (28 November 1927).

VI: 9   (1-2)

HUDSON, WILLIAM HENRY
English naturalist and author.

The Purple Land that England Lost (1885)   IV: 137 (184)

HUGHES, HERBERT
1882 - 1937. Irish composer, critic, and editor of several books on
music. Composed the music for O'Casey's play, Within the Gates. For
more on the quarrel between the two, see Letters, I.

V: 131   (171)

HUGHES, JOHN
1865 - 1941. Dublin sculptor. Hughes was a student with AE and Oliver
Sheppard at the Metropolitan School of Art, Dublin, and was a witness
to AE's wedding (1898) to Violet North. The bust of AE by Hughes (1885-
86), to which O'Casey refers, stood for years above the mantelshelf of
the outer sitting-room in AE's home on Rathgar Avenue,* and was used
as a frontispiece in Alan Denson's Letters from A.E. It is presently
in the Municipal Gallery of Modern Art, Dublin.

IV: 212   (291)

HUGHES, SEAMUS
An official of the Irish Transport and General Workers' Union. In
Fifty Years of Liberty Hall, there is a group photo of some of the
union officers, and Hughes is included. See also the article, "Sean
O'Casey and James Larkin after 1923," by Ronald Ayling, in which O'Casey
recounts some of the story surrounding Hughes.

IV: 11   (4-5)

HUGUENOTS
In the late 17th century, French Huguenots came to Ireland seeking
political and religious sanctuary. They brought with them improved
textile machinery, to which O'Casey refers. There is a Huguenot
churchyard at 10 Merrion Row, Dublin, in which are buried three French
congregations.

II: 228, 230   (354, 357)
III: 284   (427)

HUGO, VICTOR
1802 - 1885. Noted French poet, novelist and dramatist. See also
QUASIMODO.

II: 122   (187)

HUIS-CLOS
The French title of Jean Paul Sartre's play, No Exit (1946).

VI: 27   (28)

HUME, FERGUS
1859 - 1932. British writer of detective stories.

Mystery of a Hansom Cab (1887)   V: 196   (262)

HUNDINGDON
In U.S. edition only. This is John Huntington, a director of Putnam
and Co., London, Lady Gregory's* publishers. The spelling is O'Casey's
manner of portraying Lady Gregory's speech, which had a slight lisp.
U.K. see HUNTINGTON, JOHN.

V: 62

HUNT, REV. PHINEAS
Rector, St. Kevin's Church,* Dublin.

III: 148   (217)

HUNTER, REV. MR. T. R. S.
According to Martin Margulies, this is "almost certainly . . . Rev.
J. S. Fletcher of St. Barnabas, whose identity O'Casey probably dis-
guised to avoid wounding his son, Rev. Harry Fletcher.*" J. S. Fletcher
(b.1834) was rector of St. Barnabas' Church, 1872-99.

I: 91-3, 98, 104, 107-08, 109-12, 116-20, 123-5, 127, 150, 151-5, 157
     (135-8, 146, 156-7, 162, 164-7, 175-82, 185, 187, 189, 229, 232-8)

II: 41   (56)

HUNTER, TOM
Irish patriot and member of Dail Eireann. His name appears in the
"Address of Irish Commandants to the President and Congress of the
United States" (18 June 1917) as Tomas Ua Fiadhachra. See The Irish
Republic. Active in the Easter Rising at Jacob's biscuit factory.

IV: 85, 86   (110, 111)

HUNTINGTON, JOHN
See HUNDINGDON.

V: 53   (PAN)

HURLERS
In Cornwall, England, an ancient irregular group of grey stones rising
from the moor in three large and interesting circles. According to
local legend, the stones are men who were punished for playing the game
of hurling on the sabbath.

VI: 77   (103)

HURLING LEAGUE
David Krause says that O'Casey was a member of the Red Hand Hurling
Club of the Drumcondra Branch of the Gaelic League. Martin Margulies
claims that the Red Hand Branch did not have a hurling league, and that
O'Casey was a member of the Central Branch League. Saros Cowasjee
maintains that O'Casey was a member of the Ard-Chroabh, Central
Hurling Club, of the Gaelic Athletic Association.

III: 131   (191)

HUTTON'S LANE
In east Dublin, off Summerhill. III: 78 (110)

HUTTONS
John Hutton and Sons, coach builders and Dublin wheelworks, 115-19
Summerhill and 2 Dawson Place.

III: 69, 74-5, 77-8   (97, 105, 109)

HUXLEY, THOMAS
Given as HOAXLEY. 1825 - 1895. English biologist and foremost advocate
in England of Darwin's theories of evolution. The Shaw* play to which
O'Casey refers is Back to Methuselah (1921).

III: 176   (260)

HYDE, DOUGLAS
1862 - 1949. Known also as An Craoibhin Aoibhin (The Fair Branch).
Irish writer, scholar and statesman. First president (1893-1915) of
the Gaelic League*; professor of modern Irish, National University
(1909-32); president of Ireland (1938-45). Resigned from the Gaelic
League when it became too political, which Hyde felt detracted from
its goals. See also Appendix III, III: 154 (266).

III: 12, 23, 32, 77, 111, 113-15, 131, 140-2, 149-51, 153-9, 160, 236
(9, 26, 39, 108, 160, 164-7, 192, 195, 205-08, 219-22, 225-32, 234, 236,
 353)

IV: 145, 151, 159, 267   (196, 205, 216, 369)
The Illbred Child and His Mother   III: 154   (226)
The Poorhouse (1903)   IV: 145   (196)
The Marriage (1903)   IV: 145   (196)
Mise agus an Conradh (autobiography, 1938) IV: 267   (369)

HYDE PARK
Public park (346 acres) in Westminister, London. Popular meeting place
for orators of every persuasion. Scene of O'Casey's play, <u>Within the
Gates</u>. O'Casey refers to the statue of Achilles and to the Hyde Park
Memorial.

V: 61, 77, 123   (73, 97, 160)
VI: 16, 25   (12, 25)

HYDRANGEAS
Painting by Evan Walters.*

VI: 74, 85   (98, 115)

HYLAND
Appears as the head of the cutlery department at Leedom, Hampton
chandler company, Dublin.

III: 117, 120-1, 124, 126, 127, 130   (179, 183-5, 190, 192, 194, 199)

HYMDIM, LEADEM & CO.
Many spellings, including simply FIRM. Leedom, Hampton chandler company
at 50 Henry Street, Dublin, where O'Casey worked "for a year and a
half."(#) According to Cowasjee, O'Casey began work at age 14 for 3
shillings, 6 pence, weekly for a 10-hour day. He was later promoted to
dispatch clerk,and ultimately was paid 7 shillings a week.

II: 65-9, 71, 77-81#, 84-6, 92, 99, 119, 129-30, 184
    (94-101, 105, 115-21#, 125-9, 139, 150, 182, 197-8, 283)

I

IBSEN, HENRIK
1828 - 1906. Norwegian dramatist who is regarded by many as the father
of modern drama. See O'Casey's essay, "Dramatis Personae Ibsenisensis,"
in <u>Blasts and Benedictions</u>.

IV: 182, 278   (248, 385)
VI: 171, 177   (242, 250)

IGNATIUS, THE GAEL FROM COUNTY CLARE
Variant on St. Ignatius* and on the Irish song, "The Girl from the
County Clare," for which see Appendix I.

IV: 67   (85)

IMITATION OF CHRIST, THE
Famous devotional work, usually attributed to Thomas a Kempis (c.1388 -
1471).

VI: 37, 231   (43, 332)

INCAS/AZTECS
Incas were of the Quechuan people in the Peruvian highlands. Aztecs were
of the Nahuatl people in Mexico. Both were conquered by the Spanish.

III: 89-90   (127-8)

INCHICORE
Suburb south of Phoenix Park on the western outskirts of Dublin.

III: 191   (282)

INDIA
See also CLIVE, ROBERT; GANDHI, MAHATMA; and INDIAN MUTINY.

I: 68, 172   (97, 266)
III: 273   (410)
IV: 208, 211   (285, 290)
V: 36   (39)

INDIAN MUTINY
In Blasts and Benedictions (p. 252), O'Casey refers to G. W. Forrest's
book, History of the Indian Mutiny. See LUCKNOW and SEPOY.

V: 224   (300)

INIS FAIL
Irish for Isle of Destiny. Poetic name for Ireland.

III: 34   (43)

INNISFALLEN PARADE
In north Dublin, a small street running into Lower Dorset Street. The
Caseys moved to number 9 around 1881. It carried a 9 pound valuation
and a weekly rent of 6 shillings, 6 pence.

II: 48   (68)

INNISFREE
Island in Lough Gill in Co. Sligo. Celebrated by Yeats in his "Lake
Isle of Innisfree."

III: 19, 244   (20, 364)
IV: 283   (392)
V: 132   (174)

INNISKILLENERS
From Enniskillen, county seat of Co. Fermanagh. Famed for providing
the British army with two noted regiments: the 5th Inniskilling Dragoon
Guards and the Royal Inniskilling Fusiliers.

II: 230   (357)

INNS OF QUAY POLICE COURT
In   Dublin, the Inn Quay, located between Arran and Ormand quays,
is a boundary street for the Courts of Justice.

II: 39   (53)

INQUISITION
Name given to a tribunal of the Catholic Church (1229) at the Synod of
Toulouse by Pope Gregory IX. Its purpose was to discover and punish
heretics and heresy. Lasted into the 14th century. The Spanish Inquisition was an agency of the Spanish crown (1478) and functioned with
the approval of Pope Sixtus IV. It was introduced chiefly against Jews
and Moors, though its severity eventually reached into all groups which
were suspected of heretical behaviour. Not abolished until 1820.

IV: 97   (127)

INTERNATIONAL AFFAIRS ASSOCIATION OF IRELAND
A discussion and policy group concerned with Irish foreign affairs,
which hosted the "Papal Nuncio Incident" at the Shelbourne Hotel in
Dublin (31 October 1952). See BUTLER, HUBERT; O'HARA, MICKEY; and
SKEFFINGTON, OWEN. See also Blanshard, The Irish and Catholic Power,
pp. 186-91.

VI: 210   (300)

INVINCIBLES
Splinter group of Irish nationalists from the Irish Republican Brotherhood, who organized themselves (1881) for the purpose of assassinating
members of the British government shortly after the Land League* was
declared illegal, and after over 1000 men were imprisoned, including
Parnell,* Dillon,* and Davitt.* In 1882, Gladstone* and Parnell concluded the Kilmainham Treaty,* which prompted the resignation of the
chief secretary of Ireland. Cavendish* and Burke* were appointed chief
secretary and undersecretary, respectively. Both were immediately
assassinated by the Invincibles. See the article, "The Invicibles,"
Secret Societies in Ireland. In this index, see BRADY, CAFFREY, CAREY,
CURLEY, FAGEN, and KELLY.

I: 75   (108)
II: 37-9, 54   (50-3, 78)
V: 51   (59)

IPHIGENIA
In Greek legend, the daughter of Agamemnon and Clytemnestra. Subject
of dramatic poetry by Euripides, Goethe, Racine, and others.

III: 93   (134)

IRELAND OF THE VIRGINS
Probably a variant on the slogan, "Ireland of the Welcomes," and on the
old puritanical tale that Ireland was so safe that a virgin could walk
unmolested from one end of the country to the other.

III: 145   (212)

IRELAND OF THE WISE WELCOMES
From the tourist slogan, "Ireland of the Welcomes." The "wise" is
probably a reference to another title the country has often claimed:
The Land of Saints and Scholars; though, elsewhere, O'Casey called it
"the land of restraints and scollars."

III: 15   (13)

IRELAND'S FOUR BEAUTIFUL FIELDS
Ireland's four provinces: Leinster, Munster, Ulster, and Connaught.
Sometimes referred to as "Four Green Fields."

III: 24   (27)
IV: 167   (228)

IREMONGER, VALENTIN
b.1918. Irish actor, poet, diplomat, and playwright.

VI: 208   (298)

IRISH ACADEMY OF LETTERS.
Irish society of belles lettres, founded (18 September 1932) at a
meeting in the Peacock Theatre, Dublin. There were two categories of
numerical membership: academician (25) and associate (10). O'Casey
was proposed for the first category, but he declined the offer. Others
who refused to join were Joyce, Stephen McKenna, George Moore, Douglas
Hyde, and Daniel Corkery. The latter two held that membership should
consist of writers in Irish. The academy issues several awards periodically, including the Gregory Medal, the Harmsworth Award, the Casement
Award, and the O'Growney Award. See O'Casey's letter of refusal in
Letters, I, pp. 451-2. See also IRISH LITERARY ACADEMY.

VI: 179   (254-5)

IRISH AGRICULTURAL ORGANIZATION SOCIETY
Founded (1894) by Horace Plunkett* and others in the wake of Land League
agitation and the Land Acts. Plunkett's aims were simple: better farming, better business, and better living, to be accomplished primarily
through agricultural co-operatives. By 1915, there were 991 agricultural societies of one type or another (supply, farming, credit, etc.).
AE was very active in the society. George Moore described him as riding
through Ireland on a bicycle "preaching the doctrine of co-operation
and dairy farming from village to village, winning friends to the movement by his personal magnetism which he exercises wherever he goes,
and the eloquence of his belief in Plunkett."

IV: 235   (324)

IRISH CITIZEN ARMY
Formed during the 1913 Strike, the I.C.A. had the distinction of being
the first workers' army in Europe. Its purpose was to defend the strikers from the employers and police terrorism. With the demise of the
strike in January 1914, the army underwent a reorganization, initiated
largely by O'Casey. He drew up new structures, and wrote or designed
many of the important documents during his term (March-October 1914)
as secretary. The officers elected at a general meeting at Liberty
Hall (22 March 1914) were: Captain White, chairman; James Larkin,
P. T. Daly, William Partridge, Thomas Foran, Francis Sheehy-Skeffington,
vice-chairmen; Sean O'Cathasiagh, secretary; and Richard Brannigan
and Countess Markiewicz, tresurers (all *). When Larkin left for the
U.S. in late 1914, Connolly assumed command, and, with him, the direct-
ion of the army changed. O'Casey's objections to the changes and a
brief history of the army can be found in his The Story of the Irish
Citizen Army (1919), reprinted in Feathers from a Green Crow.
                                                              MORE

IRISH CITIZEN ARMY (cont.)

III: O'Casey in, in 1913 Strike   210   (312)
    and Countess Markiwicz   212, 213   (314-15)
    and reorganization of   224-5   (334-5)
    and Irish Volunteers*   225-6, 230-1,   (336-7, 343-5,
                                      263-5   395-8)
    and uniforms (see ARNOTT)   226-9   (337-42)
    and Plough and the Stars flag*   230   (342-3)
    and Bodenstown*   228, 231   (340, 344)
    and O'Casey's departure from   261   (391)
    and Howth landing*   262-6   (392-8)
    and Connolly   266-9, 270   (399-406)
    and the Easter Rising   272   (407-8)

Mentioned: 244   (365)

IRISH CONSTITUTION
In Irish, Bunreacht na hEireann (1937). Intimately associated with
Eamon de Valera,* at the time president of the executive council of
the Irish Free State. The constitution affirmed the independence of
Ireland, but acknowledged the de facto existence of Northern Ireland.
It also dismantled nearly all British functions within the Free State,
and formally changed the name of the country to Eire. The constitution
presumed Irish to be the national language, with English the official
second language. Divorce was forbidden, and "the state recognizes the
special position of the Roman Catholic Church." It is generally seen
to be a statement of liberal-democratic (albeit theocratic) principles;
a modification of English law; and Catholic principles on the individual,
the family, and the state. O'Casey referred to it as being "as revolutionary as the articles of the Church of England" (Letters, I, p. 712).

IV: 160   (217)

IRISH GODS AND FIGHTING MEN.
Variant on Lady Gregory's* Gods and Fighting Men (1904).

IV: 172   (234)

IRISH HIERARCHAELOGICAL SOCIETY OF 1842
The Irish Archaelogical Society (1840). In 1853, it merged with the
Celtic Society (1845) and became the Irish Archaeological and Celtic
Society.

III: 149   (219)

IRISH HOUSE OF PARLIAMENT
Before the Treaty,* the last quasi-independent Irish parliament was
the Grattan* Parliament (1782-1800). Dissolved by the Act of Union.*
See also BANK OF IRELAND.

I: 58   (81)

IRISH-IRELANDER
In general, those who wanted an Irish-speaking Ireland, as opposed to
an English-speaking country (cf. WEST BRITON). One of the chief ex-
ponents of this view was D. P. Moran,* who wrote in 1901: "The main
divisions in Ireland are Irish-Irelander and West Briton, and any
political papers of individual politicians that side against Irish-
Ireland are enemies of the Irish nation."   In a program note for the
Mermaid Theatre productions (1962), O'Casey wrote that he "joined the
Irish-Irelander movement in 1900."

III: 82, 106, 231, 235	(116, 153, 343, 350)
IV: 235	(324)
V: 82	(103)

IRISH JACK
O'Casey's nickname during his extreme nationalist stage.

III: 48	(64)

IRISH LITERARY ACADEMY
See IRISH ACADEMY OF LETTERS.

V: 42	(47)

IRISH LITERARY SOCIETY
In London, founded (12 May 1892) by Yeats,* Dr. John Todhunter, W. P.
Ryan, and others, at the Caledonian Hotel in the Adelphi. Sir Charles
Gavan Duffy, its president, delivered an inaugural speech on July 23 at
a garden party.

V: 38	(41)

IRISH NATIONAL FORESTERS
Fraternal, Catholic and nationalist organization which adorned itself
with elaborate costumes and uniforms. Its motto was "Unity, Nationality,
and Benevolence." Its executive offices were in Dublin at 9 Merchant's
Quay. In O'Casey's play, The Plough and the Stars, Peter Flynn is a
member of the organization. After O'Casey's satiric treatment of the
organization in the play, the Foresters were never the same, and soon
declined in membership.

III: 65, 178	(90, 263)

IRISH PARLIAMENTARY PARTY
Also given as IRISH PARTY. The primary representatives of Ireland in
the British parliament. Led by John Redmond and John Dillon (both *),
they were the Irish representatives for over 40 years until the general
election of 1918, when, in a dramatic reversal, they were almost
unanimously swept out of power and replace   by Sinn Fein.*

I: 174	(269)
II: 196	(303)
III: 150, 156	(220, 230)
IV: 150, 249	(203, 343)

IRISH PLAYERS
Group of Irish actors and actresses established (1916) as a result of
a controversy with St. John Ervine* during ,his tenure as Abbey theatre
manager. The group was headed by Arthur Sinclair* and featured most
of the Abbey players.

VI: 224   (322)

IRISH REPUBLICAN ARMY
Traces its establishment to the founding convention of the Irish Dail
(1919), though the merging of the Irish Volunteers* and the Irish Citizen
Army* for the Easter Rising was its precursor. After the Treaty,* the
army split into two groups. See FREE STATE ARMY.

IV: 52, 100, 111-12, 148   (63, 132, 146-7, 200)
VI: 184   (260)

IRISH REPUBLICAN BROTHERHOOD
Also given as REPUBLICAN BROTHERHOOD, FENIAN BROTHERHOOD, IRISH REPUB-
LICAN BROTHERS, and FENIANS.* An armed conspiratorial organization
seeking the overthrow of British rule and the establishment of an independent Ireland. Organized (c.1858) by James Stephens, the I.R.B.
was the force behind the 1867 Rising and was prominent in the Easter
Rising. Administratively, they were governed by their constitution of
1873, by which the I.R.B. was established in county and district centers,
which in turn were grouped into seven divisions: Leinster, Ulster, Munster, Connaught, north of England, south of England, and Scotland. Each
division elected one representative to sit on the Supreme Council. The
Council then elected four others whose names were known only to them.
Most of the power was concentrated in the hands of the president, secretary, and treasurer. O'Casey's references to the bishops' opposition
is an allusion to the famous sermon of Bishop David Moriarty   (1814 -
1877), when he condemned the I.R.B. with "God's heaviest curse, his
withering, blasting, blighting curse," and then informed his public that
"eternity is not long enough, nor hell hot enough" for the Fenians (10
October 1865). According to Cowasjee, O'Casey joined the I.R.B. around
1905. According to Margulies, he was in the Teeling Circle of the I.R.B.

III: and clerical opposition to   146   (214-15)
     O'Casey as Press Steward for   162   (238-9)
     and secrecy of   162-3   (239-40)
     and romanticism of   163-4   (240-1)
     and labor movement   164   (241-2)
     and O'Casey's departure from   232   (346)
     and anti-recruiting (WWI)   267   (400)
     and Easter Rising   272   (407)

Mentioned: III: 66, 114, 146, 160, 213, 266
                   (92, 165, 214, 235, 316, 399-400)
               IV: 234, 249   (323, 345)

IRISH SEA
Body of water between Ireland and England.

IV: 282   (390)
VI: 229   (329)

IRISH SOCIALIST REPUBLICAN PARTY
Also given as IRISH SOCIALIST REPUBLICANS, IRISH REPUBLICAN SOCIALISTS,
and SOCIALIST REPUBLICAN PARTY OF IRELAND. The I.S.R.P. was formed by
James Connolly* in 1896. A comprehensive outline of the party's aims
and goals can be found in Connolly's Socialism and Nationalism.

II: 179, 196   (275, 302)
III: 16, 20, 160   (16, 21, 235)

IRISH TRANSPORT AND GENERAL WORKERS' UNION
The largest trade union in Ireland. Founded (1909) by James Larkin.*
Its headquarters in Dublin are Liberty Hall,* and its organ, in Larkin's
day, was the Irish Worker,* which was published weekly before being
suppressed by the British authorities in 1914. O'Casey joined the union
in 1911, and was shortly thereafter dismissed from his job.

III: 187-8, 190, 191, 192, 193, 221, 231, 246, 265, 266
      (276-8, 281, 283-4, 286-7, 329, 343, 346, 397, 399)
IV: 11, 12, 76-8   (4-6, 97-102)

IRISH VOLUNTEERS
Irish nationalist organization, founded (25 November 1913) by Eoin
MacNeill* and others in reaction to Carson's* Ulster Volunteers.*
By July 1914, there were over 100,000 members. In late 1914, the
organization split into two groups (due, mainly, to the outbreak of
World War I): the National Volunteers and the Irish Volunteers. In
general, those who remained in the former group were caught up in the
British recruitment drive for the war; while those in the latter group
allied themselves with the Irish Citizen Army* and the Irish Republican
Brotherhood* for the Easter Rising. Their headquarters in Dublin was
at 2 Dawson Street. See the "Manifesto of the Irish Volunteers" in
Marcardle's The Irish Republic. See also O'Casey's articles in Feathers
from a Green Crow: "An Open Letter to the Volunteers," "Volunteers and
Workers," and "Irish Workers and Irish Volunteers."

III: 213, 226, 227, 230-1, 244, 261, 262, 264-6, 270, 272, 280, 282, 284
      (316, 336-7, 343-4, 364, 391, 393-7, 402, 405-07, 421, 423, 426)
IV: 18   (14)

IRVINE, GEORGE
Irish Republican Brotherhood member who was imprisoned after the Easter
Rising. Signed, under the name of Seoirse O hEireamhoin, the "Address
of Irish Commandants to the President and Congress of the United States"
(18 June 1917). See Marcardle's The Irish Republic.

III: 147-8   (215)

IRVING, HENRY
1838 - 1905. Popular English actor and theatre manager.

II: 137   (210)

IRVING, WASHINGTON
1783 - 1859. Noted American writer. See CURRAN, SARAH.

Mahomet and his Successors (1849-50)   III: 207   (308)

ISAACS, RUFUS DANIEL
1860 - 1935. British politician. O'Casey's use of the phrase, "Markoni
him well," refers to Isaacs' involvement with the Marconi Company scandal in 1912. See Frances Donaldson, The Marconi Scandal (1962).

III: 255   (381)

ISANDLWANA
Site of a South African village where British forces were annihilated
by Cetewayo's troops (1879).

I: 116   (175)

ISLE OF MAN
Island in the Irish Sea.

II: 229   (356)
VI: 214   (306)

ISLE OF THE BLEST
Generally, a generic term for any utopian south sea island. Byron*
uses it, and there is also an Irish song by Gerald Griffin, "O Brazil,
Isle of the Blest."

III: 104   (150)

ISRAELITES
I: 93   (138)
III: 18   (19)
V: 91   (116)
VI: 196   (279)

ITALY
III: 194   (287)
IV: 139, 146, 234, 261   (188, 197, 323, 361)
VI: 114, 212   (157, 304)

IVANHOE
Sir Walter Scott's* romantic hero from the village of Ivinghoe, England.

VI: 37   (43)

IVEAGH
An 11th-century Ulster kingdom.

V: 164, 165   (218, 219)

J

JACK THE JOURNEYMAN
From Yeats's* "Crazy Jane" series of poems. Number IV is entitled
"Crazy Jane and Jack the Journeyman."

VI: 229   (330)

JACKSON, SIR BARRY
1879 - 1961. English director, theatre manager and dramatist. Produced
the first performance of Shaw's* play, Back to Methuselah (1923); founded
the Malvern Festival (1929); and was director of the Memorial Theatre at
Stratford-on-Avon (1945-48).

V: 32-3, 128   (34, 167)

JACKSON, THOMAS J. (STONEWALL)
1824 - 1863. American Confederate general in the U.S. Civil War.

V: 180   (239)

JACOB'S
Prominent steam biscuit and flour stores which were owned by William
R. Jacob at 5-10 Peter's Row and 28-39 Bishop Street, Dublin. Briefly
occupied during the Easter Rising. See also BAKECOB'S.

III: 191   (283)

JAMAICA
O'Casey's reference, "a low wind in Jamaica," is a variant on the title
of Richard A. Hughes's (b.1900) novel, A High Wind in Jamaica (U.S. The
Innocent Voyage, 1929).

VI: 61, 62   (79, 80)

JAMES II, KING
1633 - 1701. Catholic king of England, Scotland and Ireland. Deposed
by English nobles in favor of his son-in-law William of Orange* for
allegedly trying to restore power to the Catholic Church. His defeat
at the Battle of the Boyne* harmed James's reputation among the Irish
people, for there was the distinct impression that he saved his own
hide at the expense of others. This earned him his popular nickname
(#), "Seumus the Shit."

II: 228-9, 231, 232#, 234-5, 239   (354-5, 358, 360#, 364-5, 371)
III: 23   (25)

JAMES STREET
In Dublin, leading up to the St. James's Gate Brewery.

II: 215   (334)

JANETHAINAYRIN, PATRON OF FACTORIES
Possibly an allusion to a Jane, a small Genoese silver coin. Spencer,*
in The Faerie Queen, used the phrase, "Because I could not give her
man a Jane." Loosely translated, then, "Jane in Erin."

III: 159   (233)

JASON
Hero of the Greek legend, who led the Argonauts to Colchis in quest of
the Golden Fleece. Son of Aeson, king of Ioleus.

III: 58   (80)

JASON, CHARLES
Charles Eason. 1823 - 1899. Owner and founder of Eason and Sons Ltd.*
The reference to "two Jasons" is an allusion to Eason's son, Charles
Eason, Jr. (#)

II: 166, 170, 171#, 180-2   (256, 261, 263#, 279-81)

JASON AND SON
Fictitous name for Eason's* distributors, 79/80 Middle Abbey Street,
Dublin. Where O'Casey worked for a short time for 9 shillings a week.
Saros Cowasjee made an effort to detail O'Casey's work experience with
Eason's, writing:

> As the story narrated by O'Casey in Pictures in the Hallway seemed
> rather highly coloured, I contacted Mr. Keath Eason, a retired
> Director of Eason's, and this is what he wrote to me in his letter
> dated 26 May 1959.

> "When Pictures in the Hallway was first published . . . it was clear
> to me reading the first three chapters about his week's employment
> at the wholesale newsagent that, however coloured it might be in the
> retrospect, it was the story by an eye-witness with a keen vision.

> "There is evidence that boys were used by us to trundle a truck with
> parcels of newspapers in the early morning from Abbey Street to G.
> N. Ry. /Great Northern Railway/ at Amiens Street well into the 20th
> century." In a private conversation, Mr. Eason told me that, after
> Johnny's dismissal, an inquiry was held into the matter, and an
> attempt was made to stop this inhuman practice of making boys trundle
> vans by bringing in the use of horse vehicles. This would be
> O'Casey's first service to the people.

O'Casey use of "Jason" stems from the Greek legend of Jason,* son of
Aeson.

II: 158-83, 184, 214   (244-81, 283, 332)
III: 172, 262   (253, 393)

JEANS, SIR JAMES HOPWOOD
1877 - 1946. English physicist and astronomer. Author of technical and
popular books on science and astronomy.

IV: 211   (289)

JEHU
From the Bible: "The watchman told saying . . . the driving is like
the driving of Jehu, son of Nimshi; for he driveth furiously." (II Kings
9: 20)

II: 64   (92)
VI: 118   (162)

JELLY ROLL/LEADBELLY
"Jelly Roll" was the nickname of Ferdinand Morton (1885 - 1941), jazz
musician. "Leadbelly" was Huddie Ledbetter (c.1888 - 1949), American
blues singer and composer.

VI: 141   (197)

JEMIMA MARY JANE
Probably a fictitious name. There is an anonymous Irish ballad, "Brother Bill and Jemima Brown."

III: 124   (180)

JENNIFER AND DUBEDAT
Jennifer Dubedat is the wife of Louis Debedat in Shaw's* play, The Doctor's Dilemma (1906).

V: 204   (273)

JERICHO
Palestinian city which was captured when the walls fell after the Hebrews marched around the city. Finally destroyed by Joshua.

I: 137   (208)

JERUSALEM
See also CHURCH OF JERUSALEM.

I: 137   (208)
II: 70   (103)
V: 238   (321)
VI: 51, 70, 81   (63, 92, 109)

JERVIS STREET
In north central Dublin. Named after Sir Humphrey Jervis, lord mayor of Dublin (1681).

II: 127   (194)
III: 195, 196   (289)

JERVIS STREET HOSPITAL
The Charitable Infirmary, 14 Jervis Street, under the care of the Sisters of Mercy.

III: 195   (289)

JESUIT CHURCH OF X XAVIERS'
See ST. FRANCIS XAVIER'S

JESUIT SOCIETY
In the Catholic Church, the Society of Jesus, founded by Ignatius Loyola* in 1534.

IV: 263   (363)

JESUS COLLEGE
Constituent college of Cambridge University.

VI: 50   (63)

JEW OF MALTA, THE
See MARLOWE, CHRISTOPHER.

JO ANDERSON/JO JOHN
Variant on Robert Burns's* poem, "John Anderson, My Jo."

VI: 115   (159)

JOAD, CYRIL EDWIN MITCHISON
1891 - 1953. English philospher and writer. A celebrated agnostic
whose conversion is documented in his God and Evil (1943).

VI: 51, 56   (64, 71)

JOB, A
Job* was the personification of poverty and patience. Of course, a job
is also the means to overcome poverty.

III: 153   (225)

JOB
Hero of the book of Job in the Old Testament.

III: 83   (118)

JOCELYN
Food ship carrying supplies to Dublin from English trade unionists
during the 1913 Strike.

III: 214   (318)

JOHN, AUGUSTUS
1878 - 1961. Welsh painter who is identified with the Impressionist
school. He painted portraits of many notable figures, including two of
O'Casey. The first, in May 1926, is in the possession of Eileen O'Casey
(1982), and was used in the second and subsequent editions of O'Casey's
play, The Plough and the Stars (see TOUHY, PATRICK). The other found
its way to the Metropolitan Museum of Art, New York. John designed the
scenery for Act II of The Silver Tassie production in London (1928).
O'Casey alludes to one of three paintings of Shaw* by John, all of which
were done in 1914. One is in the Fitzwilliam Museum, one is in the
collection of the Queen of England, and Shaw kept one. The correct
title of the "Galway" painting is Cartoon in Galway (1916). "Head of a
Gitana" is Portrait of a Spanish Gypsy.

IV:	and Coole Park tree*	142	(191)
	and Patrick Touhy*	186	(254)
	and "Count" McCormick*	282-3	(391)
V:	and Tassie premiere	33	(35)
	and portrait of O'Casey	35, 65	(38, 78)
		VI: 74	(VI: 98)
	and his gift to O'Casey	64-5	(78-9)
	and his trip to France	182	(242)
VI:	opinion of Hydrangeas*	74	(98)
	and his portrait of Shaw	172-3	(243-4)

MORE

JOHN, AUGUSTUS (cont.)

Mentioned: IV: 282   (391)
                                 VI: 85, 166   (115, 234-5)

Galway (see above)   IV: 283   (391)
Head of a Gitana (see above) V: 35, 64   (38, 79)
                                 VI: 74, 85   (98, 115)

JOHN OF AUSTRIA
Called Don John. 1547 - 1578. Spanish general who tried to conquer
Tunisia and the Netherlands. O'Casey refers (#) to Chesterton's* poem,
"Lepanto," in Poems (1915).

VI: 15#, 82   (10#, 111)

JOHNSON, SAMUEL
1709 - 1784. Celebrated English lexicographer, essayist and poet.

IV: 239   (330)
VI: 202   (288)

JOHNSTON, DENIS
b.1901. Major Irish playwright. See also the index to Appendix III.

VI: 73-80   (96-106)
The Moon in the Yellow River (1931)   VI: 73   (96)
A Bride for the Unicorn (1933)   VI: 73, 78   (96, 105)

JOLLY TOPERS
The Three Jolly Topers pub, located on the River Tolka in Finglas.

I: 80   (118)
II: 55   (78)
III: 159   (234)

JONAH
In the Bible, the Hebrew prophet who was swallowed by a whale.

III: 84, 106   (119-20, 153)

JONES, BOB
Appears as a worker with O'Casey on the Great Northern Railway of
Ireland.

III: 21   (22)

JONES, MABEL
Librarian of the Liverpool Catholic Truth Society. Her "letter to the
editor" is pasted inside one of O'Casey's notebooks (v. 14).

V: 142-3   (188)

JONES'S ROAD PARK
In north Dublin, north of North Circular Road. Now Croke Park. Site
of Pearse's* pageant on the Tain. For an indication of how much the
pageant impressed O'Casey, see his essay, "No Flowers for Films," in
The Green Crow. See also O'Casey's article, "The Irish Fete in Jones's
Road," in Letters, I, pp. 27-8. The pageant lasted a week, and it is
described in Patrick Pearse, The Triumph of Failure (Edwards).

III: 236, 241, 269   (353, 360, 404)

JONSON, BEN
1573 - 1637. Major English playwright and poet.

IV: 191   (261)

JORDAN RIVER
Chief river of Palestine, now in Lebanon, Israel and Jordan. See
Appendix III.

II: 228, 230, 239   (354, 357, 371)
III: 74   (104)
V: 73   (91)

JORDANS
In Buckinghamshire, England. A red-brick Quaker meeting house (built
1688), which has early associations with William Penn, and where Penn
is buried.

V: 147   (194)

JOSEPHUS, FLAVIUS
c.37 - 100. Noted Jewish historian.

History of the Jewish War   II: 70   (103)

JOUBERT, PETRUS JACOBUS
1831 - 1900. Boer general and politician. Commander of Boer forces
(from 1899) in the Boer War.*

II: 198   (306)
III: 164   (241)

JOYCE, JAMES A.
1882 - 1941. Celebrated Irish writer whom O'Casey greatly admired.
Commenting on Joyce's influence on him, O'Casey, in a letter to William
Maroldo, wrote (see Sean O'Casey Review, Spring 1977):

    I wasn't influenced by James Joyce any more than all who read him
    were . . . The glimpse of influence given in the /auto/biography
    were more of a desire to show my admiration for this great writer;
    as a symbol of standing by one who was attacked on all sides;
    banned by the nation and publisher, yet unshaken and supreme
    in his glorious and God-given integrity . . . Joyce's influence was
    like a bugle-call, loud and clear first, fading away as it was being
    heard; or like heavy footsteps passing by an open window, first
    driving attention to the car, then fading, very soon forgotten.
                                                        MORE

JOYCE, JAMES A. (cont.)

In 1939, O'Casey named Joyce as the author who had "presented the world with the most distinguished book or group of books" since 1918 (see Letters, I, p. 810). See also ANNA LIVIA PLURABELLE, EIREBY, MAUNSEL AND SONS, MOOKSEE/GRIPES and Appendix II (#). See also the essays by Bernard Benstock: "Sean O'Casey and/or James Joyce," Sean O'Casey, Centenary Essays, and "Sean O'Casey as Wordsmith, Essays on Sean O'Casey's Autobiographies.

V:	and German forgery	108	(140-1)
	and humor	203	(272)
VI:	"of the sad heart and		
	divine comic mind"	43	(52)
	and Adam#	56	(72)
	and the Bank of Ulster#	82	(110)
	and Ireland	120, 121	(165, 167)
	and the Seine bridge	173	(245)
	and music	174	(246)
	as saint	177-9	(251-3)
	and "Basic Joyce"	105	(144)
Mentioned:		IV: 158, 170, 278	(214, 231, 385)
		V: 46, 86	(52-3, 109)
		VI: 106, 168, 198,	(236, 237, 283, 295)
		206	

Ulysses (1922)	VI: 103, 206	(141, 295)
Finnegans Wake (1939)	III: 135, 200	(197, 297)
	IV: 250	(346)
	VI: 82	(110)

JOYCE, R.
Probably Robert Dwyer Joyce, opthalmic and aural surgeon, 73 Merrion Square.

I: 107-8   (161-2)

JUDAS
Betrayer of Jesus.

VI: 92   (125)

JUDEA
Greco-Roman name for Palestine.

III: 242   (361)

JULIAN THE APOSTATE
331 - 363. Roman emperor (from 361). Persistent enemy of Christianity; publicly announced his conversion to paganism (361).

VI: 85   (114)

JULY 12
Traditional anniversary for restaging and celebrating the Battle of the Boyne* by Protestant groups, especially the Orange Order.*

V: 89   (113)

JUNO
O'Casey's tragic mother-figure in his play, Juno and the Paycock. See also ALLGOOD, SARA.

V: 203   (272)

JUVENAL, DECIMUS JUNIUS
c.60 - c.140. Roman lawyer and satirist.

VI: 202   (298)

K

KABUL TO KANDAHAR
Kabul is the chief city and capital of Afghanistan, situated on the Kabus River. Kandahar is the chief city of South Afghanistan, and is the capital of Kandahar province. In the Afghan Wars (O'Casey's reference), both cities enjoyed strategic importance, and were occupied periodically by the British.

I: 158   (244)

KAFKA, FRANZ
1883 - 1924   Major Czech writer who dealt profoundly with the dilemma of modern man.

VI: 102   (139)

KALOMONIANS
Probably those of Kalomo, township of Rhodesia.

II: 198   (305)

KAVANAGH, PATRICK
1906 - 1967. Major Irish poet, especially in the Gaelic tradition, and novelist. See O'Casey's review article, "Melpomene in Ireland," in Blasts and Benedictions.

VI: 38, 109, 208-09   (44, 151, 298)

KEAN, EDMUND
1789 - 1833. English actor, unrivaled in his day as a tragedian.

V: 22, 181   (20, 241)

KEATING, GEOFFREY
c.1570 - c.1644. Irish historian and poet. O'Casey refers to the legend of Keating living in a cave while writing his principal work, Foras Feasa ar Eirinn (a history of Ireland). Keating was allegedly forced into the cave because of his sermons against several powerful landlords.

III: 103   (149)

KEATS, JOHN
1795 - 1821. Major English poet, one of O'Casey's favorites. See
also DARIAN.

```
I:   35                      (43)
III: 89, 278, 280           (127, 418, 420)
IV:  206, 220, 222          (282, 303, 306)
VI:  191                    (271)
"On a Grecian Urn"  V: 18   (14)
```

KEEBLE, LADY LILLAH
1875 - 1960. English actress, noted for her roles in Shakespeare and
Shaw.

```
V:  118-20                   (154-6)
```

KEEGAN, FATHER PETER
The Roscullen defrocked priest in Shaw's* play, John Bull's Other Island.
"Keegan's Dream" (#) is from the play:

> In my dreams, it is a country where the State is the Church and the
> Church the people: three in one and one in three. It is a temple
> in which the priest is the worshipper and the worshipper the wor-
> shipped: three in one and one in three. It is a godhead in which
> all life is human and all humanity divine: three in one and one in
> three. It is, in short, the dream of a madman.

```
III: 174#, 175             (256#, 258)
VI:  189                    (268)
```

KELLS
Irish town in Co. Meath on the Blackwater River. It has an ancient
monastery which was founded by St. Columba.* See BOOK OF KELLS.

```
VI: 80                       (107)
```

KELLY
A member of the Invincibles.

```
II: 37                       (50)
```

KELLY
Appears as a childhood friend of O'Casey.

```
I:  87, 135-40, 172, 175-6  (128, 206-14, 265-6, 271)
II: 10                       (5-6)
```

KELLY, BURKE, AND SHEA
From the song "The Fighting Race" (see Appendix I) by Joseph T. C.
Clarke (1846 - 1925).

```
II:  34                      (45)
III: 16, 118, 267           (15, 172, 400)
IV:  88                     (114)
VI:  10                     (2)
```

KELLY, ALDERMAN THOMAS
Dublin official and activist in the nationalist movement. Member, first
national council, Sinn Fein (1905) and organizing council (1919).
Arrested and deported to England (1919). Elected lord mayor of Dublin
while in jail (1920).

III: 278   (417)

KELLY-KENNY, SIR THOMAS
1840 - 1914. British soldier, commander of a division in the Boer
War.*

II: 201   (310)

KELTIC TWILIGHT/DAYLIGHT
Allusion to Yeats's* collection of essays, The Celtic Twilight (1893).
O'Casey emphasises the hard "C" of "Celtic" with "K." See also SELTIC
TWILIGHT.

III: 59, 123, 194   (81, 179, 286)
IV: 126, 143   (169, 194)
VI: 77   (103)

KENILWORTH HOTEL
In the Bloomsbury section of London, on Bloomsbury Street. Almost next
door to the British Museum.

V: 11   (4)

KENNA, KATIE
Probably a neighbor of the Caseys on Abercorn Road.

III: 93, 94-5, 97   (133, 135-6)

KENNY, DR.
This may be Dr. Joseph E. Kenny (1845 - 1900), Parnell's* doctor,
nationalist M.P., and a member of the National Club in Dublin. See LAMB.

IV: 273   (378)

KENSINGTON GARDENS
Park adjoining Hyde Park in London. The Round Pound there was one of
Shelley's* favorite haunts.

VI: 16   (12)

KERRY
County in western Ireland.

II: 14   (13)
IV: 114   (151)
V: 172   (229)
VI: 76   (102)

KHARTOUM
Former capital of the Egyptian Sudan. Occupied (1884) by Gordon,* and taken (26 January 1885) by troops of the Mahdi after a long siege.

V: 167   (222)

KID BOOTS
Musical comedy by W. A. McGuire, Otto Harbach, H. Tierney, and J. McCarthy. Appeared at the Winter Garden in London (2 February 1926).

V: 20   (16)

KILBURN
Section of London.

V: 65   (79)

KILCASH, TREES OF
Kilcash was the home of one branch of the Butler family. O'Casey's allusion is to the Irish poem, "Kilcash," translated by Frank O'Connor.* The first lines read:

> What shall we do for timber?
> The last of the woods is down.
> Kilcash and the house of its glory
> And the bell of the house is down.

III: 152   (224)

KILDARE
Irish county and town in Leinster province. The first church was established there by St. Brigid in the 5th century.

III: 34, 131, 144   (43, 192, 211)
IV: 276   (320)

KILDARE STREET
In south Dublin, on which is located the National Library and National Museum.

IV: 95   (125)

KILDARE STREET CLUB
Anglo-Irish Unionist club, formerly at the northern end of Kildare Street, Dublin. Martyn* was one of the founders.

III: 133   (195)

KILDARIAN GERALDINES
Variant on the Geraldines,* earls of Kildare.

III: 37   (47)

KILKENNY
Southeastern Irish county in Leinster province.

III: 159   (233)
IV: 235   (324)

KILKENNY
See ST. COINNEACH.

III: 75   (106)

KILKENNY CASTLE
One of the chief historic buildings of Kilkenny. Founded in the 12th
century, and the seat of the marquises of Ormonde.* Described in
Walter MacDonald's book, Reminiscences of a Maynooth Professor, pp.
77-8.

IV: 239   (330)

KILLALA BAY
In northwest Ireland between counties Sligo and Mayo. Site of the French
landing of about 1000 troups (1798) in support of the United Irishmen.*

III: 103   (148-9)

KILLALOE
Town and parish in west central Ireland in Co. Clare. Site of a large
hydroelectric development on the River Shannon. See also KINCORA and
SHANNON SCHEME.

II: 187   (289)

KILLARNEY
In Co. Kerry, scenic setting of three picturesque lakes. See CHRISTMAS
IN KILLARNEY and KILLARNEY in Appendix I, and III: 176 (107) in Appendix
II.

III: 179   (263)
IV: 168   (228)
V: 184   (245)

KILLASHANDRA
Irish town in Co. Cavan.

VI: 221   (317)

KILMAINHAM JAIL
The "Royal Risidence" in Pictures in the Hallway. Long a prison of
infamy. Most recently, the site of execution of the Easter Rising
leaders.

II: 27, 31-3, 39   (33, 40-3, 53)
III: 286   (490)

KILMAINHAM TREATY
An agreement (1882) between Parnell* and Gladstone.* Parnell was released from prison in exchange for a promise to control the agrarian
terrorism of the Land League.* In exchange, Gladstone agreed to push
for parliamentary action in land reform. The treaty prompted the
resignation of Earl Cowper, lord lieutenant, and W. E. Forster, chief
secretary of Ireland, who saw the agreement as a disgraceful compromise.
See also INVINCIBLES.

III: 105   (152)

KILMORE
Irish town in Co. Cavan.

III: 70   (98)

KILMORNA, GRAVES AT
The Graves at Kilmorna (1915), a novel of the 1867 Rising by Canon
P. A. Sheehan.*

III: 45   (59)

KINCHELLA, CORRY
Also given as KINSELLA. A villainous squireen in Boucicault's* play,
The Shaughraun.

II: 24, 25, 132, 135, 136, 137, 140-2   (29, 202, 211, 213, 215, 217-18)

KINCORA
Brian Boru's* home in Co. Clare, which stood on the right bank of the
River Shannon, above the bridge of Killaloe. O'Casey's allusion is to
a poem of the same name by Mangan.* See also LITTLE GREY HOME IN THE
WEST.

II: 186-8   (287-90)

KING'S COLLEGE
Constituent college of Cambridge University.

V: 24   (23)

KING'S INN STREET
In central Dublin.

I: 170   (261)

KING'S LIVERPOOL REGIMENT
In the British army, the 8th Infantry Regiment.

I: 71   (102)

KING'S ROYAL RIFLES
In the British army, the 60th Foot Regiment.

II: 211   (327)

KINGSBRIDGE
Bridge over the River Liffey, Dublin, between Wolfe Tone and Victoria
quays. Presently Sean Heuston Bridge.

II: 164   (253)

KINGSBRIDGE STATION
The Great Southern and Western Railway terminal, west of metropolitan
Dublin. Presently Sean Heuston Station.

III: 113   (164)

KINGSTON-ON-THAMES
In a letter to Harold Macmillan (Letters, II, p. 561), O'Casey identifies the writer as a "Mr. Edwards -- who, writing 20 years ago, called
me a 'Judas Iscariot,' & 'a renegade'; . . ."

IV: 128   (171)

KINGSTOWN
Dun Laoghaire, a suburb of south Dublin.

II: 34   (45)
III: 230   (343)

KINSALE
In Co. Cork. The "Head of Kinsale" refers to the cliff-walled promontory
of the Old Head of Kinsale, crowned by the ruins of a 12th-century
castle, which looks out on to the site of the sinking of the Lusitania
(1915). The "boatman of Kinsale" (#) is the title of a song by Thomas
Davis,* for which see Appendix I.

III: 156#, 200   (229#, 297)

KIRKHALA
Also given as GIRKHALA (#). Probably a variant on "Kirk," a Scottish
form of the word "church" (Kirk session = church session), and on
Valhalla, used to designate heaven.

IV: 197, 277   (270#, 384)

KIRWAN, JOHNNY
Appears as the manager of Murray, Sons and Co. Ltd.

IV: 229   (315)

KITCHENER, GENERAL HORATIO H.
1850 - 1916. British soldier (born in Ireland) who was active in the
African campaigns (1884-1902). Lost at sea in the sinking of the
cruiser, Hampshire.

II: 200-01   (309-10)

KNIGHT OF THE ROMAN SLUMPIRE
This is no order of the Roman Empire. O'Casey is alluding to the various
papal orders which designate the recipient as "Count." The figure in
question is George Noble Plunkett,* whose wife was charged with owning
many of the Dublin slums (see the article, "'Countess' Plunkett," Irish
Worker, 25 October 1913).

III: 220   (326-7)

KNIGHTS OF THE COINED CROSS OF ST. CROKER CRISPIN
In its context, the "coined cross" refers to Guinness* buying his way
into heaven by financing the reconstruction of St. Patrick's Cathedral.
"St. Croker Crispin" alludes to the brothers Crispin and Crispinian,
patron saints of shoemakers. In Henry V's address to his soldiers, he
says: "And Crispin Crispian shall ne'er go by." (Henry V). "Croker"
may be Irish folklorist, Thomas Crofton Croker (1798 - 1854).

III: 38   (49)

KNIGHTS OF COLUMBANUS
Fraternal Catholic organization with headquarters at Ely House, 8 Ely
Place, Dublin. The first spelling, "Columnbannus," is a purposeful
O'Casey misspelling (#).

III: 153#   (224#)
IV: 274   (378)

KNIGHTS OF DINGLE
Unknown. Dingle is a small Irish town in Co. Kerry.

III: 254   (380)

KNIGHTS OF THE GRAND BLACK CHAPTER
Of the Orange Order.*

III: 225, 229   (335, 341)
V: 89   (113)

KNIGHTS OF ST. PATRICK
From "The Most Illustrious Order of St. Patrick," an order of brotherhood
and knighthood. Instituted (1783) by George III, to consist of the
sovereign, the lord lieutenant of Ireland, and 15 knights companions
(increased to 22 in 1833). Their chapel is St. Patrick's Cathedral,
Dublin, and their motto is Quis separabit? (Who shall separate us). For
more references, see ORDER OF ST. PATRICK.

III: 158   (232)
IV: 91   (119)

KNIGHTSBRIDGE STREET
Forming the boundary of Hyde Park, London.

VI: 25   (25)

KNOCK
Irish village in Co. Mayo. Site of an alleged apparition (1879). Still
a popular pilgrimage site in August of each year.

IV: 197, 277, 278   (270, 384)
VI: 156   (218)

KNOX, JOHN
c.1513 - 1572. Scottish reformer. One of the principal figures of the
Reformation.

V: 219   (293)

KNOX, MONSIGNOR RONALD A.
1888 - 1957. English Catholic prelate and dabbler in detective fiction.

V: 143   (189)

KOESTLER, ARTHUR
b.1905. Journalist, political novelist, and philosopher. His most
important book, Darkness at Noon (1940), elucidates the Moscow trials.
The comments which O'Casey quotes appeared in Koestler's obituary of
George Orwell* (The Observer, 29 January 1950).

VI: 100, 101, 102   (137, 138, 139)

KOLCHAK, ALEXANDR VASILIEVICH
1874 - 1920. Russian admiral and counterrevolutionary. Organized a
Siberian army after the Russian Revolution (1917). Captured and shot
by Bolsheviks.

IV: 230   (318)

KORAN
Sacred book of the Mohammedans.

V: 127   (166)

KOREA
See also MacARTHUR, DOUGLAS

V: 223   (300)
VI: 130-1, 229, 234   (181, 328, 336)

KREMLIN
Citadel of Moscow and governing center of the USSR.*

IV: 163   (221)
VI: 113, 118   (155, 163)

KRISHNA
Hindu god of joy and voluptuousness.

V: 201   (268)
VI: 54   (68)

KRISHNAVOORNEEN
Probably a variant on AE's poem, "Krishnamurti," and on the Anglicized
Irish word, mavourneen = my darling.

III: 61   (85)

KRUGER, STEPHANUS JOHANNES
1835 - 1904. South African leader. Founder of the Transvaal state
(1852). A leader in the Boer War,* and helped to secure European allies
against the British.

II: 197, 198, 200   (305, 306, 309)

KULKIN, KIT
See McQUAID, MICK.

L

L. S. DEFENDER OF THE FAITH
Variant on L. S. D. (see ELLESDEA) and the title, "Defender of the
Faith," a personal title conferred (1521) on King Henry VIII* by Pope
Leo X* in acknowledgement of Henry's services to the church. Henry
wrote a defense of the seven sacraments and papal supremacy against the
teachings of Luther.* The title is still used as part of the style and
pomp of English sovereigns by virtue of an act of parliament (1543).

III: 112   (162)

LA GRANDE ARMEE DU VATICAN
La Grande Armee des Vatican in U.S. edition. The Grande Armee was
Napoleon's* army. The paragraph preceding this entry in the text
explains O'Casey's reference to the Vatican.

IV: 243   (336)

LABOUR PARTY (England)
Reformist socialist party which is closely allied with the trade unions
(founded 1900, present name since 1906). O'Casey is alluding (#) to
the general election of 1931, when the Labour Party's strength fell from
289 to 46 and its poll by two million. The Labour government to which
O'Casey refers (##), vis the Lane Pictures,* was in power from 1929 to
1931.

V: 87, 92#, 97##   (111, 117#, 125##)
VI: 17   (14)

LABOUR PARTY (Ireland)
One of the three major political parties in Ireland (with Fine Gael and
Fianna Fail). Founded (1914) at the suggestion of James Connolly* at
the Irish Trade Union Congress of 1912 that part of the Congress policy
should be "the independent representation of labour upon all public
boards."

IV: 169   (230)

LABOUR PRIME MINISTER
Ramsay MacDonald.*

V: 93   (119)

LACEDAEMONIANS
Ancient Spartans from the Messenian Wars (c.735 - 16 B.C.).

II: 88   (132)

LAD FROM LARGYMORE
One-act play by Seumas MacManus (1869 - 1960). Premiered (27 February 1905) at the Rotunda, Dublin.

III: 125, 126, 127   (183, 184, 185)

LADY OF SHALOTT
See TENNYSON.

LAERTES
Son of Polonius and brother of Ophelia in Shakespeare's* play, Hamlet.

III: 38   (49-50)

LAFAYETTE'S
James Lafayette, photographer, 30 Westmoreland Street, Dublin.

IV: 274   (414)

LALLANS
Dialect spoken in the southern and eastern part of Scotland. From lallan, a variant of lowland. The dialect in which Hugh MacDiarmid* wrote.

VI: 86   (116)

LALOR, FINTAN
1807 - 1849. Radical Irish Republican who advocated land nationalization and seizures of the land by Irish peasants during the early years of the Famine. Author of many articles and of the celebrated slogan, "the land of Ireland for the people of Ireland." In his article, "Literature in Ireland," in Blasts and Benedictions, O'Casey described Lalor as "the Lenin of his day, the most advanced thinker of his period."

III: 225   (335)
IV: 159   (216)

LAMB
Unknown. O'Casey uses the same description of Lamb as it is found in Five Years in Ireland (p. 73): "The Parnellites utter some plain truths about the Church -- some of them, Mr. Lamb of Newry, and the late Dr. Kenny, go so far as to say they would not take a Catholic University if the present hierarchy had anything to do with it."

IV: 273   (378)

LAMBETH WALK
In London, a thoroughfare leading from Black Prince Road to the Lambeth
Road. The name of a popular dance, featured by Lupino Lane in the musi-
cal, Me and My Gal (1937).

VI: 143   (199)

LANCASTER, ROSE OF
Allusion to the "War of the Roses," a series of dynastic English civil
wars (1455-87) between the houses of York and Lancaster, who used the
white and red roses, respectively, as their symbols. The red rose became the symbol of England when the house of Lancaster emerged victorious.

II: 20   (22)
VI: 81   (109)

LANCASTER GATE
Region of London, and the area where Yeats* maintained lodgings at 17
Lancaster Gate Terrace during the 1930s. O'Casey's visit to Yeats
occurred sometime in 1935 (see the references to Toller in O'Casey and
similar references by Yeats in a letter, 2 April 1935, to Ethel Mannin.)

IV: 194   (266)
V: 109   (142)

LAND LEAGUE
Irish association founded (1879) under the leadership of Davitt* and
Parnell.* Its purpose was to encourage peasant ownership of the land.
Declared illegal (1881), and reconstituted as the National League.*

III: 105   (152)
IV: 240   (331)

LAND OF TIR NAN NOGG
Tir na n-og, Irish for Land of Youth, a Celtic otherworld and land of
happiness. Yeats's* "Land of Heart's Desire." See also TIRNALOGIANS.

V: 81   (102)

LANDOR, WALTER SAVAGE
1775 - 1864. English poet and prose writer.

Imaginary Conversations (5 vols., 1825-29)   III: 207   (308)

LANDSDOWNE ROAD
In Ballsbridge, southeast Dublin.

III: 275   (413)

LANE, EDWARD WILLIAM
1801 - 1876. English Orientalist and eminent Arabic scholar. The book
mentioned by O'Casey is one of the world's classics.

Manners and Customs of the Modern Egyptians (1836) III: 207   (307)

LANE, HUGH/LANE PICTURES
1875 - 1915. Art collector and critic. Nephew of Lady Gregory.* Lane
was killed when the Lusitania was torpedoed (May 7). Shortly before his
death, he wrote an unwitnessed codicil to his will, which left his
collection of modern paintings to Ireland, provided that a gallery was
built for them within five years of his death. The English National
Gallery, which had possession of the paintings, refused to recognize the
codicil, and kept the paintings. A compromise was reached in 1959:
half the paintings remained in London and half went to Dublin. Both
groups would be exchanged every five years for 20 years.

IV: 128, 132, 146-7, 184, 199   (172, 177, 198, 252, 273)
V: 97   (125)
VI: 25-9, 230   (25-31, 330)

LANEHIN, KEVIN
Appears as an anti-treatyite in Inishfallen, Fare Thee Well.

IV: 103-09   (137-44)

LANGLAND, WILLIAM
c.1332 - 1400. English poet.

VI: 37   (43)

LANSBURY, GEORGE
1859 - 1940. British labor leader and politician. During the 1913
Strike, which he supported, Lansbury appointed Francis Sheehy-Skeffington* as Dublin correspondent for his Daily Herald.*

III: 214   (318)

LAOCOON AND SONS
In Greek legend, a priest of Apollo at Troy who, because he had offended
the gods, was strangled, with one of his sons, by two serpents.

VI: 198   (283)

LARKIN, DELIA
Given as LARKIN'S SISTER. 1878 - 1949. Longtime champion of women's
rights and trade union organizing in Dublin and Liverpool. O'Casey
worked at Old Forester's Hall, 10 Langrishe Place, Summerhill, Dublin,
in 1920, where Delia Larkin ran the "House Game." He was employed for
30 shillings weekly to come in every morning and clean up the hall for
nightly sessions. Delia Larkin founded the Irish Women Workers' Union
in 1912, and had a regular column for the Irish Worker.

IV: 73   (94)

LARKIN, JAMES
1876 - 1947. For several years, the leading figure in the Irish labor
movement, and for many years, a personal friend of O'Casey. Founder of
the Irish Transport and General Workers' Union (1909); founder-editor,
Irish Worker (1911-14, 1924-25, 1930-32). Larkin left Ireland (October
1914) and became an organizer for the American Socialist Party and the
Industrial Workers of the World (1915-18). He was a speaker at the
                                                              MORE

LARKIN, JAMES (cont.)

celebrated funeral of Joe Hill, who had been executed by Utah state
authorities (1915). Larkin was a founding member of the U. S. Communist
Party (1919), and was sentenced (1920) to 10 years imprisonment for
"criminal anarchy." Pardoned (1923) by Gov. Al Smith of New York, he
returned to Ireland and founded the Irish Workers' League (1923) and
the Workers' Union of Ireland (1924). He served as a member of the
executive committee of the Communist International (1924-28), and was a
delegate to its fifth congress (1924). Member, Dublin Municipal Council (1932, 1936), and a member of the Dail (1936-38, 1943-44). Larkin
visited O'Casey at Totnes (summer 1946) shortly before he died. Died
January 30; buried February 2 at Glasnevin. See O'Casey's obituaries
of Larkin in the Sean O'Casey Review (Spring 1975, Fall 1976), and the
article, "Sean O'Casey and James Larkin after 1923," Sean O'Casey Review
(Spring 1977).

III: as labor leader		187-205, 217, 220, 226, 257	(276-304, 323, 327, 336, 384)
	IV:	13, 168, 256	(IV: 5, 228, 354)
	VI:	43	(VI: 51)
O'Casey's visit for IRB		164	(242)
as speaker		187-9	(276-9)
description of		188	(278)
and Belfast strike (1907)		189	(280)
and speech, Imperial Hotel		196-9	(290-4)
	IV:	12	(IV: 5)
and AE*		211	(312-13)
and food ships		214	(318)
and Irish Citizen Army*		228, 265	(339-40, 398)
and ICA flag		230	(342-3)
and Jones's Road pageant*		236	(352-3)
and O'Casey's illness		245	(367)
and America		266	(399)
	IV:	75	(IV: 96)
linked with Connolly*		226, 257	(336, 384)
	IV:	13, 49	(IV: 7, 59)
IV: and William O'Brien*		76-9	(97-102)
and Larkin Release Comm.*		75-9, 83, 85	(96-102, 107, 108)
and clergy on		249	(345)
V: and slogan of		57	(69)
remembrance of		211-12	(283-4)
Mentioned:		IV: 285	(389)
		VI: 43, 90, 112	(51, 122, 154)

LARKIN RELEASE COMMITTEE
While Larkin* was in prison in the U.S., O'Casey helped organize the
Litir Chumainn Sheumais Ui Lorcainn (Jim Larkin Correspondence Committee)
and the Jim Larkin Release Committee (1921), which had as its officers:
Barney Conway, chairman; Michael Connolly, treasurer; Delia Larkin,*
secretary; and Seamus McGowan, Henry Dale and Michael O'Maolain. Its
offices were at 10 Langrishe Place, Dublin. See Letters, I, pp. 97-100.

IV: 75-6, 83   (96-7, 107)

LATIMER, HUGH
c.1485 - 1555. English champion of the Reformation and a Protestant
martyr.

VI: 57   (73)

LAUDER, HARRY
1870 - 1950. Scottish comedian, entertainer and ballad singer. An
ardent recruiter for the British in World War I (in which his only
son was killed), he was knighted for his services (1919). He always
ended his performances with the song he wrote, "Keep Right on to the End
of the Road" (see Appendix I). See also ST. LAUDERDAMNUSS.

V: 56, 58, 93   (66, 70, 119)

LAUGHTON, CHARLES
1899 - 1962. Successful English actor on stage and in films. In the
world premiere of O'Casey's play, The Silver Tassie, he played the role
of Harry Heegan.

V: 103   (133)

LAUZUN, ANTONIN
1633 - 1723. French soldier who led forces to Ireland to fight for
James II* at the Battle of the Boyne and at Limerick. O'Casey alludes
to Lauzun's withdrawal from Limerick to Galway, taking his French soldiers,
eight cannons, and ammunition.

V: 173   (231)

LAVERY, JOHN
1856 - 1941. Irish portrait and figure painter who studied in Paris.
The portrait (#) of Mannix* was given to the Municipal Gallery, Dublin,
in 1935.

IV: 186   (254)
VI: 26, 166#   (26, 234#)

LAW, ANDREW BONAR
1858 - 1922. British politician. Secretary of state for colonies
(1915-16); prime minister (1922-23).

III: 248   (371)
VI: 165   (233)

LAWRENCE, SIR THOMAS
1769 - 1830. English portrait painter.

V: 82   (103)

LAYE, EVELYN
b.1900. British actress. New York debut (1929) as the Marchioness of
Shayne in Coward's* play, Bitter Sweet, a role she played many times in
the 1930s.

V: 70   (86)

LAYO-TSETZE
<u>fl.</u> 600 B. C.   Chinese philosopher, founder of Taoism.

III: 59   (82)

LAZARUS
In New Testament history, the friend of Jesus who was raised from the
dead after four days.

IV: 276   (382)

LEAGUE OF NATIONS
International body which was organized (1920) for the purpose of pre-
venting wars and furthering forms of international cooperation.

IV: 208   (285)
V: 39   (43)

LEAMINGTON
English town in Warwickshire.

VI: 76   (102)

LEAR
King of Britain in Shakespeare's play, <u>King Lear</u>.

V: 36   (39)

LEARY
Laoghaire, king of Ireland (432). Responsible for the first codifica-
tion of Irish laws. Became a Christian after refusing St. Patrick*
permisssion to light a pashal fire on the Hill of Slane.*

II: 13   (12)

LECKY, W. E. H.
1838 - 1903. Anglo-Irish historian and essayist, whose balanced presentation of Irish history set him apart from his contemporaries in
Europe.

<u>History of</u> /⎺ <u>Rise of</u> - O'C. _⎺/ <u>Rationalism in Europe</u> IV: 228 (315)

LECTURER
According to Gabriel Fallon, this was Raymond Brugere, a French professor on exchange from L'Ecole Normale to Trinity College. He was a
Communist, was very familiar with the Irish dramatic movement, and
roomed at the college. The incident, which O'Casey describes, is,
according to Fallon, accurate but slightly distorted. See Brugere's
article, "Sean O'Casey et le Theatre irlandais," <u>Revue Anglo-Americaine</u>,
III (1926).

IV: 149   (201)

LEDA
From Greek mythology, the mother of Helen of Troy, Castor, Pollux, and
Clytemnestra. Subject of Yeats's* famous poem, "Leda and the Swan."

II: 120   (184)

LEDOCHOWSKI, MIEAISLAS HOLKA
1822 - 1902. Polish-born cardinal who was imprisoned and expelled from
Poland for refusing to use the German language. Prefect of the Propaganda (from 1892).

IV: 247   (341)

LEE
River in Cork. Subject of many poems and ballads.

IV: 218   (300)
V: 91   (116)

LEECH'S
Peter Leech, grocer and wine merchant, 1-2 Portland Place, Dublin.

II: 49, 55   (69, 78)

LEGION OF DECENCY
Also given as the LEGUE OF DECENCY (sic). In the United States, the
National Legion of Decency is the national film office of the Catholic
church. Established (April 1934) to protest against films which it
found to be "morally objectionable." (In 1938, 93% of all films released that year were so classified!) The Legion's "holy crusade"
(Pius XI) carried over into other areas, such as stage plays, books,
etc.

V: 202   (270)
VI: 10   (2)

LEGION OF THE PRAYGUARD
See LEGION OF THE REARGUARD, Appendix I.

LEHMKUHL, FATHER AUGUSTINE
1834 - 1918. English theologian, and author of a manual (1883) on
moral theology.

IV: 263   (363)

LEINSTER
Primarily in central Ireland, one of the four provinces.

II: 14   (12)
III: 111, 116   (161, 169)
IV: 11   (4)

LEINSTER HOUSE
On Kildare Street, Dublin. Site of Dail Eireann and Seanad.

IV: 160   (217)

LEITH
Scottish city, north of Edinburgh.

V: 58-9   (70)

LEMON'S
Confectionary store at 49 Lower Sackville (O'Connell) Street, Dublin.

III: 104   (150)

LENINGRAD
Major city in northern Russia.

VI: 176   (249)

LEO THE TENTH
1475 - 1521. Pope at age 37. Used his influence to benefit his family.
Excommunicated Luther.*

IV: 254   (351)

LEO XIII
1810 - 1903. Pope (from 1878) and energetic leader in social reform.
Author of the famous Rerum Novarum,* which deeply influenced the young
O'Casey.

V: 155   (205)

LEONARD, FATHER JOSEPH
A priest whom Shaw* consulted on Catholic ritual and theology while
writing his play, St. Joan.

VI: 169   (238)

LEONIDAS
King of Sparta (c.490-80 B. C.). Famous for his defence of Thermopylae
Pass against a vast Persian army. Slain at the pass.

II: 88, 108   (132, 164)

LET ME LIKE A SOLDIER FALL
See YES! LET ME LIKE A SOLDIER FALL, Appendix I.

LEVELLERS
One of the radical groups during the English civil war (1640), which
advocated equality and religious toleration.

IV: 275   (380-1)

LEVITES
From the tribe of Levi. A body of assistants to the priests in the
tabernacle and temple service of Jews.

IV: 233   (322)

LEWIS, SINCLAIR
1885 - 1951. American novelist and playwright. First American to be awarded the Nobel Prize for literature (1930).

V: 239   (321)

LEWIS, WYNDHAM
1884 - 1957. English artist, writer and critic. Founded, with Ezra Pound, Blast, the magazine of the Vorticist school.

VI: 228   (327)

LIBERAL PARTY
English political party. During the 1880s, the Liberal Party supported Parnell's* program of Home Rule for Ireland, and the alliance between the Party and Gladstone* was crucial to the passage of any Home Rule Bill.* When Parnell's affair with Katherine O'Shea* was made public, however, Gladstone issued a warning (24 November 1890) to Justin Mc-Carthy, vice-chairman of the Irish Parliamentary Party, that, unless Parnell resigned, the Liberals would probably lose the next election, and, with it, any chance of gaining the enactment of Home Rule.

IV: 249   (343-4)

LIBERTIES, THE
Slum area in southwest Dublin. Formerly a fashionable area which was exempt from many governmental controls (hence its name).

I: 21   (20)

LIBERTY HALL
Formerly the Northumberland Hotel (until March 1912), and meeting place of the Young Irelanders and the Land League. Located on the corner of Eden Quay and Beresford Place, it is the headquarters of the Irish Transport and General Workers' Union. It was also the headquarters of the Irish Citizen Army. The meeting (#) to which O'Casey refers took place on 22 March 1914 (see IRISH CITIZEN ARMY). Liberty Hall was one of the four symbols in O'Casey's life (##). Named after a line in Goldsmith's* play, She Stoops to Conquer: "This is Liberty Hall, gentlemen." See also RUTLAND SQUARE.

III: 188, 191, 196, 210, 212, 220, 225#, 257, 267, 268, 269
     (277, 282, 291, 312, 314, 327, 335#, 384, 400, 402, 404)
IV: 11, 12, 76##, 168, 285   (4, 6, 97-8##, 228, 395)
V: 211-12   (283-4)

LIFE GUARD RED/HORSE GUARD BLUE
British cavalry units. At Whitehall, London, the building, William Kent's Horse Guards, is the headquarters of the Army London District and the place for the morning changing of the Queen's Life Guard.

V: 36   (39)
VI: 140   (195)

LIFFEY
The River Liffey, which rises in the Wicklow mountains and flows into
Co. Kildare and through the heart of Dublin, which it divides north and
south. What the Volga is to Russians, the Liffey is to Dubliners.

I: 189-90	(291-2)
II: 188, 215	(290, 334)
III: 23, 121, 130, 187, 280	(26, 176, 189, 277, 420)
IV: 92, 264, 282	(121, 365, 390)

LIFFEY STREET
In central Dublin, north of the River Liffey.

I: 170	(261)
II: 127	(194)

LIFFORD, LORD
James Hewitt. 1709 - 1789. Lord chancellor of Ireland during the
struggle to create an independent Irish (Grattan's*) parliament. He
amassed a considerable fortune, and was a skillful lawyer and judge.
Buried at Christchurch Cathedral, Dublin.

III: 70   (98)

LIGHTWOOD, DR. JOSEPH B.
1829 - 1889. Prominent English theologian and bishop of Durham.

III: 84   (120)

LIL' ALLEGRO
Variant on L'Allegro, the first of the most famous of paired poems
(with Il Penseroso), by John Milton.* For the rest of the phrase,
see ROWLAND. Used here to describe James Agate.*

VI: 117   (162)

LILY BULLERO BULLEN A LAW
See LILLIBULLERO, Appendix I.

LILY OF KILLARNEY, THE
Operatic version of The Colleen Bawn, libretto by Boucicault* and
John Oxenford, music by Sir Julius Benedict (1862).

II: 45	(64)
III: 101, 119	(146, 172)

LIMERICK
Major Irish city, located in Co. Limerick. It has played a prominent
role in Irish history, especially in the 17th century when it was
besieged several times (1641, 1651 and 1690). In the last incident,
it was defended by Sarsfield* until its surrender (1691). The surrender
treaty, granting political and religious liberty, was almost immediately
broken by William of Orange* and Queen Anne, giving the city its title,
"City of the Violated Treaty."

I: 33, 40   (40, 51)

MORE

LIMERICK (cont.)

II: 236, 237   (367)
III: 103, 115, 189   (148, 168, 280)
V: 173   (231)

LINCOLN PLACE
In central Dublin, south of the River Liffey.

I: 20, 28   (19, 32)

LING, TOM
Thomas Lyng, one of the original members of Connolly's* Irish Republican Socialist Party.* Active in socialist circles, and an observer at
the International Socialist Congress, Paris (1900).

II: 179, 196   (275, 302)
III: 20   (21)

LIPTON'S
Dublin grocery at 59-61 Dame Street, Dublin. Owner, Thomas J. Lipton.

I: 168, 169, 170   (258, 260, 262)

LISBURN
Irish city in Co. Antrim, an important city in the linen industry.

III: 104   (149)

LITTLE BOY BLUE
Mother Goose nursery rhyme.

I: 55   (77)
VI: 38   (45)

LITTLE FLOWER, THE
St. Teresa-of-the-Child-Jesus, canonized (1925) only 28 years after her
death. In Irish legend, the "Little Flower" was Blathnad, carried off
by Cuchulain* and Cu Roi from a raid in Scotland.

IV: 48, 276   (57, 382)

LITTLE FLOWER OF LISSODELL
Eva Gore-Booth, 1870 - 1926. Sister of Countess Markiewicz. Left
Lissadell in 1897 to perform social work in Manchester (until 1913),
where she earned the title of "Little Flower." Lissadell (which
O'Casey misspells) was a grey granite house overlooking Sligo Bay,
ten miles from Sligo and five miles from Drumcliffe.

IV: 67   (85)

LITTLE JOHNS/MAID MARIONS
Used by O'Casey as a generic term for the common people. Both are from
the legendary Robin Hood* adventures.

VI: 24   (23)

LIVERPOOL
Major city in England, having the heaviest Catholic-populated region in the country.

IV: 168   (229)
V: 85, 109, 143   (108, 141, 188)
VI: 25-6, 41   (25, 27, 49)

LIVERPOOL STREET STATION
In central London, north of the Thames in Shoreditch.

VI: 44   (53)

LIVES OF THE SAINTS
By Alban Butler (1700 - 1733), English scholar,whose studies on the saints have been reprinted in many editions. See THURSTON, HERBERT.

IV: 236   (326)

LIVINGSTON, DAVID
1813 - 1873. Famous Scottish missionary and explorer in Africa.

V: 70   (87)

LLANDUDNO
Welsh city. The O'Caseys visited Penmaenmawr near Llandudno in August, 1936 and 1937, where they stayed with a Mrs. Roberts, Ardyn, Celyn Avenue.

V: 93   (119)

LOCH ERIN
Loch Erne, large scenic and historical lake in Co. Fermanagh.

II: 41   (56)

LOCKE, JOHN
1632 - 1704. English political philosopher. According to Lady Gregory's journals, O'Casey told her that Locke's Essay (see below) was the second book he read as a child.

IV: 195   (267)
Essay Concerning Human Understanding (1690)   I: 35, 36   (43, 44)

LOGUE, CARDINAL MICHAEL
Also given as LOG and LUG. 1840 - 1924. Irish Catholic prelate. Archbishop of Armagh (from 1888), and primate of all Ireland. Cardinal in 1893. In 1899, he condemned Yeats's* play, The Countess Cathleen, without having seen or read it. See also IRISH PEASANT.

III: 18, 23, 24, 59, 127, 131, 134-5, 137, 139, 140, 145
     (19, 26-7, 81, 185, 192, 196-7, 200-01, 203, 205, 213)
IV: 242, 263   (335, 363-4)

LOMONOVSKA, RAISSA
Appears as a Russian, probably an official of some sort, living in
England with whom O'Casey corresponded about the Russian Revolution.
He is not mentioned in O'Casey's letters, though he is listed in
O'Casey's notebooks in the Berg (v. 13).

IV: 162, 169   (219, 230)

LONDON COUNTY COUNCIL
Until 1 April 1945, an elected body responsible for major functions of
civic government throughout the London metropolis.

V: 24   (23)

LONDON, JACK
1876 - 1916. American socialist and writer who lived the life of
sailor, dock worker and adventurer. He wrote over 40 popular books
about those experiences. O'Casey reviewed Irving Stone's* biography
of London for the Sunday Times (30 October 1938).

White Fang (1906)   III: 207   (308)

LONDON AND NEWCASTLE TEA COMPANY
With branches in Dublin at 27 Wexford Street, 4 Talbot Street, 61a
Thomas Street, and 172 Great Brunswick Street.

I: 168   (258-9)

LONDON SCHOOL OF ECONOMICS
Founded (1895) at 9 John Street, London, by Sidney Webb* from the estate
of Fabian Society member, Henry H. Hutchinson. In 1896, the school was
located at 10 Adelphi Terrace, Shaw's* home. The main body of the school
is located near Fleet Street and Kingsway in London.

VI: 44   (53)

LONDONDERRY, LADY
Seventh Marquess Edith Helen Van-Tempest-Stewart. 1879 - 1959. Presi-
dent of Women's Legion; appointed D.B.E. (1917). First woman M.P. of
Co. Down. See O'Casey's letters to her in Letters, I.

V: 126, 159, 169   (165, 210, 224)
VI: 166   (234)

LONDONDERRY, LORD
Charles Stewart Henry. 1878 - 1949. British politician. Conservative
M.P. (1906-15). Attended Irish Convention (1917), where he opposed
nationalist demands for all-Ireland parliament. Minister of Education
in Northern Ireland government (1921-26).

V: 159, 169   (210, 224)

LONGDENE SCHOOL
In Chalfont St. Giles. A Quaker school, the headmaster of which was Joy
Clark. The school of O'Casey's son, Breon.

V: 146   (193)

LORD, REV. DANIEL
1888 - 1955. Editor, Queen's Work (from 1926), and author of hundreds
of pamphlets on social, economic and religious themes for the Catholic
Truth Society. Co-author of the restrictive "Motion Picture Production
Code" (1930) for Hollywood films.

Tolerance Thumbs Up Too Much of a Good Thing   VI: 195   (278)

LORD EDWARD STREET
In central Dublin, south of the River Liffey.

II: 215   (324)

LORD LIEUTENANT
Generic. Nominal head of the government in Ireland, their functions
were largely decorative. They were usually noblemen of great wealth
who entrusted the daily running of the country to the chief secretary,
and often to the under-secretary. In the 50 years following the
Famine (1848), the latter two positions attained a measure of power.
The chief secretary frequently carried with it a seat in the British
cabinet, and it sometimes attracted able men in British politics.

I: 137, 156, 161   (209, 240, 248)
III: 145   (214)

LORD MAYOR/LONDON
Major Sir Frank Bowater, lord mayor of London, 1938. In 1939, the
lord mayor was Sir William Coxen.

VI: 113, 114   (156, 157)

LORD'S CRICKET GROUNDS
In St. John's Wood, the headquarters of English cricket. Site of annual
matches in June and July between Eton and Harrow and Oxford and Cambridge.

V: 71   (87)

LORREQUER, HARRY
The character in the novel of the same name (1840) by Charles Lever
(1806 - 1872). See also O'Casey's essay, "Charles Lever's Stormy Life,"
in Blasts and Benedictions.

III: 133   (195)

LOSSIEMOUTH
Scottish town at the mouth of the river Lossie. Birthplace of J. Ramsay
MacDonald,* "the ragged lad of Lossiemouth."

V: 102   (131-2)

LOST ANGELES
Variant on the California city of Los Angeles, and possibly on the play,
Michael and His Lost Angels (see MICHAEL'S LOST ANGEL).

V: 183   (244)

LOST LEGION OF THE REPUBLICAN REARGUARD
See LEGION OF THE REARGUARD, Appendix I.

LOUGHREA, BARONY OF
In Co. Galway, Ireland.

IV: 139   (188)

LOUIS XIV/MLLE DE LA VALLIERE
Louis (1638 - 1715) was king of France, and had the longest reign in
European history (73 years). He was greatly influenced by his mistress,
Duchess de La Valliere (1644 - 1710), who gave him four children before
retiring (1674) to a convent.

VI: 15   (11)

LOUISIANA LOO OF THE LONG HAND
See LOUISIANA LOO, Appendix I, and LUGH OF THE LONG HAND.

IV: 200   (274)

LOURDES
French town where the Virgin Mary allegedly appeared on 18 occasions
(between 11 February and 16 July 1858) to a peasant girl, Bernadette
Sonbirous (see ST. BERNADETTE). The town has become one of the most
revered shrines in the West, and receives over a million pilgrims
annually. Found in O'Casey's play, Cock-a-Doodle Dandy.

IV: 197, 239, 276-9   (270, 330, 382-6)
V: 174   (232)
VI: 156   (218)

LOUVAIN
In Brabant province, Belgium. Its university (founded 1423 by John IV
of Brabant) is one of the world's centers of Catholic learning.

IV: 247   (341)
VI: 170   (240)

LOWNDES SQUARE
In London, off Sloane Street near Knightsbridge.

VI: 25   (25)

LUCAN, MARCUS ANNAEUS
39 - 65. Roman poet.

VI: 202   (287)

LUCE, CLAIRE
Popular American actress on stage and in films during the 1920s.

V : 181   (241)

LUCKNOW
See SEPOYS.

III: 105   (152)

LUCIFER
In the Bible, a fallen rebel archangel. See MICHAEL'S LOST ANGEL.

IV: 63   (79)

LUCRETIUS, TITUS
c.96 - 55 B.C. Roman philosophical poet and disciple of Epicurus.

VI: 200   (285)

LUGH, THE LONG HAND
The Irish Apollo. In Irish mythology, a famous chief of the Tuatha De
Danaan and the supernatural father of Cuchulain.*

III: 58, 127, 129   (80, 185, 187)
V: 114   (148)
VI: 76-7, 81   (102, 108)

LUMPKIN, TONY
Mrs. Hardcastle's son in Goldsmith's* play, She Stoops to Conquer (1773).
He is a roistering young squire who is completely spoiled by his doting
mother. O'Casey alludes to the squire-like life of Moore* at Moore
Hall, Lough Carra, Co. Mayo.

IV: 134   (179)

LURGAN
Irish town in Co. Armagh. A linen-mill center since 1619.

III: 169   (249)

LUSITANIA
The ill-fated ship which was sunk (7 May 1915) off the coast of Ireland
by German submarines with a loss of 1198 lives. See LANE, HUGH.

IV: 146   (198)
VI: 230   (330)

LUTHER, MARTIN
1483 - 1546. Leader of the Reformation in Germany.

I: 95-8   (140-6)
II: 87   (131)
III: 68   (95)

LYCURGUS
In Greek legend, a Spartan lawgiver (c.800 B.C.) who imposed upon Sparta
its characteristic institutions of able and strong warriors.

V: 184-5   (245-6)

LYDD
Municipal borough in Kent,and a maritime county in southeast England.

VI: 77   (102)

LYNCH, JUDGE
This may be Judge Richard Campbell, one of McCartan's* closest friends.
He met McCartan in the 1920s when the two were involved with the American Committee for Relief in Ireland. "Judge Lynch," in Irish history,
was famous for hanging his own son.

V: 213-14, 216-20   (285-6, 289-94)

LYNDSAY, SIR DAVID
c.1490 - 1555. Scottish poet and dramatist.

Ane Satyre of the Thrie Estaitis (c.1540)   VI: 197 (280)

LYON'S
Chain of London teashops.

V: 223   (299)
VI: 176   (249)

LYONESSE
Legendary region west of Cornwall. According to tradition, it is
40 fathoms under water between Land's End and the isles of Scilly.
Hardy's* poem, "When I Set Out for Lyonnesse" (Swinburne spelling),
deals with his trip to St. Juliot in Cornwall.

V: 168   (223)

M

MAB
See MAEVE, QUEEN.

McARTHUR, DOUGLAS
1880 - 1964. Prominent U.S. army officer. Commander of allied forces
in the Far East during World War II, and of U.N. forces during the
Korean War. McArthur is not mentioned by name in this passage, but he
is alluded to in the words, "a general." While reading the same passage
for Caedmon Records, O'Casey mentioned McArthur by name.

VI: 229   (328)

McBRIDE, JOHN
1865 - 1916. Irish patriot and martyr. Commander of the Irish Brigades
supporting the Boers in the Boer War.* Married (1903) Maud Gonne.*
Deported to France in 1904. McBride was active in the Easter Rising at
Jacob's* biscuit factory, and was executed by the British after the
Rising collapsed. III: 19 (20)

McBRIDE, SEAN
b.1904. Son of John and Maud Gonne McBride (see above). Former minister
of external affairs for Ireland (1948-51).

VI: 29   (31)

McCARTAN, PATRICK
One of the founders of Sinn Fein,* and one of the editors of Irish Freedom (1909-14). Commander, Tyrone Irish Volunteers, during the Easter
Rising. Irish representative to the U.S. during the War of Independence,
where he stayed to establish a physician's practice in New York. Active
in helping to finance the beginnings of the Irish Academy of Letters* by
organizing a series of lectures for wealthy Irish-Americans.

V: 213-14, 216-20   (285-6, 289-96)

McCARTAN'S
Hardware and crockery shop, 49 Talbot Street, Dublin. Owned by John
McCartan.

IV: 25   (23)

MacCARTHY, DESMOND
1878 - 1952. British writer and critic. For MacCarthy's comments on
AE, see the introduction of The Living Torch.

IV: 216   (297)

McCARTHY, MICHAEL
Irish writer. Described in Brown's Ireland in Fiction as having "written
and spoken against the power exercised by the Roman Catholic Church."
See also KENNY, DR.

Priests and People in Ireland (1902)   IV: 234   (323-4)

McCAULEY, REV. DR. CHARLES
Professor of sacred scripture and Hebrew, Maynooth (Thoms, 1880).

IV: 240   (331-2)

McCLONKEY, ALOYSIUS
Probably a fictitious name. The P.L.G. after his name stands for Poor
Law Guardian. There is no such name listed among the guardians in 1907,
the time of the incident. There was, however, a George McConkey, who
was an official of the Royal Irish Constabulary. In Irish fiction, there
was a humorous serial character named Darby Durkan P.L.G.

III: 121-4   (177-81)

McCLUSKEY, JACOB
Character in Boucicault's* play, The Octoroon.

II: 132   (202)

MacCOLUM, FINNAN HADDE
Fionan MacColum, early Irish folklorist and Gaelic Leaguer. With Father
Flanagan,* he represented the Gaelic League on a fund-raising tour of
the U.S. in 1910 (raising 4000 pounds). Pun on Finnan Haddock, fish dish.

III: 133   (194)

MacCONGLINNE
Historian and poet of 13th-century Ireland. Hereditary poet of the
O'Neills.* O'Casey's familiarity probably comes from the poem, "The
Vision of MacConglinne," translated by Kuno Meyer (1859 - 1919). Padraic
Colum* referred to O'Casey as "the MacConglinne of our day" (see Irish
Writing, November 1948).

VI: 203   (289)

McCOOL, FINN
In Irish legend, the central figure of the Fenian cycle. A 3rd-century
poet and leader of the Fenians.*

II: 13, 229   (11, 356)
III: 102   (147)
IV: 86, 103   (111, 136)

McCORMICK, F. J.
Peter Judge. 1891 - 1947. Major Abbey Theatre actor. Joined the Abbey
in 1918, andstayed for 29 years, performing in more than 500 plays.
Married (1925) Eileen Crowe,* and had a brief career in British films.
In O'Casey's premieres, he played the roles of Seumas Shields in The
Shadow of a Gunman; Meehawl in Kathleen Listens In; Joxer in Juno and
the Paycock; a ballad singer in Nannie's Night Out; Jack Clitheroe
in The Plough and the Stars; and Barry Derrill in The End of the Beginning.

IV: 124, 171, 173, 183, 280   (165, 232, 235, 249-50, 387)
V: 48, 121   (55, 157-8)

McCOY, BARNEY
Unknown. This may be Rev. Edward MacCoy, well known for his translations
of songs into Irish.

IV: 80   (103)

McCRACKEN & McCRACKEN
O'Casey's Dublin solicitors at 24 Upper Ormond Quay, Dublin.

V: 106-07   (137-8)

MacDERMOTT, NORMAN
b.1899. Director and designer of the premiere of O'Casey's play, Within
the Gates. For O'Casey's quarrel, see Letters, I.

V: 131   (171)

MacDERMOTT, SEAN
Or MacDiarmada. 1884 - 1916. Irish patriot, soldier, poet, and martyr.
Member, Gaelic League, Gaelic Athletic Association, Irish Republican
Brotherhood,and Sinn Fein. Manager of the I.R.B. newspaper, Irish Free-
dom, and an organizer for the Irish Volunteers. Active in the Easter
Rising. Executed May 12.

III: 164   (242)

MacDIARMID, HUGH
Pseudonym of Christopher Murray Grieve. 1892 - 1978. The leading
Scottish poet of the 20th century, and a good friend of the O'Caseys.
Founder, Scottish Nationalist Party, and editor of its organ, The Voice
of Scotland (1938-39, 1945-49, 1955-58). A leader of the Scottish
renaissance in literature. To whom Sunset and Evening Star is dedicated.
For MacDiarmid's remembrances of O'Casey, see the poet's The Company I've
Kept (1966). See also Appendix II.

VI: 86-8, 91, 92   (116-19, 124)
A Drunk Man Looks at the Thistle (1926) VI: 86, 87 (116, 118)
To Circumjack Cencrastus (1930)   VI: 86   (116)

MacDONAGH, THOMAS
1878 - 1916. Irish patriot and poet. Signatory to the Irish Proclamation,* and prominent in the Irish Volunteers. Co-founder, with Martyn*
and Plunkett,* of the Irish Theatre (1914). Executed by the British
after the Easter Rising.

III: 234   (350)

MacDONALD, RAMSAY
1866 - 1937. British socialist and politician. Prominent in the British Labour Party as its secretary (1910-12) and treasurer (1912-14).
Prime minister (1924, 1929-31, 1931-35). Author of several books on
socialism.

V: 93, 95-102   (119, 122-31)

MacDONALD, WALTER
1854 - 1920. Professor of theology, Maynooth (1880-1920). A controversial teacher, he often incurred the wrath of Irish bishops and Rome
because of his public dislike of teaching through Latin, and for
urging the laity to participate in church affairs and advocating the
entry of Catholic students into Trinity College. A number of his books
were placed on the index by Rome.

III: 136, 138-9, 142   (199-200, 203-04, 208)
IV: 158, 227, 232-67   (214, 313, 320-69)
V: 52, 142, 158, 206-07, 238   (61, 188, 209, 276, 320)
VI: 56, 92, 169, 170-2   (71, 125, 239-43)
Some Ethical Questions about Peace and War   IV: 262-3   (362, 364)
Theses on the Supernatural, Annotated   IV: 246-7   (340-1)
Motion, Its Origins and Conservation (1898) IV: 245, 258-9 (338, 357-8)
Reminiscences of a Maynooth Professor (1925) IV: 232, 235 (320, 324)

McELROY, WILLIAM
Coal merchant in London who backed the first London production of Juno
and the Paycock (1926). McElroy was best man at O'Casey's wedding
(1928), but they had a falling out over politics and other matters. It
was McElroy who often sang the "Silver Tassie" ballad, giving O'Casey's
great anti-war play its name.

V: 29-30, 63   (29-31, 76)

McENTEE, SEAN
b.1889. Irish politician and poet. Active in the Easter Rising, for
which he was sentenced to death. Sentence commuted to life imprisonment, and he was released in the general amnesty of 1917. Member of
the Dail (1918-22); minister of finance in the first de Valera government (1932) and subsequent governments (1933, 1937).

III: 234   (350)

MacEOLAIS
In Irish folklore, the son of knowledge.

III: 59   (81)

MacGILLICUDDY'S REEKS
Spelled MAGILLICUDDY in U.S. In Co. Kerry, the highest mountain range
in Ireland.

III: 164   (241)
IV: 68   (85)

McGLADE'S
Dublin newsagent and tobacconist shop at 43 Abbey Street.

III: 262   (392-3)

McGREEVY, THOMAS
1893 - 1967. Irish poet and critic. Director of the National Gallery
of Art (1950). With Joyce when he died.

IV: 207   (284-5)

MacGREGOR, ROB ROY
Pseudonym of Robert Campbell. 1671 - 1734. Freebooter and chief of
the MacGregor clan in the Scottish highlands. Sir Walter Scott's*
introduction to the novel, Rob Roy, gives details of MacGregor.

II: 154   (237)
III: 101   (146)

McGUINNESS, BENJAMIN
Benjamin Lee Guinness. 1798 - 1868. Founder of Guinness Brewery* and
benefactor (1860-65) of St. Patrick's Cathedral, Dublin.

III: 38   (48-9)

McGUINNESS, MR.
Appears as a doctor who treated O'Casey for bronchitis.

V: 70   (86)

McKAY, HERBERT KNOX
Appears as an employee of Harmsworth Irish Agency.

II: 210-13   (324-31)

McKIE, BILL
1876 - 1959. English-born member of the U.S. Communist Party who was
active in the early struggles and organizing efforts of the United Auto
Workers at Ford plants in Detroit. Central figure in a 1941 strike,
which forced Henry Ford* to accept the union contract. President, Ford
Local 600, UAW-AFL-CIO.

VI: 90   (122)

MacLIAG, GIOLLA
d. 27 March 1174. Archbishop of Armagh (from 1137) and the first primate
of all Ireland. It was with his accession that the practice of embodying
the archbishophric of Armagh with the Primacy in one person originated.

V: 165   (218)

MacLIAMMOIR, MICHAEL
1899 - 1978. Irish poet, actor and writer. One of the founders of the
Gate Theatre.*

VI: 73   (97)

MacLIR, MANANAAN
Irish legend. The patronymic means "son of the sea."

IV: 200   (274)

McLOUGHLIN, MAURICE
King of Ireland (from 1151). O'Casey repeats the error from his source
(see CASELANAGAN). On page 117, Reeves refers to Maurice O'Loughlin,
king of all Ireland, while on the same page, he quotes from a charter
naming "Mauritius Mag Lachlain." On another page (93), referring to
the same event, the king is called "Maurice Mac Lochlainn."

V: 164   (217)

McMANUS, CAPTAIN DERMOT
Frequent visitor to Yeats's* home in Riverdale. McManus was a captain
in the Free State army, and a veteran of World War I and the Irish Civil
War. He was a student of Eastern mysticism, and later became a member
of the Army Comrades Association (Blueshirts).

V: 44   (50)

McMANUS, M. J.
1888 - 1951. Irish nationalist and writer. Free-lance journalist until
1916 when he returned to Ireland from London, taking part in the Civil
War. Literary editor, Irish Press (from 1935).

VI: 120   (166)

MacMOURROUGH OF THE CURSES
Dermot MacMourrough. c.1110 - 1171. Irish king of Leinster (from 1126)
who was banished (1166) by Irish chieftains. He invoked English aid

MacMOURROUGH OF THE CURSES (cont.)
against the Irish kings and nobles, thereby introducing English rule
into Ireland. They never left. Compiled the Book of Leinster, a
collection of early Gaelic traditions.

II: 11   (8)

McNALLY, LEONARD
1752 - 1820. Playwright and political informer. Better known for the
latter than for the former. As a lawyer, he betrayed several of the
United Irishmen while supposedly defending them. A skillful informer,
his double-dealing was not discovered until after his death.

II: 196   (302)

MacNAMARA, DONNCHADH RUADH
Irish writer. Remembered chiefly for his poem, "The Fair Hills of Eire
O," an exile song which has commanded a score of translations.

III: 114   (166)

McNAMEE, JAMES
1876 - 1966. Bishop of Ardagh and Clonmacnois (from July 1927).

VI: 216   (309)

MacNEICE, LOUIS
1907 - 1963. Irish poet and playwright. Considered one of the finest
poetic chroniclers of the Spanish Civil War.* The review of Rose and
Crown to which O'Casey refers appeared in the Observer (13 July 1952).#

VI: 106, 196-7#, 203, 204-05   (146, 279-80#, 290-2)
One Eye Wild   VI: 205   (292)

MacNEILL, EOIN
1867 - 1945. Irish historian, Gaelic scholar and Irish Volunteer leader.
One of the early figures in the Gaelic League; professor of Early Irish
History, UCD (1908-45). As commander of the Irish Volunteers (1913-16),
MacNeill effectively sabotaged the Easter Rising by publishing an order
for his men not to "drill" that fateful day. Such was his reputation,
though, that he was allowed to play a role in the subsequent Free State
governments.

III: 32, 111, 131, 133, 140, 142, 155, 157, 160, 161, 226, 271-2
     (39, 161, 192, 195, 206, 208, 228, 231, 235, 236, 238, 336, 407-08)

McNEILL, JAMES
1869 - 1938. Indian and Irish civil servant who had a distinguished
career in the British service. Interested in Gaelic and cultural movements, he helped draft the constitution of the Irish Free State (1922),
and was high commissioner of the Irish Free State to London (1923-28).

V: 97   (125)
VI: 166   (234)

MacNEILL, SWIFT
John Gordon Swift. 1849 - 1926. Irish politician and historian. Author
of books on Irish constitutional and parliamentary history.

II: 57   (82)

McQUAID, JOHN CHARLES
1895 - 1973. Reactionary archbishop of Dublin (1940-72). Prominent
in the Drums of Father Ned controversy (1958). A churchman of the old
school, McQuaid extended the power of the Catholic church into all areas
of Irish life.

IV: 237, 257-60   (327, 355-9)
VI: 31   (34)

McQUAID, MICK/KIT KULKIN
"Mick McQuaid" is a popular brand of pipe tobacco that O'Casey liked to
smoke. However, it was also the name of a highly popular character in
Irish literature, created by Colonel William F. Lynam (d.1894), which
began in the pages of the Shamrock (19 January 1867). For more, see
Brown's Ireland in Fiction. Kit Kulkin is probably a similar humorous
character.

III: 120   (174)

McRORY, CARDINAL JOSEPH
1861 - 1945. Irish ecclesiastic. Vice-president of Maynooth (1912-15);
archbishop of Armagh (1928-45); cardinal (1929).

IV: 250-1   (345-6)
V: 206   (276)

MacSEAN OF THE CURSES, DONAL
Irish mythological figure.

IV: 159   (216)

MacSWEENEY, MARY
Misspelling of Mary MacSwiney, wife of Terence MacSwiney (1879 - 1920).
c.1872 - 1942. Activist in nationalist politics before, during and
after the Easter Rising. Among those who protested against O'Casey's
play, The Plough and the Stars. For more on O'Casey's troubles with
her, see Letters, I, pp. 124-8.

IV: 88, 180   (113, 245)

MacSWEENEY, PIPER TORLOGH
From the poem, "Turlough MacSweeney," by Ethna Carberry.*

III: 102   (148)

MACABIANS
The Machabees, Jewish martyrs, whose feast is celebrated throughout the
Catholic Church (1 August).

III: 153   (224)

MACMILLAN AND CO. LTD.
O'Casey's London publishers at 4 Little Essex Street. They published all
of O'Casey's plays and most of his essays over a 40-year period.

IV: 128   (171)
V: 37   (40-1)

MACMILLAN, DANIEL
1886 - 1965. Chairman and managing director, Macmillan and Co. Ltd.,
publishers (1836-63); chairman, Macmillan Holdings (from 1964).

V: 37   (40)

MACNAMARA, BRINSLEY
Pen name of John Weldon. 1890 - 1963. Irish novelist and playwright.
A director of the Abbey Theatre, he resigned because of their 1935 production of O'Casey's play, The Silver Tassie. His directorship lasted
only six months.

IV: 127, 185   (169 ,252)
The Valley of the Squinting Windows (1918)   III: 285   (428)
                                              IV: 109   (145)

MACREADY, WILLIAM CHARLES
1793 - 1873. Notable English actor.

V: 22   (20)

MADDEN, RICHARD J.
1880 - 1951. International play broker and agent for O'Casey, O'Neill,*
and others.

V: 181, 183   (241, 243)
VI: 9   (1)

MADIGAN, MAISIE
Neighbor of the Clitheroes in O'Casey's play, The Plough and the Stars.

III: 120   (174)

MADOC
Youngest son of Owain Gwynedd, king of north Wales (c.1169).

IV: 71   (89)

MADRID
O'Casey's reference is to the bitter fighting that took place in or near
the city during the Spanish Civil War.*

V: 127   (166)

MAETERLINCK, MAURICE
1862 - 1949. Belgian poet, dramatist and essayist. Nobel Prize, 1911.

Monna Vanna (1902)   IV: 125   (167)
Joyzelle (1903)   IV: 125   (167)

MAEVE, QUEEN
Legendary queen of Connaught whose armies invaded Ulster in the first
century. Central figure in the Tain.

III: 65, 237-8, 240-1   (90, 354-5, 359)
IV: 133, 141   (179, 190)

MAGDALEN COLLEGE
Constituent college of Cambridge University.

III: 248   (371)
VI: 50   (63)

MAGDENBURG
German city; a center of law during the Middle Ages.

III: 68   (95)

MAGEE, BRIAN BOY
Fire-eating nationalist recitation by Ethna Carbery* about a victim of
the 1641 Rebellion.

III: 102   (147)
IV: 159   (216)

MAGENNIS, WILLIAM
1869 - 1946. Professor of metaphysics, UCD (1909-41), and chairman,
Irish Censorship Board (1934-46) when the first two volumes of O'Casey's
autobiographies were banned in Ireland.

III: 120, 124, 176-8   (174-5, 181, 259-61)

MAGERSFONTEIN
In South Africa, site of disastrous British defeat (11 December 1899) by
the Boers under General Piet Cronje.*

II: 200   (310)

MAHDI
The expected messiah of Muslim tradition. In this case, it refers to
Mohammed Ahmed (c.1843 - 1885), the captor (1883) of Khartoum.*

I: 76   (109)

MAHON, SIR BYRON THOMAS
1862 - 1930. Irish-born British army general who distinguished himself
at the relief of Mafeking in the Boer War.* Commander-in-chief in Ireland
(1916-18).

II: 201   (310)

MAHON, CHRISTY.
Appears as a fellow worker with O'Casey. Not to be confused with the
title character of Synge's* play.

III: 7-10, 21   (1-7, 22)

MAILMURRA
There are several spellings of this, and O'Casey's is as good as any.
He was a Leinster prince, Gormlaith's* brother, and Brian Boru's* brother-
in-law.

II: 186-8   (287-90)

MALAHIDE
Ancient fortified mansion and a small Irish town 10 miles northeast of
Dublin on the inlet of the Irish Sea.   Its "silver strand" is a noted
smooth beach. Formerly the residence of the Talbot* family.

III: 8, 271   (2, 406)

MALLON, JOHN
b.1839. Noted Dublin detective. One of the chief obstacles to the Irish
Republican Brotherhood and other nationalist organizations.

II: 39   (53)

MALONE, ANDREW E.
1888 - 1939. Pen name of Laurence Patrick Byrne. For many years, the
dramatic critic for the Irish Times. Author of The Irish Drama (1929).

IV: 181   (246)

MALONE, FATHER, MONSIGNOR, BISHOP JOHN
Probably a fictional name.

III: 116   (168-9)
IV: 273   (377)

MALTA
Chief island of the former British colony of Malta in the Mediterranean
Sea.

V: 36   (39)

MANASSEH
One of the ten tribes of Israel.

II: 230, 239   (357, 371)

MANCHESTER
City, inland seaport and coal-mining town in Lancashire, England.

III: 101   (145)

MANCHESTER MARTYRS
The name given to William Allen, Michael Larkin and Michael O'Brien, who
were hanged for killing a policeman in their attempt to rescue two Fenians
in Manchester (November 1867).

III: 103   (148)

MANDALAY, ROAD TO
Allusion to Rudyard Kipling's famous poem, "Mandalay," which refers to
a Burmese girl "on the road to Mandalay."

I: 95   (142)

MANET, EDOUARD
1832 - 1883. French painter. Originator and leader of the impressionist
school. One of O'Casey's allusions (#) is to George Moore's* celebrated
friendship with Manet. Moore's most prized possession was a Manet painting, Etude pour 'Le Linge. See chapter VI of Moore's Vale.

IV: 134#, 186, 199, 282   (179#, 254, 273, 391)
V: 64   (78)

MANGAN, JAMES CLARENCE
1803 - 1849. Irish poet and translator of ancient legends. See also
KINCORA.

"Ode to the Maguire" III: 234-5   (350)
"Dark Rosaleen"   III: 15, 103, 235, 259, 266 (14, 149, 350, 388, 399)

MANHATTAN
Primary borough of New York City. See also WHITMAN, WALT.

V: 91, 121, 170, 200   (116, 157, 226, 267)
VI: 41, 201   (49, 287)

MANN, DANNY
The hunch-backed servant in Boucicault's* play, The Colleen Bawn.

II: 45   (64)

MANN, THOMAS
1856 - 1941. British labor leader, and one of the outstanding orators
and organizers of trade unions. Active in all of the major strikes in
his time.

VI: 90   (122)

MANNA
In the Bible, the miraculous food provided for the children of Israel on
their journey to the Holy Land (Exodus 16:15).

I: 167   (258)
II: 122   (188)

MANNIX, ARCHBISHOP DANIEL
1864 - 1963. President of Maynooth (1903-12); archbishop (1917). Opponent of O'Hickey,* though his nationalism was such that during the Irish
War of Independence the British forcibly forbade him to visit Ireland.
An outspoken nationalist and a religious conservative.

III: 132, 134-6, 140, 141-2   (193, 197-200, 205, 207-08)
VI: 166   (234)

MANSFIELD, FREDERICK WILLIAM
1877 - 1958. Mayor of Boston (1933-37). Banned O'Casey's play, Within
the Gates (1935).

V: 202, 205-06   (270, 275)

MANSION HOUSE
On Dawson Street, between Trinity College and St. Stephen's Green, Dublin.
In its round room was held the first session of the Dail (1919). It was
also the site of the signing of the Anglo-Irish Treaty (1922).

IV: 79   (102)

MANUAL OF MILITARY DRILL
Though O'Casey refers to the manual used by the Irish Citizen Army, it
may have been the same one that was used by the Irish Volunteers. In
Martin's The Irish Volunteers, there is an instruction from Bulmer Hob-
son's* papers: "Drill Manual -- Follow exactly the drill set out in the
British Infantry Manual, 1911 (Ponsonby, Grafton Street, Price 1s)."

III: 163   (240)

MARAT, JEAN PAUL
1743 - 1793. Swiss-born revolutionary who was active in the French
Revolution.* Assassinated 13 July.

III: 231   (344)

MARCONI
See MARKONI.

MARGATE
In northeast Kent, England, a popular seaside resort.

V: 75   (93)

MARIA DUCE
Right-wing Catholic movement founded by Rev. Dr. Denis Fahy, Holy Ghost
priest, during the 1940s. Campaigned against the Irish constitution
on the grounds that the articles were not strong enough in defence of the
Catholic Church. Protested O'Casey's play, The Bishop's Bonfire (1956).

VI: 211, 215, 230   (302, 309, 331)

MARIAN LEAGUE OF ART
Unknown. "The Marian Year" was celebrated in 1954.

V: 49   (57)

MARKELL, GEORGE BUSHAR
Producer of O'Casey's play, Within the Gates (U.S.premiere). I have not
been able to locate Markell's home in Pennsylvania where O'Casey visited,
but Markell maintained an office in New York City under the name of
"Bushar Inc." at 137 West 48th Street.

V: 181, 208-11   (241, 278-82)

MARKIEWICZ, COUNTESS CONSTANCE
1868 - 1927. Irish nationalist leader and noted orator. Founder of the
Fianna.* Sentenced to death for her role in the Easter Rising (commuted
to life, released 1917). Led the Irish Citizen Army at the funeral of
Thomas Ashe,* and was minister for labor at the first Dail (1919). I
have not been able to substantiate O'Casey's statement that she painted
a portrait of AE (#), but there was an oil portrait (1903) of him by her
husband, Casimir Dunin Markiewicz. O'Casey's criticisms of Markiewicz
have not been popular with historians and others, but a similar view was
voiced in O'Faolain's* Countess Markiewicz.

III: 211-13, 227, 228, 229-30, 261, 267   (315-16, 338, 340-2, 391, 401)
IV: 74, 82, 85, 86, 152, 180, 212#   (94, 106, 110, 205, 245, 291#)

MARKONI
Guglielmo Marconi. 1874 - 1937. Italian electrician, noted for the
perfection of a system of wireless telegraphy. For an explanation of
O'Casey's unusual spelling, see ISAAC, RUFUS DANIEL.

III: 255   (381)

MARLBOROUGH, DUKE OF
See CHURCHILL/MARLBOROUGH

MARLBOROUGH HOUSE TEACHER'S TRAINING COLLEGE
Non-denominational training college for teachers on Marlborough Street,
Dublin. Set up in 1838, it was part of the Model School system, and an
attempt by the national board of education to provide integrated education with modern teachers. Teachers were initially given a five month
course, but this was increased to two years in 1883. The college irrita-
ted Catholic authorities, and Louis Walsh* once declared that training
at the college was "an insuperable obstacle." Women were not admitted
until 1845.

II: 21   (24)

MARLBOROUGH SCHOOL
Well-known English public (U.S., private) school for boys in Marlborough,
Wiltshire. Founded (1843) for sons of the clergy.

V: 13   (7)

MARLBOROUGH STREET
In Dublin, running from Great Britain (Parnell) Street to Eden Quay.

III: 168, 175   (247, 259)
IV: 164, 168   (223, 228)

MARLOWE, CHRISTOPHER
1564 - 1593. Major English dramatist. See also the index, Appendix II.

II: 184, 185   (285)
VI: 226   (325)
The Jew of Malta (1588)   V: 110   (143)

MARMION
Narrative poem (1808) by Sir Walter Scott.*

I: 25   (26)

MARTHA/MARY
In the Old Testament, Martha is the sister of Mary and Lazurus. In
Christian allegory, she symbolizes the active life, while Mary symbolizes
the contemplative life. (Luke 10: 38-42)

VI: 29   (30)

MARTIN'S TIMBER YARD
Martin had several timber yards around Dublin, though O'Casey is probably
referring to the one at 28-30 Upper Sheriff Street, next to St. Barnabas'
Church.

II: 225   (349)

MARTINI, SIMONE
c.1283 - 1344. Italian painter. The work referred to by O'Casey is an
altarpiece.

Angel of the Annunciation   VI: 74   (98)

MARTYN, EDWARD
Also given as MYRRHTYN. 1859 - 1923. Major figure in the Irish revival.
Co-founder of the Irish Literary Theatre (1898) and the Irish Theatre
(1914). From 1885, Martyn devoted his talents to the church, writing
Morgante the Lesser (1890), a fantasy-satire that rejected the contemporary world. This, and the fact that Martyn was famous for falling
asleep at Gaelic League meetings, accounts for O'Casey coupling his name
with the Irish song, "I'm in my Sleep, and Don't Awaken Me." (#) See
also PALESTRINA.

III: 25, 111#, 120, 133#, 140,   (29, 161#, 174, 195#, 205-06,
     142, 155   208, 228)
IV: 132, 134, 144   (177, 179, 195)

MARWOOD
The hangman of the Invincibles.* Immortalized in such ballads as "The
Hangman's Grave" and "Line Written on the Execution of Joe Brady."

I: 75   (108)
II: 39   (53)

MARX, KARL
1818 - 1883. Founder of the modern socialist movement. Author, with
Frederick Engels, of several important political, social and economic
works.

V: 115   (150)
Das Kapital   III: 15   (14)
Communist Manifesto (1848)   III: 245   (366)
                               V: 78, 116   (98, 115)

MARY
In the Bible, the mother of Jesus. See also MARTHA/MARY

III: 177   (261)
VI: 41, 42   (49, 50)

MARY STREET
In central Dublin, north of the River Liffey.

I: 118   (178)

MASHONIANS
Founded Mashonaland in Africa, named after the Mashona tribe.

II: 198   (305)

MASLOVA, KATERINA
Character in Tolstoy's*Resurrection.

V: 207   (277)

MASON-DIXON LINE
Boundary line between the states of Maryland and Pennsylvania. Separated
free and slave states, and is still the traditional line between north
and south.

V: 180   (239)

MASSEY
Appears as O'Casey's classmate at St. Mary's National School.*

I: 117, 119-20, 127-35, 141-2,   (176, 180-1, 192-204, 215-18,
     145-7, 149   222-6, 228-9)
III: 86   (123)

MASSEY, RAYMOND
b.1896. Actor and director. Directed the world premiere of O'Casey's
play, The Silver Tassie, at the Apollo Theatre in London (1928).

V: 33   (34-5)

MASSILLON, JEAN BAPTISTE
1663 - 1742. French ecclesiastic. Bishop of Clermont (1717).

V: 195-6   (261)

MASSINGER, PHILIP
1583 - 1640. English dramatist.

IV: 126   (168)

MASSINGHAM, HAROLD JOHN
1888 - 1952. English journalist.

V: 136   (179)

MATAHELIANS
From Mataheleland, a region in Southern Rhodesia, proclaimed (1888) to
be within the British sphere of influence, and forcibly occupied (1893-
94) by the British South Africa Company.

II: 198   (305)

MAUNSEL AND SON
Dublin publishers at 96 Middle Abbey Street (1905 - c.1926). Publishers
of O'Casey's The Story of the Irish Citizen Army (1919), and the firm
which was to have published Joyce's* Dubliners,until the printers burned
the edition.

IV: 19, 24   (16, 22)

MAUNSEL, JAMES POOLE
Proprietor of the Daily Express and Evening Herald newspapers, Dublin.

I: 106   (159)

MAURIAC, FRANCOIS
1885 - 1970. French author, Nobel Prize (1952).

VI: 168   (237)

MAYFAIR
Fashionable locality in London. In his essay, "The Green Crow Caws,"
in Under a Colored Cap, O'Casey refers to Mayfair and St. John's Wood
as "übermensch districts."

III: 249   (373)
V: 92, 96   (117, 123)

MAYNOOTH COLLEGE
College of St. Patrick, Maynooth, Co. Kildare. Established as the
national seminary of Ireland (1795), partly to offset the effects of the
French Revolution on the Irish clergy and laymen. Their college board
of trustees was incorporated by statute in 1845, and it was invested by
the Holy See with authority to confer degrees in philosophy, theology,
and canon law in 1899. According to the autobiographies, O'Casey visited
the college at least three times (#).

III: 12, 15, 39, 131-43   (9, 13, 51, 191-209)
IV: 110, 158-9, 232#-67, 273, 284 (145, 214-16, 320#-69, 378, 393)
V: 148, 219   (196, 293)
VI: 166, 169, 170, 171, 177   (234, 239, 240, 251)

MAYO
Irish county in Connaught province.

III: 122, 152   (177, 223)
IV: 66, 277   (82, 384)
V: 177   (236)

MAZARIN, CARDINAL GIULIO
1602 - 1661. French ecclesiastic and politician. Succeeded Richelieu
as prime minister (1642).

IV: 254   (351)

MAZZINI, GIUSEPPE
1805 - 1872. Italian patriot who organized the secret Young Italy (1832).
A prime mover in the 19th-century struggle for Italian independence.

III: 244   (364)

MEALS FOR NECESSITOUS CHILDREN
Related to the "Feeding of Necessitous School Children Act" (1906), from
which Ireland was excluded because of the compromises of the Irish Parliamentary Party. In an article, "Censorship," in Blasts and Benedictions,
O'Casey mentions speaking   at meetings concerning this issue "thirty
years ago, or more." See also Krause's footnote in Letters, I, pp. 65-6.

IV: 14   (8)

MEATH
Irish maritime county in Leinster province. The reference to "Royal
Meath" (#) is an allusion to the county's former status as an ancient
kingdom.

III: 70, 154#, 188#   (99, 226#, 278#)
IV: 70   (88)
V: 54, 173, 189   (84, 230, 252)
VI: 215   (309)

MEATH, BISHOP OF
Rev. Thomas Nulty. 1818 - 1898. Trustee of Maynooth College. Bishop
(from 1866). An early supporter of the Land League,* Nulty did an about-
face in 1892, after the Parnell* revelations about Kitty O'Shea,* writing:
"No man can remain a Cathoic as long as he elects to cling to Parnellism.
The dying Parnellite himself will hardly dare to face the justice of his
Maker till he has been prepared and annointed by us for the last awful
struggle and the terrible judgement that will immediately follow it."

III: 70   (99)

MEATH STREET
In southwest Dublin, running from Thomas Street to The Coombe.

I: 21   (20)

MECHANICS THEATRE
Dublin theatre at 27 Lower Abbey Street. Remodeled (1904) and renamed
the Abbey Theatre. In 1895, O'Casey acted in a Boucicault* play in this
theatre.

II: 22, 133, 134   (26, 204, 206)
IV: 167, 285   (227, 394)

MEDDLELAND RAILWAY
Midland Railway of Ireland, with offices at 6 Eden Quay and 9 North Wall
Quay.

II: 144   (221)

MEDES
Inhabitants of Media, an ancient country in what is now Iran. Absorbed
into the Persian Empire.

V: 180   (240)

MEDUSA
In classical mythology, one of the three snake-haired monsters known as
the Gorgons.

II: 99   (150)

MEGARITHMA
In Irish legend, the brother of Brian Boru* and a leader of the 10th-
century Munster sept, Dal Cais.*

IV: 126   (168-9)

MELANCHTHON, PHILIP SCHWARTERT
1497 - 1560. German scholar and religious reformer. Drafted the Augs-
burg Confession (1530).

II: 87   (131)

MELLOR, HELEN EDNA THOMSON
Wife (m.1919) of William Mellor (1888 - 1942), English journalist and
editor of the Daily Herald (1926-31) and the Tribune (1937-38).

VI: 17   (13)

MELLOWS, LIAM
1892 - 1922. Irish military and political leader. Member, Irish
Volunteers and Irish Republican Brotherhood. Mellows led the rebellion
in the west of Ireland during the Easter Rising. He opposed the Treaty,*
was captured and executed by Free State troops.

III: 244   (365)

MELVILLE/COGHILL
Lt. Neville J. A. Coghill and Lt. Teignmouth Melville, both of the 24th
Foot in the British army. Cited for courageous action during the Zulu
Wars (21 January 1879). Posthumously awarded the Victoria Cross (1907).

I: 116, 117   (175, 176)

MEN OF EIGHTY TOO
See MEN OF EIGHTY-TWO, Appendix I.

MEN OF EIREANN
In the Tain, the warriors of Queen Maeve* who launched an attack on the
men of Ulster.

III: 236, 237, 239, 240   (353, 355, 357, 358)

MEN OF FORTY-EIGHT
Allusion to the Irish Rising of 1848. In general, it was ineffectual and
easily put down by the British authorities.

III: 128   (186)

MEN OF NINETY-EIGHT
Allusion to the Irish Rebellion of 1798. The most sustained Irish effort
to achieve independence until 1918. See EMMET, ROBERT; TONE, WOLFE;
and UNITED IRISHMEN.

III: 188, 233   (278, 348)
IV: 113   (149)

MENCKEN, HENRY LOUIS
1880 - 1956. American editor and satirist. Perhaps the most important
literary critic in the U.S. in the 1910-30 period. Founded, with Nathan,*
The American Mercury, for which he was editor (1924-33). The book to
which O'Casey refers is a collection of Mencken's views on some of the
most bizarre everyday events in the U.S.

Americana (1925)   V: 180, 230, 236   (239, 310, 317)

MENDICITY INSTITUTION
At 9 Usher's Island, Co. Dublin. Founded (1818) to "provide food and
shelter by the day for the poor and destitute."

II: 165   (254)

MERCIER, CARDINAL DESIRE JOSEPH
1851 - 1926. Belgian ecclesiastic and philosopher. O'Casey's reference
is to the controversy in which Mercier became embroiled by "his use of
biology, physiology, and neurology, to show the unity of man and to
elaborate the hylomorphic explanation of this unity." (Catholic Encyclopedia, v.9, p. 671)

IV: 246, 247, 248   (340, 341, 342)

MERCURY
In Roman mythology, the god of science and commerce.

III: 59   (81)

MEREDITH, GEORGE
1829 - 1909. English novelist and poet.

I: 35   (43)

MERRILY, OONI NI
See FEARALLY, OONA.

MERRIMAN, BRIAN
1745 - 1805. Irish poet whose reputation rests on one poem, The Midnight
Court (in Irish, Cuirt an Mheain Oidche), often praised, more frequently
banned for its controversial and humorous treatment of sex. It was
published under its Latin title in Dublin and Boston. See O'Casey's
essay, "The Gaelic Black-Headed Boy," in Blasts and Benedictions.

Mediac Noctis Consiluim (1897)   III: 201   (297)

MERRION HALL
In Dublin, on the corner of Denzille Lane (now Fenian Street) and Lower
Merrion Street. Used for religious gatherings and meetings.

II: 79, 82, 99   (118, 123, 150)

MERRION, SIR
O'Casey is punning. Merrion Square* was named for the family of 2nd
Viscount Fitzwilliam of Merrion.

IV: 187   (256)

MERRION SQUARE
One of the most fashionable areas in Dublin, having as its residents
Yeats (#82), Plunkett (#84), Wilde, and others. See also PLUNKETT HOUSE.

II: 178   (274)
IV: 187-8, 210, 269   (255-6, 288, 372)
VI: 77-9   (103-06)

MERSEY RIVER
An ocean-liner-navigable river in England, flowing into the Irish Sea.*

V: 170   (226)

METHUEN, LORD PAUL SANDFORD
1845 - 1932. English general; commander of the 1st division of the First
Army Corps in the Boer War.* See MAGERSFONTEIN.

II: 200   (310)

METROPOLITAN SCHOOL OF ART
Founded (1746) by the Royal Dublin Society as a school for drawing and
painting. In Dublin on Kildare Street.

IV: 185   (253)

MICHAEL'S LOST ANGEL
Michael and His Lost Angel, a play by Henry Arthur Jones (1851 - 1929).
See LOST ANGELES.

VI: 189   (269)

MICHAELANGELO BUONARROTI
1475 - 1564. The celebrated Italian painter.

III: 84, 136	(139, 199)
IV: 199	(273-4)
V: 111, 188, 190	(144, 250, 253)
VI: 137	(190)

MICKIEWICZ, ADAM
1798 - 1855. Polish poet who was exiled for his revolutionary activities
against the Czar. Spent the last half of his life in Paris, and his
writings were a major factor in sustaining the Polish will to survive in
the 19th century. O'Casey refers to the "Polish Legions," which were
founded in the wake of the 1848 Revolutions, and which fought against
the Austrians and the French in Rome.

III: 194   (287)

MICUIRMICK, SACRED CHOIR OF
Probably a reference to John MacCormack (1884 - 1945), world famous
Irish singer, who was a member of the choir at the Pro-Cathedral, Dublin.
He also sang with the choir at the St. Louis Exhibition (1904). The
reference to "Count" (#) stems from MacCormack's title, created (1928)
by Papal Peerage.

III: 153	(224)
IV: 283#	(391#)

MIDDLETON, GEORGE
1880 - 1927. Classmate of O'Casey at St. Barnabas National School. He
lived about a block from the dramatist, and eventually worked as a
range setter.

I: 103, 126-42, 144-7, 149, 172, 174	(154-5, 191-209, 215-25, 228, 265, 269)
II: 30, 149-53, 239	(38-9, 230-4, 371)
III: 7, 9, 86, 96-7, 99-100	(1, 5, 123, 139, 143)

MIDIANITES
Inhabitants of Midian. In biblical geography, it was a desert region
in northwest Arabia. The Midianites rescued Joseph from the pit.

V: 236   (317)

MIGNET, FRANCOIS A.M.
1796 - 1884. French historian, and author of books on the French Revolution.

Histoire de la revolution francaise de 1789 a 1814 (1824) II: 122 (187)

MILD MILLIE
One of O'Casey's Dublin street people.

III: 68-70, 72-80   (96-9, 101-12)

MILE END
In east London, about a mile from the old City Wall.

III: 250   (373)

MILE END ROAD
In London, a major thoroughfare leading out from Whitechapel toward
Stratford.

VI: 143   (199)

MILESIUS
Properly, the inhabitants of Miletus, but the name was given to the
ancient Irish because the two (sometimes five)sons of Milesius,king
of Spain, conquered the country. In mythology, they were the fifth
and last invaders of Ireland.

II: 219   (339)

MILLET, JEAN FRANCOIS
1814 - 1875. French genre and landscape painter of the Barbizan School.

IV: 199   (273)

MILLIGAN, ALICE
1866 - 1953. Irish novelist, poet and dramatist. With Ethna Carbery,*
she edited the Northern Patriot (1894-95) and Shan Van Vocht (1896-99).
One of the first to write plays for the Abbey.

III: 212   (315)

MILNER, JOHN
1752 - 1826. English vicar apostolic of the Catholic Church (1803-26).
Called "the English Athanasius."

End of Religious Controversy (1818)   I: 35   (43)

MILTON, JOHN
1608 - 1675. The celebrated blind English poet. See also ABDIEL and
HOBSON, THOMAS.

I: 35   (43)
II: 122, 126-7, 153   (186-7, 194, 235)
IV: 23, 219-20, 222   (20, 302, 306)
V: 15, 116, 132, 138, 139   (9, 151, 173, 182-3)
VI: 49, 196, 197, 203   (61, 279, 280-1, 290)
Paradise Lost (1667)   V: 111   (144)
Paradise Regained (1671)   V: 138   (182)
L'Allegro (1632)   VI: 117   (162)
Latin Elegiarum   VI: 197   (281)

MISBOURNE COTTAGES & HOUSES
Housing estate in Buckinghamshire at Chalfont St. Giles, England. The
cottage was owned by Evelyn McElroy, daughter of Billy McElroy.*

V: 133-4   (175-6)

MISHELAYMASSMORES . . . EIRAILLAS . . . SPORANGIA BELFUSSTICA
Allegorical plant-like references to various movements in Ireland.
"Mishelaymassmores" is from the Irish, mise le meas more, meaning, more
or less, "I am yours with great respect," and is probably the Gaelic
League.* "Eiraillas" may be a play on Eire, the Irish name for Ireland,
and on the German, alles, meaning "all." This is probably the Republican
movement. "Sporangia belfusstica" is the Orange Order* stronghold in
Belfast. For more on Eiraillas, see IRELAND OVER ALL, Appendix I. See
also FAIR OF FAIRS.

III: 179   (265)

MISKELL, PADDY
Michael Miskell, a pauper in Lady Gregory's* play, The Workhouse Ward
(1908).

IV: 155   (210)

MISSABIELLE
Massabielle, the grotto in Lourdes where St. Bernadette* saw the vision
of St. Mary.

IV: 55   (67, 68)

MITCHEL, JOHN
1815 - 1875. Irish patriot who was active in the Young Ireland movement.
Founded and edited the United Irishman (1847). Advocated armed
resistance, and, following the 1848 Rising, was transported to Van
Diemen's Land (Australia). He escaped (1853) and came to the U.S., where
he sided with the Confederacy during the U.S. Civil War (1861-65).
Author of Jail Journal. See also SPIKE ISLAND.

III: 225, 235   (335, 350)
IV: 158, 159   (214, 216)
V: 171, 180   (228, 240)

MITFORDS
The barons and earls of Redesdale, English politicians who were active
in Irish affairs. First baron Redesdale (1784 - 1830) was lord chancellor of Ireland (1802-06).

V: 18   (13)

MIVANT, ST. GEORGE JACKSON
1827 - 1900. English biologist who sought to reconcile science and
religion. According to Walter MacDonald,* Mivant "stimulated me in a
way I had never felt before. It was the beginning of a new life -- the
life I have led ever since."

Primer of Philosophy   VI: 170-2   (240-3)

MOBY DICK
Herman Melville's (1819 - 1891) sea classic (1851).

IV: 137   (184)
VI: 13, 38   (7, 45)

MOHAMMED
Given as MAHOMED, MAHOMMED and MUHHAMMED. c.570 - 632. The titular
name for the founder of Islam.

II: 108   (164)
V: 124, 141, 168, 221   (161, 185, 223, 296)
VI: 54, 105   (68, 144)

MOHER, CLIFFS OF
In Ireland, on the coast of Co. Clare.

III: 103   (148)

MOLD, MR.
Mr. Mould, the undertaker in Dickens's* novel, The Lives and Adventures
of Martin Chuzzlewit (1844).

V: 22   (20)

MOLIERE
Pseudonym of Jean Baptiste Poquelin. 1622 - 1673. French actor and
dramatist.

V: 181   (241)
VI: 198   (282)

MOLLSER
Tubercular young girl in O'Casey's play, The Plough and the Stars. See
CURLING, KITTY. "Mollser" was the original title of O'Casey's short
story, "A Fall in the Gentle Wind," Windfalls (1934).

V: 235   (315)

MOLYNEAUX, CAPTAIN
Young English officer in Boucicault's* play, The Shaughraun.

II: 135, 140-2   (207, 214-17)

MONASTERBOICEANS
Monasterboice, in Lough, Ireland. Site of ecclesiastical ruins, including St. Boyne's Cross, one of the oldest Christian relics in Ireland.

III: 152   (224)

MONS STAR
British army medal, given to those who served in France and Belgium in
1914. The battle of Mons was fought on 23 August 1914.

V: 57   (68)

MONTE CASSINO
Famous monastery in Italy.

IV: 257   (355)

MONTEAGLE, LORD
Thomas Spring-Rice, 2nd Baron Monteagle. 1849 - 1926. Active in rural
Irish projects, such as the Rural Library Association for Ireland
(1904). Former president of the Irish Agricultural Organisation Society.

III: 157   (230-1)

MONTGOMERY, MARSHAL BERNARD LAW
1887 - 1976. Famous British general and field marshal who attained
fame in World War II against Germany. Known for his virulent Cold War
views.

V: 27   (27)
VI: 228   (328)

MONTGOMERY STREET
Now Foley Street in central Dublin.

III: 124   (180)

MONTICELLI, ANDRE J.T.
1824 - 1886. French genre, landscape and portrait painter.

IV: 199, 206   (273, 283)

MONUMENT
In London, a 202-foot memorial to the Great Fire of 1666 which devastated
nearly four-fifths of the city.

VI: 22   (20)

MOOKSEE/GRIPES
Should be Mookse and Gripes. Shaun and Shem in Joyce's* Finnegans Wake.

V: 178   (253)

MOONEY, PADDY
Probably one of O'Casey's working class friends from Dublin.

VI: 43   (52)

MOONEY, RIA
1900 - 1973. Abbey Theatre actress. She played the role of Rosie Redmond in the premiere of O'Casey's play, The Plough and the Stars. Producer of the premiere of his play, Red Roses for Me, at the Embassy
Theatre, London (26 February 1946). See also GAIETY THEATRE.

IV: 173   (235)

MOONEY'S
Dublin pub at 1 Lower Abbey Street, near the corner of O'Connell Street.

I: 180   (278)

MOORE, GEORGE
1852 - 1933. Irish novelist and dramatist who was active in the Irish
literary revival. Best known for his autobiographical trilogy, Hail and
Farewell (1911-14). The reference to "his Anatidean lover and his lass"
(#) alludes to Moore's celebrated work, Heloise and Abelard (1921). See
also IT WAS A LOVER AND HIS LASS, Appendix I. The "Aubusson carpet" (##)
is an allusion to Middleton Murray's satire on Moore's sitting-room
elegance, Wrap Me Up In My Aubusson Carpet (1924). O'Casey also alludes
(###) to Chesterton's* essay on Moore in his Heretics (1925). See also
LUMPKIN, TONY.

IV: 63, 106#, 134##, 199, 200   (79, 139#, 179##, 273, 274)
VI: 120, 168###   (165, 237###)

MOORE, COLONEL MAURICE
1854 - 1939. Brother of George Moore,* and former commander, Connaught
Rangers.* Active in the language movement, and prominent in the Irish
Volunteers, which he led at the funeral of Thomas Ashe.* For Moore's
account of the confrontation with the Irish Citizen Army at Howth (and
possibly with O'Casey), see Fox's History of the Irish Citizen Army
(pp. 74-5).

III: 264-5   (396-8)

MOORE, MR. & MRS.
Residents with O'Casey at 422 North Circular Road, Dublin. Mrs. Moore
is Mary Moore, whose relationship with Juno is found in Letters, I, p.
188n.

IV: 97-9   (128-31)

MOORE STREET
In central Dublin, running from Great Britain (Parnell) Street to Henry
Street. A traditional site of a large open-air market.

II: 92   (138)

MOORE, THOMAS
1779 - 1852. Irish poet and national lyricist. See Appendix I, II and
III.

V: 90   (115)

MOR MUMHAN
Of doubtful historicity. The words mean only "Great Munster."

V: 86   (109)

MORAN, DAVID PATRICK
Also given as SIR GAELAHAD MORAN. 1871 - 1936. Influential enthusiast
of the Gaelic revival and vigorous champion of the Irish-Ireland* movement,
which he outlined in his book, The Philosophy of Irish-Ireland (1905).
Founder and editor of The Leader (from 1900). Opposed workers in 1913.

III: 106, 112, 113, 126, 150   (153, 162-3, 183, 221)

MORAY, EARL OF
In Scottish history, James Stewart (d.1592), who was called the "bonny earl." He was assassinated, and, according to popular ballads, was left unburied for a long time.

II: 38   (52)

MORGAN, SYDNEY
1885 - 1931. Irish actor and member of the Irish Players.* Performed in most of O'Casey's plays before his death.

VI: 53   (67)

MOROCCAN MAHOMMEDANS
In the Spanish Civil War,* North African Muslims who fought on the side of Franco.*

V: 127   (166)

MORPETH MANSIONS
In London, T. P. O'Connor's home (#5) on Victoria Street.

VI: 25   (25)

MORRIGU
In Irish mythology, a war goddess/queen who was accompanied at every battle by her four maids. In Yeats's* play, The Death of Cuchulain (1939).

II: 235   (364)
III: 244, 245   (364, 366)

MORROW, JACK
Irish artist from Belfast. Stage designer for the Irish Theatre, Hardwicke Street, Dublin (1914).

V: 29   (29)

MOSCOW
Capital of Russia. O'Casey's "holy city."

IV: 231   (318)
V: 75, 83, 186, 200   (93, 105, 247, 267)
VI: 95, 118, 143, 234   (129, 164, 199, 337)

MOSELEY, HUMPHREY
d.1661. English publisher of Milton.*

VI: 197   (281)

MOSELEY, OSWALD
1896 - 1980. English leader of British Union of Fascists.

VI: 115-16   (158-9)

MOSES
Lawgiver of the Israelites and organizer of their nation.

I: 93   (138)
V: 225   (302)
VI: 103   (142)

MOSES, MARCUS TERTIUS
I have not been able to substantiate O'Casey's claim that Moses was a
bank director. He was, however, a man of means in Dublin. In Thoms
(1896), he is listed as a wholesale tea merchant. In Thoms (1909), he
is listed as a magistrate. In between, he could be found on the welcom-
ing committee at Donnybrook Hospital during Queen Victoria's* visit
(April 1900).

III: 97-8   (140)

MOSS BROTHERS
Men's clothing store on Bedford Street, London.

V: 13   (6)

MOTHER AND CHILD BILL
A bill proposed (1951) by the Irish minister of health, Dr. Noel Browne,
which offered the introduction of a national maternity service. Browne's
concern was the tuberculosis problem in Ireland, but his proposal was
resented by the medical profession and condemned by the Catholic hierarchy. Browne subsequently resigned, and the coalition government, of
which he was a part, collapsed.

VI: 221   (316)

MOTHER OF MERCY HOSPITAL
The Mater Misericordiae Hospital on Eccles Street, Dublin.

IV: 64   (79)

MOUNT CARMEL
In Palestine, long an object of veneration. Site of the founding of the
Carmelite Order (1156).

III: 175   (258)

MT. JEROME CEMETERY
Protestant cemetery in Harold's Cross in southeast Dublin. Place of
burial of the Casey family: mother, father, sister, and brothers.
Dublin's largest Protestant burial ground.

I: 50-3   (67-73)
III: 100   (143-4)

MOUNT SINAI
In the Bible, the mountain where Moses* appeared.

III: 120   (174)

MOUNT SLEMISH
The Slemish mountains in Co. Antrim, where St. Patrick allegedly passed his youth.

II: 13   (11)
III: 104   (150)

MOUNT STEWART
House of Lord and Lady Londonderry,* Newtonard, Co. Down.

V: 109, 159, 161-2   (141, 210, 212-14)

MOUNTJOY JAIL
In north Dublin, between North Circular Road and the Royal Canal. Another of Dublin's notorious prisons (see KILMAINHAM JAIL). Site of execution of Kevin Barry.

IV: 16, 64, 100   (11, 79, 131)

MOY EALTA
Unknown.

II: 188   (290)

MOYA
Father Dolan's* niece, who is in love with Conn in Boucicault's* play, The Shaughraun.

II: 135, 141-2   (207, 217)

MOYCALLY
This is probably Moyvalley in Co. Kildare.

III: 143   (210)

MOYLE, SEA OF
Allusion to Thomas Moore's* song, "The Song of Fionnula," which begins, "Silent, O Moyle, be the roar of thy water."

II: 229   (356)

MOZART, WOLFGANG
1756 - 1791. Celebrated Austrian composer. For an example of Shaw's* criticism of Mozart (#), see Shaw on Music, pp. 67-83.

V: 190, 194   (253, 259)
VI: 174#, 175, 232   (245#, 247, 333)
Clarinet Concerto in A Major V: 162   (214)

MUINTIR NA TIRE
People of the Land, founded (May 1931) by Father John Martin Hayes, curate of Castleiney, Co. Tipperary. O'Casey partially dedicates his play, The Drums of Father Ned, to Hayes, "for bringing a sense of community life and cooperation to rural Ireland, and brightness with them."

VI: 221   (317)

MULDOON, MICHAEL
Appears to be a representative Irish figure.

VI: 120   (166-7)

MULLEN, MICHAEL
1881 - 1956. Gaelic-speaking Aran Islander, the original for Seumas
Shields in O'Casey's play, The Shadow of a Gunman. Mullen's article,
"An Ruathar Ud Agus a nDeachaigh Leis" (The Raid and What Went With It,
Feasta, 1955), gives his version of the Black and Tan raid at 35 Mountjoy Square, where he and O'Casey shared a room. The article has been
translated, and appears in Essays on Sean O'Casey's Autobiographies.

III: 228   (340)

MULLINGAR
Irish town and capital of Co. Westmeath.

VI: 80   (107)

MUNICIPAL COLLECTION
The Municipal Gallery of Modern Art, Parnell Square, Dublin.

VI: 173   (244)

MUNSTER
One of the four provinces of Ireland.

III: 111, 116, 154   (161, 169, 226)
IV: 11   (4)

MURPHY
Appears as a provisions merchant. There were several such merchants
named Murphy near O'Casey's residences.

III: 91, 281   (130, 422)
IV: 25-7, 36-7   (24-6, 40-1)

MURPHY, DR. JERIMIAH
Professor of English language and literature, University College, Galway.
See his letter to the editor, Irish Times, 3 September 1935.

V: 52   (61)

MURPHY, WILLIAM MARTIN
1844 - 1921. Irish capitalist, chief opponent of the workers during the
1913 Strike. Murphy was owner of the Irish Independent, Evening Herald,
the Imperial Hotel, and several other businesses in Dublin. He was
chairman of the Dublin United Tramway Company, and had railroad interests
in Ireland and west Africa. "Jake Jester" in O'Casey's play, The Star
Turns Red.

III: 191-4, 198   (282-7, 293)

MURRAY, REV. P. A.
Professor of dogmatical and moral theology, Maynooth, and prefect of
Dunboyne Establishment (Thoms, 1880).

IV: 237, 238, 240   (328, 329, 331)

MURRAY, THOMAS C.
1873 - 1959. Irish novelist. Regarded as one of the leading Abbey
Theatre playwrights. Murray's name is not mentioned in the latter entry
in any of the later editions of Sunset and Evening Star (#). Instead,
the words, "there is nothing to show his identity," are inserted. It is
included in all U.S. editions.

VI: 99   (136#)

The Blind Wolf (1928) VI: 77 (103)

MUSEUM
The National Museum on Kildare Street, Dublin, next to the National
Library.

III: 271   (407)

MUSSOLINI, BENITO
1883 - 1945. Italian Fascist leader.

V: 128   (167)
VI: 115, 116, 191   (158, 159, 272)

MYSTERY OF THE PELICAN, THE GREEN DRAGON, THE BLACK EAGLE, SALT,
MERCURY, ST. PATRICK'S PURGATORY, THE ROUND TOWERS, CARDINAL LOGUE'S
LEARNING, AND WHO KILLED COCK ROBIN.
All, except the first four items, are dealt with elsewhere in order in
the index. The whole phrase is a mystery, even when broken down into
parts.

III: 59   (81)

N

N.C.W.C. CO.
The National Catholic Welfare Conference, an international agency. One
branch is directly concerned with disseminating news and coordinating
the Catholic media throughout the world. Generally seen as the voice
of American bishops.

V: 137   (181)

NAAMAN
In the Old Testament, a Syrian captain who was miraculously cured of
leprosy upon bathing in the river Jordan at the command of the prophet
Elisha (2 Kings 5).

III: 74   (104)

NAGLE'S
Dublin pub at 25 North Earl Street. Owned by James J. Nagle.

I: 63, 64   (89)
II: 55, 87, 102   (79, 130, 154)

NANNY
Irish river in Co. Meath.

IV: 70   (88)

NAPLES
Italian city.

III: 285   (427)
V: 23   (21)

NAPOLEON
1769 - 1821. French emperor. It was actually Voltaire who first said
what O'Casey attributes to Napoleon (#).

III: 17#   (16#)
IV: 136, 243   (183, 335)

NASHES, TRIPPS, AND LANES
Frank Nash, Harry E. Tripp and Frederick W. Lane, prominent persons in
Chalfont St. Giles. Lane was a builder, and owned the lodging O'Casey
lived in. Nash owned several stores in Chalfont St. Giles and Gerrards
Cross.

V: 138   (181-2)

NASSAU
See HOUSE OF NASSAU.

V: 82, 88, 89, 221   (103, 112, 113, 297)

NATAL
Province in South Africa which is bounded by the Transvaal and Mozambique.

II: 197   (305)

NATHAN, GEORGE JEAN
1882 - 1958. American editor, author and dramatic critic who was a
staunch supporter of O'Casey's plays. Founder and editor, with Mencken,*
of the American Mercury; founder and editor, with others, of the American Spectator (1932). Author of many books on the theatre, one of which,
Passing Judgements (1935), was dedicated to O'Casey. See Appendix II (#).

IV: as "two Georges"   182   (248)
V: on "good drama"   20   (16)
    on the Tassie (#)   50   (58)
    on Journey's End   104   (134)
    and Within the Gates   159   (210)
    and O'Casey in N.Y.   181-2, 196, 235 (240-3, 262, 313)
                                                    MORE

NATHAN, GEORGE JEAN (cont.)

and farewell to O'Casey	238, 239	(320, 322)

VI:	and gifts to O'Casey	9	(1)
	on Purple Dust	117	(161)
	as editor	180	(254)
	and Shaw*	184	(260, 261)
	on Irish drama	189	(268-9)
	and "good plays, bad productions"	224	(322)
	and "rapidly dying theatre"	225	(323)

Mentioned:	V: 55	(V: 65)

The Critic and the Drama (1922)   IV: 182   (248)
Five Great Modern Irish Plays (1941) VI:189   (268)

NATIONAL GALLERY
Ireland's National Art Gallery on Merrion Square in Dublin. Founded in
1864. Contains classical and modern paintings. In 1914, the director
was Hugh Lane.* According to Krause, when James Stephens* gave up the
position as registrar of the National Gallery (1925), Lady Gregory*
urged O'Casey to take the job. He refused, however, and the position
was filled by Brinsley Macnamara.* (See Letters, I, p. 114.)

II:	225	(349)
III:	217	(322)
IV:	147	(198)
VI:	27, 173	(28, 244)

NATIONAL/INTERMEDIATE BOARD OF EDUCATION
The full name of the education board was the Board of Commissioners of
National Education in Ireland. Founded in 1831, the board began as
Protestant-dominated, but by 1860, there were an equal number of Catholics
and Protestants on it. In general, the board strove for a "mixed" education, but because of the suspicions of the clergy on both sides, the
plan failed. The Intermediate Board was created by the Education Act
of 1878, and was responsible for administering secondary schools. In
the early 1900s, the education board became a focal point when the Gaelic
League and others fought to have Irish taught and used in schools. By
1909, 168 schools were using it, and 3047 schools were teaching the
language. See the list of O'Casey's articles under ASSOCIATION OF TEA-
CHERS and GAELHILGE. See also NATIONAL SCHOOLS.

I:	147	(227-8)
III:	156, 241	(230, 360)

NATIONAL LEAGUE
When the Land League* was suppressed (1881), the National League rose in
its place (17 October 1882), headed by Parnell,* Dillon,* and Davitt.*
The objectives of the new body were defined as: national self-government,
land law reform, local self-government, and the development of labor and
industrial interests in Ireland.

II: 57	(82)

NATIONAL SCHOOLS
A national system of education launched in 1831. The intention was to
provide for "combined moral and literary and separate religious instruction," which would enable Catholics and Protestants to be educated together. The scheme foundered on sectarianism. Many schools refused to
become vested in the school system. In 1850, there were 3000 non-vested
and 1500 vested schools. In 1910, the respective figures were 5000 and
3400. See CENTRAL MODEL SCHOOLS and NATIONAL BOARD OF EDUCATION.

I: 65   (92)

NATIONAL THEATRE
For some of O'Casey's writings on the creation of a national theatre in
England, see "National Theatre Bunkum" in The Flying Wasp.

V: 129-30   (169-70)

NATIONAL UNIVERSITY OF IRELAND
Irish university system, with constituent colleges at Dublin, Cork and
Galway. See also NEW UNIVERSITY.

III: 133   (194)
IV: 83, 177   (107, 242)

NAVAN
Irish town in Co. Meath.

VI: 80   (107)

NAVARRE
An old kingdom (c.900-1328) which comprised the modern province of
Navarra in Spain.

III: 90   (129)

NAZIS
IV: 97   (127)
V: 234   (315)
VI: 95, 99, 113, 118, 119, 122, 127, 136, 138, 139, 144, 145, 148,
151-2, 153, 156
     (129, 135, 163, 164, 168, 170, 176, 189, 190-2, 194, 201, 202,
211-14, 219)

NEARUS
Appears as a head clerk for Leedom, Hampton chandler shop, Dublin.

II: 73-5, 77, 86, 106-11, 128, 130   (108-13, 129, 162-9, 196, 199)

NED
See OLD UNCLE NED, Appendix I.

NELSON, LORD HORATIO
1758 - 1805. British naval hero. O'Casey alludes to the amputation of
Nelson's right arm (suffered at Santa Cruz de Tenerife, 1797) and the
loss of his right eye. The Trafalgar Bay battle (1805), where Nelson
                                                           MORE

NELSON, LORD HORATIO (cont.)

won victories over the French and Spanish fleets, cost Nelson his
life. See also NELSON'S PILLAR.

I: 39, 40, 42, 66, 151   (50-1, 54, 94, 231)
II: 161   (231)
III: 208   (309)
IV: 44, 177, 183   (52, 242, 249)

NELSON'S LANE
In Dublin off North Earl Street.

III: 168   (247)

NELSON'S PILLAR
In Dublin, formerly in the middle of Sackville (O'Connell) Street. It
was a 121-foot tall column surmounted by a 13-foot statue of Lord Horatio
Nelson.* Built in 1808-09, it was destroyed during the Golden Jubilee
celebration of the Easter Rising (1966) by Irish patriots who blew off
the top part.

I: 64, 156   (89, 240)
II: 27, 71, 102, 121, 136   (34, 104, 155, 209, 248)
III: 104, 119, 153, 172, 197, 198, 199, 202-05, 223, 244, 266
     (149, 173, 225, 254, 291-3, 295, 300, 302-04, 331, 364, 398)
IV: 190   (260)
VI: 110   (152)

NEVE, GOLDEN·HAIR OF
See NIAMH (pronounced "ni-eve").

III: 179   (264)

NEW AMSTERDAM
Name given to the Dutch city of New York. Founded (1625-26) by the Dutch
East India Company on Manhattan Island. Renamed (1664) by the English;
then back to New Orange (1763); and finally New York during the American
Revolution.

V: 217   (291)

NEW DEAL
Term used by Franklin D. Roosevelt* to describe the body of relief and
reform legislation enacted under his administrations.

V: 209-10   (280)

NEW ENGLAND
Name given to the northeast section of the United States. O'Casey uses it
to signify the entire 13 states of the eastern seaboard of the U.S. to
mean the 13 colonies which rose against the British in the American
Revolution.

IV: 263   (364)

NEW ROSS
Irish town and river port in Co. Wexford. Site of a defeat of Irish
insurgents (5 June 1798) by loyalist troops.

III: 103   (148)

NEW THEATRE
On St. Martin's Lane, London. O'Casey refers to the production of the
Plough and the Stars which opened 28 June 1926.

V: 55   (65)

NEW UNIVERSITY
National University of Ireland* (founded 1908). Called "new" only in
relation to Trinity College,* founded by Queen Elizabeth in 1591.

III: 12, 31, 32, 39, 42, 115, 132,   (9, 39-40, 51, 54, 166, 191,
     134   193, 196)

NEW YORK
O'Casey left Southampton on the Majestic, 13 September 1934, and arrived
in New York on 19 September. He left New York on the Britannic, 12
December, and arrived in Liverpool on 23 December.

III: 113   (164)
IV: 75, 281   (96, 389)
V: 43, 68, 69, 75, 109, 159, 166, 170, 172, 178-98, 198-202, 206, 209,
     213, 222-3, 225, 234, 235-7, 239
     (43, 54, 83, 85, 93, 141, 210, 220, 226, 227, 229, 238-70, 275,
     280, 285, 298-300, 303, 315-18, 321)
VI: 9, 31, 117, 139, 184, 234   (1, 2, 34, 161, 194, 261, 337)

NEWGATE STREET
In central London, site of Old Bailey and Newgate Prison.

V: 74   (91)

NEWMAN, CARDINAL JOHN HENRY
1801 - 1890. Anglican leader of the Oxford Movement, and later a Catholic cardinal (1879). Rector, Dublin's Catholic University (1851-58).
Author of several literary and theological books and poems, of which his
Apologia pro Vita Sua (1864), an exposition of his spiritual history,
is considered a literary masterpiece. See index, Appendix III.

IV: 243, 245, 252   (336, 338, 348)
V: 142   (187)
VI: 51   (63)

NEWMAN, RABBI LOUIS I.
1893 - 1972. Rabbi of Rudolph Sholem temple* for 41 years. Founder,
American Friends of a Jewish Palestine (1939). Represented U.S. rabbis
at the United Nations (1946).

V: 201-02   (268-9)

NEWRY
Irish town in Co. Down.

V: 164   (217)

NEWTONARDS
Irish market town in Co. Down, near the head of Strangford Lough.

V: 161   (212)

NIALL OF THE NINE HOSTAGES
Distinguished warrior who reigned over Ireland (379-405). Noted for the
hostages he took to secure the good behavior of conquered districts.
Assassinated in 405.

III: 65   (90)

NIAMH, GOLDEN-HAIRED
From John Keegan Casey's (1847 - 1870) "Song of Golden-Haired Niamh."
Legendary Irish woman who spirited Oisin* off to the land of the young
for 300 years. From the Fenian tale, Oisin in the Land of the Young.
O'Casey uses the air to the song for his song, "The Summer Sun is
Tightly Folding," published in his Songs of the Wren No. 2 (1918).
See also NEVE.

III: 50, 92   (67, 132)

NICHOLLS
Dublin undertaker at 26-31 Lombard Street.

III: 47, 96-8   (62, 139-41)

NICHOLS, BEVERLEY
1899 - 1980. English writer. In his article, "The Public Death of
Shakespeare," in The Green Crow, O'Casey refers to Nichols as "the
Prince Charming of the English Theatre." The interview by Nichols
was printed in his book, Are They the Same at Home? Being a Series of
Bouquets Differently Distributed (1927).

V: 12-16   (6-11)

NICHOLSON'S NEK
In Natal, South Africa, a few miles north of Ladysmith, where approximately 1000 British soldiers were captured by the Boers (30 October
1899).

II: 201   (310)

NICODEMUS
In New Testament history, a member of the Sanhedrin, a disciple who
visited Jesus by night as an inquirer (John 3:1-21).

IV: 242   (334)

NIETZSCHE, FREDERICH WILHELM
1844 - 1900. German philosopher.

V: 224   (301)
VI: 54, 86   (68, 116)

NIGHTINGALE, FLORENCE
1820 - 1910. Celebrated English nurse in the Crimean War.

II: 27   (34)
IV: 277   (383)

NILE RIVER
The longest river in Africa. One of O'Casey's references alludes to the
Irish song, "Banks of the Nile," for which see Appendix I (#).

III: 116#, 205   (168#, 303)
V: 10   (3)

NINEVEH
In ancient geography, an important city which was the capital of the
Assyrian Empire. In the Bible, the residence of Sennacheuh.

II: 88   (131)

NIOBE
From Greek legend, the personification of maternal sorrow.

VI: 71   (94)

NIRVANA
In Buddhism, the final state and highest good to which the Buddhist
aspires.

IV: 192   (262)

NISSE, BERTRAM
Heart specialist on Harley Street, London, who treated O'Casey for
heart pains in the 1930s.

V: 127   (165)

NO IRISH NEED APPLY
Window signs or concluding sentences of employment advertisements that
appeared in England and the U.S. in the 19th and early 20th centuries.
In general, there were economic reasons (competition for jobs, etc.) for
this, but its practice was frequently heightened by anti-Catholicism
or Fenian "outrages." See Curtis's book, Apes and Angels.

I: 75   (108)
IV: 234   (322)

NO NO NUNETTES
Variant on the musical, No No Nanette (1925), by Otto Harbach and Frank
Mandel.

IV: 245   (338)

NO RENT MOVEMENT
The most famous movement of this sort came out of a manifesto (18 October 1881) which called upon tenant farmers to pay no rent to their landlords. The manifesto was signed by Dillon,* Davitt,* and others of the Land League.*

I I I: 105   (192)

NOAH
In the Bible, the patriarch who was ordered to build an ark for all living animals for a new world.

I: 80   (117)
II: 44   (61)
IV: 265, 272   (366, 377)
V: 201   (268)

NOBEL PRIZE
And W. B. Yeats.* For a photo of O'Casey at the dinner honoring Yeats and the prize, see Yeats and the Theatre (rpted. in Sean O'Casey Review, Spring 1978).

V: 66   (81)
VI: 103   (141)

NORA
Leading character in O'Casey's play, The Plough and the Stars. The actresses to whom O'Casey refers was Kathleen O'Regan.

V: 55   (65)

NORMANS
Invaders of Ireland in 1169. Led by Robert Fitzstephens and Maurice de Prendergast, who were accompanied by 600 soldiers.

II: 11, 185   (8, 286)
III: 103   (148)
IV: 70, 166   (88-9, 226)
V: 22, 77, 177   (20, 96, 238)
VI: 111   (154)

NORTH CIRCULAR ROAD
In Dublin, a long road, half-circling the city limits, ending at the eastern border of Phoenix Park. O'Casey's residence (#422), 1921 to April 1926. For a description of his flat, see (#).

I: 81   (118)
IV: 63, 94-5#, 190   (79, 123-4#, 260)

NORTH FREDERICK STREET
In north Dublin, connecting Upper Dorset Street with Parnell Square.

I: 176   (272)

NORTH LOTTS
O'Casey is referring to the Dublin Glass Bottle Company at 46 Sheriff Street, Upper, Castleforbes, North Lotts, almost next door to St. Barnabas' Church.

II: 225   (349)

NORTH WALL
The north bank of the River Liffey, directly opposite Sir John Rogerson's Quay, Dublin.

I: 83   (122)
II: 144, 214   (221, 332)
III: 275   (413)

NORTH WILLIAM STREET DISPENSARY
From the description, O'Casey is referring to the North City Dispensary on Clarence Street, one block south of William Street.

III: 206   (306)

NORTHAMPTONSHIRE
Midland county in central England.

VI: 77   (102)

NORTHCLIFFE PUBLICATIONS
From Vicount Northcliffe, Alfred C. Harmsworth.*

V: 58   (70)

NORTHUMBERLAND
Maritime county in northeast England.

VI: 76   (101)

NORTHUMBRIA
Former kingdom of Great Britain, reaching from the Humber to the Firth of Forth, and from the North Sea to the Celtic Strathclyde.

V: 94   (120)

NOTTING HILL GATE
O'Casey's phrase, "White Horse of the Peppers at Notting Hill Gate," is a pun on several of Chesterton's* books: The Wild Knight (1900), Ballad of the White Horse (1911), and Napoleon of Notting Hill Gate (1905). The "Peppers" is from an Irish legend about the fastest horse in the land, which belonged to a family named Pepper. Their estates were confiscated by William of Orange* after the Battle of the Boyne.* See Samuel Lover's Stories and Legends of Ireland.

III: 185   (273)

NYM, CORPORAL
Filching companion of Falstaff* in Shakespeare's* plays.

V: 23   (20)
VI: 136   (189)

O

O.G.P.U.
Initials of the secret police in the U.S.S.R. From the Russian words,
Obedinennoe Gosudarstvennoe Politicheskoe Upravlenie (United State
Political Administration).

VI: 94-5   (127-9)

O'BAWLOCHONE, ROARY
Variant on O'Casey's character in Red Roses for Me, Roory O'Balacaun,
a zealous Irish-Irelander.* O'Casey uses the words "roar" and "bawl,"
and also the Irish word, ochone, meaning a lament or wail. See also
O'FARREL, AYAMONN.

IV: 66   (83)

O'BRIEN, GEORGE
1892 - 1973. Professor of political economy and national economics,
UCD (1926-61). Appointed by the Irish government (1925) as one of the
Abbey Theatre directors. A vocal opponent of many passages in O'Casey's
play, The Plough and the Stars, including "The Song," Rosie Redmond's
song at the end of Act II. See Letters,I, pp. 144-45.

IV: 280-1   (387-9)

O'BRIEN, WILLIAM
1852 - 1928. Irish journalist and nationalist leader. Appointed by
Parnell* as editor, United Irishman (1881). Arrested and drew up
"No Rent"* manifesto while in jail. M.P. (1883-85). Organized the
United Irish League (1898) and the All for Ireland party (1910).

II: 12   (10)
III: 14, 102   (12, 146)
IV: 273   (378)

O'BRIEN, WILLIAM
1881 - 1968. Irish labor leader. President, Irish Trade Union Congress
(1913, 1918, 1925, 1941). Executive member, general treasurer and general
secretary, Irish Transport and General Workers' Union* (1918-46). Virulent opponent of Larkin.*

IV: 12, 13, 76-7, 282   (5, 6, 97-101, 391)

O'BRIEN, WILLIAM DERMOD
1865 - 1945. Irish artist and president, Royal Hibernian Academy of
Arts (1910-45). Governor and guardian, National Gallery of Ireland.
The drawing to which O'Casey refers was a portrait in oil (#), c.1914.

IV: 167, 212#   (227, 291#)

O'CAHAN, SHAUN
Early Belfast Gaelic Leaguer. Member of the executive board. Published
several articles about teaching and schools in the Gaelic League's
publications.

III: 149   (219)

O'CALLAGHAN, REV. FATHER FRANCIS (ET. AL.)
Probably a representative hypocritical priest. It is possible that
O'Casey had in mind Rev. T. A. O'Callaghan, the bishop of Cork.

III: 145   (212)

O'CASEY, BREON
b.30 April 1918. O'Casey's first child. His portrait painting of the
dramatist appeared as a frontispiece in The Bishop's Bonfire (1955). The
painting was destroyed in a fire at the home of Robert Emmet Ginna (1974).

V: 32, 33-4, 35, 39, 40, 65, 70-1, 125, 126, 133, 139-42, 144, 146-7,
    157, 169, 202, 238
    (33, 35-6, 37, 44, 79, 87, 163, 164, 174, 183-7, 190, 193-4, 208,
    225, 270, 321)

VI: 9, 17, 42, 68-9, 71, 104, 149-51, 156, 160, 175
    (1, 13, 50, 89-91, 94, 142, 208-11, 219, 224, 247)

O'CASEY, EILEEN
b.1903. Married (23 September 1927) at the Church of Our Most Holy
Redeemer and St. Thomas More, Cheyne Row, Chelsea, London. Born in
Ireland but raised in England, Mrs. O'Casey was an actress who appeared
principally in musical comedies. She played the roles of Minnie in
O'Casey's The Shadow of a Gunman, and Nora in The Plough and the Stars.
She also appeared in Noel Coward's* Bitter Sweet, and in a revival of
The Miracle. Author of Sean (1971) and Eileen (1976).

PAN

IV: 194
V: 34, 35, 39-40, 41, 55-6, 61-5, 67, 70, 75, 105, 106, 118-20, 123,
    125-7, 131, 133-6, 139-42, 144-6, 157, 169, 170, 180, 202, 238
VI: 9, 17, 22-5, 30, 33-4, 41-2, 68-9, 71, 84, 85, 86, 123, 125, 130,
    134, 138, 149-51, 156-7, 160, 161-5, 172-3, 175, 180, 182-3, 184-7,
    192, 233

U.S.

IV: 266
V: 36, 37, 44-6, 65-7, 73-8, 82, 86, 93, 136, 138, 153-7, 160-1, 163-6,
    172, 174-9, 183-7, 190-3, 208, 224-5, 227, 239, 270, 321
VI: 1, 13, 20-5, 32-3, 37-9, 49-50, 89-91, 93, 113, 114, 115, 171, 173,
    180, 187, 192-3, 208-10, 219-21, 224-5, 226-33, 243-4, 248, 255,
    260-6, 272, 335

O'CASEY, GIOLLA ODAR
Superior of Downpatrick (Dundalethglas) c.1158. In Reeves (see CASEL-
ANAGAN), O'Casey is listed as being a subscribing witness to the charter
of Newry.

V: 165   (218)

O'CASEY, NIALL
15 January 1935 - 31 December 1956. O'Casey's youngest son. Schooling
at Dartington Hall,* Devon. Two years in the British army (Royal
Artillery). Was studying geology at London University when he died of
leukaemia. See the essay, "Under a Greenwood Tree He Died," Under a
Colored Cap.

V: 33-4, 180, 188, 202, 238   (37-9, 239, 251, 270, 321)
VI: 22, 42, 68-9, 71, 104, 149-51, (20, 50, 89-91, 94, 142, 208-11,
    156, 160, 175   219, 224, 247)

O'CASEY, SHIVAUN
b.28 September 1939, Torbay Hospital, Devon, England. O'Casey's daughter.
Schooling at Dartington Hall,* Devon (until 1955). Married, 12 August
1972; son, Rueben (b.2 May 1968). Actress and teacher.

VI: 71, 123, 125, 149-51, 156, 160, (94, 171, 173, 208-11, 219,
    175, 192, 233   224, 247, 272, 335)

O'CASSIDE, CORIOLANUS
O'Casside is O'Casey's fictional name. "Coriolanus" is an allusion to
Caius Marcius Coriolanus, the hero with excessive pride in his honor,
in Shakespeare's* play, Coriolanus.

V: 12   (5)

O'CONNELL, DANIEL
1775 - 1847. Irish nationalist leader known as "The Liberator."
Founded Catholic Association (1823) for constitutional agitation for
removal of civil and religious disabilities against Catholics. As an
M.P. (1828), he forced the parliament to pass the Catholic Emancipation
Act (1829). O'Connell opposed the poor law and movements against rents,
but he led the action for the repeal of the union (see ACT OF UNION),
and he revived the Catholic Association (1842-44), holding mass rallies
throughout Ireland. Opposed by the Young Ireland organization. In
Dublin, the O'Connell monument is on O'Connell Street near O'Connell
Bridge. It was unveiled during the centenary of the 1782 Volunteers
(15 August 1882).

II: 59   (85)
III: 239-40   (357-8)
IV: 11   (4)
V: 81   (102)

O'CONNELL STREET
The main thoroughfare in Dublin. See also SACKVILLE STREET.

III: 196-7, 223, 272, 276   (291, 331, 332, 407, 409, 414)
IV: 93, 166, 196, 285   (121, 226, 268, 394)
VI: 212   (303)

O'CONNOR, FERGUS
1875 - 1952. Publisher in Dublin of song books, music, Republican and
labor pamphlets. Interned after the Easter Rising. Published O'Casey's
The Sacrifice of Thomas Ashe (1918) and his Songs of the Wren series.

IV: 16-17   (11-12)

O'CONNOR, RORY
1875 - 1922. Irish patriot and soldier. Degrees in art and engineering.
Worked in Canada (1911-15), but returned to fight in the Easter Rising.
Active in the War of Independence, and opposed to the Treaty.* Executed
in Mountjoy Prison* (8 December), along with Liam Mellows,* Joseph
McKelvey, and Richard Barrett, by Free State troops.

III: 244   (365)
IV: 92, 96   (121, 125)

O'CONNOR, RURY
RORY in U.S. edition. Ruraidh O'Conchobhar, the last king of Ireland,
was buried (c.1198) in the monastery of St. Fechin at Cong.* O'Casey
is quoting from the last and first verses, respectively, of T. W. Rolleston's poem, "The Grave of Rury."

V: 173   (230)

O'CONNOR, SEAMUS
Probably James O'Connor (Seamus O'Concubhair), whom O'Casey knew as a
fellow member of the Irish Republican Brotherhood and the Red Hand Hurling League.

III: 164   (242)

O'CONNOR, THOMAS POWER
1848 - 1929. Popularly known as "Tay Pay." Irish journalist, nationalist and politician. Called "Father of the House of Commons" because of
his unbroken service (continuously from 1885). The house which O'Casey
and Lady Gregory* visited was Morpeth Mansions at 5 Victoria Street,
London. According to a Sunday Times article (4 April 1926) by O'Connor,
the visit occurred "one day last week," or about the end of March.(#)

III: 102   (146)
V: 81   (102)
VI: 25-9#, 42   (25-9#, 50)

O'CORMAC
Probably Cormac MacDuilleanain, Irish poet, scholar and warrior. King
and bishop of Cashel (901-08). Slain at Ballghmoon (908).

V: 164   (217)

O'DALY, PATRICK
General secretary of the Gaelic League* in the early 1900s.

III: 25   (29)

O'DAY, BISHOP O'DAWN
Allusion to Bishop Thomas O'Dea.* See also THE DAWNING OF THE DAY,
Appendix I.

III: 141, 142   (207, 208)

O'DEA, JIMMY
1900 - 1965. Popular music hall comedian who used to perform pantomimes
at Christmas at the Gaiety Theatre, Dublin. The appelation O'Casey gives
to O'Dea (impudent) is an allusion to the poem, "Barney O'Hea."*

V: 48   (55)

O'DEA, THOMAS
1858 - 1923. Irish ecclesiastic. Vice-president, Maynooth (1894-1903).
Bishop of Clonfert (1903-09) and Galway, Kilmacdugh and Kilfenora (1909-
23). See also O'DAY, BISHOP O'DAWN.

IV: 241   (333)

O'DONNELL, FRANK HUGH
c.1894 - 1976. Irish playwright and author of Anti-Christ (1925).
O'Casey attended the premiere of the play at the Abbey (see Letters, I,
p. 133).

IV: 180   (245)

O'DONNELL, HUGH ROE
c.1571 - 1602. Lord of Tyrconnell. Commander at the siege of Kinsale
(1601).

I: 24   (25)
III: 105   (151)

O'DONNELL, BISHOP PATRICK
1856 - 1927. Irish ecclesiastic. Archbishop of Armagh and Catholic
prelate for Ireland (1924-27); cardinal (1925). Active in the Irish
Convention (1917-18).

III: 151   (222)
IV: 241   (333)

O'DONNELL, PEADAR
b.1893. Irish writer, socialist and trade union organizer. Active in
the War of Independence and against the pro-Treaty forces (1918-22).
Editor of the literary magazine, The Bell,* (April 1946 - 1954).
According to Freyer's Peadar O'Donnell, O'Casey first met O'Donnell in
1922 at the house of Delia Larkin.*

VI: 184   (260-1)

O'DRISCOLL
Probably from the poem, "Finneen O'Driscoll the Rover," by Robert Dwyer
Joyce (1830 - 1883). In the poem, O'Driscoll is a bold sailor "by
Cleena's green land" who repels "the Saxons of Cork and Moyallo" and
"the men of Clan London."

III: 105   (151)

O'DUFFY, BERNARD
d.31 March 1952. Irish dramatist. His one-act play, "The Coiner,"
appeared with the London premiere of O'Casey's play, The Shadow of a
Gunman (1927).

Special Pleading (one-act farce)   IV: 74   (94)

O'FAOLAIN, SEAN
b.1900. Major Irish novelist and short-story writer. Active with the
anti-Treaty forces during the Civil War (1922). O'Faolain's comments
on The Silver Tassie were published in the Irish Statesman (19 October
1929) (#).

V: 104-05#   (135-6#)
VI: 120   (167)

O'FARACHAIN, ROIBEARD
b.1909. In English, Robert Farran. Irish poet and man of letters.
Director, Abbey Theatre (from 1940). His works include both Irish and
English poetry and criticism.

VI: 208   (298)

O'FARREL, AYAMONN
Streetcar conductor in Dublin whose sympathies with Republicanism made
a deep impression on O'Casey. Finds expression in O'Casey's play,
Red Roses for Me, as the character "Roory O'Balachone", as does their
conversation regarding John Ruskin* (#).

II: 189-205#   (293-319#)
III: 120-1, 128, 224   (175-7, 186, 334)
IV: 66, 86-7, 120   (83, 111-13, 159-60)

O'FARREL, SEAN
From the first line of the Irish song, "The Rising of the Moon."

III: 103, 105   (149, 151)

O'FLAHERTY, LIAM
b.1897. Irish novelist and short-story writer. Active with the anti-
Treaty forces during the Civil War (1922). O'Flaherty's comments on
The Plough and the Stars appeared in a letter to the editor, Irish
Statesman, 20 February 1926 (#).

IV: 127, 128#, 173-4, 181#   (169, 170-1#, 236, 247#)

O'FLANAGAN, FATHER MICHAEL
1876 - 1942. Irish Republican priest. Called by Cathal Brugha* "the
staunchest priest who ever lived in Ireland." O'Casey's reference is to
O'Flanagan's actions in Sligo in 1914, when he was involved in agitation
for tenants' rights. O'Flanagan actively compaigned for the Spanish
Republicans during the Spanish Civil War.* O'Casey partially dedicated
his play, The Drums of Father Ned, to O'Flanagan.

IV: 115-17   (153-5)

O'FRIELS, LAD OF THE
Seumas MacManus' (1861 - 1960) play, <u>A Lad of the O'Friels</u> (1903).

III: 133   (195)

O'GRADY, BAGENAL
Character in Boucicault's* play, <u>Arrah-na-Pogue</u>.

II: 135   (207)

O'GRADY, STANDISH HAYES
1832 - 1915. Irish author, scholar and one of the pioneers of the Celtic
renaissance. Author of several histories and translations. O'Casey
alludes to O'Grady's father, Admiral Hayes O'Grady (1787 - 1864), brother
of Viscount Guillamore.

III: 149   (219)

O'GROWNEY, FATHER EUGENE
1863 - 1899. Professor of Irish at Maynooth (1891) and one of the
founders of the Gaelic League.* Reburied in Maynooth (1902).

III: 140-2   (205-09)
<u>Simple Lessons in Irish</u>   II: 159   (244)

O'HALLORAN
Appears as a childhood acquaintance of O'Casey.

I: 87, 135-40   (128, 206-14)

O'HANLON, DR.
O'Casey errs by indicating that O'Hanlon's notes on canon law was a book.
These notes were given to MacDonald* after O'Hanlon's death.

IV: 237   (327)

O'HANRAHAN, RED
Red Hanrahan, central figure in Yeats's* <u>Stories of Red Hanrahan</u> (1914),
an Irish poet and head schoolmaster in love with Mary Lavell.

IV: 143, 269   (194, 372)

O'HARA, MICKEY
Most Rev. Gerald Patrick O'Hara, papal nuncio to Ireland. O'Hara, an
American, was archbishop of Atlanta-Savannah, Georgia. He served as
papal diplomat in Rumania, and began his service in Dublin in March, 1952.
O'Hara was the center of what was known as the "Papal Nuncio Incident."
His reaction to a remark by Hubert Butler* set off a storm of controversy
which involved several notable Irish figures. See INTERNATIONAL AFFAIRS
ASSOCIATION.

VI: 210   (300)

O'HEA, IMPUDENT BARNEY
From the song, "Barney O'Hea," by Samuel Lover (1797 - 1868). O'Casey
is using a recurring line, as for instance the last lines of the first
verse:

> Impudent Barney
> None of your blarney
> Impudent Barney O'Hea.

In O'Casey's play, Time to Go, Barney O'Hay is a farmer-owner of five
acres. See also O'DEA, JIMMY.

III: 120   (174)

O'HICKEY, DR. MICHAEL
1861 - 1916. Irish scholar who was prominent in the Gaelic League.
Professor of Irish (from 1896), Maynooth. O'Hickey was deeply involved
in a controversy with the Irish Catholic hierarchy over "compulsory
Irish." The controversy grew so heated that he was dismissed from his
chair at Maynooth by Archbishop Mannix.* O'Casey dedicated Drums under
the Windows to O'Hickey.

III: 31-2, 39, 41, 66, 96, 115,   (39-40, 51, 54, 92, 138, 166,
131-42, 143   191-210)
IV: 233, 245, 249, 260, 267   (322, 338, 345, 359, 369)
VI: 166   (234)
Irish in the New University. . . Or Else (1909) III: 12, 31, 131
                                       (9, 39, 191, 192)

O'HIGGINS
See HIGGINS, FREDERICK ROBERT.

O'HOGAN, GALLOPING
Galloping Hogan, a famous 17th-century Irish rapparee who allegedly led
Sarsfield* to Ballyneety before the battle of Limerick.* The horse from
which Hogan derived his nickname was captured in Co. Kilkenny by the
Williamites. Hogan, however, did not surrender until the end of the war,
and then only on the condition of amnesty. General Ginkel* set Hogan to
work capturing other rapparees, but Hogan was killed in one such venture.
His former comrades gave him a soldier's funeral in recognition of past
deeds. "Galloping Hogan" is the name of a song by Percy French.

II: 236   (367)

O'KANE, ROARING
Hanna "Roaring" O'Kane, an early supporter and enthusiast of the Gaelic
League.

III: 225   (336)

O'KELLY, SEAN T.
1883 - 1966. Irish politician. One of the founders of Sinn Fein,* and
speaker of the first Dail (1919-21). President, Irish Free State (Republic after 1949), 1945-59.

III: 107, 133   (154, 194)
IV: 80-1, 154   (103-05, 214)
V: 213   (285)

O'LEARY, REV. CANON PETER
1839 - 1918. Irish scholar and vice-president of the Gaelic League.
In his time, he was described as "the greatest living master of Irish
prose." Translated into Irish the Bible, Aesop's fables, and other works.

III: 114   (166)

O'LOUGHLIN
See McLOUGHLIN.

V: 165   (219)

O'LOUGHLIN, KEVIN
Given as a Dublin civil servant and member of the O'Toole Gaelic Club
who introduced O'Casey to the writings of Shaw.*

III: 170-2   (251-3)

O'MAILLE, PATRICK
Irish member of the Dail. Wounded (1922) during the assassination of
Sean Hales.* As a reprisal, Free State troops executed four well-known
Republican prisoners. See O'CONNOR, RORY.

IV: 95   (125)

O'MALLEY, CHARLES
From the popular Irish novel (1841) of the same name by Charles Lever
(1806 - 1872). For more Lever, see LORREQUER, HARRY.

III: 133   (195)

O'MALLEY, FATHER/BENEDICT, SISTER
Characters in the film, The Bells of St. Mary, with Bing Crosby and
Barry Fitzgerald.

V: 150   (219)

O'MURACHADHA, DONAL/DONAL MacRORY/DONAL MURACHOO
These may or may not all be the same person. Their names are similar,
and they are referred to as a "boy from Tourmakeady." They all appear in
meetings or in conversations, and they may be catalysts for O'Casey's
philosophizing.

III: 114-15, 124, 126-30, 153-4,   (165-6,181, 184-90, 225-6,
     156-9   230-4)
IV: 195-215   (268-96)
VI: 105-12   (145-54)

O'MURRIES, PRINCE OF THE
Unknown.

II: 186   (288)

O'NEILL
The O'Neill family in Ireland traces its ancestry back to Niall, king of Ireland (3rd century). Their traditional base of power has been Co. Tyrone, and several of them have been prominent in the struggles for Irish independence, including Con O'Neill (1484 - 1589), Shane O'Neill (1530 - 1567), Hugh O'Neill (1540 - 1616), and Owen Roe O'Neill (1590 - 1649).

IV: 273   (378)

O'NEILL, ARTE
Arte O'Neal, a female character in Boucicault's* play, The Shaughraun.

II: 139, 140-1   (214, 215-16)

O'NEILL, EUGENE
1888 - 1953. American dramatist. Awarded Pulitzer Prize for drama (1920, 1922, 1928) and Nobel Prize for literature (1936). Greatly admired by O'Casey.

V: 239   (321)

O'NUALLAIN, PEADAR
Appears as an associate of O'Casey in the Gaelic League.

III: 66   (92)

O'PHELAN, HEAD OF THE
O'Phelan was prince of Desies (now Waterford), and one of Brian Boru's* opponents at the battle of Clontarf.*

II: 186-7   (288)

O'RAHAILLE
More properly, Aodhagan O'Rathaille. 1670 - c.1728. Irish poet famous for his laments and for his satires on the planter class of landowners.

III: 114   (166)

O'RAHILLY, THOMAS FRANCIS
1882 - 1953. Irish scholar. Professor of Irish, Trinity (1919-29); director of Celtic Studies, Dublin Institute of Higher Studies (1942-53). One of O'Casey's references (#) alludes to O'Rahilly's book, The Two Patricks (1942).

III: 202#   (298-9)
Early Irish History and Mythology (1946)   VI: 75   (100)

O'REILLY
Appears as a fellow worker with O'Casey at Leedom, Hampton chandler company, Dublin.

II: 75-6, 79-80   (110-13, 118-20)

O'REILLY, FATHER
This may be Father John O'Reilly, one of the curates at The Presbytery,
Marlborough Street, Dublin (the only such O'Reilly listed in Thoms, 1907).

III: 141   (207)
IV: 284   (393)

O'REILLY, NORA
Nora Reilly, "the only heiress of Rosscullen" in Shaw's* play, John
Bull's Other Island.

III: 175   (258)

O'RYAN, W. P.
See RYAN, WILLIAM PATRICK.

O'SHEA, KATHERINE
1845 - 1921. Wife of Captain William Henry O'Shea (1840 - 1905) who
had an affair with Parnell.* After Captain O'Shea made the matter public
by instituting divorce proceedings, Parnell's enemies used the opportunity to discredit him, causing his downfall. Parnell married her shortly
before his death.

I: 58-9   (81)
II: 10, 12, 58-9   (5, 9, 84-5)
V: 204   (273)

O'SHEA, PADDY
Early Gaelic Leaguer and writer.

III: 149   (219)

O'TOOLE GAELIC CLUB
The St. Laurence O'Toole Club, Dublin, of which O'Casey was a member.
Some of O'Casey's earliest songs were written for and sung at their
weekly meetings. His play, The Frost and the Flower, was a satire on
some of the leading members of the club.

III: 170-1   (251)
IV: 83, 229   (107, 315)

OFFALY, CHIEF OF
Unknown.

II: 186   (288)

OISIN
One of the famous warriors of the Fianna.* Perhaps the best known story
about him is the "Dialogue Between Oisin and Patrick," describing his
return from the Otherworld to Ireland, his meeting with St. Patrick,*
his sojourn with the monks, and the long discussion around paganism
and Christianity.

II: 13   (11)
IV: 103   (136)

OLD BAILEY
The famous law court on Fleet Street, London. For the context of the
first reference (#), see Appendix II.

V: 9#   (1#)
VI: 191   (271)

OLD LADIES, THE
Play adopted by Rodney Ackland from Hugh Walpole's novel.

V: 20   (17)

OLD PARLIAMENT HOUSE
See BANK OF IRELAND.

III: 175   (258)

OLD SARUM
About two miles from Salisbury, England. Site of an ancient Celtic
fortress which, later, was a Roman fortress.

V: 187   (249)

OLD VIC
Well known London theatre, located on Waterloo Road. For many years,
it was managed by Lilian Bayliss.*

V: 129-30   (168-70)

OLD WOMAN OF BEARE, THE
In Irish legend, Caillech of Beare, subject of a 10th-century anonymous
poem which tells of an old woman who had 50 foster-children and seven
periods of youth. Every man with whom she lived died of old age, though
she lived and produced grandsons and great-grandsons who became tribes
and races. The poem has been the subject of several notable translations.

III: 203, 213   (301, 315)

OLDBRIDGE
Agricultural village in Co. Meath. Site of the Battle of the Boyne.*

II: 232   (360)

OLDCASTLE
Irish town in Co. Meath.

III: 154   (226)

OLIVER, JOHN PETER
This is a noted Dublin sculptor, but it is out of place in its context.
O'Casey is quoting from MacDonald's* book, Reminiscences of a Maynooth
Professor (p. 401). Both MacDonald and O'Casey are probably referring
to Peter John Olivi (1248 - 1298), a noted medieval Franciscan philoso-
pher and theologian.

IV: 228   (314)

OLYMPIA
Formerly the Empire Theatre, Dublin. O'Casey acted there in the St.
Laurence O'Toole dramatic club's premiere of Thomas K. Moylan's play,
Naboclish (25 November 1917).

IV: 14   (8)

OMAR KHAYYAM
Fl. c.1123. Persian poet. Best known for his Rubaiyat (#), a collection
of quatrains with rhyming first, second and fourth lines.

IV: 220#, 222   (303#, 306)
V: 86   (110)

ONE BIG UNION/O.B.U.
The slogan and tactics of various revolutionary syndicalist groups during
the late 19th and early 20th centuries, including the Industrial Workers
of the World. The theory was that if workers in a nation and of the
world were organized into revolutionary unions, they would be closer to
the day when the world would be one big union, ruled by governmental
units of individual unions.

IV: 77, 78   (99, 100)

OPHELIA
Daughter of Polonius in Shakespeare's* play, Hamlet.

III: 38-9   (49-50)

ORANGE LODGES/ORANGE ORDER/ORANGEMEN
The Orange Order is an anti-Catholic organization which was founded
(1795) to "maintain the Protestant Constitution, and to defend the King
and his heirs as long as they maintain the Protestant ascendancy."
Formed after the Battle of the Diamond,* the name commemorates William
III (of Orange).* Its power through the years has been pervasive and
often blatant, especially in the north of Ireland. In Dublin, the Grand
Orange Lodge was at 10 Rutland (Parnell) Square, a short distance from
the Gaelic League (Thoms, 1896).

I: 176-7   (272-3)
II: 27, 189, 227, 230, 237-9 (34, 293, 352, 353, 357, 368-72)
III: 15, 145, 174, 225, 229   (13, 213, 257, 335, 341)
V: 89, 164   (113, 216)

ORANGE SASH/GREEN SASH
The orange sash is the most notably sash in Ireland, being an identification of the Orange Order.* O'Casey is using the "green sash" as a symbol
of narrow Irish nationalism.

IV: 160   (217)

ORDER OF THE BANNED BOOKS
See BLACK AND WHITE ASSEMBLY OF CENSORIANS.

IV: 92   (120)

ORDER OF THE BLACK PEELER AND THE GREEN GOAT
See THE PEELER AND THE GOAT, Appendix I.

IV: 92   (120)

ORDER OF THE GOLDEN EGG
From the Greek fable of a man who killed the goose to get the imagined
supply of golden eggs.

II: 89   (133)
III: 38   (48)

ORDER OF KNIGHT COMMENDATORE OF ST. GREGORY OR ST. SILVESTER
The Order of St. Gregory The Great is a pontifical order of knighthood
granted for loyal services to the papacy (four classes in 1831, three
classes from 1834). There are two papal orders dealing with St. Silvester: the Order of the Golden Spur or Milizia Aurata of St. Silvester was
a reconstitution (1841) of the medieval Knights of the Golden Spur; and
the Order of St. Silvester, which came into being as a separate entity
(1905).

III: 241   (360)

ORDER OF KNIGHTS HOSPITALLERS OF THE CLEAN SWEEP
See CONFRATERNITY OF TRUE MALTATERNIANS and HOSPITALS SWEEPS.

IV: 92   (120)

ORDERS OF LAURESTINIANS
Probably having to do with St. Laurence O'Toole.* In Joyce's* Finnegans
Wake, O'Toole doubles with Laurens.

III: 152   (224)

ORDER OF THE LITTLE GREYHOUND IN THE WEST
The "Greyhound" probably comes from AE's* poem, "The Voice of the
Waters," the first lines of which read: "Where the Greyhound River
windeth/Through a loneliness so deep." The "little greyhound in the
west" is a variant on the song," Little Grey Home in the West," for
which see Appendix I. For similar lines, see the following: II: 235
(366), III: 12 (9), and V: 66 (81).

IV: 92   (120)

ORDER OF MACHA'S BROOCH . . . ARMAGH'S RED HAT
See TAHRAHRAH BROOCH and EMAIN MACHA. Armagh is the ecclesiastical
capital of Ireland. The red hat is a symbol of that authority.

VI: 92   (120)

ORDER OF THE OLD TURF FIRE
See OLD TURF FIRE, THE, Appendix I.

IV: 92   (120)

ORDER OF ST. PATRICK
See KNIGHTS OF ST. PATRICK.

I: 22, .164   (22, 253)
III: 37, 38   (48, 49)

ORIEL, KINGS OF
Unknown.

V: 164, 165   (218, 219)

ORPEN, SIR WILLIAM
1878 - 1931. Irish painter. Appointed official artist by the British
government during World War I. He also did several sketch drawings of
the action surrounding the 1913 Strike, and was influential in the
Metropolitan School of Art.*

III: 190, 211, 212   (281, 314)
IV: 186, 199   (254, 273)

ORWELL, GEORGE
1903 - 1950. Pseudonym of Eric Blair. Author of several notable novels
about authoritarian conditions. The review of Drums under the Windows
to which O'Casey is reacting was written for the Observer (28 October
1945).

VI: 99-110   (135-152)
A Clergyman's Daughter (1935)   VI: 105 (145)
Nineteen Eighty-four (1949)   VI: 100 (137)
Animal Farm (1946)   VI: 102 (139)

OSCAR
Legendary Irish hero in the Finn cycle. Finn's* grandson and one of the
fiercest fighters in the Fianna.*

II: 219   (340)
III: 102, 246   (147, 368)
IV: 103   (136)
V: 173   (230)

OULTON, DR. HENRY J.
Physician at the North City Dispensary District, #1 Dispensary West,
Langrishe Place (Thoms, 1888). Also a medical consultant for the Dublin
Metropolitan Police (Thoms, 1909).

IV: 285   (394)

OVERSTRAND MANSIONS
Group of houses along Prince of Wales Drive, Battersea, London. After
leaving here (#49), O'Casey got into some trouble with a dispute over
a broken lease. See Letters, I, pp. 812-13.

VI: 10-11   (3-4)

OVID
43 B.C. - 17 A.D. Roman poet.

VI: 200   (285)

OXFORD
Town (#) and university in Oxford, England. See also BOAR'S HILL.

III: 143, 156, 157   (210, 230)
V: 13, 118-19#, 181   (7-8, 154#, 240)
VI: 47, 48, 53, 201   (58, 59, 66, 286)

OXFORD CIRCUS
At Oxford and Regent streets in London, one of the busiest bus and
underground centers.

V: 166   (220)

P

PADUA
One of the famous hill towns of Italy. See also ST. ANTHONY.

IV: 221   (304)

PAINE, THOMAS
1737 - 1809. American revolutionary agitator, propagandist and patriot.
Ardent supporter of the French and other revolutions.

The Rights of Man (1791-92) III: 229   (340-1)

PALESTINE
I: 137   (208)

PALESTRINA
Also PALACESTRINA. From Giovanni Palestrina (c.1526 - 1594), Italian
composer of liturgical music. Edward Martyn* left money in his will to
establish a Palestrina choir in Dublin's Pro-Cathedral.

III: 153   (224)
IV: 134   (179)

PALMERSTON PARK
In south Dublin, between Rathgar and Milltown.

II: 67   (98)

PALMIERI, FATHER DOMENICO
1829 - 1909. Jesuit philosopher who alienated Leo XIII by asserting
that hylomorphis was incompatible with the findings of natural science.

IV: 228   (314)

PANSY, PETER
From J. M. Barrie's (1860 - 1937) fantasy, Peter Pan (1904). O'Casey
is comparing the uses of Irish folklore by Lady Gregory* and Yeats.*
See Hazard Adams's Lady Gregory, pp. 89-90.

IV: 133   (178)

PAOLO AND FRANCESCA
Drama (1899) by Stephen Phillips (1868 - 1915), English poet and playwright.

V: 204   (273)

PAPAL STATES
Former realm in Italy governed directly by the papacy. Annexed to
Italy (1860-70).

IV: 243   (335)

PARIS
The siege of Paris was the Paris Commune of 1871 (March-May), which put
the city in the hands of communists. The Commune was defeated by
Versailles troops after weeks of bloody and bitter resistance (#).

III: 269#   (403#)
V: 94   (120)

PARK GATE
One of the gate entrances to Phoenix Park,* Dublin.

I: 156   (240)

PARK LANE
In London, overlooking the eastern side of Hyde Park. It is one of the
most famous London streets, having a long line of mansions, including
Londonderry House (#24).

VI: 11   (3)

PARK MAGAZINE HILL
Magazine Fort in Phoenix Park, Dublin, which Swift* characterized as:

                Behold a proof of Irish sense,
                Here Irish wit is seen,
                When nothing's left that's worth defence,
                We build a magazine.

III: 276   (415)

PARK MURDERS
See INVINCIBLES.

I: 75   (108)

PARK ROAD
The main road in Phoenix Park, Dublin.

III: 131   (192)

PARKGATE STREET
In central Dublin, north of the River Liffey.

II: 54   (78)

PARLIAMENT HOUSE
The Old Parliament House* in College Green, Dublin, where the Irish
parliament sat. See BANK OF IRELAND and IRISH HOUSE OF PARLIAMENT.

IV: 96   (126)
V: 76   (95)

PARLIAMENT STREET
In central Dublin, immediately south of the River Liffey. Where the
Grattan Bridge ends.

II: 202, 215   (313, 334)
III: 45   (60)

PARNELL, CHARLES STEWART
1846 - 1891. Irish nationalist politician and leader of the Irish
Parliamentary Party. As a member of parliament, he united the differing
Irish organizations into the Land League.* Imprisoned (1881) for
allegedly obstructing the new land act. From prison, he directed the
tenants to pay no rent as retaliation for the outlawing of the Land
League. Released under the terms of the Kilmainham Treaty.* Ruined by
allegations of adultery with Katherine O'Shea. See also:

                CONGRESS   MEATH, BISHOP OF
                HEALY, TIMOTHY   PLAN OF CAMPAIGN
                IRISH PARLIAMENTARY PARTY WESTLAND ROW STATION

I: 15-16, 21, 58-9, 74-6, 86-7, 174, 179-80
     (11-12, 20, 81-3, 107-08, 128, 268, 276-7)

II: 9-19, 28, 30-1, 33-4, 38, 56-9, 64, 196, 198
     (4-21, 35, 38-9, 43-5, 51, 81-5, 92, 302, 306)

III: 14, 19, 32, 75, 105, 128, 153, 187
     (12, 19, 39, 105, 186, 210, 225, 276)

IV: 113, 150-1, 158-9, 176, 183, 240-1, 245, 248, 249, 264, 273, 285
     (150, 203-04, 214-16, 240, 249, 331-3, 338, 343, 344, 378, 395)

V: 50, 85, 167, 204   (58, 107, 221, 273)
VI: 27, 28, 207   (28, 29, 154, 296)

PARNELL, FANNY
Frances Isabel Parnell. 1854 - 1882. Sister of Charles Stewart Parnell.*
Active in the Irish nationalist movement. Moved to the United States
where she wrote patriotic songs under the title, "Land League Songs."

I: 75   (109)
IV: 158   (214)

PARNELL SQUARE
In central Dublin, at the northern end of O'Connell Street. Formerly
Rutland Square.*

VI: 173   (244)

PARTRANE MADHOUSE
The Portrane Mental Hospital, on the peninsula of Portrane, Co. Dublin.

III: 50   (68)

PATRIDGE, WILLIAM
d.1917. Labor councilman for Kilmainham and president of the Dublin
Trades Council. Vice-chairman, Irish Citizen Army, and active in the
Easter Rising. Sent by Connolly* to organize members of the Tralee
Transport Union to transport the expected arms shipment from Germany to
Ireland shortly before the Rising (see CASEMENT, ROGER). Sentenced to
15 years after the Rising, but illness forced his early release in 1917.

III: 245-6   (367)

PASSFIELD CORNER
In Co. Surrey, England, the home of Sidney and Beatrice Webb.*

V: 40-1   (45-6)

PASTEUR, LOUIS
1822 - 1895. French chemist who pioneered studies in modern medicine.

IV: 277   (383)

PATMOS
Island of the Dodecanese in the Greek region of Calymnos. Site of a
monastery bearing the name of St. John the Divine, and a cave where,
according to legend, the apostle saw the visions of the apocalypse.

V: 73   (91)

PATON, REV. DAVID MacDONALD
b.1913. Clergyman. The lecture referred to by O'Casey was revised and
printed in Christian Missions and the Judgement of God (1953). Paton's
lecture was critical of the alliance between the churches and Third-
World capitalism.

VI: 130   (180)

PATRICK STREET
In the Coombe area of Dublin, east of St. Patrick's Park.

V: 76   (95)

PATTI, ADELINA
1843 - 1919. One of the most popular singers of her time. Her reper-
toire contained between 30 and 40 parts, including her famous "Home Sweet
Home."

V: 197   (263)

PAVELIC, ANTE
1889 - 1959. Croation fascist leader, noted as the head of the Ustasi,
an organization implicated in the assassination (1934) of Alexander I
of Yugoslavia, and as the Quisling of the Croat state under Axis
occupation (1941-44).

VI: 210   (300

PEACHUM, POLLY
Heroine of John Gay's (1685 - 1732) The Beggar's Opera (1728).

IV: 185   (253)

PEARSE, PADRAIC
1879 - 1916. Irish nationalist, leader, educator and author. Founder,
St. Enda's School,* and president of the declared Irish Republic during
the Easter Rising. One of the most revered men in Irish history.

III:	as Padruig MacPirais	111	(161)
	and Synge*	145	(213)
	as editor,	162	(238)
	as exception	235	(351)
	as educator	235-6, 241	(351-2, 360)
	and Jones Rd. festival	236-7, 240-1	(352-5, 360)
	O'Casey's tribute to	241-2	(360-1)
	and visions of	111, 244	(161, 365)
	and capitalism	268-9	(403)
	and Easter Rising	272, 283	(408, 425-6)
		IV: 157, 285	(IV: 213, 394)
	and death of	287	(430)

PECCHI, CARDINAL JOSEPH
Giacchine Pecchi (1810 - 1903) who, as Pope Leo XIII (from 1878), issued
the famous Rerum Novarum.*

IV: 248   (342)

PEEP OF DAY BOYS
Probably the play, Peep o' Day, by Edmund Falconer (1814 - 1879), which
opened in London in 1861. See "Peep o' Day at the Queen's," in Towards
a National Theatre.

IV: 184   (251)

PEG O ' MY HEART
Popular sentimental Irish novel (1913) by J. Hartley Manners.

III: 156   (229)
IV: 194   (265)

PEGASUS/POOKA
In Greek mythology, Pegasus is the winged horse which sprang from the
blood of Medusa when she was slain by Perseus. Pooka, in Irish mythology,
is a horse who awaits travelers in desolate places, rises between their
legs, and tosses them into the mud. Puck in Shakespeare's* play, A Mid-
summer Night's Dream.

V: 26   (25)

PEGEEN MIKE
Character in Synge's* play, The Playboy of the Western World.

III: 235   (350)

PEMBROKE COLLEGE
Constituent college of Cambridge University.

VI: 50   (63)

PEMBROKE PARK
In Ballsbridge, south of Dublin.

III: 156   (229)

PENAL DAYS
Those of 18th-century Ireland (to c.1770) when a new series of penal
laws were passed by England, directed primarily against Irish Catholics
and severely restricting their civil and religious rights. Lord Chancellor Bowes epitomized the spirit of the laws by writing: "the law does
not suppose any such person to exist as an Irish Roman Catholic."

III: 105   (152)

PENN, WILLIAM
1644 - 1718. Quaker founder (1682) of Pennsylvania.

II: 88   (131)
V: 147   (194)

PENNSYLVANIA
III: 113   (164)
V: 121, 208-12, 238   (157, 278-84, 320)
VI: 41   (49)

PEPPERS, WHITE HORSE OF THE
See NOTTING HILL GATE.

III: 185   (273)

PEPYS, SAMUEL
1633 - 1703. Author of a unique diary (written 1 January 1660 to 31 May 1699) portraying conduct in the naval administration, the ways of court, of everyday life, and a critical self-portrait. Portrayed in J. B. Fagan's* play, And So to Bed.

V: 26-7, 60   (26, 72)
VI: 164   (231)

PERSEUS
In Greek mythology, the son of Danae by Zeus. See also PEGASUS.

II: 110   (167)

PETER THE GREAT
Peter I. 1672 - 1725. Russian ruler (from 1682). O'Casey's reference is to Peter's world travels (1696-97), during which he visited London.

VI: 164   (231)

PETER THE PACKER
Lord Peter O'Brien. 1842 - 1914. Crown counsel and lord chief justice of Ireland. Noted for his hostility towards Irish nationalism, and for his adeptness at packing juries in such trials (hence, his name).

II: 196   (302)

PETER THE PLOUGHMAN
Variant on William Langland's (c.1332 - 1400) The Vision of Piers Plowman.

V: 189-90   (252)

PETERHOUSE COLLEGE
Also as PATTERHOUSE. Constituent college of Cambridge University.

III: 248   (371)
VI: 50   (63)

PETRARCH, FRANCESCO
1304 - 1374. Italian poet, poet laureate, Rome (1341). Minor ecclesiastic (1326).

V: 194   (258-9)

PETROGRAD
Former name of Leningrad.*

IV: 231   (318)

PETRUSHKA
Stock character in the Russian commedia (cf. Punch in England).

IV: 126   (168)

PHIBSBORO CHURCH
All Saints vicarage, Grangegorman parish church, 30 Phibsboro Road.

IV: 63   (79)

PHILADELPHIA
See also I'M OFF TO PHILADELPHIA IN THE MORNING, Appendix I.

V: 121, 169, 222, 230, 235   (157, 224, 298, 309, 315)

PHILIPPINES
Pacific Ocean islands.

VI: 142   (198)

PHILLIPSON AND SON
Bath and lamp manufacturers, 29-30 Stafford Street, Dublin.

II: 78   (116)

PHOENIX PARK
Large public park in Dublin of about 1760 acres. For many years, the
residence of the lord lieutenant. Its main entrances are the North
Circular Road gate and at Parkgate Street.

I: 9, 75, 117   (1, 108, 177)
II: 170   (261)
IV: 58   (71)
VI: 77   (103)

PICARDY
French region which saw three major battles (1914, 1918) during World
War I. See ROSES FROM PICARDY, Appendix I.

V: 197   (263)

PICASSO, PABLO
1881 - 1974. Spanish impressionist painter and founder of cubism.
See also GUERNICA.

IV: 186, 206   (254, 283)

PICCADILLY
Famous London street, running from Piccadilly Circus to Hyde Park.

VI: 143   (199)

PICKWICK
From Charles Dickens'* Pickwick Papers (1836).

VI: 136   (189)

PIGEON HOUSE FORT
Power plant in Dublin Bay. Dubliners regarded it as a less than reliable
and often erratic source of electricity.

II: 155   (238)

PIKE
Appears as a Dublin socialist.

III: 20   (21)

PIKEMEN OF NINETY-EIGHT
Allusion to the favorite (and only) weapon of Irish insurgents in the
rebellion of 1798. See also MEN OF NINETY-EIGHT.

IV: 70   (88)

PILATE, PONTIUS
Prosecutor and condemner of Jesus.

IV: 128   (171)
VI: 96   (132)

PILGRIMS
Founders of Plymouth Colony (1620).

V: 180   (239)

PINERO, ARTHUR WING
1855 - 1934. English dramatist and critic.

V: 23-5   (21-4)
The Notorious Mrs. Ebbsmith (1895)   VI: 189   (269)

PIPPA
From Robert Browning's* Pippa Passes (1841)

III: 169   (249-50)
IV: 82   (105)

PIRANDELLO, LUIGI
1867 - 1936. Italian novelist and dramatist.

Right You Are (If You Think So) (1918)   IV: 125   (167)

PISTOL
A bully, swaggerer and companion of Falstaff* in Shakespeare's* plays.

VI: 136, 216   (189, 309)

PIZARRO, FRANCISCO
c.1470 - 1541. Spanish conqueror of Peru who was noted for his brutality
toward the Incas.

III: 89   (127)

PLAN OF CAMPAIGN
First published in United Ireland (October 1886). More a campaign of
Parnell's* lieutenants than of Parnell. It was a method of collective
bargaining on individual estates. If a landlord refused to lower his
demands, the tenants combined to offer him lower rents. If he still
                                                          MORE

PLAN OF CAMPAIGN (cont.)

refused this offer, the tenants paid no rents at all. Instead, they
contributed a like amount of money to the "estate fund." This fund was
used for the maintenance and protection of tenants who were certain to
be evicted for their actions. When the funds were depleted, the
resources of the Land League were used. The campaign lasted from October,
1886, to December, 1890.

II: 38   (51)
IV: 241   (333)

PLANTAGENETS, TUDORS, GEORGES
Plantagenet is an English surname historically connected with the royal
house of Anjou.* Tudors were the English house occupying the throne
(1485-1603), founded by Owen Tudor (d.1461). The Georges were the names
of six kings of Great Britain, four from the house of Hanover and two
from the house of Windsor, formerly Saxe-Coburg-Gotha.*

VI: 205   (292)

PLATO
c.427 - 347 B.C. The celebrated Greek philosopher.

III: 203   (301)
IV: 216, 269   (297, 372)

PLAUTUS
c.254 - 184 B.C. Roman playwright.

VI: 177   (251)

PLEIADES
In classical mythology, the seven sisters of Atlas and Pleione, sisters
of the Hyades. Transformed into the constellation Taurus.

I: 26   (24)
III: 203, 204   (301, 302)

PLOTINUS
c.205 - 270. Roman philosopher.

IV: 216   (297)

PLOUGH AND THE STARS (flag)
Flag of the Irish Citizen Army, first mentioned in the April 1914 issue
of the Irish Worker as the work of "Mr. Megahy" (probably the person
carrying it). The design is of a large plough with a sword at its end,
and the stars of the Big Dipper constellation along the plough. The
original design of the flag is in the National Museum of Ireland with a
tag indicating that it was given to the museum by O'Casey.

III: 230   (342-3)

PLUNKETT, GOERGE NOBLE
1851 - 1948. Irish poet and writer on art and literature. Vice-president, Royal Irish Academy (1907-08, 1911-14), and active in the Irish
language and literary movements. The "Count" title comes from a
hereditary papal designation (Order of the Holy Sepulchre). See also
KNIGHT OF THE ROMAN SLUMPIRE.

III: 244   (364)
IV: 10, 79-80   (2, 3, 102-03)

PLUNKETT, HORACE
1854 - 1932. Irish political leader and agricultural reformer. M.P.
(1892 - 1900); commissioner of congested district board in Ireland
(1891-1918); presiding officer, Irish Convention (1917-18); senator,
Irish Free State (1922-23). The book to which O'Casey refers (#) is
Plunkett's Ireland in the New Century (1904). The Plunkett House (##)
was at 84 Merrion Square, Dublin, the headquarters of the Irish Agricultural Society.*

IV: 206, 210##, 235#   (282, 288##, 324#)

PLUNKETT, JOSEPH MARY
1887 - 1916. Revolutionary Irish poet and signatory to the Irish Proclamation. Prominent member of the Irish Volunteers,* and architect
of the military plans for the Easter Rising. Co-founder, Irish Theatre
(1914). Executed 4 May. Son of George Plunkett.*

III: 234   (350)

PLUTARCH
c.46 - c.120. Greek biographer celebrated for his studies of distinguished Romans and Greeks in pairs.

Parallel Lives   II: 122   (187)

PLYMOUTH
County borough and city in Devon, England. Important maritime center
and naval station with an extensive shipbuilding industry. Heavily
damaged in World War II, especially in 1941. The "Plymouth Road" (#)
is the major Devon route from Torquay through Totnes to Plymouth.

V: 199#, 232#   (266#, 312#)
VI: 82, 125, 151-5 (some#), 157#   (111, 173, 211-17 some#, 220#)

PLYMOUTH BRETHREN
Also as PLYMMYTH BREADIRON. Sect of evangelical Christians founded
(1828) in Ireland by J. N. Darby.

II: 79   (118)

POCAHONTAS
c.1595 - 1617. American Indian princess, noted for her alleged rescue
of Captain John Smith after his capture by Powhatan (1608).

V: 180   (239)

POIROT, HERCULE
Famous Belgian detective in Agatha Christie's (1891 - 1976) novels.

IV: 195   (267)

POLAND
The date O'Casey alludes to (#) was 1 September 1939, when Hitler* began
World War II by attacking Poland. England immediately declared war on
Germany.

V: 226-7   (304-05)
VI: 114, 119#   (156, 164#)

PONDOS
From Pondoland, territory in South Africa and a former British colony.

V: 167   (222)

POOR LAW DISPENSARY RELIEF
According to the Poor Relief (Ireland) Act (1851), or the Medical
Charities Act, the Board of Guardins divided their poor law unions into
dispensary districts. In these districts, a committee maintained a
dispensary and a medical officer. Free medical treatment was provided
those who possessed a "red ticket," but this carried with it a badge of
poverty and a certain amount of humiliation. See II: 146 (225),VI: 221
(317), and O'Casey's play, The Hall of Healing.

I: 124   (187)

POOR OUL' IRELAND
From the Irish song, "The Wearing of the Green." Part of the first verse
reads:
                    I met with Napper Tandy,
                    And he took me by the hand,
                    Saying, How is poor old Ireland,
                    And what way does she stand?

II: 35   (46)
V: 51   (59)

POOR OUL' WOMAN
Figurative title for Ireland used in Yeats's* play, Cathleen ni Houlihan.
See also SHAN VAN VOCHT.

II: 205   (317)
III: 103, 119, 174, 286   (148, 172, 257, 429)
IV: 179   (243)

POPE, ALEXANDER
1688 - 1744. English poet and leading satirist.

I: 35   (43)

POPE OF 1876
"four years before Sean was born." Pius IX (1792 - 1878), pope from 1846.

VI: 170   (240)

POPE'S BRASS BAND
Derogatory name given to the Catholic Defence Association (1851), formed
by William Keogh and John Sadlier. The association campaigned for the
right of Catholic clergy to assume titles of new sees created by the
papacy. Sadlier and Keogh alienated Protestant supporters of the
association, and eventually accepted offices from the British government,
despite membership vows to the contrary.

III: 32, 120   (39, 174)
IV: 274   (378)

POPE'S GREEN ISLAND, THE
See RYAN, WILLIAM PATRICK.

PORTADOWN
Irish market town and linen manufacturing center in Co. Armagh.

III: 65   (90)

PORTARLINGTON
Irish town in Co. Laois. The feud to which O'Casey alludes was detailed
in Ryan's* book, The Pope's Green Island (see the chapter, "The Battle
at Portarlington").

III: 143   (210)

PORTINCULA
Portiuncula, a rural chapel on the plain below Assisi, Italy, and
reputed headquarters of St. Francis.*

II: 221   (343)

PORTMARNOCK
Small Irish town north of Dublin. The "Velvet Strand" is a two-mile
stretch of sandy beach.

III: 271   (406)

POWER'S WHISKEY
John Power and Son, distillers, 98-103 Thomas Street, plus three other
distilleries in Dublin.

III: 103   (148)

POYNTER, SIR EDWARD JOHN
1836 - 1919. English historical painter and president (1896-1918), Royal
Academy. Interested in ancient Egyptian monuments. O'Casey alludes (#)
to Poynter's A Visit to Aesculapius(1880).

I: 10#   (2#)
VI: 202   (288)

PRAYACAWN DOVE DONAH
From the Irish, preachan dubh dona = bad black crow. In its context, it alludes to a prayer, but it may be related to Hyde's* poem, "An Preachan Mor."

III: 142   (208)

PRAYBOY OF THE FESTERIN' WORLD
See SYNGE, JOHN MILLINGTON.

PRESCOTT, WILLIAM
1796 - 1859. American historian. Author of several classic works on Spanish and South American history.

History of the Conquest of Peru (Everyman, 1906) III: 89, 93 (127, 133)
History of the Conquest of Mexico (Everyman, 1907)III: 89   (127)

PRIESTLY, JOHN BOYNTON
b.1894. English novelist, critic and playwright.

IV: 215   (296)

PRIMROSE HILL/LAVENDER HILL
The highest hills in London. Primrose, the highest, is 219 feet high.

VI: 121   (168)

PRIMROSE LEAGUE
Conservative party organization (1883) founded for the purpose of "the maintenance of religion, of the estates of the realm and of the imperial ascendandy." The name derives from the (mistaken) belief that the primrose was Disraeli's* flower. Celebrated on Primrose Day (19 April), the anniversary of Disraeli's death.

III: 75-6   (106-07)

PRINCE ALBERT'S OWN HUSSARS
In the British army, the 11th Hussars, nicknamed the "Cherry Pickers." In Ireland from 1857-65, 1878-1902, and 1903-07.

I: 164, 166   (252, 255)

PRINCE OF CHANG
Not mentioned in Yeats's* poetry, though the epigram to his Responsibilities (1914) has a quote from Confucius:

> How am I fallen from myself for a long time now
> I have not seen the Prince of Chang in my dreams.

VI: 178   (252)

PRINKNASH ABBEY
English Benedictine abbey three miles southeast of Gloucester. The year of O'Casey's death, work was started on a new building (1964).

VI: 70   (92)

PRINSLOO, MARTHINUS
General and Boer commander in the Boer War.*

III: 164, 264   (241, 403)

PRO-CATHEDRAL
St. Mary's Pro-Cathedral in Dublin at Marlborough and Cathedral streets.
Originally St. Mary's Metropolitan Catholic Chapel, it is the seat of
the Catholic archdiocese of Dublin and was the first great church for
Dublin Catholics as a district denomination.

III: 24, 160, 168, 172, 176, 200, 245, 271
    (28, 235, 247, 254, 259, 295, 365, 407)
IV: 164-5   (223-4)

PROCLAMATION OF THE IRISH REPUBLIC
Historical document from the Easter Rising in Dublin (1916). In world
history, it has a national status comparable to America's Declaration of
Independence and France's Declaration of the Rights of Man. On the
first day of the Rising, Pearse* read the document on the steps of the
General Post Office on O'Connell Street. The signatories to the
proclamation (all executed after the Rising): Thomas J. Clarke,* Sean
MacDermott,* Patrick Pearse,* James Connolly,* Thomas MacDonagh,*
Joseph Plunkett,* and Eamon Ceannt. O'Casey quotes from the first
paragraph of the document (#).

III: 272   (408)
IV: 157#   (213#)

PROFESSOR TIM
Play (1925) by George Shiels (1886 - 1949).

III: 125, 204   (182, 302)
V: 121   (157)

PROMETHEUS
In Greek mythology, celebrated as the benefactor of mankind. O'Casey
refers (#) to the statue of Prometheus in Rockefeller Center in New
York City. It is a gilded bronze statue, weighs eight tons, is 18 feet
high, and was installed in 1934, the same year O'Casey visited New York.
The sculptor was Paul Manship. See also SHELLEY.

III: 162   (238)
V: 114, 187#   (148, 248#)

PROPERTIUS /CYNTHIA
Sextus Propertius (c.50 - c.15 B.C.), Roman elegiac poet who dedicated
several poems and books to his mistress, Cynthia (real name Hostia).

V: 176   (234)
VI: 199, 200, 203   (285, 289)

PROSPERO
Rightful Duke of Milan in Shakespeare's* play, The Tempest.

VI: 227   (325)

PROTESTANT ORPHAN SOCIETY
Founded 1828. Located at 17 Upper Sackville (O'Connell) Street, the
society's aims were "to provide diet, lodging, clothing,and Scriptual
education for the destitute orphans of deceased Protestants."

III: 215-19   (319-25)

PROUDHON, PIERRE JOSEPH
1809 - 1865. Regarded as the father of anarchism. O'Casey's quote is
from Proudhon's Qu'est-ce que la Propriete (1840), which viewed
bourgeois property as theft.

V: 67   (83)

PRUFROCK
From Eliot's* "The Love Song of J. Alfred Prufrock." See also ETERNAL
FOOTMAN.

VI: 136-7   (189-90)

PTOLEMY
Alexandrian astronomer, geographer and mathematician. See EBLANA.

II: 235   (364)

PUBLIC LIBRARY
In 1896, there were two main libraries in Dublin: 106 Capel Street
and 22 Thomas Street.

III: 81, 85   (116, 122)
IV: 229   (315)

PUCK
Mischievous household spirit of English folklore.

IV: 122   (163)

PUFFING DICK, KING OF THE BEGGARS
Historically, the "king of the beggars" was Bampfylde Moore Carew
(1693 - 1770), a famous English vagrant who held the title for forty
years (from 1730).

IV: 161   (218)

PURCELL, HENRY
c.1658 - 1695. English musician and composer of large amount of church
music and scores for many plays.

V: 27   (27)

PUREFOY, MR.
This could be either Rev. Amyrald D. Purefoy, curate of Christchurch
Cathedral, or Richard Dance Purefoy, M.D., Dublin obstetrician on Rutland
Square. Probably the former.

I: 186   (287)

PURSER, SARAH
1848 - 1943. Irish illustrator from a family of illustrators. Famous
for her portrait of Roger Casement.* O'Casey refers (#) to her oil
painting of AE (c.1902).

IV: 212#   (291#)
VI: 176   (249)

PURSUIVANTS SORROY AND NORROY
A pursuivant is an attendant to a herald whose duty it is to proclaim
war and peace, carry messages to other sovereigns, and look after the
heraldic arms. Edward III (1312 - 1377) appointed two heraldic king-
at-arms for the south and north of England, Surroy and Norroy. See
also BORRIS-IN-OSSARY THING AT ARMS.

III: 151   (221)

PUSHA DEEN INGE
"Deen Inge" is William Ralph Inge (1860 - 1954), "the gloomy dean of
St. Paul's," London (1911-34). Pusha may be Pasha.

III: 185   (273)

Q

QUASIMODO
The hunchback of Notre Dame in Hugo's* novel (1831).

VI: 191   (271)

QUEEQUEG
Queequeg, Starbuck's veteran harpooner in Melville's novel, Moby Dick.*

VI: 13   (7)

QUEEN WAS IN THE PARLOUR, THE
Play (1926) by Noel Coward.* Opened at St. Martin's Theatre, London,
August 1926.

V: 20   (16)

QUEEN'S HALL
In London on Regent Street, seating 3000 people. Where is held most
of the city's principal concerts.

III: 157   (230)

QUEEN'S LANCERS
In the British cavalry of the line, the 9th (Queen's Royal) Lancers and
the 16th (The Queen's) Lancers.

I: 164   (252)

QUEEN'S OLD TOUGHS
See ROYAL DUBLIN FUSILIERS.

I: 68, 69   (97, 99)
III: 105   (152)

QUEEN'S SAPPERS AND MINERS
In the British army, the Royal Engineers.

I: 68   (97)

QUEEN'S THEATRE
In Dublin at 209 Great Brunswick (Pearse) Street. Home of the Abbey
Theatre (1951-66) after the old theatre burned down. "Where Sean had
seen his first play" (#). The revival of the Silver Tassie (##) was
directed by Ria Mooney* (24 September to 6 October 1951).

II: 45, 131   (63, 201)
IV: 285#   (395#)
V: 53##   (62##)

QUICKLY, MISTRESS
Housekeeper of Dr. Caius in Shakespeare's* play, The Merry Wives of
Windsor. In 1, 2 Henry IV and Henry V, she is the hostess of Boar's
Head, the tavern frequented by Falstaff* and his companions.

V: 18   (14)

QUIDNUNC
Pen name of Seamus Kelly, dramatic critic of the Irish Times, Dublin.

VI: 210   (301)

QUIDQUOD DE PARNELLIO
O'Casey errs by calling this an encyclical. It was a Papal Rescript
(20 April 1888) that condemned the Plan of Campaign* and the practice
of boycotting, and forbade the clergy from taking part in either.

IV: 241   (332-3)

R

RACHEL
In the Bible, the daughter of Laban, sister of Leah, and wife of Jacob.
The prophet Jeremiah represents Rachel as weeping for her children, the
descendants of her son Joseph, the people of Ephraim and Manasseh
(Jeremiah 31:15).

VI: 37   (44)

RACINE, JEAN BAPTISTE
1639 - 1699. French tragic poet and dramatist.

Andromaque (1667)   III: 51   (70)
Iphigenie (1674)   III: 51   (70)

RADCLIFFE
Prestigious U.S. women's college in Cambridge, Massachusetts.

V: 205-06   (274-5)

RADICAL CLUB
Loose organization of writers which was organized in the mid-1920s by
Liam O'Flaherty* to counter the influence of Yeats,* Gogarty,* and AE.*
Some of the members included Cecil Salkeld, Austin Clarke,* F.R.
Higgins,* and Brinsley Macnamara.*

IV: 127   (104)
VI: 78   (104)

RAFFERTY, BLIND
Anthony Raftery. c.1784 - 1835. Famous blind poet from Co. Mayo whose
works were discovered by Hyde* and Lady Gregory.* Best known for his
masterpiece, a dirge on the "Anach Cuan." Lady Gregory erected a tomb-
stone over his grave (1900). See also DONOUGH, YELLOW-HAIRED.

IV: 230   (317)

RAHILLY, PROFESSOR
See O'RAHILLY, THOMAS F.

RAMSDEN, ROEBUCK
"A president of highly respectable men," "an advanced thinker and a
fearlessly outspoken reformer" in Shaw's* play, Man and Superman. The
description is tongue-in-cheek. Ramsden is a pompous reactionary.

IV: 183   (249)

RAMSGATE
Popular seaside resort in Kent, England. O'Casey's quote is from
Ward's* book on Chesterton,* a letter to Chesterton's close friend,
E. C. Bentley.

VI: 15   (10)

RANNS ROUND RASNAREE
Rann in Irish is a verse, saying, rhyme, or a song, though not the whole
work. The Battle of Rosnaree is an 11th-century Red Branch saga,
describing the battle in which the North was avenged after the main
struggle in the Tain.*

IV: 68   (85)

RAPHAEL
1483 - 1520. Celebrated Italian painter.

III: 136, 217   (199, 322)
IV: 199   (273)
VI: 173   (244)

RATHFARNHAM
Small village four miles from the center of Dublin.

IV: 105, 231   (138, 319)
V: 43   (48)

RATHGAR
Neighboring village of Dublin, south of the Grand Canal.

III: 13, 275   (10, 413)
IV: 105   (138)

RATHGAR AVENUE
A reference to AE's* house at #17 (1906-33). Norah Hoult described the
house as
    a modest two-storied house, the long narrow room divided by folding
    doors, which was one part studio and one part study and sitting
    room . . . you would follow him into the first room where his
    pictures were kept, many of them still unframed and stacked against
    the wall, and from there into the room at the back which opened out
    of it, where there were more pictures hung on the walls and where
    his books stood on three low shelves that ran the length of the
    room.

AE's home was a gathering spot for many Dubliners in the arts, literature
and theosophy every Sunday evening at 7:30.

IV: 216   (297)

RATHMINES
Neighboring village of Dublin south of the Grand Canal.

II: 84   (125)
III: 22, 124, 172, 275   (23, 181, 253, 413)
IV: 105, 155   (138, 210)

READE, CHARLES
1814 - 1884. English novelist and dramatist. O'Casey refers to his
masterpiece, the story of the father of Erasmus.*

Cloister and the Hearth (1861)   II: 122   (187)

READING
County borough in Berkshire, England, and the site of the prison which
was immortalized in Wilde's* Ballad of Reading Gaol (1898). It was
also one of the prisons where many Irish men and women were interned
after the Easter Rising.

IV: 9   (1)

RED ARMY
The army of the U.S.S.R., which bore most of the fight against Nazi
Germany in World War II.

IV: 162-3   (220)
VI: 75, 118, 119, 142-3   (99, 163, 164, 199-200)

RED BOOK OF THE EARLS OF KILDARE
Collection of title deeds and other documents regarding the land and
property of the Geraldines* of Co. Kildare, compiled by Philip Flattis-
bury (c.1470 - c.1570).

III: 285   (427)

RED BRANCH KNIGHTS
Irish legend of a body of champion warriors, chosen for their strength
and bravery, specially trained in the art of warlike deeds.

III: 65   (90)
IV: 68, 133   (86, 179)
V: 50-1, 165   (59, 218)

RED FLAG
Symbol of labor and revolution since the 19th century, and a 20th-century
symbol of socialism. The song, "The Red Flag," was the official song
of the British Labour Party. O'Casey also uses the term as a symbol
of the Soviet Union. O'Casey's reference (#) to red flags in Ireland
alludes to events during the War of Independence when several "soviets"
were declared in various parts of the country. For more on O'Casey
and flags, see "The Flutter of Flags" in his The Green Crow.

III: 259   (388)
IV: 12, 116#   (6, 154#)
V: 162, 226   (214, 303)
VI: 127   (176)

RED GUARDS
There was a small organization called the Red Guards during the Russian
Revolution, but they disappeared as casualties of the civil war (1918-
22). O'Casey uses the term more as a symbolic description.

IV: 230   (318)
VI: 176   (249)

RED HAND
Heraldic symbol of Ulster (#) and of the O'Neills.* It was also found
in the union badge of the Irish Transport and General Workers' Union (##).

III: 211, 265###   (313, 398##)
V: 163#, 169   (215#, 224)

RED SQUARE
In Moscow, adjoining the Kremlin walls and the Cathedral of St. Basil.

VI: 119   (164)

REDMOND, JOHN
1856 - 1918. Major Irish political leader and chief of the Parnellites
after the death of Parnell.* Supported England during World War I, and
promoted recruitment in Ireland. Opposed Sinn Fein,* the Irish Volunteers,* and the Irish Citizen Army.* O'Casey wrote a six-stanza poem,
"John Redmond: Dead 1918," which may be found in Letters, I, p. 76.
The lines, "telling him that he had the opportunity of his life in
MORE

REDMOND, JOHN (cont.)

setting an unforgettable example to the Carsonites if he would go to
the House of Commons and on Monday, and in a great speech, offer all
his soldiers to the Government?" (#) is a direct quote from The Autobiography of Margot Asquith, reprinted and edited by Mark Bonham
Carter, Boston, 1963.

II: 196, 229, 232   (303, 356, 360)
III: 14, 102, 156-7, 254#, 267   (12, 146, 230-1, 380-1#, 400)

REDMOND, ROSIE
Prostitute in O'Casey's play, The Plough and the Stars. For its premiere,
the role was played by Ria Mooney.*

IV: 176   (239)

REFORM ASSOCIATION
Organization of landlords who sought the devolution of governmental
power in Ireland following the 1903 Land Act for the purpose of under-
mining the nationalist movement. William O'Brien* supported the
association in the hope that "conference plus business" would replace
nationalist agitation and parliamentary maneuver as the strategy for
achieving nationalist goals.

III: 105   (152)

REFORMATION
Relgious revolution in the 16th century which led to the establishment
of Protestant churches. There were substantial alterations in discipline
and doctrine in some countries, particularly in Germany by Luther* and
in Switzerland by Zwingli.*

I: 91-8   (135-46)
IV: 254, 265   (351, 366)
V: 226, 230   (303, 309)

REGENT'S PARK
One of the largest (472 acres) London parks, situated in the northwest
section of the city, and containing the Zoological Gardens.

V: 71   (87)

REGNON, FATHER THEODORE DE
Jesuit theologian and author of an extensive and detailed patristic
study, Etudes de theologie positive sur la Sainte Trinite (1892).
With Father Baudier,* one of the foremost 19th-century theologians.

IV: 248   (342)

REILLY, WILLIE
Title of a novel (1855) by William Carleton (1794 - 1869). See also
RODDY THE ROVER.

III: 18, 118   (18, 172)

REMBRANDT
1606 - 1669. Celebrated Dutch painter. O'Casey alludes (#) to his
Self-Portrait in a Plumed Hat (1629).

III: 61   (84)
VI: 52#   (65#)

REMNANTS OF THE GREAT FEAST
Probably an allusion to Bricriu's Feast, the longest narrative of the
Ulster cycle.

III: 57   (79)

REMUS AND ROMULUS, UNCLE
Allusion to (a) the legendary twin brothers, Romulus and Remus, who
founded the city of Rome (753 B.C.), and (b) the character, Uncle Remus,
created by American short-story writer, Joel Chandler Harris (1848 -
1908).

VI: 201   (287)

RENOIR, PIERRE AUGUSTA
1841 - 1919. Leading French impressionist painter.

IV: 186, 199, 282   (254, 273, 391)
V: 64   (78)
VI: 173   (244)
Umbrellas   IV: 147   (198)
                 VI: 23   (331)

RERUM NOVARUM
Papal encyclical (1891) by Leo XIII* outlining the Catholic Church's
position on the rights and duties of capital and labor. Generally seen
to be an important encyclical, though it was also seen as merely an
attempt by the church to co-opt socialist programs and delay and defuse
any revolutionary attempts to establish socialism.

III: 230   (326)
IV: 75   (96)
V: 116   (151)

RESURGAMISE UPSADAISEUM HUNGARIUS
See GRIFFITH, ARTHUR and next entry.

III: 15, 16   (14)

RESURRECTION OF HUNGARY, THE
Series of newspaper articles by Arthur Griffith,* published (1904) in
book form. It outlined Griffith's "Hungarian Policy," which he saw as
a successful model for Ireland to emulate. Basically, it was the policy
successfully pursued by Franz Deak, who organized a massive abstention
of Hungarian representatives from the Imperial Diet in Vienna to secure
the re-establishment of a separate Budapest parliament.

III: 234   (350)

REUBEN
In the Bible, one of the tribes of Israel, descended from Reuben, son of
Jacob.

II: 230, 239   (357, 371)

REVENUE
Commissioners of Inland Revenue in England. O'Casey's tax problems were
similar to other writers who had to live month to month. See his letter
to J. R. Storey, Letters, I, p. 445.

V: 65   (80)

REVERE, PAUL
1735 - 1818. American patriot famous for his ride from Boston to
Lexington to warn the colonists of the arrival of British troops.

II: 65   (96)
V: 180   (239)

REYNARDINE
Described in songs as "an outlawed man in a land forlorn." Subject of
the Irish ballads, "Renardine" and "Mountains of Pomeroy."*

III: 103   (148)

REYNOLDS, HORACE
b.1896. Writer and teacher at Harvard and Brown universities. There
are several letters by O'Casey to Reynolds, and one in particular gives
valuable biographical details (Letters, I, pp. 696-700).

V: 233-4   (314-15)

RHINE RIVER
Major river in central Europe.

III: 285   (427)
IV: 17   (12)
VI: 119   (164)

RIBBENTROP, JOACHIM VON
1893 - 1946. Minister of foreign affairs (1938-45) in Nazi Germany.
Hanged as a war criminal.

VI: 22, 116   (20, 160)

RICE, ELMER
1892 - 1967. American playwright. The play to which O'Casey refers is
Judgement Day (1934), which paralleled the Reichstag trial.

V: 239   (321)

RICHARD THE THIRD
1452 - 1485. Last of the Yorkist kings of England. In Shakespeare's*
plays, 2 and 3 Henry VI and Richard III. Killed at the Battle of Bosworth.*

II: 20   (22)
V: 188   (250)

RICHARD'S POOR QUEEN
From Shakespeare's* play, Richard II. The exact line is "go bind thou
up yon dangling apricocks."

III: 260   (390)

RICHMOND
Residential district in Surrey, England.

VI: 12   (5)

RICHMOND BRIDGE
In central Dublin, between Wolfe Tone and Victoria quays. Presently
the Sean Heuston bridge.

IV: 92   (121)

RICHMOND HOSPITAL
In northwest Dublin, now St. Lawrence hospital.

V: 36   (39)

RICKETTS, CHARLES
1866 - 1931. English painter, sculptor, wood engraver, and critic.

VI: 173   (244)

RINGSEND
Small village east of Dublin on the River Liffey.

II: 83   (124)
III: 191   (282)

RINN
Irish town in Co. Leitrim.

III: 25   (28)

RISING OF THE MOON
Title of a play by Lady Gregory,* but in this case see Appendix I.

III: 103   (149)

RIVERSDALE
Yeats's* home in Rathfarnham, Co. Dublin, which he leased in 1933.
O'Casey visited Yeats there in mid-September 1935.

V: 43   (48)

ROBARTES, MICHAEL
See AHERNE, JOHN.

IV: 269   (372)
V: 87   (110)

ROBERTS, GENERAL FREDERICH SLIGH
First earl Roberts of Kandahar, Pretoria, and Waterford. 1832 - 1914.
British soldier. Crushed   the Sepoy Mutiny* winning Victoria Cross.
Commander in chief, Ireland (1895-99) and in the Boer War,* forcing
Boers to surrender (1900). O'Casey's reference (#) to Roberts being
Irish-born was a popular error. Roberts was born in India.

II: 200-01#   (309-10#)
III: 87, 94   (124, 135)

ROBERTS, HILDA
b.1901. Irish painter and illustrator. The painting of AE* was a
portrait in oils (1929).

IV: 212   (291)

ROBERTSON, THOMAS WILLIAM
1829 - 1871. English dramatist, founder of the "cup and saucer" drama,
the drama of realistic, contemporary, domestic interior.

V: 24   (22)

ROBESPIERRE, MAXIMILIAN
1759 - 1794. French revolutionary and radical in the Constituent
Assembly (1789-91). The best known of French revolutionaries.

II: 177   (273)
III: 231   (344)

ROBIN HOOD
Legendary English outlaw. See also MAID MARION.

II: 127   (194)

ROBINSON CRUSOE
Novel (1719) by Daniel Defoe (c.1659 - 1731).

IV: 236   (326)

ROBINSON, LENNOX
1886 - 1958. Irish playwright, novelist and stage manager. Manager,
Abbey Theatre (1910-14, 1919-23), and director (1923-56). Directed the
premieres of O'Casey's The Shadow of a Gunman, Kathleen Listens In, and
The Plough and the Stars.

IV: and The Harvest Festival   115   (153)
    and The Crimson in the Tri-Colour 117   (156)
    and the "Thirteen Club"*   124-6   (166-9)
    and Juno premiere   171   (232)
                                                   MORE

ROBINSON, LENNOX (cont.)

IV:	and <u>Plough</u> premiere casting	173, 279	(235-6, 387)
	and Shaw's <u>Man and Superman</u> row	183	(250)
	O'Casey's second thoughts about	184	(252)
	and Patrick Touhy*	185	(253)
	at Yeats's* house	270	(373)
V:	and <u>Tassie</u> rejection	31-2, 34	(32-3, 37)
	at Yale <u>vis</u> Ward Costello*	53	(62)
	and U.S. Abbey tour	108, 121	(140, 157-8)
Mentioned		IV: 122	(163)
		V: 105	(136)

ROBINSON, REV. PASCHAL
1870 - 1948. Professor of medieval history, Catholic University (U.S.,
1913-19), and apostolic nuncio to Ireland (from 1929). First papal
nuncio to Ireland in 300 years.

V: 231   (310)

ROCHE, SIR BOYLE
1743 - 1803. Called by Froude* "the buffoon of the Conservative party"
in the Irish House of Commons. M.P. (1776-1800). Voted for the Act of
Union* and was rewarded with Master of Ceremonies at Dublin Castle.

III: 166   (244)

ROCKEFELLER CENTER
Collective name for group of buildings from West 48th Street to West
51st Street along Fifth and Sixth avenues, New York City.

V: 186-7   (248-9)
VI: 9   (1)

RODDY THE ROVER
Agrarian terrorist and hero of the novel (1845) by Irish writer, William
Carleton (1794 - 1869). Spelled "Rody" in the original.

III: 120, 125, 202, 286   (174, 182, 359, 428)

RODEAN
Prestigious English girls' school in Brighton. Founded 1885.

VI: 24   (24)

ROENTGEN, WILHELM KONRAD
1845 - 1923. German scientist, discoverer of X-rays (1895). Nobel
prize in physics (1901).

IV: 214   (294)

ROMAN EMPIRE/ROMANS/ROME
II: 47, 70, 221   (67, 103, 342)
III: 32, 116, 130, 136-9, 194   (39, 168, 189, 199-204, 287)
IV: 89, 164, 218, 228, 234, 241, 243, 245, 247-8, 254, 261, 265
      (116, 223, 300, 314, 323, 332, 335, 338, 341-2, 351, 363, 366)
V: 77, 86, 116, 161, 178, 217, 238   (96, 109, 151, 213, 238, 291,
                                               321)
VI: 81, 110, 115, 168, 179, 196, 199, 201, 202
      (108, 152, 158, 237, 254, 279, 283, 286, 287)

ROMEO AND JULIET
The two lovers in Shakespeare's* play.

V: 204   (273)

ROONEY, WILLIAM
1873 - 1901. Irish poet and Gaelic enthusiast. Co-founder, with
Griffith,* Celtic Literary Society (1889). His works were published
posthumously by Griffith.

III: 235   (350)

ROOSEVELT, FRANKLIN D.
1882 - 1945. Thirty-second president of the U.S. (1933-45). The fireside chats which O'Casey refers to (#) evolved from Roosevelt's earlier
campaign use of the radio for political purposes. It established a
direct link for him to the people and was enormously popular. See
also NEW DEAL.

V: 195, 209-10#   (260, 280#)
VI: 142   (199)

ROSCOMMON
Irish county in Connaught province.

V: 177   (236)
VI: 80   (107)

ROSCULLEN
Scene of events in Shaw's* play, John Bull's Other Island.

III: 174   (257)
IV: 220   (303)

ROSE ALCHEMICA
Variant and allusion to Yeats's* "Rosa Alchemica," The Secret Rose.

IV: 143   (194)

ROSE AND CROWN
In a review of Rose and Crown, Paul Carroll wrote: "The title of the
book is an ironic allusion to the poetic names by which British pubs
are so often called. O'Casey sees all Britain as a pub where poetry --
the Rose -- can be heard if you listen; but where political authority
-- the Crown -- is always present to see that the poetry doesn't get

ROSE AND CROWN (cont.)
out of hand." (Theatre Arts, December 1952) See also LANCASTER, ROSE OF.

I: 16   (12)
V: 78, 90, 94, 96, 230   (98, 114, 121, 122, 309)
VI: 107, 108, 110, 143   (147, 149, 150, 152, 200)

ROSE MARIE
Operetta (1924), with book and lyrics by Otto Harbach and Oscar Hammerstein II, music by Rudolf Friml and Herbert Stothart. During its long
run in London (1925), Eileen O'Casey,* under the name of Eileen Carey,
performed in the chorus.

V: 20, 55   (16, 65)

ROSEBUD, MR. AND MRS.
Characters in O'Casey's play, The Crimson in the Tri-Colour. In a
play critique, however, by Lady Gregory (Letters, I, pp. 95-6), the
name "Budrose" is used.

IV: 117   (155)

ROSSA, JEREMIAH O'DONOVAN
1831 - 1915. Renowned Irish Republican Brotherhood leader. Active in
the 1867 Rising, for which he was arrested, sentenced to life imprisonment, but amnestied. He went to the U.S. where he edited nationalist
newspapers and wrote two well-known accounts of prison life. Rossa
died in New York, and his body was returned to Ireland. His funeral
occasioned Pearse's* famous funeral oration (1 August 1915).

III: 103   (148)

ROSTAND, EDMOND
1868 - 1916. French poet and playwright. Author of Cyrano de Bergerac.

V: 124   (161)

ROTARIANS
From the Rotary Clubs (established 1922). Each club consists of one man
from each business, profession or institution in the community. The
original club held its meetings in the offices of its members in rotation.

V: 235-7   (316-18)

ROTHENSTEIN, SIR WILLIAM
1872 - 1945. English painter and an official artist with British and
Canadian armies during World War I. One of the drawings of AE* to which
O'Casey refers was done in 1914 (published in Twenty-four Portraits,
1920). The other was done in 1921.

IV: 212   (291)

ROTTERDAM
Dutch city. In World War II, its center was almost devastated by Nazi
bombs in a one-day raid (14 May 1940) which killed 30,000 people.

VI: 123   (170)

ROTUNDA
Eighteenth-century building on Rutland (Parnell) Square housing a
theatre, concert halls, and other rooms for meetings and exhibitions.
Formerly a hospital.

I: 15, 40, 178, 180   (11, 50, 275, 278)
III: 162, 226, 235   (239, 336, 351)

ROUND TOWERS
Pre-Norman monasteries built in 9th-12th century Ireland. Used as
watchtowers and forts.

III: 59   (81)

ROUSSEAU, JEAN JACQUES
1712 - 1778. Celebrated French philosopher.

V: 226   (303)
Social Contract (1762) III: 15   (14)

ROWE
Henry Roe, Dublin distiller, who spent 200,000 pounds for the restora-
tion of Christchurch cathedral in the 1870s. After the restoration,
Roe went broke, lost his Thomas Street distillery, and left Dublin.

III: 70   (99)

ROWLAND
From Shakespeare's* play, King Lear: "Child Rowland to the dark tower
came." For a variant, see LIL' ALLEGRO. VI: 23 (21)

ROXBOROUGH HOUSE
Lady Gregory's* family home near Loughrea, Co. Galway. Destroyed during
the Irish Civil War (1922).

IV: 132, 133   (177, 179)

ROYAL ACADEMY OF ARTS
Founded (1768) by George III for the establishment of a school of design,
and for holding an annual exhibition of works by living artists.

I: 10   (2)
V: 114   (149)

ROYAL DUBLIN FUSILIERS
In the British army, the 102nd and 103rd Foot regiments. Known as the
"Queen's Old Toughs."*

I: 69   (98)
II: 47, 197, 201   (66, 305, 311)
III: 34, 45, 105, 163   (43, 59, 152, 240)
IV: 173   (236)
V: 36   (39)

ROYAL EYE AND EAR HOSPITAL
In Dublin on Adelaide Road. Amalgamation of St. Mark's Opthamology
Clinic and the National Eye and Ear Infirmiry (1897). See also CUMMINS,
DR. JOSEPH.

IV: 170   (231)

ROYAL FIELD ARTILLERY
In the British army, one of three (with Horse Artillery and Garrison
Artillery) royal regiments of artillery.

I: 83   (121)

ROYAL HOSPITAL
In Kilmainham, Dublin. Built in 1860. Presently a folk museum.

II: 31   (40)

ROYAL IRISH ACADEMY
In Dublin at 19 Dawson Street. Founded in the late 17th century for the
purpose of "promoting the study of science, polite literature and
antiquities."

III: 145   (231)

ROYAL IRISH CONSTABULARY
One of the two main police forces (see also DUBLIN METROPOLITAN POLICE)
before 1922. They had numerous barracks throughout the country, enabling
them to respond to any "emergency." Headquartered in Dublin Castle.*

I: 65-7, 75   (92-5, 108)
II: 56   (80-1)
III: 65   (90)
IV: 232   (321)

ROYAL OAK
Dublin pub on Parkgate Street.

I: 44   (58)
II: 54   (78)

ROYAL THEATRE
Should be Theatre Royal, better known as the Drury Lane Theatre, London.

V: 11   (4)

ROYALTY THEATRE
In London on Portugal Street. The play O'Casey refers to was Juno and
the Paycock, which opened at the Royalty (16 November 1925), and was
transfered to the Fortune* (8 March 1926). O'Casey missed the Royalty
opening, but he was present for opening night at the Fortune, during
which he made a curtain speech.

V: 11   (3)

RUBENS, PETER PAUL
1577 - 1640. Celebrated Flemish painter.

IV: 199   (274)

RUDOLPH SHOLEM TEMPLE
Jewish temple at 7 West 83rd Street, New York City. See also NEWMAN,
LOUIS I.

V: 201-02   (268)

RUISDAEL, JACOB
c.1628 - 1682. Dutch painter.

VI: 80   (108)

RUSKIN, JOHN
1819- 1900. English art critic and sociological writer. One of
O'Casey's favorites. Prolific writer of volumes of his views on the
principles of art, and author of a series of 96 essays in the form of
letters to the working class on the remedies for poverty and misery.
O'Casey is reading (#) from Ruskin's "War" and "Traffic" in his Crown
of Wild Olive. Later, he alludes (##) to a collection of Ruskin's
poetry, edited (1908) by Chesterton.*

I: 10   (2)
II: 185, 190, 191-2#, 197   (285, 293, 295-7#, 304)
IV: 149, 212   (202, 291)
VI: 168##   (237##)
Seven Lamps of Architecture (1849) II: 122   (187)
Sesame and Lilies (1865)   II: 122   (187)
Ethics of the Dust (1866)   II: 122   (187)
The Crown of Wild Olive (1866)   II: 122, 184, 191 (187, 284, 294-5)
Unto This Last (1860)   II: 122   (187)

RUSSELL, GEORGE
1867 - 1935. Nearly always given as AE. Irish writer, editor and theo-
sophist. Author of mystical poems and essays, and one of Dublin's
noted personalities. Editor, Irish Homestead and Irish Statesman. AE
was apparently the kind of person whom one either liked or didn't, and
O'Casey had almost no use for him. Nobody has written about AE the way
O'Casey did, and a clash of values pervades O'Casey's criticism. The
first references only allude to AE; his name is not mentioned. The
letter (#) on behalf of the workers appeared in the Irish Times, 7 October 1913, and later in the Freeman's Journal. It has been widely reprinted in anthologies of the period. See also:

AEOLIAN   MARKIEWICZ, COUNTESS CONSTANCE
ANCIENT OF DAYS   ORDER OF THE LITTLE GREYHOUND
BIRDS OF DIAMOND GLORY   RATHGAR AVENUE
GIBBON, MONK   ROTHENSTEIN, SIR WILLIAM
GREGORY, LADY AUGUSTA   SOLOMONS, ESTELLA
GILBERT, DONALD   SPICER, THEODORE
HUGHES, JOHN   TITTLE, WALTER
IRISH ACADEMY OF LETTERS   TREE OF LIFE
IRISH AGRICULTURAL SOCIETY   TYNAN, KATHERINE

MORE

RUSSELL, GEORGE (cont.)

III: 59-65, 162, 190, 211#, 230, 244   (81-90, 238, 281, 312-13#, 343, 364)

IV: 143-4, 172, 180, 184, 185, 195-216, 268, 282
   (194, 234, 245, 252, 268-98, 371, 391)

V: 38-9, 104, 136	(42-3, 135, 179)	
VI: 161, 164	(227, 230)	
Homeword Songs by the Way (1894)	IV: 191	(262)
The National Being (1916)	IV: 206, 208	(284, 285)
Thoughts for a Convention (1917)	IV: 208	(285)
The Candle of Vision (1918)	IV: 210	(289)

RUSSELL, THOMAS
1767 - 1803. United Irishman* leader and frequent contributor to their newspaper, Northern Star. Arrested (1796) and sent to Fort George. Joined Robert Emmet* (1802). Hanged at Downpatrick.

III: 103   (148)

RUSSIAN BASILICA
Probably the Russian Cathedral at Fifth Avenue and 97th Street, New York City.

V: 186   (248)

RUSSIAN REVOLUTION
The revolution of October 1917 in Russia, setting up the first socialist state.

IV: 14, 16, 162, 230-1   (8, 10-11, 219-21, 318)
V: 36, 219   (39, 294)
VI: 174   (246)

RUTH, ET. AL.
Ruth is the chief character in the Old Testament book of Ruth. She was a Moabitess who, after the death of her husband, accompanied her mother-in-law, Naomi, to Bethlehem where she became the wife of Boaz, a relative of her first husband, and through him an ancestress of David.

III: 48-9   (65-6)

RUTHERFORD, ERNEST
1871 - 1937. British physicist who investigated the nature of radioactive transformations and the nature of the atom. Nobel prize for chemistry (1908).

IV: 277   (383)
V: 13   (8)
VI: 49   (61)

RUTLAND SQUARE
Now Parnell Square, at the northern end of O'Connell Street. In 1920,
the Irish Transport and General Workers' Union moved its head offices
to 35 Parnell Square, leaving Liberty Hall free for use by its Dublin
branches. (#)

II: 227   (353)
III: 88   (126)
IV: 12#, 76#   (6#, 97#)

RYAN, FRANK
1902 - 1944. Irish Republican Army leader and Spanish Civil War
commander. Active in the Irish War of Independence (1918-22) and against
the Free State in the Civil War (1922-23). Founder and secretary of the
Irish Republican Congress (1934); commanded first Irish contingent in
Spain (December 1936); adjutant, Abraham Lincoln 15th International
Brigade. Buried in the German Democratic Republic. Ryan was a student
when he and O'Casey first met, and he was among those protesting the
opening of The Plough and the Stars. The debate which O'Casey refers to
was held by the "Literary and Historical Society" of University College
Dublin, and took place in a hall attached to Mills' Restaurant in
Merrion Row. It was presided over by Arthur E. Clery, professor at
UCD.

IV: 177   (242)

RYAN, PROFESSOR J. L.
Should be L. J. Ryan, head teacher, Male Model Schools, of the Central
Model Schools,* Dublin.

I: 65   (92)

RYAN, WILLIAM PATRICK
1867 - 1942. Irish journalist and author of several books on the labor
and literary movements. Ryan's "Boyne Valley Project," an effort to
bring industrialization to the area, was condemned by Cardinal Logue*
because the financier of the project also financed Ryan's newspaper,
The Irish Peasant.*

III: 23, 135, 145, 174   (25-6, 197, 212-13, 259)
The Pope's Green Island (1912) III: 23 (25)
                                IV: 182 (249)

S

SACKVILLE STREET
Former name of O'Connell Street, Dublin.

I: 22, 178, 180   (22, 275, 278)
II: 66, 86, 88, 90, 102, 126, 127   (97, 129, 132, 135, 155, 193-4)
III: 63, 146, 154   (87, 88, 215, 226)
IV: 153, 285   (207, 394)
V: 217   (291)
VI: 206-07   (295)

SACRED CONGREGATION OF THE PROPAGANDA
Catholic congregation in Rome established by Pope Gregory (1622) which
is concerned with all matters regarding missions throughout the world.

IV: 234, 247, 279   (323, 341, 386)

SACRED ROTA
Catholic tribunal first set up in the 13th century and re-established
by Pope Pius X (1908). It is a court of first instance, appeal, or
final appeal, according to the history and origin of the case.

III: 136, 138   (200, 203)

SACRED SODALITY OF RUDDY ROVERIANS
See RODDY THE ROVER.

III: 152   (224)

SADLIER AND KEOGH
See POPE'S BRASS BAND.

III: 32   (39)

ST. AIDAN
Also AIDAUN. c.626. Irish saint from Ferns who founded a famous
monastery in Co. Wexford.

III: 97, 242   (140, 361)
IV: 234   (323)
V: 161   (213)

ST. ALLSUP OF SHELMEXHAM
"Alsop" is a brand of British ale. Shell-Mex House is the home of the
British Council on The Strand, London, which published Chesterton's*
book, G. K. Chesterton Explains the English (1935), O'Casey's allusion.

III: 201   (298)

ST. ALOYSIUS GONZAGA
Italian Jesuit saint whose death at the age of 23, while attending
victims of a plague, makes him a patron saint of youth.

III: 159, 242   (233, 361)

ST. ALPHONSO DE'LIGUORI
1696 - 1787. Italian prelate and founder of the Redemptionist Order
(1732).

Meditations   VI: 132   (183)

ST. ANDREW
Brother of St. Peter and the first of Christ's apostles in order of
time. Patron saint of Scotland, old Russia and Greece.

III: 147, 219   (216, 325)
VI: 191   (271)

ST. ANDREW'S CHURCH
In Dublin, the All Hollows' Catholic Church on Westland Row.

II: 18   (19)

ST. ANTHONY
1195 - 1231. One of the most popular saints in the Catholic Church.
Said to give help finding lost articles.

II: 90   (136)
III: 159   (233)
IV: 15, 48, 97-8, 155, 161, 276   (10, 57, 128, 210, 218, 382)
V: 164   (217)
VI: 91   (124)

ST. ANTHONY GUIDE
Found as "S.A.G." on letters and parcels to insure their safe passage
through the mails. See ST. ANTHONY.

VI: 209   (299)

ST. AUGUSTINE
354 - 430. Early Christian Church father and philosopher who exercised
a powerful influence over later church doctrine. The book O'Casey
refers to is an autobiography.

IV: 265   (367)
V: 193   (258)
Confessions   VI: 132   (183)

SSSSSSS BARA, BECCAN COMAN, DIMA, DALUA, FLAN, AND GARVAN
These are all Irish saints. More about them may be found (in Latin) in
Carolus Plummer, Vitae Sanctorum Hiberniae (Oxford, 1910, rptd. 1968).

III: 177   (262)

ST. BEDE THE VENERABLE
673 - 735. English scholar and theologian. Author of an ecclesiastical
history of England (731).

VI: 204   (291)

ST. BENEDICT
c.480 - c.550. Founder of the Benedictine Order, though little is known
of him other than what is found in St. Gregory's Dialogues.

IV: 257   (355)
V: 164   (218)

ST. BERNADETTE
1844 - 1879. French peasant girl who had visions of the Virgin Mary at
Lourdes which led to the establishment of the town as a shrine.

IV: 273, 276-7   (377, 382, 384-5)
V: 163   (217)

ST. BERNARD
1091 - 1153. French saint who established 68 Cistercian monasteries and
wrote many treatisies and sermons. Doctor of the Church.

IV: 257   (355)
V: 194   (259)
VI: 37, 133   (43, 184)

ST. BRENDAN
d.577. Irish saint and reputed discoverer and seafarer. O'Casey
alludes (#) to the popular legend that St. Brendan discovered America and (##) to his feast day (May 16).

III: 285##   (427##)
IV: 71#   (89#)

ST. BRIDGET
One of the three patron saints of Ireland,known widely as "Mary of the
Gael."

III: 92, 94, 97, 159, 242   (133, 135, 140, 233, 361)
IV: 144, 147, 234, 276, 281 (195, 199, 323, 382, 389)
V: 161   (213)

ST. BRONACH
c.500. Irish saint. Many stories surround his bronze bell in Kilbroney,
Co. Down, and its mysterious unaided ringing.

III: 158   (232)

ST. BURNUPUS
St. Barnabas Church, Upper Sheriff Street, North Wall, Dublin. One of
the four symbols (#) of O'Casey's life. It supported a national school,
which O'Casey attended sporadically (1890-94), and it was also where he
taught Sunday School (1900-03). Featured in his play, Red Roses for Me.
The church was built in 1870. It was designed by A. G. Jones in Perpen-
dicular Gothic, and its tower rose to a height of 135 feet. The church
cost 4000 pounds to build,and was one of three churches built from the
will of a Miss Shannon.

II: 144, 223, 225-6, 231, 237   (222, 346, 349, 351, 358, 368)
IV: 76#   (98#)

ST. CANICE
Given as KILKENNY and ST. KIERAN OF KILKENNY. c.517 - 600. Irish
saint and founder of Kilkenny, named from his church of Cainneach.

III: 75, 159   (106, 233)

ST. CATHERINE'S CHURCH
On Thomas Street, Dublin. Place of marriage of O'Casey's parents (27
January 1863), and also the site of Robert Emmet's* execution.

II: 27   (34)

ST. CATHERINE'S COLLEGE
Constituent college of Cambridge University.

VI: 44, 46, 51   (53, 56, 64)

ST. CHARLES BORROMEO
1538 - 1584. Italian nobleman and ecclesiastic who was known for his
ecclesiastical reforms. Re-assembled the Council of Trent.*

IV: 254   (351)

ST. CLEMENT'S
St. Clement Dane Church in London. Built (1691) from the designs of
Christopher Wren. Its tower rings out the famous peal which gave rise
to the nursery rhyme, "The Bells of London," to which O'Casey alludes
(#) and which he quotes (##).

V: 9##   (1##)
VI: 191#   (271#)

ST. COLMCILLE
521 - 597. One of the most venerated Irish saints, Colmcille was also
the apostle of Scotland, founder of the Scottish nation, founder of the
dynasty of Ulster kings that continued to 1610, and the bearer of
Christianity to Iona and to most of northern England. O'Casey refers
to him as the "Dove of Iona," from colm, the Irish word for "dove."

II: 218   (338)
III: 97, 189, 241, 242   (140, 280, 361)
IV: 234   (323)
V: 161   (213)

ST. COLUMBANUS
d.651. Irish saint and upholder of Celtic customs.

III: 242   (361)
IV: 234   (323)

ST. CYPRIAN
c.200 - 258. Early Christian Church father who was beheaded at Carthage.

IV: 265   (367)

ST. DAMNAMMAN CHURCH
St. Laurence O'Toole Catholic Church, Seville Place, Dublin. O'Casey's
pun is obvious, though he may also be alluding to the Irish saint, St.
Adamnan.

II: 144, 238   (222, 370)
III: 92   (132)

ST. DOMINIC
1170 - 1221. Spanish saint who founded (1216) the Dominicans. Known
for his concern for the poor.

II: 221   (343)

ST. ENDA
c.535. Enda of Aran, the patriarch of Irish monasticism. Known for his
austere life on the Aran Islands.

III: 242   (361)

ST. ENDA'S SCHOOL FOR BOYS
Patrick Pearse's* school, which offered a celebrated curriculum in
Irish history and studies. Founded in 1908, the school was moved
(1910) from Cullenswood House to The Hermitage, Rathfarnham, Co.
Dublin.

III: 235, 269, 287   (351, 404, 430)

ST. FINBARR
c.600. Irish saint venerated as the founder of the city of Cork. Established a monastery at the mouth of the River Lee.

III: 159, 242   (233, 361)
IV: 68   (85)

ST. FOWNES, ABBEY OF
O'Casey pun. Reference to the United Irishman newspaper offices at 17
Fownes Street, Dublin.

III: 16   (15)

ST. FRANCIS OF ASSISI
1181 - 1226. Celebrated saint, a scholar and founder of the Franciscans (1209).

I: 29   (32-3)
II: 133, 221   (204, 343)
III: 260   (389, 390)
IV: 160   (218)
V: 194   (259)

ST. FRANCIS DE SALES
1567 - 1622. French saint and patron saint of Catholic writers (since
1922). Known as a converter of Protestants.

III: 242   (361)

ST. FRANCIS XAVIER'S CHURCH
Given as JESUIT CHURCH OF X XAVIER'S. Jesuit church on Upper Gardiner
Street, Dublin.

III: 168   (247)

ST. FULGENTIUS
468 - 533. Early Christian bishop whose extant letters treat of the
various virtues.

IV: 265   (367)

ST. FURZE
St. Fursey, c.600, whose feast day is observed throughout Ireland.

III: 285   (427)

ST. GABRIEL
The Archangel and the angel of the Annunciation (Luke 1:26).

I: 55   (77)
III: 104, 123   (150, 179)
IV: 80   (103)

ST. GEORGE
Patron saint of England. Subject of many legends, of which the dragon
story is comparatively recent.

III: 147, 208, 219, 243   (216, 308, 325, 363)
VI: 139, 191   (194, 271)

ST. GEORGE'S CHURCH
On Lower Temple Street (Hill Street, post-1886), Dublin.

I: 70, 77   (101, 111)
II: 133   (204)
IV: 285   (394)

ST. GREGORY THE GREAT
c.550 - 604. The first monk to become pope, and considered to be the
outstanding pope of the first 1000 years of Christianity.

VI: 51   (63)

ST. IGNATIUS LOYOLA
1491 - 1556. Spanish nobleman who, after being wounded in battle with
the French, offered his services to the church. Founder of Jesuits.

III: 159, 242   (233, 361)
IV: 67   (85)
V: 185   (251)

ST. ITA
c.570. After St. Bridget,* the most popular woman saint. Founded a
large community of maidens near Limerick.

VI: 203   (290)

ST. JAMES OF COMPOSTELLO
Also known as St. James the Greater, brother of St. John the Apostle.

V: 127   (166)

ST. JAMES'S SQUARE
In London, north of Pall Mall, site of several historical houses.

V: 131   (172)

ST. JEROME
c.342 - 420. Famous early translator of the Latin Bible. Noted for
his outspokenness.

V: 191   (255)

ST. JOAN OF ARC
1412 - 1431. French heroine who was condemned as a heretic and burned
at the stake. See also SHAW, GEORGE BERNARD.

IV: 166, 243   (226, 336)

ST. JOHN THE BAPTIST
New Testament forerunner of Jesus.

I: 167   (258)
III: 62   (86)
V: 51   (60)

ST. JOHN OF BOSSCO
1815 - 1888. Italian ecclesiastic from Piedmont who was known for his
youth schools and boys' clubs in Turin.

IV: 236   (326)

ST. JOHN OF THE CROSS
John de Pepes. 1542 - 1591. Established reform among the Carmelite
friars, for which he suffered persecution and imprisonment at Toledo.

V: 191   (255)
VI: 132   (183)

ST. JOHN LATERAN
Church of the Holy Savior, popularly known as the Lateran. The cathedral
church of the Pope in Rome.

VI: 191   (271)

ST. JOHN'S COLLEGE
Constituent college of Cambridge University.

VI: 51, 59-61, 65   (64, 76-8, 84-5)

ST. JOHN'S OF MORNINGSIDE HEIGHTS
St. John's Cathedral in upper Manhattan, New York City. It is a large
Episcopalian cathedral on the northwest corner of Central Park.*

V: 186   (248)

ST. JOHN'S WOOD
Residential district of St. Marylebone metropolitan borough, London.
Once a popular artists' residence.

V: 71-5   (87-93)

ST. JOSEPH
Husband of Mary and foster-father of Jesus.

III: 177   (261)
IV: 57   (70)
V: 151-4   (200-05)

ST. JOSEPH'S FREE NIGHT SHELTER
St. Joseph's Night Refuge for Homeless Women and Children on Brickfield
Lane and Cork Street, Dublin. Founded in 1861. Capacity 145 beds.

III: 168   (248)

ST. JUST, LOUIS ANTOINE LEON DE
1767 - 1794. French revolutionary leader. An intimate associate of
Robespierre* with whom he was arrested and guillotined (28 July).

III: 231   (344)

ST. KEVIN
c.550. One of the great Irish saints.   Founder of the monastery of
Glendalough. His feast day (3 June) is celebrated throughout Ireland.

III: 102, 242   (147, 361)

ST. KEVIN'S CHURCH
On South Circular Road, Dublin. Built 1892. In his Memoirs, Desmond
Fitzgerald wrote that he knew of O'Casey's "enthusiasm for High Angli-
canism, /and/ of the visits he had paid with Blythe to Church of Ireland
dignitaries to get them to have a service in Irish on St. Patrick's
Day."

III: 148   (217)

ST. KIERAN COLLEGE
In Co. Kilkenny, Ireland. Founded 1782. Long one of the chief Irish
seminaries. Walter MacDonald* entered the college at age 11 in July
1870. The college was under the supervision of the Lord Bishop of
Ossary.

IV: 236, 237, 238   (326, 328)

ST. KIERAN OF KILKENNY
See ST. CANICE.

ST. LAUDERDAMNUS, FEAST OF
Variant on Harry Lauder,* Scottish ballad singer and comedian, who was
an ardent recruiter for the British during World War I, a task O'Casey
greatly disliked. The feast day O'Casey mentions, November 13, is that
of St. Francis Xavier Cabrini, patron saint of emigrants.

III: 87   (125)

ST. LAURENCE O'TOOLE
1128 - 1180. Popular Irish saint by virtue of his position of archbishop of Dublin (from 1162) during the invasion by Normans (1169).
Mediated between Roderick O'Connor* and McMurrough* (1170), but submitted
to Henry II of England (1171). Used as a go-between by Henry and the
Irish chieftains.

III: 172, 176-8, 190, 200-01 (254, 259-63, 281, 297)
IV: 164-6   (223-6)

ST. LAURENCE O'TOOLE SISTERS OF CHARITY/SEE/WARD
For the Sisters of Charity, see ST. VINCENT'S HOSPITAL (#). The St.
Laurence O'Toole See was the see (##) of Dublin. The ward was in
St. Vincent's Hospital.*

III: 246-7, 258 (all#)   (368-9, 386, all#)
IV: 14#, 281##   (9#, 389##)

ST. LAWRENCE
Famous Christian martyr and one of the seven deacons of Rome under
Pope St. Sixtus II. Roasted on a gridiron (258). Many date his death
as the death of idoltry in Rome.

III: 62   (86)

ST. LOUIS
Louis IX. 1214 - 1270. King of France (from 1226). Went on Sixth
Crusade (1248-54), but had a relatively peaceful reign.

V: 188   (250)

ST. LUKE
From the Bible. Companion of St. Paul and traditionally regarded as
the author of the third gospel.

III: 49, 177   (66, 261)
V: 153   (202)

ST. MAC CUA
One of the followers of St. Columkille.* Closely associated with the
early Irish church.

II: 218   (337)

ST. MARGARET'S
Small village one mile northeast of Finglas, outside of Dublin. In
1907, the curate was Rev. James MacDonnell, to whom O'Casey may be
referring.

III: 145   (213)

ST. MARK'S OPTHALMIC HOSPITAL
On Lincoln Place, Dublin. Built 1844 and absorbed (1898) by the National
Eye and Ear Infirmary,* Adelaide Road. Chief surgeon, John B. Story.*
Capacity, 50 beds, with an extensive outpatient service.

I: 20, 22, 28-33   (19, 21, 32-9)
IV: 285   (395)

ST. MARTIN
c.316 - 297. Venerated saint of Europe during the Middle Ages who also
had considerable influence on the Celtic churches.

IV: 161   (218)

ST. MARTIN'S
Probably the church at Ludgate, London. O'Casey's usage of the term is
from the famous nursery rhyme, "Bells of London."

VI: 191   (271)

ST. MARY
Virgin mother of Jesus.

III: 242   (361)
IV: 100   (132)

ST. MARY/ST. GEORGE AND ST. MARY
Anglican and Catholic churches in Totnes, Devon. St. Mary, on High
Street, was rebuilt during the Middle Ages (1432-60).

VI: 69-70   (92)

ST. MARY'S NATIONAL SCHOOLS FOR BOYS AND GIRLS
At 43 Lower Dominick Street, Dublin. Where O'Casey attended school in
the late 1880s.

I: 115   (173)

ST. MARY'S PARISH CHURCH
At 25 Lower Dominick Street, Dublin. Where O'Casey was baptised (28
July 1880) by Rev. T. R. S. Collins ("T. R. Hunter"), and where his
sister ("Ella") and her husband were married. Housed St. Mary's
Infant School where O'Casey's sister taught and which he attended for a
brief period.

I: 71-2, 78   (103, 114)

ST. MERCURIUS
c.250. Said to have been a Scythian officer in the Roman army who was
beheaded for the faith. Revered as a "warrior-saint."

VI: 84   (114)

ST. MICHAEL
Regarded as the chief of the archangels, protector of the church and
her members from Satan's attacks.

III: 123, 220, 246, 258   (179, 327, 369, 386)
IV: 80   (103)

ST. NOCNOC OF DUENNADURBAN
Variant on the Irish word for hill, cnoc (pronounced, roughly, "knock");
the Mayo town of Knock*; and Deanna Durban, French actress of the 1930s
and 1940s, who starred in several films, including It Started with Eve.

III: 199   (295)

ST. ODO OF CLUNY
c.879 - 942. French ecclesiastic who undertook monastery reforms in
France and Italy.

V: 191-2   (255-6)

ST. OSMOND
d.1099. English saint who was prominent in building Salisbury Cathedral.*

V: 189   (252)

ST. PATRICK
c.389 - c.461. Apostle and patron saint of Ireland.

I: 174, 176   (268, 271, 272)
II: 13, 16, 133, 195, 214, 237   (10, 16, 204, 302, 331, 368)
III: 97, 103, 125, 134, 147, 148, 158, 162, 173, 176, 190, 200-05, 227,
     229, 240, 242, 248, 266
     (140, 148, 182, 196, 216, 217, 232, 238, 255, 260, 281, 296-304,
     338, 341, 358, 361, 372, 398)
IV: 67, 113, 122, 151, 165, 177, 183, 278, 281
     (84-5, 150, 162, 205, 223, 242, 249, 372, 378)
V: 164, 189, 217   (216, 218, 252, 290, 291)
VI: 25, 177, 179, 191, 215   (25, 251, 254, 271, 309)

ST. PATRICK'S CATHEDRAL
On Patrick Street, Dublin.

III: 37, 70, 147   (47, 99, 216)

ST. PATRICK'S DAY/PARADE
March 17, every year.

I: 65   (92)
III: 101, 123, 157, 202   (145, 178, 179, 230, 299)
VI: 10, 25, 26   (2, 25, 27)

ST. PATRICK'S IN FIFTH AVENUE
The famous St. Patrick's Cathedral on Fifth Avenue in New York City.

V: 186   (248)

ST. PATRICK'S PURGATORY
An old superstition surrounding a cavern on Saints Island in Lough
Derg, Co. Donegal. Where St. Patrick* allegedly prevailed upon God to
show him the entrance to purgatory in Ireland.

III: 59   (81)
V: 194   (258)

ST. PAUL
Apostle of the Gentiles who made three famous journeys over western
Asia Minor and Greece, facing hostile populations and other obstacles
(I Timothy 2:7). O'Casey quotes (#) from I Timothy 6:10.

I: 35   (43)
III: 208#, 220   (308#, 327)
IV: 246, 265   (340, 366)
V: 86   (109)

ST. PAUL OF THE CROSS
1694 - 1775. Popular Italian preacher, founder (1737) of the Barefoot
Clerks of the Cross and Passion (Passionists). Said to have gifts of
prophecy and healing.

V: 49   (57)

ST. PAUL'S CATHEDRAL
In London, one of the most famous cathedrals in the world. One of
Christopher Wren's masterpieces.

V: 92, 190   (117, 253)

ST. PETER
Simon Peter, a disciple of John the Baptist* and Jesus, and the vicar
of Christ on earth. One of O'Casey's allusions (#) involves Peter
holding "the keys of the kingdom of Heaven" (see Matthew 16:19).
The "Order of St. Peter" (##) is a fictitious metaphor for priests.

I: 35   (43)
II: 221   (342)
III: 116##, 220   (168##, 327)
IV: 91#, 265   (119#, 367)
V: 218-19   (291)
VI: 179   (254)

SS PETER AND PAUL
Saints Peter* and Paul,* often linked together because of their position
as co-founders of the Church of Rome, and because of their power and
influence in the early church. Both are allegedly buried in Rome.

I: 35   (43)
III: 220   (327)

ST. PETER OF ALCANTARA
1499 - 1562. Spanish Franciscan who instituted(1554) severe reforms.
One of the great Spanish mystics.

III: 159   (233)

ST. PETER'S
In Vatican City, the domed church built by Constantine I, supposedly
over the grave of St. Peter.* Contains the famed Sistine Chapel.

V: 190   (253)
VI: 169   (238)

ST. RUTH, GENERAL
French general who was sent by Louis XIV to command the Irish army
(May 1691) during the Jacobite wars. He previously led regiments of
the famous French Irish Brigade at Savoy.

III: 37   (48)

ST. SAMUEL
In the Bible, a Hebrew judge and first of the great prophets.

IV: 265   (366)

ST. SAVIOUR'S CHURCH
Dominican church on Dominick Street, Dublin.

I: 113   (171)
III: 168   (247)

ST. STEPHEN
The first deacon and the church's first martyr for Christ. O'Casey's
reference is to St. Paul's participation in the stoning death of
St. Stephen.

IV: 247   (340)

ST. STEPHEN'S GREEN
On the south side of Dublin, St. Stephen's Green is one of the city's
ancient commons. It is a quarter-mile square, and was made a public
park in 1880 by a gift of 20,000 pounds by Sir Arthur Guinness.*

III: 103, 106, 259   (149, 154, 387)
IV: 102, 103, 104, 129, 170   (134, 136, 137, 138, 172, 231)

ST. THOMAS AQUINAS
c.1225 - 1274. Italian scholastic philosopher and systematizer of
Catholic theology.

IV: 160, 227, 246   (218, 313, 340)
V: 193-4   (258)
Summa Theologica   VI: 202   (288)

ST. THOMAS' CHURCH
In Dublin on Marlborough Street.

III: 165   (242)

ST. UISKEBAHA
Variant on the Irish words for whiskey, uisce beatha.

III: 178   (263)

ST. URSULA
Early Christian saint whose abhorrence of marriage led her on a
pilgrimage with 11,000 virgins through Europe to celebrate virginity.
Her name is used in connection with convents and Catholic girls' schools.

IV: 82   (106)

ST. VINCENT DE PAUL
1580 - 1660. Patron saint of all charitable societies.

IV: 276   (382)

ST. VINCENT DE PAUL'S SOCIETY
In Dublin, the society was located at 50 Upper Sackville (O'Connell)
Street. Its purpose was "giving relief to the poor with no religious
distinction." In 1895, there were 168 branches in Ireland.

III: 73, 217   (102, 323)

ST. VINCENT'S HOSPITAL
Founded in 1834 and operated by the Sisters of Charity. In Dublin, the
hospital was located on St. Stephen's Green, and had a capacity of 160
beds. O'Casey was a patient there (August 15 to September 1, 1915) for
an operation on his neck for tubercular glands.

III: 246-59   (368-87)
IV: 190   (260)
V: 36   (39)

SALAMANCA
City in Western Spain. Site of bitter fighting during the Spanish
Civil War.*

V: 127   (166)

SALIMBENE, FRA
c.1221 - c.1289. Italian monk who was known chiefly for his religious
chronicles.

V: 193   (258)

SALISBURY, EARL OF
Robert Cecil, 1st Earl of Salisbury and 1st Viscount Cranborne. 1563 -
1612. British politician who secured the accession of James VI of Scotland to the English throne (1603) as James I. Buried at Westminister
Abbey.

V: 187   (249)

SALISBURY, MARQUIS OF
Robert Arthur Talbot Gascoyne-Cecil, 3rd Marquis of Salisbury. 1830 -
1903. British politician and an implacable foe of Irish Home Rule.

I: 75   (109)
III: 248   (371)
V: 91   (116)

SALISBURY PLAIN
An undulating chalk plateau north of Salisbury, England. Extends for
20 miles.

V: 36   (39)

SALISBURY'S CATHEDRAL
Also given as CHURCH OF SALISBURY. The great English cathedral in
Salisbury, England. Built (1220-80) with the tallest (404 feet) spire
in England, the cathedral contains many valuable manuscripts, including
Christopher Wren's report on the spire.

III: 285   (428)
V: 138, 187-9   (181, 249-52)

SALKELD, CECIL
Dublin artist and conversationalist. His daughter, Cecila, was the
wife of Brendan Behan.

IV: 127   (169)

SALMON, DR. GEORGE
1819 - 1904. Irish mathematician and theological writer. Provost
(1888-1902), Trinity College, Dublin. The book O'Casey refers to
was a series of lectures delivered in the Divinity School at Trinity.

The Infallibility of the Church (1888)   IV: 237   (327)

SALOME
In the Bible, the wife of Zebedee and mother of the apostles, James
and John. One of the women who watched the crucifixion of Jesus and
went to the sepulcher on the resurrection morning.

III: 168   (247)

SALVATION ARMY
Religious organization founded (1878) by William Booth.* Its activities
are directed against the sufferings of the poor and destitute.

II: 171, 178   (263, 274)
III: 243, 279   (363, 418)
V: 230   (309)

SAMEKH
Fifteenth letter of the Hebrew alphabet. Often found in mythological
symbolism as representing Mars, fate, the Devil, and Aquarius and
Sagittarius.

IV: 126   (168)

SAN FRANCISCO
Major California city having a large Irish-American population.

III: 150   (220)
IV: 210   (309)

SANDYMOUNT
Neighboring village of Dublin, south of the Grand Canal.

I: 189   (291)
II: 67, 83   (98, 124)
IV: 66   (83)

SANKO PANKO
Sancho Panza, the squire and faithful follower of Don Quixote in
Cervantes' (1547 - 1616) masterful novel.

III: 211   (313)

SANKEY AND MOODY
Ira David Sankey (1840 - 1908) and Dwight Moody (1837 - 1899), American
evangelists known for their mass rally sermons. Visted Dublin in 1875.
In a letter to William Maroldo (Sean O'Casey Review, Spring 1977), dated
26 February 1963, O'Casey wrote:

> Yes, indeed, Sankey and Moody came to Dublin, bringing the erring
> protestants of Dublin to their knees, making loud lamentation for
> their sins, swearing allegiance to the service of heaven, and
> bravely keeping their vows intact for a day or two. I never heard
> these evangelists, for I may not have been born at the time; and
> my knowledge of them came from my mother who liked a few of their
> hymns, but kept true to the episcopal church all the same. I
> remember reading a marginal note made by my father in a book of
> his which refuted the "Romish" doctrine of Invocation of Saints
> and Angels; the note saying "Crowds mobbed Sankey and Moody,
> tearing buttons from their coats, seizing their hankerchiefs and
> tearing them into small pieces as sacred souveniers, and yet we
> denounce the practive of invoking saints through their relics,
> bits of bone, etc., while we invoke buttons and strips of cloths
> called hankerchiefs!"

I: 40   (52)
III: 148   (217)
IV: 216   (298)

SANTRY
Neighboring village north of Dublin.

IV: 223   (307)

SARAGOSSA
City in northern Spain. Augustina, the "Maid of Saragoza," was celebrated in Byron's* Childe Harold.

III: 90   (129)

SARATOGA
New York village where a 1777 battle marked a turning point in the
American Revolution.

II: 12, 88   (9, 131)
V: 180   (240)

SARSFIELD, PATRICK
Earl of Lucan. c.1650 - 1693.   Irish national hero active in the
Jacobite Wars. Assisted James II's* reorganization of Irish forces
(1686); fled with James to France, but returned for several decisive
battles, including the battle of the Boyne* and the siege of Limerick.*
After the capitulation at Limerick, Sarsfield joined the French. Killed
shortly afterwards at Landen, Belgium.

I: 21   (21)
II: 229, 230, 236-7, 239   (355, 357, 367-8, 371)
III: 102, 105   (148, 152)
IV: 67   (85)
V: 173   (231)

SASSENACH
See CLAN SASSANACH.

II: 235   (365)

SATO, JUNZO
b.1897. Japanese journalist, diplomat and literature enthusiast who
met Yeats* in Portland, Oregon (20 March 1920) where he presented the
poet with an ancient sword. See Sato's article, "A Sketch of My Life,"
W. B. Yeats and Japan. For Yeats's references to Sato, see the poems,
"My Table" and "Self and Soul."

V: 45, 46   (50, 52)

SATOLLI, FRANCESCO
1838 - 1910. Italian theologian. In the controversy referred to by
O'Casey (see REGNON, THEODORE DE), Satolli opposed the writings of
Baudier* and Regnon.

IV: 248   (342)

SAUL
First king of Israel (c.1025 B.C.); succeeded by David.*

IV: 265   (366)

SAUL
Irish town in Co. Down.

V: 164   (216)

SAVAGE CLUB
London literary club at 8 Adelphi Terrace (until 1936) and Carleton
House Terrace.

V: 25   (24)

SAVED FROM THE SEA
Play by Arthur Shirley and Ben Landech.

II: 133, 160, 209   (204, 246, 324)

SAYERS, DOROTHY
English writer of detective fiction. See also WIMSEY, LORD PETER.

IV: 195   (266)
V: 143   (189)
The Mind of the Maker (1941)   VI: 58   (74)

SCARABS
Variant. See VI: 115 (159), Appendix III.

SCHACKLETON'S
George Schackleton and Sons, 35 James Street and Anna Liffey Mills,
Lucan.

III: 191   (283)

SCHULTE, JOHANN FRIEDRICH VON
1827 - 1914. German Catholic composer of works on ecclesiastical law.

Ueber Kirchenstrafen   V: 151   (199)

SCOTLAND
V: 93   (119)
VI: 86, 103, 219   (117, 142, 314)

SCOTS OF THE HIGHLAND BRIGADE
Allusion to the battle of Magersfontein,* during which the Highland
Brigade, commanded by Major General Andrew Wauchope (1846 - 1899),
suffered great casualties, including a quarter of their officers. Said
one soldier, "we were led into a butcher's shop and bloody well left
there."

II: 200   (310)

SCOTS WHA HAE AT BANNOCKBURN
From Robert Burns's* poem, "Bruce's March to Bannockburn." At the
Battle of Bannockburn (1314), Robert the Bruce defeated the English
under Edward II.

III: 32   (40)

SCOTT, SIR WALTER
1771 - 1832. Scottish poet, novelist, historian, and biographer. See
also IVANHOE.

I: 35   (43)
II: 122   (187)
IV: 21, 23   (18, 20)
Lady of the Lake (1810)   III: 51   (70)
Marmion (1808)   I: 25   (26)

SCOTTISH BORDERERS
King's Own Scottish Borderers, 25 Regiment, in the British army, a com-
pany of which was responsible for indiscriminate shooting at Bachelor's
Walk.*

III: 261-3   (392-4)

SCUDAMOUR
Figure in Edmund Spenser's* Faerie Queene.

V: 77   (97)

SCUDDER, SALEM
Character in Boucicault's* play, The Octoroon.

II: 132, 134   (202, 206)

SEABHAC NA CEITHRE CAOILE (THE HAWK OF THE SLENDER QUARTERS)
Four-act play by Tomas O hAodha, published (1906) by the Gaelic League.

III: 235   (351)

SEGONZAC, ANDRE DUNOYER DE
1884 - ? . French painter of landscape and figures.

V: 64   (78)
VI: 85   (115)

SEINE RIVER
In northcentral France, flowing through Paris where Joyce* lived for
many years.

VI: 173   (245)

SELT/SELTIC TWILIGHT
See KELTIC TWILIGHT. O'Casey frequently used this spelling to
characterize the British, who commonly used a soft rather than a hard
"C." Used also in his play, The Shadow of a Gunman (Act II).

V: 80, 81, 85, 86   (101, 102, 108, 109)

SELWYN, ARCHIE
Edgar Selwyn. 1875 - 1944. American theatrical producer. Author of
several plays.

V: 69-70   (85-6)

SEMIRAMIS/NINUS
In Assyrian legend, Semiramis was the wife of Ninus and the founder of
Nineveh.

II: 88, 108   (131, 164)

SEMPE, FATHER/ABBE PEYRAMALE
In Werfel's* play, The Song of Bernadette, Pere Sempet is a chaplain,
and Marie Dominique Peyramale is the dean who refused to build a chapel
on the site of Massabielle grotto until he had evidence of the miracle.

IV: 277-8   (384)

SENECA, LUCIUS
c.4 B.C. - 65 A.D. Roman statesman, philosopher and playwright.

VI: 202   (287)

SEPHIROTH TIPPERETH
In theosophic philosophy, a cosmogony from the Kabbalah, a collection of ancient Hebrew writings treasured for centuries by occultists. See Ellmann's books, Yeats - The Man and the Mask and The Identity of Yeats. See also GOLDEN DAWN.

IV: 126   (168)

SEPOYS
The Sepoy Revolt (1857-58) against British authority in India. The most immediate cause was the introduction into the native (Sepoy) army of a new rifle whose use required the touching of grease on the cartridge. The principal result of the mutiny was the abolition of the East India Company and placing India under Crown rule. See INDIAN MUTINY.

V: 224   (301)

SEUMAS THE SHIT
Common Irish nickname for James II.*

II: 57, 232   (82, 360)

SEVEN WOODS OF COOLE
Allusion to Yeats's* poem of the same name.

IV: 140, 284   (189, 393)

SEVERN
River flowing through England and Wales.

IV: 215   (295)

SEVILLE PLACE
In central Dublin, leading south from Amiens Street. Site of the O'Toole Piper's Club headquarters.

III: 261   (391-2)

SHAFTESBURY
Athony Ashley Cooper, 7th earl of Shaftesbury. 1801 - 1885. Advocate of social legislation for mental institutions (1845), shorter working hours for factory workers (1847), abolition of women and child labor in coal mines (1842), and housing reform.

V: 168   (223)

SHAKESPEARE, WILLIAM
For more of O'Casey on Shakespeare, see his essays in The Flying Wasp and in Blasts and Benedictions. See also:

ANTHONY	ELSINORE	LAERTES	RICHARD THE
BARDOLPH	FALSTAFF	LEAR	THIRD
BRUTUS	GLOUCESTER, DUKE OF	NYM	ROMEO AND JULIET
CALIBAN	HAMLET	OPHELIA	SHALLOW, MASTER
CARDINAL	HENRY THE SIXTH	QUICKLEY	TEARSHEET, DOLL
			TYBALT

MORE

SHAKESPEARE, WILLIAM (cont.)

```
I:    34, 76                         (42, 110)
II:   24, 108-11, 114-16, 123-4, 127, 132, 137, 153, 156, 185
      (28-9, 164-70, 173-7, 187, 189, 195, 211, 235, 240, 285)
III:  11, 168, 183, 193             (8, 247, 270, 285)
IV:   23, 125, 182, 208, 222, 278   (20, 167, 248, 286, 306, 385)
V:    15, 18, 26, 27, 33, 36, 37, 52, 84, 116, 124, 128, 129, 181
      (9, 14, 27, 35, 39, 40, 61, 107, 151, 161, 167, 169, 241)
VI:   57, 64-5, 66, 88, 105, 197, 200   (73-4, 84-7, 120, 144, 281, 282,
                                         284)
```

Shakespeare's Works	I: 35	(43)
	IV: 75	(95)
Globe Edition	II: 122	(187)
Macbeth (1605-06)	II: 23	(28)
King Henry VI (1590-92)	II: 23	(28)
Richard The Third (1592-93)	II: 23	(28)
Coriolonius (1607-09)	V: 12	(5)

SHALLOW, MASTER
Justice Robert Shallow in Shakespeare's* plays, King Henry IV, part II,
and The Merry Wives of Windsor.

```
V: 234                              (315)
```

SHAN VAN VOCHT
Also given as SEAN BHEAN BOCHT. Corruption of the Irish words, an
t-sean bhean bhocht, the poor old woman, a euphemism for Ireland.

```
II:   170                           (261)
III:  156                           (229)
```

SHAN VAN VOGUE, LADY
Variant on Shan Van Vocht.*

```
VI: 108                             (149)
```

SHANNON, EARL OF
Henry Boyle. 1682 - 1764. British parliamentary leader (1707-56).
Leader of the Irish Whig party who resisted British attempts to drain
Irish resources. O'Casey mistakes the amount of Boyle's pension. It
was an annual pension of 2000 pounds for 31 years (given 1756), with
titles of Baron of Castlemartyr, Viscount Boyle of Bandon, and Earl of
Shannon.

```
III: 70                             (98)
```

SHANNON RIVER
In southeast Ireland, the best known of all Irish rivers.

```
II:  187, 237                       (289, 367)
V:   91, 180                        (116, 239)
```

SHANNON SCHEME
Project undertaken by the Irish Free State government (1927) to develop
the River Shannon for electrical power. A 60-megawatt station was built
at Ardnacrusha.

IV: 151   (205)

SHARPHAN/SHARPHAN HOUSE
The Sharpham estate in the parish of Ashprington, Devon, England, lying
on the River Dart.* Sharpham House is a late Georgian house designed
by Sir Robert Taylor for Captain Philemon Powall, R.N., in 1826.

VI: 135   (187, 188)

SHAUN THE POST
Character in Boucicault's* play, Arrah na Pogue.

II: 132, 135   (203, 207)

SHAW, CHARLOTTE
d.1943. Wife (from 1898) of George Bernard Shaw.* It was to Mrs. Shaw
that O'Casey made his famous statement (#): "God be my judge that I
hate fighting" (see Letters, I, pp. 433-4).

V: 41-2, 103, 107-08#   (46-7, 133, 139-40#)
VI: 161-91   (226-70)

SHAW, GEORGE BERNARD
1856 - 1950. Celebrated Irish dramatist, and a close friend of the
O'Caseys. The production of Androcles and the Lion which O'Casey refers
to opened at the Abbey on 4 November 1919. For more on the Blanco
Posnet controversy, see Robinson's Ireland's Abbey Theatre, pp. 59-65.
For more of O'Casey on Shaw, see several of his essays in The Green Crow
and in Blasts and Benedictions. See also the interesting letter from
O'Casey to Ronald Ayling in Cowasjee's Sean O'Casey. See also:

ABBEY THEATRE	DEMPSEY, FATHER	KEEGAN, FATHER
ADELPHI TERRACE	DORAN, BARNEY	KEEGAN'S DREAM
AYOT ST. LAWRENCE	DOYLE, JUDY AND CORNY	O'REILLY, NORA
BONNINGTON, BLOMFIELD	EVANS, FEEMY	RAMSDEN, ROEBUCK
BRIEUX, EUGENE	FARRELL, PATSY	ROSCULLEN
BRITOMART, LADY	HAFFIGAN, MATT	TANNER, JACK
BROADBENT, TOM	IRISH ACADEMY OF LETTERS	WAYNEFLETE, LADY
	JENNIFER AND DUBEDAT	

III: and O'Casey's talent/criticism   164   (242)
      and O'Casey's "introduction" to   171-3   (252-5)
      and Ireland   174-8   (255-61)
      and children   216-17   (322)
                                          VI: 32-6, 68-9   (VI: 35-41, 90)
      and military affairs   227   (338)

IV: and Three Shouts on a Hill   30   (31)
      and the Coole Park tree   142   (191)
      criticism, and importance of   182   (248)
      and sheepdogs   224   (309)

                                                           MORE

SHAW, GEORGE BERNARD (cont.)

V: and The Silver Tassie	40-2, 103	(45-7, 133)
	VI: 161, 180	(VI: 226, 254)
and letter to Lady Gregory* vis the Tassie	103	(133)
and letter to O'Casey vis amateur rights (23 July 1932)	118	(139)
and Jesuits	205	(274)
and British critics and O'Casey	222-3	(299)
and nationalism	226	(303)
	VI: 106	(VI: 141)
VI: and Chesterton*	15	(10)
and comparison with T. P. O'Connor*	25	(26)
and limitations of the Bible	37	(42)
and O'Casey's children's education	68-9, 180	(90, 255)
and "Shaw's Corner"	161-91	(226-70)
and death of	186-7	(263-6)
Mentioned:	III: 186	(275)
	IV: 125, 220	(167, 303)
	V: 204	(273)
	VI: 43, 45,	(52, 55, 165,
	120, 121, 219	167, 314)

Works:

Androcles and the Lion (1912)	IV: 114	(152)
John Bull's Other Island (1904, Home Rule edition, 1912)	III: 171, 204	(252-3, 302)
	VI: 167, 189	(236, 268)
The Shewing-Up of Blanco Posnet (1909)	IV: 138	(186)
Dramatic Criticism (probably Dramatic Opinions and Essays, 1907)	IV: 182	(248)
Man and Superman (1903, see ABBEY)	IV: 183	(249)
Back to Methuselah (1921)	VI: 30	(33)
Heartbreak House (1917)	VI: 175-6, 189	(248, 268)
Caesar and Cleopatra (1900)	VI: 188	(267)
Candida (1898)	VI: 188	(268)
The Devil's Disciple (1900)	VI: 188, 189	(268, 269)
Saint Joan (1923)	VI: 175, 188	(248, 267)

SHEBA, QUEEN OF
In Biblical history, the Sabaens were the most important people in Arabia. From this region came a queen to test Solomon's* wisdom (I Kings 10:1). In Arabic legend, her name was Balkis. She bore a son to Solomon, and from this son the Ethiopians claim descent.

III: 92, 94   (133, 135)

SHEED, FRANCIS JOSEPH
1897 - 1981. Publisher and husband of Maisie Ward.* Co-founder of Sheed and Ward Publishers, London and New York. O'Casey is quoting from Sheed's book, Man and Sanity (1946)

IV: 223-4, 227   (307-09, 313)

SHEEDY, DR. MORGAN
1853 - 1939. Rector, Cathedral of the Blessed Sacrament, Altoona,
Pennsylvania. To whom O'Casey partially dedicated his play, The
Drums of Father Ned. Editor-publisher, The Altoona Monthly, and author
of Christian Unity (1895) and Social Problems (1896). In a letter to
Dr. Irma Lustig (29 November 1951), O'Casey wrote:

> I wonder do the friends you mention know anything about what goes on
> in Altoona? A priest there, Father Sheedy, sent me his blessing
> when I was in New York in 1934. He was a life-long friend of Dr.
> /Walter/ MacDonald of Maynooth. I was so busy with Rehearsals that
> I had time only to write and thank him. I mislaid his letter, &
> forgot his address. Then it came to me suddenly, when I saw the
> name of the Town in an American journal. He was an old man then;
> &, I fear, must be dead now. He wrote to me several times while
> I was in N.Y., & I replied as well as I could in the midst of the
> furors of a new production. How sorry I am now, I didn't go down
> to Altoona.

V: 238   (320)

SHEEHAN, CANON PATRICK AUGUSTINE
1852 - 1913. Irish writer and novelist. Known as a "Catholic" novelist
for his writings on episodes on Irish clerical life, Catholic adolescence,
and other Catholic subjects.

Graves at Kilmorna (1915)   III: 45   (59)
Luke Delmege (1901)   III: 133   (195)

SHEEHY-SKEFFINGTON, FRANCIS
1878 - 1916. Pacifist, socialist, champion of women's rights, and a
vice-chairman of the Irish Citizen Army.* Executed during the Easter
Rising on orders of an English officer, Captain Bowen Colthurst. To
O'Casey, Skeffington was the socialist embodiment of the Rising. See
his comments in The Story of the Irish Citizen Army.

III: 273   (409)

SHEEHY-SKEFFINGTON, HANNAH
1877 - 1946. Zealous Republican and widow of Francis Sheehy-Skeffington.* Active in nearly all Irish nationalist groups. Leader of the
protesters at the premiere of O'Casey's play, The Plough and the Stars.
Ardent supporter of Republican Spain during the Spanish Civil War.*

IV: 177-9   (242-4)

SHEEMSA, PATRON OF MARRYMAKERS
From the Irish word, siamsa, a merry gathering.

III: 159   (233)

SHELLEY, PERCY BYSSHE
1792 - 1822. English romantic poet. The "Irish Declaration" which
O'Casey refers to was An Address to the Irish People, given during
Shelley's visit to Dublin (February-March 1812). Shelley campaigned
actively "for the purpose of obtaining the emancipation of the Catholics,
from the Penal Laws that aggrieve them, and a Repeal of the Legislative
Union Act." (#)

II: 122		(187)
III: 197(#)		(292#)
V: 15, 116		(9, 151)
VI: 49, 105		(61, 144)
Prometheus	V: 18	(14)
	VI: 37	(43)
The Skylark	III: 39	(50)
Queen Mab	III: 39	(50)

SHELLY, SEAN (also SHAWN)
Appears as a Dublin associate of O'Casey and a former member of the
Irish Citizen Army Council.

III: 228	(346)
VI: 43	(52)

SHENTEE OHKAY
See KELLY, SEAN T.

III: 286   (428)

SHEPPARD, OLIVER
1865 - 1941. British sculptor and a member of the Royal Hibernian
Academy. Sheppard's marble bust of AE* is now in the National Gallery
of Ireland. There is a picture of it on the title page of The Living
Torch. Sheppard's first bust of AE was destroyed in the fire of the
R.H.A. during the Easter Rising.

IV: 212   (291)

SHERIDAN, MARY
Lady Gregory's* nurse and companion for 40 years. She was an Irish
speaker, Roman Catholic, and an encyclopedia of Irish folklore and
fairy tales. She was alive during the 1798 Irish Rebellion, and was
once in service to a leading United Irishman, Hamilton Rowan.

IV: 133   (178-9)

SHERIDAN, RICHARD
1751 - 1816. Celebrated Irish dramatist and parliamentary orator.

Plays   II: 122   (187)

SHERIFF STREET
In Dublin, east of Amiens Street Railway Terminal. On which St. Barnabas' Church was located.

II: 143, 150   (219, 230)

SHERRIFF, ROBERT CEDRIC
b.1896. English dramatist. The play which O'Casey refers to opened in
December at the Criterion Theatre, London (1929).

Journey's End (1929)   V: 20, 103-04   (16, 17, 134)

SHIELDS, ARTHUR
1897 - 1970. Abbey theatre actor. Brother of Barry Fitzgerald.* In
the premieres of O'Casey's plays, he played the roles of Donal Davoren
in The Shadow of a Gunman; The Free-Stater in Kathleen Listens In;
Johnny in Juno and the Paycock; The Young Man in Nannie's Night Out;
and Lt. Langon in The Plough and the Stars.

IV: 125   (166)

SHILLISHALLIUCKS OF THE WHITE NILE
Variant on the Shilluk tribe of the White Nile (one of three principal
streams forming the Nile River), and on the word, "shillyshally."

III: 181   (267)

SHINN FANE
Corruption of the Irish words, sinn fein* = ourselves alone.

VI: 194   (275)

SHIVA
Third god of the Hindu triad. In later mythology, regarded as the
destroyer, with Brahma* as the creator and Vishnu as the preserver.

V: 144   (190)

SHOCKING, SILAS K.
Silas Kitto Hocking. 1850 - 1935. English Free Church (Methodist)
minister and novelist.

III: 148   (217)

SHONELLY, DR.
Appears as a doctor who attended O'Casey's brother, Tom.

II: 146-7   (225-6)

SHOREDITCH
Metropolitan borough and parish in London. The "bells" which O'Casey
refers to is from the nursery rhyme, "Bells of London."

V: 9   (1)

SHORNCLIFFE CAMP
Major English military camp during World Wars I and II in Sandgate, Kent.

V: 36   (39)

SHREWSBURG
Town in Shropshire, England.

VI: 79   (107)

SHROPSHIRE LAD
Title of a collection of verse (1896) by Alfred E. Housman (1859 -
1936), English classical scholar and poet.

V: 23, 27   (21, 26)

SHYLOH
In Old Testament geography, Shiloh is a town in Ephraim, Palestine.
It was a meeting place the Israelites, and for centuries contained the
sanctuary of the ark of the covenant.

VI: 44   (54)

SIBERIA
Traditional prison camp region and exile location in Russian history.

V: 78   (98)
VI: 214   (306)

SIDNEY, SIR PHILIP
1554 - 1586. English poet and author of romantic prose.

VI: 67   (87)

SIDNEY, SYLVIA
See SYDNEY, SYLVIA

SIEGFRIED
Hero of Wagner's* The Ring of the Nibelung.

III: 58   (80)

SIERRA, GREGORIO MARTINEZ
1881 - 1947. Spanish playwright, poet and novelist.

Two Shepherds (1931)   IV: 274   (379)

SILVER KING, THE
Play (1907) by Henry Arthur Jones (1851 - 1929), English dramatist.

V: 26   (25)

SIMMS
Probably the Simms brothers, Robert and William, who were on the fringes
of the United Irishman movement. Assisted Tone* and Russell*
financially.

III: 103   (148)

SIMON, SIR JOHN
1873 - 1954. English lawyer and politician. M.P. (1906-18, 1922-40).
The incident O'Casey refers to was a speech in May 1926 on the floor of
the House of Commons which, according to the D.N.B., "indubitably had
some effect in bringing it /the General Strike*/ to an end."

V: 58, 94   (69, 120)

SINBAD
The sailor. Chief figure in The Arabian Nights.*

IV: 235   (325)

SINCLAIR, ARTHUR
1883 - 1951. Abbey theatre actor, husband of actress Maire O'Neill.
Co-director, with her, and actor with the Irish Players.* In O'Casey's
notebooks, he wrote:

> Arthur Sinclair had a company touring England with Irish plays . . .
> It was a fine company of actors, and Sinclair, though a comparative-
> ly ignorant man, was really a great actor, though given to taking
> too much drink at times. (Sean, p. 279)

For an account of the Abbey's attempts to block a production of Juno
by the Irish Players, see Cowasjee's Sean O'Casey, pp. 98-100.

V: 105   (136)

SINGASONGA OF NOTACHAGPUR
"Singasonga" is a variant on (a) sing a song of a, and (b) Singalang
Burong in Frazier's* book, The Golden Bough. Notachagpur, also in
Frazier, is Chota Nagpur, a region in India.

III: 181   (267)

SINGER COMPANY BUILDING
At 149 Broadway in New York City. Erected in 1908, named for the per-
fecter of the sewing machine, Isaac Singer (1811 - 1875).

V: 190   (254)

SINGING JAIL BIRDS
Play (1924) by Upton Sinclair (1878 - 1968), American author and social-
ist. According to Lady Gregory's journals, the event described by
O'Casey took place in the Abbey office, not her home.

IV: 137   (184)

SINN FEIN
Founded (1905) by Arthur Griffith* as an Irish political organization
to be inclusive of all Irish traditions. Griffith wrote:

> It is the declaration of the Irish Protestant Parliament and Pro-
> testant Volunteers of 1782, it is the declaration of the Irish
> Catholic Parliament and Catholic army of 1689, and the meaning
> and justification of every nationalist movement in Ireland since 1172.

MORE

SINN FEIN (cont.)

The name came from the Irish words for, loosely translated, "ourselves
alone." It was allegedly suggested to Griffith by Maire Butler, an
Irish nationalist and Gaelic Leaguer, who was a cousin of Sir Edward
Carson.* In Dublin, the Sinn Fein building was at 6 Harcourt Street.
The Sinn Fein Ard Fheis (#) was the 10th Sinn Fein convention, held at
the Mansion House in Dublin (25 October 1917).

III: 20, 21, 134-6, 144, 166, 242-3, 266, 276, 280, 281, 286
     (21, 22, 195-9, 212, 244, 362-3, 399, 414, 420, 422, 429)
IV: 10#, 30, 61, 169, 268   (2#, 31, 75, 76, 230, 370)

SITWELL, OSBERT
1892 - 1969. English poet, playwright and novelist.

The Scarlet Tree (autobiography, 1946)   V: 205   (274)

SKAGERRACK
Arm of the North Sea between Norway and Denmark.

VI: 114   (157)

SKEFFINGTON, DR. OWEN
1909 - 1970. Son of Francis and Hannah Sheehy-Skeffington* and a
liberal member of the Irish Senate. The first reference by O'Casey has
become known as the "Papal Nuncio Incident" (for which see BUTLER,
HUBERT; INTERNATIONAL AFFAIRS ASSOCIATION; and O'HARA, MICKEY). The
second incident involved Skeffington's scheduled appearance at the
Rathmines Town Hall in November 1952, a month after the papal nuncio
affair. Shortly before his appearance, Skeffington received a note
from the students saying that the Vocational Education Committee
(administrators of the Dublin technical schools) had forced them to
withdraw the invitation. Skeffington, who had been invited in August,
found that he had been linked with the "insult" to the papal nuncio
because he had invited Butler. Throughout his distinguished life,
Skeffington was an eloquent defender of liberal and unpopular causes
in Ireland.

VI: 210-11   (300-02)

SKIBBEREEN
Irish town in Co. Cork. Site of the ruins of a Cistercian Abbey where
victims of the Famine (1846-50) are buried.

III: 101   (145)
IV: 91, 212   (119, 291)

SKUMBERG, DUKE OF
Frederich Hermann, duke of Schomberg. c.1615 - 1690. Soldier of
fortune and mercenary. Accompanied William of Orange* to Ireland,
and commanded the expedition against James II.* Killed at the Battle
of the Boyne.*

II: 230, 232   (358, 359)
III: 37   (48)

SKYE
See SKYE BOAT SONG, Appendix I.

SLANE, HILL OF
Legendary site in Co. Meath associated with St. Patrick's* arrival in
Ireland in the 4th century.

II: 13-14   (12)

SLANEY
Irish river in the Wicklow mountains.

IV: 70   (88)

SLEEVENAMONITES
Variant on the Irish song, "Slievenomon," for which see Appendix I.

III: 153   (224)

SLIEVE MISH
Irish mountain range in Co. Kerry.

IV: 68   (85)

SLIGO
Irish city and county in Connaught province.

III: 15, 155, 213   (14, 227, 316)
IV: 116   (153)
VI: 216   (309-10)

SLOANE STREET/SQUARE
In Chelsea, London. On Sloane Square stands The Royal Court Theatre.*
There is also The Queen's, a restaurant where Sean and Eileen O'Casey
often went before and after they were married.

VI: 25   (25)

SLOGAN
In real life, John Hogan, schoolteacher and native Irish speaker from
Galway. He taught at St. Barnabas National School and was nicknamed
"Bosch" for his strict discipline and readiness to use a cane.

I: 99, 103-04, 109, 125, 130, 131, 141-50, 153, 155, 157
     (147, 153-5, 164, 189-90, 197, 198, 216-30, 234, 238, 241)
II: 41   (56)

SMILLIE, BOB
1859 - 1940. British labor leader. President, Miners' Federation (1912-
21). As president, Smillie pledged 1000 pounds a week to the Dublin
workers during the 1913 Strike.

VI: 90   (122)

SMITH, NED
Appears as a fellow worker with O'Casey.

III: 21   (22)

SNOWDEN, PHILIP
1864 - 1937. British politician. Bitter critic of Ramsay MacDonald.*

V: 95-7, 100   (122-4, 128)

SOCIAL CREDIT PARTY
Canadian political party (1935), which based its program on reform of
the monetary system along the lines of social credit.

V: 146   (193)

SOCIALISM
See also COMMUNISM, RUSSIAN REVOLUTION and SOVIET UNION.

II: 179   (275)
III: 213   (315)
IV: 160, 162-4, 220, 224   (217, 219-22, 303, 308)
V: 83, 97   (105, 125)
VI: 55, 58, 94-6, 98, 220-3   (69, 75, 127-31, 133, 316-20)

SOCIALIST PARTY OF IRELAND
Cumannacht na hEireann. Formed in 1904. In 1921, it became the
Communist Party of Ireland. O'Casey was a member of the S.P.I. for a
brief time after the Easter Rising.

IV: 14, 77   (8, 98)

SOCIETY OF AUTHORS
The Incorporated Society of Authors, Playwrights, and Composers, 11
Gower Street, London. O'Casey applied for membership on 19 June 1924
(see Letters, I, p. 110).

V: 39, 108   (43, 140)

SOCIETY OF ST. CATHERINE'S COLLEGE
The Shirley Society of St. Catherine's College.*   Mr. Alfred A. K.
Arnold, in behalf of the society, invited O'Casey to give a talk at
Cambridge (although see HENN, THOMAS R.).

VI: 44-6, 53   (53-6, 68)

SOCRATES
c.470 - 399 B.C. Celebrated Greek philosopher.

III: 62   (85-6)
IV: 212, 216   (291, 297)
VI: 57   (73)

SODALITIES OF THE GUILD OF MATTHEWISONS OF TALBUTTAMIA
See TALBOT, MATTHEW.

III: 153   (224)

SOLID MEN OF THE MULDOON CLAN
See MULDOON, THE SOLID MAN, Appendix I.

SOLOMON
King of Israel (c.973-933 B.C.), son of David and Bathsheba.

I: 144   (220)
II: 238   (370)
III: 83   (118)

SOLOMON'S SONG
In the Bible, one of the books of the Old Testament. Also known as
the Song of Songs.

V: 192   (256)

SOLOMONS, ESTELLA FRANCIS
First name also given as ESTELLE. 1902 - 1965. Irish artist. The
portrait of AE (#) was a portrait in oils (1930).

IV: 212#, 271   (291#, 374)

SOMERSETSHIRE
English county bounded by Devon, the Bristol Channel, Wiltshire, Dorset,
and Gloucester.

VI: 77   (102)

SONG OF BERNADETTE
See WERFEL, FRANZ. Also alluded to as BERNADETTE OF BALLYVOURNEY and
. . . OF MISSABIELLE.

III: 160   (235)
IV: 48, 67, 278   (57, 85, 384)

SONG OF THE SHIRT
Poem of social protest by Thomas Hood (1799 - 1845), English poet,
artist and journalist. O'Casey uses a variant of this for the title
of a chapter in Drums under the Windows (see "Song of a Shift").

VI: 115   (158)

SOPHOCLES
c.496 - 406 B.C. Greek tragic poet.

IV: 269   (372)

SORRASAINT
Appears as the manager of Leedom, Hampton chandler company, Dublin. A
pun on the words, "sorry saint."

II: 80-1, 85-6, 111-12   (120, 127-8, 170-2)

SOUDAN
In O'Casey's youth, it was known as the French Sudan, accounting for his
statement about the "tricolour in the Soudan" (#).

I: 76   (109)
II: 170#   (261#)

SOUTH KENSINGTON
In southwest London between Kensington and Chelsea. The flat which
O'Casey refers to was on Clareville Street.

V: 31   (32)

SOUTH WALES BORDERERS
In the British army, the 24th Foot Regiment.

I: 116   (175)

SOUTHWARK CATHEDRAL
St. Saviour's Church in Southwark, residential district of London.

VI: 31   (34)

SOVIET UNION/RUSSIA/SOCIALIST FEDERATION OF STATES/U.S.S.R.
See also COMMUNISM and SOCIALISM.

IV:	revolution,* mentioned	14	(8)
	revolution, O'Casey's support for	16	(10)
	revolution, as one of two fights		
	for liberty	16, 162	(10-11, 220)
	atheism of	89	(116-17)
	O'Casey's support of	128, 162-4	(171, 219-22)
		VI: 94, 95, 98	(VI: 127, 129-30, 133-4)
	and books as present for	128	(171)
	and Civil War	162	(220)
V:	and Stanley Baldwin*	78	(97-8)
	and Eamon de Valera*	83	(105)
	and detective stories	227	(305)
VI:	and education	38	(45)
	and "The Dree Dames"	94-6	(126-30)
	and World War II	113, 118, 142-4	(155, 163-4, 199-201)
	and""invasion of Ireland"	212-16	(303-09)
	and World War III potential	234	(336-7)

Mentioned: IV: 44, 169, 211, 253   (51, 230, 290, 350)
                  VI: 203   (290)

SPAIN
References to the Spanish Civil War (#) and the Spanish Armada (##).

I: 169   (260)
V: 127#   (166#)
VI: 82###   (111###)

SPANGLER SBUNGLER
Variant on Oswald Spengler (1880 - 1936), German philosopher whose
chief work, Decline of the West (1918-22), predicted the eclipse of
Western civilization, a favorite subject of theosophists.

III: 59   (82)

SPARTA
The leading Greek state in the 6th century. Dowling's study, A History
of Irish Education, quotes James Nash, a Waterford school teacher,
"I flog the boys every morning to teach them to be Spartans."

I: 143, 145, 148   (220, 222-3, 226)
V: 184   (245)

SPEAIGHT, ROBERT
1904 - 1976. Noted English Shakespearean actor and dramatic critic for
the Catholic Herald. His letter, "In Defence of Sean O'Casey," appeared
in the Catholic Herald (30 August 1935), and is reprinted in Krause's
Sean O'Casey.

V: 52   (60)

SPEECHES FROM THE DOCK
Anthology of Irish patriotic speeches and appeals, edited by T. D.,
A. M., and D. B. Sullivan. Reprinted in many editions.

II: 190   (293)
III: 15   (14)

SPELLMAN, CARDINAL FRANCIS
1899 - 1967. Right-wing U.S. Catholic clergyman. Bishop (1932) and
archbishop (1939) of New York; cardinal (1946). Spellman's name is not
mentioned in the first entry in the PAN edition. In the last paragraph
on page 358 of the U.S. edition, there should be inserted between the
words " . . . themselves. Catholics . . . " the following:

    'The Federal Council of Christian Churches who have persuaded
    President Truman to withdraw the American envoy, Myron Taylor,
    from the Holy See, are guilty of intolerance,' said Cardinal
    Spellman. This is a kettle black as hell calling another
    as black as night.

IV: 259
VI: 10, 31   (2, 34)
Road to Victory (1943) IV: 262 (362)

SPENCER DOCK
In west central Dublin, north of the River Liffey.

III: 275   (413)

SPENSER, EDMUND
c.1552 - 1599. English poet. Also served as sheriff of Cork. See
GOG/MAGOG and JANETHAINAYRIN.

MORE

SPENSER, EDMUND (cont.)

Faerie Queen (1590, 1596)   III: 284   (427)
View on the Present State
of Ireland (allusion to)   V: 201   (269)

SPERANZA
Pseudonym of Jane Francisca Elgee, Lady Wilde. 1826 - 1896. Oscar
Wilde's mother. Active in the Young Ireland movement and author of
several articles in the Nation.*

IV: 158   (214)

SPICER-SIMSON, THEODORE
1871 - 1959. The wax medallion of AE* which O'Casey refers to was
done in 1922. Spicer-Simson also did medallions of James Stephens,*
Yeats* and Lady Greogory.*

IV: 212   (291)

SPIKE ISLAND
In Cork Harbour. Site of Westmoreland Prison which was used as a
British prison (1847-85). Reclaimed by Ireland in 1938.

V: 171   (228)

SPINOZA
See SPUNOOZA.

SPION KOP
Natal mountain, site of an important Boer victory over the British
(24 January 1900).

III: 105   (152)

SPRING-RICE, MARY
British novelist, daughter of Lord Monteagle.* Participated in the
gun-running venture for the Irish Volunteers with Erskine Childers.*

III: 157   (231)

SPUNOOZA
Baruch Spinoza. 1632 - 1677. Dutch philosopher who was regarded as
one of the most eminent expounders of Pantheism.

III: 59   (82)

SQUEERS, MRS.
In Dickens's* Nicholas Nickleby (1838), the wife of Wackford Squeers,
the brutal predatory proprietor of Dotheboys Hall.

VI: 193   (274)

STACK, AUSTIN
1879 - 1929. Minister for home affairs during the Irish War of Independence, which also included being in charge of Irish Republican courts.
See his letter to O'Casey (Letters, I, pp. 94-5) for one of the sub-plots
of The Shadow of a Gunman.

IV: 85, 86   (110, 111)

STAFFORD STREET
In west central Dublin, running from Parnell Street to Upper Abbey
Street. Now Wolfe Tone*(born #44) Street. The Irish Worker* was
printed by the "Stafford Street Printers."

II: 78   (116)
III: 236   (352)

STALIN, JOSEPH
1873 - 1953. Russian dictator.

V: 93   (119)
VI: 119, 121, 142   (165, 167, 264, 265)
Life of Lenin (1931)   IV: 165 (225)

STALINGRAD
O'Casey's reference is to the decisive battle (February 1943) which
marked a halt to the Nazi advance into the U.S.S.R.

VI: 143   (200)

STANDARDARIANS
Probably those of the Catholic newspaper, The Standard.* See also
DARIAN.

III: 152   (224)

STARKIE, WALTER FITZWILLIAM
1894 - 1976. Irish writer, conversationalist, and friend of artists
and statesmen. Author of many books and articles. As one of the
directors of the Abbey Theatre* (1927-42), he favored presentation of
O'Casey's play, The Silver Tassie.

V: 40, 132   (45, 173-4)

STATUE OF LIBERTY
American national monument located on Bedloe's Island off New York
City. Officially titled Liberty Enlightening the World.

V: 177-8   (237)

STEPHENS, JAMES
c.1882 - 1950. Major Irish poet, essayist, short-story writer, and
critic. In a letter to Ronald Ayling (22 May 1957), O'Casey wrote that
he had hoped that dedicating Cock-a-Doodle Dandy to Stephens would help
Stephens out his "then lethargic condition of mind which prevented him
from writing anything; . . . it didn't." The one-act play which O'Casey
refers to (#) was The Wooing of Julia Elizabeth, based on Stephens's
MORE

STEPHENS, JAMES (cont.)

The Charwoman's Daughter. The play opened at the Abbey Theatre, 9
August 1920.

III: 190   (281)
IV: 115#, 184-5, 191, 198, 204-05, 207, 209
     (152#, 252, 262, 271, 280-2, 284-5, 288)

STEPINAC, CARDINAL ALOYSIUS
b.1898. Yugoslav Catholic leader. Imprisoned by Tito (1946), freed
(1951), made cardinal in 1952. See also BUTLER, HUBERT.

IV: 252   (349)
VI: 210   (300)

STERN, CREDA
According to Granville Hicks (New Leader, 29 November 1954), this is
Freda Utley (1898 - 1978), a prominent member of the British Communist
Party. Her husband, Acradi Berdichevsky, was a Soviet citizen whom she
met while working as a senior scientific worker at the Institute of
World Economy and Politics, Moscow (1930-36). He was arrested by the
O.G.P.U. and died in a concentration camp.

VI: 92-5   (125-30)

STEYN, MARTINUS T.
1857 - 1916. South African lawyer and politician. President, Orange
Free State (1896-1900).

II: 198   (306)

STOBART, JOHN CLARKE
English author of several anthologies of Latin poetry and books on
Roman and Greek culture.

VI: 202-03   (289)

STOCK EXCHANGE
In London's Capel Court, Throgmorton Street.

V: 77   (96)

STOKE GABRIEL
In Devon, England, a short distance from O'Casey's home in Torquay.
Home of John Davis, the navigator.

VI: 80   (107)

STOKER, DR. GRAVES
Dublin surgeon at 46 Rutland (Parnell) Square. Surgeon, Drumcondra
Hospital and Great Northern Railway.

III: 88   (126)

STONE, IRVING
b.1903. American writer and biographer.

V: 227-8   (306-07)
Lust for Life (1934, Van Gogh - O'C) V: 225   (302)

STONEHENGE
Circular grouping of stones standing on the Salisbury Plain.* A "sun-
stone" stands outside the outer circle at a point where a viewer in the
center of the inner circle can see the sun rise at the summer solstice.
The significance of Stonehenge is still subject to archeological study
and debate.

V: 61, 186, 239   (73, 248, 321)
VI: 25   (24)

STONEYBATTER
Suburb west of Dublin.

I: 160   (246)

STORE STREET
In central Dublin, behind the Custom House.

II: 170   (262)

STORY, DR. JOHN B.
1850 - ? . Dublin eye surgeon with Royal Victoria Eye and Ear Hospital and to St. Mark's Opthalmalic Clinic.* Resided at 6 Merrion Square.

I: 21, 29, 30-2   (19, 33, 35-8)
III: 53   (72)

STRANGFORD LOUGH
Land-locked inlet of the Irish Sea in Co. Down.

V: 161, 169   (212, 224)

STRINDBERG, AUGUST
1849 - 1912. Swedish playwright and novelist. See O'Casey's review of
The Strange Life of August Strindberg by Elizabeth Sprigge in New
Theatre, February 1949.

IV: 125, 278   (167, 385)
VI: 87   (118)

STRONGBOW, RICHARD
Second earl of Pembroke. c.1184. Early leader of the invasion of
Ireland. Captured Waterford and Dublin.

IV: 93   (121)

STUART KING
See JAMES II.

V: 174   (231)

SUALTAM'S SIN
Should be Sualtam's Son, Cuchulain,* from several lines in Yeats's*
play, At the Hawk's Well (the play in question).

IV: 270   (373)

SUBLIME ORDER OF EXCOMMUNICATION FOR CATHOLIC I COLLEGIO TRINITATIS
Variant on the Catholic Church's order forbidding, on pain of excommunication, Irish Catholics from attending Trinity College,* Dublin.

IV: 92   (120)

SUGAR LOAF MOUNTAIN
In the Wicklow Mountains at Kilmacanogue.

IV: 80   (103)

SUGRUE
Padraig O Siochfhradha (O'Sugrue). 1883 - 1964. Irish writer of
short stories and children stories. Pen name, "An Seabhac." Gone is
Gone, another version of the story referred to by O'Casey, was published
by Faber and Faber, London.

An Baile Seo 'Gainne-ne (This Town is Ours) (1913) VI: 222   (319)

SUIL-A-BEG
Cottage of Arte O'Neal in Boucicault's* play, The Shaughraun.

II: 139   (214)

SUIL-A-MORE CASTLE
Unknown.

II: 140   (214)

SULLISANLAY, PATRON OF SLUMS
Unknown.

III: 159   (233)

SULLIVAN, CHARLIE
Well-known Dublin actor of the 1890s who often appeared in Boucicault's*
plays. His sister, a Dublin actress,was married to Frank Dalton, whom
O'Casey calls Tommie Talton.*

II: 132-3, 134-5, 142   (203-04, 206-07, 218)

SULLIVAN, ROBERT
Dublin barrister and Irish education board member. Author of several
popular school books which ran into many editions.

Spelling Book Superseded (1858, 53rd ed.)   I: 187   (288)
Geography Generalised (1861, 27th ed.)   II: 87   (131)

SULLIVAN, FATHER RUSSELL
Head of the Legion of Decency* and the Boston Council of Catholic
Organizations. One of the chief opponents of a Boston production of
O'Casey's play, Within the Gates.

V: 202-03, 205-06   (270-1, 274-6)

SUMMERHILL
Section of north central Dublin, east of O'Connell Street.

II: 65   (96)
III: 66   (93)

SUTRO, ALFRED
1863 - 1933. English playwright and translator of Maeterlinck.

V: 24   (22)

SWAFFER, HANNEN
1879 - 1962. British journalist, dramatic critic of Daily Express
(1926) and Daily Herald (from 1931).

V: 25   (24)

SWANN'S WAY
Autobiographical novel (Du Cote de Chez Swann, 1913) by French novelist,
Marcel Proust (1871 - 1922).

V: 141   (186)

SWEENY
From an anonymous Irish poem of the 12th or 13th century, "Sweeny the
Mad." Sweeny, king of Dal Araidhe (c.634), was angry over the proposed
site of a church and tried to bodily expel the cleric. His wife,
Eorann, ripped off his clothes trying to stop him. Sweeny was cursed,
and wandered around Ireland for seven years, living in trees with wild
birds. His sanity returned when he was told that his son had died.
O'Casey's reference to the "apple tree" stems from one of the verses
in the poem: "O Apple tree, little apple tree/ Much thou art shaken
. . ."

VI: 62, 128, 207   (81, 178, 295)

SWIFT, JONATHAN
1667 - 1745. Famous Irish satirist, poet, and a generous benefactor
of charities and hospitals. Swift's Hospital (#) is St. Patrick's
Hospital for Imbeciles, Dublin, to which Swift bequeathed several thousand pounds. Opened 19 September 1757.

II: 31#   (40#)
III: 21, 37   (22, 48)
V: 45, 76   (51, 95)
VI: 101, 102   (138, 140)

SWISS SWINGILLIANS
See ZWINGLI, HULDREICH.

II: 228   (354)

SWORD OF LIGHT
Symbol of the Easter Rising and the Irish literary renaissance, which
dates from early literature. In later literature, it symbolized
intuitive knowledge, education and progress. Taken up by scholars of
the literary movement, and, in 1966, it was chosen as a symbol for the
1916 Easter Rising. See also SWORD OF LIGHT, Appendix IV.

II: 196-7, 219   (303, 339)
III: 21, 22, 142   (23, 25, 209)

SYDNEY, SYLVIA
Nee Sophia Kosow. b.1910. Broadway and film actress whom O'Casey met
in New York in 1934. Visited the O'Caseys in Battersea.

VI: 9   (1)

SYMONS, ARTHUR
1865 - 1945. Welsh poet and literary critic.

IV: 138   (186)

SYNGE, JOHN MILLINGTON
1871 - 1909. Major Irish playwright. Most of the chapter, "Song of a
Shift," in Drums under the Windows, refers to the premiere of Synge's
play, The Playboy of the Western World, at the Abbey Theatre (26 January
1907). For more of O'Casey on Synge, see "John Millington Synge" in
Blasts and Benedictions.

III: 39, 41, 120-1, 126, 130, 135, 145, 234, 243
     (51, 54, 175-6, 178, 183-4, 189, 213, 350, 362)
IV: 158, 176   (214, 240)
The Playboy of the Western World (1907) IV: 167   (227)
                                         V: 47   (53)
Riders to the Sea (1904)   IV: 138   (186)

SYRIA
VI: 110   (152)

T

TACITUS, CORNELIUS
c.55 - c.117. Roman orator, politician and historian.

Germania   II: 122   (187)
Life of Agricola   II: 122   (187)

TAGORE, RABINDRANATH
1861 - 1941. Hindu poet, painter and musician. Nobel Prize for literature (1913). Yeats met Tagore in 1912, and produced Tagore's play, The
Post Office, at the Abbey Theatre in 1913. He published it at the Cuala
Press one year later. The theme of one of Yeat's poems, "An Image from

TAGORE, RABINDRANATH (cont.)
a Past Life," is taken from Tagore's "In the Dusty Path of a Dream."
Yeats also wrote an introduction to Tagore's _Gitanjali_ (1912).

IV: 208   (285)

TAHRAHRAH BROOCH
The Tara Brooch, an ancient Irish medallion of great fame. It is made
of white bronze wrought in an Irish filigree of very delicate workman-
ship.

III: 201   (298)

TAILLTIN
See FAIR OF TELLTOWN.

III: 242   (361)

TAILTE, QUEEN
In Irish mythology, queen of the Firbolog and foster mother of the sun
god, Lugh.*

III: 65   (90)

TAIT, HARRY
Appears as a classmate of O'Casey.

I: 113-16   (171-5)

TALBOT, MATTHEW
1856 - 1925. Celebrated Dublin figure. A former alcoholic, Talbot
became a feverent religious convert. He forced himself to lead a severe
and austere life, denying his need for personal necessities to the point
of chaining himself to control the urges.

III: 245   (365)
IV: 165-7, 273   (224-6, 377)
VI: 40-1   (48)

TALBOT STREET
In central Dublin, running into Amiens Street heading east.

II: 78   (116)

TALBOTS
Norman family of English aristocracy in Ireland. Included the earls of
Waterford and Shrewsbury. The most prominent was Richard Talbot (1630 -
1691), who was active in struggles against England. Wounded at the
siege of Drogheda, escaped to France, created peer by James II,* and
was Lord Lieutenant (1687). Fought at the battles of Aughrim and Boyne.*

III: 8   (2)

TALTON, TOMMIE
Probably Frank Dalton,* a well-known Dublin actor who appeared in many
of Boucicault's* plays at the turn of the century. Dalton was the
father of Louis Dalton, the Irish playwright, and was married to Charlie
Sullivan's* sister.

II: 22, 24-5, 131-9, 142   (25-9, 209-12, 218)

TANDY, NAPPER
1740 - 1803. Co-founder, with Tone* and Russell,* of the Society of
United Irishmen.* Tandy was given command of a French corvette with
soldiers for the attempted (abortive) landing in Donegal during the
1798 Rebellion. Hero of the ballad, "The Wearing of the Green."*

II: 28   (35)
VI: 182, 194   (258, 276)

TANNER, JACK
An anarchist, author of the Revolutionists' Handbook, and a satire
on H. M. Hyndman, British labor leader, in Shaw's play, Man and Superman.

IV: 183   (249)
VI: 45   (55)

TARA
In Co. Meath, near the Boyne River. The Hill of Tara (#) was the seat
of Irish kings from ancient times to the 16th century. See also THE
HARP THAT ONCE THROUGH TARA'S HALLS, Appendix I.

I: 65   (92)
II: 14   (12)
III: 104, 112, 173#, 238, 239, 242, 266
     (150, 162, 255#, 356, 361, 398)
IV: 67, 276, 285   (84, 381, 395)
V: 81, 86, 173   (103, 109, 230)
VI: 179#, 212#   (254#, 303#)

TARA STREET
In central Dublin, south of the Custom House.

III: 221   (329)
IV: 285   (395)

TATE GALLERY
Art gallery in Millbank, London. Opened (21 July 1897) by the Prince
of Wales (later King Edward VII). Named for Sir Henry Tate (1819 -
1899), who gave the building as a museum, and, with it, 65 pictures and
two important bronzes.

VI: 28   (30)

TATTER JACWELSH, PATRON OF HOBOES
Variant on "Tatter Jack Walsh," an Irish jig.

III: 159   (233)

TAWN BO COOLEY
Tain Bo Cuailgne, the greatest of all Celtic tales and the central epic
of the Ulster cycle. Popularly known as the Cattle Raid of Cooley, the
Tain tells the story of Queen Maeve* of Connaught seeking to equalize
her wealth with that of her husband, Ailill. He has the famous white-
horned bull of Connaught, and she is determined to acquire the equally
famous brown bull of Cooley. Unable to get the bull on loan, she tries

MORE

TAWN BO COOLEY (cont.)

to take it by force. She agrees to a combat whereby Cuchulain* will
meet a Connaught warrior each day from winter until spring. The Men of
Eireann* invade Ulster and carry off the brown bull, but they are defeated later by the men of Ulster after a ferocious battle. The brown
bull slays the white-horned bull, and returns to Ulster. His heart
bursts and he finally dies.

III: 111, 239   (161, 357)

TAYLOR, MIMSIE
American actress, friend of George Jean Nathan.*

V: 238   (320)
VI: 9   (1)

TAYLOR, MYRON C.
Not found in U.S. editions. See SPELLMAN, CARDINAL FRANCIS. 1874 -
1959. American lawyer, business executive and diplomat. Associated with
U.S. Steel Co., and was Roosevelt's* personal representative to the
Vatican.

IV: 259

TAYLOR, WILLIAM COOKE
1800 - 1849. Irish scholar, author of several historical, educational
and religious works for students. Died of cholera in the Famine.

Epitome of Classical Geography (n.d.)   II: 122   (187)
Aeneid (trans.)   II: 122   (187)

TEARSHEET, DOLL
Prostitute and intimate of Falstaff* in Shakespeare's* play, 2 Henry IV.

V: 18   (14)

TEL-EL-KEBIR
Village in Egypt where British troops, under Garnet Wolseley, defeated
the Egyptians (13 September 1882).

V: 85   (108)

TELL, WILLIAM
Legendary hero of Switzerland in the struggle for independence of the
Schwyz Uri and Unterwalden cantons.   See Appendix III, this page.

III: 33   (41)

TEMPLE STREET
In central Dublin, running from Gardiner's Place to Hardwicke Place.

II: 133   (204)

TEN DAYS THAT SHOOK THE WORLD
The now-classic treatment of the first few days of the Russian Revolution (1917), written (1919) by John Reed (1887 - 1920), with an introduction by Lenin.* What the book lacked in historical accuracy was overshadowed by the stimulus it gave revolutionary groups around the world when accurate news of the revolution was difficult to gauge. The book has been translated into many languages.

V: 49   (57)

TEN LOST TRIBES
Part of the legend of the twelve tribes of Israel. Used by O'Casey in his play, Oak Leaves and Lavender.

V: 201   (268)

TENNYSON, ALFRED
1809 - 1892. Popular English poet. For more references, see Appendix II and III. O'Casey refers (#) to a short biography of Tennyson by Chesterton, The Bookman Biographies, no. 6.

II: 122		(187)
III: 168		(247)
VI: 168#, 232		(237#, 333)
Maud (1855)	I: 9	(2)
	VI: 104-5	(143-4)
Voyage of Maeldune	III: 144	(212)
Lady of Shalott	II: 97, 99	(147, 149)
	VI: 100	(137)

TENTER'S FIELD
Area southwest of central Dublin, immediately south of the Coombe.

I: 20   (19)
II: 43   (60)

THACKERAY, WILLIAM M.
1811 - 1863. Celebrated English novelist and satirist.

I: 35   (43)

THAMES EMBANKMENT
In London, the Victoria Embankment on the River Thames, running from Blackfriar Bridge to Westminister.

III: 249   (372)

THAMES RIVER
Principal river in England, approximately 228 miles long.

VI: 10, 17, 129   (3, 13, 179)

THANKSGIVING DAY
American national holiday, the fourth Thursday in November.

V: 185   (246)

THE POCKET
George's Pocket, a cul-de-sac at the back of St. George's* Church on
Temple Street, Dublin.

II: 133   (204)
IV: 285   (394)

THEATRE ROYAL
The Queen's Royal Theatre, 209 Great Brunswick (Pearse) Street, Dublin.
Built 1884.

II: 209   (324)

THEEBAW
Thebaw or Thibaw. 1858 - 1916. Last king of Burma (1878-85). Defeated
in the Third Burmese War (1885). I: 158 (244)

THERMOPYLAE, PASS OF
Narrow pass from Thessaly to Locris, between Mount Octa and a marsh
bordering the Maliacus Sinus. Site of the famous (480 B.C.) conflict of
the Persian War.

II: 88   (132)

THERSITES
Pen name of Thomas Woods (1923 - 1961), columnist for the Irish Times.

VI: 210   (301)

THESEUS
In Greek legend, the chief hero of Attica.

II: 110   (167)

THIRD ORDER OF ST. FRANCIS/ST. FORMULUS
In the Catholic Church, third orders are lay orders of men and women
pursuing ordinary avocations of secular life. ST. FORMULUS (#) is a
variant. The Franciscans are the most numerous.

III: 171   (252)
IV: 274#   (378#)

THIRTEEN CLUB
A select dining club near the Moira Hotel, Trinity Street. Yeats was
one of its leading members. In his book, Sean O'Casey, Gabriel Fallon*
gives more details of the occasion (pp. 47-9)

IV: 124   (166)

THIRTY-NINE ARTICLES
Points of doctrine agreed upon by archbishops, bishops and clergy of the
Church of England at a convocation held in London (1652). The articles
relate to the doctrine of the Trinity, the rule of faith, doctrine of
sin and redemption, and other religious matters.

V: 219   (293)

THIS WOMAN BUSINESS
Play (1925) by Noel Coward.* O'Casey is referring to a Haymarket
Theatre production of this play in London which opened in April, 1926.

V: 20   (16)

THOMAS, JAMES HENRY
1874 - 1949. English labor leader and politician. General secretary,
National Union of Railwaymen (1918-24, 1925-31). For an account of
his troubles with de Valera,* see Bromage, De Valera and the March of
a Nation, pp. 237-40 (#).

IV: 160#   (217#)
V: 94-7, 100, 101, 228   (120-4, 128, 131, 307)

THOMAS STREET
In southwest Dublin near the Coombe district and the Guinness Brewery.

I: 21   (20)
II: 27   (34)

THOMPSON, DR.
This may be Captain Wade Thompson, secretary of Adelaide Hospital,
Dublin.

III: 246   (368)

THOMPSON, FRANCIS
1859 - 1907. British poet and prose writer of mystical prepossessions.
Best known for his poem, "The Hound of Heaven."

IV: 209   (288)

THOMPSON, JAMIE
Appears as an Orangeman from the Portadown Orange lodge.

III: 65   (90)

THOOR BALLYLEE
Yeats's* home in Co. Galway, a Norman castle and cottages which he
bought in 1917 for 35 pounds, and in which he and his family spent
their summers until 1929. The bridge that O'Casey refers to is found
in Yeats's poem, "Meditations in Time of Civil War."

IV: 96   (126-7)

THOR
In Old Norse mythology, the god of thunder, champion of gods, and the
friend of mankind.

II: 188   (291)
III: 58   (80)
V: 232   (312)
VI: 119   (165)

THORWALDSEN, BERFEL
1768 - 1844. Danish sculptor.

<u>Venus</u>   IV: 95   (124)

THREE HUNDRED AND THREE MEN
From the first verse of Thomas Davis's* song, "A Nation Once Again,"
for which see Appendix I.

III: 155   (229)

THREE ROCK MOUNTAIN
One of the Dublin mountains.

III: 205   (303)

THREE SORROWS OF STORYTELLING
Related to Lady Gregory's* sorrows, but also the title of a publication
by Douglas Hyde.* (1895).

IV: 146   (197)

THRONE ROOM
In the State apartments of Dublin Castle,* a ceremonial room decorated
in white and gold with pilasters and chandeliers. Presented by William
of Orange.*

IV: 91   (119)

THURSTON, FATHER HERBERT
1856 - 1939. English writer and prolific contributor to the Catholic
journal, <u>Month</u>, and to the <u>Catholic Encyclopedia</u>. Co-editor, with
Attwater,* of a revision (1926-38) of Butler's* <u>Lives of the Saints</u>.

IV: 260   (359)

THYATIRA
In ancient geography, a city in Lydia, one of the seven cities mentioned
in the Book of Revelation.

II: 118   (180)

TIBULLUS, ALBIUS
c.54 - c.18 B.C. Roman elegiac poet. See Appendix II for source and
translation of the passage quoted by O'Casey.

VI: 199   (284)

TILLET, BENJAMIN
1860 - 1943. Celebrated British labor leader.

III: 214   (317)

TILLYRA CASTLE
See TULLYRA CASTLE.

TIMES SQUARE
Tourist attraction at 42nd Street and Broadway in New York City.

V: 185   (246)

TINKERBELL
Character in J. M. Barrie's (1860 - 1937) fantasy, Peter Pan (1904).

IV: 77   (99)

TIPPERARY
Irish county in Munster province.

III: 47, 103, 285   (64, 149, 427)
V: 177   (236)
VI: 80, 110   (107, 151)

TIR FHIACHRACH AIDHNE
Tir is the Irish word for land. The whole phrase is related to Ui
Fhiachrach, one of the three early sections of Connaught. See O'Rahilly,
Early Irish History and Mythology, p. 405.

V: 173   (230)

TIRCONNELL
See TALBOTS.

I: 24   (25)
V: 173   (231)

TIRNALOGIANS
See LAND OF TIR NA N-OG.

III: 153   (224)

TITIAN
1477 - 1576. Italian painter and chief master of the Venetian school.

III: 61, 217   (84, 322)
IV: 199   (273)

TITTLE, WALTER
1883 - ? . American-born artist and member of the Royal Art Society
in London. His dry-point etching of AE* was published in Fine Prints
of the Year, 1933.

IV: 212   (291)

TOBIN, RICHARD FRANCIS
1843 - ? . Distinguished Dublin surgeon. Surgeon to St. Vincent's
Hospital, and probably the same doctor who attended Connolly's* wounds.
Resided at 60 St. Stephen's Green.

III: 252   (376, 377)

TOLKA BRIDGE/RIVER
The Tolka River enters Dublin at Glasnevin and flows southeast through
Drumcondra and Ballybough. The Tolka Bridge (#) is the bridge over the
river at Drumcondra Road.

I: 189   (291)
II: 50#, 63#, 206   (72#, 91#, 318)

TOLLER, ERNST
1893 - 1939. German poet, dramatist and political revolutionary. One
of the best writers from the expressionist school. Banished (1933)
from Germany by the Nazis.

Hoppla, Wir Leben (1927)   V: 116   (151)

TOLSTOY, LEV NIKOLAEVICH
1828 - 1910. Famous Russian novelist, philosopher and religious mystic.
O'Casey alludes (#) to Chesterton's* work, Simplicity and Tolstoy (1912).

IV: 278   (385)
VI: 168#   (236-7#)
Resurrection (1899-1900)   V: 207   (277)

TOM BROWN'S SCHOOLDAYS
Celebrated novel (1857) by Thomas Hughes (1822 - 1896), English novelist
and Christian Socialist activist.

VI: 131   (182)

TOM, UNCLE
This is O'Casey's uncle. His last name may have been Casey, although
O'Casey refers to him as "Mr. Hall." (See II: 29 PAN, 37 US.)

II: 27-37, 40   (33-48, 54)

TOMMIES
Slang for British soldiers. From Kipling's poem, "Tommy Atkins."

III: 258, 278, 284   (386, 418, 422)
IV: 51, 52, 60, 62   (61, 63, 74, 77)
V: 36   (39)

TONE, THEOBALD WOLFE
1763 - 1798. Irish revolutionary leader and father of the modern Irish
democratic movements. Co-founder, with Tandy* and Russell,* of the
Society of United Irishmen.* Tone organized French assistance for the
1798 Rebellion, gathering an expedition of 43 ships and 15,000 men, but
the ships were dispersed by a storm. Two years later, he tried again,
but was captured by the British after a fight off Lough Swilly. Imprisoned, he was refused a soldier's death and committed suicide. Buried
at Bodenstown.* The reference to Tone's views on property is from his
famous statement:

    If the men of property will not support us they must fall. We can
    support ourselves by the aid of that large and respectable class
    of the community: the men of no property.

                                                         MORE

TONE, THEOBALD WOLFE (cont.)

The reference to Tone's internationalism is from Connolly's* Labour in Irish History. In the chapter, "United Irishmen as Democrats and Internationalists," Connolly referred to the Society's founding document (June 1791), writing:

> It would be hard to find in modern Socialist literature anything more broadly International in its scope and methods, more definitely of a class character in its methods, or more avowedly democratic in its nature than this manifesto . . .

The Tone monument was a foundation stone, laid on Grafton Street, Dublin, during the 1898 Commemorations. The monument was never completed. The book which O'Casey refers to (probably the same one despite different titles) was edited by Tone's son. It was printed in the U.S. (1828), and reprinted in several editions between 1876 and 1920.

I:	as leader of the United Irishmen	177-8	(273-4)
		III: 158	(III: 233)
		IV: 273	(IV: 377)
II:	as Protestant	28	(35)
	memorial stone for	161	(249)
		III: 108	(III: 156)
III:	grave of	34, 162, 175,	(43, 239, 259,
		228, 242	340, 361)
		V: 164	(V: 217)
	as Internationalist	229	(340-1)
	and "Boys of Ormand Market"*	231	(344)
		IV: 256	(IV: 354)
	and rights of property	265	(297)
Mentioned:		II: 159	(244)
		III: 75, 102	(106, 148)
		IV: 100, 158,	(132, 214, 216,
		159, 177, 183	242, 249)
		V: 79	(100)
Life of Theobald Wolfe Tone (1828)		II: 190, 212	(293, 328)

TOPHET
Old Testament hell where corpses were burned and human sacrifices performed in the worship of Moloch (Isaiah 30:33).

II: 215   (333)

TORBAY
Tor Bay, inlet of the English Channel in Devon. Tor Bay hospital was where Shivaun O'Casey* was born.

VI: 84, 125   (113, 173)

TORNA
Pseudonym of Tadh Ua Donnchadha. 1874 - 1949. Irish writer in Gaelic.
Editor, Gaelic Journal (1902-09). Author of many textbooks on Irish
grammar, and translator of several old Irish studies.

III: 144   (212)

TORQUAY
Mid-Victorian borough of 6244 acres in Devon, England, with three ancient
parishes: Tor Mohun, St. Marychurch and Cockington. O'Casey moved to
3 Villa Rosa Flats, 40 Trumlands Road, St. Marychurch on 9 June 1954 and
remained there until his death.

VI: 82, 125   (111, 173)

TORRES VEDRAS
Town in western Portugal. Site of a major battle by Wellington against
the French (1810-11) in the Peninsular War.

III: 105   (152)

TOSTAL
Gaelic for "a hosting." In 1958 (after the autobiographies), the Dublin
Tostal Council organized a spring festival which was to feature the
premiere of O'Casey's play, The Drums of Father Ned, an adaptation of
Ulysses, and some of Beckett's plays. Archbishop McQuaid* refused to
bless the festival because of O'Casey's play. O'Casey withdrew the play
(as did Beckett).   See "The Drums of Father Ned" in A Paler Shade of
Green.

VI: 212   (303)

TOTNES
In Devon, England, a small town on a hill rising from the west bank of
the River Dart. Part of the town extends across the river to the
suburb of Bridgetown. O'Casey lived in Totnes for 17 years (September
1938 - June 1954).

V: 70, 232   (87, 312)
VI: 69, 73-5, 79-81, 128, 135, 137-8, 140-3, 149-51, 157, 192
    (91, 97-9, 106-09, 177, 187, 191-2, 195-9, 209-10, 220, 272)

TOUHY, PATRICK
1894 - 1930. Dublin artist and teacher at the Metropolitan School of
Art.* His portrait of O'Casey for the first edition of The Plough and
the Stars was replaced by one by Augustus John.* O'Casey ordered the
change in a letter to Macmillan (19 May 1926).

IV: 185-6   (253-4)

TOURIST ASSOCIATION
Bord Failte Eireann, a public enterprise responsible for the development
of the Irish tourist industry.

VI: 215   (309)

TOURMAKEADY
Irish town in Co. Mayo.

III: 25, 124, 126, 127, 129, 130   (28, 181, 184, 185, 188, 190)

TOURNEUS, CECIL
c.1575 - 1626. English dramatist. Author of an allegorical lament on
political and ecclesiastical corruption.

V: 110   (143)

TOWNSHEND DRAMATIC SOCIETY
Appears as a dramatic society in Dublin which was organized by O'Casey
and his brothers.

II: 131-2   (201)

TOWNSHEND STREET
In south central Dublin, running parallel to the River Liffey.

II: 20, 132   (22, 203)
III: 190   (281)

TRAFALGAR BAY
Off the coast of Spain where the famous battle between Nelson* and the
French and Spanish fleets was waged (1805).

III: 205   (303)
IV: 44   (52)

TRAFALGAR SQUARE
One of the principal squares in London. The National Gallery faces on
it.

V: 77   (96)
VI: 106   (145-6)

TRANSVAAL
Province of South Africa and a former British colony. Conquered and
annexed by England during the Boer War.*

II: 198   (306)

TRANSVAAL COMMITTEE
Irish organization which was formed during the Boer War * to support
the Irish Brigades. The committee supplied volunteers under the guise
of maintaining an ambulance for the Boer wounded, and was also instrumental in hindering British recruiting efforts. The Irish Brigades were
led by Colonel Arthur Lynch and Colonel J. Y. F. Blake, whose second-
in-command was John MacBride.*

II: 198   (306)

TREASURE ISLAND
Famous novel (1883) by Robert Louis Stevenson (1850 - 1894).

VI: 37, 38   (43, 45)

TREATY
See ARTICLES OF ASSOCIATION.

IV: 79, 82-6, 88, 90, 152   (102, 106-11, 115, 205)
V: 50   (58)

TREATY STONE
When Sarsfield* capitulated after the siege of Limerick,* the Treaty of
Limerick was signed (3 October 1691) on this stone, now a monument beside
Thomond Bridge, Limerick. The treaty guaranteed equality of treament
to Catholics, but this provision soon disappeared by the institution of
Penal Laws.*

III: 105   (152)

TREE OF LIFE
In its context, the Tree of Life was a symbol of the Order of the Golden
Dawn (see GOLDEN DAWN). It is also found in AE's* poem, "On a Hill-Top,"
and in many of Yeats's* poems.

IV: 126   (168)

TRENTIAN CREED
There is no creed as such, although the reference is clearly to the
Tridentine Catechism, the catechism of the Council of Trent.

V: 219   (293)

TREVELYAN, GEORGE M.
1876 - 1962. British historian and author of several noted books on
England and Europe.

V: 13   (7)

TRINITY COLLEGE
In Dublin, founded 1591.

I: 21, 58   (19, 81)
III: 12, 21, 113, 115, 143, 145   (9, 23, 163, 166, 210, 213)
IV: 24, 92, 149, 158, 237, 243, 255-6, 257, 260, 264
     (22-3, 120, 201, 214, 327, 335, 353-5, 359, 364)
V: 76   (95)

TRINITY COLLEGE
Constituent college of Cambridge University.

III: 248   (371)
VI: 50   (63)

TRISTAN AND ISOLDE
Metrical romance (c.1210), written by Gottfried von Strassburg, and an
opera (1865) by Richard Wagner. The story is popular in several national
mythologies, although it is particularly close to old Irish folklore.

III: 147   (216)
V: 204   (273)

TRUCE
In Irish history, the truce between the Irish Republican Army and British authorities, signed on 9 July and going into effect on 11 July 1921 at noon. Despite several breaches, it remained in effect until the Treaty* was signed.

IV: 64   (80)

TRUMAN, HARRY S.
Not found in U.S. editions. See SPELLMAN, CARDINAL FRANCIS. 1884 - 1972. Thirty-third president of the U.S. (1945-52).

IV: 259

TRUMPET MAJOR
Novel (1880) by Thomas Hardy.*

V: 23, 27   (21, 26)

TUAM
Archbishopric in Co. Galway. Site of an ancient church and the metropolitan see of the province of Connaught.

III: 132   (194)

TUAM, ARCHBISHOP OF
John Healy. 1841 - 1918. Bishop of Clonfert (1884-1903) and archbishop of Tuam (1903-18). Known as a "Castle Bishop" during the land agitation of the 1880s.

III: 132   (194)

TUATHA DE DANAAN
In Irish mythology, "the people of the goddess Dana." Their king was Dagda* the good, and, in the Book of Invasions, they are described as descendants of the Nemedians who invaded Ireland (c.15th century B.C.). They in turn were defeated by the Milesians* and disappeared into the hills of Ireland.

III: 57   (79)

TUBERNEERING
In Co. Wexford. A symbol of the 1798 Rebellion. Site of a major Irish victory over the British army (June).

IV: 91   (119)

TUERK, JOHN
1892 - 1951. With George Bushar Markell,* producer of the U.S. premiere of O'Casey's play, Within the Gates.

V: 181, 208   (241, 278)

TUFTS COLLEGE
American university in Medford, Massachusetts.

V: 205-06   (275)

TUGELA, BATTLE OF
In Natal, South Africa, on the Basutoland border. Site of a major campaign during the Boer War* in which the Royal Dublin Fusiliers* played a prominent part, suffering many (30%) casualties (February 1900).

II: 197, 201   (309, 310)
III: 41   (54)

TULLYRA CASTLE
Tullira or Tulira. Edward Martyn's home in Co. Galway, five miles north of Gort. There is a photo of the castle in Smythe's A Guide to Coole Park.

III: 133   (195)
IV: 132   (177)

TUNBRIDGE WELLS
Fashionable district in Kent, England.

V: 111   (145)

TURF BOARD
In Ireland, Bord na Mona, a government agency which is responsible for harnassing the peat-bog complexex.

VI: 215   (309)

TURNER, JOSEPH
1775 - 1851. English landscape painter, chiefly a water-colorist. The Turner Room (#) is in the Tate Gallery.*

III: 61   (84)
IV: 30, 199, 206   (31, 274, 283)
VI: 28#, 80, 164   (30#, 108, 231)

TUXEDO
O'Casey is punning on the sort of people whom Douglas Hyde* spoke to in the U.S on his tour, and also on Tuxedo Park, an affluent section of New York.

III: 113   (164)

TWO JOHNS
According to Margulies's The Early Life of Sean O'Casey, a son named John was born to O'Casey's mother (c.1870) and died two years later. Another, also named John, suffered a similar fate shortly before O'Casey was born.

IV: 22   (20)
VI: 71   (94)

TWO NATIONS OF ENGLAND
The other half of the title of Disraeli's* novel, Sybil, or The Two Nations (1845).

V: 57   (67-8)

TYBALT, FIERY
In Shakespeare's* play, <u>Romeo and Juliet</u>, a fiery member of the Capulet clan who challenges Romeo at the Capulet feast.

II: 109   (165)

TYBURN
Allusion to an execution place at Marble Arch, London, that stood until 1783. Since moved to Newgate Prison.*

III: 271   (407)

TYLER, WAT
d.1381. English leader of peasants' revolt against the repressive "Statutes of Labourers" and imposition of poll tax (1381). Demanded abolition of serfdom, removal of restrictions of labor and trade, and amnesty for rebels.

III: 188   (278)
VI: 102   (140)

TYNAN, KATHERINE
1861 - 1931. Irish poet and novelist. Among the leaders of the Irish literary renaissance. O'Casey is quoting from her statement in the introduction to <u>The Living Torch</u> (p. 7):

> I have known in my time some few undoubted geniuses -- three certainly in literature -- W. B. Yeats, Francis Thompson, and George Russell (A.E.) to which I have a fourth in James Stephens. In none of these have I found the beauty of genius as I find it in George Russell.

IV: 209   (288)

TYRONE
Irish county in Ulster province.

IV: 273   (378)

TYRONE, EARL OF
Richard Power. 1630 - 1690. One of the Power family singled out for special protection by Cromwell.* Power was a minor, though important, figure during the Restoration struggles in England. A frequent member of the Irish parliament.

III: 70   (98)

U

ULSTER
Northeast province of Ireland. Comprises the nine counties of Antrim, Armagh, Down, Fermanagh, Derry, Tyrone, Cavan, Donegal, and Monaghan. The first six form Northern Ireland.

ULSTER (cont.)

II: 235	(364)
III: 111, 116, 168, 237, 240	(161, 169, 248, 354, 358)
IV: 11, 66, 68, 160	(4, 83, 86-7, 217)
V: 51, 82, 88, 163-5, 216-20	(60, 103-04, 112-13, 215-18, 289-95)
VI: 111, 121, 169	(154, 167, 239)

ULSTER VOLUNTEERS
Armed miliatary organization formed (1912) to protest Home Rule for
Ireland. Led by Orangemen, it was composed primarily of Ulster
Protestants. The arms landing, referred to by O'Casey, occurred 24-25
April 1914. It was countered by the Irish Volunteers* at Howth.*

III: 226   (337)

ULSTER'S HOUND
See CULLEN'S HOUND.

V: 50   (59)

ULYSSES
Latin name of Odysseus. In Greek legend, a king of Ithaca, one of the
heroes of the Trojan War, especially famous for his wanderings and
exploits on a ten-year homeward voyage.

II: 88   (131)

UNCLE TIM'S CABIN
Popular term used by Dubliners as a reference to the vice-regal lodge
while Tim Healy* was governor-general of Ireland.

III: 244	(365)
IV: 150	(203)

UNCROWNED KING OF IRELAND
Title bestowed upon Parnell* in recognition of his popularity and power.
Another "uncrowned king" of the period was Gordon,* who, as governor-
general of the Sudan, received the popular title by the British.

I: 179	(276)
II: 18, 19	(19, 20)
III: 75	(106)

UNION JACK
Flag of Great Britain. See (#)for O'Casey's ideas of what the flag
represents.

I: 67, 74, 176, 182	(96, 108, 241, 272)
II: 23, 73, 76	(27, 107, 113)
III: 68, 89#, 102, 147	(95, 127#, 146, 216)
IV: 176	(240)

MORE

UNION JACK (cont.)

V: 90   (115)
VI: 117   (162)

UNIONISTS
In Irish history, those supporters of the union of Great Britain and
Ireland (see ACT OF UNION).

III: 106   (153)
IV: 208   (285)

UNITED IRISHMEN
Revolutionary society formed (1791) after the French Revolution* for
the purpose of overthrowing British rule in Ireland. Although burdened
with a bourgeois leadership, the society infused a European democratic
ideology into the Irish nationalist movement. Their strongest following
was from shop keepers and artisans in urban areas, and they had few
ties to the peasantry, a fact which hindered them during the 1798
Rebellion. See also TONE, THEOBALD WOLFE.

III: 103   (148)

UNITED STATES/AMERICA
II: 19   (20)
III: 156   (230)
IV: 71, 210, 211, 264, 282   (89, 288, 290, 365, 390)
V: 107, 109, 121, 172, 178   (139, 141, 157, 229, 237)
VI: 9, 38, 103, 139-42, 147, 212, 233, 234
      (1, 44-5, 142, 194-9, 206, 303, 334, 336)

UNIVERSALISTS
In its context, from the Catholic newspaper, The Universe and Catholic
Weekly.*

III: 152   (224)

UPANISHADS
Philosophical treatises and metaphysical commentaries of the Hindus.
In his youth, AE* spent his evenings studying the Upanishads and the
Books of the Vedas.*

IV: 216   (297)

URSULINE CONVENT, BURGESS HILL
At Brentwood, Essex, England. In her biography, Sean, and her autobiog-
raphy, Eileen, Eileen O'Casey mentions that she was sent to the Ursuline
Convent. She frequently attended Mass at a convent in nearby Burgess
Hill.

V: 140   (184)
VI: 24, 36   (24, 42)

USNACH
In Irish mythology, the sons of Usnach -- Naisi, Ardan and Ainle -- were
a famous band of the Red Branch knights* at the court of Connor MacNessa.
Samuel Ferguson* translated a famous poem, "Deirdre's Lament for the Sons
of Usnach."

III: 242   (361)

USSHER, ARCHBISHOP JAMES
1581 - 1656. Irish theologian who propounded a Biblical chronology which
was long inserted into the margins of the Authorized Versions of the
Bible. According to Ussher, the creation took place in 4004 B.C.. He
was despised in Ireland for using his power to condemn the use of the
Irish language in the Church of Ireland.

III: 84   (120)

UTRILLO, MAURICE
1883 - 1955. French painter; best known for his paintings of cathedrals,
villages and Parisian street scenes.

V: 64   (78)

UTUMARA
Probably Kitagawa Utamaro. c.1754 - 1806. Japanese engraver and designer of color prints.

IV: 125   (167)

V

VALENCIENNES
Town in northern France, site of a famous lace industry (died out in the
19th century).

I: 23   (24)

VALENTINE, MISS
Appears as a teacher at St. Mary's National School.

I: 115-19, 124   (174-9, 187-8)

VALLOMBROSA
Benedictine abbey in the valley of the same name, east of Florence,
Italy.

IV: 258   (356)

VAN GOGH, VINCENT
1853 - 1890. Celebrated Dutch painter. See also STONE, IRVING.

IV: 75, 170, 186, 282   (95, 231, 254, 391)
V: 64   (78)
White Roses   VI: 85   (115)

VANITY FAIR
Fair described in Bunyan's Pilgrim's Progress. Used as a synonym for
the present world and its worldliness.

IV: 257   (355)
VI: 65   (85)

VANNUTELLI, CARDINAL VINCENZO
1836 - 1930. Papal nuncio, Belgium (1866); curator of the Rota (1878);
cardinal (1900). Visited Ireland on a special mission representing
Pope Pius X at the consecration and reopening of St. Patrick's Cathedral,
Armagh (21 July 1904).

III: 140   (205)

VARIAN, DR.
The O'Casey family physician for over 20 years.

V: 70   (87)

VARIAN'S
At 90-93 Talbot Street, Dublin. One of the largest brush makers in
Ireland.

II: 78, 224   (116, 347)
III: 104   (149)

VATICAN
City-state enclave in Rome, Italy, whose ruler is the Pope, who is also
bishop of Rome and the head of the Roman Catholic hierarchy.

III: 111, 173   (160, 255)
IV: 113, 159, 160, 218, 241-3, 245, 246, 252, 265, 279
     (150, 216, 300, 333, 334-5, 338, 339, 348, 367, 386)
V: 219, 221, 236   (293, 297, 317)
VI: 120   (165)

VAUGHAN, BERNARD JOHN
1842 - 1922. Jesuit priest known for his popular orations and sermons
which were published in several forms. Active in work among the poor.

VI: 176   (248)

VAUGHN, MISS
Appears as a fellow worker with O'Casey at Leedom, Hampton chandler
company, Dublin.

II: 112, 113   (171, 172)

VAYNUS
In the Dublin dialect, this is Venus, and is probably a replica of The
Sleeping Venus by Giorgione.*

II: 208   (322)

VERMEER, JAN
1632 - 1675. Dutch landscape and portrait painter and colorist.

IV: 199   (274)

VELASQUEZ, RODRIGUEZ
1632 - 1675. Considered one of the leading representatives of naturalism.
Painted many portraits of dwarfs, court jesters, and the insane.

III: 55   (76)

VENICE
Major city in northeast Italy.

VI: 89-90   (121)

VERDI, GIUSEPPE
1813 - 1901. Renowned Italian operatic composer.

Il Trovatore (1845)   IV: 103   (136)
"Oh Leonora" (from the above) V: 219   (294)

VERJIL
See VIRGIL.

VERONA/MONTAGUE/CAPULET
In Shakespeare's* play, Romeo and Juliet, the Capulet family is that of
Juliet; Montague is the family name of Romeo; Verona is an ancient
Italian city, once part of the Republic of Venice.

II: 108   (165)

VICE-REGAL LODGE
In Phoenix Park, Dublin, where was held the social functions of the
Viceroyalty, an officer of the British crown before 1922. Later, it
was the governor-general's residence. See UNCLE TIM'S CABIN.

II: 38   (51)
III: 34, 116, 244   (43, 169, 365)
IV: 91, 150   (119, 203)

VICTORIA CROSS
Premiere British award for bravery in the presence of the enemy. Instituted by Queen Victoria* (1856).

IV: 17   (12)

VICTORIA PARK
In east London, near Victoria Park station, a park of over 200 acres
with a boating lake.

VI: 50   (62)

VICTORIA, PRINCESS MAY, OF TECH
Queen Mary. 1867 - 1953. Queen of George VI, Princess May of Teck.

III: 75   (106)

VICTORIA, QUEEN
1819 - 1901. Queen of Great Britain and Ireland and empress of India
(1876). O'Casey's use of "Famine Queen" comes from the Irish famine
(1840s) when, by her inaction, she doomed millions to emigration or
starvation. The visit of Victoria to Dublin (1900), described in "The
Red Above the Green," occasioned protests, but also many festivities.

I: 15, 37, 39, 40, 42, 66, 75, 86, 105, 151, 164, 172-4, 176-7, 181
      (11, 46, 51, 54, 94, 108, 127, 158, 231, 266-8, 272, 279-80)
II: 26, 30-1, 198   (32, 38-9, 305)
III: 75, 208   (106, 309)
IV: 44   (52)

VICTORIA STATION
In London, north of the Thames, near Buckingham Palace.

V: 182   (242)

VICTORIAN ORDER
The Royal Victorian Order, one of the nine existing British orders of
knighthood. Ranks eighth in order of precedence. Founded (1896) for
personal services rendered to the sovereign.

III: 208   (309)

VIENNA
O'Casey alludes to a 1952 production of The Silver Tassie (translated by
Elisabeth Freundlich and Gunther Anders) that caused a great deal of
polarization among newspaper reviewers and theatre-goers.

VI: 195   (277)

VIGILANCE COMMITTEE
W. P. Ryan's* book, The Pope's Green Island, mentions (p.100) that
several "Vigilance Committees" were established in 1911 to deal with
socialist newspapers.

III: 116, 152   (169, 224)

VIGILIOS, DON
Papal representative at Constantinople (536-c.538), and Pope (c.538-55).

III: 136   (199)

VIKING TOOLES/VIKINGS
For Viking Tooles, see ST. LAURENCE O'TOOLE. The Vikings invaded Ireland
periodically from c.800-c.1200, and founded many cities, including Dublin.
For many years, Irish chieftains levied tribute to the Shetlands, the
Orkneys, and the Faroes. In Irish history, the battle of Clontarf* is
usually regarded as a turning point in the Norse occupation. After the
battle, they assimilated into the Irish population, although their impact
was made on the Irish language and on her customs and mythology.

II: 185, 188   (286, 290)

VILLON, FRANCOIS
1431 - c.1463. France's greatest lyricist. Author of many ballads and
poems.

VI: 53   (66)

VINEGAR HILL
In Co. Wexford, site of a major defeat for Irish forces in the 1798
Rebellion (21 June). Celebrated in many songs.

III: 101   (145)
IV: 70   (89)

VIRGIL
70 - 19 B.C. Regarded as Rome's greatest poet.

III: 183   (270)
IV: 80   (103)
V: 23, 85-6   (20, 108-09)
VI: 198-9, 200, 201, 202   (282, 283, 285, 286, 287)

VIVANI, RENE RAPHAEL
1863 - 1925. French politician. Socialist deputy for Paris (1893-1902,
1906-10); premier (1914-15).

III: 243   (363)

VOLUNTEERS OF 1782
Originally formed to defend Ireland from possible French invasion after
regular troops had been withdrawn for service against the American
Revolution, the Irish Volunteers were raised at a time when Irish national
aspirations were oriented towards full legislative independence. In 1782,
they gathered at Dungannon* and elected delegates who resolved that "a
claim of any body of men other than the King, Lords, and Commons of
Ireland, to bind this kingdom is unconstitutional, illegal, and a
grievance." Arthur Griffith* claimed the 1782 Constitution as the basis
for Sinn Fein.* This constitution assumed a federal arrangement in the
British Isles, but it had been attained after the American Revolution,
and was swathed in some of the romance of that era.

III: 226   (337)

VON KLUCK, ALEXANDER
1846 - 1934. German soldier and right-wing commander of three main
armies invading France (1914), directed against Paris.

III: 266   (399)

W

WADDELL, HELEN
b.1899. British author of several books on medieval subjects.

VI: 201, 203   (286, 289)
The Wandering Scholars (1927) VI: 162 (227)
Medieval Latin Lyrics (1929)   VI: 162 (227)

WAGNER, RICHARD
1813 - 1883. German tone poet, composer and writer on music. One of
Shaw's* best known books (#) was The Perfect Wagnerite (1898).

VI: 174#, 177   (245#, 250)
Der Ring des Nibelungen (1848-74) VI: 37   (43)

WAKEFIELD
Prison site in Yorkshire, England, and one of the places of internment
for Irish men and women following the Easter Rising. Over 750 prisoners
were received there (6 May-1 June 1916).

IV: 9   (1)

WAKE OF WILLIAM ORR
Poem by William Drennan (1754 - 1820) that praises the life of Orr
(1766 - 1797), a United Irishman* who was hanged at Carrickfergus "just
to frighten the Presbyterians."

III: 233   (348)

WALES
V: 9, 93   (1, 119)
VI: 77, 219   (102, 314)

WALES, PRINCE OF
Albert Edward, Edward VII of England. 1841 - 1910. King of Great
Britain and Ireland (from 1901). Eldest son of Queen Victoria.*

I: 76, 181   (110, 279)

WALKER, JOHNNY
A brand of Scotch whiskey. O'Casey is alluding to George Walker. 1618 -
1690. Bishop-designate and governor of Derry during (1688) the siege
of Derry.* For many years, there was a tall monument to him in Derry,
but it was destroyed by the Provisional Irish Republican Army (28 August
1973).

II: 232, 237   (359, 369)

WALKER'S ENGLISH DICTIONARY
John Walker. 1732 - 1807. English lexicographer. His dictionary was
first printed in 1791. Re-issued and revised many times. In Twentieth
Century Authors, O'Casey is quoted: ". . . with the help of an old
Walker's Dictionary / I _/ taught myself to read and write fairly
well."

II: 88   (132)

WALLACE, EDGAR
1875 - 1932. English author of popular thrillers and detective stories.

IV: 194   (266)
V: 19, 138   (16, 182)

WALLER, DR. HAROLD
Leading London gynecologist and close friend of the O'Caseys. He delivered O'Casey's first son, Breon, and often accompanied the family to
the theatre. In a letter to Jack Daly, O'Casey wrote of Waller: "He is
one of my few friends." (Letters, I, p. 512)

V: 70   (87)

WALLER, HAROLD
1840 - 1910. English clergyman and author of several theological works.

V: 70   (87)

WALLIS, COLM
Colm de Bhailis. 1796 - 1906. Irish folk poet whose collected verses
were published by the Gaelic League, Dublin (1904). In 1903, he was
a cause celebre of Pearse,* who urged Gaelic League members to contribute
money to ease the poet's poverty-stricken plight.

III: 115   (166-7)

WALLS OF DERRY
See DERRY'S WALLS, Appendix I.

WALPOLE, HUGH SEYMOUR
1884 - 1941. English novelist. Author of several autobiographical works
detailing his experiences with the Russian Red Cross during World War
I.

VI: 99   (135)

WALPURGIS
In German folklore, the night before May 1 when witches are said to ride
to some appointed rendezvous where they observe the witches' sabbath.
Utilized by Goethe* in Faust.

V: 136   (178)

WALSH, EDWARD
1805 - 1850. Irish schoolteacher and author of several poems, ballads
and articles for the Nation.* Schoolmaster to convicts on Spike Island*
until he was dismissed for bidding farewell to John Mitchel.*

V: 171-2   (228)

WALSH, LOUIS J.
1880 - 1942. Identified by Richard Ellmann as a "district justice in
Donegal from 1923 until his death. Known in his youth as 'the boy
orator,' he wrote several books of no consequence."

III: 120, 133   (174, 195)
The Pope at Killybuck V: 51 (59)

WALSH, PADDY
Probably a dockworker friend of O'Casey in the labor movement. Mentioned
in Letters, I.

VI: 43   (52)

WALSH, WILLIAM JOSEPH
1841 - 1921. Irish theologian and nationalist. Archbishop of Dublin
(from 1885) and a supporter of the Land League* until Parnell's* diffi-
culties with the Catholic hierarchy. Advocated trade unionism and women's
suffrage, but condemned the strikers in 1913.

III: 138   (202)
IV: 241, 242   (332, 334, 335)
VI: 170   (241)

WALTERS, EVAN
1893 - 1951. Welsh painter. Painted the portrait of O'Casey for the
first edition of The Silver Tassie (1928). He also did the Madonna,
hanging on the hospital wall, for Act III of the play's premiere (1929).
See HYDRANGEAS.

VI: 46, 50   (57, 63)

WANDSWORTH COMMON
An elongated common in Wandsworth, south of London.

VI: 16   (12)

WARD, MAISIE
1889 - 1975. Writer and co-founder of Sheed* and Ward Publishers,
London and New York.

IV: 264   (365)
VI: 16, 167-70   (11, 235-40)
Gilbert Keith Chesterton (1943) VI: 15   (10)

WARWICKSHIRE
Island county in central England.

VI: 76   (102)

WASHINGTON, GEORGE
1732 - 1799. First president of the United States.

II: 88   (131)
IV: 263   (364)
V: 178, 180   (238, 239)

WATERFORD
Irish city and county in Munster province.

III: 189   (280)

WATERFORD, BISHOP OF
Richard A. Sheehan. 1845 - 1915. Bishop of Waterford and Lismore (from 1892). Active in archaelogical, literary and art societies.

III: 138, 139   (202, 204)

WATERLOO
Decisive battle (18 June 1915) in Belgium between the forces of Wellington* and Napoleon.* The word is proverbial (O'Casey's use) for a final or deciding blow.

III: 252   (376)

WATERLOO ROAD
In south Dublin, connecting Upper Leeson Street and Upper Baggot Street.

IV: 105   (138)

WATERLOO ROAD
In central London, south of the River Thames, on which is located the Old Vic* Theatre.

V: 129, 130   (168, 170)

WATLING STREET
In south Dublin, running from Thomas Street to the intersection of Victoria Quay and Usher's Island.

II: 215   (334)

WATTS, RICHARD
1898 - 1981. American dramatic critic. Motion picture critic (1924-36) and dramatic critic (1936-42), New York Herald Tribune. O'Casey alludes to Watts's lifelong bachelorhood and the critic's reputation as a lady's man.

V: 239   (321-2)

WAUGH, EVELYN
1903 - 1966. English writer.

VI: 36, 168   (42, 237)

WAYNEFLETE, LADY CICELY
Famous woman traveller and sister-in-law of Sir Howard Hallman in Shaw's* play, Captain Brassbound's Conversion.

VI: 189   (269)

WEBB'S
George Webb, bookseller, 5 Crampton Quay, Dublin.

IV: 232   (320)

WEBBS
Sidney, first baron Passfield (1859 - 1947),and Beatrice (1858 - 1943)
Webb. Married 1892. Founders of the Fabian Society and the New Statesman, influential British publication. Joint authors of several important
socialist studies.

VI: 40, 173   (45, 244-5)

WEBSTER, JOHN
c.1580 - c.1625. Noted English dramatist. See COROMBONA, VICTORIA.

IV: 126   (168)
The Duchess of Malfi (1614) III: 260   (390)
                             V: 110, 113, 163 (143, 147, 216)

WEEJODAVLIN
Wee Joe Devlin.*

III: 153   (224)

WEHRMACHT
Official name of the combined army, navy and air force in the Third
Reich under Hitler's reign.

VI: 119, 143, 146   (164, 165, 199, 204)

WELL OF INDRA
In Hinduism, Indra is the son of Dyaus and Nistigri, and the bringer of
rain and harvest.

IV: 196   (269)

WELLER, SAM
Mr. Pickwick's* quick-witted servant in Dickens's* Pickwick Papers (1836).

VI: 136   (189)

WELLESLEY
American women's college at Wellesley, Massachusetts.

V: 205-06   (274-5)

WELLINGTON, LORD
Arthur Wellesley. 1769 - 1852. British (b. Ireland) general and politician. Irish M.P. (1790-95); Irish secretary (1807-09). Best known
for his crushing defeat of Napoleon* in the Waterloo Campaign (1815).
Opposed Catholic emancipation for Ireland as P.M. (1828-30); organized
miliary against the Chartists.

II: 84   (125)
III: 70   (98)

WELLS, H. G.
1866 - 1946. English essayist, novelist and historian. Best known for
his series of scientific and speculatory futurist novels. Ardent femi-
nist. For more on the Chesterton-Belloc (#) reference, see "About

MORE

WELLS, H. G. (cont.)

Chesterton and Belloc" in The Works of H. G. Wells, v. 9 (1925).

IV: 250, 252, 259	(346, 349, 358)
V: 118-21	(154-7)
VI: 169-72#	(239-43#)
Mr. Britling Sees it Through (1916) VI: 76	(102)

WERFEL, FRANZ
1890 - 1945. Expressionist poet, dramatist and novelist. The references
to Werfel's war-time activities are explained in the introduction to
his most famous book (cited below).

The Song of Bernadette (1941)	III: 160	(235)
	IV: 278	(384-5)

WESLEY, JOHN
1703 - 1791. English clergyman, founder of Methodism.

V: 230   (309-10)

WEST
Appears as a printing firm on Stafford Street, Dublin, which printed
some items for Pearse's* festival. There were two printing shops on
Stafford Street (nos. 13 and 47-8), but neither were named West (Thoms,
1909). This may have been the same firm which printed the Irish Worker,
also on Stafford Street but not named West.

III: 236   (352)

WEST BRITON
Derogatory label for those Irish who aped the English ways, and, by
their actions, who would have turned Ireland into a "West Britain."
See also IRISH-IRELAND.

III: 32	(39)
IV: 235	(324)

WEST COUNTRY
Generally, the southwest counties of England, including Cornwall, Devon,
Somerset, Goucestershire, and northwestern Wiltshire. O'Casey's play,
Oak Leaves and Lavender, is "a war-time fantasy of the West Country."
See also his article, "Totnes of Gentle Mien," written for West Country
magazine (Winter 1946, reprinted in Sean O'Casey Review, Fall 1975).

VI: 82, 128   (110, 178)

WESTLAND ROW/WESTLAND ROW STATION
In south Dublin, now Pearse Station. Parnell's*remains were sent
here on 17 October 1891. Received by a bodyguard of 2000 Gaelic Athletic
Association members, who proceeded to Glasnevin* cemetery with the body.

IV: 285   (395)

WESTMINISTER
Used as a symbol of British authority.

III: 175   (258)

WESTMINISTER ABBEY
World famous church in Parliament Square, Westminister, London.
England's national Valhalla, the chief burial spot of her distinguished
men. Where British monarchs have been crowned since William the
Conqueror.

III: 249   (372)
V: 92, 138, 185, 187   (117, 181, 246, 249)
VI: 156, 202   (219, 288)

WESTMINISTER CATHEDRAL
The primary Catholic church in England. Built 1895-1903.

VI: 27, 28, 56, 156, 177   (28, 30, 71, 219, 250)

WESTMINISTER CONFESSION
A 33-chapter document (1646) presenting a comprehensive outline of
Calvinism.

II: 13   (10)
V: 219   (293)

WESTMORELAND BRIDGE
The Cross Guns Bridge.*

II: 54, 63   (78, 92)

WESTMORELAND STREET
Formerly College Lane. In southeast Dublin, an adjunct to O'Connell
Street.

I: 22, 181, 184   (22, 280, 284)

WEXFORD
Irish county having several historical sites, including a 9th-century
Danish settlement which was captured (1169) by Diarmid MacMurrough.*
Wexford was also the southern headquarters of the United Irishmen.*
See BOYS OF WEXFORD, Appendix I.

III: 189   (280)
IV: 70, 90   (88, 118)

WHITE, CAPTAIN J. R.
1879 - 1947. Chairman of the Irish Citizen Army* and its drillmaster.
Former British army officer (D.S.O. winner) and son of Sir George White,
hero of Ladysmith (Boer War*). Autobiography, _Misfit_ (1930).

III: 212, 224, 227-30   (315, 334, 338-42)

WHITE HART OF THE HOLLANDS
The White Hart was the badge of Richard II, who was the half-brother of
Sir Thomas Holland, 1st earl of Kent. Coincidentally, the White Hart
was also the name of the student cafeteria at Dartington Hall* where
O'Casey's children were educated.

VI: 81   (109)

WHITE STAR LINES
Shipping firm whose ships included the ill-fated Titanic.

V: 170, 172   (227, 229)

WHITEBOYS
Anti-landlord Irish agrarian organization (c.1761) whose members wore
white frocks over their clothes as a disguise. Sometimes known as
Levelers for their tactics of breaking over fences of leveled enclosures.

V: 90   (115)

WHITEHALL
Suburb of Dublin, north of Drumcondra.

III: 13   (10)

WHITEHALL COURT
In London, the flat (#4) of Shaw* where he and Mrs. Shaw* lived from
October 1927.

V: 41   (47)
VI: 161, 180-1   (227, 257)

WHITMAN, WALT
1819 - 1892. Celebrated American writer and one of O'Casey's favorites.
Whitman was born on Long Island, New York, and worked for many years in
Brooklyn and Manhattan. See Appendix II and III.

III: 25, 82, 283, 284   (29, 116, 425, 426
IV: 54, 213   (65, 292)
V: 79, 98, 170, 178, 200, 213 (99, 125, 226, 238, 267, 286)
VI: 13, 171, 201, 227   (11, 242, 287, 326)
Drum Taps (1865)   III: 142   (208)
Leaves of Grass (1855)   IV: 35   (37)
"When Lilacs Last in the Doorway Bloom'd"   III: 193   (286)
                                      V: 125   (163)

WHITTINGTON, RICHARD
c.1358 - 1423. English mercer and philanthropist. Lord mayor of London
(1397-98, 1406-07, 1419-20). Left legacies for rebuilding Newgate*
prison, founding an almshouse, and for organizing Whittington College.

V: 74   (91)

WHO KILLED COCK ROBIN?
Mother Goose nursery rhyme. Also a song and the title of poems, essays
and books.

I: 56, 58   (78, 80)
III: 59   (81)

WICKLOW
Irish maritime county and city in Leinster province. A "Wicklow wedding"
is an allusion to Boucicault's* play, <u>Arragh-na-Pogue, or a Wicklow
Wedding</u> (#). O'Casey reference to it being "Parnell's place"(##)
alludes to Charles Stewart Parnell* who was raised in Wicklow, was an
officer in the Wicklow militia, and was high sheriff of Co. Wicklow
(1874). The Wicklow mountains (###) are part of the Leinster chain,
extending from Dublin Bay through Wicklow and Wexford to the Barrow
River.

II: 13, 38###   (11, 51##)
III: 147#, 162###, 269, 285   (216#, 238###, 404, 427)
IV: 12   (6)
V: 107   (139)

WILBUR, RAY LYMAN
Spelled WILBUT in PAN edition. 1875 - 1949. Physician, college president (Stanford), and, under Herbert Hoover,* secretary of the interior
(1929-33).

IV: 212   (292)

WILD GEESE
The name given to thousands of Irish men and women who fled Ireland
after 1691 to continental Europe. Many served in the armies of France,
Spain, Austria, and Italy, and several attained distinction. It has been
estimated that 500,000 refugees served in the French army from 1691 to
1789.

III: 19, 105   (20, 152)

WILD SWANS OF COOLE
Yeats's* collection of poems (1919).

III: 19   (20)
IV: 136   (183)

WILDE, OSCAR
1856 - 1900. Celebrated Irish poet, dramatist and novelist.

IV: 30, 182   (31, 248)
<u>The Picture of Dorian Gray</u> (1891)   IV: 40   (45)

WILLIAM AND WOODS
Dublin confectionary manufacturers, 205-206 Great Britain (Parnell)
Street.

II: 55   (79)

WILLIAM OF ORANGE
Also given as KING BILLY and WILLIAM III. 1650 - 1702. King of England
(1689-1702) and stadholder of the United Netherlands (1672-1702). Head
of the House of Orange. Landed at Tor Bay, Devon (1688); crowned king
of England (1689). Defeated Irish and French forces during the Jacobite
wars, and was prominent at the Battle of the Boyne.* The Dublin statue
which O'Casey refers to (#) stood opposite Trinity College. It was
done by Grinling Gibbons, and, after many mutilations, was blown up
in 1929. The Brixham statue (##) stands on the quay, and commemorates
William's landing in 1688.

II: 27, 50, 228-33, 237   (34, 72, 355-61, 368)
III: 23, 37, 276#   (25, 47, 428#)
V: 23#, 94, 193   (21#, 120-1, 230-1)
VI: 80##, 202#   (107##, 288#)

WILLIAMS
This may be Benjamin Williams (1889 - 1953), American novelist and
detective story writer. According to information supplied by Irving
Stone (present at the occasion), the person in question worked with him
on a magazine, Detective Dragnet, but he is not certain of the man's
first name.

V: 225, 227   (302, 305)

WILLOGOD, PATRON OF WORKERS
Variant on the "render-unto-Caesar-that-which-is-Caesar's" game.

III: 159   (234)
VI: 55   (71)

WILLOUGHBY, INSPECTOR
Well-known member of the Dublin Metropolitan Police. During the 1913
Strike, he was a prominent figure in several places where riots occurred.

III: 223   (331)

WILTSHIRE
County in southern England.

V: 189   (252)
VI: 77   (102)

WIMBORNES
Probably a reference to Sir Ivor Churchill Guest, 1st viscount Wimborne.
Liberal lord lieutenant or Ireland (1915-18). Opposed conscription for
Ireland (1918), for which he was removed from office. First president,
Liberal Party (1931).

IV: 274   (380)

WIMSEY, LORD PETER
Also given as WHIMSEY. Private detective in many novels and short
stories by Dorothy Sayers.*

IV: 195   (267)
V: 143   (189)

WINDERMERE'S LAKE
In northwest England in the Lake District.

VI: 200   (285)

WISEMAN, MONSIGNOR NICHOLAS PATRICK STEPHEN
1802 - 1865. English theologian. Archbishop of Westminister, and
greatly influential in the Catholic revival in England. Cardinal, 1850.

VI: 40   (48)

WITTENBERG
German city; site of a 15th-century castle-church where Martin Luther*
nailed his 95 Theses(1517), launching the first phase of the Reformation.

I: 95   (140)
V: 219   (293)

WOEMAN OF THE PIERCING WAIL
Variant on the first line of the poem, "Lament for the Princess of Tir-
Owen and Tirconnell," by Mangan.* The first line reads: "O Woman of the
Piercing Wail."

III: 115   (168)

WOGAN, YOUNG CAPTAIN JACK
Appears as a victim of the Irish Civil War. Perhaps a model for Johnny
Boyle in O'Casey's play, Juno and the Paycock.

IV: 120, 121   (159, 160, 162)

WOLFE TONE MEMORIAL COMMITTEE
An Irish Republican Brotherhood* front organization that was initially
formed to commemorate the 1798 Rising and Tone (see the Grafton Street
entry under TONE). The committee lasted well into the 20th century,
largely due to the efforts of Tom Clarke* and his widow, Kathleen.
Tone's monument was finally erected in November 1967. O'Casey served
as secretary to the committee for a brief time, probably in 1912 or
1913. Located at 41 Parnell Square, Dublin. Other members included
Willie Pearse, Bulmer Hobson,* Sean MacDermott, Patrick McCartan,*
and Clarke as chairman.

III: 162, 231   (238, 344)

WOLSELEY, LORD GARNET JOSEPH
1833 - 1913. British army officer who distinguished himself at Sebasto-
pol, during the Sepoy Mutiny,* and in Egypt.

III: 87, 94   (124, 135)

WOLSEY, THOMAS
c.1475 - 1530. English prelate and politician, one of the major figures
in Shakespeare's* play, Henry VIII.

II: 131   (202)
IV: 161   (218)

WOOD/WOODS, DR.
It is not certain that these are the same person. There was a Dr.
F. J. Woods at 69 Lower Gardiner Street, Dublin (Thoms, 1912).

III: 53, 207   (73, 306-07)

WOOD, SIR EVELYN
1839 - 1919. British army officer who distinguished himself during the
Sepoy Mutiny* (Victoria Cross) and during the Zulu Wars (1878-79).

III: 87, 94   (124, 135)

WOODS
Appears as a fellow worker with O'Casey at Leedom, Hampton chandler
company, Dublin.

II: 117, 119-21   (179, 182-5)

WORCESTERSHIRE REGIMENT
In the British army, either the 29th or 36th Infantry regiments.

IV: 90   (118)

WORDSWORTH, WILLIAM
1770 - 1850. English poet laureate (1843-50). O'Casey alludes (#) to
Wordsworth's schooling at St. John's College, Cambridge University.

IV: 49   (59)
VI: 61#   (79#)

WORONZOW ROAD
In St. John's Wood, London. O'Casey moved there (#19) in January 1928,
staying until October 1931.

V: 34   (36)

WREN, CHRISTOPHER
1632 - 1723. World famous English architect. Designer of St. Paul's
cathedral, the Monument, Drury Lane theatre, the towers of Westminister
Abbey, etc. (all *)

V: 190   (253)

X

XERXES
c. 519 - 465 B.C. King of Persia (from 486). Leader at the battle of
Thermopylae.*

II: 88   (131)

Y

YALE UNIVERSITY
Prestigious American university at New Haven, Connecticut.

V: 53, 181   (62, 240)

YEAR OF ONE
Allusion to the French Revolution,* after which their calendars listed 1789 at "Year One." The words were used on French documents that circulated in Ireland during the 1798 Rebellion.

IV: 9   (2)

YEATS, ANNE
Given only as ANNE. b.1919. Dublin artist and daughter of W. B. Yeats.* For whom he wrote "A Prayer for my Daughter" (1919).

V: 44   (50)

YEATS, GEORGE
Nee Hyde-Lees. 1894 - 1968. Wife of W. B. Yeats* (m. 21 October 1917). Interested in spiritualism (see Yeats's poem, "A Vision"), and believed by Yeats to have mediumistic powers.

V: 43, 109   (48, 142)

YEATS, JACK BUTLER
1871 - 1957. Irish painter, brother of W. B. Yeats.*

IV: 201   (276)

YEATS, JOHN BUTLER
Given only as YEATS'S FATHER. 1839 - 1922. Irish painter, member of the Royal Hibernian Academy. The painting of AE* which O'Casey refers to was a portrait in oils (1903), formerly in the John Quinn Collection, New York.

IV: 212   (291)

YEATS, WILLIAM BUTLER
1865 - 1939. Celebrated Irish poet. Most of O'Casey's relationship is detailed under separate entries throughout this index. O'Casey also quotes liberally from Yeats's works, for which see Appendix II and III. See also:

BYZANTIUM	GOLDEN DAWN	MORRIGU
CATHLEEN NI HOULIHAN	GREGORY, ROBERT	O'HANRAHAN, RED
CLAN OF FERGUS	HIGGINS, F. R.	PRINCE OF CHANG
DECTORA	HOLY ROOD	ROSE ALCHEMICA
DONOUGH, YELLOW-HAIRED	IRISH ACADEMY OF	SUALTIM'S SIN
DRUMCLIFFE	LETTERS	TAGORE, RABIN.
DULAC, EDMUND	IRISH LITERARY	YEATS, ANNE
EMER	SOCIETY	YEATS, GEORGE
FARR, FLORENCE	JACK THE JOURNEYMAN	YEATS, JACK BUTLER
	LEDA	YEATS, JOHN BUTLER
		MORE

MORE

YEATS, WILLIAM BUTLER (cont.)

YOEMAN OF THE GUARD
Allusion to an operette by Gilbert and Sullivan.

YORK
Mansion group along Prince of Wales Drive in Battersea,* London.

YORKE, FATHER PETER C.
1864 - 1925. Irish-born priest in the archdiocese of San Francisco.
Active in the west coast labor movement and a crusader against bigotry.
                                                            MORE

YORKE, FATHER PETER C. (cont.)

Founder (1902) and editor, Leader, a weekly newspaper devoted to Irish
nationalism and the rights of labor. Vice-president, Sinn Fein, in
the U.S. O'Casey partially dedicated his play, The Drums of Father Ned,
to Yorke, writing: " . . . Father Yorke of San Francisco who warned
Irish-Ireland of fond delusions many years ago, and who told Dr. Mc-
Donald, his friend, that in the Rerum Novarum, the Church was offering
the workers no more than platitudes."

III: 150   (220-1)

YORKTOWN
Historic town in the U.S. on the York River near Williamsburg, Virginia.
Site of Cornwall's surrender at the end of the American Revolution.

II: 12, 88   (9, 131)
V: 180   (240)

YOUGHAL
Irish seaport town in Co. Cork.

IV: 233   (321)

YOUNG MEN'S CHRISTIAN ASSOCIATION
The Dublin Y.M.C.A. was at the Christian Union building.* O'Casey also
gives a variety of other names, only two of which are real.The Catholic
Young Men's Society was at 29 North Frederick Street, Dublin. The
names O'Casey gives are:
   CATHOLIC YOUNG MEN'S SOCIETY*   III: 118   (172)
   YOUNG MEN'S CATHOLIC ASSOCIATION   VI: 221   (317)
   YOUNG MEN'S CATHOLIC ASSOCIATION OF THE CROSS III: 126   (183)
   YOUNG MEN'S CATHOLIC CHRISTIAN CROSS ASSOCIATION III: 122 (178)
   YOUNG MEN'S CHRISTIAN ASSOCIATION   II: 211   (327)

YPRES
French for the Flemish Ieper, town in west Flanders. An important battle
site in World War I.

III: 285   (427)

Z

ZEUS
In Greek mythology, king of all gods, the supreme and all-powerful
deity.

II: 88   (131)
IV: 157, 212   (213, 291)
V: 94   (120)

ZIBLIARA, CARDINAL TOMMASO
1833 - 1893. Dominican theologian and philosopher. One of the important
people in the revival of Thomism.

IV: 228   (314)

ZION
In the Bible, Mount Zion was the site of the royal residence of David.

II: 15, 32, 221   (13, 41, 342)

ZOLA, EMILE
1840 - 1902. French naturalist novelist and courageous champion of
Dreyfus.*

La Debacle (1892)   III: 82   (116)

ZULUS
Bantu-speaking people of the Northern Nguni group of South Africa.
Defeated by the British (1880), and divided into 13 kingdoms.

I: 116   (175-6)
II: 198   (305)
V: 167   (222)

ZWINGLI, HULDREICH
1484 - 1531. Swiss religious reformer. Established the Reformation*
in Switzerland.

II: 87   (131)

APPENDIX I:
SONGS AND TUNES

A

A-HUNTING WE WILL GO
Folk song attributed to Thomas A. Arne.

VI: 193   (275)

ABIDE WITH ME
Church hymn, words by Henry Francis Lyte, music by William H. Monk.

II: 223   (346)

ADESTES FIDELES
Traditional 18th-century Latin hymn. See the line, "Oh, come let us
adore him"(#).

IV: 278   (385)
VI: 39#   (45#)

AFTER THE BALL
Popular song (1892) by Charles K. Harris.

I: 23   (23)
IV: 240   (331)

AIN'T GONNA RAIN
Old midwestern American folk song. O'Casey uses the first line: "It
ain't gonna rain no more."

VI: 114   (157)

ALICE, WHERE ART THOU?
Popular song (1861), words by Wellington Guernsey, music by Joseph
Ascher. See the chapter of the same name in Pictures in the Hallway.

II: 116-17   (178)
V: 193   (257)

ALL GOD'S CHILLUN GOT WINGS
Traditional Negro spiritual. O'Casey uses variants of the title: "without the wings" (#) and "got stings" (##). Also the title of a Eugene O'Neill* play.

V: 88#   (111#)
VI: 40##   (48##)

ALL I WANT IS A LITTLE BIT OFF THE TOP
Popular music hall song by Murray and Leigh. O'Casey uses a variant of the first line of the chorus: "Carve a little bit off the top for me, for me."

III: 176   (260)

ALLILIU NA GAMHNA"
Traditional Irish children's folk song.

III: 253   (379)

ALPINE ECHOES
Traditional instrumental by Karl Merz.

I: 73   (106)

AN CAILIN DEAS
Given as COLLEEN DYAS. Traditional allegorical Irish ballad. Cailin deas is the Irish phrase for "nice girl."

III: 15   (14)

AN IRISHMAN'S GLORY SHINES BRIGHTER THAN GOLD
Unknown; probably an Irish-American Tin Pan Alley song.

III: 141   (207)

ANCHOR'S WEIGHED
Popular song by Arnold and Braham. O'Casey gives the words to verse one.

I: 79   (114)

ASPERGES ME
"Cleanse Me," a Catholic hymn sung during the sprinkling of holy water.

V: 186   (247)

AULD LANGE SYNE
Famous farewell song (1799) by Robert Burns.*

I: 77   (113-14)
IV: 282   (390)
V: 109   (142)

AWAKE AND LIE DREAMING NO MORE
Unknown.

III: 57   (78)

B

BAA BAA BLACK SHEEP
Children's nursery song.

VI: 47   (58)

BALLAD OF FREEDOM
See ABDEL-KADAR ,primary index.

BALLYHOOLEY BLUE RIBBON ARMY
Irish song about an abstentionist organization founded in the U.S. By
1878, it had extended to Great Britain. Members wore a blue ribbon to
demonstrate their pledge. Ballyhooley is in Ireland near Mallow.

II: 40   (56)

BANKS OF THE NILE
Anonymous Irish street ballad about an Irishman leaving home to "join
the British army on the Banks of the Nile."

III: 116   (168)

BANKS OF THE TWEED
Old Scottish ballad about one of Scotland's most famous rivers.

VI: 103   (142)

BARD OF ARMAGH
Anonymous Irish song about Phelim Brady, the famous Bard of Armagh, a
wandering balladmaker.

III: 16   (15)

BARNEY O'HEA
See O'HEA, IMPUDENT BARNEY , primary index.

BATTLE OF LIMERICK
Irish song by Thomas Davis.* O'Casey gives lines from verses five and
six.

I: 33-4   (40-1)

BAY OF BISCAY
English song, words by Andrew Cherry, music by John Davy. From the
English ballad opera, Spanish Dollars.

II: 106   (161)

BELLS OF SHANDON
Well-known Irish song, words by "Father Prout" (Rev. Father S. Mahoney,
d.1866), to the air of "The Groves of Blarney."* Shandon steeple is on
the northern bank of the River Lee in Cork.

IV: 283   (391)

BILL BAILEY, WON'T YOU PLEASE COME HOME
Popular American song (1902) and an early ragtime classic by Hughie
Cannon.

III: 57   (78)

BLACKBERRY BLOSSOM
Traditional Irish reel, perhaps based on the old Irish folk song, "Si
Blath Geal Na Smeur" (She is the Blackberry's Fair Blossom).

IV: 147   (199)

BLUE BUTTERFLY DANCING
Probably an Irish country song or a reel or jig.

IV: 136   (183)

BLUE-TAILED FLY
American classic of minstrel shows. Words and music by Dan Emmett (1846).

V: 191   (255)

BOATMAN OF KINSALE
Irish song by Thomas Davis.*

III: 156   (229)

BOLD ROBERT EMMET
Anonymous Irish song of the leader of the 1803 Rising. O'Casey uses the
first line of verse one.

III: 283   (425)

BOLL WEEVIL SONG
A 19th-century American folk song of farmers' woes with the pesty,
crop-destroying insect.

V: 237   (319)

BONNIE EARL OF MORAY
An old Scottish ballad about James Stewart, called the "bonny earl."

II: 38   (52)

BONNY BUNCH OF ROSES O
Irish ballad of Napoleon, on whose fortunes Ireland's hopes seemingly
depended. The roses are a symbol of England.

III: 156   (229)
IV: 273   (377)

BONNY TYNESIDE
Scottish folk song.

V: 94   (120)

BOUND FOR CAANAN
Church hymn by John Leland. O'Casey gives the chorus.

II: 21   (23)

BOUND FOR THE RIO GRANDE
Old American capstan chantey.

VI: 29   (31)

BOWLD SOJER BOY
Irish song by Samuel Lover, Irish poet and novelist.

II: 67   (99)

BOYS OF KILKENNY
Anonymous song about the men and women of Kilkenny.

III: 118   (233)

BOYS OF OLD ERIN THE GREEN
Irish street song. O'Casey gives several lines.

II: 230   (356)

BOYS OF SANDY ROW
Song of the Orange Order.*

II: 228, 229, 230, 236   (354, 355, 357, 367)

BOYS OF WEXFORD
Irish nationalist song by R. Dwyer Joyce recalling the 1798 Rebellion.
Often sung at Parnell's* rallies.

III: 118, 155   (172, 229)

BRAVE SONS OF HIBERNIA
Irish folk tune.

III: 101   (145)

BRENNAN OF THE MOOR
Irish song of a famous highwayman who roamed the countryside following
the Irish defeat in 1691. Sometimes found under the title, "Lament on
the Execution of Captain Brennan." Also the name of a character in
O'Casey's play, Red Roses for Me.

VI: 71, 217   (94, 311)

BRIAN BORU'S MARCH
Traditional Irish martial tune.

III: 113   (165)

BRIAN O'LINN
Anonymous Irish street ballad. Often found in collections of Mother
Goose.

III: 156   (229)

BRING BACK MY BONNY TO ME
Sentimental Scottish song from which O'Casey gives two lines. Written
by H. J. Fuller.

VI: 152   (213)

C

CARRY ME BACK TO OLD VIRGINIA
Popular (1878) song of American minstrel shows,words and music by James
A. Bland.

IV: 35   (38)

CATHLEEN MAVOURNEEN
Sometimes found as "Kathleen Mavourneen." Words by Annie Crawford,
music by Frederick William Nichols (c.1840).

III: 243   (364)

CELTS AND SAXONS
Irish song by Thomas Davis.* O'Casey uses lines from the first and
last verses. He used these same lines in an article he wrote for the
Irish Worker (10 May 1913), for which see Feathers from a Green Crow.

III: 108   (158)

CHEER, BOYS, CHEER
Words by Charles MacKay, music by Henry Russell (1850). It is not
certain that this is the song referred to by O'Casey.

III: 249   (373)

CHERRY RIPE
Song based on the poem of the same name by Robert Herrick. Music
(1825) by Charles Edward.

III: 51   (70)

CHRISTMAS IN KILLARNEY
Popular song (1950), words and music by John Redmond, James Cavanaugh,
and Frank Weldon.

V: 184   (245)

CLARE'S DRAGOONS
Irish song by Thomas Davis,* evoking memories of the "Wild Geese"*.

III: 110, 118   (160, 172)

COME BACK TO ERIN
Irish exile song, words by Charlotte Allington Barnard, music by
"Claribel."

IV: 90   (118)

COME TO THESE YELLOW SANDS
Well-known song from Shakespeare's* play, The Tempest.

III: 51, 111   (70, 160)
IV: 163   (222)

COME WITH ME AND BE MY LOVE
Perhaps from "The Passionate Shepherd to His Love," Christopher Marlowe.

VI: 162   (227)

COMING THROUGH THE RYE
Folk song by Robert Burns.*

I: 23   (23)
IV: 125, 163   (167, 222)

CRUISKEEN LAWN
Irish folk song. The title means "The Little Full Jug."

IV: 152   (206)

D

DAISY BELL
Popular song (1892), words and music by Harry Daire. The first line is
the recognizable, "Daisy, Daisy, give me your answer, do."

III: 21, 119   (23, 172)

DAN MURPHY
This may be an allusion to the popular Irish song, "The Stone Outside
Dan Murphy's Door."

III: 114   (165)

DANCE THEM AROUND
Probably an English country dance.

VI: 76   (101)

DANNY BOY
Old Irish song which is also known as "Londonderry Air." Popular (1913)
adaptation by Frederick E. Weatherly.

III: 156   (229)
V: 32   (33)

DARK WOMAN OF THE GLEN
Traditional Irish song, written by P. Touhy. Known by its Irish name,
"Moll Dhubh an Gleanna."

III: 15   (14)

DAWNING OF THE DAY
Old Irish love song, words by Edward Walsh. Known by its Irish title,
"Fainne Geal an Lae."

III: 141, 142, 164   (207, 208, 241)

DEAR LAND
Irish song by John O'Hagan. O'Casey gives the words to verse four.
See the chapter, "I Strike a Blow for You, Dear Land," Pictures in the
Hallway.

II: 199   (307-08)

DEAR LITTLE SHAMROCK
Popular Irish song by Andrew Cherry. Sometimes known as "The Green Little
Shamrock."

I: 26   (29)
VI: 133   (185)

DEAR OLD GIRL
Popular American song (1903), words by Richard Bush, music by Theodore
Morse.

V: 237   (319)

DEER'S CRY
Also found as "Holy Patrick's Cry of the Deer" and "St. Patrick's Breast-
plate." An old Irish hymn from the late 7th or early 8th centuries.
Allegedly composed by St. Patrick* to protect him from his enemies. Also
given as "dear's cry" (#), and alluded to with the phrase, "the deer are
coming back to Ireland" (##).

II: 178   (275)
III: 105##   (151##)
V: 189   (252)
VI: 194#, 203   (275#, 289-90)

DERRY'S WALLS
Song of the Orange Order,* evoking memories of the Siege of Derry.*

II: 237   (369)

DEUTSCHLAND UBER ALLES
National anthem of Germany.

III: 266   (400)

DOWN WENT McGINTY
One of the celebrated comic songs of the 1890s, words and music by
Joseph Flynn (1889).

V: 175   (234)

DYING COWBOY
Also known by the titles, "The Cowboy's Lament" and "The Streets of
Laredo." O'Casey gives the words to the chorus.

V: 237-8   (319)

E

EHREN ON THE RHINE
American ballad by William Hutchinson describing the parting of a soldier
and his love.

I: 86   (126-7)

EILEEN ALLANNAH
Sentimental Irish love song, words by E. S. Marble, music by J. R. Thomas
(1873). There is another, "Eileen Alanna Asthore," words by Henry
Blossom, music by Victor Herbert (1917). III: 119 (172)

EIN FESTE BURG IS UNSER GOTT
"A Mighty Fortress in Our God," famous hymn by Martin Luther.*

V: 142   (187)

EILEEN AROON
Old Irish love song, also found under the title, "Eibhlin a Ruin,"
ascribed to Carol O'Daly, a 14th-century bard, translated by Gerald
Griffin.

III: 119   (172)

EXILE OF ERIN
Irish exile song by Thomas Campbell.

III: 119   (172)

F

FAITH OF OUR FATHERS
Well-known church hymn by Frederick William Faber. O'Casey gives the
words to verse one (#).

III: 125, 219#   (182, 326#)
V: 90#   (114#)

FAREWELL BUT WHEN E'ER YOU WELCOME THE HOUR
Irish song by Thomas Moore.*

I: 165   (254)
IV: 91   (119)

FATHER O'FLYNN
Irish song by Alfred Percival Graves, one of his most famous songs.

III:	119, 220, 280	(172, 327, 421)
VI:	169, 178	(238, 252)

FELONS OF OUR LAND
Irish nationalist song by Arthur M. Forrester. O'Casey gives the words
to the last verse (#). See also (##): "the felon's cap became the noblest
crown an Irish head could wear," a slight misquote of the second line
in the last verse.

III:	190#	(294#)
IV:	9##	(1##)

FIGHTING RACE
Given as "Kelly, Burke, and Shea," a recurrent line in the song which
O'Casey uses for his representative Irishmen. Written by Joseph I. C.
Clarke. O'Casey quotes the last two lines in the song (#).

II:	34	(45)
III:	16, 118, 267	(15, 172, 400)
IV:	88	(114)
VI:	10#	(2#)

FINNEGAN'S WAKE
Traditional 19th-century Irish-American song.

III:	129	(188)

FLANNIGAN TO FINNIGEN
Probably an Irish-American Tin Pan Alley song. There is a well-known
light poem, "Finnigin to Flannigan," by Strickland W. Gillilan.

III:	58	(80)

FLOWER OF FINAE
Irish song by Thomas Davis* about one of the "Wild Geese."*

III:	101, 156	(146, 299)

FOGGY DEW
One of the oldest Irish tunes which is frequently given new words for
each rebellion. The latest, about the Easter Rising, was written by
Rev. P. O'Neill. See also IV: 70 (88), Appendix III.

III:	285	(428)

FOLLOW ME UP TO CARLOW
Irish song by P. J. McCall about Feagh MacHugh O'Byrne (1544 - 1597), a
hero of the 16th century Irish wars against Queen Elizabeth. For an
apparent variant of the song, see (#), which resembles James Stephens'*
poem, "Follow, Follow, Follow."

II:	38	(51)
III:	63#	(88#)

G

GARRYOWEN
Well-known tune in the U.S. as the official marching song of the New York National Guard Regiment (165th Infantry), known as the "Fighting Irish."

III: 268   (402)

GERALDINES, THE
Irish song by Thomas Davis.* O'Casey gives (#) the words to the first four lines of verse four.

III: 139   (204)
IV: 232-3#   (321#)

GIRL FROM THE COUNTRY CLARE
Probably "The Darling Girl from Clare," an Irish song by Percy French. Two of the verses end with "the girl from County Clare." O'Casey wrote a song, "The Girl from the County Kildare."

III: 101, 156   (146, 229)
IV: 67   (85)

GLEN OF AHERLOW
Irish ballad by Charles Joseph Kickham. Also found under the title, "Patrick Sheehan," a soldier from Aherlow who goes blind in the Crimean War.

III: 103   (148)

GO WHERE GLORY WAITS THEE
Irish song by Thomas Moore.*

IV: 92, 200   (120, 274)

GOD REST YOU MERRY GENTLEMEN
An 18th-century English carol, popularly sung during the Christmas season. O'Casey uses several variants of the title.

II: 130   (199)
III: 201   (297)
IV: 54   (65)
V: 162   (214)
VI: 39   (46)

GOD SAVE IRELAND
Patriotic Irish ballad by T. D. Sullivan, Tim Healy's* father-in-law. For over sixty years, the Irish national anthem.

I: 75   (108)

GOD SAVE THE QUEEN
National anthem of England. O'Casey gives (#) part of the words.

I: 156, 162, 176, 182#   (240, 250, 272, 281#)

GOODBYE DOLLY GRAY
Popular (1900) Boer War song by Will D. Cobb and Paul Barnes.

III: 118   (172)

GRAIN OF WHEAT
Irish country dance.

III: 77   (109)

GREEN ABOVE THE RED
Patriotic Irish ballad by Thomas Davis.* O'Casey gives (#) the words to
the last two verses. See the chapter title, "The Red Above the Green,"
I Knock at the Door.

I: 15, 182-3#   (11, 281-2#)

GREEN BUSHES
Folk song from which O'Casey gives one of the verses.

V: 169   (224)

GREEN GREW THE RUSHES
Scottish folk song by Robert Burns.*

VI: 25   (25)

GREEN HILLS OF HOLY IRELAND
Anonymous Irish folk song.

III: 119   (174)
IV: 177   (241)

GREENSLEEVES
English ballad of antiquity. Mentioned twice in Shakespeare's plays.

VI: 53   (66)

GROVES OF BLARNEY
Satirical Irish song, words by R. A. Milliken, to a tune adopted from
"Slan cois Maighe" (Farewell to Margire).

III: 45   (59)
IV: 150   (203)

H

HALLELUJAH, I'M A BUM
American folk song, possibly by Joe Hill, celebrated union organizer
and balladeer. O'Casey gives the words to verse one (#). See also
"bum song" VI: 101 (139).

III: 249, 257#   (372, 384#)

HARD TIMES COME AGAIN NO MORE
American folk song by Stephen Foster. O'Casey gives the first verse.

I: 171   (263)

HARK THE HERALD ANGELS SING
Popular Christmas hymn. Words by Charles Wesley, music by Felix
Mendelssohn. O'Casey gives it as "herald angels are singin'" (#) and
"herald angels didn't sing" (##).

I: 74#   (107#)
II: 223   (346)
V: 74##   (92##)

HARP THAT ONCE THROUGH TARA'S HALLS
Famous Irish song by Thomas Moore.* O'Casey gives the words to the first
part of verse one (#).

I: 65   (92)
III: 76#, 112, 128   (107#, 162, 187)
IV: 276   (381)

HAS ANYBODY HERE SEEN KELLY?
Popular American version of "Kelly from the Isle of Man",* written by
C. M. Murphy and Will Letters. American version by William J. McKenna.

III: 57   (79)

HAS ANYONE SEEN MY LORD?
Old Negro spiritual from Tennessee.

VI: 192, 193   (273, 274)

HASTE TO THE WEDDING
Traditional Irish jig, attributed to Thomas Arne, and sometimes found
under the title, "Come, Haste to the Wedding." There is also a song of
O'Casey's title by P. J. McCall.

VI: 52   (66)

HEART BOWED DOWN, THE
From the opera, The Bohemian Girl (1843), words by Edward Fitzball, music
by Michael W. Balfe. See also (#): "my heart bowed down."

I: 45   (60)
V: 125#   (163#)

HEARTS OF OAK
Old English ballad dating from the Seven Years War (1759), written by
David Garrick.*

I: 27   (29)

HIELAND LADDIES
Traditional Scottish ballad which was very popular during World War II.

I: 160   (245)

HOME SWEET HOME
Popular American ballad, written (1822) by John Howard Payne. See also
"Rome Sweet Rome" III: 153 (224) and "Romewards" III: 125 (182).

IV: 274   (379)
V: 197, 210   (263, 282)

HOME TO OUR MOUNTAIN
Popular song from Verdi's* opera, Il Trovatore.

IV: 103   (136)

HOLY PATRICK'S CRY OF THE DEER
See DEER'S CRY, this appendix.

HOOSH THE CAT FROM UNDER THE TABLE
Probably the Irish dance, "Uis an Cat" (Hoosh the Cat).

III: 271   (406)
VI: 148, 173   (207, 245)

I

I COME, I COME,ME HEART'S DELIGHT
From the opera, The Lily of Killarney (1862), libretto by Dion Boucicault,* music by Sir Julius Benedict.

II: 45   (64)

I HEAR YOU CALLING ME
Popular John McCormack* recording, words by F. K. Harford, music by
Leonard B. Marshall.

II: 154   (237)

I KNOW MY LOVE BY HIS WAY OF WALKING
A west Irish air, words from an old song.

II: 111   (170)

I WANT TO GO TO IDAHO
Probably an Irish-American Tin Pan Alley song.

III: 58   (80)

I'M GOING HOME TO DIXIE
Probably "I'm Going Back to Dixie," a minstrel show ballad by A. C.
White.

IV: 71   (90)

I'M IN MY SLEEP AND DON'T WAKEN ME
Traditional Irish ballad. Irish title, "Ta me i mo chodradh is na dui-
sigh." See also III: 122 (177), "waken up the deep sleepers."

II: 229   (355)
IV: 67   (84)

I'M OFF TO PHILADELPHIA IN THE MORNING
Famous Irish song of an emigrant going to America.

V: 169   (224)

I'M THE MAN YOU DON'T MEET EVERYDAY
Anonymous Irish song.

III: 16   (15)

IF YOU WERE THE ONLY GIRL
Popular song (1925), words by Clifford Grey, music by Nat D. Ayer. Afterwards introduced in the film, The Vagabond Lover (1929).

VI: 115   (159)

IN DUBLIN'S FAIR CITY
Popular Irish song of Dublin's Mollie Malone, a fishmonger who died of
a fever. O'Casey uses part of the chorus ("alive, alive, Oh") in III:
69 (97) and V: 127 (166).

II: 40   (55)

IN THE SHADE OF AN OLD APPLE TREE
One of the most popular American songs of its time (1905). Words by
Harry Williams, music by Egbert van Alstyne.

III: 151, 241   (222, 359)

IRELAND OVER ALL
Irish patriotic ballad by Eamonn Ceannt, one of the signers of the Irish
Proclamation and one of the martyrs of the Easter Rising. Sung to the
tune of "Deutschland über alles".* Though O'Casey does not explicitly
mention this song, it is implied in the made-up word "Eiraillas"
(Ireland over All). Elsewhere, O'Casey notes that German songs were
popular among Irish nationalists in World War I (see the VON KLUCK
entry).

III: 179   (265)

IRISH HURRAH
Irish song by Thomas Davis.*

IV: 9   (1)

IT WAS A LOVER AND HIS LASS
Also given by O'Casey as "a lad and his lass" (#). From Shakespeare's*
play, As You Like It.

IV: 106, 141   (139, 190)
V: 192#   (256#)
VI: 80, 226   (108, 325)

IT'S A LONG WAY TO TIPPERARY
Popular (1912) song, words by Jack Judge, music by Harry Williams.

III: 252, 267   (377, 400)

J

JACKETS   GREEN
Irish song by Michael Scanlon of a girl's hero-worship of Patrick Sarsfield.* To a traditional air.

II: 196   (303)

JOHNNY, I HARDLY KNEW YE
Famous Irish song of the 19th century. O'Casey gives lines 5-7, verse five.

III: 164   (241)
VI: 227   (326)

JOHNNY MY OWN TRUE LOVE
Popular English folk song.

V: 27   (27)
VI: 76   (102)

K

KEEP RIGHT ON TO THE END OF THE ROAD
Popular song, words and music by Harry Lauder,* who used to end his performances with this song.

III: 87   (125)
V: 93   (119)
VI: 145, 168   (203, 237)

KELLY FROM THE ISLE OF MAN
See HAS ANYBODY HERE SEEN KELLY, this appendix.

III: 61, 156   (85, 229)

KELLY OF KILLANNE
Sometimes found under the title, "Kelly, the Boy from Killanne," an Irish song by P. J. McCall. John Kelly was one of the leaders of the Wexford rising in the 1798 Rebellion, leading a charge through Three-Bullet Gate at Ross.

III: 103, 156   (148, 229)

KILLARNEY
Popular Irish song, words by Edmund Falconer, music by Michael Balfe (1862). O'Casey gives (#) the words to part of verse one.

III: 76#, 179   (107#, 263)

KITTY OF COLERAINE
Anonymous Irish courting song.

III: 45, 119   (59, 172)

L

LAMBETH WALK
Popular song and dance from Me and My Gal, words and music by Noel Gay
and Douglas Furber (1937).

VI: 143   (199)

LAMENT OF THE IRISH EMIGRANT
See III: 18 (18) and 120 (174), Appendix III.

LAMENTATION OF AUGHRIM
Old Irish tune of the sigh for Ireland's perished hopes. It gave Thomas
Moore the inspiration for his song, "Forget Not the Field."

VI: 120   (165)

LAND OF THE LEAL
Popular Scottish song by Lady C. Naire.

II: 39   (53)

LANNIGAN'S BALL
Cheery tune originating from Athy, Ireland. Words by George Cavan to
the tune of "Hurry the Jug."

III: 129   (188)

LARK IN THE CLEAR AIR, THE
Anonymous popular Irish folk song.

III: 277   (415)

LAST GLIMPSE OF ERIN WITH SORROW I SEE, THE
Irish song by Thomas Moore.*

IV: 91   (119)

LAST POST
The Irish "Taps," the mournful dirge played over the graves of the dead.

I: 77   (112)
III: 142   (208)
VI: 82, 224, 225   (111, 322, 323)

LEATHER AWAY THE WATTLE
Irish song by F. O'Neill. O'Casey gives the words to one of the verses.

III: 151-2   (223)

LEGION OF THE REARGUARD
Also LEGION OF THE PRAYGUARD (#) and LOST LEGION OF THE REPUBLICAN REAR-
GUARD (##). Irish song from sometime after the Easter Rising. In de
Valera's* address to the Irish Republican Army at the end (24 May 1923)
of the Civil War, he began: "Soldiers of the Republic, Legion of the
Rearguard."

IV: 113##, 274#   (150##, 378#)

LESBIA WITH HER BEAMING EYE
Irish song by Thomas Moore.* Sometimes known as "Nora Creina."

III: 118   (172)

LET ERIN REMEMBER THE DAYS OF OLD
Irish song by Thomas Moore* which invokes remembrances of Ireland's
"faithless sons."

III: 268   (402)
IV: 152   (206)
VI: 10   (2)

LET HIM GO, LET HIM TARRY
Given as WILL IT GO, WILL IT TARRY. Anonymous boy vs. girl Irish song.

IV: 281   (388)

LET THE PEOPLE SING
From the review, Lights Up! (1940), words by Ian Grant and Frank Eyton,
music by Noel Gay.

VI: 193   (274)

LIFT THE ROOF HIGHER
Irish country dance.

III: 271   (406)

LIGHT OF OTHER DAYS, THE
Irish folk song, music by Michael W. Balfe, words by A. Bunn.

II: 185   (285)

LILLIBULLERO
Political folk song which satirizes James II, who made an unwelcome
nomination to the position of lord lieutenant of Ireland. Words (c.1686)
by Thomas Wharton. Given by O'Casey in variants.

II: 229   (355)
III: 132   (192)

LILY OF LAGUNA
Popular song (1942), words by Paul Webster, music by Ted Rito.

V: 98   (126)

LINCOLNSHIRE POACHER, THE
Anonymous Lincolnshire county (England) folk song.

V: 23, 27   (21, 26)

LITTLE ALABAMA COON
American folk song, words and music by Hattie Starr (1893).

III: 118   (172)
V: 231-2   (311)

LITTLE BROWN JUG
Popular drinking song, probably written by Joseph Winner (1869) under
the name of Eastburn. O'Casey gives the words to several verses.

I: 25-6   (27)

LITTLE GREY HOME IN THE WEST
English folk song, words by W. D. Eardley-Wilmot, music by Herman Lohr
(1911). See also ORDER OF THE LITTLE GREYHOUND IN THE WEST, primary
index.

II: 235   (366)
III: 12, 61   (9, 84)
IV: 92   (120)
V: 66   (81)

LITTLE MARY CASSIDY
Irish song by Francis A. Fahy to the tune of "An Staian Ornan."

VI: 211-12   (303)

LOCH LOMAND
Famous Scottish folk song telling of the disastrous retreat of the Highland Army from England after the 1745 Rising.

IV: 17, 218   (13, 300)
VI: 200   (285)

LOUISANA LOU
Given in variants. The is probably the song, "Lou-Lou-Louisana." I
have not been able to locate the composer, but it was recorded by Norman
Brooks (b.1928) on Zodiak labels (#109).

I: 27   (30)
IV: 200   (274)
V: 190   (253)

LOVE'S OWN SWEET SONG
Given by O'Casey as SOME OLD SWEET SONG. Words by C. C. S. Cushing and
E. P. Heath, music by Emmerich Kalman (1914).

IV: 34   (36)

M

MAIRE OF BALLYHAUNIS
Popular Co. Mayo Irish song, composed by a friar named Costello, about
the ancient abbey of Ballyhaunis. According to tradition, the friar
fell in love with a beautiful girl, wrote this love-sick song, and left
for a foreign land. O'Casey frequently sang this song at Gaelic League
meetings.

III: 101, 254   (146, 379)

MAN FROM GOD KNOWS WHERE, THE
Long Irish ballad by Florence M. Wilson about a mysterious man hanged
at Downpatrick Gaol.

V: 164, 216   (217, 289)

MAN ON THE FLYING TRAPEZE, THE
Circus song, first published in 1867-68.   O'Casey gives it in variants.

IV: 159, 197   (216, 270)
V: 236   (318)

MAN THAT BROKE THE BANK AT MONTE CARLO, THE
Music hall song (1892) by Fred Gilbert about the misfortunes of Charles
Wells who broke the bank six times but, trying one more time, lost it
all.

III: 119   (172)

MAN WHO STRUCK O'HARA, THE
Irish folk song. O'Casey uses it in his play, Time to Go.

I: 158   (243)
III: 119   (172)
VI: 210   (301)

MARSEILLAISE, LA
French national anthem, words and music by Claude Joseph Rouget de
l'Isle. Composed during the French Revolution.*

II: 170   (261)
III: 141   (206)
IV: 12   (6)

MARY OF ARGYLE
English folk song, words by Charles Jeffreys, music by Sidney Nelson
(c.1838).

III: 118   (172)

MASTER McGRATH
Irish folk song of a greyhound who became a national hero by beating an
English dog,"White Rose," three times, carrying the coveted Waterloo Cup
to Ireland. There is a monument to him in Co.Waterford.

III: 155, 262   (229, 392)

MEN OF EIGHTY-TWO
Irish patriotic song by Thomas Davis.*

III: 156   (229)

MEN OF HARLECH
The national Cambrian war song, "The March of the Men at Harlech,"
originating from the sieges of Harlech Castle in the Welsh village of
Harlech.

III: 32   (40)

MEN OF THE WEST
Irish national song by William Rooney,* with allusions to the 1798 Rising.
Sung to the tune of the American Civil War song, "Sherman's March to the
Sea."

III: 118, 266   (172, 399)

MI NA-MEALA
Irish song by Thomas Davis.*

III: 245   (365)

MICK McGILLIGAN'S DAUGHTER, MARY ANNE
Irish song by Louis A. Tierney about a father's bragging of the talents
of his daughter.

III: 157   (231)
IV: 279   (386)
V: 81   (102)
VI: 231   (331)

MINSTREL BOY, THE
Celebrated song (1813) of a lad gone to war by Thomas Moore.*

III: 18, 120   (18, 174)
IV: 92, 275   (120, 381)
VI: 10   (2)

MISS O'HARA AND HER EMERALD TIARA
Probably an Irish-American Tin Pan Alley song.

III: 58   (80)

MOONCOIN, THE
Traditional Irish reel.

III: 45   (59)

MOTHER MACHREE
Sentimental and popular (1910) Irish song, words by Rida Johnson, music
by Chauncey Olcott and Ernest R. Ball.

III: 118, 154, 204   (172, 266, 302)
VI: 10   (2)

MOUNTAINS OF MOURNE
Irish song by Percy French of an Irish laborer in London who prefers his
Mary living near the Mountains of Mourne.

III: 58, 164   (80, 241)
IV: 69   (87)
V: 161   (213)
VI: 212   (303)

MOUNTAINS OF POMEROY
Irish ballad from the 19th century by George Sigerson which chronicles
the loves of the Irish outlaw, Renardine.* O'Casey gives the words to
one verse (#).

III: 21#, 103   (22#, 148)

MULDOON THE SOLID MAN
American folk song. Can be found in the book, The Flying Cloud and 150
Other Old Time Songs and Ballads of Outdoor Men, Sailors, Lumberjacks,
Men of the Great Lakes, etc., by Michael C. Dean (1922).

III: 101, 118, 119-20, 155   (145, 172, 173-5, 229)
IV: 234, 279   (323, 386)
VI: 212   (304)

MY HANDSOME GILDEROY
Anonymous song of the famous outlaw, Gilderoy.* O'Casey gives the words
to the first verse.

VI: 143-4   (201)

MY HEART'S IN THE HIGHLANDS
Folk song by Robert Burns.*

V: 125   (163)

MY LODGING, IT IS ON THE COLD GROUND
English folk song from the 18th century which is frequently found in
collection of Negro spirituals.

II: 104   (157-8)
IV: 151, 218   (205, 300)

MY LOVE IS LIKE A RED, RED ROSE
Folk song by Robert Burns,* and one of O'Casey's favorites.

III: 183   (270)
IV: 197, 222   (271, 306)

MY LOVE, SHE'S BUT A LASSIE YET
Folk song by Robert Burns.*

III: 183   (270)

MY OLD KENTUCKY HOME
American folk song (1853), words and music by Stephen Foster.

IV: 205   (282)
VI: 147   (205)

N

NATION ONCE AGAIN, A
Still one of the most popular Irish nationalist songs. Written by Thomas
Davis,* and often sung at Irish Parliamentary Party* rallies under
MORE

NATION ONCE AGAIN, A (cont.)

Parnell's* leadership. See also THREE HUNDRED AND THREE MEN, primary
index.

III: 65   (89)
IV: 89, 280   (116, 387)

NEARER MY GOD TO THEE
Church hymn, words by Sarah Adams, music by Lowell Mason (1859).

I: 116   (174)

NED OF THE HILL
In Irish, Eamon an Chnuic. Written by Samuel Lover about Edmond O'Ryan,
an outlaw minstrel whose property was confiscated after the Jacobite
Wars. O'Casey uses this air for his own song, "Red Roses for Me."*

VI: 129   (179)

NELL FLAHERTY'S DRAKE
Sometimes found under the title, "Ned Flaherty's Drake," anonymous 19th-
century Irish ballad, said to be a code name for Robert Emmet.*

III: 119   (182)

NINE HUNDRED AND NINETY-NINE MEN
Perhaps a variant on the famous hymn, "Ninety and Nine Men" (1876),
words by E. C. Clephane and Ira D. Sankey.*

I: 158   (243)

NORA CREENA
Boy-meets-girl song, also found under its Irish title, Nora Crionna.
Crionna means wise, with an overtone of sly.

III: 18, 101   (18-19, 146)
V: 176   (234)

NOW THAT DAYLIGHT FILLS THE SKY
Traditional 6th-century Latin hymn.

II: 223   (346)

NUNC DIMITTIS
The Song of Simeon (Luke 1:29), sung at Evening Prayer in the Church of
England.

IV: 21   (18)
VI: 189   (269)

O

O BAY OF DUBLIN
Irish song by Helen Selena (Lady Dufferin).

II: 63, 185, 186, 188   (91, 286, 287, 290)

OH FOR A STEED
Irish song by Thomas Davis.* In both entries, O'Casey has altered one
word in the seventh verse. It should read:

> Oh! for a steed, a rushing steed, on the Curragh of Kildare,
> And Irish squadrons skilled to do what they are ready to dare -
> A hundred yards, and <u>Holland's</u> guards,
> Drawn up to engage me there.

The repeat of the last line in the first entry (#) is also added.

II: 51#   (73#)
III: 163   (240)

OH FOR THE WINGS OF A DOVE
Processional hymn, words by W. Bartholomew, music by Felix Mendelssohn
(1844).

III: 153   (225)

O GOD, OUR HELP IN AGES PAST
Hymn from the poem of the same name by Isaac Watts. Rung daily on the
bells of St. Clement's Church, London.

VI: 127   (176)

OH NO, JOHN
English folk song.

V: 146   (193)

O'DONNELL ABU
Stirring Irish marching song by Michael J. McCann (1843).

I: 24   (25)

OFT IN THE STILLY NIGHT
Popular Irish song by Thomas Moore.* O'Casey gives the words to one
verse (#).

II: 183#   (282#)
IV: 119   (158)

OLD BOG ROAD
Irish exile song by Teresa Brayton.

VI: 194   (276)

OLD COMRADES
There are several songs with this title, and it is difficult to tell
which one O'Casey is thinking of.

V: 32   (33)

OLD GREY MARE
Probably the popular American song by Frank Panella (1915), although
there is an Irish song with the same name.

V: 233   (314)

OLD HUNDRETH
Popular psalm tune, first published (1551) by Lord Bourgeois.

VI: 154   (216)

OLD MAN RIVER
Broadway, and later a film, tune from Showboat (1927), words by Oscar
Hammerstein II, music by Jerome Kern. See also VI: 145 (203), Appendix
III.

IV: 205   (281)

OLD UNCLE NED
American folk song by Stephen Foster. O'Casey twice uses a line from
it: "went away where the good niggers go," I: 40, 159 (52, 244).

I: 76   (110)

ONWARD CHRISTIAN SOLDIERS
Popular processional hymn, words by Sabine Baring-Gould, music by Sir
Arthur Sullivan (1871).

III: 125   (182)

ORANGE AND GREEN WILL CARRY THE DAY
Irish song by Thomas Davis* to the air of "The Protestant Boys." O'Casey
gives the words to the last verse.

II: 159   (245)

OULD PLAID SHAWL
Street ballad by Francis Fahy of a young man taken in by "the damsel with
the ould plaid shawl."

III: 120, 204   (174, 302)

OUR LADY
Hymn by J. Richardson. O'Casey gives the words to the middle of the
first verse.

VI: 122   (170)

OUR OWN AGAIN
Irish song by Thomas Davis.* O'Casey gives the words to the first half
of verse one.

IV: 80   (102)

P

PACK UP YOUR TROUBLES IN YOUR OLD KIT BAG AND SMILE, SMILE, SMILE
Popular English and American song (1915), words by George Asaf, music by
Felix Powell.

IV: 62, 122	(77, 162)
V: 173	(231)
VI: 131	(182)

PADDY HAGGERTY
Sometimes known as "Old Leather Breeches." A Co. Tipperary ballad, words
and music traditional.

III: 101   (146)

PALATINE'S DAUGHTER, THE
Irish love song emanating from the culture of German immigrants from
Palitinate to the Irish districts around Ardare and Rathleale, Co.
Limerick (1709).

III: 253, 284   (379, 427)

PEELER AND THE GOAT, THE
Irish song of ridicule. "Peelers" is Irish slang for police. In 1918,
O'Casey wrote a song, "Sinn Fein Election Song. Hurrah! for Ireland and
Sinn Fein," to the tune of "The Peeler and the Goat" (see Letters, I,
pp. 86-7). O'Casey gives the words (#) to verses one and two.

II: 60-1#	(87-8#)
III: 156	(229)

PEG OF MY HEART
Popular sentimental song (1913), words by Alfred Bryan, music by Fred
Fisher.

III: 156   (229)

POLLY, PUT THE KETTLE ON
Children's song and popular nursery rhyme.

V: 146   (193)

PRIDE OF PETRAVORE, THE
Sometimes known as "Eileen Og," an Irish ballad by Percy French.

III: 101   (146)

PULSE OF THE BARDS AWAKEN
Irish folk song.
IV: 136   (183)

Q

QUICK! WE HAVE BUT A SECOND
Irish song by Thomas Moore.*

II: 228   (354)

R

RAKES OF MALLOW, THE
An 18th-century Co. Cork song, words attributed to Edward Lysaght.

III: 45, 101   (59, 145)

RATTLING BOYS FROM PADDY'S LAND, THE
Anonymous Irish song about the glories of the Irish Brigades.

III: 101   (145)
VI: 108   (149)

RED-CAPPED CONNACHTMAN, THE
Probably an Irish country dance.

IV: 136   (183)

RED FLAG, THE
Socialist song written by Irish journalist Jim Connell for the London
Dock Strike of 1889. The official song of the British Labour Party.
O'Casey uses the song in his play, The Star Turns Red.

IV: 12   (6)

RED ROSES FOR ME
Dublin street song which O'Casey uses as the title and as a song (Act I)
in his play, Red Roses for Me (1944). The words are almost surely by
O'Casey.

II: 142-3   (219)

REMEMBER THE GLORIES OF BRIAN THE BRAVE
Irish song by Thomas Moore.* See also BRIAN BORU, primary index.

II: 228   (355)
III: 24   (27)

REVEILLE
Traditional wake-up call in the military forces.

VI: 82, 224, 225   (111, 322, 323)

RICH AND RARE WERE THE GEMS SHE WORE
Irish song by Thomas Moore,* alluded to by O'Casey with just the words,
"rich and rare."

III: 123, 124   (178, 180, 181)
IV: 196   (266)

RING THE BELL, WATCHMAN
Rousing American song by abolitionist Henry Clay Work. The line used by
O'Casey is from the chorus.

IV: 82   (105)

RISING OF THE MOON, THE
Irish nationalist song of the 1798 Rising, written sixty years after the
event by John Keegan Casey while he was in prison for Fenian activities.
The title is proverbial for an Irish rising.

III: 103   (149)

ROAMIN' IN THE GLOAMIN'
Popular song (1911), words and music by Harry Lauder.*

VI: 97   (132)

ROCK OF AGES
Well-known church hymn (1832), words by Augustus M. Toplady, music by
Thomas Hasting.

II: 2   (7)
III: 19   (19)
V: 29   (29)

ROCKY ROAD TO DUBLIN
Sometimes found under the title, "Along the Rocky Road to Dublin," words
by Joe Young, music by Bert Grant (1915).

I: 161   (247)
IV: 71   (90)

ROLL OUT THE BARREL
Sometimes found under the title, "Beer Barrel Polka," words and music
by Lew Brown, Wladimir A. Timm, and Jaromir Vejvoda (1939). The original title of O'Casey's play, Oak Leaves and Lavender.

III: 71   (99)

ROSE OF TRALEE, THE
Popular Irish song from Co. Kerry, words and music by William Pembroke
Mulchinoc. O'Casey gives the words to the second half of verse one(#).

I: 108-09#   (163#)
III: 18, 119, 156   (18, 182, 229)
IV: 55   (67)

ROSES OF PICARDY
Popular World War I song (1916), words by Frederick E. Weatherly, music
by Haydn Wood.

V: 197   (263)

S

SACRED HEART
Old (1613) church hymn, words by Aloys Schlor. O'Casey gives the words
to verse one.

II: 122   (334)

SAIL ON, SAIL ON
Irish song by Thomas Moore.* O'Casey gives the words to part of verse
one.

IV: 286   (396)

SALUTARIS HOSTIA
Traditional Latin church hymn.

VI: 198   (282)

SAY 'AU REVOIR' BUT NOT 'GOODBYE'
Popular song (1893), words and music by Harry Kennedy.

IV: 151   (204)

SCANDALIZE MY NAME
Old Negro spiritual. Alluded to by O'Casey's use of a line from the
chorus: "Do you call this religion?"

III: 39   (51)
V: 205   (274)

SCOTCH BLUEBELL
Sometimes found as "The Blue Bell of Scotland," popular anonymous song
(1800).

V: 56   (66)

SHAMUS O'BRIEN
Irish song by J. M. Crofts. A favorite of Pearse.*

III: 118   (172)

SHAN VAN VOCHT
For derivation, see this entry under primary index.

II: 170   (261)
III: 156   (229)

SHE IS FAR FROM THE LAND
Irish song by Thomas Moore.*

III: 51   (70)

SHE LIVED BESIDE THE ANNER
Sometimes found as "The Irish Peasant Girl," words and music by Charles
Joseph Kickham.

IV: 218   (299)

SHENADOAH
Capstan chantey with many versions. O'Casey gives one.

I: 50   (70-1)

SILENT, O MOYLE
See MOYLE, primary index.

SILVER TASSIE, THE
Folk song by Robert Burns* which became the title of O'Casey's famous
anti-war play.

V: 30-1   (31)

SKYE BOAT SONG
Scottish exile song which invokes memories of the extermination of
Scottish clans at Culloden (1745).

IV: 17   (13)
V: 94   (120)
VI: 147   (205)

SLATTERY'S MOUNTED FUT
Comic Irish song by Percy French about a buffoon militia (Mounted Foot)
organized by Slattery's eldest son.

III: 119   (182)

SLIEVENAMON
Irish song by Charles Joseph Kickham.

III: 153   (224)

SMITH'S SONG
See DING DONG DEDERO, primary index.

SNOWY BREASTED PEARL
Also found under its Irish title, "Pearla an Bhrollaigh Bhain," an old
Irish melody, translated by George Petrie.

III: 15   (14)

SOGGARTH AROON
Irish song by John Banim. Irish for "my beloved priest."

VI: 178   (251)

SOFT DEAL BOARD
Also found under its Irish title, "An Clar Bog Deil." Irish song by
Edward Walsh.* IV: 136 (183)

SOLDIER'S SONG, THE
National anthem of Ireland, written by Pearder Kearney (see CEARNEY).
O'Casey also uses (#) the first line of the third verse: "Sons of the
Gael, Men of the Pale."

III: 164, 188#   (241, 242, 277#)
IV: 175   (239)

SONG OF THE BOYNE WATERS
Irish song by Thomas Davis.* O'Casey has altered one word in the last
two lines. It should read:

> Ireland awoke - Dungannon spoke -
> With fear was <u>England</u> shaken.

III: 160   (236)

SONG OF O'RUARK
See FAIR OF THE VALLEY LAY SMILING BEFORE ME, primary index.

SOUTH DOWN MILITIA
Popular Orange Order song. Written by William Blacker.*

II: 236   (367)

STAR OF THE COUNTY DOWN, THE
Anonymous boy-meets-girl Irish song of "Rose McCann from the banks of
the Bann, she's the Star of the County Down."

III: 158   (232)

STAR SPANGLED BANNER, THE
National anthem of the United States. Written by Francis Scott Key.

V: 210, 225   (282, 303)

STEER MY BARQUE TO ERIN'S ISLE
Old Irish exile song.

IV: 268   (370)

STEP TOGETHER
Irish patriotic song by M. J. Barry.

III: 105, 229   (152, 341)

STONE OUTSIDE DAN MURPHY'S DOOR, THE
See DAN MURPHY, this appendix.

STORMY WEATHER -- KEEPS RAINING ALL THE TIME
Popular song (1933), words by Ted Kohler, music by Harold Arlen.

V: 146   (192)

SUMMER IS ICUMEN IN
One of the oldest musical compositions extant. O'Casey gives it in
several variants.

III: 111, 176   (160, 260)
V: 209   (278)
VI: 182   (259)

SWANEE RIVER
Better known as "Old Folks at Home," written by Stephen Foster (1851).

III: 20   (21)

SWEET BYE AND BYE
Well-known church hymn by Ira D. Sankey.* Given as "sour bye and bye."

IV: 15   (9)

SWEET INNISFALLEN
Irish song by Thomas Moore.* Inspiration for the title of O'Casey's
Inishfallen, Fare Thee Well.

IV: 286   (396)

SWEET MARIE
Irish song by Percy French about a racing mare.

III: 118   (172)

SWING LOW, SWEET CHARIOT
Old Negro spiritual. Alluded to by O'Casey with the following lines:

"Came to carry him home"	II: 38	(52)
"Swing low, swing high"	V: 234	(315)
"He looked over Jordan"	VI: 226	(325)

VI: 44   (54)

T

TANTUM ERGO
Traditional Latin hymn.

VI: 198, 203   (282, 289)

TE DEUM LAUDAMUS
We Praise Thee, O God, a long and joyful hymn from the Catholic and
Anglican churches.

IV: 66, 206, 260   (83, 283, 359)
VI: 131   (181)

TELL ME THE OLD, OLD STORY
Well-known church hymn (1866) by Katherine Hankey.

VI: 51   (63)

THERE'S A FRIEND FOR LITTLE CHILDREN
Hymn by Albert Midlare.

I: 27   (30)

THORA
Popular song, recorded by John McCormack.*

III: 119   (172)

THOU ARE NOT CONQUERED YET, DEAR LAND
Irish song by The O'Rahilly, martyr and one of the first to be killed
during the Easter Rising.

III: 245   (366)

THOUGH THE LAST GLIMPSE OF ERIN WITH SORROW I SEE
Irish song by Thomas Moore.*

III: 287   (431)
IV: 91, 285   (119, 395)

TOBY JUG
Old English folk ballad by Henry Harrington.

V: 87   (110)

TONE'S GRAVE
Irish song by Thomas Davis.* O'Casey gives the words to the second,
fourth and seventh verses.

I: 177-8   (274-5)

TRAMP, TRAMP, TRAMP
Famous American Civil War song, words and music by George F. Root.

II: 237   (368)
VI: 114   (156)

TREE IN THE WOOD, THE
Anonymous Nova Scotian folk song.

V: 237   (319)

V

VENI CREATOR SPIRITUS
Latin hymn from the 9th century.

II: 160   (246)

VICAR OF BRAY
Irish song about a clergyman whose sympathies and loyalties changed with
the fortunes of successive rulers.

III: 133   (195)

W

WACHT AM RHEIN, DIE
Popular German song, words by Schneckenburger, music by Karl Wilhelm
MORE

WACHT AM RHEIN, DIE (cont.)

(1854). It became a national song during the Franco-Prussian War.

III: 266   (400)

WALLS OF LIMERICK
Irish set dance.

II: 237   (367)

WAS IST DAS DEUTSCHEN VATERLAND
German song, words by E. M. Arndt.

III: 266   (400)

WE ALL GO THE SAME WAY HOME
Unknown. See the chapter title of the same name in I Knock at the Door.

I: 56   (78)

WE ARE ALL NODDING
Scottish folk song.

III: 141   (247)
V: 148, 149, 158   (195, 197, 209)

WE LIFT OUR HEARTS TO GOD ON HIGH
Anonymous church hymn.

II: 223   (346)

WE WON'T GO HOME UNTIL MORNING
Famous celebration song, more popularly known as "For He's A Jolly Good
Fellow," words by William Clifton (1842).

III: 38, 111   (48, 160)

WE'LL CROWN DE VALERA KING OF IRELAND
According to Holt's Protest in Arms (p.155, who also gives the words),
this anonymous Irish song was popular in the south of Ireland after
1918.

IV: 10   (3)

WE'LL HANG JEFF DAVIS ON A SOUR APPLE TREE
O'Casey uses an Irish variant of this Union song of the American Civil
War. For some of the words, see (#).

II: 10#   (6#)
III: 118   (171)
VI: 92   (125)

WEARING OF THE GREEN
Irish song of the 1798 Rising.

VI: 182, 194   (258, 276)

WEDDING OF GLENCREE
"The Wedding Above in Glencree," a cheery Irish song about the affairs
at the wedding of Larry M'Grane and Judy M'Shane.

IV: 271, 272   (375, 376)
V: 46, 142   (52, 187)

WELCOME, THE
Irish song by Thomas Davis.* O'Casey gives a variant of one of the
verses (one or four).

III: 58   (80)

WEST'S ASLEEP, THE
Irish song by Thomas Davis.* O'Casey's "The West's Awake" alludes to the
last verse.

III: 103   (148)
IV: 132   (176)

WHEN THE BLUE OF THE NIGHT MEETS THE GOLD OF THE DAY
Bing Crosby's* most popular recorded song (1931), words and music by
Crosby, Roy Turk and Fred E. Ahlert.

VI: 61   (79)

WHEN FIRST I MET THEE WARM AND YOUNG
Irish song by Thomas Moore.*

IV: 200   (274)

WHEN IRISH EYES ARE SMILING
Popular Irish song (1912), words by Chauncey Olcott and George Graff Jr.,
music by Ernest R. Ball.

III: 121   (176)

WHEN SHALL THE DAY BREAK IN EIREANN
Irish song by D. J. Dowling.

III: 114   (165)
IV: 50   (61)

WHERE THE RIVER SHANNON FLOWS
Popular Irish song (1905), words and music by James J. Russell.

II: 235   (365)
III: 60   (83)
V: 180   (239)

WHISKEY JOHNNY
Popular drinking song with several versions.

III: 130   (189)

WHO FEARS TO SPEAK OF NINETY-EIGHT
Irish song by John Kells Ingram invoking "The Memory of the Dead" (alternate title) of the 1798 Rising. O'Casey gives the words to verse two and four (#).

II: 140, 190-1#   (214, 294-5#)

WIDDECOMBE FAIR
See FARMER OAK, primary index.

WIDOW MALONE
Irish song by Charles Lever.

III: 18   (18)
VI: 207   (296)

WILD IRISH BOY
Unknown. This may be "The Wild Boy," an Irish tune by M. L. Baum.

V: 105   (136)

WILLY REILLY
Irish folk song. The song ends with "And away goes Willy Reilly and his own dear Colleen Bawn." Used in the famous last scene of O'Casey's play, Juno and the Paycock.

III: 18, 118   (18, 172)

WIND THAT SHAKES THE BARLEY, THE
Irish song by Robert Dwyer Joyce.

III: 156   (229)

WRAP THE GREEN FLAG AROUND ME
Irish nationalist song.

IV: 276   (381)

Y

YES! LET ME LIKE A SOLDIER FALL
From the English opera, Maritana (1845), words by Edward Fitzball, music by Vincent Wallace.

I: 73   (105)

YOUR TINY HAND IS FROZEN
Famous song from Giacomo Puccini's opera, La Boheme (1896).

V: 32   (34)

SELECTED INDEX TO APPENDIX I

APPENDIX II:
O'CASEY'S USE OF EXTRACTS
FROM OTHER SOURCES

This is the least complete of all the appendices. It identifies those quotes from songs, poems and prose which O'Casey set apart from the text. It is incomplete because O'Casey is drawing on several decades of exposure to thousands of poems and songs. He often begins the quotation in the middle of the work, making conventional indices and concordances useless. It is also apparent that O'Casey improvised a great deal. In a letter to his publishers (Letters, I, p. 746), he wrote: "I have seen the published versions of these songs, & find my own is better." Readers should not be surprised to find that his versions do not always square with others. All of the songs in this section are, for the most part, given in fuller detail in Appendix I.

I. I KNOCK AT THE DOOR

21	(21)	See CLAN OLIVER, primary index.
25-6	(27)	From "Little Brown Jug."*
33-4	(40-1)	From "The Battle of Limerick."*
56	(78)	From "We All Go the Same Way Home."*
63	(88-9)	Appears to be a variant of a street song.
67	(95-6)	Unknown, probably a British military song.
69-70	(99)	Perhaps a variant on "William and James on the Banks of the Clyde."
79	(114)	From "The Anchor's Weighed."*
86	(126-7)	From "Ehren on the Rhine."*
86	(128)	Unknown, possibly a street song.
89-90	(132-3)	From a children's party game.
90	(133)	From "Round and Round the Village," a popular nursery rhyme.
108-09	(163)	From "The Rose of Tralee."*
157	(241)	Probably from a children's nursery rhyme.
158	(243)	From "The Man Who Struck O'Hara."*
171	(263)	From "Hard Times Come Again No More."*
177-8	(274-5)	From "Tone's Grave."*
181	(279)	Chorus of "Ehren on the Rhine."*
182	(281)	From "God Save the Queen."*
182-3	(281-2)	From "The Green Above the Red."*
188	(290-1)	From Tennyson's* poem, "The Brook."
191	(294)	From Tennyson's* poem, "The Brook."

II. PICTURES IN THE HALLWAY

10	(6)	From "We'll Hang Jeff Davis on a Sour Apple Tree."*
21	(23)	From "Bound for Canaan."*
21	(24)	From Shakespeare's* play, 3 Henry VI.
22	(25)	Ibid
23	(27)	Ibid
24-5	(29)	From Boucicault's* play, The Shaughraun.
25	(30)	From Shakespeare's* play, 3 Henry VI.
35	(46)	Unknown, probably a street song.
36	(47-8)	Unknown.
47	(67)	Unknown, probably an old Fenian ballad.
50	(70-1)	From "Shenandoah."*
50	(71)	From "The Light in the Window."*
51	(73)	From "Oh, for a Steed."*
54	(77)	Last line of Shelley's* poem, "Love's Philosophy."
55	(80)	Unknown.
56	(80)	The first two lines are from T. D. Sullivan's song, "Thirty-Two Counties." The rest is probably a variant.
60-1	(87-8)	From "The Peeler and the Goat."*
67	(99)	From "The Bowld Sojer Boy."*
77	(113-14	From "Auld Lang Syne."*
100	(151)	Lines 100-109 of Tennyson's* poem, "The Lady of Shalott."
112	(171)	Parody of Song of Solomon 2: 10-13.
116-17	(178)	From "Alice, Where Art Thou."*
121	(186)	From Milton's* poem, Paradise Lost.
130	(200)	Unknown, possibly an O'Casey variant.
132	(202)	From Shakespeare's* play, Henry VIII.
138	(212)	O'Casey composition.
142-3	(219)	From "Red Roses for Me."*
159	(245)	From "Orange and Green Will Carry the Day."*
167	(257-9)	Unknown, perhaps an O'Casey composition.
176	(271)	Last verse (ceangal) to "Oidhche Bhios ag Luighe im Shuan" (An Evening I Lay in Repose) by Sean Clarach MacDomhnaill (1691 - 1754), chief of Munster poets. In English (translated by Maureen Murphy):

Pain and gripping fever in the heat of hellfire,
Without friend, without physician, without food, without the
        slackening of great thirst.
Without bed, without way, without God, without people's affection
This on the foreigners for the years they have oppressed our people.

183	(282)	From "Oft in the Stilly Night."*
190	(294)	From "Felons of Our Land."*
190-1	(294-5)	From "Who Fears to Speak of Ninety-Eight."*
199	(307-08)	From "Dear Land."*
217-18	(336-7)	O'Casey composition.
222	(334)	From "The Sacred Heart."*
224	(348)	O'Casey composition.
230	(356)	From "Boys of Old Erin the Green."*

III. DRUMS UNDER THE WINDOWS

19	(20)	According to a letter from O'Casey to Irish Writing (Feb. 1949), this song can be found in Griffith and His Times by George Lyons (Talbot Press: 1923).
21	(22)	From "The Mountains of Pomeroy."*
38	(49)	From the preface to Burns's* poem, "Address to the Unco Guid, or the Rigidly Righteous."
57	(78)	Unknown, probably an O'Casey composition.
58	(80)	Variant on "The Welcome."*
60	(83)	O'Casey composition.
63	(88)	Variant on "Follow Me up to Carlow."*
64	(88-9)	Variant on AE's* poem, "The Dream of the Children."
64	(89)	O'Casey compositon.
76	(107)	From "Killarney."*
76	(108)	From "The Harp That Once Through Tara's Halls."*
82	(116)	From Eithne Carbery's* poem, "Four Winds of Eireann."
83	(117-18)	Combination of five Biblical verses: Job 5: 15; Psalms 9:18; Psalms 34-6; Psalms 132: 15; and Proverbs 22:2.
100	(144)	O'Casey composition.
108	(156)	From "Celts and Saxons."*
127	(185)	From Yeats's* poem, "Red Hanrahan's Song About Ireland."
129	(187)	From Yeats's* poem, "To His Heart, Bidding It Have No Fear," last five lines.
141	(207)	Variant on "We are all Nodding."*
148	(217)	Unknown, probably a Dublin street song.
152	(223)	From "Leather Away the Wattle."*
160	(236)	Variant on "Song of the Boyne Waters."*
161	(237)	Last two lines in the first three verses of Yeats's* poem, "September 1913."
163	(240)	From "Oh, for a Steed."*
169	(249)	From Browning's* poem, "Pippa Passes."
174	(256)	Unknown.
178	(262)	See BINNS, BENJAMIN, primary index.
185	(273)	From "Spring."*
189	(280)	Unknown.
192	(284)	From Chaucer's* "Prolog of the Canterbury Tales."
197	(292)	From Shelley's* poem, "The Masque of Anarchy."
219	(326)	From "Faith of Our Fathers."*
225	(335)	From Lalor's* Irish Felon, serialized in the Irish Worker.
225	(335)	Ibid. This particular quote was found on the left side of the Worker's title page in each issue.
238	(355)	Unknown.
241	(361)	From Pearse's* essay, "The Murder Machine."
244	(364)	Variant on AE's style of writing.
244	(365)	Unknown.
244	(365)	From Allan Seegar's poem, "I Have a Rendez-

MORE

IV: INISHFALLEN, FARE THEE WELL

184	(251)	Line 18, scene one, Act III of Milton's* Cymbeline.
185	(252)	Last line of Yeats's* poem, "To a Poet, Who Would Have Me Praise Certain Bad Poets, Imitators of His and Mine."
196	(269)	From AE's* poem, "By the Margin of the Great Deep."
197	(270)	Lines six and seven of AE's* poem, "The Dream."
206	(282-3)	Slight misquote of the last paragraph in AE's* essay, "Blake's Designs."
206	(283)	From AE's* short essay, "Derivations."
208	(286)	Three quotes from AE's* essay, "Shakespeare and the Blind Alley."
209	(288)	See GIBBON, MONK, primary index.
209	(288)	See TYNAN, KATHERINE, primary index.
210	(288)	See CURRAN, CONSTANTINE, primary index.
210	(289)	Misquote of two lines of AE's* poem, "A Call."
212	(292)	Unknown.
220	(302-03)	From Milton's* poem, Paradise Lost.
220	(303)	See OMAR KHAYYAM, primary index.
223-4	(307-08)	See SHEED, F. J., primary index.
231-2	(319)	Unknown.
233	(321)	From "The Geraldines."*
240-1	(332)	O'Casey variant on "Soldier's of Christ, Arise."
245-7	(338-41)	From Walter MacDonald's* book, Reminiscences of a Maynooth Professor.
258	(357)	From Patrick Kavanagh's poem, "Through the Open Door."
269	(379)	From Yeats's* poem of 185 (252).
275	(381)	Possibly an O'Casey composition.
279	(386)	O'Casey composition.
280	(387)	O'Casey composition.
283	(392)	Unknown.
286	(396)	From "Sail On, Sail On."*

V: ROSE AND CROWN

9	(1)	Unknown.
9	(1)	From "The Bells of London," nursery rhyme.
10	(3)	Variant on a similar poem in Joyce's Portrait of the Artist as a Young Man:

Stephen Dedalus is my name,
Ireland is my nation.
Clongowes is my dwelling place,
And heaven my destination.

16	(12)	From Yeats's* poem, "The Moods."
18	(14)	From Act I of Marlowe's play, The Jew of Malta.
19	(15)	From Yeats's* essay, "The Irish Dramatic Movement," in his Plays and Controversies.
21	(18)	Ibid, p. 200.

21	(18-19)	Ibid, p. 178.
22	(19)	Ibid, p. 177.
24	(22-3)	From Archer's* The Old Drama and the New.
27-8	(27)	Combination of three sentences from Yeats's* essay, "The Irish Dramatic Movement," in his Plays and Controversies, pp. 72, 171, & 191.
30-1	(31)	From "The Silver Tassie."*
34-6	(36-9)	From Yeats's* letters to Lady Gregory (25 April 1928) and to O'Casey (20 April 1928). See Letters, I, pp. 267-9, 271-3.
40-1	(45)	From Shaw's letter to O'Casey (19 June 1928).
41-2	(46-7)	From Charlotte Shaw's* letter to Eileen O'Casey (8 July 1928). See Letters, I, p. 298.
45	(50)	From Yeats's* poem, "The Tower."
45	(51)	From Yeats's* poem, "Blood and the Moon."
46-7	(53)	Unknown.
47-8	(54-5)	See MACNAMARA, BRINSLEY, primary index.
49	(56-7)	Unknown.
49-50	(57)	See IRISH CATHOLIC, Appendix IV.
50	(58)	From Nathan's* foreward to Five Great Modern Irish Plays (1941), p. xi.
50	(58)	See THE STANDARD, Appendix IV.
50	(58-9)	See CU ULADH, primary index.
51	(59)	Unknown.
51-2	(60)	Unknown.
52	(60-1)	See SPEAIGHT, ROBERT, primary index.
54	(63)	Unknown.
54	(64)	From the anonymous poem, "A Song of Winter."
57	(67-8)	From book two, chapter five of Disraeli's* Sybil.
58	(69)	From Sarah N. Cleghorn's poem, "The Golf Links."
68	(83)	From Tennyson's* poem, "Northern Farmer, New Style."
72	(80)	Unknown.
78	(98)	From book five of Spencer's* Faerie Queene.
79	(99)	From Yeats's* poem, "To His Heart, Bidding it Have No Fear."
81	(102)	Unknown.
83	(106)	From Yeats's* poem, "The Collar-Bone of a Hare," last four lines.
84	(106)	Unknown.
87	(111)	Last two lines, second verse, of Yeats's* poem, "Under the Round Tower."
90	(114)	From "Faith of Our Fathers."*
98	(126)	From Tennyson's* poem, "A Character."
100	(129)	From Tennyson's* poem, "The Princess."
100	(129)	From Tennyson's* poem, "Day Dream, L'Envoi."
100	(129)	From the beginning of chapter five, "The Locust Years," in Churchill's* The Gathering Storm.
101	(130)	Unknown, probably from the same (above).
101	(130)	Unknown, from Disraeli.
102	(131)	Unknown.
110	(143)	From Webster's* play, The White Devil or Vittoria Corombona.

112	(145)	Unknown.
112	(146)	From Yeats's* poem, "The Lover Tells of the Rose in His Heart," the middle lines of verse one.
131	(172)	Probably an O'Casey composition.
135	(178)	From "How Many Miles to Babylon," a Mother Goose nursery rhyme.
136	(179)	Second line, verse one of AE's* poem, "The Great Breath."
141	(186)	O'Casey composition.
147	(193)	Unknown.
148, 149	(195, 197)	From "We Are All Nodding."*
150	(198)	O'Casey composition.
154	(204)	Unknown.
155	(206)	O'Casey composition.
158	(209)	From "We Are All Nodding."*
161	(213)	O'Casey composition.
163	(215)	From Shakespeare's* play, Richard II.
163	(216)	From the tenth verse of the poem, "Alfrid's Itinerary through Ireland,"translated by Mangan.*
169	(224)	From "The Green Bushes."*
172	(229)	From "The Shores of Amerikay."*
173	(230)	See O'CONNOR, RURY, primary index.
174	(232)	O'Casey composition.
176	(235)	O'Casey composition.
178	(237)	From a poem by Emma Lazarus which is found on the Statue of Liberty.*
184	(244)	From Shakespeare's* play, A Midsummer Night's Dream.
193	(257)	O'Casey composition.
194	(259)	From any one of numerous American square dance songs, most of which have the same or similar refrains.
194	(259)	Line 21 of William Dunbar's* poem, "The Ballad of Kynel Kittoh."
218	(292-3)	O'Casey compositions.
221	(296)	Unknown.
223	(300)	From T. S. Eliot's* poem, The Hollow Men.
229	(308)	From Whitman's* poem, "Song of Myself."
230	(310)	From H. L. Mencken's* book, Americana.
232	(311)	From "Little Alabama Coon."*
232-3	(312-13)	O'Casey composition.
236	(318)	From "The Man on the Flying Trapeze."*
237	(319)	From "Dear Old Girl."*
238	(319)	From "The Dying Cowboy."*
240	(322)	Unknown.

VI: SUNSET AND EVENING STAR

9	(1)	From Robert Louis Stevenson's poem, "Underwoods."
25	(24)	Probably a children's song.
30	(32)	From "Oats, Peas, Beans, and Barley Grow," a children's song.
33	(37)	O'Casey composition.

43	(52)	See I: 86 (128), this appendix.
56	(72)	Misquote of a passage (p. 47) from Joyce's* Finnegans Wake.
66	(86)	Unknown.
74	(99)	O'Casey composition.
74-5	(99)	See Irish Writing, Appendix IV.
77	(102)	From Shakespeare's* play, Richard III.
81	(109)	Unknown.
82	(110)	Misquote of a passage (p. 398) from Joyce's* Finnegans Wake.
86	(116)	From Hugh MacDiarmid's* poem, To Circumjack Cenrastus.
86	(117)	Ibid.
86	(117)	Ibid.
87	(117)	From MacDiarmid's* poem, "Better One Golden Lyric."
87	(118)	From MacDiarmid's* poem, "Ballad of the Crucified Rose."
88	(119)	From MacDiarmid's* poem, "Poet's Pub."
88	(119)	From MacDiarmid's* poem, "Metaphysical Pictures of the Thistle."
88	(120)	From T. S. Eliot's* poem, "The Love Song of J. Alfred Prufrock."
91	(123)	O'Casey composition.
104	(143)	From Tennyson's* poem, "Maud."
111-12	(153-4)	O'Casey's variant on "The Tri-Colour Ribbon."*
117	(162)	Unknown.
122	(170)	From "Our Lady."*
123	(171)	Last four lines of the last verse of Bartholomew Dowling's poem, "Revelry for the Dying."
127	(176)	From "O God, Our Help in Ages Past."*
127	(176)	From Tennyson's* poem, "The Princess."
137	(191)	Lines 73-4 of Eliot's* poem, "The Love Song of J. Alfred Prufrock."
144	(201)	From "My Handsome Gilderoy."*
148	(206)	Unknown.
152	(213)	From "Bring Back My Bonny to Me."*
157	(221)	Appears as a simple newspaper rhyme.
172	(243)	From "Old Mother Hubbard," a Mother Goose nursery rhyme.
183	(259-60)	O'Casey composition.
191	(271)	From Keats's* poem, "Lines Written in Disgust of Vulgar Superstition."
194	(276)	O'Casey composition and variant on "The Wearing of the Green."*
199	(284)	From Tibullus,* Elegy I (Book I:I), lines 59-62. In English (trans. Jack Lindsay):

When my last hour comes, may I look on you
and, dying, hold you with my failing hand.
You'll lament me, Delia, set on the funeral
    pyre
and kisses mingled with grieving tears you'll
    shed.

201	(287)	From Whitman's* poem, "The Muse in the New World."
201	(287)	From Byron's* "Beppo."
203	(290)	Fourth verse of "St. Ita's Fosterling," translated by Robin Flower.
203	(290)	From "The Song of Crede, Daughter of Gooary," translated by Kuno Meyer.
207	(295)	O'Casey composition.
211	(302)	According to James Carens, this is probably by James Montgomery; not by Gogarty. The first two lines read:

They've closed our ports to English goods;
On Irish beef we'll gorge.

216	(309)	Unknown.
217	(310)	Last four lines of the last verse in Yeats's* poem, "Two Songs from a Play."
217	(311)	Probably an O'Casey composition. It is paritally repeated in VI: 229 (330).
220	(315)	Unknown.
225-6	(324)	"The Ruin'd Rowan Tree," a song written by O'Casey for the revised version of his play, Purple Dust. First used in 1957.
227	(326)	From "Johnny, I Hardly Knew You."*
227-8	(326-7)	O'Casey composition.
232	(333)	From the prologue to Tennyson's* play, Becket. In the U.S. edition, the section is set in quotation marks.
232	(333)	Proverbial; listed in the Oxford Book of English Proverbs (p. 662).
232	(334)	From John Webster's* play, The Duchess of Malfi.

SELECTED INDEX TO APPENDIX II

MORE

SELECTED INDEX TO APPENDIX II (cont.)

Walt Whitman			IV:	134	(180)		21	(18)
III:	284	(426)		141	(190-1)		21	(18-19)
IV:	54	(65)		147	(199)		22	(19)
V:	229	(308)		148	(200)		27-8	(27)
VI:	201	(287)		150	(203)		34-6	(36-9)
				151	(204)		79	(99)
William Butler Yeats				179	(244)		83	(106)
III:	127	(185)		185	(252)		87	(111)
	129	(187)		269	(379)		112	(146)
	161	(237)	V:	16	(12)	VI:	217	(310)
	287	(431)		19	(15)			

APPENDIX III:
O'CASEY'S USE OF
QUOTATIONS FROM
OTHER SOURCES

This appendix lists and annotates O'Casey's use of other works which he incorporates <u>into</u> (rather than <u>apart</u> from) the text. From his many years of reading, he picked up phrases from hundreds of sources: poems, plays, essays, the Bible, and even the streets. Some of these phrases are colloquial while others are quite identifiable. The Bible, Yeats's poems, and Shakespeare's plays constitute the largest source of phrases, and this is no accident because those were his favorite pieces of literature. I have also included allusions to occasions which are described by O'Casey which are not indexable in the conventional sense, and which, because of the manner of their use by O'Casey, might otherwise go unnoticed. A selected index is at the end of this section.

I. I KNOCK AT THE DOOR

10   (3)   "Peace be still." From Mark 4:39: "And he arose, and rebuked the wind, and said unto the sea, Peace, be still."

23   (23)   "Coming through the rye." See Appendix I.

26   (29)   "Garrison i neirinn of the saints and scholars." "I neirinn" is a loose variant on the Irish words for "in Ireland." For many centuries, Ireland was known as the "Land of Saints and Scholars," a reference to their alleged piety and scholarship.

27   (29)   "Sun burst of Ireland." Old emblem in Irish history, and the emblem of the flag of <u>Na Fianna Eireann</u>, the Irish Boy Scouts.

36   (41)   "An abomination in the sight of the Lord." Found in several biblical verses including Deuteronomy 7:25, 23:18, 28:4, and 27:15.

39   (50)   "Come in the evening, come in the morning . . ." See "The Welcome," Appendix I.

39   (51)   "The boy stood on the burning deck." Opening line of the poem, Casabianca.*

40   (52)   "Went away where the good niggers go." From "Old Uncle Ned."*

41   (53)   "Folds shall be full of sheep." From Numbers 32:24: "Build you cities for your little ones, and folds for your sheep . . . "

41   (54)   "Wherever two or three are gathered in his name." From Matthew 18:20: "For wherever two or three are gathered in my name; there am I in the midst of them."

64   (91)   "The old man was dead, the old man was buried." From an old English nursery rhyme.

68   (97)   "The fifth of November,of gunpowder, treason and plot." From an anonymous poem about the plan of Guy Fawkes to blow up the British House of Parliament.

70   (101)   "His mouth is most sweet: yea, he is almost lovely. " From Song of Solomon 5:16: "His mouth is most sweet, yea, he is altogether lovely. This is my beloved, and this is my friend, O daughter of Jerusalem."

72   (104)   "O be joyful in the Lord . . . song of sixpence." Variant of Psalms 100:1-2, and of the anonymous rhyme, "Sing a Song of Sixpence."

73   (106)   "Whither thou goest I will go." From Ruth 1:16: "And Ruth said, Intreat me not to leave thee, or to return from following after thee: for whither thou goest, I will go; . . ."

74   (106)   "The broad way that leadeth to destruction." From Matthew 7:13: "Enter ye in at the strait gate: for wide is the gate, and broad is the way that leadeth to destruction, . . ."

74   (107)   "Herald angels are singing." See HARK THE HERALD ANGELS SING, Appendix I.

78   (113)   "Something old and something new." Allusion to the well-known nursery rhyme.

87   (129)   "Idolators shall not inherit the kingdom of God." Variant on 1 Corinthians 6:9: "Knew ye not that the unrighteous shall not inherit the kingdom of God? Be not deceived: neither fornicators, nor idolators, nor adulterers, nor effeminate, nor abusers of themselves with mankind."

87   (129)   "God is not the God of the dead." Variant on Luke 20:38: "For he is not a God of the dead, but of the living: for all live unto him."

87   (129)   "Blessed are the dead." From Revelation 14:13: "And I
heard a voice from heaven saying unto me, Write, Blessed
are the dead which die in the Lord from henceforth: . . ."

92   (137)   "The idle soul shall suffer hunger." From Proverbs 19:
15: "Slothfulness casteth into a deep sleep; and an idle
soul shall suffer hunger."

97   (144)   "Sore afraid." Found in several passages in the Bible.

101   (150)   "Let not your heart be troubled." From John 14:1: "Let
not your heart be troubled: ye believe in God, believe
also in me."

145   (221)   "Conscience doth make cowards of us all." A line in
Shakespeare's* play, Hamlet.

151   (232)   "If God be with us . . . who can be against us." Variant
on Romans 8: 31: "What shall we then say to these things?
If God be for us, who can be against us."

152   (233)   "Cursed be he that perverteth the judgement of the
stranger." From Deuteronomy 27: 19: "Cursed be he that
perveteth the judgement of the stranger, fatherless, and
widow. And all the people shall say, Amen."

159   (244)   "Where the good niggers go." See I: 40 (52), this
appendix.

159   (245)   "I had a good job but I left it." From an old Army
marching chant.

164   (252)   "Wasn't theirs to reason why." Variant on the line,
"Theirs not to reason why," in the second stanza of
Tennyson's* famous poem, The Charge of the Light Bri-
gade.

169   (261)   "Wash ye, make ye clean." From Isaiah 1:16: "Wash ye,
make ye clean; put away the evil of your doings from
before mine eyes; cease to do evil."

169   (261)   "Sit in darkness." From Isaish 42:7: "To open the blind
eyes, to bring out the prisoners from the prison, and
them that sit in darkness out of the prison house."

189   (292)   "Bread cast upon the waters." Variant on Ecclesiastes
11:1: "Cast they bread upon the waters: for thou shalt
find it after many days."

II. PICTURES IN THE HALLWAY

7   (2)   "Their rock of ages and their morning star." See ROCK OF
AGES, Appendix I. "Morning star" is found in Job 38:7 and
Revelations 2:28 and 22:16.

9   (5)   "Beyond the pale." In Irish history, the Pale was those counties where "the Queen's writ ran," i.e., where English rule held sway. In the 14th century, the Pale included the counties of Louth, Meath, Trim, Dublin, Kilkenny, Wexford, Waterford, and Tipperary. By the late 15th century, however, it included only the counties of Louth, Meath, Dublin, and Kildare.

9   (5)   "A golden bowl was broken, a silver cord loosened, and a wheel broken at the mighty cistern." Variant on Ecclesiastes 12:6: "Or ever the silver cord be loosed, or the golden bowl be broken, or the pitcher be broken at the fountain, or the wheel broken at the cistern."

10   (6)   "Valley of the shadow of life." Variant on Psalms 23: 4: "Yea, though I walk through the valley of the shadow of death, I will fear no evil: for thou art with me; thy rod and thy staff they comfort me."

11   (8)   "In room 15 they slew the man that made them." It was in Committee Room #15 that the fateful meeting was held that decided the political future of Parnell.*

12   (9)   "Island of scuts and schemers." Variant on I: 26 (29), this appendix.

14   (13)   "It is marvellous in our eyes." From Psalms 118: 23: "This is the Lord's doing; it is marvellous in our eyes."

15   (14)   "Plan of campaign." See primary index.

26   (31)   "Let not your heart be troubled." From John 14: 27: "Peace I leave with you; my peace I give unto you: not as the world giveth, give I unto you. Let not your heart be troubled, neither let it be afraid."

33   (43)   "Lead kindly light, amid the encircling gloom." The first line of John Henry, Cardinal Newman's* The Pillar of Cloud (1833).

37   (50)   "God moves in mysterious ways, his wonders to perform." From the Olney hymns (1779, no. 35), "Light Shining Out of Darkness," by William Cowper.

38   (51)   "Vale of tears." Possibly a variant on a line from Shakespeare's* play, Othello: "for I am declined into the vale of years."

38   (51)   "Parnell is his name, me lord, Ireland is his station, Wicklow is his dwellin' place, an' jail his destination." See Rose and Crown, 10 (3), Appendix II.

38   (51)   "Plan of campaign." See primary index.

38   (52)   "Came to carry him home." See SWING LOW, SWEET CHARIOT, Appendix I.

39   (53)   "Where the Queen's writ ran." See II: 9 (5), this appendix.

41   (57)   "He made man in His own image." Variant on Genesis 1:27: "So God created man in His own image, in the image of God created he him; male and female created he them."

42   (58)   "I lift up mine eyes unto the hills." Variant on Psalms 121: 1: "I will lift up mine eyes unto the hills, from whence cometh my help."

76   (112)   "Let your light so shine before men that they may see your good words, and glorify your Father which is in heaven." Exact quote of Matthew 5: 16.

77   (114)   "To sleep, perchance to dream." Line from Shakespeare's* play, Hamlet.

80   (120)   "Jesus wept." John 11: 35, the shortest verse in the Bible.

81   (121)   "Silver cords were loosened and their bowls were broken." See II: 9 (5), this appendix.

83   (124)   "Muzzle the ox that treadeth on corn." Variant on Deuteronomy 24: 4: "Thou shalt not muzzle the ox when he treadeth out the corn."

103   (157)   "Follow, follow, I will follow Jesus." From the hymn, "Down in the Valley," by William O. Cushing.

106   (161)   "White man's burden." Title of a famous poem by Rudyard Kipling.

107   (163)   "They were called; but he had been chosen." Variant on Matthew 20: 16: "So the last shall be first, and the first last: for many are called, but few chosen."

117   (179)   "Cleave to his wife." From Genesis 2: 24: "Therefore shall a man leave his father and his mother, and shall cleave unto his wife: and they shall be one flesh."

123   (189)   "To thine own self be true." Line from Shakespeare's* play, Hamlet.

127   (195)   "Screw your courage to the sticking-place." Line from Shakespeare's* play, Macbeth.

130   (199)   "Farewell, a long farewell to all your greatness." Variant on a line from Shakespeare's* play, Henry VIII: "Farewell, a long farewell to all my greatness."

156   (240)   "Night's candles are burnt out." Line from Shakespeare's* play, Romeo and Juliet.

160   (247)   "With the walk of a queen." From the last lines of Yeats's* play, Cathleen ni Houlihan: " 'Did you see an old woman going down the path?' 'I did not; but I saw a young girl, and she had the walk of a queen.'"

162   (249)   "Kiss me hardy, kiss me quick." From surgeon Beatty's account of Lord Nelson's* death (21 October 1805): "And take care of my dear Lady Hamilton, Hardy, take care of poor Lady Hamilton. Kiss me, Hardy."

170   (261)   "For more than these cometh of evil." From Matthew 5: 37: "But let your communication be, Yea, yea; Nay, nay: for whatsoever is more than these cometh of evil."

178   (275)   "Born of the water and the spirit." Variant on John 3: 5: "Jesus answered, Verily, verily, I say unto thee, Except a man be born of water and of the Spirit, he cannot enter into the kingdom of God."

179   (276)   "Humblest Roman of them all." Variant on a line from Shakespeare's* play, Julius Caesar: "This was the nobelest Roman of them all: . . ."

183   (283)   "He was the light of the world." Variant on John 8: 12: "Then spake Jesus again unto them, saying, I am the light of the world: he that followeth me shall not walk in darkenss, but shall have the light of life."

183   (283)   "Let your light so shine before men that they may see your good works and glorify your Father which is in heaven." Exact quote of Matthew 5: 16.

183   (283)   "The light that lighteth every man that came into the world." Variant on John 1: 9: "That was the true Light, which lighteth every man that cometh into the world."

185   (285)   "The light that lighteth every man coming into the world." See entry immediately above.

185   (285)   "The light of other days would light the days to come." Variant on Thomas Moore's* song, "Oft in the Stilly Night,"* verse one, lines three and four: "Fond memory brings the light/ Of other days around me."

188   (290)   "Bell, book, . . . candlelight." Variant on a line in Shakespeare's* play, King John: "Bell, book and candle shall not drive me back."

188   (291)   "The light of God shone round the soul of Brian." Variant on Luke 2: 9: "And, lo, the angel of the Lord came unto them, and the glory of the Lord shone round about them; and they were sore afraid." See also I: 97 (144), this appendix.

197   (304)   "A tall, white, holy candle." Perhaps an allusion to Yeats's* poem, "Red Hanrahan's Song about Ireland," for which see III: 127 (185).

212   (329)   "Come, let us reason together." Variant on Isaiah 1:
18: "Come now, and let us reason together, saith the
Lord; though your sins be as scarlet, they shall be as
white as snow; though they be red like crimson, they
shall be as wool."

214   (332)   "A man's a man for a' that." Fourth line, second verse,
of Burns's* poem, "For A' That and A' That."

214   (332)   "Go in pride, my sin." Variant on John 8: 11: "She
said, No man, Lord. And Jesus said unto her, Neither
do I condemn thee: go and sin no more."

215   (333)   "Dublin's three castles." Dublin's city crest has
three castles.

215   (333)   "The glory that was Greece and the grandeur that was
Rome." Last two lines of the second verse of the poem,
"To Helen," by Edgar Allan Poe.

215   (333)   "Stoops to conquer." Variant on the title of the play,
She Stoops to Conquer (1773), by Oliver Goldsmith.*

224   (347)   "I was born in iniquity, and in sin hath my mother
conceived me." Variant on Psalms 51: 5: "Behold, I was
shapen in iniquity; and in sin did my mother conceive
me."

236   (366)   "Under a spreading chestnut tree." Variant on the
opening line of the poem, "The Village Blacksmith," by
Henry Wadsworth Longfellow: "Under the spreading chestnut tree."

236   (366)   "One more river to cross." From a recurring line
("There's one more river to cross") in the old Negro
spiritual, "One More River."

III. DRUMS UNDER THE WINDOWS

12   (9)   "Oh, silver trumpets, be ye lifted up and call to the
great race that is to come." From the last passages
in Yeats's* play, The King's Threshold (1904).

12   (9)   "Four Winds of Eirinn." Variant on the title of Eithna
Carbery's* poem, "Four Winds of Freedom."

12   (9)   "Waken up your courage, O Ireland." Slogan of the
Cumann na mBan (Irish Women's Council), commonly found
as Musgail do Mhisneach a Bhanba!

12   (9)   "Long-hidden Ireland." See CORKERY, DANIEL, primary
index.

13   (10)   "Whenever two or three are gathered together." See
I: 41 (54), this appendix.

14	(15)	"The red-haired man's wife." Probably the Irish song, "The Red Man's Wife."
18	(18)	"Walk of the queen." See II: 160 (247), this appendix.
18	(18)	"Wrapping of . . . the green flag." See WRAP THE GREEN FLAG AROUND ME, Appendix I.
18	(18)	"Mary sitting on a stile." From the song, "The Lament of the Irish Emigrant."*
19	(20)	"Dunkirk to Belgrade." See primary index.
19	(20)	"Cathleen ni Houlihan, your way's a thorny way." From Eithna Carbery's* poem, "The Passing of the Gael." Used several times in O'Casey's play, The Shadow of a Gunman.
19	(20)	"Let Yeats arise now and go to Inisfree." Variant on the first lines of Yeats's* poem, "The Lake Isle of Innisfree": "I will arise and go now,and go to Innisfree,/ And a small cabin build there, of clay and wattles made."
21	(23)	"Cathleen ni Houlihan, your way's a thorny way." See III: 19 (20), this appendix.
21	(23)	"Alumna licentiae quam stulti libertatem vocabunt." Loosely, "the child of freedom which the foolish call liberty."
24	(28)	"No sound of a linnet's wings." Variant on lines in Yeats's* poem, "The Lake Isle of Innisfree."
33	(41)	"Hofer, Brian, Bruce, and Tell." O'Casey quotes several lines which are out of order from Thomas Davis's* song, "A Song for the Irish Militia." The first four lines of verse three should read: "The rifle brown and sabre bright/ Can freely speak and nobly write --/ What prophets preached the truth so well/ As Hofer, Brian, Bruce,and Tell?"
34	(42)	"Through the harp blows the cold wind." Variant on a line from Shakespeare's* play, King Lear: "Through the hawthorn blows the cold wind."
36	(45)	"Happier are the dead who are already dead." Perhaps a variant on a line from Emerson's* Beauty: "He thought it happier to be dead/ To die for Beauty, than live for bread."
37	(48)	"Quiz seberrabbit." Variant on the motto of the Knights of St. Patrick*: "Quis Separabit?" (Who Shall Separate?), and on the fictional character, Brer Rabbit, created by Joel Chandler Harris, American story teller. For more Harris, see REMUS AND ROMULUS, UNCLE, primary index.

38	(50)	"I tell thee, churlish priest, a ministering angel shall my sister be." A line from Shakespeare's play, <u>Hamlet</u>.
39	(50)	"The boy stood on the burning deck." See CASABIANCA, primary index.
39	(51)	"The Word was made flesh." From John 1: 14: "And the Word was made flesh, and dwelt among us, and we beheld the glory, the glory as of the only begotten of the Father, full of grace and truth."
45	(59)	"He will be remembered for ever." Variant on the famous lines in Yeats's* play, <u>Cathleen ni Houlihan</u>: "They shall be remembered for ever,/ They shall be alive for ever,/ They shall be speaking for ever,/ The people shall hear of them for ever."
45	(60)	"Rose and crown." See primary index.
48	(65)	"Fair waved the corn in Canaan's pleasant land." From the hymn, "Fair Waved the Golden Corn."
48	(65)	"Parable of the wheat and the tares." Found in Matthew 13: 24-30.
60	(83)	"Dree in one." Variant on "Keegan's Dream."* O'Casey also uses the word, dree, in his chapter, "The Dree Dames," <u>Sunset and Evening Star</u>.
61	(84)	"Little grey home in the south." See LITTLE GREY HOME IN THE WEST, Appendix I.
61	(85)	"Derry down." A nonsense word-filler, frequently found in Irish songs.
62	(86)	"Crowds of wild olives." See RUSKIN, JOHN, primary index.
62	(87)	"Very well then -- I contradict myself." From Whitman's* poem, "Song of Myself," stanza 51.
63	(87)	"Now let us arise." See III: 19 (20), this appendix.
69	(97)	"Alive, alive-o." See IN DUBLIN'S FAIR CITY, Appendix I.
82	(116)	"Twenty thousand welcomes." Variant on the common Irish greeting, <u>cead mile failte</u> (one hundred thousand welcomes).
84	(119)	"Point-counter-point." Title of an Aldous Huxley novel (1928).
85	(121)	"Farewell, a long farewell to all your greatness." See II: 130 (190), this appendix.
86	(123)	"Battle royal." Cf. the title of one of the chapters in O'Casey's <u>Pictures in the Hallway</u>.

87   (124)   "Are ye not more precious than very many sparrows?"
Variant on Luke 12: 7: "Fear not therefore: ye are of
more value than many sparrows."

87   (125)   "His daily work for bread, and his nightly work for the
lily." In the New Statesman and Nation (2 August 1941),
O'Casey wrote: "There is a Persian proverb which says:
'If you have two pennies, with one buy bread, and with
the other a lily.' But if we have but one penny, we can
only buy bread. It has been my fight for a long span of
years now to try to bring about a condition in which the
worker spending his penny on bread will have one left to
buy a lily."

89   (128)   "Domino woebescums . . . Query eileisons." Variant on
the Latin, Dominus vobiscum (The Lord be with you), and
the Greek,Kyria eleison (The Lord have mercy).

96   (138)   "Lillies of the field." From Canticles 2:1: "I am the
rose of Sharon and the lily of the field."

104   (150)   "Herself alone." Variant. See SINN FEIN, primary index.

104   (150)   "Lemons and oranges." Since O'Casey quotes from the
poem, "The Bells of London" (V: 9 (1)), this may be
another reference to it.

105   (152)   "Stepped together." See STEP TOGETHER, Appendix I.

105   (152)   "Old, unhappy, far-off things and battles long ago."
From Wordsworth's* poem, The Solitary Reaper (1803).

111   (160)   "Rings on her fingers and bells on her toes." The third
line of a well-known nursery rhyme, "Ride a Cock Horse."

111   (161)   "An tawn bo cooly." See TAWN BO COOLEY, primary index.

111   (161)   "Annals of the four musters." Variant on the Annals of
the Four Masters, an important book of Irish history,
compiled (1632-36) by a number of historians who were
led by Micheal O Clerigh.

114   (165)   "For the people . . . with the people . . . but not of
the people." Variant on the concluding lines of Abraham
Lincoln's famous Gettysburg Address (19 November 1863):
"This government of the people, by the people, and for
the people shall not perish from the earth."

115   (168)   "Wall of weeping." Suggests the famous Wailing Wall
in Palestine.

120   (174)   "No sitting on a stile for him." See III: 18 (18), this
appendix.

120   (174)   "Seven pillars of wisdom." Title of T. E. Lawrence's
account of the Arabs' revolt against the Turks.

120   (174)   "Declenda est syngestoria et defendi senserationem
                  Hibernicombactoerin." O'Casey's version of "The story
                  (or star) of Synge* must be destroyed to defend the
                  rational/good sense of Hibernia come back to Erin."
                  "Come Back to Erin" is an Irish song.

120   (174)   "Vox Macgenniscensorensis is a vox pupuli." O'Casey's
                  version of "The Voice of Macgennis* the censor is the
                  voice of the people."

120   (174)   "The light of other days." See II: 185 (285), this
                  appendix.

122   (177)   "Waken up the deep sleepers." See I'M IN MY SLEEP AND
                  DON'T AWAKEN ME, Appendix I.

123   (179)   "Dunkirk to Belgrade." See III: 19 (20), this appendix.

125   (182)   "Canons to the right of us, canons to the left of us,
                  volleyin' an' thunderin' out th' thruth." Double
                  allusion: first, to canons of the church, and second,
                  to the first part of verse three of Tennyson's* poem,
                  "The Charge of the Light Brigade."

127   (185)   "A play . . . about an Irish queen." Yeats's* play,
                  The Countess Cathleen.

132   (192)   "Chasubulleros bullen a law." See LILLIBULLERO,
                  primary index.

133   (194)   "Nulla tremulato antea profundi cranuimalis omnibusiboss
                  episcopalitia." O'Casey's version of, loosely, "Do
                  not tremble before the deep, evil mind of the big boss
                  bishops."

136   (199)   "Athanasius contra junta episcopolican hibernica."
                  Allusion to St. Athanasius (c.293 - 373), known as
                  "Athanasius contra mundum, " a Latin phrase alluding to
                  Athanasius's war against Arianism. O'Casey's version,
                  then, of "Athanasius against the junta of Irish bishops."

141   (207)   "Noble six hundred." From the last line of Tennyson's*
                  poem, "The Charge of the Light Brigade."

141   (207)   "The quick and the dead." From the Apostles' Creed, part
                  of which reads: "From then he shall come to judge the
                  quick and the dead."

142   (208)   "Waken up your courage O Ireland." See III: 12 (9),
                  this appendix.

153   (225)   "Religion is the hope of the workers." Variant on the
                  oft-quoted (and misquoted) line from Marx's* essay,
                  "Contribution to the Critique of Hegel's Philosophy of
                  Right" (1844): "Religion is the sigh of the oppressed
                  creature, the heart of the heartless world, just as it is
                                                                          MORE

153   (225)   (cont.) the spirit of a spiritless situation. It is the
              opium of the people." (Emphasis in original.)

155   (228)   "Cumonora nah erreann." Pun on the Irish words,
              cumann na hEireann (literally, the club of Ireland, but
              with broader meanings).

164   (241)   "Guns and drums." See JOHNNY, I HARDLY KNEW YE, Appendix
              I.

169   (250)   "Way of all flesh." From John Webster's* play, Westward
              Hoe (1607), act two, scene two: "I saw him now going
              the way of all flesh."

169   (250)   "The word of the modern, the word En-Masse." Allusion
              to Whitman's* poem, "Song of Myself": "And mine a word
              of the modern, the word En-Masse."

174   (256)   "Hewing wood and drawing water." Variant on Joshua 9:
              21: "And the princes said unto them, Let them live; but
              let them be hewers of wood and drawers of water unto all
              the congregation; as the princes had promised them."

174   (256)   "Butcher, baker, and cnadlestick maker." From the
              nursery rhyme, "Rub-a-Dub Dub."

180   (266)   "The mild knight of the little man . . . of God's tre-
              mendous trifles; . . . grand chief arranger of the gray-
              bards at play; awethor of the misuses of divorsety;
              . . . suborned into life to make right what's wrong with
              the world, and to lead the fiat of heretics to the end
              of the roaman road." Variant on several of Chesterton's*
              works: The Wild Knight (1900), The Napoleon of Notting
              Hill ("little man" 1904), Tremendous Trifles (1900);
              The Uses of Diversity (1920), The Superstition of Di-
              vorce ("divorsety" 1920), What's Wrong with the World?
              (1910), The Queer Feet ("fiat" 1911), Heretics (1905),
              and The End of the Roman Road (1924). With thanks to
              William Maroldo.

181   (268)   "The following lines are found in Chesterton's* "The
              Secret Garden," The Father Brown Omnibus (1951 edition),
              pp. 40-1: " . . . his temples tight like a man in sudden
              and violent pain. _Stop, stop, stop! he cried; stop talk-
              ing for a moment /minute/ . . . Will God give me
              strength? Will my brain give one /make the one/ jump and
              see all? Heaven help me! I used to be fairly good at
              thinking. Will my head split - or will it see? I see
              half, I only see half! He buried his face /head/ in his
              hands, and stood in a sort of rigid torture of thought
              and prayer." With thanks to William Maroldo.

183   (270)   "When her hair has turned to silver, he will love her
              just the same; he will only call her sweetheart, that
              will always be her name." From the famous song, "When
              Your Hair has Turned to Silver."*

186   (275)   "Those who are about to die, salute you." Variant on a
line in the <u>Life of Claudius</u> by Seutonius: "Hail emperor,
we who are about to die salute you."

188   (277)   "Sons of the Gael, Men of the Pale." See SOLDIER'S SONG,
THE, Appendix I.

188   (278)   "Here was the word of the modern, the word En-Masse"
(twice). See III: 169 (250), this appendix.

189   (279)   "Flower in a vase . . . as well as a loaf on a plate."
See III: 87 (125), this appendix.

189   (279)   "To sleep, perchance to dream." See II: 77 (114), this
appendix.

191   (283)   "Per ardua add fastra." O'Casey's version of "through
difficulty to the stars," the slogan of the R.A.F. From
Virgil's* <u>Sic itur ad astra</u> (This is the way to the
stars).

193   (286)   "When lilacs bloomed in the doorway." See WHITMAN, WALT,
primary index.

200   (296)   "Borne into the narrow way that led unto life." Variant
on Matthew 7: 14: "Because strait is the gate, and
narrow is the way which leadeth unto life, and few there
be that find it."

203   (301)   "Hitchin' your flagon to a bar." Variant on a line from
Emerson's* <u>Civilization</u> (1870): "Hitch your wagon to a
star."

203   (301)   "Shinin' shift." Cf. the chapter title, "Song of a
Shift," in <u>Drums under the Windows</u>.

204   (303)   "Hibernica salubrio,este pesta quaesta essentia terrifica
tornadocum." Mostly just word sounds, although some
items are discernible. "Salud y pestas" (health and
money) is a Spanish toast.

211   (313)   "All gone, now, but not forgotten." Cf. the dedication
to O'Casey's <u>Pictures in the Hallway</u>.

211   (313-14) "Yeats . . . passed by, and looked up at the windows."
The first part is an allusion to Yeats's* epitaph,
"Horseman, pass by." The latter may be an allusion
to Yeats's famous rejection of <u>The Silver Tassie</u>, during
which the poet wrote to O'Casey: "you were exasperated
almost beyond endurance by what you had seen or heard
as a man is by what happens under his windows, . . ."
With thanks to Ronald Ayling.

212   (314)   "Beebeesee." B.B.C., the British Broadcasting Corporation.

221   (329)   "Two comrades." O'Casey is alluding to the events
                surrounding the murder of James Nolan, who was beaten
                by police during their baton charge on striking workers
                at Liberty Hall during the opening days of the 1913
                Strike.

222   (330)   "Captains and the kings." Title of a poem by Rudyard
                Kipling.

224   (334)   "Despair came to sup with him." Suggests the line: "Not,
                I'll not, Carrion Comfort, Despair, nor feast on thee,"
                in Carrion Comfort by Gerard Manley Hopkins.

230   (343)   "Sons of the morning." Found in the hymn, "Star of the
                East" (which was also a metaphor for the Russian Revolu-
                tion   and in Isaiah 14:12.

241   (361)   "Not for Pearse the glory that was Greece, nor the grand-
                eur that was Rome." See II: 215 (333), this appendix.

242   (361)   "You came before the swallow dared." Line from Shakes-
                peare's* play, The Winter's Tale.

245   (365)   "Mea na meala culpas." O'Casey pun on mea culpa (through
                my fault), and on the Irish words, Mi na-meala (honeymoon),
                the title of an Irish song by Thomas Davis.*

245   (366)   "Workers of all lands, unite." Variant on the last lines
                of the Communist Manifesto (1848) by Karl Marx:* "Working
                men of all countries, unite!"

245   (367)   "What is the pleasure of life . . . but the good hours
                of an ague." Variant on lines from John Webster's* play,
                The White Devil (1612): "The pleasure of life, what is
                it but the good hours of an ague?"

249   (373)   "How can men die better than facing fearful cods for
                the cashes of his fathers and the temples of his goods!"
                Pun on the lines from Thomas Babington, Lord MacAulay's
                poem, Lays of Ancient Rome: "And how can man die better/
                Than facing fearful odds/ For the ashes of his fathers,/
                And the temples of his gods?"

252   (382)   "The good hours of the ague are over." See III: 245 (367)
                above.

259   (388)   "Peace came dropping slow, dropping from the veils of the
                morning." Lines from Yeats's* poem, "The Lake Isle of
                Innisfree."

261   (390)   "Three cheers for the red, white, and blue." Line from
                the American ballad, "Columbia, The Gem of the Ocean."

265   (397)   "Writ . . . doesn't run here." See II: 39 (53), this
                appendix.

267   (400)   "To the ships that go down to sea." Variant on Psalms 107: 23: "They that go down to the sea in ships, that do business in great waters."

268   (402)   "They served neither king nor kaiser." Allusion to the banner which Connolly* hoisted over the entrance to Liberty Hall in Dublin: "We Serve Neither King Nor Kaiser."

271   (407)   "Remember for ever boys." Satiric statement on lines in Yeats's* play, Cathleen ni Houlihan, for which see III: 45 (59), this appendix.

271   (407)   "The silver trumpets that had lifted themselves up to call to the great race that was to come." See III: 12 (9), this appendix.

281   (422)   "Group of innocents." In its context, suggests the "Slaughter of Innocents."

283   (425)   "On his cornet." Suggests lines from Whitman's* poem, "Song of Myself": "With music I come, with my cornets and my drums,/ I play not marches for accepted victors only, I play marches/ for conquer'd and slain persons."

284   (426)   "The fools, the fools." Suggests Pearse's* famous oration at the gravesite of O'Donovan Rossa* in 1915: "They /the British/ think they have foreseen everything, think they have provided against everything; but -- the fools! the fools! the fools!"

285   (428)   "A place fit for heroes." From a speech by David Lloyd George* at Wolverhampton (24 November 1918): "What is our task? To make Britain a fit country for heroes to live in."

287   (430)   "They who shall speak to her people for ever." See III: 45 (59), this appendix.

287   (430)   "He will be remembered for ever." See III: 45 (59), this appendix.

287   (431)   "Lost leaders." Cf. the chapter title of the same name in Drums under the Windows.

287   (431)   "A last glimpse of Erin." See THOUGH THE LAST GLIMPSE OF ERIN WITH SORROW I SEE, Appendix I.

IV: INISHFALLEN, FARE THEE WELL

9   (1)   "Things had changed, but not utterly; and no terrible beauty was to be born." Variant on the last lines of Yeats's* poem, "Easter 1916": "Now and in time to be,/ Wherever green is worn,/ Are changed, changed utterly:/ A terrible beauty is born."

9   (1)   "Felon's cap became the noblest crown an Irish head could wear." See FELONS OF THE LAND, Appendix I.

12   (6)   "Far from the madding crowd." Variant on a line in Thomas Gray's* poem, <u>Elegy Written in a Country Churchyard</u>: "Far from the madding crowd's ignoble strife."

14   (8)   "Sin of idleness." See I: 92 (137), this appendix.

15   (9)   "Sour bye and bye." See SWEET BYE AND BYE, Appendix I.

16   (11)   "Who would be remembered, if not for ever, for awhile anyhow." See III: 45 (59), this appendix.

18   (13-14) "They shall not grow old as we who are left grow old." Except for transposing the words "not" and "grow," this is the first line, fourth stanza, of the poem, "For the Fallen," by Laurence Binyon.

18   (14)   "Life to a whimper." Suggests the celebrated lines from Eliot's* <u>The Hollow Men</u> (1925): "This is the way the world ends/ Not with a bang but a whimper."

21   (17)   "His comforter, his rod, and his staff." Variant on Psalms 23: 4: "Yea, though I walk through the valley of the shadow of death I will fear no evil, for thou art with me; thy rod and thy staff they comfort me."

21   (18)   "Screw up his courage." See II: 127 (195), this appendix.

29   (30)   "Hail and farewell." Cf. the chapter title of the same name in <u>Inishfallen, Fare Thee Well</u>.

31   (32)   "Not a mouse stirring." Line from Shakespeare's* play, <u>Hamlet</u>.

31   (33)   "All the perfumes of Arabia . . ." Suggests the line from Shakespeare's* play, <u>Macbeth</u>: "All the perfumes of Arabia would not sweeten this."

34   (36)   "The great only appear great because the workers are on their knees." Radical aphorism which is usually attributed to Proudhon.* It appeared in James Connolly's* paper, <u>The Workers' Republic</u>, with regularity.

34   (36)   "Some old sweet song." See LOVE'S OWN SWEET SONG, Appendix I.

34   (37)   "The rest was silence." Line from Shakespeare's* play, <u>Hamlet</u>.

35   (37)   "Never morning wore to evening, but some heart did break." Line from Tennyson's* poem, "In Memoriam."

35   (38)   "All for the forbidden bite of an apple." Allusion to the biblical fable of Adam and Eve's explusion from the Garden of Eden.

47   (55)   "Red badge of courage." Title (1895) of Stephen Crane's
                 realistic study of the common man under fire in battle.

48   (57)   "Upon these stones I will build my church." Variant on
                 Matthew 16: 18: "And I say unto thee, That thou art
                 Peter, and upon this rock I will build my church; and the
                 gates of hell shall not prevail against it."

49   (58)   "Gathered up the fragments." Cf. the chapter title in
                 Pictures in the Hallway.

50   (60)   "Eire's five beautiful green fields." Poetic allusion
                 to Ireland's four provinces (Ulster, Munster, Connaught,
                 and Leinster), and to Royal Meath (see MEATH, primary
                 index).

50   (61)   "When will the day break in Eirinn, when will her day
                 star arise." See WHEN SHALL THE DAY BREAK IN EIREANN,
                 Appendix I.

52   (62-3)   "Two boys." O'Casey is alluding to Patrick Kennedy and
                 James Murphy who were arrested on the night of 9 Feb-
                 ruary 1921 by British forces. They were taken to Dublin
                 Castle and interrogated. Around midnight, they were
                 put into a car and taken to a field in Drumcondra with
                 two other cadets. The next morning, the two cadets and
                 Kennedy were found dead. Murphy claimed that they had
                 been made to stand against a wall in the field. Buckets
                 were put over their heads and they were shot.

54   (65)   "Merry gentlemen." See GOD REST YE MERRY GENTLEMEN,
                 Appendix I.

63   (79)   "Brave in another world." Suggests the book, Brave
                 New World (1932), by Aldous L. Huxley.

63-4   (79)   "Lucifer and his lost angels." See LUCIFER and MICHAEL'S
                 LOST ANGELS, primary index.

65   (81)   "Good to be merry for tomorrow we die." Variant on 1
                 Corinthians 15: 32: "Let us eat and drink; for tomorrow
                 we die."

65   (82)   "Peace was dropping now from the veils of the morning."
                 See III: 259 (388), this appendix.

70   (88)   "Long-barrelled gun." Suggests a line from the Irish
                 song, "The Foggy Dew": "While Britannia's sons with their
                 long-ranged guns/ Sailed in by the Foggy Dew."

72   (90)   "The mists rolling down the bog." Usually found as "the
                 mist that does be on the bog," a satiric parody of
                 Synge's* romantic description of Irish rural life.

71   (90)   "Look out for war; immediate and terrible war." See
                 CHURCHILL, WINSTON, primary index.

73 (92) "Valley of the shadow of anxiety." See II: 10 (6), this appendix.

73 (93) "Gone in the wind." Suggests the title of the celebrated novel, <u>Gone with the Wind</u> (1936), by Margaret Mitchell.

77 (99) "Voice of labour." Title of the newspaper of the Irish Transport and General Workers' Union (from January 1918).

88 (114) "The terrible beauty." See IV: 9 (1), this appendix.

88 (115) "Gathered from the fragments." See IV: 49 (58), this appendix.

89 (116) "While tailors worked night and day making uniforms for the new Free State Army." Cf. the line in O'Casey's play, <u>Juno and the Paycock</u>, Maisie Madigan to Needle Nugent: "I'd call you a real thrue Die-hard an' live-soft Republican, attendin' Republican funerals in the day, an' stopping up half the night makin' suits for the Civic Guards."

89 (116) "Making their land a nation once again." See NATION ONCE AGAIN, A, Appendix I.

89 (116) "Clap hands, clap hands, till Daddy comes home." From a traditional English nursery rhyme.

91 (119) "The dragon had conquered the knight." Suggests the popular legend of St. George* and the dragon.

91 (119) "Farewell but whenever you welcome the hour of the flight of the earl." See FAREWELL BUT WHENEVER YOU WELCOME THE HOUR, Appendix I, and FLIGHT OF THE EARL, primary index.

94 (123) "Lift your heart up, Mother Erin." Perhaps a variant on the song, "Lift up your Heart," by Thomas Moore, or on a hymn of the same name by John Masterman.

100 (132) "Ireland's terrible beauty." See IV: 9 (1), this appendix.

100 (132) "Sure 'twas for this that Emmet fought, and Wolfe Tone sunk serene." Line from verse four of Thomas Davis's* song, "The Green Above the Red."*

106 (139) "Lover and his lass." See IT WAS A LOVER AND HIS LASS, Appendix I.

109 (145) "Valley of the squinting windows." See MACNAMARA, BRINSLEY, primary index.

110 (145) "Episcopal declaration." On 10 October 1922, the Irish hierarchy, in a meeting at Maynooth, issued a "Joint Pastoral Letter" to the priests and people. The letter condemned resistance to the Provisional Government by

MORE

110   (145)   (cont.) Republicans, whom they termed as "morally only a system of murder and assassination of the National forces."

110   (146)   "One of the Free State ministers." Richard Mulcahy, minister for defense in the Provisional Government. The statement quoted by O'Casey was delivered in the Dail following the executions of Joseph Spooner, Patrick Farrelly, and John Murphy who were charged with illegal possession of revolvers and bombs (30 November 1922).

118   (157)   "Whom the Lord loveth, he chasteneth." Variant on Hebrews 12: 6: "For whom the Lord loveth he chasteneth, and scourageth every son whom he receiveth."

119   (158)   "How often in the stilly night." See OFT IN THE STILLY NIGHT, Appendix I.

119   (159)   "Thirty pieces of silver." Allusion to the biblical tale of Judas's betrayal of Jesus. See Matthew 26: 14-15.

125   (167)   "Coming through the rye." See Appendix I.

134   (180)   "His letters defending the workers." Yeats* wrote an article, "Dublin Fanaticism," for the Irish Worker on 1 November 1913, denouncing the capitalists of Dublin for their oppression of Irish workers.

135   (180-1) "A silver cord was sundered or a golden bowl was broken." See II: 9 (5), this appendix.

135   (182)   "One and twenty welcomes." Line from A. E. Housman's A Shropshire Lad.*

144   (194)   "Great Breath." Title of a poem by AE.*

148   (200)   "Walk of a queen." See II: 160 (247), this appendix.

151   (205)   "Blue shirts." Name of a fascist organization in Ireland which was popular in the 1930s. The group, small in number, was led by General Eoin O'Duffy, a former commander of Free State forces during the Irish Civil War (1923).

151   (205)   "Lodgins in the cowld, cowld ground." See MY LODGINGS, IT IS ON THE COLD, COLD GROUND, Appendix I.

152   (205)   "Sound and a fury." Variant on the title of a popular novel, The Sound and the Fury (1929) by William Falkner.

154   (208)   "Seventy-seven dead men." The number of Republicans executed by the Irish Free State during the Civil War in 1923. A complete list can be found in Macardle's book, The Irish Republic.

154   (209)   "The terrible beauty of a tall-hat is born to Ireland."
                For "terrible beauty . . . is born," see IV: 9 (1), this
                appendix. The tall-hat reference may be an allusion to
                the chapter, "Tall Hats and Churns," in Gogarty's* As
                I Was Going Down Sackville Street.

155   (210)   "Three of her four beautiful fields." See IRELAND'S FOUR
                BEAUTIFUL FIELDS, primary index.

156   (212)   "The taking of the oath could be done without taking the
                oath." This piece of madness was formulated by de Valera*
                as a method by which he and his party, Fianna Fail, could
                enter the Dail in 1927. See Bromage, De Valera and the
                March of a Nation, p. 218.

159   (216)   "Heaven, and all that." Cf. the chapter title, "All
                Heaven and Harmsworth Too," in Pictures in the Hallway.

162   (220)   "A world in arms against them." Allusion to the Allied
                intervention against the Soviet Union after the October
                Revolution (1917). Over 14 nations sent troops to support
                the counter-revolutionaries. The term, "world in arms,"
                is from On Frederick the Great (1842), by Thomas Babing-
                ton, Lord Macaulay.

162   (220)   "The terrible beauty that had been born there." See IV:
                9 (1), this appendix.

163   (222)   "Yellow sands." See COME TO THESE YELLOW SANDS, Appendix
                I.

163   (222)   "Coming through the rye." See Appendix I.

165   (225)   "Workers of Dublin, and the world." See III: 245 (366),
                this appendix.

165   (225)   "You've nothing to lose but the world, and you've the
                holy chains to gain." See III: 245 (366), this appendix.

165   (225)   "Make the world safe for bosses." Variant on Woodrow
                Wilson's famous comments in an address to Congress (2
                April 1917): "The world must be made safe for democracy."

168   (228)   "All changed, now, changed utterly." See IV: 9 (1), this
                appendix.

174   (238)   "Swearing he could never consent, consented." Variant on
                a line in Byron's* Don Juan: "And whispering 'I will ne'er
                consent' -- consented."

177   (241)   "Green hills of holy Ireland." See III: 119 (174), this
                appendix.

177   (241)   "His famous apotheosis." Allusion to Yeats's* speech
                before the rioting crowd at the Abbey Theatre on the
                fourth night of the opening run of O'Casey's play,
                                                            MORE

177   (241)   (cont.) The Plough and the Stars (11 February 1926): "Is
                 this going to be a recurring celebration of Irish genius?
                 Synge first, and then O'Casey! The news of the happen-
                 ings of the last few minutes will flash from country to
                 country. Dublin has once more rocked the cradle of a
                 reputation. From such a scene in this theatre went forth
                 the fame of Synge. Equally the fame of O'Casey is born
                 here tonight. This is his apotheosis."

178   (243)   "Walk of a queen." See II: 160 (247), this appendix.

179   (243)   "Changed, changed utterly." See IV: 9 (1), this appen-
                 dix.

182   (249)   "The mist that does be on the bog." See IV: 72 (90),
                 this appendix.

184   (251)   "Quoth the raven. Nevermore." From Edgar Allan Poe's
                 poem, The Raven.

194   (266)   "Rich and rare." See RICH AND RARE WERE THE GEMS SHE
                 WORE, Appendix I.

203   (278)   "Earth breath." Probably an allusion to one of AE's*
                 collection of poetry, The Earth Breath and other poems
                 (1897).

205   (281)   "At Home." Name given to weekly gatherings at AE's*
                 home. See RATHGAR AVENUE, primary index.

205   (281)   "His Journal." See IRISH STATESMAN, Appendix IV.

214   (295)   "To die with a whimper." See IV: 18 (14), this appen-
                 dix.

218   (300)   "Lodgings on the cold, cold floor." See IV: 151 (205),
                 this appendix.

224   (308)   "Sans sight, sans smell, sans taste, sans everything."
                 Construction suggests similar lines from Omar Khayyam's
                 Rubaiyat which O'Casey quotes in IV: 220 (303).

228   (315)   "The scarlet pimpernel." Title of a celebrated novel
                 (1905) of romances of the French Revolution by Baroness
                 Orczy.

231   (318)   "O silver trumpets be ye lifted up and call to the great
                 race that is to come." See III: 12 (9), this appendix.

245   (338)   "Disturber of the peace." A phrase found in several
                 places but also in Shakespeare's* play, Titus Andronicus.

246   (339)   "Rest, rest, perturbed spirit." Line from Shakespeare's*
                 play, Hamlet.

248   (343)   "It is far better to know about the things that are
Caesar's than to know about the things that are God's."
Variant on Mark 12: 17: "And Jesus answered saying unto
them, Render Caesar the things that are Caesar's, and
to God the things that are God's. And they marvelled
at him."

257   (355)   "Writ of excommunication doesn't run here." See II: 39
(53), this appendix.

260-1   (360)   "Professional catholic lecturer." Allusion to the events
of 6-20 August 1938 when O'Casey quarrelled with Maurice
Lehy. See Krause's notes in Letters, I, pp. 731-5, 749.
The time gap was ten years, not a few months.

262   (362)   "The word that wasn't with God." Variant on John 1: 1:
"In the beginning was the Word, and the Word was with
God, and the Word was God."

268   (371)   "Ancient order of chivalry." In its context, a variant
on the Ancient Order of Hibernians.*

271   (375)   "Bone of their bone, flesh of their flesh." Variant on
Genesis 2: 23: "And Adam said, "This is now bone of my
bones, and flesh of my flesh; she shall be called Woman,
because she was taken out of Man."

272   (377)   "Ding-dong-dedero." See this entry in primary index.

275   (380)   "The sign of things to come." Variant on a line from
Shakespeare's* play, Troilus and Cressida: "The baby
figure of the giant mass/ Of things to come."

282   (390)   "Lead kindly light, amid the encircling gloom." See II:
33 (43), this appendix.

282   (390)   "An' seas betune us braid hae roared, sin auld lang
syne." See AULD LANG SYNE, Appendix I.

283   (392)   "Standing pensively at the door of his small cabin."
See III: 19 (20), this appendix.

283   (392)   "Ireland's red-rose-border hem." Allusion to the last
lines of Yeats's* poem, "To Ireland in the Coming Times":
"May know how my heart went with them/ After the red-rose-
bordered hem."

284   (395)   "Peep of day." See DIAMOND, BATTLE OF, primary index.

285   (395)   "Last glimpse of Eireann." See THOUGH THE LAST GLIMPSE
OF EIREANN WITH SORROW I SEE, Appendix I.

V: ROSE AND CROWN

9   (2)   "Faith, her privates we." Line from Shakespeare's* play,
Hamlet.

11   (5)   "And so to bed." Title of a play by J. B. Fagan.*

12   (5)   "Photographed talking to a policeman." This photograph appears in a collection of O'Casey's early political writings, Feathers from a Green Crow, edited by Robert Hogan.

17   (13)   "Twilight of the goods." Variant on the title, Twilight of the Gods, a novel by Richard Garnett (1888).

17   (13)   "Noble six hundred." See III: 141 (207), this appendix.

29   (29)   "The things that belong to Caesar." See IV: 248 (343), this appendix.

40   (45)   "Rose of Sharon and the lily of the valley." See III: 96 (138), this appendix.

46   (53)   "Seven years after." O'Casey is referring to seven years after the Tassie was published (1928). The world premiere was not until 1929.

47   (54)   "Hearseman, pass by." In O'Casey's notebooks, he wrote: "Hearseman is one who drives a hearse, the car carrying a corpse to the cemetery. The words are a play on the last few words of the epitaph written by Yeats himself for his headstone. They are Horseman, Pass by. My term tries to show the wide difference between horseman and hearseman." (Eileen O'Casey, Sean)

47   (54)   "Not a mouse stirring." See IV: 31 (32), this appendix.

52   (61)   "The light of other days." See II: 185 (285), this appendix.

53   (62)   "The old lady had said yes." Variant on the title of Denis Johnston's* play, The Old Lady Says No. The "old lady" was Lady Gregory.*

53   (63)   "Peace, be still." See I: 10 (3), this appendix.

54   (64)   "Brekkek Kekkek . . ." This line, found in Aristophanes' The Frogs, is identical to one found in Joyce's* Finnegans Wake.

56   (67)   "Now is the accepted time, now is the day of salvation." Variant on II Corinthians 6: 2: "For he saith, I have heard thee in a time accepted, and in the day of salvation have I succoured thee: behold, now is the accepted time; behold, now is the day of salvation."

58   (69)   "Home fit for heroes." See III: 285 (428), this appendix.

66   (81)   "Little gray home in the north-west." See LITTLE GREY HOME IN THE WEST, Appendix I.

71   (88)   "Quick and the dead." See III: 141 (207), this appendix.

72   (89)   "Words upon the window pane." Title of a one-act play (1934) by Yeats.*

73   (90)   "Eight and twenty phases of the moon." Variant on the title of Yeats's* poem, "Twenty and Eight Phases of the Moon."

73   (90)   "Not a mouse stirs." See IV: 31 (32), this appendix.

73   (91)   "Homes of clay and wattles made." See III: 19 (20), this appendix.

73   (91-2) "Am I nothing to all ye who pass by." Variant on Lamentations 1: 12: "Is it nothing to you, all ye that pass by? . . ."

74   (92)   "Herald angels didn't sing." See HARK THE HERALD ANGELS SING, Appendix I.

81   (102)   "It is marvellous in our eyes." From Psalms 118: 23.

83   (105)   "Four winds of Eireann." See III: 12 (9), this appendix.

95   (121)   "Jimmy there and Jimmy here." Probably a variant on the first lines of Rudyard Kipling's famous poem, "Tommy Atkins": "Oh, it's Tommy this, an' Tommy that, an' Tommy go away."

95   (122)   "The cupboards were bare." Allusion to "Old Mother Hubbard," traditional nursery rhyme.

95   (122)   "Out of the deep we cry unto thee." Variant on Psalms 100: 1: "Out of the deep have I called unto thee, O Lord: Lord hear my voice."

95   (122)   "The bells were tolling." Variant on John Donne's famous lines in his <u>Devotion</u>: "Any man's death diminishes me, because I am <u>involved</u> in Mankind. And therefore never send to know for whom the bell tolls; it tolls for thee."

96   (123)   "For whom the bells toll." See entry immediately above. Also the title of an Ernest Hemingway novel (1940).

97   (125)   "First few letters of Socialism's alphabet." Suggests <u>The ABC of Communism</u> (1922), a famous theoretical work by Nikolai Bukharin, one of Stalin's* victims.

105   (136)   "A letter from Lady Gregory." See <u>Letters</u>, I, pp. 368-9.

109   (141)   "Sean the proud." In Irish history, Shane O'Neill was known as "The Proud." He was a leader of Irish forces in the 16th-century wars against Elizabeth I. This is also a reference to O'Casey's fierce pride.

109   (141)   "To them the things that are theirs." See IV: 248 (343), this appendix.

109   (142)   "Then here's a hand, my trusty frien', an' gi'e's a hand of thine! Seas between us braid ha'e roared sin' auld lange syne." Lines from the song, "Auld Lang Syne" (see Appendix I).

112   (146)   "Brave old world." See IV: 63 (79), this appendix.

116   (151)   "All the glory that was Greece, the grandeur that was Rome." See II: 215 (333), this appendix.

116   (151)   "The last mask." Allusion to Yeats's* theories of acting, whereby the actors wore masks and depended on body movements to convey the meaning and style of plays.

117   (152)   "Remember him for ever." See III: 45 (59), this appendix.

118   (153)   "In a letter to Sean." The Shaw* letter was dated July 23, 1932 (see Letters, I, p. 449n).

119   (154)   "Lord, I am not worthy." Variant on Luke 7: 6: "Then Jesus went with them. And when he was now not far from the house, the centurion sent friends to him, saying unto him, Lord, trouble not thyself: for I am not worthy that thou shouldest enter under my roof."

119   (155)   "Out of encircling gloom." See II: 33 (43), this appendix.

120   (156)   "Through a dark cloud of fears the time redeem the well-read vision in the lower dream; to put new money in the fading purse, the time redeem." Variant on lines 19-21, part four, of T. S. Eliot's* poem, Ash-Wednesday (1930).

125   (163)   "When lilacs in the dooryard bloomed." See WHITMAN, WALT, primary index.

126   (164)   "To give us our daily bread." Variant on lines in "The Lord's Prayer."

129   (168)   "For ever amber." Forever Amber, a "flagging erotic Restoration novel" (1944) by Kathleen Winsor.

131   (171)   "Shooting an arrow into the sky." Variant on the opening line of Henry Wadsworth Longfellow's poem, "The Arrow and the Song" (1845).

137   (181)   "Candle, bell, or book." See II: 188 (290), this appendix.

139   (183)   "They no longer serve who only stand and wait." Variant
                 on lines from Milton's* poem, On His Blindness: "They also
                 serve who only stand and wait."

139   (183)   "England hath no longer any need of thee." Variant on
                 a line in Wordsworth's* poem, London (1802): "England
                 hath need of thee; she is a fen" (written about Milton).

141   (186)   "Way of all flesh." See III: 169 (250), this appendix.

144   (190)   "To be or not to be." Celebrated line from Shakespeare's*
                 play, Hamlet.

146   (192)   "Welcome as the flowers in May; come into the parlour,
                 dear; stormy weather." For "stormy weather," see Appen-
                 dix I. "Come into the parlour" is from the Irish song
                 of the same name, beginning with "If you're Irish, come
                 into the parlour." "Welcome as the flowers in May" is
                 a line from the chorus of the Irish song, "Dear Old
                 Donegal."

145   (191)   "O Paradise, O Paradise, who doth not long for rest."
                 Variant on a line in Frederick William Faber's song,
                 "Paradise": "Who doth not crave for rest."

149   (197)   "What is the stars, Joxer, what is the stars?" Celebrated
                 lines from O'Casey's play, Juno and the Paycock.

155   (204)   "Rung the bell, lit the candle, read from the book, and
                 made the place fit for friars to live in." Variants. See
                 II: 188 (290) and III: 285 (428), this appendix.

170   (226)   "The last -- which shall be first." Variant on Matthew
                 19: 30: "But many that are first shall be last; and the
                 last shall be first."

174   (231)   "Men of Aran." Suggests the famous film, Man of Aran
                 (1935) by Pat Mullen.

183   (243)   "Valley of the shadow of life." See II: 10 (6), this
                 appendix.

183   (244)   "Lady of shallow." See TENNYSON, primary index.

186   (247)   "Come unto me all ye who labour and we will give you
                 work." Variant on Matthew 11: 28: "Come unto me, all
                 ye that labour and are heavy laden, and I will give you
                 rest."

188   (251)   "Them were the days when knights were bold." Colloquial
                 phrase.

191   (255)   "How does your garden grow." From the nursery rhyme,
                 "Mary, Mary, Quite Contrary."

192   (256)   "Lad and a lass." See IT WAS A LOVER AND HIS LASS, Appen-
                 dix I.

196   (261)   "Lady on a white horse, rings on her fingers and bells on her toes." The lady on a white horse is Lady Godiva (wife of Earl Leofric) who allegedly rode through the city at noon in the nude to protest oppressive taxes. For the rest, see III: 111 (160), this appendix.

202   (270)   "Point-counter-point." See III: 84 (119), this appendix.

205   (274)   "D'ye call dis religion." See SCANDALIZE MY NAME, Appendix I.

205   (274)   "Dope?" In Act II of O'Casey's play, The Plough and the Stars, the Covey remarks: "Dope, dope. There's only one war worth having: the war for th' economic emancipation of th' proletariat."

206   (275)   "The stuff that dreams are made on." Variant on lines from Shakespeare's* play, The Tempest: "We are such stuff/As dreams are made on, and our little life/Is rounded with a sleep."

209   (278)   "Summer was icumen in." See SUMER IS ICUMEN IN, Appendix I.

212   (284)   "Old and happy, far-off things, and battles long ago." See III: 105 (152), this appendix.

215   (288)   "Tanglewood." Site in Berkshire, Massachusetts, of a famous music festival.

223   (300)   "UnAmerican." O'Casey is referring to the House Committee on UnAmerican Activities, a legislative committee of the House of Representatives, which conducted hearings into alleged Communist influences in the entertainment, labor union, and educational areas in American life. Many of O'Casey's American friends suffered at the Committee's hands.

226   (303)   "Calling on the workers of all lands to unite together." See III: 245 (366), this appendix.

231   (310)   "Lead kindly light." See II: 33 (43), this appendix.

231   (310)   "Workers of all lands." See III: 245 (366), this appendix.

234   (315)   "Swing low, swing high." See SWING LOW, SWEET CHARIOT, Appendix I.

237   (319)   "Some got Drunk, and some got Boozy, an' all got stuck on Black-eye'd Susy." Opening lines of the song, "Black-eyed Susan."

240   (323)   "Hail and farewell." See IV: 29 (30), this appendix.

VI: SUNSET AND EVENING STAR

10   (2)   "Thank God for the race and sod" and "Sign your name, Kelly, sign your name, Burke, sign your name, Shea." See THE FIGHTING RACE, Appendix I.

11   (4)   "One more river to cross." See II: 236 (366), this appendix.

11   (5)   "Her kingdom had come." Variant on a line in the "Lord's Prayer."

15   (10)   "The white horse." See NOTTING HILL GATE, primary index.

16   (11)   "Bow of burnished gold." Variant on a line in Blake's* Milton: "Bring me my bow of burning gold."

21   (19)   "Valley of the shadow of death." See II: 10 (6), this appendix.

22   (20)   "Unto us a child is born, unto us a son is given." Lines from Isaish 9:6.

31   (33)   "I will greatly multiply." Line from Genesis 3:16.

31   (34)   "Pie from the sky." Allusion to the last line of the chorus of a famous labor song, "The Preacher and the Slave," by Joe Hill: "You'll get pie in the sky when you die."

31   (35)   "Gold and silver have I none." Variant on Acts 3: 6: "Silver and gold have I none; but such as I have give I thee."

39   (45)   "Ring out wild bells; ring out the old, ring in the new, ring out the false, ring in the true." Variant on lines in Tennyson's poem, In Memoriam, stanzas one and two:

> Ring out, wild bells, to the wild sky . . .
> Ring out the old, ring in the new,
> Ring, happy bells, across the snow:
> The year is coming, let him go;
> Ring out the false, ring in the true.

39   (45)   "Oh, come let us adore him." See ADESTES FIDELES, Appendix I.

39   (46)   "God rest you merry men." See GOD REST YE MERRY GENTLEMEN, Appendix I.

39   (47)   "Suffer the little ones to come to me." Variant on Mark 10: 14: "But when Jesus saw it, he was much displeased, and said unto them, Suffer the little children to come unto me, and forbid them not; for of such is the kingdom of God."

41   (49)   "Sign of the three kindles." In Dublin, there is a
              publishing firm, Sign of the Three Candles.

41   (50)   "Battles long ago." See III: 105 (152), this appendix.

42   (50)   "Casting of bread upon the waters." Variant on
              Ecclesiastes 11: 1: "Cast thy bread upon the waters: for
              thou shalt find it after many days."

42   (50)   "The land thou tillest shall be plundered with thistle
              and with thorn, and in the sweat of thy face shalt thou
              eat bread." Variant on Genesis 3: 18-19: "Thorns also
              and thistles shall it bring forth to thee; and thou shalt
              eat the herb of the field; In the sweat of thy face shalt
              thou eat bread."

43   (52)   "O'Casey of the pick and shovel." Cf. the chapter title,
              "At the Sign of the Pick and Shovel," Drums under the
              Windows.

44   (53)   "Swearing he'd never consent, consented." See IV: 174
              (238), this appendix.

44   (53)   "Rose of sharon and the lily of the valley." See III:
              96 (138), this appendix.

45   (54)   "Don a mask, like Yeats." See V: 116 (151), this
              appendix.

45   (55)   "Of every idle word man shall speak, he shall give an
              account thereof in the day of judgement." Variant on
              Matthew 12: 36: "But I say unto you, That every idle
              word that men shall speak, they shall give account there-
              of in the day of judgement."

46   (56)   "The reds and the blacks." English title of a novel
              by Stendhal (1831).

46   (57)   "A young Welsh artist." Evan Walters.*

51   (63)   "Then only the chosen few." See II: 107 (163), this
              appendix.

52   (66)   "Am I nothing to ye all, Professors, who pass me by?"
              See V: 73 (91-2), this appendix.

57   (73)   "Even the flask of wine would have to wait till they
              could easily handle a loaf." See III: 189 (279), this
              appendix.

60   (78)   "Earth with her thousand voices." From Coleridge's*
              poem, Hymn in the Vale of Chanouni (1802): "Earth with
              her thousand voices, praises God."

61   (78)   "Like a thief in the day." See II: 81 (120), this
              appendix.

61	(79)	"A sound of revelry by night." From Byron's* <u>Childe Harold's Pilgramage</u>, canto III, stanza 21.
61	(79)	"'Tis now the witching hour of the morning." Variant on a line from Shakespeare's* play, <u>Hamlet</u>: "'Tis now the witching hour of the night."
61	(80)	"No pictures in the hall here . . . no drums under the window either." Cf. O'Casey's <u>Pictures in the Hallway</u> and <u>Drums under the Windows</u>.
71	(93)	"For tomorrow he would die." See IV: 65 (81), this appendix.
71	(94)	"Bow of burnished gold." See VI: 16 (11), this appendix.
79	(105)	"She said no too often." See V: 53 (62), this appendix.
79	(106)	"Hail and farewell." See IV: 29 (30), this appendix.
80	(108)	"Lover and his lass." See IT WAS A LOVER AND HIS LASS, Appendix I.
83	(112)	"The rose of sharon and the lillies of the valley." See III: 96 (138), this appendix.
89	(121)	"Religion is the dope of the workers." See III: 153 (225), this appendix.
90	(122)	"Though Eliot hadn't been chosen, maybe not even called." See II: 107 (163), this appendix.
101	(139)	"Bum song." See HALLELUJAH, I'M A BUM, Appendix I.
102	(139)	"Abandon hope, ye who enter here." Variant on the famous line from Dante's* <u>The Divine Comedy</u>: "All hope abandon, ye who enter here!"
103	(141)	"A poem written by Yeats, and dedicated to 'a poet, who would have me praise certain bad (Irish) poets, imitators of his and mine.'" With the exception of the word in parenthesis, this is the title of the poem.
104	(143)	"Voice by the cedar tree." Line from Tennyson's* poem, <u>Maud</u>.
105	(145)	"Honour set in one eye and death i' in the other." Variant on a line in Shakespeare's* play, <u>Julius Caesar</u>: "Set honor in one eye and death i' the other."
113	(155)	"Couldn't screw their courage to the sticking place." See II: 127 (195), this appendix.
113	(155)	"Had so many children he didn't know what to do." See 95 (122), this appendix.

113	(156)	"The shape of things to come." Title of a book by H. G. Wells* (1933).
114	(156)	"A continent fit for zeros to live in." See III: 285 (428), this appendix.
115	(158)	"The Flash within the Circle." Symbol of fascism which O'Casey used in his play, The Star Turns Red.
115	(158)	"The egg and I." Title of a notable book by Betty MacDonald (1945).
115	(159)	"Song of a shift." Cf. the chapter title of the same name in O'Casey's Drums under the Windows, and SONG OF A SHIRT, primary index.
116	(159)	"Fold their taunts like Scarabs and silently steal away." Variant on lines from Henry Wadsworth Longfellow's poem, "The Day is Done": "Shall fold their tents, like the Arabs,/And as silently steal away."
116	(160)	"Heavily hangs the broad sunflower over its grave i th' earth so chilly." Lines from Tennyson's* poem, "The Princess."
119	(165)	"Whom the gods would destroy, They first make mad." Lines from Henry Wadsworth Longfellow's poem, The Masque of Pandora.
120	(166)	"A country where so many are afraid to live." Cf. one of the final lines in O'Casey's play, Cock-a-Doodle Dandy: "To a place where life resembles life more than it does here."
122	(169)	"Like a thief in the day." See II: 81 (120), this appendix.
123	(170)	"Imaginot line." Variant on the Maginot Line, a fortified border between Germany and France on which France foolishly depended to repel invasions.
124	(172)	"Twilight of the cods." See V: 17 (13), this appendix.
128	(177)	"Not a drum was heard, though something like a funeral note was sounding." Variant on lines from Charles Wolfe's poem, "The Burial of Sir John Moore at Corunna": "Not a drum was heard, not a funeral note."
128	(178)	"He maketh me lie down in green pastures." Variant on Psalms 23: 2: "He maketh me to lie down in green pastures; he leadeth me beside the still waters."
131	(182)	"Smile, smile, smile." See PACK UP YOUR TROUBLES IN YOUR OLD KIT BAG . . . ., Appendix I.

135   (188)   "These little ladies were not for burning." Variant on
the title of the Christopher Fry play, The Lady's Not
for Burning (1949).

135   (188)   "Deep valley of the shadow of death." See IV: 21 (17),
this appendix.

136   (189)   "The waste land." See ELIOT, THOMAS STEARNS, primary
index.

136   (190)   "Blood, sweat, and tears." In PAN, given as "toil,
sweat, and tears." From Churchill's* first statement
as prime minister in the House of Commons (13 May 1940):
"I have nothing to offer but blood, toil, tears, and
sweat."

137   (190)   "Home they brought her warrior dead." Line from
Tennyson's* poem, "The Princess."

137   (191)   "Things were changed, changed utterly." See IV: 9 (1),
this appendix.

140   (195)   "Puppet passes." See PIPPA, primary index.

141   (197)   "The innocents abroad." Title of a book by Mark Twain
(1869).

145   (202)   "Kings and captains." See III: 222 (330), this appendix.

145   (203)   "Long river of wearied men mus' just keep rolling along."
See OLD MAN RIVER, Appendix I.

145   (203)   "Let the dead bury the dead." From Matthew 8: 22.

145   (203)   "A long journey through long days without end." Variant
on plays by Eugene O'Neill*: Days Without End (1934) and
Long Day's Journey into Night (1955). Although the
latter was not published until after Sunset and Evening
Star, it was written much earlier.

145   (203)   "Keep right on left right to the end of the road." See
KEEP RIGHT ON TO THE END OF THE ROAD, Appendix I.

146   (204)   "Our Father which art in heaven." Opening line of the
"Lord's Prayer."

147   (205)   "Oh, when shall my head rest on a pillow at home while
the vacant midnight passes." Variant on lines from
Whitman's* poem, "The Artilleryman's Vision": "And my
head on the pillow rests at home, and the vacant midnight
passes."

149   (208)   "The heavens were hung with black." Variant on lines
from Shakespeare's* play, 1 King Henry VI: "Hung be the
heavens with black, yield day to night."

155   (217)   " Vengeance is mine." From Romans 12: 19: "Dearly beloved, avenge not yourselves, but rather give place unto wrath; for it is written, vengeance is mine; I will repay, saith the Lord."

156   (218)   "Harder times than those of Dickens." Allusion to the celebrated work, Hard Times (1854), by Charles Dickens.*

158   (221)   "Nothing dies but something mourns." From Byron's* Don Juan: "Ah, surely nothing dies but something mourns."

166   (234)   "Remembrance of things past." If O'Casey read Proust, it's an allusion to the English title of A la Recherche du Temps Perdu. If not, then to Shakespeare's* "I summon up remembrance of things past" (Sonnet 30).

167   (235)   "Bind up each other's wounds." Suggests a line from Shakespeare's* play, King Richard III: "Give me another horse!/Bind up my wounds."

168   (236)   "His /Chesterton's/ sister-in-law." Ethel Oldershaw.

168   (237)   "Like the title of one of them." Unknown.

168   (237)   "Cosmos of cosmic comprehension." Satiric use of Chesterton's* belief in the cosmos, as in his "Introduction to the Book of Job": "A cosmic philosophy is not constructed to fit a man; a cosmic philosphy is constructed to fit a cosmos."

168   (237)   "Tremendous trifles." See III: 180 (266), this appendix.

168   (237)   "Old woman who lived in a shoe." From the famous nursery rhyme of the same name.

168   (237)   "See the conquering zero come." Variant on the opening line of a poem by Thomas Morell which was used by Handel in his oratorio, Joshua (1747): "See, the conquering hero comes!"

168   (237)   "Kept right on to the end of the road to Rome." See KEEP RIGHT ON TO THE END OF THE ROAD, Appendix I, and III: 180 (266), this appendix.

171   (242)   "White horse." See NOTTING HILL GATE, primary index.

175   (247)   "Woeman of the guard." Variant on the title of the light opera, Yoeman of the Guard (1888), by Gilbert and Sullivan.

175   (247)   "State for a long star." In the U.S., the state of Texas is known as "The Lone Star State."

176   (248)   "What voice had shouted Dope." See V: 205 (274), this appendix.

176   (249)   "War-cry." See this entry in Appendix IV.

176   (249)   "Lo, I am with you always." Variant on Matthew 28: 20:
"Teaching them to observe all things whatsoever I have
commanded you: and lo, I am with you alway, even unto
the end of the world. Amen."

177   (251)   "Come blow your horn." Line from the nursery rhyme,
"Little Boy Blue."

178   (252)   "Dies irae erin on all shinners." Translated loosely as
"Ireland's Day of Wrath on all sinners." Further,
"shinners" was a popular name for members or sympathizers
of Sinn Fein.* See also DIES IRAE, primary index.

188   (266)   "Indomitably Irishry." From Yeats's* poem, "Under Ben
Bulben."

191   (272)   "Ring out wild bells to the wild skies" (twice). See
VI: 39 (45), this appendix.

194   (275)   "Burn everything except English coal." From Swift's*
reply to the British embargo on Irish goods, "Proposal
for the Universal Use of Irish Manufacture" (1720).
The Celtic version of "Burn baby burn."

194   (275)   "The dear's cry." See DEER'S CRY, Appendix I.

198   (281)   "Hovels of clay and wattles made." See III: 19 (20),
this appendix.

199   (284)   "Footman, pass on." See V: 47 (54), this appendix, and
ETERNAL FOOTMAN, primary index.

200   (284)   "Sad sight, sad sound, sad sense." Suggests verse 24 of
the Rubaiyat of Omar Khayyam, quoted by O'Casey in IV:
220 (303).

203   (289)   "Fifty years agrowing." Suggests the title, Twenty
Years Agrowing, by Maurice O'Sullivan.

204   (292)   "The rust was silence." Variant on a line in
Shakespeare's* play, Hamlet: "The rest was silence."

204   (292)   "We shall not quench the smoking flax." Variant on
Isaiah 42: 3: "A bruised reed shall he not break, and
the smoking flax shall he not quench."

218   (312)   "Strange interlude." Title of a Eugene O'Neill* play.

220   (315)   "'The pleasure of life,' yells out a rebellious Elizabethan, 'what is it but the good hours of an ague?'"
See III: 245 (367), this appendix.

220   (316)   "'The red flare of dreams.'" From Yeats's* play, The
Land of Heart's Desire.

220   (316)   "'All things declare that struggle hath deeper peace than sleep can bring.'" From William Vaughn Moody's play, The Masque of Judgement.

221   (317)   "Building there a small cabin of clay and wattles made." See III: 19 (20), this appendix.

227   (326)   "Twinkle, twinkle mighty bomb." Variant on the traditional nursery rhyme, "Twinkle, Twinkle Little Star."

SELECTED INDEX TO APPENDIX III

MORE

SELECTED INDEX TO APPENDIX III (cont.)

APPENDIX IV:
NEWSPAPERS AND JOURNALS

ALLY SLOPER
General interest magazine out of London. Known as Ally Sloper's Half-Holiday (1884-1923); later as Half Holiday.

II: 64, 175   (94, 270)

AMERICAN SPECTATOR
Monthly American periodical (November 1932-May 1937), started by Ernest Boyd, Theodore Dreiser, James Branch Cabel, George Jean Nathan,* and Eugene O'Neill.* The articles to which O'Casey refers -- his contributions -- include:
        "Laurel Leaves and Silver Trumpets" December 1932
        "Dramatis Personae Ibsenisensis" July 1933
        "A Protestant Kid Thinks of the Reformation" July 1934
        "Why I Don't Wear Evening Dress" November 1934

V: 181   (240)
VI: 180   (254)

ANSWERS/ANSWERS TO CORRESPONDENTS
Weekly journal of instruction from London. Published as Answers to Correspondents (June 1888-December 1889); then as Answers.

II: 175, 210, 214, 215, 223 (270, 325, 331, 333, 345)
V: 58   (70)

BEALTAINE
Organ of the Irish Literary Theatre (1899-1900), edited by Yeats.*

VI: 79   (105)

BELL, THE
Irish literary magazine of poems, short stories, reviews, and book and play reviews. Founded in Dublin with Sean O'Faolain* as literary editor and Peadar O'Donnell* as managing editor (1940).

VI: 184, 208   (260, 297)

BOY'S FRIEND
Weekly magazine with articles on subjects of interest to boys. Published
by Fleetway House, London.

II: 210   (325)

BOYS OF LONDON AND NEW YORK
Weekly magazine with articles on subjects of interest to boys. Published
in London (1879-99).

I: 187   (289)
II: 20, 64, 78   (23, 94, 116)

CATHOLIC HERALD
In Ireland, the Irish Catholic Herald, a weekly newspaper of general
news on Ireland and the Catholic Church. Published by New Catholic
Press, Ltd., London, with different editions for Tyneside, Liverpool,
Birmingham, Leeds, Manchester, Wales, and Ireland. See also CATHOLIC
HERALDANGELISTS, primary index.

VI: 178   (252)

CATHOLIC TIMES
The Catholic Times and Catholic Opinion, a weekly newspaper of Catholic
interest, published (from 1859) in London at 33 Chancery Lane with
editions for Liverpool, London, and Manchester. See also CATHOLIC
TIMERIANS, primary index.

VI: 178   (252)

CELTIC CHRISTMAS
The Christmas number of the Irish Homestead* (1897-1910).

III: 211   (313)

CHIPS
Described as "Melanesian news for boys and girls." Published in London
(March 1906-December 1911).

II: 210   (325)

CHURCH TIMES
Weekly newspaper of general and ecclesiastical interest. Founded in
1863, published by G. J. Palmer and Sons Ltd., London.

V: 191   (254)

COMIC CUTS
Comic magazine published in London (from May 1890). Absorbed The Golden
Penny Comic and Merry and Bright.

II: 210   (325)

CORK EXAMINER
Daily nationalist newspaper, published in Cork (from 1841).

IV: 111   (147)

CRITERION, THE
Founded and edited for its life by T. S. Eliot.* Began as a quarterly
review (1922-25), then New Criterion (1926-27), then Monthly Criterion
(1927-28), and finally The Criterion (September 1928-January 1939).

V: 175   (234)

CROSS, THE
Irish religious monthly, published (from 1910) by the Passionate Fathers,
Mount Argus, Dublin.

V: 48-9   (56-7)

DAILY EXPRESS
Daily Unionist and Protestant newspaper, published in London and Manchester and in Dublin by Maunsel and Co. Ltd. H. S. Doig, editor.

I: 106   (159)
II: 7, 8, 11, 18, 64-6, 132   (2, 3, 8, 19, 94-6, 203)
III: 153   (226)

DAILY HERALD
Daily labour newspaper which started as a strike sheet of London
printers (from 1911). For the cartoon which O'Casey refers to, see
DYSON, WILL, primary index.

III: 214   (318)

DAILY SINN FEIN
Daily nationalist newspaper, published (1909-10) by Arthur Griffith.*

III: 243   (363)

DANA
Subtitled "An Irish Magazine of Independent Thought." Edited (May 1904-
April 1905) by John Eglinton and Frederick Ryan.

III: 154   (226)

DUBLIN PENNY JOURNAL
"Legends, tales, and stories of Ireland." Four volumes, 1832-34.

IV: 236   (326)

DUBLIN REVIEW
Quarterly review, published in London (1836-to date). O'Casey's
reference is to Chesterton's book, The Superstition of the Sceptic
(1925), which included correspondence between Chesterton and Coulton.*
The discussion was continued by Chesterton in the Dublin Review (January-
March 1925) and by Coulton in the Review of Churches* (July 1925).

V: 193   (258)

EVENING HERALD
Evening edition of the Irish Independent (from 1891). Daily Dublin
nationalist-independent newspaper. O'Casey alludes to an article,
                                                            MORE

EVENING HERALD (cont.)

"O'Casey's Obscenity: Play That May Shock Christians," by M.B. (13 August 1935).

V: 51-2, 53-4   (60, 62-3)

EVENING MAIL
Daily Dublin evening newspaper (from 1823), 37-38 Parliament Street.

VI: 99-100   (136)

EVENING TELEGRAPH
Daily Dublin newspaper, published (from 1876) by The Freeman's Journal Ltd. Generally considered nationalist and pro-Home Rule.

II: 26   (32)

EIRE
Eire, The Irish Nation, a weekly Irish Republican journal (January 1923-25 October 1924). Its address was given as Progress Press, 127 Stockwell Street, Glasgow, Scotland; but it was quite clearly the paper of de Valera.* It featured articles by Childers,* Markiewicz,* and others who praised de Valera's "Document No. 2."* For the quote used by O'Casey, see COCKADOO, REV. DR., primary index.

IV: 111   (147)

FAR EAST
Monthly magazine, published at St. Columban's, Navan, Co. Meath. It was the official organ of the Maynooth Mission to China Inc.

VI: 130   (181)

FORGET-ME-NOT
Later called Forget-Me-Not Novels. Published in London and Liverpool (1891-April 1918) by Fleetway House.

II: 175, 210   (270, 325)

FREEMAN'S JOURNAL
One of Ireland's oldest (from 1763) daily newspapers. Published in Dublin, its policies were constitutional-nationalist. Organ of the Irish Parliamentary Party.* The review (#) O'Casey refers to appeared in the 24 June 1913 issue.

II: 163, 164   (251, 253)
III: 150, 156   (221, 230)
IV: 251#   (347#)

GOLDEN STORIES
Popular children's adventure magazine from London (June 1898-March 1913). As Golden Hours from March 1913.

II: 210   (325)

HARMSWORTH MAGAZINE
Monthly pictorial magazine (July 1898-July 1901) from London.

II: 210, 215   (325, 333)

HOLY LEAVES
Holly Leaves in U.S. edition (the correct title). The special Christmas
number of Illustrated Sporting and Dramatic News (1874-1945).

II: 206   (319)

HOME CHAT
Weekly women's magazine published in London (from 1895) by Fleetway
House.

II: 210   (325)

HOME CIRCLE
Weekly family magazine published in London (1894-97).

II: 210   (325)

IRIS
Full title: An Iris, an Irish language magazine, published at 2 Upper
O'Connell Street, Dublin. Seamus O'Neill, editor (from 1945).

VI: 222   (319)

IRISH CATHOLIC
Weekly Catholic newspaper (from 5 May 1888) published in Dublin. Owned
by William Martin Murphy.* Patrick Fogarty, editor. The article which
O'Casey refers to appeared in the 7 September 1935 issue.

V: 49-50   (57)

IRISH DEMOCRAT
Leftist Republican newspaper published in London. It began as a bulletin
of the Republican Congress (1934). Taken over by the Connolly Association
(1938) with Leslie Daiken, the poet, as editor. Printed in January
1939 as Irish Freedom. Name changed to Irish Democrat in 1945 under the
editorship of Dr. Flann Campbell. Present (1982) editor, C. Desmond
Greaves (since 1948).

VI: 220   (316)

IRISH ECCLESIASTICAL RECORD
Organ of the Catholic clergy in Ireland. Owned and published by Browne
and Nolan Ltd., Nassau Street, Dublin (1864-1922).

IV: 258, 259, 262   (357, 358, 363)

IRISH FREEDOM
Weekly organ of the Irish Republican Brotherhood (1909-14). Some of its
editors were Thomas Clarke,* Patrick McCartan,* P. S. O'Hegarty, and
Bulmer Hobson.*

III: 160, 161, 164, 208, 232, 234, 267   (236, 242, 308, 346, 350, 400)

IRISH HOMESTEAD
Weekly organ of the Irish agricultural and industrial movement (1895-
1923). Merged into the Irish Statesman.* Some of its editors included
Father Tom Finley, H. F. Norman, and AE.*

III: 211   (313)

IRISH INDEPENDENT
Daily Dublin newspaper (from 1891) published by Independent Newspapers
Ltd., 111 Middle Abbey Street. Generally supportive of Parnell.*

II: 163, 164, 198   (251, 253, 306)

IRISH NATION / IRISH PEASANT
The Irish Peasant was published at Navan in the Boyne Valley, 20 miles
from Dublin, by James McCann, M.P. for the College Green division of
Dublin, and was connected with his industrial schemes in Meath. It was
edited by William Patrick Ryan* who restarted it in Dublin as the
Peasant (1907-08) where it became the Irish Nation (1909-10). The paper
was suppressed in 1906 by the efforts of Cardinal Logue* who, in a letter
to McCann's son, wrote that it "was becoming a most pernicious spirit"
which opened its columns to anti-clerical views. Should this continue,
said Logue, he would denounce. See the introduction to Ryan's book,
The Pope's Green Island.

III: 23   (25, 26)

IRISH PRESS
Daily Dublin newspaper published (from 1931) by Irish Press Ltd., Burgh
Quay. De Valera* and his family were the principal shareholders.

VI: 10, 13, 120   (3, 8, 166)

IRISH PROTESTANT
Daily Dublin independent (anti-Orange Order*) newspaper published
(August 1901-January 1915) and edited by Lindsay Crawford* and Frank
Donaldson.

III: 233   (348)

IRISH ROSARY
Religious journal published (from April 1897) on alternate months by
the Dominican Fathers, St. Saviour's Priory, Dublin. See O'Casey's
letter vis the Silver Tassie (11 September 1930).

III: 122   (178)
V: 51   (59)

IRISH STATESMAN
Weekly journal of literature, art and politics (1919-30), edited by
Warren Wells and AE.* Official organ of Sir Horace Plunkett's* Irish
Dominion League. Published several significant O'Casey letters and
documents (See Letters, I).

IV: 127, 174, 180, 195, 207, 210, 269   (170, 236, 245, 268, 285, 289,
                                          372)
V: 38   (42)

IRISH THEOLOGICAL QUARTERLY
Religious journal published (from 1906) by the faculty of theology,
St. Patrick's College, Maynooth.*

IV: 259, 262, 264   (357, 363, 364-5)

IRISH TIMES
Daily Dublin newspaper (from 1859); one of the most influential in
Ireland. Generally seen as the voice of the Anglo-Irish ascendancy.

I: 181   (280)
II: 163, 164   (251, 253)
III: 197   (291)
V: 39, 53   (43, 44, 62)
VI: 130, 208, 221   (180, 297, 316)

IRISH WORKER
Socialist and labor weekly newspaper, and for many years the voice of
the Irish Transport and General Workers' Union.* Larkin was its founder
and editor (1911-14, 1924-25, 1930-32). Its Chicago editor was Jack
Carney, a close friend of O'Casey.

III: 164, 208   (242, 308)

IRISH WRITING
"The Magazine of Contemporary Irish Literature" (1946-57). Published in
Cork, edited by David Marcus and Terence Smith. The correct title of
the article on O'Casey (#) was "Joxer in Totnes: A Study in Sean
O'Casey," December 1950.

VI: 73#, 209   (96#, 298)

LEADER, THE
Nationalist, Catholic Dublin weekly, founded by D. P. Moran* who was
its editor until his death (from 1900). Self-described as "A Review of
Current Affairs, Politics, Literature, Art, and Industry." Published
at 32 Lower Abbey Street.

III: 150   (221)
IV: 236   (326)

LONDON STORY PAPER
Adventure story magazine for boys, published in London (1888-99).

I: 62   (87)

MARVEL
Adventure stories out of London. Published as Halfpenny Marvel Library
(1893), as Halfpenny Marvel (1893-98), and as The Marvel (1898-1922).

II: 210   (325)

MESSENGER, THE
American Roman Catholic monthly journal, published by the Church of the
Brethren, Elgin, Illinois (from 1851).

VI: 85   (114)

MONTH, THE
Catholic magazine of literature, science and art. Published six times
yearly (from 1863) by Longmans, Green, and Co., London.

IV: 260, 262   (359, 362)

NEW REPUBLIC
American weekly magazine of literary and political reviews. The article
O'Casey refers to is "The Silver Tassie, by Sean O'Casey," by Stark
Young (27 November 1929).

V: 107   (139)

NEWS OF THE WORLD
Popular newspaper in London, published three times weekly.

III: 24   (28)

OBSERVER, THE
General interest London publication (from 1791) which printed the
Silver Tassie correspondence by O'Casey, Yeats, Lennox Robinson, and
Walter Starkie in an article, "Mr. O'Casey's New Play. Why it was
Rejected. Mr. Yeats on the Dramatist's Job. The War and the Stage,"
3 June 1928 (#). See also ORWELL, GEORGE, primary index.

V: 38#   (42#)
VI: 102, 104, 204   (140, 146, 292)

PEARSON'S WEEKLY
"To Interest. To Elevate. To Amuse." Published by C. Arthur Pearson
Ltd., 18 Henrietta Street, London.

II: 175   (270)

PICTURE POST
Weekly London magazine (from 1938) which became Hilton's National Weekly
of London. Published by Hilton Press, Ltd., 43-44 Shoe Lane.

V: 223   (300)

PLAIN PEOPLE, THE
Weekly Republican and anti-treaty paper, published and circulated in
Dublin during the Civil War (1922). A thorough search of the paper has
failed to produce O'Casey's play.

IV: 114   (151)

PLUCK
"A high-class weekly library of adventure at home and abroad, on land
and sea." Published in London as Stories of Pluck (1895) and as Pluck
(to 1916).

II: 210   (325)

RADIO TIMES
Organ of the British Broadcasting Corporation (from 1923).

VI: 205   (292)

REVIEW OF THE CHURCHES
Published in London (1891-1930). See DUBLIN REVIEW, this appendix.

V: 193   (258)

REVIEW OF REVIEWS
Reviews of periodical literature, published at 189 Temple Chambers,
Temple Avenue, London (1890-1936), then as World Review of Reviews.

III: 207   (307)

ST. ANTHONY ANNALS
Illustrated monthly magazine, official organ of the Association of St.
Anthony. Established at the Convent of the Sisters of Charity, Temple
Street, Dublin.

IV: 182   (249)

SCRAPS
Literary and pictorial ("curious and amusing") magazine out of London
(1883-1910).

II: 175   (270)

SINN FEIN
Irish nationalist weekly owned and edited by Arthur Griffith.* Published (5 May 1906-22 August 1914) in Dublin at 49 Middle Abbey Street.

III: 34, 234, 243, 267   (43, 350, 363, 400)

SPECTATOR, THE
Weekly journal of literary and political reviews (from 1828), published
by Spectator Ltd., 99 Gower Street, London.

V: 151   (199)

STANDARD, THE / EAGLE, THE
The Eagle (as Standard from 1938) was a weekly Catholic periodical
which was published in Dublin by Standard Ltd., Pearse Street. In
"Tender Tears for Poor O'Casey" (The Green Crow), O'Casey wrote of the
Standard: "A weekly journal whose editorial office is in the porchway
of heaven's doorway." The article on the Dublin production of Tassie
(#) appeared on 30 August 1935. O'Casey also alludes (##) to the involvement of Peadar O'Curry, editor of the Standard, as the chief
speaker at the International Affairs Association* meeting which spawned
the "Papal Nuncio Incident."

V: 50#   (58#)
VI: 210##   (300##)

STUDIES
Irish quarterly review of letters, philosophy and science. Published by
Talbot Press, Ltd., Dublin. See also GANNON, REV. P. J., primary index.

IV: 263   (363)
V: 226   (304)

SUNDAY COMPANION
Weekly "stories and articles of a religious tone." Published by Fleetway House, London (from 1895).

II: 175, 210   (270, 325)

SUNDAY TIMES
In London (from 1882).

V: 20, 26   (17, 25)
VI: 46, 117, 196, 204   (56, 162, 278, 291)

SWORD OF LIGHT, THE
Known by its Irish name, An Claidheamh Soluis. Weekly organ of the
Gaelic League* (from 1899). Edited by Eoin MacNeill,* Sean MacGiollar-
nath, Padraic Pearse,* Manus O'Donnell, J. Ford, and Piaras Beaslai.
Reached its maximum circulation in 1904 with over 3000 copies weekly.

III: 162   (238)

TABLET, THE
Weekly Catholic newspaper on current topics, published by Tablet Publishing Co., London.

IV: 260   (359)
V: 51   (59)

TIME AND TIDE
Weekly newspaper (from 1920), owned and edited by Lady Rhondda (1883-
1958), 2nd Viscountess Margaret Haig Thomas. Published several O'Casey
articles in the 1930s.

V: 130   (169)

TIMES LITERARY SUPPLEMENT
Influential weekly literary review, published by Times Newspapers Ltd.,
London (from 1902).

V: 54   (63)

TITBITS
Popular short-story magazine (from 1881), published on alternate Fridays
by George Newnes Ltd., Tower House, London.

II: 175   (270)

TRIBUNE, THE
Socialist weekly newspaper (founded 1937), published by Tribune Pub-
lications Ltd., 24 St. John Street, London. Editor, Raymond Postgate.
See also GALVIN, PATRICK, primary index.

VI: 17, 220   (14, 316)

UNION JACK
"Tales for British Boys!"(January 1880-September 1883). Later as
Union Jack Library of High Class Fiction (1894-1933).

II: 210   (325)

UNIVERSE, THE
Weekly Catholic newspaper with stories on current topies (1860-1909),
then as The Universe and Catholic Weekly (from 1909). Published by
Catholic Newspapers, Ltd., London.

III: 177   (260)
IV: 260   (359)
V: 137, 144   (180, 190)
VI: 97, 178   (132, 252)

VOGUE
Magazine of fashion, art and stage reviews. Published in London at Rolls
House Publishing Co. Ltd., Bream's Building.

V: 191   (255)

VOLUNTEER, THE
Weekly newspaper (from 1914) and organ of the Irish Volunteers.* Editors
included Lawrence de Lacy, Bulmer Hobson,* and Eoin MacNeill.*

III: 269   (403)

WAR CRY
Official gazette of the Salvation Army.*

III: 243   (363)

WARDER, THE
Adventure stories published in Dublin (January 1823-May 1909).

II: 11, 18   (8, 19)

WEEKLY BUDGET
London paper (1861-1912).

II: 175   (270)

WONDER
Weekly London magazine of adventure and comic stories (1892-93). Later
as The Funny Wonder (1893-1901), then as The Wonder (1901-02). II:210(325).

WORKER'S REPUBLIC
Socialist and labor newspaper founded by James Connolly (from 1898).

III: 266   (399)

APPENDIX V:
WORKS BY O'CASEY

See also:

ASHE, THOMAS	GOOD, FLUTHER
BOYLE, CAPT. JACK	JUNO
BOYLE, MARY	MOLLSER
BRENNAN, CAPT.	MADIGAN, MRS.
DALY, JOXER	NORA
FLYNN, PETER	O'BAWLOCHONE, ROARY
GOGAN, MRS.	REDMOND, ROSIE
	ROSEBUD

CALL OF THE TRIBE
O'Casey ballad which he wrote shortly after the famous Sinn Fein* Ard
Feis (25 October 1917). According to Sean McCann (The World of Sean
O'Casey), the dramatist discarded his own copy, but he gave one to
Maire Keating. The ballad was published in McCann's book (pp. 36-7).

IV: 11   (4-5)

CATHLEEN LISTENS IN
Given in printed texts as Kathleen. One-act play. First printed in
Feathers from a Green Crow. In the last reference (#), it is given as
the "second play," i.e., after The Shadow of a Gunman.

IV: 123, 169, 190#   (164-5, 230, 260#)

COOING OF THE DOVES
An early short play which became Act II of The Plough and the Stars.

IV: 123   (164-5)

CRIMSON IN THE TRICOLOUR, THE
An early play which was rejected by the Abbey (28 September 1922). See
Yeats's* critique of the play in Letters, I, pp. 102-03. The work is
considered lost.

IV: 117   (155)

DRUMS UNDER THE WINDOWS
Volume three of the autobiographies. Published in October, 1945. See
O'HICKEY, MICHAEL and ORWELL, GEORGE, primary index.

VI: 99, 102, 106, 149, 151, 195, 203   (135, 140, 146, 208, 212, 277, 289)

END OF THE BEGINNING, THE
A Comedy in One-Act. First published in Windfalls (October 1934, banned
in Ireland in December). See Letters, I, pp. 651-2, and GALVIN, PATRICK,
primary index.

VI: 222   (318-19)

FROST IN THE FLOWER, THE
With The Harvest Festival,* one of the first plays submitted by O'Casey
to the Abbey Theatre (1919). See the letter of rejection in Letters, I,
pp. 91-2. The play is considered lost.

IV: 114   (152)

GREEN GATES
Original title of O'Casey's play, Within the Gates.

V: 123   (160)

HALL OF HEALING
"A Sincerious Farce in One Scene." See also the chapter, "The Hill of
Healing" in I Knock at the Door.

VI: 221-3   (316-20)

HARVEST FESTIVAL, THE
With The Frost in the Flower,* one of the first plays submitted by
O'Casey to the Abbey Theatre (1919). See letter of rejection in Letters,
I, pp. 91-2. This is the earliest play of O'Casey's in existence.
Published in 1980.

IV: 115   (153)

I KNOCK AT THE DOOR
Volume one of the autobiography. Published in March, 1939 (banned in
Ireland 16 May, ban revoked 16 December 1947). See also AMERICAN
SPECTATOR, Appendix IV, and GOGARTY, OLIVER, primary index.

VI: 42, 70-2, 113, 119-20, 196,   (50, 93-6, 155, 165-6, 278,
    203-04   289, 290)

JUNO AND THE PAYCOCK
"A Tragedy in Three Acts." The third play (#) of O'Casey's to be pro-
duced at the Abbey Theatre (3 March 1924). See also FILM COMPANY, FOR-
TUNE THEATRE, HUDSON THEATRE, and SINCLAIR, ARTHUR, primary index.

IV: 123-4#, 170-2, 177, 180, 187#, 190 (165#, 231, 241, 245, 255#, 260)
V: 105, 108, 121, 203   (136, 140, 157, 272)
VI: 9-10   (1-2)

NANNIE'S NIGHT OUT
One-act play. Originally entitled "Irish Nannie Passes." The review
which O'Casey refers to was in the Irish Statesman, 11 October 1924.

IV: 172   (234)

OAK LEAVES AND LAVENDER
"Or a Warld on Wallpaper"(a reference to Yeats's* criticism of The Silver
Tassie). Not given by title; only alluded to. The premiere (O'Casey's
allusion) was at the Lyric Theatre, Hammersmith, London (13 May 1947).
See also GRAYBURN, JOHNNY, primary index.

VI: 225   (322-3)

PICTURES IN THE HALLWAY
Volume two of the autobiographies. Published in March, 1942 (banned in
Ireland 16 December, ban revoked 16 December 1947). See GRIFFIN, EDWARD,
primary index.

VI: 116, 203   (160-1, 289)

PLOUGH AND THE STARS, THE
"A Tragedy in Four Acts." See COOING OF THE DOVES, this appendix, and
NEW THEATRE and TOUHY, PATRICK, primary index.

IV: 127-8, 172-81, 279-81   (169-71, 235-47, 387-9)
V: 50, 55, 235   (39, 65, 315)

PURPLE DUST
"A Wayward Comedy." In O'Casey's papers, there is a fragmentary draft
of the play with the title, "Stay in Country." See also AGATE, JAMES,
primary index.

VI: 116-18, 120   (161-2, 166)

RED ROSES FOR ME
"A Play in Four Acts." Originally entitled "A Rich Bunch of Roses."
See CUMMINS, DR. JOSEPH, primary index.

VI: 149   (208)

ROBE OF ROSHEEN
Early play which was written in 1918. Rejected by the Abbey Theatre
(15 April 1922).

IV: 114   (151)

ROSE AND CROWN
Volume five of the autobiographies. See also MacNEICE, LOUIS and
ROSE AND CROWN, primary index.

VI: 196-7, 203-04   (279-81, 290-1)

SHADOW OF A GUNMAN, THE
"A Tragedy in Two Acts." Not given by title; only alluded to. The first
O'Casey play to be produced at the Abbey Theatre (12 April 1923).

IV: 94, 122-3, 168-9   (123, 163-4, 229)

SILVER TASSIE, THE
"A Tragi-Comedy in Four Acts." Premiere (#), 11 October 1929. See also
GAIETY THEATRE; JOHN, AUGUSTUS; NATHAN, GEORGE JEAN; QUEEN'S THEATRE;
SHAW, GEORGE BERNARD; WALTERS, EVAN; YEATS, WILLIAM BUTLER, primary
index.

V: 31-42, 43-4, 46-52, 53, 66, 103-05#, 107, 122, 132
    (31-47, 48-9, 53-61, 62, 80, 133-6#, 138-9, 159, 173)
VI: 78, 120, 195, 224   (104, 166, 277, 322)

SOUND THE LOUD TRUMPETS
One of O'Casey's earliest articles. Published (25 May 1907) in The
Peasant and Irish Ireland under the pseudonym, An Gall Fada (The Tall
Foreigner). See also BIRRELL, AUGUSTINE, primary index.

III: 23   (26)

STAR TURNS RED, THE
One of O'Casey's most proletarian plays (published 1940). In the play-
wright's papers, there is an early draft of the play with the title,
"The Red Star," in Irish.

VI: 120   (166)

STORY OF THE IRISH CITIZEN ARMY, THE
Published in 1919. O'Casey's first publication in book form.

IV: 19-20   (16-17)

THREE SHOUTS ON A HILL
Early O'Casey essay (considered lost). See also IV: 66 (82), "three
shouts on two hills."

IV: 30   (31)

TIME TO GO
"A Morality Comedy in One-Act." First published in volume four of
Collected Plays (1951).

VI: 222   (318)

WITHIN THE GATES
"A Play of Four Scenes in a London Park." Published in 1933.

V: London production (premiere)   109, 131   (141, 171)
    New York premiere   131, 159, 181,   (171, 210, 241,
                                    183, 198, 202   264, 269, 270)
    Boston banning (15 January 1935) 202-07   (270-7)
    Irish banning   VI: 120   (VI: 166)

APPENDIX VI: CHAPTER-BY-CHAPTER DATA ON O'CASEY'S LIFE

I. I KNOCK AT THE DOOR

From 1880-c.1892. From 85 Upper Dorset Street to (from 1883) 9 Innis-fallen Parade to (from 1888) a two-room attic flat in St. Mary's School, Lower Dominick Street, to (from 1889) 22 Hawthorn Terrace, North Wall, in the parish of St. Barnabas, Dublin.

Age, to about 12-13. The title is from Matthew 7: 7: "Ask, and it shall be given you; seek, and you shall find; knock, and it shall be opened to you," part of which O'Casey quotes on the title page. The original title was "First the Green Blade" (Letters, I, p. 721), which became the title of chapter two. Alluding to the dust jacket, which shows a small boy knocking at a door, O'Casey wrote: "it is the door of life that he is supposed to be knocking at" (Letters, I, p. 773).

"A Child is Born"
1880, 85 Upper Dorset Street. Some of the events take place in earlier O'Casey residences before O'Casey was born. See TWO JOHNS, primary index. The chapter title is from Isaish 9: 6: "For unto us a child is born, unto us a son is given . . ."

"First the Green Blade"
1880-85, 85 Upper Dorset Street and 9 Innisfallen Parade. Briefly attended St. Mary's Infant School. The chapter title is from Mark 4:28: "For the earth bringeth forth fruit of herself; first the blade, then the ear, after that the full corn in the ear . . . ," and from p. 64 (90): "green must be a great favourite of God's, for look at the green grass, and the leaves of bushes and trees; and teacher said that green stands for life, and God loves life."

"The Hill of Healing"
After O'Casey's father's death, probably sometime in 1886 or early 1887, 9 Innisfallen Parade, ages 6-7. See also HALL OF HEALING, Appendix V.

"His Da, His Poor Da"
1886, 9 Innisfallen Parade, age 6.

"His Father's Wake"
1886, 9 Innisfallen Parade, age 6. O'Casey's father died on September 6 at the age of 59. This chapter is an expanded version of "His Father's Dublin Funeral" which appeared in English: Magazine of the English Association (v.1, no.1, 1936).

"His Father's Funeral"
1886, 9 Innisfallen Parade, age 6. O'Casey's father was buried in Mount Jerome cemetery.

"We All Go the Same Way Home"
1886, 9 Innisfallen Parade, age 6. The chapter title is from the song of the same name (see Appendix I).

"R.I.P."
1886, 9 Innisfallen Parade, age 6. The original title was "Plans gang agley."

"Hail, Smiling Morn"
1888-89, from 9 Innisfallen Parade to an attic flat in St. Mary's School, Lower Dominick Street, to 22 Hawthorn Terrace. O'Casey's sister was married on March 7, 1889. O'Casey attended St. Mary's School until February 1889. The chapter title may be a variant on a line from Robert Burns's* song, "Blythe and Merry": "Her smile was like a summer morn."

"The Tired Cow"
c.1889-90, 22 Hawthorn Terrace, ages 9-10. Attending St. Barnabas' National School.

"The Street Sings"
c.1890, 22 Hawthorn Terrace, age 10. Attending St. Barnabas' National School.

"The Protestant Kid Thinks of the Reformation"
c.1890, 22 Hawthorn Terrace, age 10. Attending St. Barnabas' National School.

"The Dream School"
c.1890-91. 22 Hawthorn Terrace, ages 10-11. Attending St. Barnabas' National School.

"Pain Parades Again"
c.1890-91, 22 Hawthorn Terrace, ages 10-11. Attending St. Barnabas' National School.

"A Child of God"
c.1890-91, 22 Hawthorn Terrace, ages 10-11. Although O'Casey mentions St. Mary's National School in this chapter, the description of the surrounding streets more closely describes the area around St. Barnabas' National School.

"Battle Royal"
c.1890-91, 22 Hawthorn Terrace, ages 10-11. Attending St. Barnabas' National School.

"Vandhering Vindy Vendhor"
c.1890-91, 22 Hawthorn Terrace, ages 10-11. Attending St. Barnabas'
National School.

"Crime and Punishment"
c.1890-91, 22 Hawthorn Terrace, ages 10-11. Attending St. Barnabas'
National School.

"The Lord Loveth Judgement"
c.1890-91, 22 Hawthorn Terrace, ages 10-11. The chapter title is from
Psalms 37: 28: "For the Lord loveth judgement, and forsaketh not his
saints, they are preserved for ever: . . . "

"The Dream Review"
c.1890-91, 22 Hawthorn Terrace, ages 10-11. Attending St. Barnabas'
National School. The "Sham battle" which is described by O'Casey may
have been in honor of Queen Victoria's* visit to Dublin in April 1886.

"Life Is More Than Meat"
c.1890-91, 22 Hawthorn Terrace, ages 10-11. The chapter title is from
Matthew 6: 25: "Therefore I say unto you, be not solicitous for your life,
what you shall eat, nor for your body, what you shall put on. Is not
the life more than the meat: and the body more than the raiment."

"The Red Above the Green"
c.1890-91, 22 Hawthorn Terrace, ages 10-11. The chapter title is a
variant on the title of a song, "The Green Above the Red," for which
see Appendix I.

"I Knock at the Door"
c.1890-91, 22 Hawthorn Terrace, ages 10-11.

II. PICTURES IN THE HALLWAY

From c.1891-92 to c.1900-03. From 22 Hawthorn Terrace to (from 1897)
18 Abercorn Road. Age 11-12 to 20-23. Employed for about 18 months
as a stock boy at Leedom-Hampton, wholesale chandlers in Henry Street
(1894-95), and as a van boy for Eason and Son (see JASON), wholesale
newsagents in Lower Abbey Street. Dismissed from Eason's after one
week for disobedience (1896). The quote on the title page is from
chapter 24 of Nathaniel Hawthorne's novel, The Marble Faun.

"A Coffin Comes to Ireland"
1891, 22 Hawthorn Terrace, age 11. Parnell's* coffin arrived in Ireland
on 17 October.

"Shakespeare Taps at the Window"
c.1891-92, 22 Hawthorn Terrace, ages 11-12.

"Royal Risidence"
c.1891-92, 22 Hawthorn Terrace, ages 11-12. O'Casey uses the chapter
title on page 181 (280), which is derived from Daniel 4: 30: "The king
spake, and said, Is not this Babylon which have built as a royal residence for the house of the kingdom of the might of my power, and for the
honour of my majesty?" In Latin, ris = laughter.

"The Hawthorn Tree"
c.1891-92, 22 Hawthorn Terrace, ages 11-12. The original title of this
chapter was "Dungdodgers over the Border" (Letters, I, p. 812). In
Christian legend, the Hawthorn formed the Crown of Thorns on Christ's
head.

"Cat 'n Cage"
c.1892, 22 Hawthorn Terrace, age 12. See CAT AND CAGE, primary index.

"Coming of Age"
c.1893, 22 Hawthorn Terrace, age 13. The title may be from a line in
Shakespeare's* play, Romeo and Juliet: "thou wilt fall backward when
thou comest of age."

"Bring Forth the Best Robe"
1894, 22 Hawthorn Terrace, age 14. Employed at Leedom, Hampton chandlers.
The chapter title is from Luke 15: 22: "But the father said to his servants, Bring forth the best robe, and put it on him; and put a ring on
his hand, and shoes on his feet."

"Work Made Manifest"
1894-95, 22 Hawthorn Terrace, ages 14-15. Employed at Leedom, Hampton
chandlers. The chapter title is from 1 Corinthians 3: 13: "Every man's
work shall be made manifest: for the day shall declare it, because
it shall be revealed by fire: . . . "

"The Shame Is a Thief and a Robber"
1894-95, 22 Hawthorn Terrace, ages 14-15. Employed at Leedom, Hampton
chandlers. The chapter title is derived from two verses: "As the thief
is ashamed when he is found . . ."(Jeremiah 2:26) and "Verily, verily,
I say unto you, He that entereth not by the door into the sheepfold,
but climbeth up some other way, the same is a thief and a robber" (John
10:1).

"Gather Up the Fragments"
1894-95, 22 Hawthorn Terrace, ages 14-15. Employed at Leedom, Hampton
chandlers. O'Casey uses the chapter title in IV: 49 (58). The title
is from John 6: 12: "When they were filled, he said unto his disciples,
Gather up the fragments that remain that nothing be lost."

"Alice, Where Art Thou ?"
1894-95, 22 Hawthorn Terrace, ages 14-15. Employed at Leedom, Hampton
chandlers. The chapter title is from a song of the same name (see
Appendix I).

"To Him That Hath Shall Be Given"
1894-95, 22 Hawthorn Terrace, ages 14-15. Fired from Leedom, Hampton
chandlers. The chapter title is derived from Matthew 13: 12: "For whosoever hath, to him shall be given, and he shall have more abundance:
but whosoever hath not, from him shall be taken away even that he hath."

"Touched by the Theatre"
1895, 22 Hawthorn Terrace, age 15. Acts the role of Father Dolan in
Boucicault's* play, The Shaughraun, at the old Mechanics Theatre in
Abbey Street, Dublin.

"Death on the Doorstep"
c.1897-98, 18 Abercorn Road, ages 17-18. The chapter is out of place.
O'Casey's brother, Tom, did not die until 1914. He may, however, have
had an earlier serious illness.

"Work While It Is Not Yet Day"
1896, 22 Hawthorn Terrace, age 16. Works as a van boy for Eason and
Son. O'Casey's confirmation (p.160 PAN, p. 246 US) took place at Clontarf Parish Church (29 March 1898). At that time, O'Casey lived at 18
Abercorn Road. The chapter title is derived from John 9: 4: "I must work
the works of him that sent me, while it is day: the night cometh, when
no man can work."

"Cap in the Counting House"
1896, 22 Hawthorn Terrace, age 16. Dismissed from Eason and Son.

"The Sword of Light"
c.1897, moved to 18 Abercorn Road, age 17. For derivation of chapter
title, see primary index.

"I Strike a Blow for You, Dear Land"
c.1898, 18 Abercorn Road, age 18. For derivation of chapter title, see
DEAR LAND, Appendix I.

"All Heaven and Harmsworth Too"
c.1900-01, 18 Abercorn Road, ages 20-21. The chapter title is a variation
of the title of a popular book, All This and Heaven Too (1938) by Rachel
Field (Warner Brothers film, 1940).

"Pictures in the Hallway"
c.1900-03, 18 Abercorn Road, ages 20-23. Teaches Sunday School at St.
Barnabas Church (1900-03).

III. DRUMS UNDER THE WINDOWS

From 1903 to 1916. Lived at 18 Abercorn Road for the entire period.
Ages 23-36. Employed (1903-11) as a laborer on the Great Northern Railway of Ireland (GNRI). Learns the Irish language, joins the Drumcondra
Branch of the Gaelic League, and gaelicizes his name to Sean O Cathasaigh (c.1906). Joins the St. Laurence O'Toole Club, and writes first
stories and articles for the club's journal (c.1907). First publication,
an article, "Sound the Loud Trumpet," for The Peasant and Irish Ireland
(25 May 1907). Joins the Irish Republican Brotherhood, and also becomes
secretary of the local branch of the Gaelic League (c.1908). Founder-
member and secretary of the St. Laurence O'Toole Pipers' Band (1910).
Joins the Irish Transport and General Workers' Union (1911),which leads
to his dismissal from the railroad (December 1911). Begins to write
articles for the Irish Worker (1912). Secretary of the Wolfe Tone
Memorial Committee (July 1913) and of the Women and Children's Relief
Fund (from October 1913) during the General Strike. Brother, Tom, dies
(6 February 1914) at age 44. Secretary of the Irish Citizen Army (March-
October 1914), writing a regular column for the Irish Worker, "By the
Camp Fire"(from May 1914). Enters St. Vincent's Hospital, Dublin, for an
operation on his neck for tubercular glands (15 August 1915). The quote
on the title page is from Yeats's* Purgatory.

"At the Sign of the Pick and Shovel"
c.1903-11, 18 Abercorn Road, ages 23-31. Working on the GNRI. See his
articles about some of the practices on the railroad in Feathers from a
Green Crow.

"Poor Tom's Acold"
1914, 18 Abercorn Road, age 34. Parts of the chapter refer to earlier
events. The chapter title is from a line in Shakespeare's* play, King
Lear: "Poor Tom's a-cold. I cannot daub it further."

"House of the Dead"
c.1907, 18 Abercorn Road, age 27. Parts of the chapter refer to the
death of O'Casey's brother-in-law (see BENSON, NICHOLAS, primary index).
Employed at the GNRI.

"Behold My Family is Poor"
c.1907, 18 Abercorn Road, age 27. Employed at the GNRI. The chapter
title is from Judges 6: 15: "And he said unto him, Oh my Lord, wherewith
shall I save Israel? Behold, my family is poor in Manasseh and I am the
least in my father's house."

"Home of the Living" (US: "House of the Living")
c.1908-09, 18 Abercorn Road, ages 28-29. Parts of the chapter refer to
the death of O'Casey's sister (1 January 1918). The chapter title may
be derived from Job 30: 23: "For I know that thou wilt bring me death,
and to the house appointed for all living."

"Drums under the Windows"
c.1906, 18 Abercorn Road, age 26. Employed at the GNRI.

"Song of a Shift"
26 January 1907 and following, 18 Abercorn Road, age 27. Employed at
the GNRI. For derivation of chapter title, see SONG OF THE SHIRT,
primary index.

"Lost Leader"
1910, 18 Abercorn Road, age 30. Employed at the GNRI. The chapter
title is from Robert Browning's* poem of the same name.

"Gaelstroem"
c.1905-10, 18 Abercorn Road, ages 25-30. Some of the chapter deals
with "Language Week," an annual festival around St. Patrick's Day when
the Gaelic Leauge held nationwide celebrations which culminated with a
large procession through Dublin. The Hyde "dinner" incident is documented in The Shaping of Modern Ireland, O'Brien, ed., p. 56.

"Hora Novissima"
c.1905-10, 18 Abercorn Road, ages 25-30. Employed at the GNRI. The
chapter title is from the famous poem by St. Bernard of Cluny*: "Hora
Novissima, tempora pessima sunt, vigilemus."

"Green Fire on the Hearth"
1912, 18 Abercorn Road, age 32. Semi- or unemployed from this chapter on.
The chapter title is derived from Jeremiah 36: 22: "Now the king sat in
the ninth month; and there was a fire on the hearth burning before him."
The "green" is from the color of the cover of Shaw's Home Rule edition
of John Bull's Other Island.

"Prometheus Hibernica"
1913, 18 Abercorn Road, age 33. Part of the chapter refers to O'Casey's
dismissal from the GNRI (December 1911). Some of the titles which he
considered for this chapter were "Irish Prometheus" and "Red Prometheus."

"Dark Kaleidoscope"
1913-14, 18 Abercorn Road, ages 33-34. Part of the chapter refers to
the care of O'Casey's nieces and nephews (1918). On page 219 (325),
O'Casey uses the sentence: "Ireland was rather more of a kaleidoscope
than a shadow-show: always re-shaping itself to a different pattern."

"Under the Plough and the Stars"
1914, 18 Abercorn Road, age 34. O'Casey was secretary to the Irish
Citizen Army from March to October.

"In this Tent, the Rebubblicans"
c.1915, 18 Abercorn Road, age 35. Parts of the chapter refer to events
occurring one or two years before and after 1915. The chapter title is
an allusion to Lady Gregory's speech mannerism which had a slight lisp
(see p. 244 PAN, p. 364 US). For more on this, see HUNDINGDON, primary
index.

"St. Vincent's Provides a Bed"
1915, 18 Abercorn Road, age 35. O'Casey was a patient on St. Vincent's
Hospital from August 15 to September 1.

"Prepare, Everyone with Weapons"
July 1914, 18 Abercorn Road, age 34. See BACHELOR'S WALK, primary index.

"The Bold Fenian Men"
Easter Week, 24-29 April 1916, 18 Abercorn Road, age 36. The chapter
title is from an Irish song of the same name by Michael Scanlan.

IV: INISHFALLEN, FARE THEE WELL

From 1917 to early 1926. Lived at 18 Abercorn Road, 35 Mountjoy Square
(briefly in 1920), and 422 North Circular Road (from 1921). Employed
only sporadically and for a brief time as a janitor at the Old Forrester's
Hall, 10 Langrishe Place (1920). O'Casey's publications for this time
span include:

1918	The Story of Thomas Ashe; The Sacrifice of Thomas Ashe; Songs of the Wren, No. 1; Songs of the Wren, No. 2; More Songs of the Wren.
1919	The Story of the Irish Citizen Army
1925	(February) Two Plays (The Shadow of a Gunman and Juno and the Paycock
1926	(April) The Plough and the Stars

Several of O'Casey's plays were rejected during this period, including:

1920	(January 26) The Harvest Festival and The Frost in the Flower.
1922	(April 15) The Seamless Coat of Kathleen
	(September 28) The Crimson in the Tri-Colour

For the dates of the premieres of O'Casey's plays, see ABBEY THEATRE,
primary index. For a time (from November 1921), O'Casey was secretary of
the "Release Jim Larkin Committee" and the "Jim Larkin Correspondence
Committee."

"High Road and Low Road"
1917-18, 18 Abercorn Road, ages 37-38. The chapter title is from the
chorus of the famous Scottish song, "Loch Lomand."*

"Mrs. Casside Takes a Holiday"
November 9, 1919, and after, 18 Abercorn Road, age 38. On page 31 (33),
O'Casey uses the sentence: "She had taken a holiday from life at last."
O'Casey's allusions to the deaths in Dublin refer to the Spanish Flu
which claimed thousands of lives during the winter of 1918-19. He
mentions the epidemic in his essay, "The Green Crow Caws," Under a
Colored Cap, p. 75. Title based on Death Takes a Holiday.

"Hail and Farewell"
1919-20, 18 Abercorn Road, ages 39-40. O'Casey uses the chapter title
in VI: 79 (106). The original title came from Catullus, Carmina XCIC:
"atque in perpetuum, frater, ave atque vale."

"The Raid"
1920, 35 Mountjoy Square (rooming with Micheal O Maolain), age 40.

"Pax"
1920-21, 422 North Circular Road, ages 40-41. Employed at Old Forrester's
Hall (see LARKIN, DELIA, primary index). The meeting between Lloyd
George* and de Valera* occurred on 12 July 1921.

"Drifting"
1921, 422 North Circular Road, age 41.

"Into Civil War"
1922-23, 422 North Circular Road, ages 42-43.

"Comrades"
1922-23, 422 North Circular Road, ages 42-43.

"The Clergy Takes a Hand"
1923, 422 North Circular Road, age 43. Cf. the chapter title with the
sentence in III: 194 (287): "Sean wondered why the clergy didn't stand
with the men . . . "

"Blessed Bridget o'Coole"
1922-23, 422 North Circular Road, ages 42-43. Some of the chapter refers
to events in 1924. The chapter title is an allusion to Lady Gregory's*
The Story Brought by Brigit (1924). One of the titles which O'Casey
considered was "The Old Lady Says Yes," a variant on one of Denis Johnston's* plays.

"Where Wild Swans Nest"
The week beginning 7 June 1924 when O'Casey arrived at Lady Gregory's*
home at Coole Park, Galway; 422 North Circular Road, age 44. The chapter
title is an allusion to Yeats's* poem, "The Wild Swans at Coole."

"A Terrible Beauty Is Borneo"
1923-24, 422 North Circular Road, ages 43-44. O'Casey uses the chapter
title on p. 157 (213) which is a variant on the famous last line of
Yeats's* poem, "Easter 1916": "A terrible beauty is born."

"The Temple Entered"
1924-26, 422 North Circular Road, ages 44-46. O'Casey also recounts
some earlier events regarding his plays.

"Dublin's Gods and Half-Gods"
1924-25, 422 North Circular Road, ages 44-45.

"Dublin's Glittering Guy"
Mid-1920s, 422 North Circular Road, ages 44-45. The chapter title is
probably an allusion to the last line of AE's* poem, "Transformations":
"Seeing nowhere a glimmer of the Glittering Gate." The title of scene
one of O'Casey's play, The Bishop's Bonfire, is "The Jittering Gate."

"The Girl He Left Behind Him"
c.1917-23, 18 Abercorn Road and 422 North Circular Road, ages 37-43.
The chapter title is from the Irish song, "The Girl I Left Behind."

"Silence"
O'Casey's account of Walter MacDonald's* career is from MacDonald's
book, Reminiscences of a Maynooth Professor, published (1925) posthumously.

"Inishfallen, Fare Thee Well"
Early 1926 (April), 422 North Circular Road, age 46. The chapter title
is from the Irish song, "Sweet Innisfallen," by Thomas Moore, which
begins: "Sweet Innisfallen, fare thee well."

V: ROSE AND CROWN

From April 1926 to December 1934 (three of the chapters cover events
that occurred in 1935). Lived at 7 Lansdowne Terrace and 2 Trafalgar
Chambers, Chelsea Square, London (to July 1926); at 32 Clareville Street,
South Kensington (to January 1927); at 19 Woronzow Road, St. Johns Wood
(to September 1931); to 2 Misbourne Cottages, Chalfont St. Giles, Buck-
inghamshire (to October 1931); to Hillcrest, Chalfont St. Giles (to
January 1935). Married Eileen Reynolds Carey in the Roman Catholic
Church of the Holy Redeemer and St. Thomas More, Chelsea (23 September
1927). First child, Breon, born 30 April 1928. Publications for this
period include:
        1928   (June) The Silver Tassie
        1933   (December) Within the Gates
        1934   (October) Windfalls
See APOLLO THEATRE and ROYALTY THEATRE, primary index, for premiere dates.
The single line on the dedication page is from John Dryden's play, Don
Sebastian (1690). The poem is from Byron's* play, The Deformed Trans-
formed (1822).

"London Apprentice"
April 1926 to c.December 1926, 7 Lansdowne Terrace, 2 Trafalgar Chambers
(off Chelsea Square), and 32 Clareville Street, all in London; age 46.

"The Silver Tassie"
1927-28, 19 Woronzow Row, ages 47-48. See also SILVER TASSIE in appendices one and five.

"The Friggin Frogs"
Mostly August through October. 1935, during which O'Casey lived at 49
Overstrand Mansions, Prince of Wales Road, Battersea (London); age 55.
The chapter title is a derivation of The Frogs by Aristophanes (also
used by Joyce in Finnegans Wake).

"Feathering His Nest"
Late 1927-28, 19 Woronzow Road, ages 47-48.

"Rose and Crown"
c.1932-33, Hillcrest, ages 52-53. See ROSE AND CROWN, primary index.

"Black Oxen Passing By"
Spring, 1935, 49 Overstrand Mansions, Prince of Wales Road, Battersea
(London), age 55. The chapter title is from a line in Yeats's* play,
The Countess Cathleen: "the years like great black oxen tread the world."

"A Long Ashwednesday"
c.1932-33, Hillcrest, ages 52-53. There are also allusions to earlier
and later events. The title is derived from T. S. Eliot's* poem, Ash-
Wednesday, paraphrased by O'Casey on page 120 (156).

"A Gate Clangs Shut"
September 1931 to c.1934, 2 Misbourne Cottages and Hillcrest, ages 51-
54. The chapter was originally published in Irish Writing (December
1950).

"A Friar by the Fireside"
c.1932, Hillcrest, age 52.

"The Star of the County Down"
September 1934, Hillcrest, age 54. The chapter title is from an Irish
song of the same name (see Appendix I).

"Ship in Full Sail"
September 13-19, 1934; Hillcrest; age 54. O'Casey left Southampton on
the Majestic and arrived in New York on 19 September.

"In New York Now"
September-October 1934. In New York, O'Casey stayed at the Royalton
Hotel, 44 West 44th Street; the Devon Hotel, 70 West 55th Street; the
Dorset Hotel, 30 West 54th Street; and the Biltmore Hotel, 43rd Street
and Madison Avenue (Letters, I, p. 769). Age 54.

"Within the Gates"
October 1934, in New York and Philadelphia, age 54. The latter half of
the chapter deals with the banning of O'Casey's play, Within the Gates,
in Boston (15 January 1935) after O'Casey's return to England.

"Pennsylvania Visit"
October or November 1934, age 54.

"Wild Life in New Amsterdam"
November or December 1934, age 54. See NEW AMSTERDAM, primary index.

"Hearts and Clubs"
November or December 1934, Devon Hotel (New York), age 54.

"Only Five Minutes More"
December 1934, Devon Hotel (New York), age 54. O'Casey delivered the
Morris Gray Poetry Talk at Harvard University on the subject, "The Old
Drama and the New" (16 November 1934). He left New York on the
Britannic on December 14 and arrived in Liverpool on December 23. The
chapter title is from the song, "Five Minutes More," lyrics by Sammy
Cahn, music by Jule Styne (1946).

VI: SUNSET AND EVENING STAR

From 1935 to 1952-53. Lived at 49 Overstrand Mansions, Prince of Wales
Road, Battersea, London (to September 1938) and at Tingrinth, Totnes,
Devon (to June 1954). Second son, Niall (15 January 1935) and first
daughter, Shivaun (28 September 1939), born. Publications for this
period include:

1937	The Flying Wasp
1939	I Knock at the Door
1940	The Star Turns Red and Purple Dust
1942	Red Roses for Me and Pictures in the Hallway
1946	Oak Leaves and Lavender and Drums under the Windows
1949	Cock-a-Doodle Dandy and Inishfallen, Fare Thee Well
1951	The Hall of Healing and Time to Go
1952	Rose and Crown

His Collected Plays were published in four volumes from 1949 (2) to
1951 (2). The title, Sunset and Evening Star, is from the first line of
Tennyson's* poem, "Crossing the Bar."

"A Drive of Snobs"
c.1935-37, 49 Overstrand Mansions, ages 55-57. The original title
was "Street of Snobs."

"Childermess"
c.1938-39, Devon, ages 58-59. Part of the chapter refers to a visit to
T. P. O'Connor's* home (1928). Part of this chapter appeared in Time
and Tide. It is reprinted in Letters, I (6 July 1935), as "A Letter
of Thanks." See CHILDERMASS, primary index.

"Cambridge"
February 1936, 49 Overstrand Mansions, age 56. O'Casey's talk, The
Holy Ghost Leaves England, was delivered to the Shirley Society of St.
Catherine's College, Cambridge University.

"Deep in Devon"
1938-39, Devon, ages 58-59. See IRISH WRITING, Appendix IV.

"The Dree Dames"
1940, Devon, age 60. The date is derived from O'Casey's comment that
he had "been a comrade to the Soviet Union for twenty-three years,"
i.e., since 1917 (p. 94 PAN, p. 128, US).

"Rebel Orwell"
1945, Devon, age 65. Orwell's review of <u>Drums under the Windows</u> appeared
in the <u>Observer</u> (28 September 1945). The chapter title is derived from
Cyril Connolly's comment: "I was a stage rebel, Orwell a true one,"
quoted in Arthur Koestler's* obituary of Orwell (<u>Observer</u>, 29 June 1950).

"Heavily Hangs the Broad Sunflower"
1940-41, Devon, ages 60-61. The chapter title is from Tennyson's* poem,
"The Princess."

"Orphans of the Storm"
c.1940, Devon, age 60. The title is identical to the title of a D. W.
Griffith silent film (1922). O'Casey's original title was "Orphans
of the Sturm."

"Red Laugh of War"
c.1942-43, Devon, ages 62-63. O'Casey uses the sentence: "Red laughter
of war was echoing over the graves" on page 143 (200). The title is
from Alfred Noyes's poem, "Love Will Found Out the Way."

"In Cellar Cool"
c.1940-41, Devon, ages 60-61.

"Shaw's Corner"
c.1949-50, Devon, ages 69-70. Shaw's Corner was the name of George
Bernard Shaw's estate.

"Sunset"
1945, Devon, age 65. Some of the events which O'Casey refers to occurred
in 1952 and 1953.

"Outside an Irish Window"
1952-53, Devon, ages 72-73.

"And Evening Star"
1952-53, Devon, ages 72-73.

SELECT BIBLIOGRAPHY

BOOKS

A.E. (George W. Russell), Collected Poems, London, 1920
          , Letters from A.E., Alan Denson, ed., London 1920
          , The Living Torch, Monk Gibbon, ed., New York
     1937 (rpt. 1970)
Ayling, Ronald, and Michael Durkan, Sean O'Casey: A Bibliography, London
     1978.
Bell, J. Bowyer, The Secret Army, New York, 1971.
Benstock, Bernard, Paycocks and Others: Sean O'Casey's World, Dublin, 1976.
Blanshard, Paul, The Irish and Catholic Power, Boston, 1953.
Boucicault, Dion, The Dolmen Boucicault, David Krause, ed., Dublin, 1964.
Browne, Kevin, They Died on Bloody Sunday, Ennis, n.d. (pamphlet).
Brooke, Stopford, et. al., A Treasury of Irish Poetry in the English
     Tongue, New York, 1900.
Cleeve, Brian, Dictionary of Irish Writers, 3 vols., Cork, 1967-71.
Colum, Padraic, ed., Anthology of Irish Verse, New York, 1948.
Connolly, James, Labour and Easter Week, Desmond Ryan, ed., Dublin, 1949.
Cooke, John, ed., Dublin Book of Irish Verse, 1728-1909, Dublin, 1909.
Cowasjee, Saros, Sean O'Casey, The Man Behind the Plays, London, 1964.
Coxhead, Elizabeth, Daughters of Erin, London, 1965.
          , Lady Gregory, London, 1961.
Crone, John S., A Concise Dictionary of Irish Biography, Dublin, 1937.
Curtis, Edmund, and R. B. McDowell, ed., Irish Historical Documents, 1172-
     1922, New York, 1943.
Delancey, John J., and James E. Tobin, Dictionary of Catholic Biography,
     New York, 1961.
Dictionary of National Biography (British)
Edwards, Ruth Dudley, Patrick Pearse, The Triumph of Failure, London,
     1977.
Eglinton, John, A Memoir of A.E., London, 1937.
Ellmann, Richard, Yeats - The Man and the Mask, New York, 1948.
          , The Identity of Yeats, New York, 1964.
Ervine, St. John, Bernard Shaw: His Life, Work and Friends, New York, 1956.
Fallon, Gabriel, Sean O'Casey, The Man I Knew, London, 1964.
Feeney, John, John Charles McQuaid: The Man and the Mask, Cork, 1974.
Fox, Ralph, History of the Irish Citizen Army, Tralee, 1944.
Greyer, Grattan, Peadar O'Donnell, Lewisburg, Pa., 1973.
Gifford, D. C., Notes for Joyce: An Annotation of James Joyce's Ulysses,
     New York, 1974.

Glasheen, Adaline, A Census of Finnegans Wake, London, 1957.
        Second Census of Finnegans Wake, Evanston, Il., 1963.
Gogarty, Oliver St. John, Collected Poems, New York, 1954.
Greaves, Desmond, The Life and Times of James Connolly, London, 1961.
Gregory, Augustus, Lady Gregory's Journals, Lennox Robinson, ed., New
        York, 1947.
Gregory, Padraic, ed., Modern Anglo-Irish Verse, London, 1914.
Hartnoll, Phyllis, ed., The Oxford Companion to the Theatre, London,
        3rd. ed., 1967.
Havlice, Patricia Pate, ed., Popular Song Index, New Jersey, 1975.
Healy, James N., ed., Ballads from the Pubs of Ireland, Cork, 1965.
        Mercier Book of Old Irish Street Ballads, v. 1
        (1967), v. 2 (1969).
        The Second Book of Irish Ballads, Cork, 1962.
Herbert, Ian, ed., Who's Who in the Theatre, 16th ed., London, 1977.
Hoagland, Kathleen, ed., 1000 Years of Irish Poetry, New York, 1947.
Hobson, Bulmer, Ireland Yesterday and Tomorrow, Tralee, 1968.
Hodgart, Matthew J., and Mabel P. Worthington, Song in the Work of
        James Joyce, New York, 1959.
Holt, Edgar, Protest in Arms, New York, 1960.
Hone, Joseph, W. B. Yeats, New York, 1943 (rpt. 1967).
Hoskins, W. G., Devon, London, 1964.
Hyde, Douglas, A Literary History of Ireland, New York, 1899.
Iris-Leabhair na bhFiann, The Fianna Handbook, 3rd ed., Dublin, 1964.
Jackson, George P., ed., Down-East Spirituals and Others, New York, 1953.
Jackson, Robert W., The Story of Limerick, Cork, 1973.
Jackson, T. A., Ireland Her Own, New York, 1947 (rpt. 1970).
Jeffares, A. Norman, A Commentary on the Collected Poems of W. B. Yeats,
        Stanford, Calif., 1968.
        and A. S. Knowland, A Commentary on the Collected
        Plays of W. B. Yeats, Stanford, Calif., 1975.
Joyce, Weston St. John, The Neighborhood of Dublin, Dublin, 1921.
Kain, Richard M., Dublin in the Age of William Butler Yeats and James
        Joyce, Norman, Okla., 1972.
Kee, Robert, The Green Flag, London, 1972.
Kennelly, Brendan, ed., The Penguin Book of Irish Verse, London, 1970.
Kenny, Herbert A., Literary Dublin, A History, New York, 1974.
Kent, William, ed., An Encyclopedia of London, London, 1937.
Kilroy, James, ed., The Playboy Riots, Dublin, 1971.
Krause, David, Sean O'Casey, The Man and His Work, New York, 1960.
        , The Profane Book of Irish Comedy, Cornell, 1982.
Kunitz, Stanley J., and Howard Haycraft, ed., Twentieth Century Authors,
        New York, 1942.
Larkin, Emmet, James Larkin, Irish Labour Leader, Cambridge, Mass., 1965.
Lovelace, Austin, and William C. Rise, Music and Worship in the Church.
Lyons, F. S. L., Charles Stewart Parnell, New York, 1977.
        Ireland Since the Famine, London, 1971.
McCann, Sean, ed., The World of Sean O'Casey, London, 1966.
McCarthy, Michael, Five Years in Ireland, 1895-1900, London, 1901.
McCormick, Lily, I Hear You Calling Me, Milwaukee, 1949.
McHugh, Roger, ed., Dublin 1916, New York, 1966.
MacManus, Seumas, The Story of the Irish Race, New York, 1944.
Macardle, Dorothy, The Irish Republic, Dublin, 1937.
Manning, Maurice, The Blueshirts, Dublin, 1971.
Margulies, Martin, The Early Life of Sean O'Casey, Dublin, 1970.
Martin, F. X., ed., The Irish Volunteers, 1913-1915, Dublin, 1963.
        and F. J. Byrne, The Scholar Revolutionary, New York, 1973.

Mason, Redfern, The Song Lore in Ireland, Ann Arbor, Mich., 1971.
Mikhail, E. H., Sean O'Casey: A Bibliography of Criticism, London, 1972.
Miller, Liam, The Dolmen Press Centenary Papers, Dublin, 1968.
Mitchell, Arthur, Labour in Irish Politics, 1890-1930, Dublin, 1974.
Moody, T. W., and F. X. Martin, eds., The Course of Irish History,
    Cork, 1967.
Moore, Thomas, Moore's Poetical Works, New York, 1869.
Nevin, Donal, ed., 1913 - Jim Larkin and the Dublin Lock-Out, Dublin,
    1964.
New Catholic Encyclopedia, New York, 1967.
O'Brien, Conor Cruise, ed., The Shaping of Modern Ireland, Toronto, 1960.
O'Brien, Nora Connolly, James Connolly: Portrait of a Rebel Father,
    Dublin, 1935 (rpt. 1975).
O Broin, Leon, Revolutionary Underground, The Story of the Irish Repub-
    lican Brotherhood, 1854-1924, Dublin, 1976.
O'Casey, Eileen, Sean, London, 1971.
          , Eileen, London, 1976.
O'Casey, Sean, Blasts and Benedictions, Ronald Ayling, ed., London, 1967.
          Feathers from a Green Crow, Robert Hogan, ed., London,
    1962.
          The Flying Wasp, London, 1937.
          The Letters of Sean O'Casey, David Krause, ed., v. 1,
    London, 1975; v. 2, London, 1980.
          Under a Colored Cap, London, 1963.
          Windfalls, London, 1934.
O'Connor, Frank, Short History of Irish Literature, New York, 1967.
O'Connor, Thomas Power, and Robert McWade, Gladstone and Parnell and the
    Great Irish Struggle, London, 1886.
O'Faolain, Sean, Countess Markievicz, London, 1934.
O Fearail, Padraig, The Story of Conradh na Gaeilge, Dublin, 1975.
O'Hegarty, P. S., A History of Ireland Under the Union, London, 1952.
O Hehir, Brenden, A Gaelic Lexicon for Finnegans Wake, Berkeley, Calif.,
    1967.
Opie, Iona and Peter, ed., The Oxford Dictionary of Nursery Rhymes,
    New York, 1951.
O'Rahilly, Thomas I., Early Irish History and Mythology, Dublin, 1946.
Oxford Dictionary of Quotations, 2nd ed., London, 1954.
Pakenham, Thomas, The Year of Liberty, The Great Irish Rebellion of 1798,
    New Jersey, 1969.
Parrish, Stephen, ed., A Concordance to the Poems of W. B. Yeats, New
    York, 1963.
Partridge, Eric, A Dictionary of Slang and Unconventional English, New
    York, 1937 (rpt. 1970).
Phillips, W. Alison, The Revolution in Ireland, London, 1926.
Ragan, David, Who's Who in Hollywood, 1900-1976, New York, 1976.
Reeves, William, Ecclesiastical History of Down, Connor, and Dromore,
    1847.
Reid, J. B., ed., A Complete Word and Phrase Concordance to the Poems
    and Songs of Robert Burns, Glasgow, 1889.
Reynolds, John J., Statement of the Claim for the Return to Dublin of
    the 39 Lane Bequest Pictures Now at the Tate Gallery, London,
    Dublin, 1932.
Robinson, Lennox, ed., Golden Treasury of Irish Verse, New York, 1925.
          Ireland's Abbey Theatre, London, 1951.
Rodgers, W. R., Irish Literary Portraits, New York, 1973.
Rumpf, E., and A. C. Hepburn, Nationalism and Socialism in Twentieth-
    Century Ireland, Liverpool, 1977.

Ryan, Desmond, <u>Remembering Sion</u>,
Ryan, William Patrick, <u>The Pope's Green Island</u>, Boston, n.d.
Shannon, Cathal, ed., <u>Fifty Years of Liberty Hall, 1909-1959</u>, Dublin, n.d.
Smythe, Colin, <u>A Guide to Coole Park, Co. Galway</u>, Gerrards Cross, 1973.
<u>Songs and Recitations of Ireland</u>, books 1-5, Cork, 1967-72.
Stephens, James, <u>Collected Poems</u>, New York, 1954.
          , <u>The Insurrection in Dublin,</u> New York, 1916.
Summerfield, Henry, <u>That Myriad-Minded Man</u>, Gerrards Cross, 1975.
Taylor, Geoffrey, ed., <u>Irish Poets of the Nineteenth Century</u>, Conn., 1951.
<u>Thoms</u>, 1880, 1888, 1896, 1907, 1912, 1919, 1924.
Thornton, Weldon, <u>Allusions in Ulysses</u>, Chapel Hill, 1961.
<u>Tri-Coloured Ribbon: Walton Songs</u>, book 2, Dublin, 1969.
<u>Walton's 132 Best Irish Songs and Ballads</u>, Dublin, n.d.
<u>Walton's New Treasury of Irish Songs and Ballads</u>, 2 v., Dublin, 1968.
Webb, Alfred, ed., <u>A Compendium of Irish Biography</u>, New York, 1879.
Williams, T. Desmond, ed., <u>Secret Societies in Ireland</u>, Dublin, 1973.
<u>Who was Who</u>, selected volumes, 1897-1970, London.
Wright, Arnold, <u>Disturbed Dublin</u>, London, 1914.
Yeats, William Butler, ed., <u>A Book of Irish Verse</u>, London, 1894 (4th ed.,
          1920).
                         <u>Collected Plays</u>, New York, 1934 (10th ed., 1973).
                         <u>Collected Poems</u>, New York, 1933 (14th ed., 1967).
                         <u>Essays</u>, New York, 1924.
                         <u>The Letters of W. B. Yeats</u>, Allan Wade, ed.,
          London, 1954.
                         <u>Plays and Controversies</u>, New York, 1924.
                         <u>The Senate Speeches of W. B. Yeats</u>, Donald R.
          Pearce, ed., Bloomington, 1960.
                         <u>Uncollected Prose</u>, John Frayne, ed., New York,
          1976.
Younger, Carleton, <u>Ireland's Civil War</u>, London, 1968.
Zimmerman, Georges-Denis, <u>Songs of Irish Rebellion</u>, Hatboro, 1967.

ARTICLES

Armstrong, William, "Sean O'Casey, W. B. Yeats, and the Dance of Life,"
          <u>Sean O'Casey</u>, Ronald Ayling, ed., London, 1969, 131-42.
                    "The Sources and Themes of <u>The Plough and the Stars</u>,"
          <u>Modern Drama</u>, IV, 1961, 232-42.
Ayling, Ronald, "Feathers Finely Aflutther," <u>Modern Drama</u>, VII, 1964,
          135-47.
               "Sean O'Casey and the Abbey Theatre," <u>The Dalhousie
          Review</u>, Spring 1972, 21-33.
               "O'Casey's Words Live On," <u>New World Review</u>, XXXIV,
          November 1966, 52-9.
               "Feathers Flying: The Politics in the Early Life and
          Thought of Sean O'Casey," <u>Dubliner</u>, III, Spring 1964, 54-67.
               "Sean O'Casey: Fact and Fancy," <u>The Massachusetts Review</u>,
          VII, 1966, 603-12 (review of Fallon's book).
               "Sean O'Casey and Jim Larkin After 1923," <u>Sean O'Casey
          Review</u>, III, Spring 1977, 99-104.
               "The Autobiographies of Sean O'Casey," <u>Research Studies</u>,
          37, June 1969, 122-29.
               "Sean O'Casey, The Writer Behind His Critics," <u>Drama
          Survey</u>, III, 1964, 582-9.
               " /Review of Cowasjee's book/, <u>Drama Survey</u>, III, Fall
          1965, 582-91.

Blaghd, Earnan de (Ernest Blythe), "Hyde in Conflict," The Gaelic League Idea, Sean O Tuama, ed., Dublin, 1972.

Bowen, B. P.,"Dublin Humourous Periodicals of the 19th Century," Dublin Historical Record, XIII, March/May 1952, 2-11.

Bromage, Mary C., "The Yeats-O'Casey Quarrel," Michigan Alumnus Quarterly Review, LXIV, 1958, 135-44.

Burca, Seamus de, "Pea ar Kearney (1883-1942)," Dublin Historical Record, XXVIII, no. 2, 42-56.

Colum, Padraic, "The Narrative Writings of Sean O'Casey," Irish Writing, no. 6, 1948, 60-9. See also O'Casey's reply, ibid, no. 7, 1949, 87.

Edwards, A. C., "The Lady Gregory Letters to Sean O'Casey," Modern Drama, VIII, May 1965, 95-111.

Elistratova, A., "Sean O'Casey," Soviet Literature, November 1952, 164-69.

Esslinger, Patricia M., "Sean O'Casey and the Lockout of 1913: Materia Poetica of the Two Red Plays," Modern Drama, VI, 1963, 59-63.
                    "The Irish Alienation of Sean O'Casey," Eire-Ireland, I, Spring 1966, 18-25.

Henchy, Deirdre, "Dublin 80 Years Ago," Dublin Historical Record, XXVI, December 1972, 18-33.

Hughes, Marie, "The Parnell Sisters," Dublin Historical Record, XXI, March/May 1966, 14-27.

Johnston, Denis, "The Dublin Trams," Dublin Historical Record, XII, August,1951, 99-113.
                    "Sean O'Casey, A Biography and An Appraisal," Modern Drama, IV, 1961, 324-8.

Kavanagh, Jim, "My Friend O'Casey," Sean O'Casey Review, II, Fall 1975, 58-63.

Keating, Edgar F., "Colourful, Tuneful Dublin," Dublin Historical Record, IX, Sept./Nov. 1947, 73-83.

Krause, David, "Some Truths and Jokes About the Easter Rising," Sean O'Casey Review, III, Fall 1976, 2-23.
                    "Sean O'Casey, 1880-1964," Massachusetts Review, VI, 1965, 233-51.
                    and Anthony Butler, "A Storm in the Fair City," Sean O'Casey Review, III, Spring 1977, 127-43.

Larkin, Emmet, "Socialism and Catholicism in Ireland," Church History, XXXIII, no. 4, 462-83.

Lindsay, Jack, "Sean O'Casey as a Socialist Artist," Sean O'Casey, Ronald Ayling, ed., London, 1969, 192-203.

Moya, Carmela, "The Mirror and the Plough," Sean O'Casey Review, II, Spring 1976, 141-53.

O'Casey, Breon, "Sean O'Casey - A Portrait," Sean O'Casey Review, III, Fall 1976, 53-7.

O'Casey, Sean, "O'Casey's letters," Sean O'Casey Review, III, Fall 1976, 50-2 (letters to Helen Kiok).

Porter, Raymond J.,"O'Casey and Pearse," Sean O'Casey Review, II, Spring 1976, 104-14.

Reeves, William F., "Dublin Quays and Shipping, 1886-1896," Dublin Historical Record, XI, December 1949, 32.

Sato, Junzo, "A Sketch of My Life," W. B. Yeats and Japan, Shotaro Oshima, ed., 1965, 131-33.

About the Author

ROBERT G. LOWERY is Editor/Publisher of the *Irish Literary Supplement* and *Sean O'Casey Review*, and editor of *An O'Casey Annual* and *ACIS Newsletter*. He has written *Sean O'Casey: Centenary Essays; Essays on O'Casey's Autobiographies; Sean O'Casey: From Times Past by Brooks Atkinson; An O'Casey Annual;* and *"My Very Dear Sean," George Jean Nathan's Letters to Sean O'Casey.*